SAINT GERMAIN
PROPHECY TO THE NATIONS

B O O K II

ELIZABETH CLARE PROPHET

PEARLS OF WISDOM
TEACHINGS OF THE ASCENDED MASTERS
Mark L. Prophet • Elizabeth Clare Prophet
VOLUME THIRTY-ONE • 1988

SUMMIT UNIVERSITY PRESS®

Saint Germain
Prophecy to the Nations
Elizabeth Clare Prophet

Pearls of Wisdom 1988
Volume Thirty-One Book Two

Published by
The Summit Lighthouse®
for Church Universal and Triumphant®

LIBRARY OF CONGRESS CATALOG CARD NUMBER: 89-61842

INTERNATIONAL STANDARD BOOK NUMBER: 0-922729-01-8

Printed in the United States of America

Summit University Press®
First Printing

Page *xvi:* The Messenger Elizabeth Clare Prophet,
photograph by Harry Langdon
Page *xv:* The Ascended Master El Morya
Chief of the Darjeeling Council of the Great White Brotherhood

The Ascended Master Saint Germain

The Ascended Master Jesus Christ

Contents

Saint Germain Stumps Canada

FREEDOM 1988
June 29 – July 4, 1988
Heart of the Inner Retreat, Royal Teton Ranch, Montana

The Ascended Master Kuthumi

The Harvest
October 5 – 10, 1988
Royal Teton Ranch, Montana

I

Letters to the Field

Appendix

Letters and Articles on the
Montana Department of Health and Environmental Sciences'
Environmental Impact Statement
on Church Universal and Triumphant

Contacting his amanuensis Mark L. Prophet in Washington, D.C., the Ascended Master El Morya, Chief of the Darjeeling Council of the Great White Brotherhood, founded The Summit Lighthouse in August 1958 for the purpose of publishing the teachings of the Ascended Masters. The anointed Messengers Mark L. Prophet and Elizabeth Clare Prophet were trained by their Guru El Morya to receive the Word of the LORD in the form of both spoken and written dictations from the Ascended Masters. Since 1958, the personal instruction of the Masters to their chelas in every nation has been published in weekly letters called *Pearls of Wisdom.*

Before his ascension on February 26, 1973, Mark transferred the mantle of the mission to Elizabeth, who continues to set forth the mysteries of the Holy Grail in current *Pearls of Wisdom,* Keepers of the Flame Lessons, and at Summit University. These activities, headquartered at the New Age community at the Royal Teton Ranch in Montana, are sponsored by the Brotherhood as the foundation of the culture and religion of Aquarius. For information on other volumes of *Pearls of Wisdom* published since 1958 and numerous books and audio- and videocassettes distributed by The Summit Lighthouse, write for a free catalog.

II

PROPHECY FOR THE 1990s
by
Elizabeth Clare Prophet

1

Whether There Be Prophecies, They Shall Fail:
By Free Will and the Violet Flame

Saint Germain has given me a vision of the future. As stated by the Archangel Zadkiel on November 25, 1987, in Washington, D.C., we have two choices:

I cast before you now a vision of violet flame, as over the land a sacred fire does burn: all of America covered by violet flame. This is the vision whereby you see what destiny America can deliver unto the nations. It is a future of hope, prosperity and light, and an inner walk with God. This is the vision of Saint Germain. . . .

This is Option the First whereby you the Lightbearers, by Holy Amethyst's ray, determine that the all-consuming fire of God shall be for transmutation and transformation in the earth body and element, in the sea and the waters, and in the air. . . .

The scene of violet flame covering the land is one that can be accomplished by you. And if it is not, beloved, then you will see Option the Second. You will see coming to pass the third vision of George Washington:

N.B. "Prophecies for the 1990s II" is based on a lecture given by Elizabeth Clare Prophet February 13, 1988, Sheraton-Palace Hotel, San Francisco, California, up-dated for publication in 1988 *Pearls of Wisdom.*

You will see a cloud coming forth out of the East and out of the West and over the seas. You will see warfare and bloodshed upon this very continent and soil. You will see, beloved, cities of the nation overcome and burdened, a people rising up by the call of Micah, the Angel of Unity, to be one and to turn back the Adversary. And you will see as hope against hope the failing of those of America to turn back that nightmare of the Great War.

You will see, then, that the only deliverance that can come to a people so unprepared as this to face a world war is Divine Intervention. And yet, beloved, though the angelic hosts descend, some among you must be pillars of fire whereby to anchor that Divine Intercession.

Therefore, see and know, beloved, that what kind of victory shall be your own is truly your choice and choosing in this hour.[1]

Our generation is ill-equipped to meet the challenges of personal and planetary karma. Events and conditions in our time have gone too far. How can we, as the one or the many, deal with such monumental problems as drugs, which have impaired the minds of several generations? As toxic and radioactive waste spoiling the earth, the air, the water and animal life? As the last plagues, signaled by cancer and the AIDS epidemic? As the "great chastisement" and the "great, great war," which Mother Mary prophesied at Fátima for the second half of the twentieth century? As child abuse inside or outside the womb? As manipulation of people and money at every hand by the power elite? And as the loss of human dignity through one euphoric escape after another— until people would rather succumb to nuclear death than summon the will to live?

Let us contemplate the prophecy of an age. In 1986 I published the book *Saint Germain On Prophecy,* which contains the Master's prophecies for the 1980s and beyond and his step-by-step interpretations of the quatrains of Nostradamus. Since then I have spoken Saint Germain's message to audiences from coast to coast. "Prophecy for the 1990s II" adds an important chapter to the series of lectures I have delivered from the Great White Brotherhood on the signs of the times.

The 30-year ministry of The Summit Lighthouse began with the earliest dictations of the Ascended Masters through my late husband, the beloved Messenger Mark L. Prophet, who founded this movement in 1958 in Washington, D.C., under the direction of the Ascended Master El Morya. In 1964 I also received the mantle of Messenger, which includes the gifts of the Holy Spirit. And throughout my ministry, by God's grace, I have built upon the foundation of prophetic teachings already laid.

These teachings outline a path of personal Christhood leading to the soul's reunion with God through the ascension. The Ascended Masters' dictations shed light on the ancient mysteries of Christ and Buddha and illumine the everlasting gospel for the New Age of Aquarius. They provide an analysis of current issues and the consequences of mankind's violation of Cosmic Law outpictured in the return of personal and planetary karma.

Saint Germain has shown me what the future holds but he has sealed my lips so that I may not speak of what I have seen. He has not, however, forbidden me to talk about the prophecy of astrology, which I call the handwriting in the skies. Astrology is a means of anticipating the future as a series of probabilities that are still subject to change by free will. It behooves us to study the stars and read what the heavens are telling for the United States, for the Soviet Union, for our planet and personally for each one of us. For the handwriting in the skies is unmistakably clear.

All astrology is the prophecy of karma, of causes we have set in motion and effects we will reap from those causes. Your birth chart tells you exactly what karma and what talents, attainments and blessings you are bringing with you from your past lives. It tells you the initiations, the soul testings and trials that are before you in this life, the strengths you can build on and the weaknesses you can surmount—and the challenges to your individuality in God, which you must face and conquer. Your birth chart is not a predestination. It is simply what you have written, for better or for worse, on your karmic record. Omar Khayyám wrote of the Moving Finger of karma, as I would interpret it:

> The Moving Finger writes; and, having writ,
> Moves on: nor all your Piety nor Wit
> Shall lure it back to cancel half a Line,
> Nor all your Tears wash out a Word of it.[2]

But you must not look at your astrological chart with the sense that it is signed, sealed and delivered and there is nothing you can do about it. There is everything you can do about it! Because the handwriting on the wall is *your* handwriting! And what Omar Khayyám didn't know is that because it is yours *you can erase it*. Why, you have a Mighty I AM Presence, a Holy Christ Self, a divine spark and free will! You are a co-creator with God! This means you can create, and once you have created you can decide to either preserve your creation because it is worthy of God and man or you can decide to destroy it because it is not worthy. These three options are ours under the offices of the Trinity as defined in Hinduism: Creator, Preserver and Destroyer.

I have seen Keepers of the Flame deter or diminish the impact of impending karma by directing the mighty light rays of God and the fullness of the Cosmic Christ consciousness into the negative astrological configurations which signaled that karma, thereby transmuting it before it could manifest in their worlds. I have seen them dissolve their diseases and lengthen their allotted lifespan by good works, obedience to cosmic law, prayer and fasting, and forgiving and loving all life free. I have seen that when people determine to walk a path of discipleship under Jesus Christ and Mother Mary and Saint Germain and the Ascended Masters, they gain a self-mastery that enables them to ride the wave of their karma instead of being inundated by it, to ride the bull of their human creation instead of being trampled by it.

I have seen and therefore I believe that in all things, with God and through his Christ, we can emerge the living conqueror—whether in this life or the next, whether on earth or in heaven—as long as we merge with the shaft of Light from the heart of the beloved Mighty I AM Presence, the Pure Person of the living God who is with us, that descends even in this moment into the place prepared, our waiting heart-chalice here below.

Therefore, it is necessary to understand that whether there be psychic predictions or prophecies or astrologies or quatrains of Nostradamus or the readings of Fátima and Medjugorje, we the people of earth turning to our God can make them fail before the mist of the Fates becomes the crystal (i.e., the crystallization) of karma.

The mist is the unformed, the uncongealed. It is the thought-form suspended in the mind not yet clothed with physical form. Before it crystallizes, the mist can be read and known as a record of nonresolution whose time for resolution has not yet run out. But when it does run out we say the mist has become the crystal—the sands have fallen in the hourglass.

Therefore, time and space are our God-given opportunity to balance karma before that karma falls due. And that's precisely what being in embodiment on planet earth is all about! It's our opportunity, by the grace of God, to undo the unrighteous deeds we have done and to do righteous deeds in their place—before the karma becomes an indelible record on the Book of Life and we are judged for our words and our works before the judgment seat. God in his infinite mercy has given to every living soul not one but many incarnations in which to balance her karma before the mist becomes the crystal.

Unless we invoke this violet flame under the law of forgiveness to erase the cause, effect, record and memory of our past violations of the Great Law, sooner or later we will be compelled to balance our personal and planetary karma (a) by serving the individuals or institutions we have injured or dealt unjustly with or (b) by bearing that karma in our bodies as diseases, disorders, debilitation, aberration, accident or death.

What we have to come to grips with is that once the mist becomes the crystal, it is impossible to turn it back.

I am delivering the warning in this "Prophecy for the 1990s II" to tell the world the worst and the best that can happen in the decade of the 1990s and beyond. And I tell it as I see it in the heavenly signs of astrology, in the earthly signs of the Four Horsemen and in the handwriting on the wall of karma, karma everywhere telling us to hurry up and do something about the mess we have made of the blessed earth and our blessed earth bodies before it is too late. A lot of people see the karma and hear what it's telling us but they don't know what to do about "the mess we've made."

When Moses said, "Our God is a consuming fire,"[3] he was telling us what we could do for our time and for all time: When we misuse God's fire to create unjustly, only God's fire will suffice to uncreate our unjust creations. The sacred fire of the LORD's Spirit, when invoked by his sons and daughters on earth, will pass through and "uncreate" any and all of our untoward creations, as well as our thoughts and feelings, our words and deeds.

The karma of the planet has been held in abeyance for thousands of years by the Light, i.e., the God consciousness, of the saints and Christed ones of all ages. Unless we foresee the due dates of karma as prophesied by the Ascended Masters and direct God's gift of the violet flame into the mist of the negative karma of planet earth, it will descend with the Chaos and old Night of ancient cataclysm recorded only in the memory of the race.

Therefore I recommend the following:

1) Read this book and underline the Ascended Masters' warnings and prophecies and the astrological predictions.

2) Send for my four violet flame tapes, *Save the World with Violet Flame! by Saint Germain 1–4,* and invoke the violet flame daily. On each 90-minute cassette you can join me with 800 voices in giving dynamic decrees and songs to the violet flame. Implore divine intercession and violet flame transmutation for the karmic

conditions outlined in the astrology notes and charts in this book and for the problems affecting you and your loved ones.

3) Call daily for the mitigation or the complete transmutation of all prophecies and astrological predictions foretold and expect God's miracle and his victory in your life.

4) Meanwhile, take practical physical steps to move your family out of harm's way and follow Saint Germain's explicit directives for physical preparedness in the face of a potential nuclear war and/or earth changes.

A million or 10 million people invoking the violet flame could, according to God's mercy, turn back the karma earth's evolutions have created, while it will take centuries or millennia to undo that karma if it descends physically on planet earth to satisfy the law of retribution wherever mankind do not repent of their deeds.

That's why we have to transmute this karma now—while there is yet time. No one can live half-slave and half-free, as we do while under the cudgel of our karma and the threat of its swift and sudden descent. Therefore we can decide to make our lives count for one purpose, the victory of the age; and we together, one-times-one-times-one in the Divine One, can beat the Fates. Yes, we can in God's name transmute past-present-future by the violet flame and move on to fulfill the cycles of the fiery destiny of our calling in God!

This is the day when we must make our decision to live in reality, to choose to be and to enter the mainstream of life as God intended us to live it. If we do not make that choice today, if we just let ourselves bob along on the waves of human emotion in and out with the tides of the moon and the astral sea, we will witness at some level of our psyches the disturbances in the earth body that Saint Germain showed me in his vision of the future.

If I didn't *believe* with all my heart and soul that God has placed within us the will to change, the power to change, the wisdom to know when change is possible and when it is not, and the love of change when it is ordained, then I would not be speaking to you this evening in San Francisco in the Grand Ballroom of the Sheraton-Palace Hotel.

If I didn't *know* with all of my mind and spirit that God has placed in us his divine spark whereby his all-consuming fire is kindled within us for alchemical change in the microcosm and the macrocosm of our worlds, then there would be no point in placing before you the prophecies of Saint Germain. Because I know there is time and space to turn the tide of karma, I *must* deliver this the Lord's message. For he has not only empowered me with his mantle, he has impelled me with his Fiery Spirit.

Today, then, is our day of decision. It is not an altar call. It is a call from the heart of God to your soul to *remember.* Let the divine memory unfold this night as you remember your beginnings in the Great Central Sun with your beloved twin flame. Remember the foreknowledge you had that one day you would be at this crossroads in time and space on a planet in distress called Earth, and that you would be told *how you could make all the difference.*

Belshazzar's Feast

Then Daniel spoke up in the presence of the king. Keep your gifts for yourself, he said, and give your rewards to others. I will read the writing to the king without them, and tell him what it means.

O king, the Most High God gave Nebuchadnezzar your father sovereignty, greatness, glory, majesty.

He made him so great that men of all peoples, nations and languages shook with dread before him: he killed whom he pleased, spared whom he pleased, promoted whom he pleased, degraded whom he pleased.

But because his heart grew swollen with pride, and his spirit stiff with arrogance, he was deposed from his sovereign throne and stripped of his glory.

He was driven from the society of men, his heart grew completely animal; he lived with the wild asses; he fed on grass like the oxen; his body was drenched by the dew of heaven, until he had learned that the Most High rules over the empire of men and appoints whom he pleases to rule it.

But you, Belshazzar, who are his son, you have not humbled your heart, in spite of knowing all this.

You have defied the Lord of heaven, you have had the vessels from his Temple brought to you, and you, your noblemen, your wives and your singing women have drunk your wine out of them. You have praised gods of gold and silver, of bronze and iron, of wood and stone, which cannot either see, hear or understand; but you have given no glory to the God who holds your breath and all your fortunes in his hands.

That is why he has sent the hand which, by itself, has written these words.

The writing reads: *Mene, Mene, Tekel and Parsin.*

The meaning of the words is this: *Mene:* God has *measured* your sovereignty and put an end to it;

Tekel: you have been *weighed* in the balance and found wanting;

Parsin: your kingdom has been *divided* and given to the Medes and the *Persians.*

At Belshazzar's order Daniel was dressed in purple, a chain of gold was put round his neck and he was proclaimed third in rank in the kingdom.

That same night, the Chaldaean king Belshazzar was murdered, and Darius the Mede received the kingdom, at the age of sixty-two.

Daniel 5:17-31 Jerusalem Bible

2

The Astrology of World Karma:
An Ascending Series of Challenges

Today we are about to enter an era that is unprecedented in this century and perhaps in all of recorded history—both in its potential for spiritual and scientific progress and in its potential for destruction.

All destruction is self-destruction. This we must remember. Nothing can destroy us from without unless we are first self-destroyed from within. And we do have the power to destroy ourselves from within, make no mistake about it. For we have been co-creators with Life for aeons. But as I have said, what man has done, man can undo. Therefore we must learn to exercise the power of the spoken Word to deliver ourselves from our self-destructive creations of the past.

Ours is to decide what of our human creation is constructive, leading to world and individual acceleration, hence Good. This we must preserve. Ours is also to decide what of our human creation is destructive, leading to world and individual deceleration, hence Evil. This we must not preserve.

In order to "destroy" our miscreations, or "transmute" them, as the Ascended Masters say, we must first call upon the law of forgiveness for having miscreated, i.e., for having misused God's Power, Wisdom and Love given to us to create after the patterns of Elohim. Then we must invoke the violet flame of forgiveness and transmutation to forgive and transmute our miscreations, even as we must go about replacing them with renewed soul creations patterned after the divine.

We are gathered on the shores of the Motherland* this evening to consider these truths and to apply them directly to the

---

*The California coast was part of the "Motherland," a term used to refer to Lemuria, or Mu, the lost continent that once existed in the Pacific Ocean. According to the findings of James Churchward, Lemuria was made up of three land masses stretching more than 5,000 miles from east to west and was destroyed by earth changes approximately 12,000 years ago.

portent of coming events. We as a planetary evolution have sown
the wind of our collective misqualified energies and we are about
to reap the whirlwind.[4] For the karma for these miscreations, held
in abeyance for centuries, is returning to our doorstep daily at a
stepped-up rate because we are living at the end of the age of
Pisces on a world in transition. If we decide to apply the alchemy
of the Seventh Ray by invoking the violet flame and directing it
into the karma of a planet and a people, we just might set the earth
on a course of victory.

The astrological configurations of the next 12 years tell us that
we will face an ascending series of karmic challenges, including
the possibilities of war, revolution, economic upheaval and major
earth changes.

Saint Germain was embodied as Roger Bacon (1214–1294),
one of the greatest scientific minds of the thirteenth century.
Already in this life the soul of Saint Germain was internalizing
the spiral of Aquarius, and the age of which he was to become
hierarch.

Bacon believed that it was possible to avoid wars through the
study of astrology. He said that if the leaders of the Church had
read the astrological warnings, such as the comet of 1264, which
preceded the battles that broke out all over Europe, they might
have averted the wars of their times.

In his *Opus Majus* he wrote: "Oh, how great an advantage
might have been secured to the Church of God, if the characteristics of the heavens in those times had been discerned beforehand
by scientists, and understood by prelates and princes, and transferred to a zeal for peace. For so great a slaughter of Christians
would not have occurred."[5]

All who, like Roger Bacon, have the alchemist's heart know
the truth of this statement: As long as the mist is still the mist and
not the crystal, no future is inevitable. Nevertheless, in the final
decade of this century we the people of planet earth will write and
sign our destiny with the future—not in the mist, but in the
crystal. And this time, having writ, nor all our Piety nor Wit shall
lure it back to cancel half a line—nor all our tears wash out a word
of it. And we may weep and reap an opportunity lost. Therefore
this evening we shall read the destiny of our untransmuted karma
written in the skies, that on the morrow we may write the destiny
of our transmuted karma and seal it in the sacred fire of God.

First let us examine in detail what will happen if we the
people do nothing.

On February 13, 1988, at exactly 3:53 p.m., Saturn entered the sign of Capricorn.* It will remain there until February 6, 1991, except during the period between June 9 and November 12, 1988, when it will retrograde into Sagittarius. When the slow-moving outer planets (Saturn, Uranus, Neptune and Pluto) shift from sign to sign or form major aspects, they usually trigger important political, economic, social, cultural and geophysical changes on earth.

Of itself, Saturn's movement into Capricorn could do much to depress the world economy and place severe stress on the government of the United States and a number of other nations. But Uranus will also enter the sign of Capricorn on February 14 at 4:31 p.m. It will remain there until January 11, 1996, with a comparatively brief period of retrogradation into Sagittarius between May 26 and December 2, 1988.[6]

What Saturn-Uranus Conjunctions Mean

Thus, on February 14, 1988, Saturn and Uranus, separated by just 5 minutes of arc, formed a nearly exact conjunction at 0° Capricorn. Saturn-Uranus conjunctions are relatively rare. They occur about every 45 years. They last formed a conjunction— that is, lined up at the identical point in space as seen from earth— in 1942.

Saturn-Uranus conjunctions have coincided with momentous events throughout history. In an excellent summary of the 60 conjunctions of Saturn and Uranus between 600 B.C. and 2400 A.D., astrologer Richard Nolle points out that they have marked important turning points in three areas: (1) economic change, especially periods of inflation or deflation; (2) global or regional military conflict, primarily along east-west lines; (3) religious persecution and changes in the status of religious institutions.[7]

The Saturn-Uranus conjunction of 598 B.C. at 14° Aquarius, for example, coincided with the first stage of the Babylonian captivity—the Babylonian invasion of Judah, capture of Jerusalem and exile of the king and key officials. The conjunction of 326 B.C. at 2° Taurus coincided with the military zenith of the Greco-Macedonian empire—Alexander the Great's invasion of India. But that victory marked the end and not the beginning of further greatness. In fact, as Nolle points out, it was "the last gasp for ancient Greece: within four years the classic period in Greece was at an end."[8] The next Saturn-Uranus conjunction, which occurred in Sagittarius, took place in 281 B.C. and coincided with the collapse of the Greek economy.[9]

---

*All times are given in Pacific Standard Time unless otherwise noted.

Hard Saturn-Uranus aspects (conjunctions, squares and oppositions) have long been associated with wars. The pattern holds in modern times. The Saturn-Uranus conjunctions of 1897 in Sagittarius coincided with the Spanish-American War. The Saturn-Uranus opposition of 1918 and 1919 in Leo-Aquarius and Virgo-Pisces coincided with the Russian Revolution and with World War I.

The Saturn-Uranus square of 1930 and 1931 in Capricorn-Aries coincided not with a major war but with the Great Depression, which was one of the social forces that created the climate for World War II. This was hardly a peaceful time, however. In 1930 there were revolutions in Argentina and Brazil, and Gandhi began his campaign of civil disobedience in India. In 1931 King Alfonso of Spain was deposed, and Mao Tse-tung established the first Chinese Soviet Republic in a remote area of China.

The Saturn-Uranus conjunction of 1942 in Taurus coincided with World War II. The Saturn-Uranus square of 1951–52 in Cancer-Libra coincided with the Korean War. The Saturn-Uranus opposition of 1965 and early 1967 in Virgo-Pisces coincided with the escalation of the Vietnam War.

The Saturn-Uranus squares of 1975 through 1977 in Leo-Scorpio coincided with worldwide conflict, including the takeover of Cambodia by the Khmer Rouge in 1975 and the start of a holocaust that would claim three million to four million lives within two years; the takeover of Laos by the Communist-led Pathet Lao; a military coup in Peru; heavy fighting in Lebanon with Lebanese Christians opposed to Palestinian guerrillas and Lebanese Moslems; the takeover of Beirut and Tripoli by the Syrian Army; conflict between Ethiopia and Somali-backed guerrillas; and the civil war in Angola.

Even though events triggered by Saturn-Uranus conjunctions tend to be predictable, not all Saturn-Uranus conjunctions have the same influence or strength. Much depends on the sign in which the conjunction occurs.

The Saturn-Uranus conjunctions of 1988 in Capricorn are extremely powerful, which is an anomaly since they are not exact conjunctions. (In addition to the nearly exact Saturn-Uranus conjunction at 0° Capricorn on February 14, 1988, Saturn and Uranus formed another nearly exact conjunction at 2° and 0° Capricorn on December 2, 1988.)

A conjunction is one of the major aspects planets form with one another. The term aspect refers to the angular separation between planets. The major aspects in astrology are the conjunction

(0° separation), sextile (60°), square (90°), trine (120°), and opposition (180°). Although aspects are most powerful when exact, they do not need to be exact to be operative. The arc of space, expressed in degrees, in which an aspect is operative is called the orb of influence, or "orb." There is a good deal of controversy over how large an orb should be allowed. A number of astrologers agree that an aspect is effective 5° to 8° from the point at which it is exact, and in mundane charts perhaps as much as 10°.

The exact conjunctions of Saturn and Uranus in 1988 take place in Sagittarius: the first on February 12, 1988, at 29°55′ Sagittarius; the second on June 26, 1988, at 28°47′ Sagittarius; and the third on October 18, 1988, at 27°49′ Sagittarius.

We can get an idea what to expect from a Saturn-Uranus conjunction in Sagittarius by reviewing what took place during past conjunctions in this sign.

There have been four Saturn-Uranus conjunctions in Sagittarius since 600 B.C. The first, as noted, marked the collapse of the Greek economy. The second took place 309–311 A.D. and coincided with a period of bitter persecution of Christians by Diocletian and the joint Roman emperors Constantius and Galerius, which finally ended with Galerius' edict of toleration that legalized the practice of Christianity within the Roman Empire. The third Saturn-Uranus conjunction in Sagittarius occurred between 1397 and 1399, close to the beginning of the Renaissance.

The fourth Saturn-Uranus conjunction in Sagittarius since 600 B.C. takes place in 1988. Based on past history, this conjunction may be expected to coincide with war, economic collapse, religious persecution and/or toleration, and the renewal of culture and learning.

The exact Saturn-Uranus conjunction in Sagittarius has a good deal of power. But the nearly exact conjunctions of Saturn and Uranus in Capricorn in 1988 are even more powerful because the influences of this conjunction in the abstract sign of Sagittarius are carried over and more easily (and powerfully) expressed in the concrete sign of Capricorn.

Saturn rules Capricorn and is naturally powerful when it is in its own sign, where it can easily express its characteristics, including the capacity to crystallize or precipitate planetary energies (both good and bad karma) in the Capricornian environment. Moreover, the influences signified by the *exact* Saturn-Uranus conjunction in Sagittarius—war, economic collapse, et cetera—tend to be more concrete and physically expressed when these planets move into Capricorn.

It is structurally easy to transfer the energies of the Saturn-Uranus conjunction from Sagittarius to Capricorn. The first conjunction in Sagittarius takes place within five minutes of the Capricorn cusp, giving the aspect a Capricorn character to start with. In other words, the Sagittarius conjunction is really more of a Sagittarius-Capricorn conjunction and already carries part of the Capricorn vibration.

As an earth sign governed by the planet Saturn, Capricorn rules political, governmental, economic and social power in both their positive and negative manifestations. Because it is ruled by Saturn, it tends to limit or bring to an end unrealistic behavior. Saturn is not a "bad" or "unlucky" planet even though it is traditionally known as a "malefic" and is often associated with unfortunate circumstances. Saturn's influence, particularly when in Capricorn, is supportive when a person or groups of people have acted wisely, practically and responsibly. It is then associated with wealth, honors, freedom of action, respect, justly gained and/or administered power, good government and an orderly society.

But Saturn is a teacher and a tester. And since human nature is often marked by human folly, Saturn is associated with hard times, difficult challenges, recessions and depressions, delays, misfortune, debt, loss of honor or respect, periods of little or no opportunity, the limitation or loss of freedom due to increased governmental authority, and dictatorships and repressive regimes. Under its influence people are often pessimistic, gloomy, depressed, despondent and victims of their own sense of limitation.

Saturn and Uranus Conjoin the Galactic Center

There is another element to consider. The Saturn-Uranus conjunctions of 1988 in Sagittarius conjoin a point in space known as the Galactic Center. Simply speaking, the Galactic Center is the center of gravity of our galaxy around which our Sun orbits about every 250 million earth years in the same way the earth orbits our Sun every 365 or so days. Astronomers are not certain what the Galactic Center really is. Some think it may be a black hole. One thing is certain: the Galactic Center emits huge quantities of energy.

The astrological influence of the Galactic Center is not completely understood. Astrologers are in the early stages of researching its astrological importance.[10] Nevertheless, some influences have already been observed. Theodor Landscheidt, for example, accurately predicted a period of economic recession and uncertainty in 1982 due to the conjunction of Neptune with the Galactic Center.[11]

In gauging the influence of the Saturn-Uranus conjunction with the Galactic Center, we can look at the one previous Saturn-Uranus conjunction with the Galactic Center since 600 B.C. This Saturn-Uranus conjunction took place over a two-year period between 400–402 A.D. and was exact at 16°21′ Capricorn on February 1, 401. The position of the Galactic Center, which precesses backwards at the rate of about 1 degree every 72 years, was then about 18° Capricorn.

The conjunction of Saturn and Uranus with the Galactic Center in 401 coincided with the breaking up of the mightiest political and social entity the world had known to that time— the Roman Empire. Upon the death of Theodosius I in 395, the Roman Empire permanently split into eastern and western divisions. The Eastern Empire was called the Byzantine Empire. Alaric, leader of the Visigoths, invaded the Western Empire in 401 (just as Saturn and Uranus were making their conjunction in alignment with the Galactic Center) and sacked Rome in 410.

Today Saturn and Uranus are again making their conjunctions with the Galactic Center. This knowledge should at least give us pause and compel us to consider whether we will allow their potential influence to cause momentous changes in our time— changes on the same scale as the fall of the Roman Empire. The influence of these 1988 conjunctions in Sagittarius, which will include the economic, military, social and religious changes that normally mark Saturn and Uranus conjunctions, will also be carried over into Capricorn.

Enter Neptune

George Santayana said, "Those who cannot remember the past are condemned to repeat it."[12] Our times mandate that we learn from our astrological history: the configurations of the planets, the events that coincided with them, and the consequences of the choices made by the players on the historical stage. We must also learn from the karmic portents of that astrology, which were evident in the social, economic and political signs of the times and to a greater or lesser extent circumscribed the choices of those involved.

Will we forever ignore the warnings of our sages and our prophets (or of the insane who also contact the psychic depths) or of the little child who in holy innocence would lead us when we choose to ignore the prompting of the Inner Self?

Knowing what we know about the past, and seeing what we

see in these correlations, we can hypothesize by the geometric coordinates of the heavens that there is the possibility of a major international conflict in the next few years.

But the Saturn-Uranus conjunction is only a part of the picture. Enter Neptune, which on February 22, 1988, was in the early degrees of Capricorn, 9° to be precise, forming a wide-orbed conjunction with Saturn and Uranus. When Neptune transits through earth signs—that is, Virgo, Capricorn or Taurus—it tends to trigger downturns in the economy. This is partly because the illusions and illusory behavior associated with Neptune become grounded in the earth signs.

Two preliminary but significant events indicate what we may expect from the rest of Neptune's transit of Capricorn—the fall of oil prices and the decline of the dollar. Neptune rules a number of commodities, most notably oil.

After Neptune's transit from Sagittarius into Capricorn in 1984, oil prices fell.* This is because Sagittarius is a fire sign that tends to be optimistic and expansive, while Capricorn is an earth sign that tends to be pessimistic and deflationary. This drop in prices surprised many experts who believed that oil prices could only continue to rise. They were victims of their own illusory thinking about oil, which was stimulated by Neptune in Sagittarius. Shortly after Neptune entered Capricorn the dollar also began to decline.

Although Neptune's entry into Capricorn began to depress the dollar and oil prices, the world economy did not begin to rapidly implode because Uranus was still in Sagittarius, and Saturn had entered Sagittarius on November 16, 1985. Thus there was enough optimism to keep the international financial system afloat. Huge quantities of debt, made possible in large part by the Federal Reserve Board's double digit expansion of the U.S. money supply, burdened both the U.S. economy and the international financial system. But the markets ignored the debt overhang and economies continued to expand.

Confidence in the health of the economy began to wane in the fall of 1987, as Saturn and Uranus neared the end of their transit in Sagittarius. Other astrological factors (which I will explain in a moment) entered the picture and exposed the inherent weaknesses of the U.S. and world financial systems. These portents triggered the great stock market crash of October 19, giving us a small fore-taste of things to come.

---

*Neptune entered Capricorn in two phases. It first entered the sign on January 18, 1984, but retrograded back into Sagittarius on June 22, 1984, and stayed there until November 21, 1984, when it entered Capricorn the second time. It will remain there until January 29, 1998.

The Portents of Saturn-Uranus-Neptune Conjunctions

Before we look at how those economic events are synergistically related to coming astrological challenges, I would like to point out that Saturn-Uranus-Neptune conjunctions are extremely rare. The last time these three planets were conjoined was in 1307. The last time before that was in 234 B.C. In other words, Saturn-Uranus-Neptune conjunctions come about every 700 to 1500 years.

It is difficult to quantify the impact of these three planets except to say that it is great. Saturn-Uranus conjunctions can trigger wars and are related to the onset of depressions. Saturn-Neptune conjunctions can trigger events equally as momentous. We will see multiple conjunctions of these three planets in the next several years: Saturn and Uranus, Saturn and Neptune, and Neptune and Uranus. But in February 1988 all three were grouped together.*

The effects of multiple planet alignments whose conjunctions are spread out over a long period of time may take years to appear. The long-term consequences may take decades or centuries to become fully apparent. Later astrological events, such as an eclipse or an important conjunction in aspect to the original conjunction, may bring into manifestation, for better or worse, the potential long-term influences released at the time of the original conjunction.

For example, the conjunction of Saturn, Uranus and Neptune in Scorpio in 1307 was the primary astrological impulse that resulted in the Black Death (bubonic plague) of 1348–50, which wiped out half the population of England and at least one-third of the population of Europe. Later astrological events drew on and brought into manifestation the potential influences of the Saturn-Uranus-Neptune conjunction.

The Medical Faculty of Paris ascribed the plague to a conjunction of Mars, Jupiter and Saturn in Aquarius on March 20, 1345. Astrologer Dylan Warren-Davis recently argued that the portents of that conjunction certainly showed the potential for an epidemic.[13] But that conjunction could not have been the sole or even the primary astrological cause of the Black Death, which was the worst disaster in history. It simply wasn't powerful enough.

The Mars-Jupiter-Saturn conjunction of 1345 formed a square to and activated a portion of the energy potential of the

---

*The three 1988 Saturn-Uranus conjunctions occur on February 12, 1988, at 29°55′ Sagittarius; on June 26, 1988, at 28°47′ Sagittarius; and on October 18, 1988, at 27°49′ Sagittarius. Saturn will conjoin Neptune on March 3, 1989, at 11°55′ Capricorn; on June 23, 1989, at 11°15′ Capricorn; and on November 13, 1989, at 10°22′ Capricorn. Uranus will conjoin Neptune on February 2, 1993, at 19°34′ Capricorn; on August 19, 1993, at 18°49′ Capricorn; and on October 24, 1993, at 18°33′ Capricorn.

Saturn-Uranus-Neptune conjunction of 1307. Of course, the Medical Faculty of Paris could not have known about the earlier Saturn-Uranus-Neptune conjunction since Uranus and Neptune had not yet been discovered.

There may have been other astrological factors related to the virulent spread of the Black Death that the Medical Faculty of Paris was unaware of. Astrologer Diana Rosenberg points out that the Jupiter-Saturn conjunction of 1345 occurred at the time of the "Great Mutation,"[14] i.e., the point in the cycle of conjunctions between Jupiter and Saturn when they move from a series of conjunctions in astrological signs of one element (fire, air, water or earth) to a series of conjunctions in another. The ancients paid careful attention to the "Great Mutation" in their mundane predictions and considered it to be particularly powerful. The fourteenth century was a remarkable but tragic period, a time of troubles with historical and astrological parallels to our own. In *A Distant Mirror: The Calamitous 14th Century*, Barbara W. Tuchman suggests that we have much to learn about the present by studying the events of the fourteenth century and contemporaries' reactions to them. In effect, we can put our time in some sort of perspective by viewing them in the "distant mirror" of that century.

Tuchman wrote that she undertook the study of the fourteenth century in order to

> find out what were the effects on society of the most lethal disaster of recorded history—that is to say, of the Black Death of 1348–50, which killed an estimated one third of the population living between India and Iceland. Given the possibilities of our own time, the reason for my interest is obvious. The answer proved elusive because the fourteenth century suffered so many "strange and great perils and adversities" (in the words of a contemporary) that its disorders cannot be traced to any one cause; they were the hoofprints of more than the four horsemen of St. John's vision, which had now become seven—plague, war, taxes, brigandage, bad government, insurrection, and schism in the Church. . . .
>
> Although my initial question has escaped an answer, the interest of the period itself—a violent, tormented, bewildered, suffering and disintegrating age, a time, as many thought, of Satan triumphant—was compelling and, as it seemed to me, consoling in a period of similar disarray. If our last decade or two of collapsing assumptions has been a

period of unusual discomfort, it is reassuring to know that the human species has lived through worse before.[15]

Now, for the first time since the fourteenth century, we face the challenge of a Saturn-Uranus-Neptune conjunction. As we embark on a perilous journey into the future, let us remember that the fourteenth century was more than a time of misery, although there was an abundance of misery. In addition to the Black Death, the Saturn-Uranus-Neptune conjunction triggered the Hundred Years War, which broke out in 1337, and the Ottoman invasion of Europe in 1354.

These disastrous events ultimately changed economic, political and sociological patterns. As astrologer Richard Nolle points out, the Saturn-Uranus-Neptune conjunction caused a revolution in military technology that brought the feudal period to a close and hastened the rise of the monarchies, and catalyzed the power struggles that resulted in the exile of the papacy to France.[16] And the widespread mortality caused by the Black Death started an economic revolution by consolidating wealth in fewer hands.

By acting in time and space we can anticipate events just as momentous in our time and, as Roger Bacon prophesied, we can forestall the tellings and foretellings of the Four Horsemen that ride across the celestial window before our gaze.

The Black Death, or bubonic plague, is a bacterial disease which has been largely under control since the development of antibiotics such as tetracycline.[17] In our time the condition that thus far best meets the criteria of a plague is the acquired immunodeficiency syndrome, or AIDS.

AIDS and Astrology

According to the currently accepted theory, AIDS is caused by a virus that attacks an important part of the immune system—the white blood cells known variously as T-4 leukocytes, T-helper, or simply T-cells, which are essential for the neutralization of viruses and certain foreign bacteria. With a decline in the number of T-cells, the body is not able to fight off otherwise controllable infections. Thus, the AIDS patient gets one or more opportunistic infections that would normally be suppressed by his immune system. These infections, rather than the AIDS virus itself, ultimately kill the AIDS victim.

Like the Saturn-Uranus-Neptune conjunction in Scorpio of 1307 (which was related to the Black Death), the Saturn-Uranus-Neptune conjunction in Capricorn of 1988–89 is related to the rise of diseases of the immune system and other epidemics, including Lyme disease. Both the planet Saturn and the sign it rules, Capricorn, have partial rulership of the immune system. Negative Saturn-Capricorn energies can have a depressing effect, hence they may be associated with a depressed immune response. Uranus rules new conditions, circumstances or technologies as well as diseases of the blood and circulatory system—all characteristics of AIDS, particularly if one looks at AIDS as a blood-borne disease.

Neptune can have a degenerative effect on the immune system and is also associated with hard-to-define problems and elusive causes, something unquestionably related to AIDS. The combined effect of Saturn, Uranus and Neptune conjoined in Capricorn suggests that a modern plague would be characterized by a degenerative condition related to a weakened or debilitated immune system due to hard-to-define, novel causes. AIDS, of course, is precisely that, a previously unknown degenerative condition in which a depressed immune system leaves the body vulnerable to opportunistic infections.

There are several other astrological influences related to AIDS and other kinds of epidemics that act synergistically with the influences of the Saturn-Uranus-Neptune conjunction in Capricorn. Pluto is now transiting in the sign of Scorpio, where it has been since November 5, 1983, and where it will remain until January 17, 1995. Pluto in Scorpio is also related to plagues. The areas of life that Pluto and Scorpio rule are especially related to AIDS. Scorpio rules or is related to sex, sexuality, medicine, the healing arts, the drug industry, joint financial affairs and matters of life and death. Pluto rules or is associated with decay, death and regeneration, investigation, power and its misuses, secret and underhanded dealings, destruction and the threat of annihilation, and annihilation itself. In conjunction with Neptune in Capricorn (conjoined Saturn and Uranus), Pluto in Scorpio indicates the strong possibility of deception or intrigue with long-term consequences.

During the Capricorn megaconjunction of January 11, 1994, Saturn in Aquarius will square Pluto in Scorpio. Among other things, this could precipitate widespread plagues and famines, the plagues being either an expansion of the existing AIDS epidemic, something entirely new, or both.

On January 28, 1998, Neptune will enter Aquarius. According to astrologer John Townley, "Neptune in Aquarius . . . is quite consistently associated with the great plagues, extending all the way back into Roman times."[18] Again, it is not clear whether this might relate to an expansion of the AIDS epidemic, something new, or both.*

Mars, the Trigger Horse

On February 22, 1988, Mars entered Capricorn and made an exact conjunction with Uranus at 0 degrees 18 minutes Capricorn and a wide-orbed conjunction with Neptune at 9 degrees Capricorn. The following day it made an exact conjunction with Saturn at 0 degrees 45 minutes Capricorn (fig. 1). Mars is the fourth horseman of the famous four that ride neck and neck in Capricorn in February 1988.[19] These four riders—Mars, Saturn, Uranus and Neptune—as harbingers of our karma and our karmic destiny, have contradictory influences that make it difficult for individuals to deal with them, and even more difficult for entire nations of peoples to do so.

Saturn rules institutions, the state, land, legal systems, tradition and authority. It tends to limit freedom. It gives you freedom only by your own self-discipline and the path of your soul's initiation under the Great White Brotherhood. Saturn is our tester. You might see it as the instrument of the Ascended Master Lord Maitreya, the Cosmic Christ, testing you; or you might see it as Antichrist, depending upon your perspective. It doesn't really matter, because Saturn will get you coming or going. Under its influence you will be tested by forces of Light and forces of Darkness *and* by your own returning karma, positive and negative.

Once you earn your freedom under Saturn, you have earned it by self-mastery and you hold on to it by self-mastery. Without that self-mastery you don't make it either way with Saturn.

Uranus, on the other hand, governs progress, revolution, economic and political change, scientific and social innovation, aspects of warfare, civil unrest, strikes, the breakdown of authority, and the wise (or unwise) use of nuclear energy. It gives the impulse for freedom.

Neptune rules enlightenment, spiritual inspiration and intuition, drugs, subversion, disillusionment, treachery and scandal. It gives the impulse for illumination.

Mars, although it is part of the conjunction for only a matter of days, gives the entire configuration a warlike character and acts as a trigger to release or activate its energies.

*See Appendix A for "A Startling Thesis on the Origin of AIDS," a summary of my Summit University Forum in which Dr. Robert Strecker, an expert on the origins of AIDS, unveils his theory that AIDS is a man-made virus.

Conjunction of Mars, Saturn, Uranus and Neptune in Capricorn
February 22–23, 1988

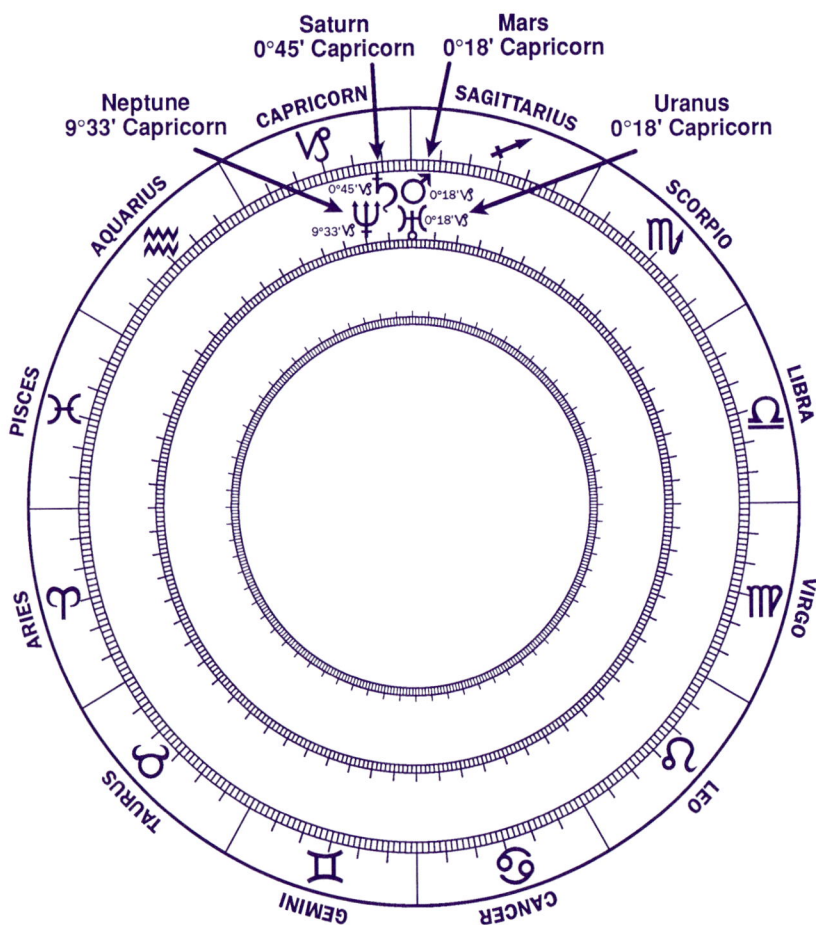

FIGURE 1   On February 22–23, 1988, Mars, Saturn, Uranus and Neptune formed a conjunction that marked the formal beginning of a period of upheaval and change on the planet. This conjunction occurred in two steps. On February 22 at 6:49 p.m. PST, Mars made an exact conjunction to Uranus at 0°18′ Capricorn. Then, at 11:01 a.m. PST on the 23rd, Mars made an exact conjunction to Saturn at 0°45′ Capricorn. Neptune was at 9°33′ Capricorn. A conjunction occurs when two or more planets occupy the same degree of the zodiac, although aspects need not be exact to be within the "orb of influence." A rare Saturn-Uranus-Neptune conjunction is the core of this configuration. The last one occurred in 1307 and was the primary astrological impulse for the Black Death.

The Four Planetary Horsemen in Capricorn
Mark a Period of Upheaval and Change

This conjunction of Mars, Saturn, Uranus and Neptune, signaling the ride of the Four Horsemen of the Apocalypse in Capricorn, marks the formal starting point of a period of upheaval and change on the planet. Unless the Lightbearers can and will call forth the violet flame with renewed fervor, the era of financial expansion related to oil and international finance will come to a halt and, with the exception of one last brief expansionary period when Saturn and Uranus retrograded into Sagittarius between May and December of 1988, national economies will contract.

This is a time when nations will become conservative and reactionary, there will be massive debt liquidation, the real price of commodities will fall (as has already occurred since Neptune entered Capricorn in January 1984), and a crash in the real-estate market is likely. A pessimistic mood will sweep the earth, war is likely to break out and the United States government will be in danger of being destroyed or reformed beyond recognition.

In short, this Capricorn conjunction and other imminent astrological phenomenon show that the period between late February 1988 and the year 2000 will be a time of karmic summing up. And not one of us will be exempt from that karmic summing up. For the Twenty-Four Elders have said, "The time has come for the people of earth to balance their personal as well as their planetary accounts."

During this period we are likely to see the reform, disruption or dissolution of economic and political systems, revolution, major cataclysm and war. Moreover, if the psyche of the nation does not collectively integrate with the Inner Self, we will see a national schizophrenia, a schism so wide as to be irreparable absent total conversion of the soul by the Holy Spirit to the Universal Christ.

3

Cataclysm: Nature's Transmutation
The Nature Kingdom Needs the Violet Flame to Save the Earth

Virgo and Pelleur, hierarchs of the gnomes, the Nature spirits who serve God and man in the earth element, delivered a warning of planetary upheaval through me on April 6, 1980. Their message was part of a series of dictations by the four hierarchs of the Nature kingdom delivered April 6 through 27, 1980. They said:

In past ages when the discord, death and disease self-created by mankind have reached proportions greater than that which the elementals could bear, Nature herself has convulsed; and earth in upheaval (through the conscious cooperation of the hierarchs of the gnomes, the sylphs, the undines and the fiery salamanders) has overturned mankind's misguided and malicious mechanization of life. . . . Thus it was elemental life who unleashed the fountains of the deep, causing the great deluge that resulted in the sinking of the continent of Atlantis and the flood of Noah. . . .

We come therefore to state our case on behalf of elemental life, to implore and to plead that Keepers of the Flame increase and intensify their invocations to the violet flame, standing shoulder to shoulder with the beings of the elements to transmute all human discord lest it become a burden too hard to bear and the pendulum of the Great Law swing again toward retribution through planetary cataclysm.

We send forth the warning to hearts of gold that if and unless there is a great intensification of the saturation of the earth body with the violet flame through the multiplication of the calls of Keepers of the Flame, there will be in this decade major planetary upheavals, changes in weather conditions and earthquakes that result in great loss of life as well as permanent changes in the geographical surface of the earth. . . .

We alert you, beloved ones, while there is yet adequate time and space for you to comply with the Law and provide the necessary counterbalance of God's consciousness and his sacred fire.[20]

On April 13, 1980, Oromasis and Diana, hierarchs of the salamanders, the Nature spirits who serve God and man in the fire element, underscored the need for the violet flame: "Again we say, the violet flame is the most effective and intense means of erasing the wrongs and hurts of the past."[21]

On May 18, 1980, just three weeks following the last in this series of dictations by the Hierarchs of the Elements, Mount St. Helens erupted. The massive explosion generated by this volcano, located in the Cascade Range in the state of Washington, had approximately 500 times the force of the atomic bomb dropped on Hiroshima.

In his June 1, 1980 dictation, Saint Germain told us that the amount of violet flame invoked by the evolutions of the planet had not been sufficient to completely transmute the residue of karma that the Law therefore required to precipitate physically for redemption:

The beings of the elements react in the fury and the fire from on high. And there comes out of the earth the message and the warning that is already come to Keepers of the Flame that unless sufficient quantity of violet flame be invoked, elemental life will no longer bear the burden of the cross of planetary karma and there will be in this decade significant changes in the very surface of the earth.

I had supposed that a greater response would be forthcoming from all of you to this message of Virgo and Pelleur in the *Pearls of Wisdom.* But it did not evoke immediately that sufficiency of light to stay the hand of this catastrophe but rather allowed it to manifest for all the world to see that coming upon them are those days that indeed ought to be feared by those who have not the fear of the LORD.

Now with the sounding of the rumblings in the earth as added warning as the adjustments continue, Keepers of the Flame are quickened and vitalized to the realization that it is indeed the requirement of the hour to increase their gift of the violet flame upon the altar of God . . . .

Once and for all, then, let Keepers of the Flame *know*—as I stand before you the Knight Commander and the Father of the Church and the one in whom is entrusted the balance of this two-thousand-year cycle—*know*, I tell you, that every word of every child of my heart, every dynamic decree is of ultimate import in these most trying hours!. . .

The question is: Can the sacred fire be so injected, can the enlightenment and the comfort of the Holy Spirit be so spread abroad by dedicated hearts that, indeed, further cataclysm at all levels of manifestation can be stayed?[22]

When the evolutions of a planet do not invoke enough violet flame to transmute their transgressions against Nature, karmic law decrees that Nature's form of "transmutation" must act. For when the time for resolution is upon the planetary spheres, only Mercy can stay the hand of impending karma. And Mercy is as Mercy does. It works through the merciful hearts of those in embodiment who keep the flame of Life and know that the daily invocation of mercy as the transmutative action of the violet flame is the means to "act in time to save nine."

In addition to the eruption of Mount St. Helens, the 1980s were marked by considerable upheaval. Even though natural disasters come regularly throughout the centuries, this decade had more than its share.

1980

October 10. An earthquake measuring 7.3 on the Richter scale in northwest Algeria killed 4,500 people.

November 23. An earthquake measuring 7.2 on the Richter scale in Naples, Italy, killed 4,800.

1981

July 12–15. Floods in Sichuan, China, killed 1,300 and caused $1.14 billion in property damage.

1982

May 12. The worst floods in 30 years in Guangdong, China, killed 430 and left 450,000 homeless.

August and September. Floods in northeastern India left 600 dead and 2.2 million homeless.

September 17–21. Floods in El Salvador and Guatemala killed 1,300.

December 13. An earthquake measuring 6.0 on the Richter scale in North Yemen killed 2,800.

1983

June. Monsoon rains in India killed 900.

October 30. An earthquake measuring 7.1 on the Richter scale in eastern Turkey killed 1,300.

1984

September 2. Typhoon *Ike* killed 1,363 and left 1.2 million homeless in the southern Philippines.

1985

May 25. A cyclone in Bangladesh killed 10,000.

May 31. Tornadoes in New York, Pennsylvania, Ohio and Ontario killed 90.

September 19–21. An earthquake registering 8.1 on the Richter scale struck the central and southwestern regions of Mexico, killing 25,000, destroying part of Mexico City and devastating three coastal states.

November 13. The Nevado del Ruiz volcano, 85 miles northwest of Bogotá, Colombia, catapulted fireballs into the air and sent an avalanche of mud, snow and trees into the towns of Armero and Chinchina, killing 25,000. About 90 percent of Armero was inundated, some places by as much as 30 feet of mud. It was the third most deadly volcanic eruption ever and the worst since the eruption of Mount Pelée killed 30,000 in Martinique in 1902.

1986

August 21. A cloud of poisonous gas released from Lake Nios in Cameroon swept through nearby villages and killed more than 1,700. The lake is situated in a volcanic crater. It is believed that the gas, probably composed of carbon dioxide and hydrogen sulfide, was released by an underground earthquake or landslide.

October 10. In El Salvador, an earthquake measuring 5.4 on the Richter scale caused extensive damage in San Salvador and killed at least 1,000.

1987

March 5–6. An earthquake measuring 7.3 on the Richter scale in northeast Ecuador killed more than 4,000.

1988

Spring. A severe drought across the United States caused more than $30 billion in agricultural losses and brought a heat wave that contributed to 10,000 deaths, making it the nation's worst natural disaster. The damage from drought-related forest fires was the greatest on record. During the late summer fires destroyed about 4 million acres of forest, including about half of Yellowstone National Park's 2.2 million acres.

August 2. Flash floods along China's east coast killed thousands and left tens of thousands homeless.

August–September. Monsoons caused flooding that inundated three-fourths of Bangladesh, killed 1,300 and left 30 million homeless.

August 21. An earthquake measuring 6.5 on the Richter scale killed at least 1,000 in remote areas of Nepal and India.

September 13. Hurricane Gilbert, one of strongest storms to hit the Caribbean, killed hundreds and left 500,000 homeless in Jamaica. 39 tornados spawned by Gilbert hit Texas. Gilbert did more than $10 billion worth of damage.

November 6. An earthquake measuring 7.3 on the Richter scale in southwest China near the Burmese border killed 1,000.

November 29. The worst cyclone to hit Bangladesh and eastern India in 20 years killed 1,300 and left 200,000 homeless. It destroyed 500,000 tons of crops and 50,000 houses.

December 7. An earthquake in Armenia measuring 6.9 on the Richter scale killed 25,000 and left 500,000 homeless. This was the worst earthquake to hit the Caucasus mountain region in 80 years.

1989

April 26. A tornado in central Bangladesh destroyed 20 villages, killed 1,000 and injured another 12,000.

July 9. Two earthquakes measuring 5.5 on the Richter scale hit the Izu Peninsula in Japan, triggering landslides and injuring at least 18 people. These were the strongest of 20,000 tremors that hit the peninsula in the previous 10 days. Also, an underwater volcano erupted off the shore of Ito, a resort town on the Izu peninsula.

September 17–22. Hurricane Hugo, with winds gusting up to 160 miles per hour, struck a dozen islands in the Caribbean, killed 33 and left 150,000 homeless. The storm destroyed about $2 billion worth of property and devastated the tourist economies of a number of the islands. Hugo then hit the Carolinas and Virginia, where it killed 28 and caused $4 billion in property damage. Charleston, S.C., was the worst hit, and many of its historic buildings were destroyed.

October 17. An earthquake measuring 7.1 on the Richter scale in the San Francisco Bay area killed 65, injured 3,000 and caused $8 billion in property damage.

October 18–19. A series of earthquakes jolted northeastern China in mostly rural areas west of Beijing. At least five of the quakes registered 5.0 or more on the Richter scale, the strongest one measuring 6.1. Twenty-nine people were killed and an estimated 60,000 left homeless.

December 14–15. Redoubt Volcano, 115 miles southwest of Anchorage, Alaska erupted, sending a column of volcanic ash 7 miles into the air.

December 27. An earthquake measuring 5.5 on the Richter scale in Newcastle, Australia, killed at least 9 and caused $1 billion in property damage.[23]

The calamities of the eighties are an index of just how much Nature can and cannot take of mankind's karma. These calamities marked the decade with more than ordinary upheaval and human suffering. While the number of disasters did not increase, the strength of hurricanes and volcanic eruptions as well as the severity of droughts did; and the loss of life and damage to economies was much greater than normal.

If only mankind knew they had the ability to work with elemental life to transmute the karmic causes of cataclysm brewing just beneath the surface of everyday life before it breaks out with such violence in the physical plane! Our invocation of Mercy's violet flame on behalf of the elementals must go hand in hand with our judicious care of the ecosystem and a profound respect and reverence for the laws governing Nature's cycles of self-renewal.

Though Mother Nature ever prefers the gentler way, when the sons and daughters of God fail to hold the balance of the yang and yin forces in the earth, cataclysm becomes Nature's only recourse to restore it. As I said before, when the people fail to do their part to clean up the mess they have made of the earth body and their own bodies, the Lords of Karma send forth the decree to all elemental life transmitted through their hierarchs, "The Great Law has pronounced: 'Thus far and no farther!'"

Thus, for want of man's communion with the sacred fire and his intercession on behalf of the Nature kingdom, for want of Divine Justice brother to brother, nation to nation, and for the desecration of Woman and the Child in society, major earth cataclysms have been unleashed at the end of cosmic cycles and they will be unleashed again ere we see the dawn of a golden age of Aquarius, if the people do not abandon their selfish and short-sighted violation of our planet's resources.

4

The United States of America
and the Union of Soviet Socialist Republics:
El Morya Unlocks the Mystery of Their Identities

Since I am going to be talking a good deal about the conjunctions of Mars, Saturn, Uranus and Neptune in Capricorn and other configurations in relation to the charts of the United States and the Soviet Union, I would like to introduce you to these charts.

In order to correctly interpret the astrological portents involving the United States and the Soviet Union, we must have the correct date and time for the birth of these nations. The first problem to be solved is: Which events marked the birth of each nation? The second: What is the precise hour of each event?

Official records were not kept for the times of key events in the birth of either the United States or the Soviet Union. The *Journals of the Continental Congress,* for example, do not record the time that resolutions were passed, the time debates began or ended, the time Congress adjourned—or even the time it commenced in the morning. Because official records provide limited information, historians and astrologers have had to rely on unofficial records such as letters and diaries as well as circumstantial evidence to argue for various times.

There is an ongoing debate among astrologers about the United States birth chart. Most astrologers assume that the United States was born July 4, 1776, the date the Declaration of Independence was signed.[24] Since 1987 I have explained to my audiences that according to the Ascended Master El Morya, the Fourth of July is not the birth date of the United States but the date of her conception. The nation's birth date, El Morya told me, was the occasion of the inauguration of George Washington as our first president.

It is clear from the history of the American Revolution that the United States was not born at the signing of the Declaration, but mightily conceived. It is a matter of record that the states did not intend to form a new nation concurrent with the adoption of the Declaration. The instructions the state legislatures sent to their delegates in Congress leave no doubt that the states intended to retain sovereignty and form a union later.

North Carolina, for example, authorized its delegates to vote for independence providing they reserved "to this colony the sole and exclusive right of forming a constitution and laws for this colony."[25] Virginia, in its instructions to its delegates, supported independence "provided that the power of forming government. . . be left to the respective colonial legislatures."[26] In fact, a company of militia volunteers from New Jersey initially refused to take an oath to the United States when they reported for duty to George Washington at Valley Forge on the grounds that "our country is New Jersey."[27] Men from other states felt the same.

In short, upon declaring their independence, the thirteen states considered themselves to be—and were—separate countries that looked forward to a time when they would be united in a confederation. It was not until the Constitution had been framed and ratified and George Washington was inaugurated as the nation's first president that the United States had a functioning national government.

Some astrologers even argue that other events that occurred days or years before the signing signified the birth. Helen Boyd and Jim Lewis claim the United States was born July 6, 1775, at 11 a.m. when Congress, sitting in Philadelphia, approved the Declaration of the Causes and Necessity of Taking Up Arms against the British. Julian Armistead argues that the United States was born on July 2, 1776, when Congress adopted a resolution that read in part: "That these United States are, and, of right, ought to be, Free and Independent States. . . ."[28] Both of these dates can be shown to be inaccurate on historical grounds.

Those who do see the signing of the Declaration as the birth of the nation argue over the time of day it occurred. The proposed times of birth range from 2:13 a.m. to 5:13:55 p.m. and the proposed Ascendants for the conceptional chart range from 7°14' Gemini to 13°10' Sagittarius. Most astrologers believe that the July Fourth chart has either a Gemini or a Sagittarius Ascendant. But there is support for a Virgo, Libra and Scorpio rising as well.

British astrologer Ebenezer Sibly, who in 1787 published the first-known astrological chart for the signing, was alive when the document was signed and thus was in the best position to research the time. Like many of the men who signed the Declaration, he was a Mason. Astrologer Michael Baigent argues that it is reasonable to assume that Sibly's Masonic brethren told him the time the document was signed.[29] Sibly said that the Declaration was signed at

5:10 p.m. Dane Rudhyar, a well-known twentieth century astrologer, rectified Sibly's chart for 5:13:55.*

What time, then, *was* the Declaration of Independence signed? Although the historical evidence is inconclusive, having reviewed the arguments, I believe that the existing evidence, combined with some inductive logic based on the character of the nation and the chart's response to transiting planets, strongly suggests a Sagittarius rising.

On November 14, 1989, I asked El Morya to solve the problem of the dates and times of the major historical events in the birth of the United States and the Soviet Union. The Master obliged by opening up the akashic records.

El Morya pegged the hour and the minute of the signing of the Declaration of Independence at exactly 5:13 p.m. on July 4, 1776. Therefore we now know for certain that America's conceptional Sun is at 13°19' Cancer, her conceptional Ascendant is at 12°59' Sagittarius and her conceptional Moon is at 27°12' Aquarius (fig. 2).

El Morya called the signing of the Declaration of Independence "the bravest conception there ever was."

Now let us turn to the United States birth chart. Sometime before he was inaugurated, George Washington had been anointed by Saint Germain to wear the mantle of the Great White Brotherhood in the highest office in the land. Both as general and as president, George Washington was destined to bear the flame of Liberty for America.

Therefore, on April 30, 1789, by the vote of the people as well as by divine approbation, the Christed one George Washington was officially given the mantle of the leadership of the nation. America was truly born that day and the people gained a sense of the national unity through the man God had sent to embody all they had fought for and won under his leadership.

Although Washington was scheduled to take the oath of office at noon, the ceremony was delayed for at least an hour. Historians' estimates range from 1:00 p.m. to 1:20 p.m. to 1:30 p.m.

El Morya has confirmed that the time of the birth of the United States of America is 1:30 p.m., April 30, 1789. Knowing this, we can precisely calculate her birth chart: her natal Sun is at 10°46' Taurus, her natal Ascendant is at 7°37' Virgo, and her natal Moon is at 16°35' Cancer (fig. 3).

I use the conceptional chart to study economic and political

*Rectification is a method of attempting to find the unknown moment of birth of a person or nation. The usual procedure is to compare the dates of known events in that person or nation's life with transits and progressions to the natal chart and then to adjust the birth time so that the key transits and progressions coincide with the events.

The United States of America
Conceptional Chart
July 4, 1776, 5:13 p.m.

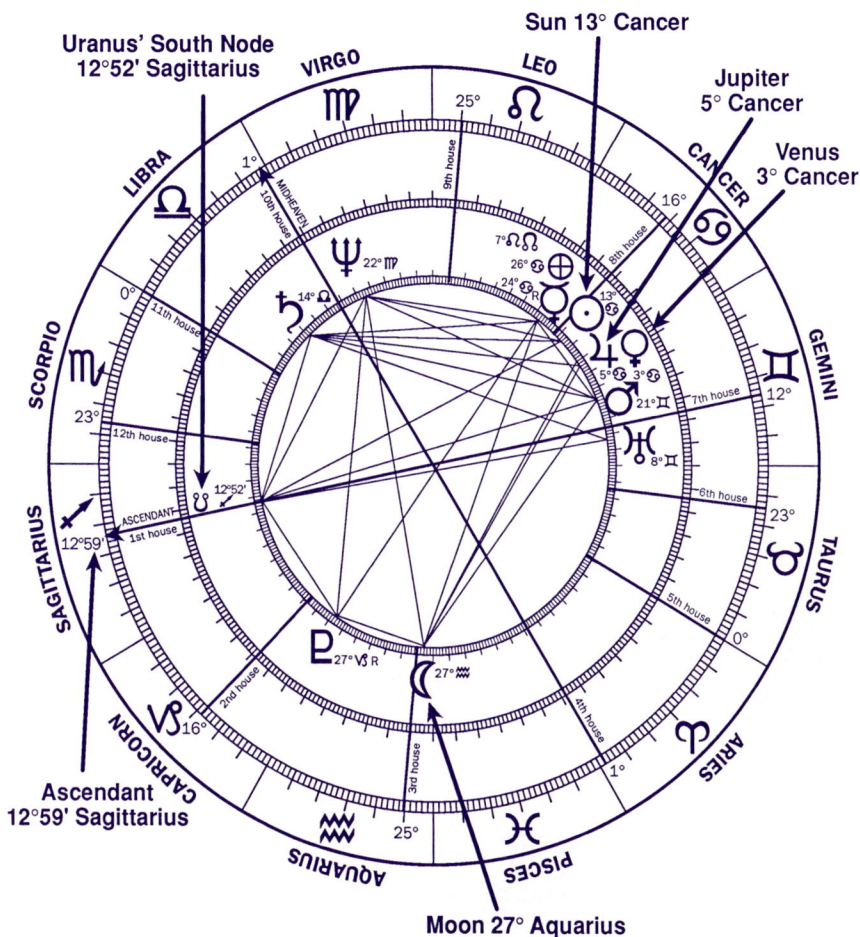

FIGURE 2 The United States was *conceived* at 5:13 p.m. Local Mean Time (LMT), July 4, 1776, in Philadelphia, Pennsylvania, at the signing of the Declaration of Independence. The United States conceptional Sun is at 13°19′ Cancer, the Moon is at 27°12′ Aquarius, and the Ascendant is at 12°59′ Sagittarius. The Sun forms a conjunction with Jupiter at 5° Cancer and Venus at 3° Cancer, which finds expression in the United States' expansive maternal nature and the impulse to nurture and protect. This conjunction also gives rise to the American people's deeply felt patriotism and strong sense of family. The Moon in Aquarius shows that the American family was destined to evolve to a higher level—but that the family is subject to fragmentation if the process of evolution takes place without commensurate spiritual growth. The Sagittarius Ascendant endows the nation with a philosophical, adventurous, freedom-loving temperament.

The United States of America
Birth Chart
April 30, 1789, 1:30 p.m.

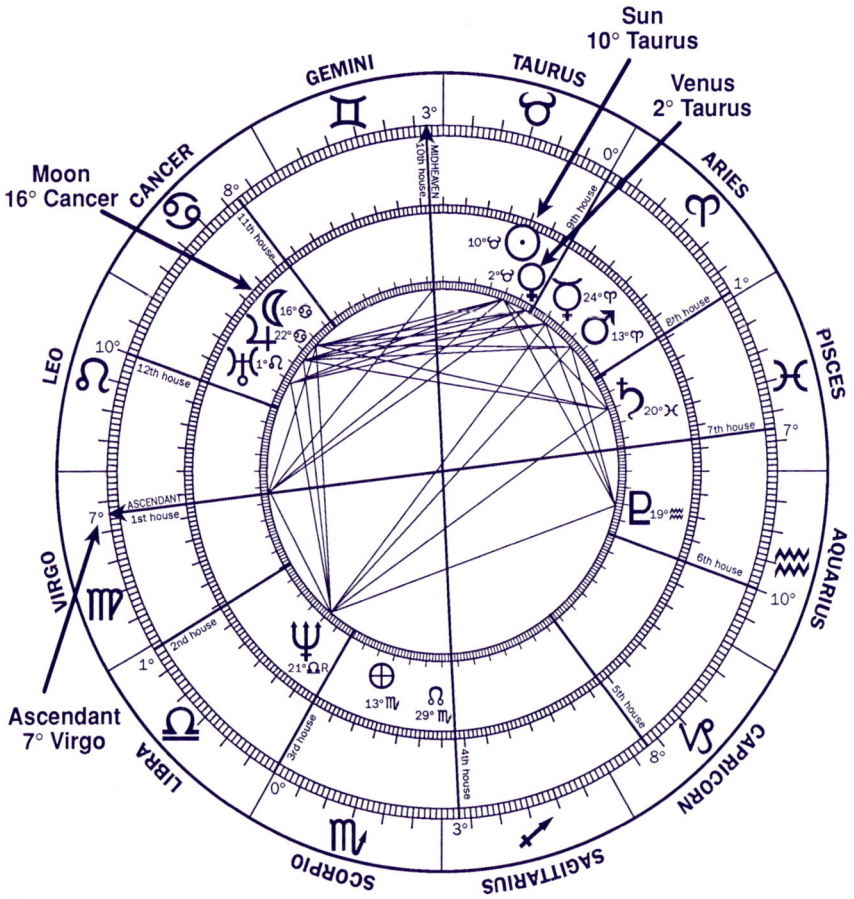

FIGURE 3 The United States of America was born at 1:30 p.m. LMT on April 30, 1789, when George Washington took the oath of office as her first president at Federal Hall in New York City. The Sun in the birth chart is at 10°46′ Taurus, the Moon is at 16°35′ Cancer and the Ascendant is at 7°37′ Virgo. The Sun is conjoined Venus at 2° Taurus, sextile the Moon and trine the Ascendant. This configuration is the basis for a stable, practical government. The Sun-Venus conjunction shows the nation's capacity to mobilize its agricultural, financial and commercial resources to generate great wealth. But it is also associated with conspicuous consumption, the concentration of wealth in a few hands, recessions or depressions, deficit spending and debt accumulation.

cycles and other national trends, and I use the birth chart to study the behavior of the economy and the psychology and conduct of American foreign policy, especially U.S.-Soviet relations.

Like the U.S. natal chart, the birth chart for the Soviet Union is subject to debate. Charts have been proposed for various hours of the day on the sixth, seventh, eighth and ninth of November 1917, the confused period when the Bolsheviks seized power over Mother Russia.

When El Morya opened up the akashic records to confirm the U.S. charts, he also revealed that the Soviet Union was born at 3 p.m., November 7, 1917. At that precise hour Lenin took the platform and delivered his famous speech proclaiming the triumph of the Bolshevik Revolution to the Petersburg Soviet with the words "Now begins a new era in the history of Russia, and this third Russian revolution must finally lead to the victory of Socialism. . . . Long live the worldwide Socialist revolution!"[30] The Soviet Union's Sun is at 14° 33′ Scorpio, her Moon is at 23° 37′ Leo, and her Ascendant is at 6° 48′ Aries (fig. 4).

El Morya called the Bolshevik Revolution "the most infamous act in the history of the world."

The Portents of the United States Conceptional Chart

One of the notable features of the United States conceptional chart is the conjunction of the binary star Sirius to the Sun at 13 degrees Cancer.[31] (fig. 5)

Sirius is the brightest star in the night sky. It was known by the ancients as the "Royal One." Its name has generally been derived from the Greek word for "sparkling" or "scorching." However, its name in Arabic, *Al Shi'ra,* and its name in Egyptian, Persian and other languages is so similar that the nineteenth-century German astronomer Christian Ideler thought they might have had a common ancient source, possibly the Sanskrit *Surya,* meaning "the Shining One, the Sun."[32]

Various astrologers say that when well-placed in a chart, Sirius gives honors, wealth, fame and commercial success. But it is also associated with danger and violence.

What the ancients knew we confirm. Sirius is the seat of galactic government of the Great White Brotherhood and the retreat of the Sun god Surya, one of the greatest gods in the Hindu pantheon, who was known to self-contain the God consciousness of the Sun and the all-power of that Presence.

The judgments of God meted out through the Cosmic Council of Sirius can be either sparkling or scorching, depending on whether you have exercised your free will to glorify the living God

Union of Soviet Socialist Republics
Birth Chart
November 7, 1917, 3:00 p.m.

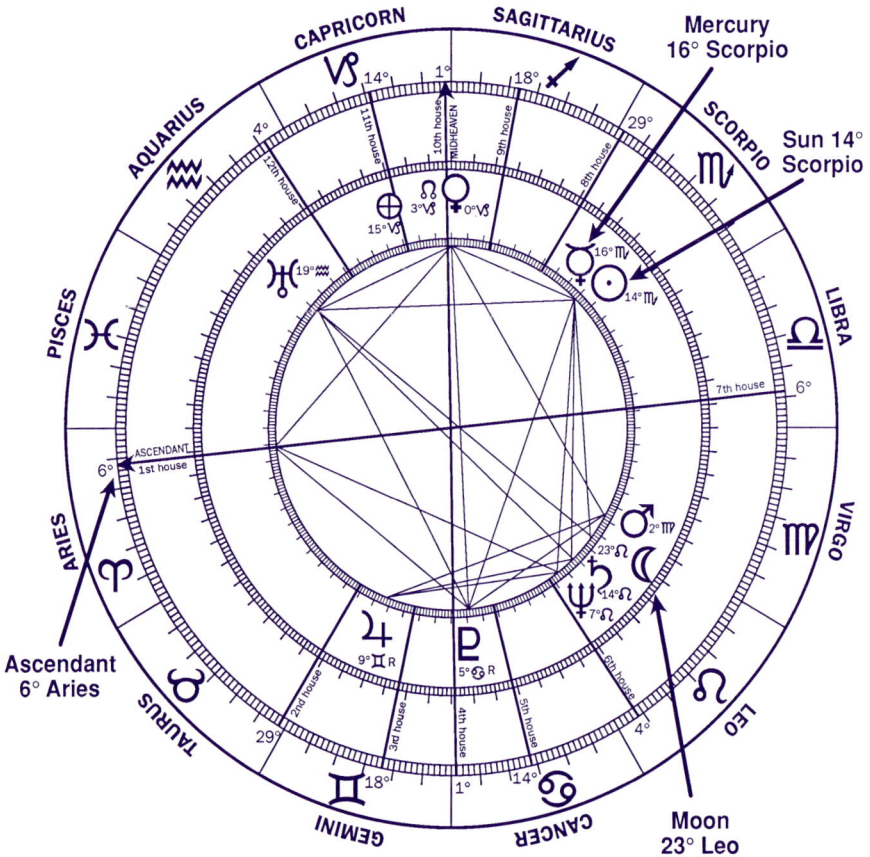

FIGURE 4   The Union of Soviet Socialist Republics was born following a nearly bloodless coup at 3:00 p.m. Eastern European Time (EET) in Saint Petersburg, Russia, on November 7, 1917. The Soviet Union's Sun is at 14° 33′ Scorpio, its Moon is at 23° 37′ Leo, and its Ascendant is at 6° 48′ Aries. Scorpio rules death and regeneration, science, engineering, military combat and joint economic relations. Because of the inherently secretive nature of the unevolved Scorpio, the Soviet Union is a closed society whose leaders restrict the information that reaches their people and the outside world. They have a need both to dominate and to protect themselves from domination, which drives them to view all other nations as enemies to be conquered. Scorpio secrecy leads to deception, which the Soviets have fashioned into a state policy and raised to a fine art.

The United States Conceptional Sun Conjoined Sirius

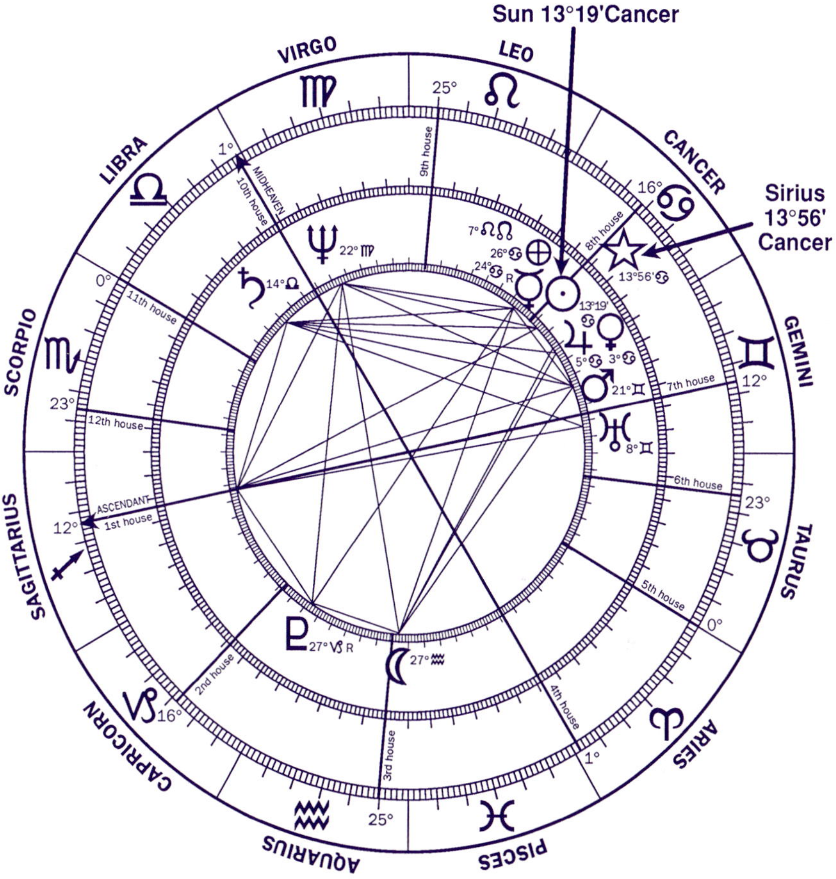

FIGURE 5 In 1776, Sirius, the brightest star in the night sky, was at 11°0′ Cancer conjoined the United States conceptional Sun at 13°19′ Cancer. Since fixed stars move forward in the zodiac at the rate of about 1 degree every 72 years, Sirius is now at 13°56′ Cancer but still conjoined the conceptional Sun. Sirius was known by the ancients as the "Royal One." Well-placed, Sirius gives honors, wealth, fame and commercial success. It is also associated with danger and violence. Its name is thought to be derived from the Greek word for "sparkling" or "scorching." It could also be traced back to the Sanskrit *Surya*, meaning "the Shining One." Sirius is the seat of galactic government of the Great White Brotherhood and the Sun god Surya. The judgments of God through the Cosmic Council can be either sparkling or scorching, depending on your past use of free will.

in all your houses and members (i.e., in the astrological opportunities of all lifetimes) or to espouse a cause fomenting the denial of
that God in his sons and daughters.

Thus the intensity of the light of Sirius multiplies our posi-
tives and brings to final judgment our negatives—and us with
them. To spawn an illusory energy veil, called "evil," for the
glorification of the lesser ego, to promote the denial of the Divine
One, is indeed the means of canceling out the self that was made
in the image of the God Self. For we are not separate from our
creations, as God is not separate from his. In truth we are what we
create and we create ourselves. Thus our star rises or falls by our
works as well as by our words.

Sun-Jupiter-Venus Conjunction

The U.S. conceptional chart has several other distinguishing
characteristics. Her conceptional Sun at 13° Cancer forms a conjunction with Jupiter at 5° Cancer and Venus at 3° Cancer. The Sun,
the most important body in the conjunction, gives life, identity,
vitality and will power. In mundane astrology it is associated with
the national identity and leadership. The sign of Cancer rules home,
mother, family, land, food, the people, women and patriotism.

This conjunction finds expression in our country's expansive
maternal nature and the impulse to nurture, feed and protect. It
shows the American people's deep attachment to the land of their
birth, strong patriotism and their healthy concern for or not so
healthy preoccupation with the material world. It also shows the
potential for great wealth and abundance as well as extravagance,
waste, indulgence and overexpansion.

The Sun-Jupiter-Venus conjunction in Cancer is the primary
source of the strong American sense of home and family and the
tendency to withdraw into home and family as a place of refuge in
time of trouble. The family has become an idealized institution in
the United States. But because of the placement of the Moon
(which rules Cancer) in the evolutionary sign of Aquarius, the
institution of the family (and more broadly, the concept of community) was destined to evolve in America. We have seen this
occur particularly as new technologies have made life easier, as
women have gained greater social and political freedom, and as
new legislation has affected the family for better or worse.

The Challenge of an Aquarius Moon

The Moon in Aquarius gives the United States the opportunity to create a new model or mode of expression for the family on

a higher level. It shows the possibility of establishing Aquarian communities based on an evolved family unit. But such developments require much inner growth. Absent spiritual development, the innovations that were likely under its influence could impede or reverse the evolutionary process and fragment the family.

Right now the family is under stress—if not assault. "Fifteen million American children, one quarter of the population under 18, are growing up today without fathers," writes social commentator Nicholas Davidson. "This is the greatest social catastrophe facing our country. It is at the root of the epidemics of crime and drugs, it is deeply implicated in the decline in educational attainment, and it is largely responsible for the persistence of widespread poverty despite generous government support for the needy."[33]

We are all aware of the symptoms of the besieged family— high divorce rates, teenage pregnancy, increased welfare, rising crime and drug abuse, battered wives, child abuse and so on. Throughout the eighties both political parties have pledged to "save the family."

But there is no consensus about how to do it. Some say that Congress (a Uranian/Aquarian institution) is partially to blame for the breakup of the family. According to Davidson, legislation that made divorce and welfare much easier also increased the number of single women managing frequently impoverished households with children. Children who grow up without fathers are statistically more likely to get involved in drugs and crime and to demonstrate lower achievement in school than children from two-parent homes.

It is tempting to try to define the problems facing the family with an abundance of statistics and sociological rationales. But statistics measure effects, not causes. First and foremost, the problem of the family is spiritual. The astrology of the United States conceptional chart requires spiritual growth as a prerequisite to maintaining family health and cohesion while the institution evolves.

And the challenges to the family are certain to increase. Pluto, transiting in Scorpio, begins to form a square to the conceptional Moon in Aquarius in January of 1990. As the square grows tighter and becomes exact on January 4 and April 24, 1994, the family unit will be under far greater stress than we have seen thus far.

Jupiter, Ruler of the United States Conceptional Chart

The United States conceptional Ascendant is 12°59′ Sagittarius. The planet which rules the sign on the Ascendant is considered to be the ruler of the chart. Jupiter rules Sagittarius, hence it rules the U.S. conceptional chart. This greatly amplifies the Jupiterian/Sagittarian influence in the life of the nation.

Jupiter is a planet that tends to amplify or magnify whatever it touches. It rules philosophy, religion, higher education, the judiciary and the nation's legal theory, church/state relations, great wealth, ambassadors and foreign affairs.

A Sagittarius Ascendant shows a temperament that is philosophical, religious and abstract, expansive and international, optimistic, just, prophetic, adventurous and freedom loving. If you take our national/international profile as individuals and as "Uncle Sam," that description fits.

Talking about the Sagittarius Ascendant in the U.S. chart, Dane Rudhyar points out that "the Sagittarian temperament is also usually considered to have the following characteristics: self-righteousness, the desire to be loved, dependence on intuition rather than on strictly intellectual logic, an outspoken, impulsive and demonstrative temperament, good fellowship, generosity, humanitarianism, joviality and philosophical optimism, love of sports and of distant journeys or adventures. Our ambitious schemes and passionate desire for expansion and for 'bigger and better' results [are also Sagittarian]."[34] But the Sagittarius temperament can also be hypocritical, tyrannical, bigoted, hard-hearted, bombastic, blunt, undiplomatic and shortsighted.

Sagittarius gives the urge to develop one's world view, to bring it into manifestation and to live by it. Between 1760–1775, when an ideological revolution took place in America, this urge was a preoccupation. This period of philosophical ferment, and not the war, was the real revolution. "The Revolution," observed John Adams, "was in the minds of the people, and this was effected from 1760 to 1775, . . . before a drop of blood was shed at Lexington."[35]

Uranus and the Impulse for Freedom

For the most part, astrologers have been unsuccessful in discovering the astrological impulse for the American Revolution. Some have tried to explain the fervor for revolution by theorizing that the U.S. conceptional chart (they call it the birth chart) has Gemini rising. Then Uranus (the planet of revolution) would conjoin the U.S. Ascendant. However, they disregard the fact that the Declaration of Independence would have had to have been signed between 2 a.m. and 4 a.m. for this to be correct.

In any case, we can find the drive for revolution right in the U.S. conceptional chart with a Sagittarius Ascendant. The heliocentric south node of Uranus* is conjoined the U.S. conceptional Ascendant in Sagittarius. Uranus' heliocentric south node is now at 13°59' Sagittarius. In 1776 it was at 12°52' Sagittarius conjoined the U.S. conceptional Ascendant at 12°59' Sagittarius. This conjunction combines the impulse for freedom, innovation and revolution (Uranus' south node) with the drive to externalize and expand a way of life built on a philosophical, religious and legal world view (Sagittarius).

Rudhyar writes of the effect of the conjunction of the U.S. conceptional Ascendant with Uranus' south node, "When the [Ascendant is conjoined] to the line of Uranus' nodes there is an absolutely basic, karmic or structural identification between the person's individuality and Uranus. Indeed the individual person [or nation] is born indelibly stamped with Uranus' power, and fated to act as a transforming force in society, as an 'agent' of Uranus."[36]

Since Jupiter is the ruler of Sagittarius, which is conjoined Uranus' south node, it picks up the revolutionary impulse from the node. And since Jupiter is conjoined the Sun, representing the national identity, this revolutionary-philosophical influence is an integral part of the American identity. The Moon (ruler of Cancer, the sign where the Sun and Jupiter are placed in the U.S. conceptional chart) is in Uranus-ruled Aquarius, indicating that the impulse for freedom is an essential element of the political culture.

Jupiter-Sagittarius-Uranus' South Node Bungling

The influences of Jupiter, Sagittarius, and Uranus' south node may not always be positively expressed. In their negative expression, they are associated with incompetent or militant foreign relations, religious intolerance, inflation, the misuse of foreign aid, an inflated sense of self-importance, and inattention to detail, sudden, unpredictable, eccentric and tyrannical actions, anarchic or repressive behavior, radical ideology, guerrilla warfare and alliances of war.

It also shows that the United States has the propensity to launch out in international matters—military, diplomatic and economic—without thinking through the details of her plan or the consequences of her actions.

It is easy to catalog modern U.S. military misadventures, from the conduct of the Vietnam War to Jimmy Carter's abortive

---

*Every planet has heliocentric nodes. They are the two points—the north, or ascending node, and the south, or descending node—where the planet's orbit intersects the plane of the earth's orbit around the Sun. The nodes are 180° apart.

rescue of U.S. hostages held in Iran to the Iran-Contra scandal. Even one of the most "successful" U.S. military adventures of the eighties, the invasion of Grenada, was an embarrassing tangle of small disasters.

From start to finish, it was typical of Jupiter-Sagittarius-Uranus' south node bungling. On October 25, 1983, the United States invaded the tiny island of Grenada. President Reagan told the nation, still feeling the effects of failed attempts to rescue Americans in Iran, that the armed forces "are standing tall again."[37] Yet twenty thousand American soldiers had difficulty defeating a handful of Cubans and a small detachment of Grenadians.

To begin with, the entire operation was planned in four days. That in itself created considerable confusion. The CIA had no agents on the island, hence intelligence was understandably thin. Nor did the military have any up-to-date maps. The U.S. Defense Mapping Agency finally came up with a complete set on November 2, a week after the fighting ended. Soldiers, however, fought with tourist maps and antiquated British charts. Vice Admiral Joseph Metcalf, a U.S. commander, used one dated 1895.

But this was not the least of the difficulties. Troops were unable to communicate effectively because there were not enough batteries to run their secure voice radios. A shipment of batteries finally arrived after the fighting was over. But while U.S. troops were fighting, the Army couldn't talk to the Navy or the Air Force to the Marines. The commanders couldn't even communicate from land to ships they could see offshore.

And then there was the problem of attacking the wrong targets. An A-7 attack jet destroyed an insane asylum, killing seventeen people. Another A-7 mistakenly attacked a command post of the 82d Airborne Division, wounding seventeen U.S. soldiers, one of whom later died.

But what borders on astonishing is that the military did not know the location of the six hundred American students at St. George's University Medical School. This is almost beyond comprehension because, as writer James Perry points out,

> President Reagan had told the nation the prime reason for the invasion was to safeguard more than 600 young Americans attending the island's St. George's University Medical School. The invading force was informed that all these U.S. students were living at the school's Grand Anse campus. In fact, most of them were at the True Blue campus and living

on the Lance aux Epines peninsula. Their parents knew that. A phone call could have confirmed it, for the school's switchboard was in full operation.[38]

Economic Influences in the U.S. Conceptional Chart

The United States has a number of indicators of material well being and financial success in both her conceptional and her birth chart. However, her astrology indicates that her economy is subject to periods of boom and bust, and to being dominated by a power elite.

The Sun-Jupiter-Venus conjunction in Cancer in the U.S. conceptional chart shows an abundance of resources, a tendency to inflate the currency, and a strong drive for material success and comfort. But it does not explain the American capacity to efficiently produce large quantities of crops through successfully harnessing technology. Nor does it explain her sophisticated business and financial structure. We find these in her birth chart. However, this conjunction is a good indicator of periods of boom and bust.

Saturn at 14° Libra is square to the Sun-Jupiter-Venus conjunction in Cancer. Saturn is the planet of crystallization and precipitation and provides the concrete element to the conjunction of the Sun, Jupiter and Venus in Cancer in the seventh house. It facilitates the physical precipitation of the potential wealth of the Cancer planets.

The square of Saturn helps make this expansive and somewhat impractical grouping practical and organized. Saturn has the tendency to constrict flow, in this case of the nation's money and economic activity. At times the square of Saturn to these planets decreases or blocks the flow of abundance. Since Jupiter rules expansion and Saturn rules contraction, it is one of several indicators of the inflation-recession/depression cycle.

Pluto at 27° Capricorn in the second house of the nation's wealth, banks, stock exchanges and currency is opposed to Mercury at 24° Cancer in the eighth house of the national debt and interest rates. This is the principal indicator for domination of the economy by a power elite. Pluto in Capricorn also has the capacity to reduce or destroy the nation's supply of money. Therefore, since Saturn rules Capricorn, the square of Saturn to Jupiter and the opposition of Pluto in Capricorn to Mercury in Cancer may at times interact to seriously reduce economic activity in the United States.

Saturn's square to Jupiter and its trine to Uranus are crucial to understanding the economic dynamics and financial success of the United States (fig. 6). The square of Saturn (system and

Saturn Square Jupiter and Trine Uranus
in the United States Conceptional Chart

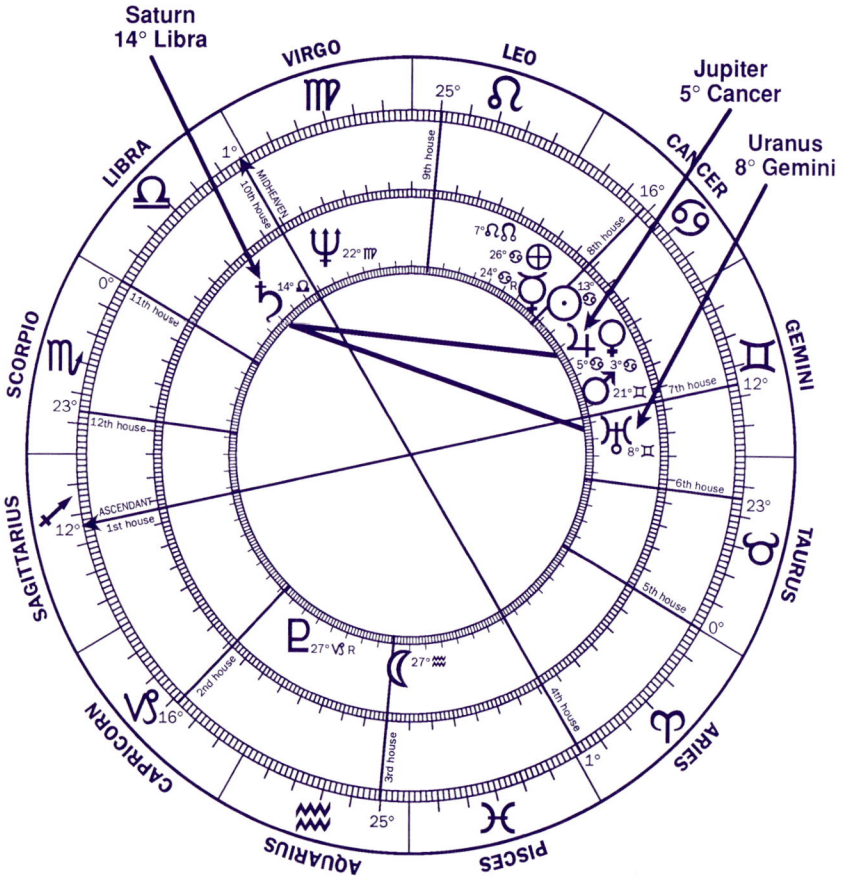

FIGURE 6 Saturn at 14° Libra, Jupiter at 5° Cancer and Uranus at 8° Gemini in the United States conceptional chart are the astrological foundation of the nation's economic system. Saturn (system and organization) square Jupiter (wealth and expansion) establishes a framework for producing wealth through a free market economy (Uranus). Saturn trine Uranus shows a skilled labor force, technological development and advanced methods of agriculture. Saturn (political power and the form of government) has the power to limit, divide or separate. In Libra (law), Saturn points to a system of government based on the separation of powers and checks (Saturn) and balances (Libra). Saturn (order) trine Uranus (freedom and innovation) are the basis for a new form of government that establishes political liberty and "a new order of the ages"—the words inscribed on the Great Seal of the United States, *Novus Ordo Seclorum.*

organization) to Jupiter (wealth and expansion) establishes a theoretical (Jupiter) and practical (Saturn) framework for a dynamic economic system capable of producing wealth through a free market economy (Uranus) and property rights.

The Saturn-Uranus trine indicates innovations in the work place, a skilled labor force, technological development and advanced agricultural methods. It also holds the possibility of economic and political freedom for the working man.

A New Order of the Ages

When considering the organization of a national economy, it is important to remember that a nation's economic system is dependent on her political system. The form of the United States government is clearly described, in principle, by the square of Saturn in Libra to the Sun conjoined Jupiter in Cancer and the trine of Saturn to Uranus in Gemini. This configuration anticipates—and is the astrological underpinning for—the framing, adoption and activation of the Constitution as the supreme law of the land.

Saturn rules the national administration, political power and the form of government. In the conceptional chart it is placed in the tenth house, which it rules, and in the sign of Libra, where it is exalted.* Since Libra rules the law, Saturn in Libra in the tenth house is a sign that the United States was destined to elevate and revere the law. As Thomas Paine said, "In America, the Law is King."[39]

Saturn, which has the capacity to precipitate also has the power to limit, divide or separate. Hence we see the astrological matrix for the separation of powers, a concept imported from Europe (Jupiter in the seventh house) and applied (Saturn) for the benefit of the people (Cancer) in a practical (Saturn) legal (Libra) framework.

Libra rules equality, justice and cooperation. In simple terms, we are describing an equitable (Libra) system of government (Saturn/tenth house) that depends on checks (Saturn) and balances (Libra) in order to divide power and protect liberty—and where all are equal (Libra) before the law (Saturn in Libra).

Because Saturn rules order and Uranus rules newness, freedom and innovation, the Saturn-Uranus trine is the basis for a new form of government, a "new order" that establishes political liberty. The nation's founders inscribed the words *Novus Ordo Seclorum*, "a new order of the ages," under the unfinished pyramid that appears on the reverse side of the Great Seal of the United States.

---

*When a planet is exalted, its influence is strengthened and it easily expresses its highest characteristics.

The conceptional chart contains many of the potentialities that eventually came into being once the Constitution was framed, ratified and went into effect and George Washington was inaugurated. But many aspects of the national life and personality that are not explained by the conceptional chart are explained by the birth chart.

The Portents of the United States Birth Chart

The conceptional chart shows a national temperament that is philosophical, idealistic, revolutionary and freedom loving. The United States birth chart, with its Sun at 10° Taurus, shows a temperament that is stable, practical, patient and materialistic (fig. 3).

Venus rules the sign of Taurus, and the United States Sun is conjoined Venus at 2° Taurus. Venus and Taurus rule banks, stock exchanges, the nation's currency, commercial affairs, trade, fertile fields and grain. The conjunction of the Sun and Venus in Taurus indicates a strong economy, equitable distribution of wealth and budget surpluses.

The Sun-Venus conjunction also shows ardent appreciation and support for the arts and a love for music. On the negative side, it shows a propensity for government and nationally known figures to become involved in sex scandals.

The United States birth chart carries forward the potential for wealth found in the conceptional chart and gives it practical expression. The natal Sun at 10° Taurus conjoined Venus at 2° Taurus, sextile the Moon at 16° Cancer and trine the Ascendant at 7° Virgo forms the basis for a stable, practical government and a strong economy with intricate technology. It shows the nation's capacity to mobilize her agricultural, financial and commercial resources to generate great wealth. But it is also associated with conspicuous consumption, the concentration of wealth in a few hands, recessions or depressions, deficit spending and debt accumulation.

The United States natal Saturn at 20° Pisces in the seventh house of foreign affairs is quincunx Neptune at 21° Libra in the second house of money and banking (fig. 7). This is the basis for the nation's tendency to be cautious, isolationist, idealistic and compassionate in her relations with other nations, in contrast to influences in the United States conceptional chart that indicate a bold, opportunistic and internationalist approach to foreign affairs.

Saturn quincunx Neptune denotes American generosity to other nations; but it also shows that U.S. foreign policy tends to be

Saturn Quincunx Neptune in the
United States Birth Chart

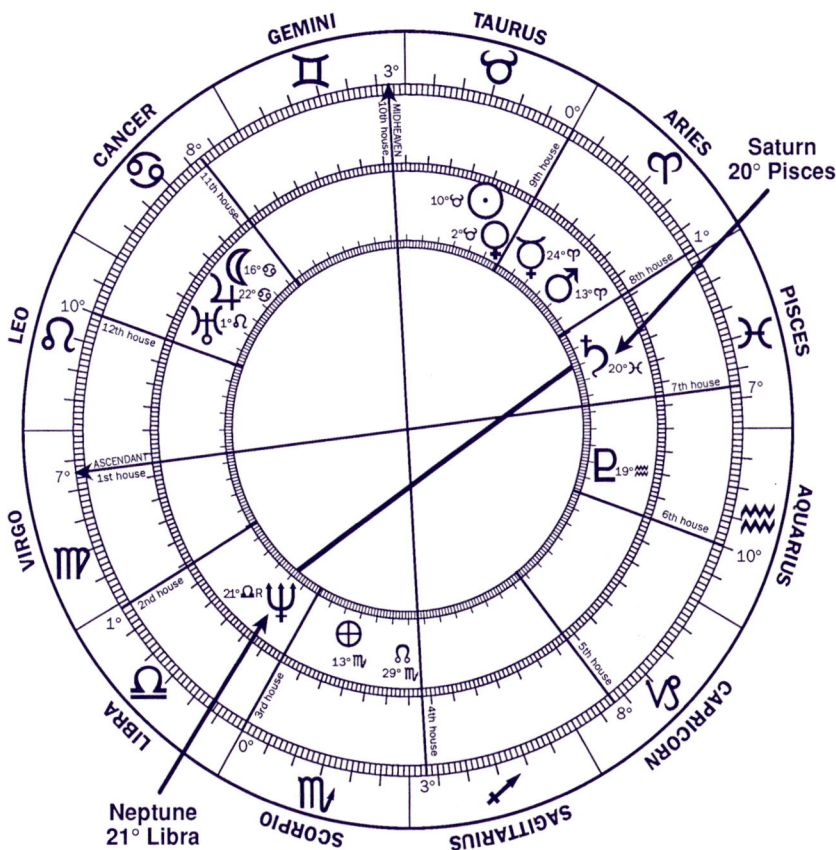

FIGURE 7 The United States natal Saturn at 20° Pisces in the seventh house of foreign affairs is quincunx (150° apart from) Neptune at 21° Libra in the second house of money and banking. This is the basis for the United States' tendency to be cautious, isolationist, idealistic and compassionate in its relations with other nations (in contrast to influences in the United States conceptional chart that indicate a bold, opportunistic and internationalist approach to foreign affairs). The Saturn quincunx Neptune shows that U.S. foreign policy tends to be bureaucratic and plagued by confusion, deception, false idealism and a lack of resolve. This aspect denotes American generosity to other nations. But it also shows the potential to form alliances based on international trade and finance that serve the interests of the business community but not of the nation.

bureaucratic and plagued by confusion, deception, false idealism and a lack of resolve. It indicates the potential to form alliances based on international trade and finance that serve the interests of the business community but not of the nation. And it shows false expectations related to the capacity of foreign aid to influence other nations.

The United States natal Neptune at 21° Libra in the second house (of money and finance) makes an opposition to Mars at 13° Aries and Mercury at 24° Aries in the eighth house (of taxes and interest rates). These planets square the Moon at 16° Cancer and Jupiter at 22° Cancer in the eleventh house (of Congress), forming a T-square (fig. 8).

The configuration shows an expansive economy and great wealth. But Neptune in the second house shows deception in the management of the nation's currency. And its square to Pluto in Capricorn in the United States conceptional second house shows that the nation's finances (and thus the government) could be dominated by a financial elite.

There are a few elements in the United States birth chart that indicate the potential for innovations in government which restrict freedom rather than enhance it. Even though the impulse for freedom exists in the conceptional chart—signaled by Uranus trine Saturn and Uranus' south node conjoined the Ascendant—it may not be expressed through the birth chart without enlightened leadership.

Uranus in the U.S. birth chart is at 1° Leo in the eleventh house of Congress and legislation square the Sun and Venus in Taurus. It also indicates conflicts and power struggles between Congress and the president. This indicates the potential for a power-hungry Congress to pass oppressive legislation that increases the power of the federal government.

Pluto is at 19° Aquarius (the sign ruled by Uranus) in the sixth house (of the civil service, the armed forces, the labor force, and the national food supply). Because Pluto is in the sign ruled by Uranus, there is a relationship between the two planets. This shows the potential for the loss of freedom through a congressionally created, unelected bureaucracy. It also shows that Americans are vulnerable through an unhealthy diet which could compromise a strong, decisive national identity.

As Pluto transiting in Scorpio makes its square to the U.S. natal Pluto at 19° Aquarius (exact on December 16, 1990, May 5, 1991, and October 13, 1991) we can expect to see an increase in labor unrest, food shortages or famine, and the destruction or disintegration of our armed forces.

The Moon, Mercury, Mars, Jupiter and Neptune Form a T-Square in the United States Birth Chart

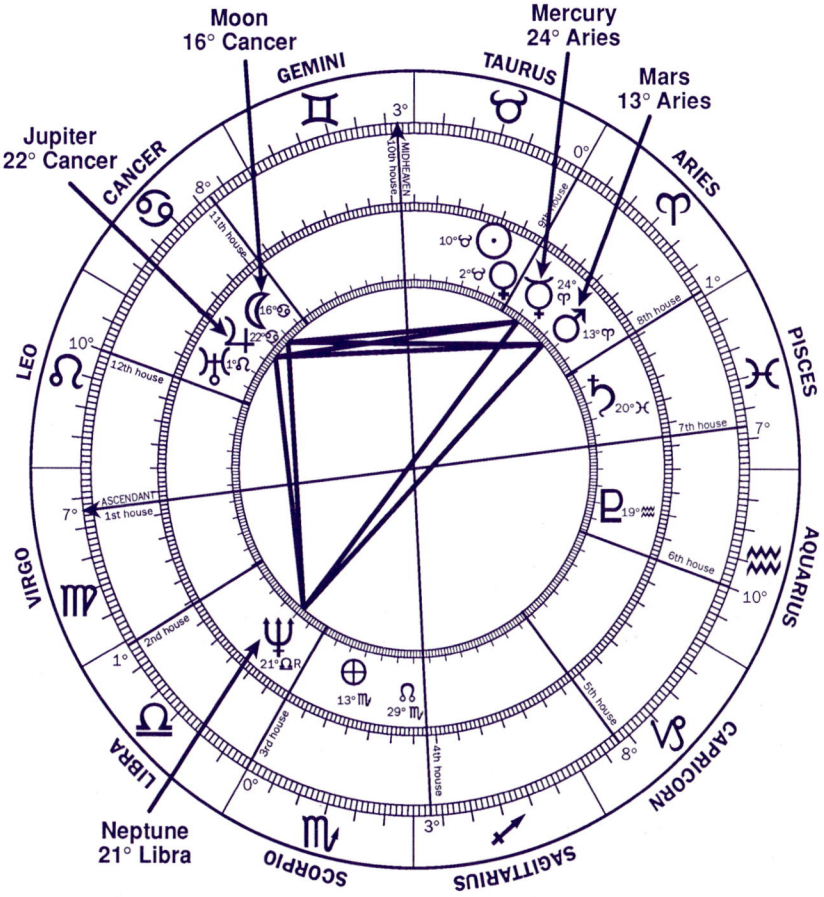

FIGURE 8 The United States natal Neptune at 21° Libra in the second house (of money and finance) makes an opposition to Mars at 13° Aries and Mercury at 24° Aries in the eighth house (of taxes and interest rates). These planets square the Moon at 16° Cancer and Jupiter at 22° Cancer in the eleventh house (of Congress), forming a right triangle called a T-square. The configuration shows an expansive economy and great wealth. But Neptune shows deception in the management of the nation's currency and squares Pluto in Capricorn in the United States conceptional second house, showing that the nation's finances (and thus the government) could be dominated by a financial elite.

The Portents of the Birth Chart of the Soviet Union

The Soviet Union's Sun is at 14° 33′ Scorpio, the sign which rules death and regeneration, science, engineering, military combat and joint economic relations. Because of the inherently secretive nature of the unevolved Scorpio, the Soviet Union is a closed society whose leaders restrict the information that reaches their people and the outside world. The Sun in Scorpio gives them a need both to dominate and to protect themselves from domination and inclines them to view all other nations as enemies to be conquered. Scorpio secrecy leads to deception, which the Soviets have fashioned into a state policy and raised to a fine art.

The Soviet Union's Neptune at 7° Leo, Saturn at 14° Leo and Moon at 23° Leo (in the sixth house of the work force, the armed forces and the national food supply) oppose her Uranus at 19° Aquarius (in the twelfth house of prisons, espionage and the secret police). These planets square the Soviet Sun at 14° Scorpio conjoined Mercury at 16° Scorpio (in the seventh house of foreign affairs, treaties and war), forming a T-square (fig. 9).

This configuration shows that the Soviets are clever strategists and indefatigable propagandists, but that they are unable to use their indigenous pool of scientific and engineering talent to establish a productive economy. It also shows the Soviet tendency to use political repression, espionage, secrecy, deception and military force to solve their economic and political problems.

Pluto, the planet of power and control, at 5° Cancer (in the fourth house of the people) at 1° Capricorn shows systematic domestic repression, the use of secret police, poor agricultural production and intentionally created famines.

The United States natal Sun at 10°46′ Taurus and the Soviet Union's natal Sun at 14°33′ Scorpio are in polarity (fig. 10). In astrological terms they form an opposition, an aspect that can show either union and cooperation or separation and conflict. Since this polarity involves the nations' Suns (which represent the national identity and leadership), it shows that at times the United States and the Soviet Union are cooperative and at other times not. In general, however, the superpowers are likely to be cooperating *and* competing, at once friends *and* enemies. For example, on October 24, 1973, during the heyday of detente, the threat of direct Soviet intervention in the Yom Kippur War between Israel and a coalition of Arab states nearly provoked a nuclear exchange.

In the late 1980s and early 1990s, transiting planets will severely impact the United States and Soviet charts, a subject we will take up in succeeding chapters.

The Sun, Moon, Mercury, Saturn, Uranus and Neptune Form a T-Square in the Soviet Union's Birth Chart

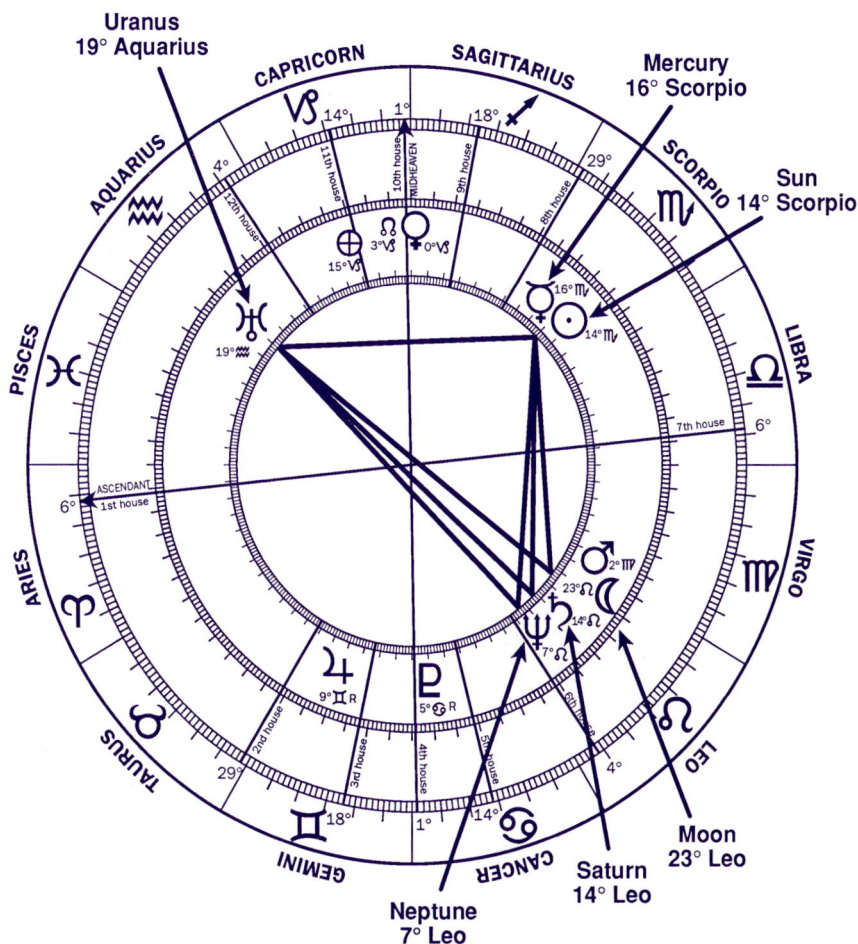

FIGURE 9 The Soviet Union's Neptune at 7° Leo, Saturn at 14° Leo and Moon at 23° Leo (in the sixth house of the work force, the armed forces, and the national food supply) oppose her Uranus at 19° Aquarius (in the twelfth house of prisons, espionage and the secret police). These planets square the Soviet Sun at 14° Scorpio conjoined Mercury at 16° Scorpio (in the seventh house of foreign affairs, treaties and war), forming a right triangle called a T-square. This configuration shows that the Soviets are clever strategists and indefatigable propagandists, but that they are unable to use their indigenous pool of scientific and engineering talent to establish a productive economy. It also shows the Soviet tendency to use political repression, espionage, secrecy, deception and military force to solve their economic and political problems.

The Soviet Union's Sun
Opposed the United States Sun

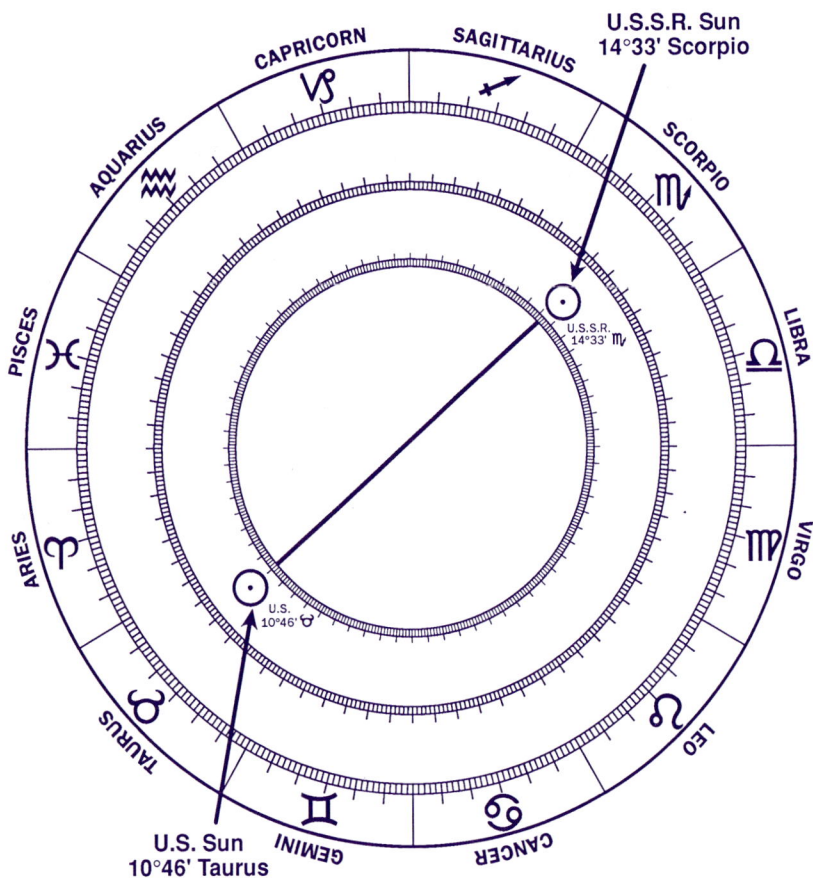

FIGURE 10 The United States natal Sun at 10°46′ Taurus and the Soviet Union's natal Sun at 14°33′ Scorpio are in polarity. In astrological terms they form an opposition, an aspect that can show either union and cooperation or separation and conflict. Since this polarity involves the nations' Suns (which represent the national identity and leadership) it shows that at times the United States and the Soviet Union are cooperative and at other times not. In general, however, the superpowers are likely to be cooperating *and* competing, at once friends *and* enemies. For example, on October 24, 1973, during the heyday of detente, the threat of direct Soviet intervention in the Yom Kippur War between Israel and a coalition of Arab states nearly provoked a nuclear exchange.

The Mars-Saturn-Uranus-Neptune Conjunction:
The Four Horsemen in Capricorn Influence Economic Affairs

War is related to economic affairs and often follows or is triggered by problems in national economies. Therefore, let us return to our discussion of the February 22 and 23, 1988, conjunction of Mars, Saturn, Uranus and Neptune in Capricorn and follow the development of these astrological influences in economic affairs.

This is not the first time a powerful Capricorn conjunction has strongly affected the United States. On December 30, 1929, Venus, Mars, Saturn, the Sun and the Moon formed a conjunction between 0° and 10° in Capricorn (fig. 11) just as the United States was sliding into the Great Depression. This conjunction spanned the same area of the zodiac (0°–10° Capricorn) as the conjunction for February 22 and 23, 1988 (0°–9° Capricorn). On December 31, 1929, Mercury was at 27° Capricorn conjoined to the U.S. conceptional Pluto and opposed to her conceptional Mercury at 24° Cancer.

The Capricorn conjunction of December 30, 1929, also made an opposition to the U.S. conceptional Sun, Jupiter and Venus in Cancer. Neptune was in the earth sign Virgo at the time. The effect of this configuration was dramatic: it constricted the national economy, reduced personal wealth and created a state of psychological depression that prolonged the downturn. This configuration also predicted the restructuring of the federal government in an increase and concentration of power. The New Deal legislation did just that.

The Capricorn conjunction of 1929 also influenced the Federal Reserve System (fig. 12). Congress passed legislation that established the Federal Reserve System (the Fed) on December 23, 1913, at 6:02 p.m. EST in Washington, D.C. The Fed's Sun at 1° Capricorn shows that the System is supposed to be prudent and provide long-term economic stability. But its Sun makes an opposition to Pluto

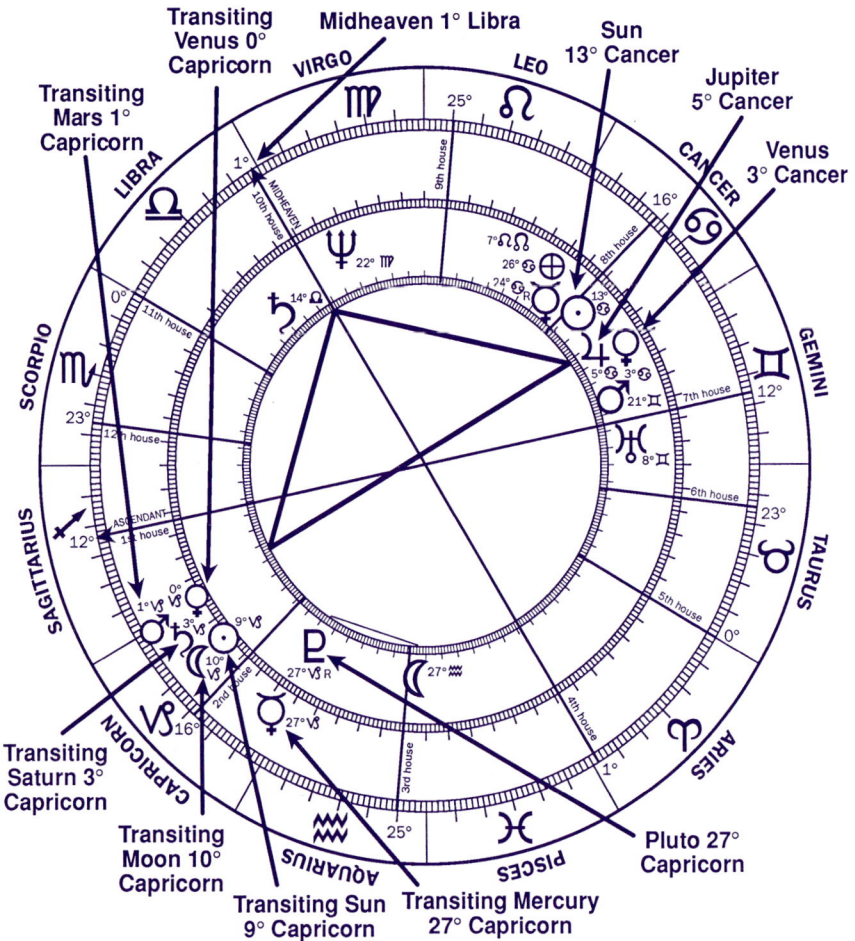

Conjunction of Five Planets in Capricorn Forms
a T-Square in the United States Conceptional Chart
December 30, 1929

FIGURE 11 On December 30, 1929, five planets—Venus, Mars, Saturn, the Sun and the Moon—formed a conjunction between 0°0′ and 10°50′ Capricorn, at the start of the Great Depression. These planets formed an opposition to the United States conceptional Sun at 13° Cancer, Jupiter at 5° Cancer and Venus at 3° Cancer and a square to the Midheaven at 1° Libra, forming a T-square (right triangle). On December 31, 1929, Mercury made an exact conjunction to the United States conceptional Pluto at 27° Capricorn in the second house of money and banking. These configurations constricted the economy, created a state of psychological depression, and prompted the federal government to increase and concentrate its powers. New Deal legislation did just that.

Conjunction of Five Planets in Capricorn
Activates the Federal Reserve System's Birth Chart
December 30, 1929

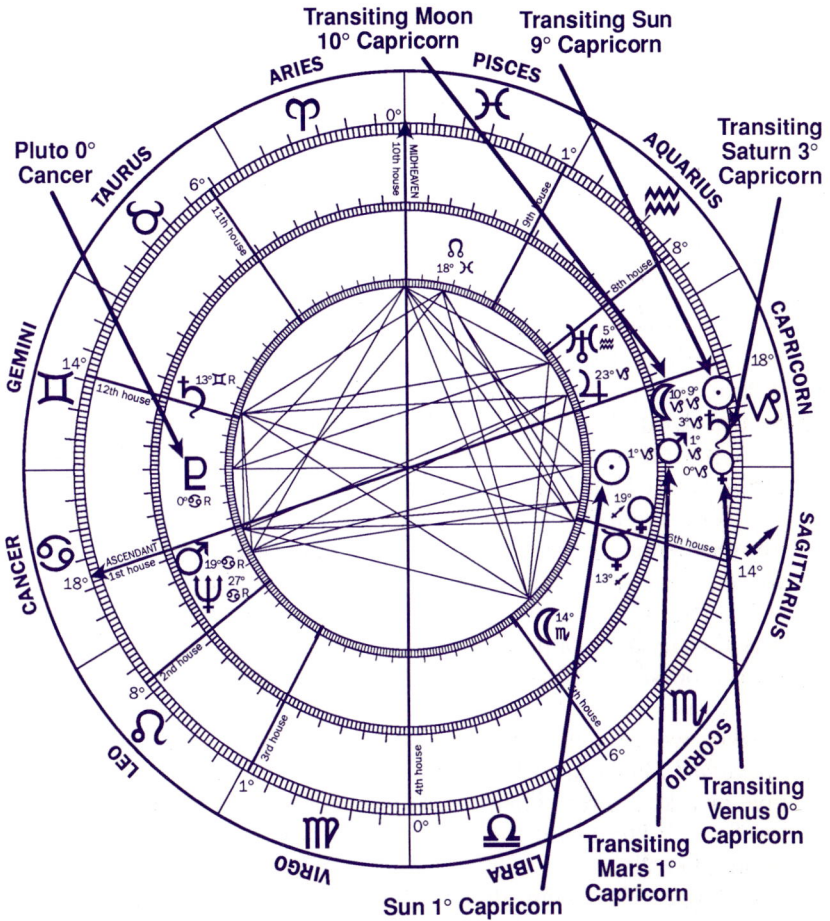

FIGURE 12 The Federal Reserve System (Fed) was established by an act of Congress on December 23, 1913, at 6:02 p.m. EST in Washington, D.C. The Fed's Sun at 1°33′ Capricorn shows that the system is supposed to be prudent and provide long-term economic stability. But the Sun is opposed to Pluto at 0°5′ Cancer in the twelfth house of deception and self-defeating behavior; this is indicative of the fact that the system was the secret creation of plutocrats and that the Fed periodically creates recessions and depressions. The five planets that formed a conjunction in Capricorn on December 30, 1929—Venus, Mars, Saturn, the Sun and the Moon—also conjoined the Fed's Sun and opposed its Pluto. This explains the failure of the Fed to fine-tune the economy. Instead, the Fed constricted the money supply and caused the economy to sink into the depression.

at 0° Cancer in the twelfth house of deception and self-defeating behavior, which is indicative of the fact that the System was the secret creation of plutocrats and that the Fed periodically creates recessions and depressions.

The 1929 conjunction of Venus, Mars, Saturn, the Sun and Moon between 0° and 10° Capricorn is conjoined the Fed's Sun and opposed its Pluto. This indicates the failure of the Fed to fine-tune the economy in order to forestall the Great Depression (if indeed it had any real intention of doing so). Instead, the Fed constricted the money supply at the wrong time, exacerbated the already dire financial situation and caused the economy to sink into the depression.

As influential as the 1929 Capricorn conjunction was, it was not as powerful as the Capricorn conjunction of February 1988. For one thing, the conjunction in 1929 had only one outer planet in it, Saturn. The conjunction of 1988 involves three outer planets— Saturn, Uranus and Neptune. But there are other reasons why it is more powerful and potentially more destructive than the indicator of the Great Depression.

Two events took place in the late summer of 1987 that were unprecedented in this century. On August 24, 1987, the Sun, Moon, Mercury, Venus and Mars were located between 0° and 5° Virgo (fig. 13). According to astroeconomist Arch Crawford, this was the tightest conjunction of any five planets in more than 100 years—possibly 400 years.

Crawford used this conjunction to predict the date the stock market would reach its top. In the August 8, 1987 edition of *Crawford Perspectives* he wrote, "We pick the top for August 24, give or take 3 days. Then a horrendous Crash into the Eclipse of the Sun."[40] He meant the eclipse of the Sun that would occur on September 22.

August 25, the day after the conjunction, the Dow Jones Industrial average reached its highest point at 2722 and started down, setting the stage for the record drops of last October, including the 508-point drop on October 19, known as Black Monday.

I don't know if Mark Twain was an astrologer, but he has some homespun wisdom on the subject: "October. This is one of the peculiarly dangerous months to speculate in stocks in. The others are July, January, September, April, November, May, March, June, December, August, and February."[41]

The Harmonic Convergence

While we are on the subject of this August conjunction, I should like to add that Arch Crawford looked at the chart drawn

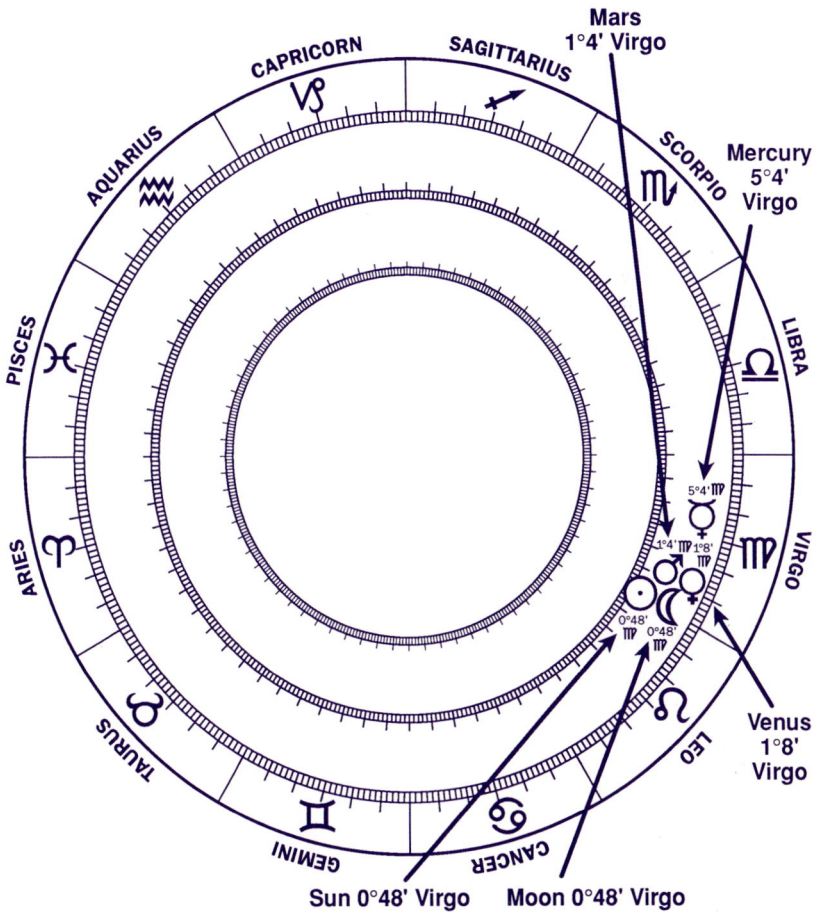

Five Planet Conjunction in Virgo
August 24, 1987

Mars
1°4' Virgo

Mercury
5°4'
Virgo

Venus
1°8'
Virgo

Sun 0°48' Virgo   Moon 0°48' Virgo

FIGURE 13 On August 24, 1987, the Sun, Moon, Mars, Mercury and Venus formed the tightest conjunction of any five planets in over one hundred years. They were all between 0°48′ Virgo and 5°4′ Virgo. Astro-economist Arch Crawford used this configuration to predict the date the Dow Jones industrial average would reach its peak. In the August 8, 1987 edition of *Crawford Perspectives* he wrote, "We pick the top for 24 August, give or take 3 days. Then a horrendous Crash into the Eclipse of the Sun." He was referring to the eclipse of the Sun at 29° Virgo on September 22, 1987. On August 25, the Dow reached its top at 2722 and started down, setting the stage for the record drops of October 1987 including the 508-point plunge on October 19.

for the Harmonic Convergence of August 16 and 17 of last year and
concluded as I did that there wasn't anything about those dates
likely to herald an age of enlightenment. He believes as I do that
Dr. José Argüelles et al. picked the wrong day.[42] While we're
always hopeful for influences that could bring peace and enlightenment, we think the dates the Mayans must have calculated were
August 22 to 24, not August 16 to 17, and that the portents were
quite negative.

The planetary changes and the breakdown of institutions and
situations on the planet that José Argüelles predicts are not
consistent with earth's vibration or her destiny.

At 2:46 a.m. on November 27, 1989, beloved Cyclopea, the
Elohim of the Fifth Ray, announced the real Harmonic Convergence. He said:

> For by the momentum [of your service to this hour] and
> the [timing of the] moment, we may see heaven and earth
> meet in an extraordinary way, beloved. You have heard
> these words before, but I say to you, the convergence of
> heaven and earth in this hour is truly in the capstone that
> I now place on the pyramid of the United States of America
> at the etheric octave.
>
> O the wonders of the Love of the Chela unascended
> and the Guru ascended! O the wonders of the Love of
> heaven and earth! It is a Love story, beloved. For it has been
> the great desiring of those above to visit those below in this
> tangible way[—through the *real* "harmonic convergence":
> the meeting of souls ascended and unascended in the Eye of
> the capstone]! And it is truly the desiring of those below to
> enter in to the hearts of the saints robed in white.[43]

The chart for the date and time of Cyclopea's dictation, "The
Placing of the Capstone on the Pyramid of the United States of
America: The Convergence of Heaven and Earth" (fig. 14), is
dominated by a cardinal T-square. The cardinal signs, Aries,
Libra, Cancer and Capricorn, initiate action and deal with the use
or abuse of power.

The anchor of the T-square is a conjunction of Uranus at
3°44′ Capricorn, Neptune at 10°47′ Capricorn, and Saturn at
11°43′ Capricorn with a point known as the Lowest Heaven (or
IC) at 11°2′ Capricorn. The IC is the point in every chart that is
opposite the Midheaven. It is beneath the feet of the observer and
represents the lowest descent of a planetary influence into the
planes of matter. It is also the cusp, or line that marks the

The Placing of the Capstone on the Pyramid of the United States of America
The Convergence of Heaven and Earth
November 27, 1989, 2:46 a.m.

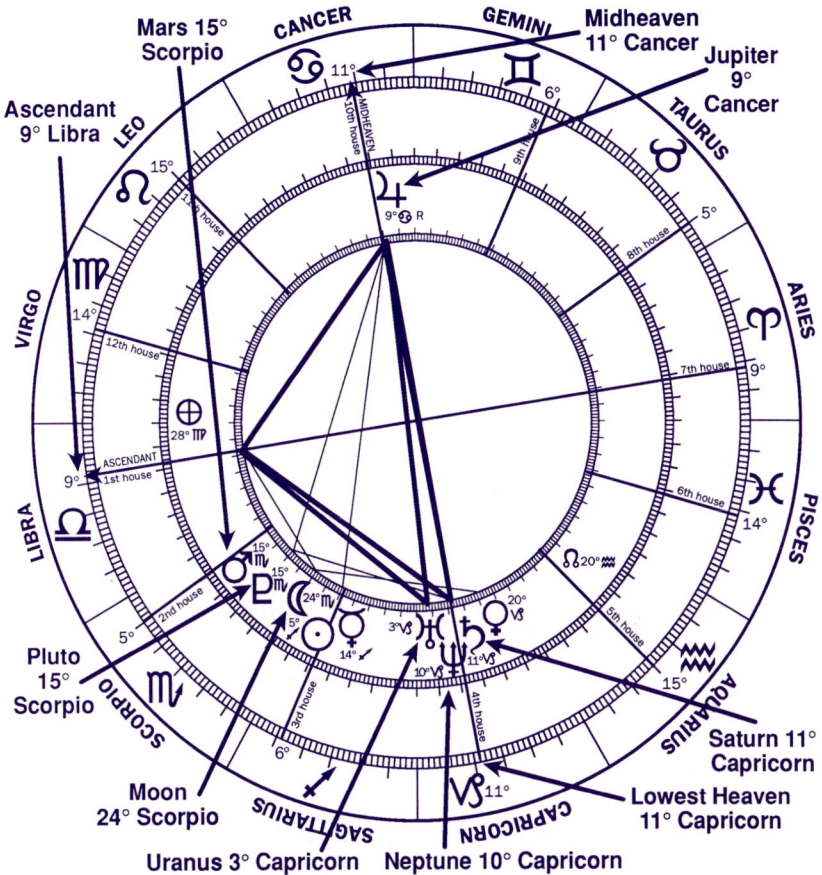

FIGURE 14   At 2:46 a.m. on November 27, 1989, Cyclopea, the Elohim of the Fifth Ray, announced, "The convergence of heaven and earth in this hour is truly in the capstone that I now place on the pyramid of the United States of America at the etheric octave....For it has been the great desiring of those above to visit those below in this tangible way[—through the *real* "harmonic convergence": the meeting of souls ascended and unascended in the Eye of the capstone]!" The chart for this true Harmonic Convergence is dominated by a T-square made up of Uranus at 3° Capricorn, Neptune at 10° Capricorn, and Saturn at 11° Capricorn conjoined the Lowest Heaven at 11° Capricorn opposed to the Midheaven at 11° Cancer conjoined Jupiter at 9° Cancer square the Ascendant at 9° Libra. This configuration shows the descent of the spiritual world to the lowest possible level while the children of the Mother on Earth achieve the highest attainable plane of consciousness.

beginning, of the fourth house, the house of the Mother.

These Capricorn planets and the IC make an opposition to the Midheaven (the point overhead) at 11°2′ Cancer conjoined Jupiter at 9°28′ Cancer. And all of the planets, the Midheaven, and IC square the Ascendant at 9°7′ Libra, thereby forming a T-square (or right triangle).

T-squares are the most dynamic astrological configuration. The power and intensity of this particular T-square is increased by the presence of four outer planets and by the fact that all the aspects are very close and that all the planets and the Ascendant, Midheaven and IC are in cardinal (power) signs.

This T-square shows the converging of heaven and earth. According to the teachings of the Ascended Masters, Capricorn is the highest spiritual sign of the zodiac. But it is also an earth sign with the capability of anchoring its spiritual potential in matter. The fact that the Capricorn planets are on the IC shows that Capricorn's spiritual potential can be anchored at the lowest possible level. And Saturn (the planet of crystallization) helped concretize and unite the influences of Uranus (the planet of freedom) and Neptune (the planet of spirituality and transcendence). In other words, heaven descended to the lowest level possible.

The Capricorn planets are in polarity with Jupiter (the planet of religion) in Cancer (the sign of children of the Mother) conjoined the Midheaven (representative of the highest attainable plane of consciousness). The Capricorn-Cancer planets square the Ascendant in Libra (the sign of balance, which in this case represents a plane of equilibrium where heaven descending and earth ascending can meet).

There is another dimension to this chart—a nearly exact conjunction of Mars at 15°40′ Scorpio and Pluto at 15°55′ Scorpio loosely conjoined the Moon at 24° Scorpio. The conjunction of Mars and Pluto in Scorpio shows either penetrating vision or the opposition to it. This Mars-Pluto conjunction has a warlike influence and will impact the U.S. and Soviet natal charts, as we shall see in chapter 8.

The planets in the T-Square of November 27 are close to the position they occupied on November 13, a peak date for economic difficulties (see fig. 18).

The fact that the two major configurations in this chart show the potential for economic turmoil and war shows that the Light-bearers were in a race with converging karmic circumstances to achieve the harmonic convergence of heaven and earth—and that they won! They were able to create the conditions that made it possible for Cyclopea to place the capstone on the pyramid before war and economic collapse made it impossible.

Saint Germain's Prophecies and the October 1987 Crash

The drop in the market came as no surprise to me. On Thanksgiving 1986 Saint Germain said:

> Economic debacle is foreseen. Prepare. Setbacks will be sudden. Be not lulled by the heyday. Many Band-Aids upon the economy, the money system, the banking houses— these will not prevent the collapse of nations and banking houses built on sands of human greed, ambition, and manipulation of the lifeblood of the people of God. . . .
>
> The mitigating factor in economic debacle, in nuclear war, in plague untold and death is the nucleus of Light-bearers and the quotient of sacred fire they invoke.[44]

On Saturday night, October 3, 1987, speaking in New York City, Saint Germain gave a dictation through me that included a fiery condemnation of the manipulators of God's people:

> Thus, the "spiritual wickedness in high places" of this city. . .is a manipulation in money matters beyond conception.
>
> And therefore I say, Woe! Woe! Woe! Let the judgments descend upon those who manipulate the abundant Life of a people of God and subject them to a slavery untold far beyond that of the Egyptian taskmasters!. . .
>
> I say unto all purveyors of drugs and all who poison the minds and souls and bodies of youth eternal everywhere:
>
> Woe! Woe! Woe!
>
> So the pronouncement of the judgment of Almighty God be upon you. So by the spirit of the Prophet does there descend now that karma upon those who are the destroyers in the earth!
>
> And let the archdeceivers of the people in their nests in the nations' capitals now tremble, for the LORD God Almighty does walk the earth!
>
> For the LORD God Almighty is come and the Divine Mother does enter and does take dominion in the Matter universe.[45]

On this unprecedented occasion I heard these words pour from my lips as I delivered "The Speaking of the LORD God":

Hear me, people of earth! I say to you, bind, then, the oppressor! For the hour is come for the judgment of the fallen ones in the earth who would push you to the brink of war and economic collapse and famine and plague. . . .

And the golden-calf civilization does go down! And the Cain civilization is judged! For no longer is the Cain civilization protected by the mark of Cain. It is no more.

And therefore, let the fallen ones know that the hour is come that they must pay the price for the shedding of the blood of the holy innocents and of the sons of God and of the prophets and of the Christs. Therefore, let them tremble! For I come into their citadel of international power and moneyed interests. And I AM, of the LORD God, do declare unto you that through my Archangels they shall know the judgment.[46]

With scarcely a delay factor from the spoken Word 'from on high' to the crystallization of these judgments, on Tuesday, October 6, three days hence, the Dow fell a record 91.55 points. In the two weeks following Saint Germain's dictation, the Dow registered back-to-back its two biggest weekly declines, falling a record 158 points October 5 to 9 and then dropping another 235 points October 12 to 16.

Then on Black Monday, October 19, the market crashed. The DJIA fell more than 508 points, the largest decline since the crash of October 29, 1929, that had signaled the onset of the Great Depression.

On the night of October 19, I took a dictation from the Goddess of the Sun, Vesta, Divine Complement of Helios, in Toledo, Ohio. She said, "Yes, there can be a rise again [in the stock market], beloved, but never as steady as before. Thus, the sudden setbacks are experienced. Prepare, then. . . "[47]

When you hear the *Woe! Woe! Woe!*—the deprecatory woes—pronounced three times as they are in the Book of Revelation, this is the LORD's pronouncement of the descent of the karma of the people involving their sins against the Father, the Son and the Holy Ghost. And whatever the people have done to violate the Light-Energy-Consciousness and the Power-Wisdom-Love of the Trinity is also considered a sin against the divine spark, the threefold flame, which is the individualized focus of the Trinity God placed within the hearts of his sons and daughters. And so when the karma descends, the three woes are the decree that the Presence of the Trinity be reduced in each lifestream proportionate to the severity of their karma.

In all the years of my Messengership, whenever I have checked the judgments and the prophecies of the LORD delivered through the Holy Spirit in the Ascended Masters' dictations against the astrology of the hour, I have found confirmation in the handwriting in the skies. The October 3 dictation is a stunning example of the correlation between these two sources of the LORD's judgments and his prophecies: on October 6 the judgments and the prophecies descended upon America.

God has not left us comfortless. Not only has he written his signs of warning in the heavens, in our hearts and in our souls, not only has he sent his angels to warn us, but he has also established the office and the mantle of the Messenger to warn those who read neither the signs in the heavens nor those of the heart, the soul and the angels.

Therefore we who read and run with the message of our deliverance in time and in space may escape those things that may come upon the earth. They may not necessarily come upon ourselves but upon those fallen angels whose time in space is up, the oppressors of the people who through their materialistic civilizations and their world totalitarian movements exercise their factors of control. Their karma is already descending.

Therefore again and again God has said to his people what he said through Joshua: "Come apart and be a separate and chosen people, elect unto God." God wants us to separate ourselves out from the vibration of the fallen angels. He wants us to cut the ties we have to their money and power systems, to their godless materialism and their totalitarian controls. He wants us to get out from among them and to expose their International Capitalist/Communist Conspiracy. God wants us to separate ourselves out from them so that when their karma descends it does not fall upon our families and our households. Therefore, let us also accept the admonishments of Joshua, who said, "As for me and my house, we will serve the LORD":

> Now therefore fear the LORD, and serve him in sincerity and in truth: and put away the [Nephilim][48] gods which your fathers served on the other side of the flood, and in Egypt; and serve ye the LORD.
>
> And if it seem evil unto you to serve the LORD, choose you this day whom ye will serve; whether the [Nephilim] gods which your fathers served that were on the other side of the flood, or the [Nephilim] gods of the Amorites, in whose land ye dwell: but as for me and my house, we will serve the LORD.

And the people answered and said, God forbid that we should forsake the LORD, to serve other [Nephilim] gods;

For the LORD our God, he it is that brought us up and our fathers out of the land of Egypt, from the house of bondage, and which did those great signs in our sight, and preserved us in all the way wherein we went, and among all the people through whom we passed:

And the LORD drave out from before us all the people, even the Amorites which dwelt in the land: therefore will we also serve the LORD; for he is our God.

And Joshua said unto the people, Ye cannot serve the LORD: for he is an holy God; he is a jealous God; he will not forgive your transgressions nor your sins.

If ye forsake the LORD, and serve strange [Nephilim] gods, then he will turn and do you hurt, and consume you, after that he hath done you good. . . .

And Joshua said unto the people, Ye are witnesses against yourselves that ye have chosen you the LORD, to serve him. And they said, We are witnesses. . . .

So Joshua made a covenant with the people that day, and set them a statute and an ordinance in Shechem.

And Joshua wrote these words in the book of the law of God, and took a great stone, and set it up there under an oak, that was by the sanctuary of the LORD.

And Joshua said unto all the people, Behold, this stone shall be a witness unto us; for it hath heard all the words of the LORD which he spake unto us: it shall be therefore a witness unto you, lest ye deny your God.[49]

The September 22, 1987 Eclipse of the Sun
at 29° Virgo or 0° Libra

The decline in the market since August 25, 1987, is only the first leg of its descent. The second leg will be related to the Capricorn conjunction of February 22–23, 1988, and to the eclipse of the Sun that occurred on September 22, 1987, at 29° Virgo or (as some astrologers prefer to designate it) at 0° Libra.

That eclipse was destined to influence the economy, the government and the course of peace and war on the planet. It fell the closest of any eclipse in this century to one of the equinox, or solstice, points—a very powerful placing. This is quite probably the most intense eclipse of the century. At 29° Virgo, the eclipse falls within 2° of the Midheaven of the United States conceptional chart at 1° Libra. The Midheaven rules the nation's government, purpose and reputation. Therefore, the eclipse had an overwhelming effect on the United States.

In the astrology of nations, eclipses often show a loss of power, a death or a disaster. An eclipse of the Moon conjoined Pluto triggered the Chernobyl disaster, as I showed in Book Two of *Saint Germain On Prophecy.*

Pluto is often associated with death and destruction. President John F. Kennedy's assassination on November 22, 1963, was preceded by a total solar eclipse earlier that year. That eclipse was exactly conjoined his natal Saturn at 27° Cancer in his tenth house of career and public standing and opposed the U.S. conceptional Pluto at 27° Capricorn.

Had he been a student of astrology and a practitioner of the science of the spoken Word under the Ascended Masters, President Kennedy could have, by the grace of God, defeated that astrology. As I have said again and again, it is entirely within our power, as sons of God on earth, when the Lord so ordains it, to transmute the negative effects of our karma by violet flame invocations.

In the fall of '87, prior to the stock-market crash, when I was stumping the East Coast, I said:

> A solar eclipse falling on the U.S. Midheaven at a time when the nation is headed into progressively more difficult circumstances does not augur well. It could be extremely detrimental to the nation's public standing and institutions, including the Congress and the office of the president— especially to Ronald Reagan. If played out to its extreme it could lead to the fall of the government, the "death" of our form of government, the fall or death of the president, literally or figuratively, and the onset of a major economic catastrophe.

As we all know, the economic catastrophe, or at least the very first part of it, took place on October 19. I believe that the other elements may soon play themselves out as the sequence of astrological events unfolds.

At the time of the solar eclipse of September 22, 1987, Neptune was at 5° Capricorn square to the eclipse and United States Midheaven. This indicates that things are not what they seem in the United States today. The potential for treachery and intrigue is exceptionally high. This eclipse puts every aspect of our nation at risk. In other words, the eclipse is the sign of the descent of karma.

This cyclic descent of karma often belies the astrological times—degrees, minutes, seconds. For it would appear that if nothing happened on that day and date, we're home free.

Not so. Astrology is precise, and so is the law of karma. Astrology tells us when the button of karma was pressed. But karma takes its time, moving invisibly yet inexorably: first through the etheric plane, then the mental, then the astral and finally the physical. Like an avalanche, it appears as that "sudden destruction" that Paul wrote about, "as travail upon a woman with child"; and, the apostle added, "they shall not escape [their karma]!"[50] This is the true meaning of that passage of scripture. Though karma may be on its way for centuries, when it finally comes upon us, it is too late.

President Reagan Meets the Fates

The configurations we are examining may have an effect on President Ronald Reagan.

Ronald W. Reagan was born February 6, 1911, in Tampico, Illinois. Astrologer Frances McEvoy says that Reagan and his mother, Nelle, consulted astrologer Ralph Kraum soon after they arrived in Hollywood. Kraum used 2 p.m. CST for Reagan's time of birth. It was probably based on Nelle's recollection and gives Reagan an Ascendant of 7°47′ Cancer (fig. 15). Reagan's Sun is at 16°56′ Aquarius.

Aquarius and Uranus rule revolution and are the astrological underpinnings of the "Reagan Revolution." Reagan's Uranus at 26° Capricorn (the sign that rules the past) shows that Reagan wanted to return the nation to former glory. Neptune (the planet of illusion) at 19° Cancer is quincunx to Reagan's Sun and opposed to his Uranus; this shows that the Reagan Revolution was largely illusion. Detachment (distorted into overdetachment by Neptune) is an Aquarian trait at the heart of Reagan's "management style."

A number of astrologers were of the opinion that it was by no means certain that Ronald Reagan would finish his term of office.

First of all, early in his presidency he experienced a severe astrological challenge. The arc of the zodiac between 29° Virgo and 9° Libra is critical to the United States. Between October 28, 1980, and mid-September 1981, Jupiter and Saturn were closely conjoined in the early degrees of Libra. They formed exact conjunctions on December 31, 1980 (9° Libra), March 4, 1981 (8° Libra) and July 23, 1981 (4° Libra).

A conjunction of these two planets occurs every 20 years and was anticipated by astrologers because since 1840 it has coincided

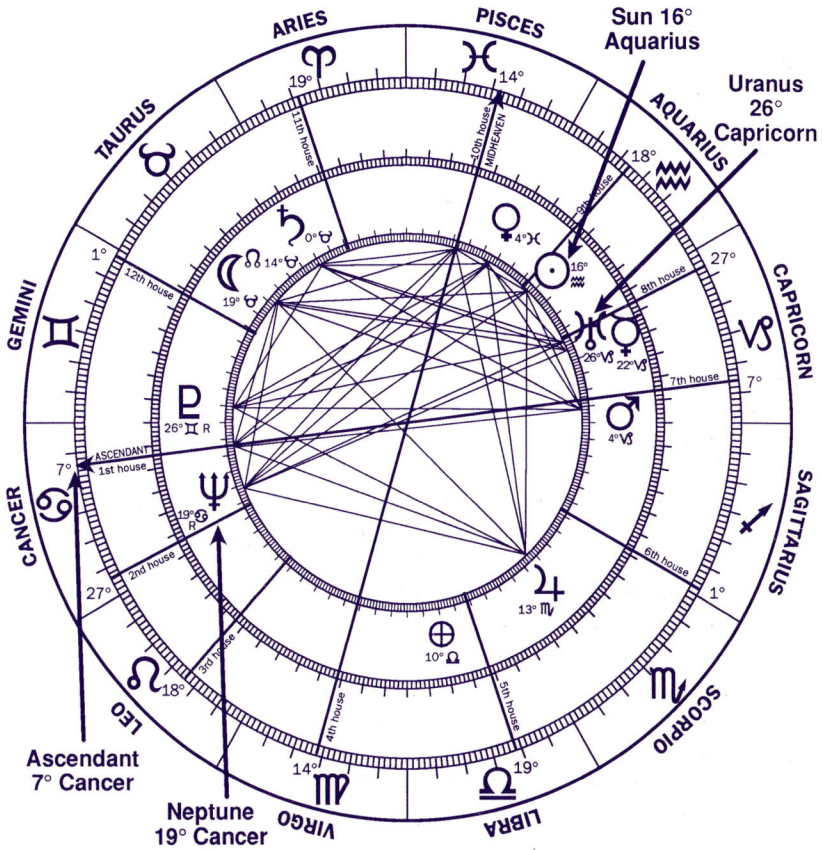

Ronald W. Reagan
Birth Chart
February 6, 1911, 2:00 p.m.?

FIGURE 15 Ronald W. Reagan was born February 6, 1911, in Tampico, Illinois. Astrologer Frances McEvoy says that Reagan and his mother, Nelle, consulted astrologer Ralph Kraum soon after they arrived in Hollywood. Kraum used 2 p.m. CST for Reagan's time of birth. It was probably based on Nelle's recollection and gives Reagan an Ascendant of 7°47′ Cancer. Reagan's Sun is at 16°56′ Aquarius. Aquarius and Uranus rule revolution and are the astrological underpinnings of the "Reagan Revolution." Reagan's Uranus at 26° Capricorn (the sign that rules the past) shows that Reagan wanted to return the nation to former glory. Neptune (the planet of illusion) at 19° Cancer is quincunx to Reagan's Sun and opposed to his Uranus; this shows that the Reagan Revolution was largely illusion. Detachment (distorted into over-detachment by Neptune) is an Aquarian trait at the heart of Reagan's "management style."

with the death of an American president, usually by assassination: Harrison, Lincoln, Garfield, McKinley, Harding, Roosevelt and Kennedy. This repetitive cycle will either make you superstitious or a believer in astrology as the mathematics of destiny.

Popular belief also attributed the cyclic death of American presidents to the curse of the Shawnee Indian chief Tecumseh on President William Henry Harrison. Harrison was a General in the U.S. Army and governor of the Indiana Territory who presided over a steady encroachment onto Indian lands. At the Battle of Tippecanoe in 1811 he led U.S. forces in a bloody defeat of the Shawnee Indians led by Tecumseh's brother, the Shawnee Prophet. Tecumseh joined the British to fight against the United States in the War of 1812 and was killed in the Battle of the Thames, October 5, 1813. Either he or his brother reputedly pronounced a curse on Harrison and on the White House. Harrison, elected president in 1840, died of pneumonia after only a month in office.

As you know, Ronald Reagan was shot but not killed by John Hinckley March 30, 1981. Heretofore, the Jupiter-Saturn conjunctions that coincided with deaths of presidents had been in earth signs (the sure sign of physical karma) but the 1980–81 conjunction occurred in Libra, an air sign, which would not necessarily indicate the crystallization of this cyclic national karma in the physical. However, the air sign, corresponding to the mind and mental activity, would show the crystallization of the intent and the attempted assassination in the mind of the would-be assassin. Because of this some astrologers speculated that the president would not be assassinated in office.

I believe the president survived an attempted assassination because Saint Germain's Keepers of the Flame throughout the world held a weekend prayer marathon of dynamic decrees to thwart and transmute the predicted assassination (which Saint Germain made me aware of before the fact) and to break the curse of Tecumseh. And so they gathered in their sanctuaries on January 25, 1981, invoking the protection of the Seven Archangels and the action of the violet flame delivered by the heavenly hosts to mitigate the effects of individual and national karma according to the will of God.

I wish I could tell you that this is the end of the matter, but it is not. Major configurations in years to come can activate a sensitive point in the zodiac. The planets move on to other positions but, as Saint Germain has taught me, these planets leave what he calls a "ghost" of themselves on the computer screen of the skies, which can then be reactivated by the tug and pull of future astrological events.

The ghost of the 1980–81 Jupiter-Saturn conjunction will influence and be influenced by later events. There is a never-ending play of energy as worlds seem to collide before our eyes, only to separate and move on, having cast the spell of their combined potions upon billions of microcosmic entities who know not the destiny of their stars—and who plunge headlong to a destiny not of their choosing, but of their making. The forces are invisible but the causes can be known. And so we study the ancients' interpretations of the planets to discover what they have to tell us about the signs of our times.

The solar eclipse of September 22, 1987, revisited the sensitive degrees of Libra, 1° through 9°, where the Jupiter-Saturn conjunction took place from October 28, 1980, to mid-September 1981. This catalyzed and brought to completion the unmanifest energies of the conjunction.

Furthermore, on March 18, 1988, there was an eclipse of the Sun at 28° Pisces. This eclipse was a mirror image of the eclipse at 29° Virgo but slightly less powerful since it was not quite as close to the equinox point at 0° Aries as the other was to the equinox point at 0° Libra. The difference between the eclipses is likely to be minor, however, since this eclipse squared Saturn and Uranus in Capricorn and opposed the U.S. conceptional Midheaven. Therefore, this eclipse could produce effects similar to the Virgo eclipse that triggered the crash of October 19, 1987.

There are a number of ways that the effects of the solar eclipse at 29° Virgo can manifest. The first effects started to become noticeable after October 8, 1987, when the transiting Sun made its conjunction with the U.S. conceptional Saturn. President Reagan and the nation lost prestige because of the administration's inability to carry out a credible policy in the Persian Gulf, the stock market crash, and the rejection of Reagan's nominee Judge Robert Bork for the Supreme Court. But these are only the first of a series of effects that are likely to unfold over the next six months to two years.

The Capricorn conjunction of February 22–23, 1988, also impacted Reagan's chart. It fell on his natal Mars at 4° Capricorn and opposed his Pluto at 26° Gemini. This shows the loss of political power (Capricorn planets) and mental power (Pluto in Gemini). In addition, transiting Pluto at 12° Scorpio activated a T-square formed by Reagan's natal Jupiter at 13° Scorpio, his Moon at 19° Taurus and his Sun at 16° Aquarius (fig. 16). The

Conjunction of Mars, Saturn, Uranus and Neptune
Activates Ronald Reagan's Birth Chart
February 22–23, 1988

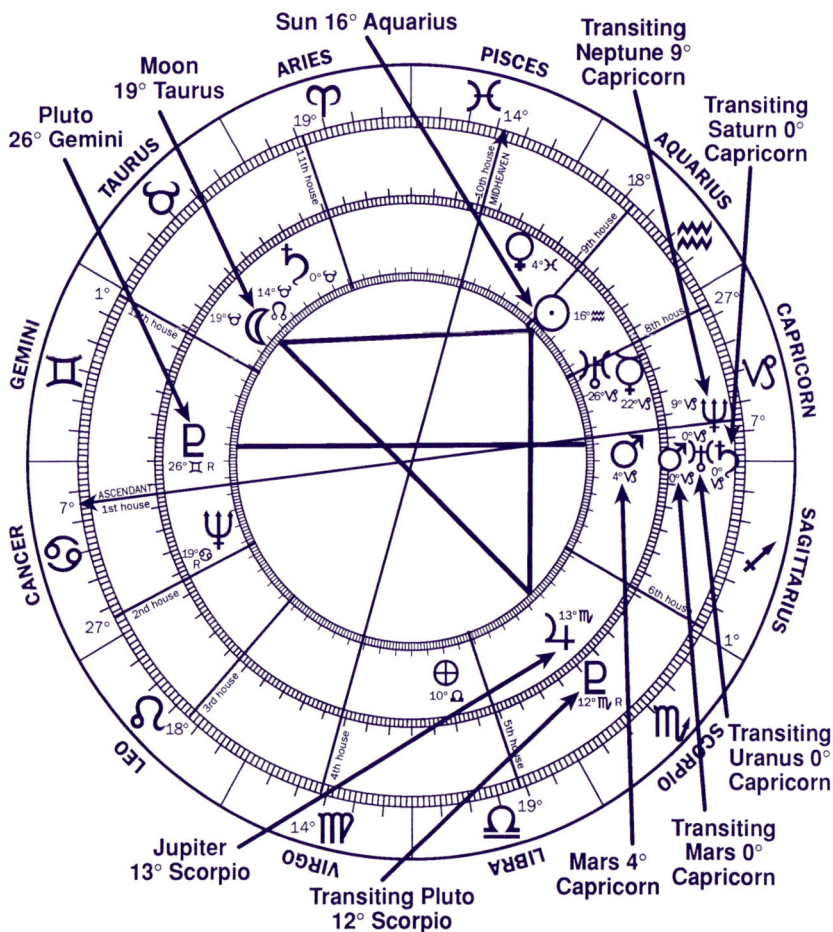

FIGURE 16 On February 22–23, 1988, transiting Mars, Saturn and Uranus at 0° Capricorn and Neptune at 9° Capricorn formed a conjunction to Ronald Reagan's Mars at 4° Capricorn and an opposition to his Pluto at 26° Gemini. This shows the loss of political power (Capricorn planets) and mental power (Pluto in Gemini). At that time transiting Pluto at 12° Scorpio activated a T-square (right triangle) formed by Reagan's Jupiter at 13° Scorpio, his Moon at 19° Taurus and his Sun at 16° Aquarius. The combined effect of these configurations could have been politically or physically fatal. In *Landslide: The Unmaking of the President 1984-1988*, Jane Mayer and Doyle McManus report that Reagan had effectively abdicated his office and was briefly in danger of being involuntarily retired under the Constitution's 25th Amendment, which allows the Cabinet to remove a President who is "unable to discharge the powers and duties of his office."

combined effect of these configurations could have been politically or physically fatal.

According to some, Reagan almost didn't finish his last two years in office. In a book called *Landslide: The Unmaking of the President 1984–1988*,[51] Washington reporters Jane Mayer and Doyle McManus reveal startling facts that portray Reagan in 1987 as incompetent and uninterested in running the country.

Just before Howard Baker took over as chief of staff in March 1987, two of his aides went on a secret fact-finding mission to the White House, according to Mayer and McManus. After interviewing White House staff and aides, they discovered that the "ex-actor," as he once opted to be called, often went home at 4:00 p.m., sometimes never came to work at all, spent most of his time watching videos and TV, and would sign papers without reading them. The *Los Angeles Times Book Review* observed that "by the second term, Reagan had crossed over from delegating authority to abdicating his duties as President."[52]

Baker and his aides were so shocked at what they learned that they considered invoking Section Four of the 25th Amendment, a provision that allows for the removal of the president if he is no longer competent to govern. All it takes is the agreement of the vice president and a majority of the cabinet. Fortunately for Reagan, neither Baker, the vice president nor the cabinet took action.

At the end of his second term Ronald Reagan was scrambling to defeat his chart by establishing for himself "a place in history" when he should have been establishing for himself a place in the Sun of his I AM Presence. His choice of emphasis on self-importance has dealt a fatal blow to the nation.

In truth Ronald Reagan did not finish his term in office either as keeper of the flame of the Presidency and the White House or as keeper of the flame of the people and the nation. And the lights went out all over the world. And they won't come on again until we the citizens of Terra are enlightened from within.

Effects of the February 22–23, 1988 Conjunction on the United States

The conjunction of Mars, Saturn and Uranus at 0° Capricorn and Neptune at 9° Capricorn on February 22–23, 1988, will have a number of effects on the United States. It squared the U.S. conceptional Midheaven at 1° Libra as well as the point of the solar eclipse of September 22, 1987, at 29° Virgo, which completes a T-square (right triangle in space), and it could initiate the second leg of the stock market crash of October 1987.

The conjunction also opposed the U.S. conceptional Sun at 13° Cancer, Jupiter at 5° Cancer and Venus at 3° Cancer (fig. 17). This is reminiscent of the conjunction of five planets in Capricorn on December 30, 1929, that helped trigger the Depression. But this Capricorn conjunction, barring some x-y-z unknowns, could have an even greater impact on the economy.

The Saturn-Uranus conjunction at 0° Capricorn, which occurred as part of the larger conjunction, is particularly noteworthy. A Saturn-Uranus conjunction alone can ignite international political and economic upheaval in the affairs of the nations, even without any of the complicating and amplifying factors in this configuration. As I pointed out earlier, it is a primary indicator of war.

This is one of several cycles that link economic turmoil and war. Saint Germain's interpretation of Nostradamus's quatrains also points to the linking of war and economic turmoil.

The Federal Reserve System has an opposition between its Sun at 1° Capricorn and its Pluto at 0° Cancer, and will therefore also be powerfully influenced by the Capricorn conjunction of Mars, Saturn, Uranus and Neptune, February 22–23, 1988. This Capricorn conjunction was conjoined the Fed's Sun and opposed its Pluto. All of these planets squared the U.S. conceptional Midheaven at 1° Libra conjoined the eclipse of the Sun of September 22, 1987, at 29° Virgo, forming a T-square.

T-squares are dynamic configurations. This one indicates that the Federal Reserve System has been acting, and will probably continue to act, in a manner that is harmful to the nation and ultimately harmful to itself, even though what the Fed is doing may be of immediate value to those who created it—the financial and industrial powers of this nation. The records show that one cause of the October crash was the Fed's tight money policy. Under this heavy Capricorn influence the Fed has followed a generally deflationary policy.

On November 13, 1989, transiting Saturn made an exact conjunction to Neptune at 10°22′ Capricorn and both made an exact opposition to Jupiter at 10°29′ Cancer (fig. 18). This configuration could herald the next big drop in the market. Since Saturn and Neptune are slow-moving planets, their conjunctions occur about every 36 years and have a three- to six-month period in which their direct effects may be felt. While most astroeconomists expected more dramatic events on or around November 13, there have been signs of economic weakness and debt liquidation, including the Savings and Loan bailout and the big drop in the

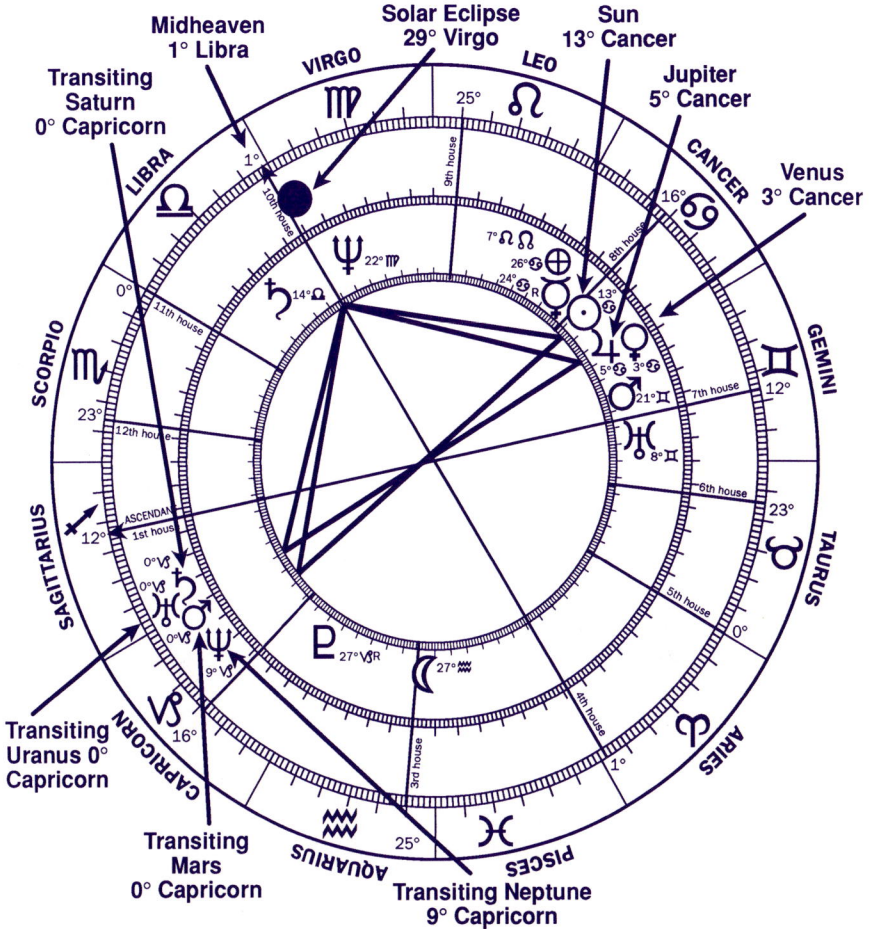

Conjunction of Mars, Saturn, Uranus and Neptune
Forms a T-square in the United States Conceptional Chart
February 22–23, 1988

FIGURE 17 On February 22–23, 1988, Mars, Saturn and Uranus at 0° Capricorn and Neptune at 9° Capricorn formed a conjunction with each other and an opposition to the United States conceptional Sun at 13° Cancer, Jupiter at 5° Cancer and Venus at 3° Cancer. This is reminiscent of the five-planet Capricorn conjunction of December 30, 1929, that helped trigger the Depression—but now it could have an even greater impact on the economy. This conjunction forms a square to the conceptional Mid-heaven at 1° Libra and the solar eclipse of September 22, 1987, at 29° Virgo, which completes a T-square (right triangle) and could initiate the second leg of the stock market crash of October 1987. The Saturn-Uranus conjunction at 0° Capricorn, which is part of the larger conjunction, can ignite international political and economic upheaval. Since it is also a primary indicator of war, it is one of several cycles that link economic turmoil and war.

Transiting Saturn, Neptune and Jupiter Form a T-Square in the U.S. Conceptional Chart
November 13, 1989

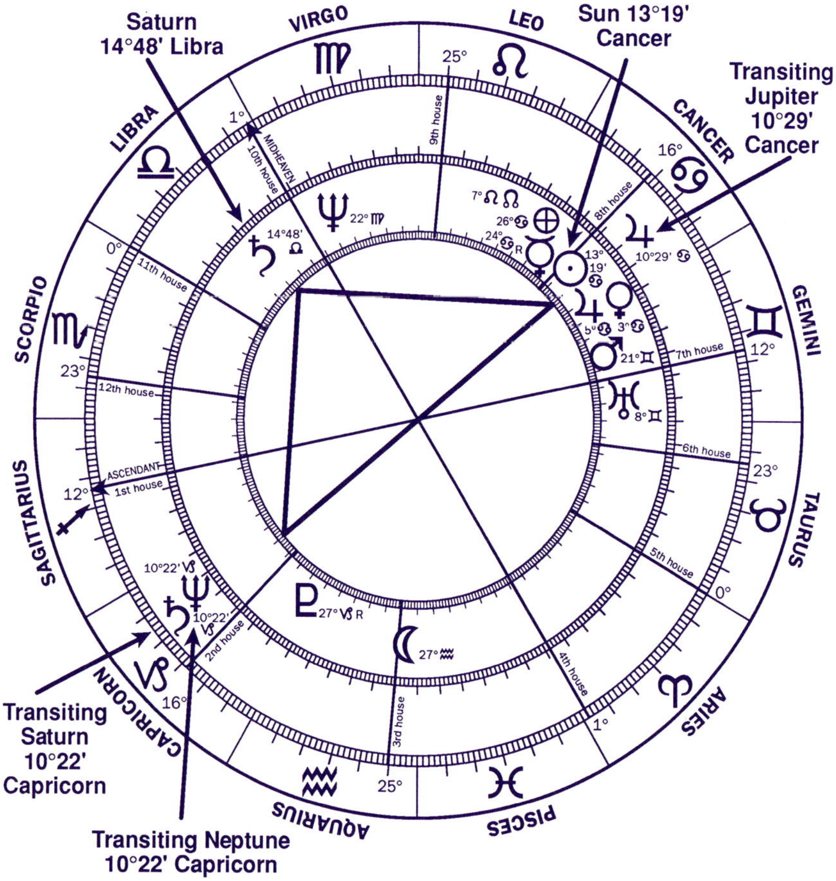

FIGURE 18 On November 13, 1989, transiting Saturn and Neptune formed a conjunction at 10°22′ Capricorn and an opposition to transiting Jupiter at 10°29′ Cancer conjoined the United States conceptional Sun at 13°19′ Cancer. These planets squared the U.S. conceptional Saturn at 14°48′ Libra, thereby forming a T-square (a right triangle) in the U.S. conceptional chart. This T-square is likely to activate major debt liquidation in the United States. Since Saturn and Neptune are slow-moving planets, their conjunctions occur about every 36 years and have a three- to six-month period in which their direct effects may be felt. While most astroeconomists expected more dramatic events on or around November 13, there have been signs of economic weakness and debt liquidation, including the Savings and Loan bailout and the big drop in the stock market on October 13, 1989. The pace of debt liquidation is likely to increase as the economy moves into a recession.

stock market on October 13, 1989. The pace of debt liquidation is likely to increase as the economy moves into a recession.

The opposition of transiting Saturn and Neptune to transiting Jupiter will affect more than the New York Stock Exchange and other stock, bond and commodity markets. It will be a critical factor in triggering major debt liquidation and could lead to the dissolution of much of the Western banking system. It could precipitate an economic crisis so severe as to provoke revolution or lead to the dissolution of the U.S. government.

Jupiter, Saturn and Neptune will also square the U.S. conceptional Saturn, forming a T-square. Saturn, which represents the federal government and the Constitution, is the focal point of the T-square. This is another indication that the government as well as the Constitution that gave it life could be strained to the point of collapse by national and international karma coming to bear upon the people.

The Violet Flame for the Healing of the Economy and Everything Else!

If American citizens do not collapse under this weight, if each of us uses any of the violet flame cassettes 1–4, *Save the World with Violet Flame! by Saint Germain,* daily, we will see a mitigation of this projected economic debacle that could be the pulling of the rip cord of war between the superpowers.

This doesn't mean that the karma that cast the configuration in the skies would simply disappear like snow at Camelot. It means the mist wouldn't become the crystal. It means some of it would have been transmuted at etheric, mental or astral levels before it ever manifested, and the rest would have to be consumed day by day as we continue to faithfully give our calls for divine intercession.

What we can do for ourselves and our families and our children, we can do for the nation. And what we can do for the nation, we can do for the world. But we must do it! Or these things will come to pass, thus saith the LORD.

Keepers of the Flame throughout the world, including behind the Iron Curtain, are giving their violet flame decrees daily. Called by the Darjeeling Council of the Great White Brotherhood, we are mounting a worldwide effort to saturate planet earth with the violet flame. And this astrology of the Four Horsemen that I am laying before you is the compelling reason why we must run with the message of Saint Germain and the violet flame and tell the Lightbearers of the world that this karmic cycle coming upon planet earth is our challenge and our call to arms for the LORD's victory in the final decade of the twentieth century.

Saint Germain said at the beginning of the decade, on February 17, 1980:

> There are some economists in America who have seen the dangers for years. They wonder why the collapse has not already occurred. I will tell you, my beloved. A little violet flame goes a long, long way. Legions of Light multiply your calls to the violet flame hour by hour and apply the sacred alchemy of the law of transmutation to the problems of the economy. . . .
>
> We repeat that it is in the influx of the sacred fire in an accelerated and rolling momentum of the violet flame invoked by Keepers of the Flame, as well as in specific calls for the economy, that the answer is given.[53]

In a dictation given that same year Saint Germain emphasized the efficacy of the violet flame:

> A half hour to the violet flame in invocation three times a day will result in—you know what? A holding of the balance for the earth *and* your own balance of personal karma.
>
> Some of you have come to me for many years in wonder and consternation that you make not further progress on the Path. And somehow you have overlooked the universal solvent of the violet flame. . . .
>
> Use the violet flame to go beyond yourself, to exceed yourself. It is the law of self-transcendence.
>
> See what it can do.[54]

In 1986, the Master said:

> We must have the physical sounding of the Word. This is the purpose of the dynamic decree as the most efficient and accelerated means of forestalling those things coming upon the earth or the individual as the outplaying of karma.[55]

On February 7, 1987, Saint Germain said that through the violet flame we could transcend the cycles of our karma:

> Indeed, it is possible for you to transcend all of the cycles of your karma in this age. But whatever the calling or the choosing of your soul, remember it cannot be accomplished without the Holy Spirit's gift to you of the violet

flame. And truly it is given in this hour. And there is no mantra more necessary to your deliverance and survival—for the violet flame is a physical flame!. . .

When you apply the spiritual science and the true path of the balancing of karma to the problems of the economy, to the problems of defense, education, drugs in America, you can make all the difference. For God is no respecter of persons.[56]

Saint Germain spoke of the chime of an ancient bell in his May 30, 1987 dictation:

I AM hopeful, in the profoundest sense of the word, that you will hear my cry and know this: that God our Father has truly entrusted to my heart an opportunity to save this nation under God, not I alone but many Masters of Light. . . .

The chime of an ancient bell now sounds. One of my angels called by Portia does begin this chiming. It will sound in the ear of every true son and daughter of Liberty as though he or she does hear a liberty bell that long ago rang on other spheres. This chiming, beloved, shall continue as the inner Call. And if it [stops] its chiming, beloved, Cosmos shall know that I, Saint Germain, have no longer opportunity to rescue the [Lightbearers].

Therefore, beloved, let the giving of the violet flame on behalf of those who respond and hear be continuous as a vigil unto the seventh age. So long as there are those who respond, even a single heart reciting my violet flame mantra in each twenty-four-hour cycle, Opportunity's door shall remain open and the chime shall be heard.[57]

From the moment I heard that dictation Saint Germain's promise began to grow in my heart—and the chime itself grew as a flame of hope. And then I said to myself, "What are you doing about this? You are not doing enough." That's when I decided I had to put out the *Save the World with Violet Flame!* decree and song cassettes with words and send them all over the world. My goal was to get the Lightbearers of the world together, regardless of their religious focus, to recognize the violet fire—and Saint Germain—as *the key* to their passage through the uncharted seas of the astral plane that every soul must navigate, here or hereafter, to get to the octaves of Light.

God's people, facing the karmic forces of self-destruction that are set in motion on planet earth today, also need the intercession of the Seven Archangels led by Archangel Michael for their 24-hour protection by angelic legions of blue lightning. These warriors of the mighty angel of the LORD sustain the protection of God's Presence round the righteous who praise his name I AM THAT I AM and call upon him daily. I have also released two cassettes to Archangel Michael: *Decrees and Songs to Archangel Michael* and *Archangel Michael's Rosary for Armageddon.*

It thrills me no end to be able to put in the hands of thousands of people the option, which they now have with these tapes, to make a daily decision to offer dynamic decrees. But even if I were to give the tapes to ten thousand souls of Light, it is still not enough. Because if there is a slip 'twixt the cup and the lip, the "cares of this world" may cause the few and the many to say, "Well, I think I'll just skip my decrees today. I gave them yesterday and I'll give them tomorrow, but I'll get by today and get these things done that I just haven't been able to get to lately."

And that's the beginning of the wedge that gets wider and wider. And pretty soon you've neglected your decrees for two and three days a week! Then the first thing you know a whole month has gone by and you've lost your momentum. And it's hard to get back into it.

I say, "Whistle *while* you work." Recite your mantras mentally or hold them in your heart. Play your tapes in the background rather than not at all. And get your decrees in while driving to and from wherever. Choose *your* call—the one you like the best and that works the best for you—and then give it whenever the mind or voice can utter it.

By calling on the name of God, I AM THAT I AM, you can invoke the immediate intercession of your beloved I AM Presence and Holy Christ Self. The Word of God is power. And a little goes a long way. Speak the mantra: "I AM the Resurrection and the Life!"[58]—and be it!

Those who remember to make the call and understand the supreme importance of doing so must shepherd those who do not. We must make the calls to the Seven Archangels daily for the protection of the Lightbearers that they remember the importance of the mission—and the means to fulfill it: the call. Yes, the call compels the answer. Make the call! "I will call upon the Lord and he will answer me," said the psalmist and the prophets.[59]

6

Capricorn Conjunctions
in 1989, 1990, 1991 and 1994:
Saturn Challenges All in Its Path

The conjunction of February 22–23, 1988, is not the only major grouping of planets in Capricorn we will see in the next 12 years. There will be more. For those who love to serve and know the Brotherhood's axiom "The reward for service is more service," there are plenty of opportunities ahead.

On December 27, 1989, the Sun, Moon, Mercury, Saturn, Uranus and Neptune were in Capricorn, with the Sun and Moon at 6° Capricorn making a close conjunction to Uranus at 5° Capricorn and a looser conjunction to Neptune at 11° Capricorn and Saturn at 15° Capricorn. Only Mercury, at 25° Capricorn, was outside of this conjunction (fig. 19). This is the first of several groupings of six planets in Capricorn that take place in 1989 and 1990. It occurs on the New Moon—when by definition the Sun and Moon are always conjoined, in this case at 6°22′ Capricorn—and will have a profound effect on the Soviet Union.

The Sun and the Moon, as mentioned, will be conjoined transiting Uranus at 5° Capricorn in the Soviet Union's tenth house (of the nation's leaders) and opposed the Soviet Union's Pluto conjoined transiting Jupiter at 5° Cancer in the Soviet Union's fourth house (of the people). Transiting Venus at 6° Aquarius and Mars at 6° Sagittarius are each quincunx (150° apart from) the Jupiter-Pluto conjunction, forming an acute isosceles triangle, called a Finger of God, which is bisected by the Sun-Moon-Uranus conjunction. This shows the likelihood that extraordinary pressure on Soviet leaders from violently unstable political and economic conditions could prompt them to use repressive measures throughout the empire and alter their timetables for war.

In late December 1990, there will be six planets* in Capricorn: the Sun, Mercury, Venus, Saturn, Uranus and Neptune.

*Astrologers acknowledge that the Sun and Moon are not planets, but they sometimes refer to them as such for convenience.

Capricorn New Moon Forms a Bisected Finger of God in the Soviet Union's Birth Chart
December 27, 1989

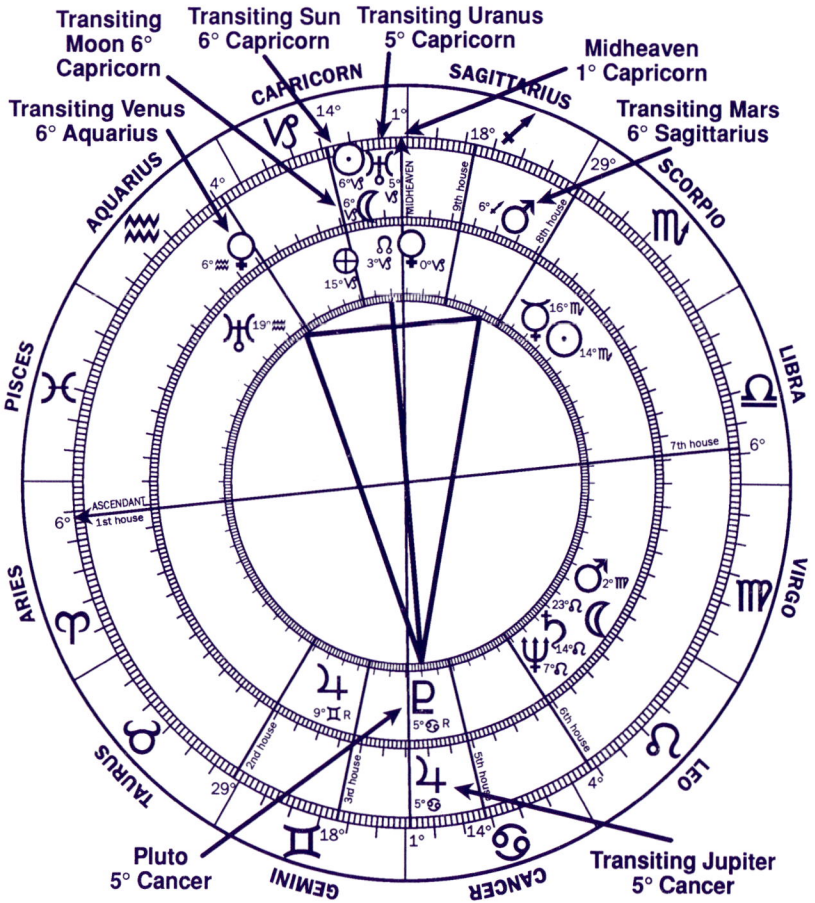

FIGURE 19 The first of several groupings of six-planets in Capricorn that take place in 1989-90 occurred December 27, 1989, on the New Moon. The Sun and Moon at 6°22′ Capricorn conjoined transiting Uranus at 5° Capricorn in the Soviet Union's tenth house (of the nation's leaders) and opposed the Soviet Union's Pluto conjoined transiting Jupiter at 5° Cancer in the Soviet fourth house (of the people). Transiting Venus at 6° Aquarius and Mars at 6° Sagittarius were quincunx (150° apart from) the Jupiter-Pluto conjunction, forming an acute isosceles triangle called a Finger of God, which is bisected by the Sun-Moon-Uranus conjunction. This could put extraordinary pressure on Soviet leaders from violently unstable political and economic conditions, which could prompt them to use repressive measures throughout the empire and alter their timetables for war.

While these planets do not form a conjunction, they will tend to have a depressing effect on the government, the economy and the people. Economist Ravi Batra, in his book *The Great Depression of 1990*, uses well-established U.S. economic cycles to argue convincingly that we are due for a "great depression" in 1990 that will last for seven years.[60]

On February 6, 1991, Saturn, the planet that rules Capricorn, will leave Capricorn and enter Aquarius. This will lighten the load somewhat, but with Uranus and Neptune remaining in Capricorn there will still be a major Capricorn challenge.

On January 11, 1994, seven planets—Mars, Venus, Neptune, the Moon, the Sun, Uranus and Mercury, in that order—will form a tight "megaconjunction" between 17° and 26° Capricorn (fig. 20). The unusually large number of planets in one sign and their proximity to each other gives this conjunction extraordinary power. But what makes this conjunction even more intense than the ones I have already discussed is that Saturn at 28° Aquarius forms a tight square with Pluto at 27° Scorpio. This increases the potential for the negative Capricorn characteristics to manifest. Under this conjunction we could experience economic and military challenges in the extreme.

In addition to heralding war and depression, the megaconjunction may well be the primary influence that produces major earthquakes. Further, we are apt to see the dramatic loss of political liberty in the United States and throughout the world, the establishment of dictatorships, an increase in spy and secret police activity, widespread plague and famine, the rise and fall of nations and power blocs, and danger from radioactivity, possibly from nuclear war.

These negatives will not be the sudden result of this conjunction only. Should they appear, they will be the logical manifestation of influences that began on the portentous day of February 13, 1988.

The Power Elite and Their Hidden Agenda

A behind-the-scenes feature of American history is the role played by a financial elite that has gained control of the U.S. monetary system. One of the major causes of the American Revolution was the desire for economic freedom. The war eliminated political tyranny but it did not automatically establish economic freedom.

The U.S. conceptional chart has Pluto at 27° Capricorn in the second house of money and finance (fig. 21). This indicates the probability of a powerful banking elite dominating the nation's

Megaconjunction of Seven Planets in Capricorn
January 11, 1994

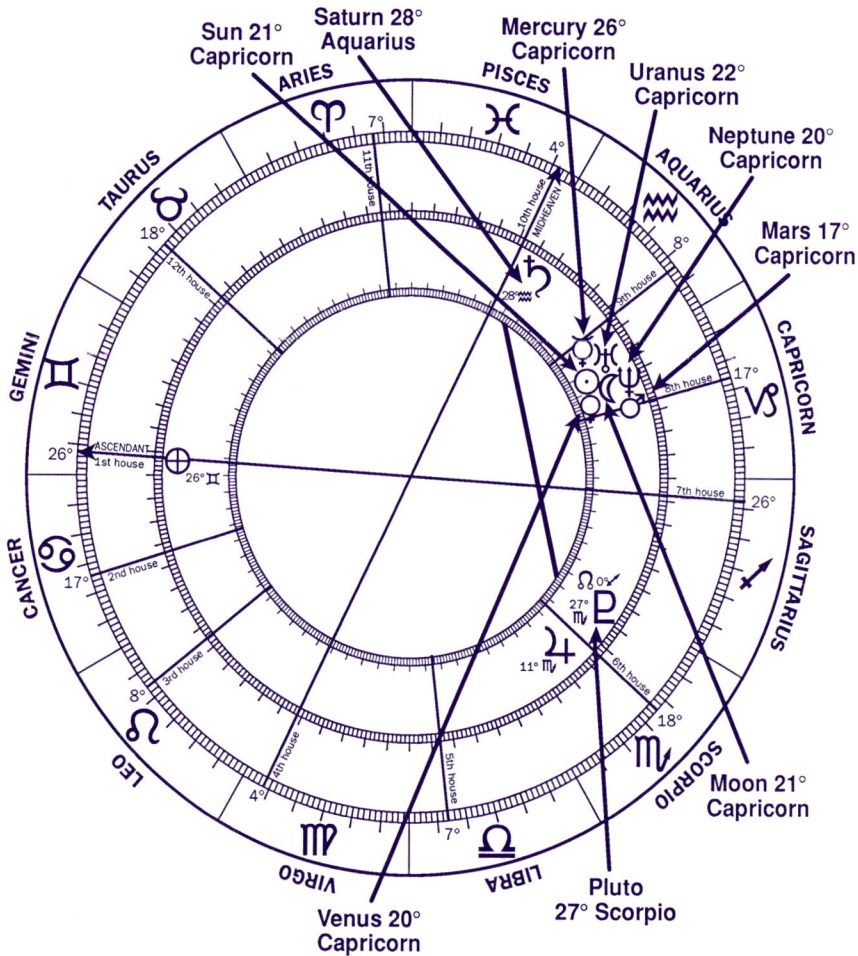

FIGURE 20 On January 11, 1994, seven planets—Mars, Venus, Neptune, the Moon, the Sun, Uranus and Mercury—will form a very tight "megaconjunction" in Capricorn. All seven planets will fall between 17° and 26° Capricorn. A nearly exact square of Saturn, the ruler of Capricorn, at 28° Aquarius to Pluto at 27° Scorpio is likely to intensify the conjunction's negative potential. This conjunction could trigger economic and military challenges in the extreme, the dramatic loss of political liberty throughout the world, the establishment of dictatorships, widespread plague and famine and danger from radioactivity, possibly from nuclear war.

Pluto in the Second House
of the United States Conceptional Chart

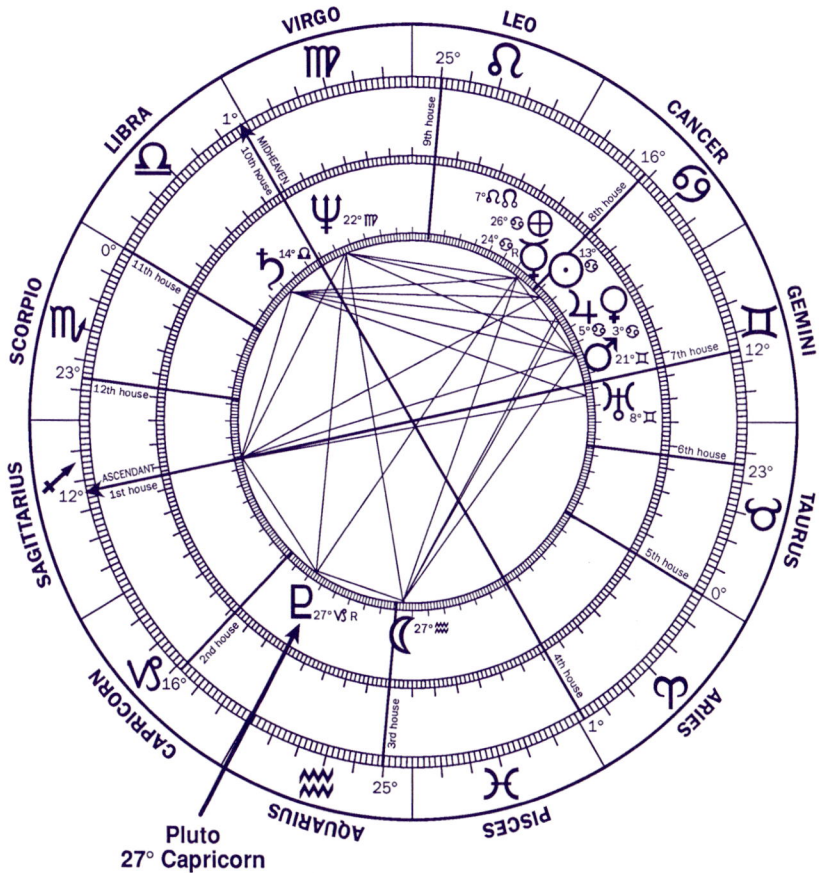

FIGURE 21 Pluto (which rules secrecy, power from wealth, and the need to control) is at 27° Capricorn (which rules political power) in the United States conceptional chart. It is in the second house of the Treasury, the Gross National Product, money, finance, banks and commerce. This shows the probability of a powerful banking elite dominating the nation's finances and thereby the government. On December 23, 1913, Congress created the Federal Reserve System and turned over to it the non-transferable money powers granted to Congress by the Constitution. The plan for the Fed was worked out in 1910 at a secret meeting of bankers held at J.P. Morgan's estate on Jekyll Island, Georgia. The Fed functions as a government-within-a-government on behalf of the banking community. Responsible only to itself, it is omnipotent. The Fed, with no Congressional supervision, can unilaterally create economic policy.

finances and thereby the government. To a greater or lesser degree this has happened, and we are all living under the black umbrella of their reign.

The power elite have attempted to exempt themselves from every possible responsibility or liability to the people. But they will not escape their judgment through the coming astrological configurations. They will face their karma, but they will not face it like everyone else. They will face it like "the kings of the earth and the great men and the rich men" who "hid themselves in the dens and in the rocks of the mountains; and said to the mountains and rocks, Fall on us, and hide us from the face of him that sitteth on the throne, and from the wrath of the Lamb: For the great day of his wrath is come; and who shall be able to stand?"[61]

Through their establishment of the Federal Reserve System on December 23, 1913, the power elite institutionalized their control of America's finances. By the Federal Reserve Act, which created the Federal Reserve System, Congress, on behalf of the banking and business community, turned over to a private corporation the nontransferable money powers granted to Congress in Article I, Section 8 of the Constitution. The plan for the Federal Reserve System was worked out in 1910 at a secret meeting of bankers held at J. P. Morgan's estate on Jekyll Island, Georgia.[62]

Few today understand the system's origins or how it works. In effect, the Federal Reserve System functions as a government-within-a-government on behalf of the banking community, which created it under the guise of acting in the public interest. Responsible only to itself, the Fed is omnipotent. With no Congressional supervision, it can, through its power to set interest rates and expand or contract the supply of money and credit, influence economic activity enough to unilaterally create economic policy. The Fed's chart, which has Pluto at 0° Cancer in the twelfth house of hidden influences, making an opposition to its Sun at 1° Capricorn, shows that it was created surreptitiously to serve the interests of hidden power blocs.

During the next 12 years the power of the financial elite may come to an end or be greatly diminished. Unfortunately, the influences that could cause the demise of the power elite could also cause the destruction of the U.S. economy, so intertwined are they. "How are the mighty fallen!"[63]

When the Fed was born, Neptune (the planet of deception and illusion) was at 27° Cancer, forming an exact opposition to the U.S. conceptional Pluto (the planet of secrecy, power and control) at 27° Capricorn (fig. 22). This shows the hidden but critical tie between

The Federal Reserve System's Neptune
Opposed Pluto in the United States Conceptional Chart

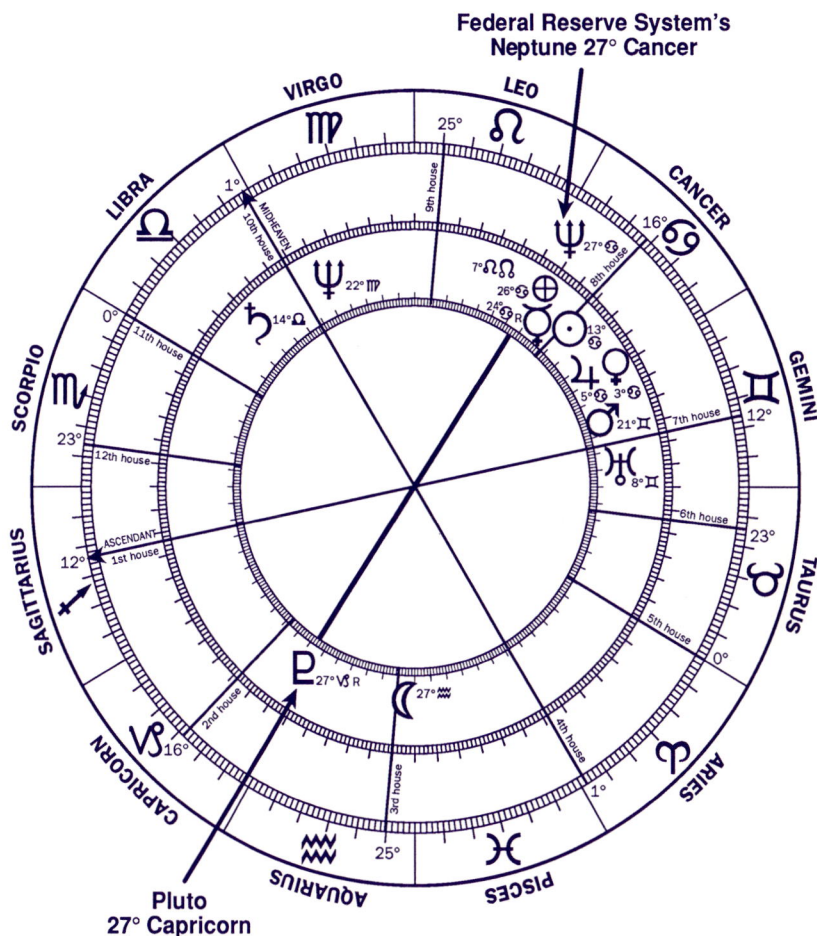

FIGURE 22   The Federal Reserve System's Neptune at 27° Cancer forms an opposition to the United States conceptional Pluto at 27° Capricorn in the second house of money and banking. This shows the hidden but critical tie between the Fed and the power elite and that the Fed could dissolve should the power elite lose power. Four eclipses forming hard (stressful) aspects to the U.S. conceptional Pluto could "eclipse" the financial elite's power: solar eclipses at 29° Cancer (July 21, 1990), 25° Capricorn (January 15, 1991), and 28° Aries (April 17, 1996); and a lunar eclipse at 25° Libra (April 15, 1995).

the Fed and the power elite. But because Neptune also rules the process of dissolution, the power elite's hold on the economy is potentially tenuous, and the Federal Reserve System could well dissolve if and when the power elite should lose their power.

The power elite are represented in the U.S. conceptional chart by Pluto at 27° Capricorn in the second house of money and finance. During the next eight years a series of eclipses will fall in close aspect to the U.S. conceptional Pluto: a solar eclipse at 29° Cancer on July 21, 1990, will oppose the U.S. conceptional Pluto; a solar eclipse at 25° Capricorn on January 15, 1991, will conjoin it; a lunar eclipse at 25° Libra on April 15, 1995, will square it; and a solar eclipse at 28° Aries on April 17, 1996, will also square it. These could have the effect of "eclipsing" the power elite's power.

Then, on February 5, August 14 and November 25, 1995, transiting Uranus (the planet of freedom and violent and unpredictable change) will make exact conjunctions to the U.S. conceptional Pluto at 27° Capricorn, shaking and perhaps breaking the power elite's grip on the U.S. economy (fig. 23).

Finally, on January 20, August 31 and November 14, 1997, after Uranus has shaken up the financial powers that be, transiting Neptune will make exact conjunctions with the U.S. conceptional Pluto at 27° Capricorn (fig. 23) and oppositions to the Federal Reserve System's Neptune at 27° Cancer. During this transit, the nation's financial system stands to dissolve and with it the power of the financial elite—if it has not already been destroyed or perhaps restructured along more enlightened lines, of, by and for the people, by the influence of Uranus. It is at this time that the Federal Reserve System is also likely to be restructured or dissolved, depriving the financial elite of their most powerful mechanism of control over the government and economy, hence the people of the United States.

The Fed is the Achilles' heel of the Establishment's control of this nation's money system. Through the Fed's vulnerability by their betrayal of the people their downfall is assured. For these "financial powers that be" are to be counted as archdeceivers amongst the fallen angels who were cast out of heaven by Archangel Michael and his hosts in the war that was fought and won in heaven that must now be fought and won on planet earth.[64]

The fallen angels had betrayed the Universal Christ in all of God's people. Therefore their karmic judgment was to be banished from heaven. They were forced to descend to the level of their dark deeds and take physical embodiment until they should repent of their wickedness and turn and serve the Light of God

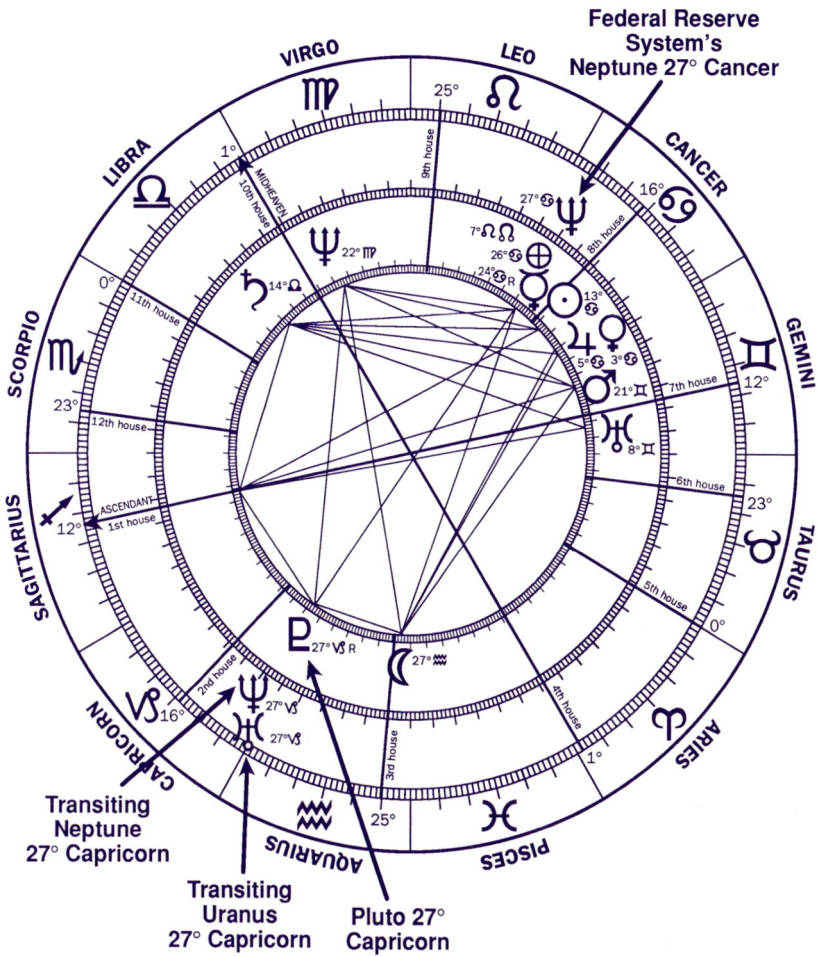

Transiting Uranus and Neptune Conjoined the
United States Conceptional Pluto
1995 and 1997

FIGURE 23 On February 5, August 14 and November 25, 1995, transiting Uranus (the planet of freedom and unpredictable change) will make exact conjunctions to the United States conceptional Pluto (the planet of power and control) at 27° Capricorn in the second house of the nation's money and may signal a break in the power elite's grip on the United States economy. Then, on January 20, August 31 and November 14, 1997, transiting Neptune (the planet of dissolution) will make exact conjunctions with the U.S. conceptional Pluto and nearly exact oppositions to the Federal Reserve System's Neptune at 27° Cancer. This transit of Neptune could dissolve the power of the financial elite. It could also lead to the dissolution of the nation's financial system, if it has not already been destroyed or restructured along more enlightened lines.

in his people. And when their time of opportunity for atonement is up, if they still refuse to bend the knee before the Christed ones, they will stand trial before the Court of the Sacred Fire and pass through the second death.[65]

These are the godless who extinguished their own divine spark by their denial of the Christ Presence in the issue of God and their defiance before the LORD God himself, which has not ceased to this very hour. With no God flame burning in their breasts, these hollowed-out ones must devise ways and means to steal the Light of the people. At the top of the list are multiple methods of stealing people's money or getting them to part with their earnings, which represent their lifeblood, their labor and their self-worth.

And they have succeeded in manipulating the people by manipulating their Light; for the Light of the people goes into the goods and services that are the products of their labor. And it is the people's money that the power elite then concentrate in the money systems to keep their corporate power and their controls in international commerce alive.

The only way out for the children of the Light is for the Sons of God in the earth to lead them (by the Teachings of the Ascended Masters and by example) to come out from among the power elite, to withdraw their monies from their investments in international establishment banking houses and corporations. To withdraw support from the financial elite will no doubt contribute to their decline, for the only power and money they have is the people's; but most importantly it will rescue the people from being destroyed along with the financial elite when they meet their karma that will surely descend according to the signs in the heavens and the signs in the earth.

The power elite believe that they are the gods in the earth who hold our destiny in their hands. Therefore they do not acknowledge Almighty God. And for their crimes against every son and daughter of God, their karma will descend. And they will go down.

But the people do not have to go down with them. This nation does not have to be destroyed by the power elite, although that is the direction in which it is headed. And unless the people wake up and denounce the golden calf consciousness, that's the way it's going to end up.

But if shepherds will rise up in the midst of the people to teach them what is happening, what is bound to happen, and show them how to set up their own investment systems and their own banking houses and how to invest in those things that are not going to fall when the economy falls, the people will survive and only the fallen ones will go down.

Abraham Lincoln stood firm in his defense of America from takeover by the banking establishment, and he was assassinated by their interests because they were determined to bring in this system that we are under today and this yoke that is upon us.[66]

Today, more than a century later, we can see that we the people of the United States of America, "in order to form a more perfect union," must take our stand based on our union with God and manifest the Light of our Christhood that will see to it that a nation and her sacred labor and her monetary system survive out from under the control of these fallen ones.

The Correlation between the Sunspot Cycle and the Onset of Wars and Earthquakes

There are other indicators of war for the 1990s. First, there is a correlation between the sunspot cycle, which peaks about every 11 years, and the onset of wars. The term "sunspot cycle" refers to the cyclic increase and decrease in the number of sunspots on the surface of the sun. The cycle reaches its peak (i.e., maximum) about every 11 years. Biologist Marsha Adams, an expert on the relationship between sunspots and earthquakes, compared the outbreak of wars with sunspot cycles going back to the 1700s. She found that wars tend to occur about three years after the peak of a sunspot cycle, although they occasionally occur before.

Adams also found that two years after the sunspot cycle peaks, very large-magnitude earthquakes (those eight and above on the Richter scale) occur for a two- to three-year period.

The current cycle, which is expected to reach its maximum in late 1989 or early 1990, is rising faster than previous cycles and indications are that it may be the largest on record.

There are other astrological cycles that indicate a high probability of war in the late 1980s and early 1990s. French astrologers Henri-Joseph Gouchon and Claude Ganeau discovered three major cycles of peace and war based on the zodiacal proximity of the five outer planets, Jupiter through Pluto, to each other. As astrologer Charles Harvey explains, Gouchon "found that by calculating the total angular separation between each of the pairs of the outer planets" (Jupiter-Saturn, Jupiter-Uranus, et cetera) on an annual basis "and then plotting the results on a graph, the resulting curve showed a striking correspondence with the main periods of international crisis and, most impressively, major and sustained 'lows' for the period 1914–18 and 1940–45."[67] Astrologer André Barbault called this the "Cyclical Index." The Korean War, the Suez Crisis and the Vietnam War also correlate with a negative slope on the graph.

Ganeau developed two cycles—the "Index of Cyclic Equilibrium" and the "Index of Cyclical Variation"—which are variations of the Cyclical Index. All three indexes have successfully predicted positive periods of harmony, growth, optimism and peace and negative periods of destabilization, disruption and decay. In the late 1980s and early 1990s these indexes will be in the depths of their negative cycle, indicating conflict of the magnitude of past world wars.[68]

The Great Divine Director:
Initiator of the Sons and Daughters of God under the Hierarchy of Capricorn

Capricorn 'initiations' do not have to be negative. They can and do appear to be negative since they have the power to collapse all that is not founded on the bedrock of reality.

But for those of such foresight as our father Abraham, Capricorn influences can be and are beneficial. If peoples and nations build on the foundation of Truth with the Universal Christ and his flame within the heart as the chief cornerstone, then the ascended beings who are part of the hierarchy of Capricorn will empower those builders with the vision of the city which hath eternal foundations in the law of the Logos "whose builder and maker is God."[69]

The hierarchs of Capricorn help us to solidify our gains and to organize our resources, including long-term planning and building in areas that supersede the last round of self-mastery. They also teach us to enter spirals of self-transcendence in ever-new and spiritually exalting realms.

The Great Divine Director is the Ascended Master known as the hierarch of Capricorn. He holds the focus of the hierarchy of Capricorn and its flame of God-power for the evolutions of this world. This means that when our initiations come under this hierarchy, we face the Great Divine Director and receive our instruction and examinations under his rod. The Seven Archangels assist him in this discipline of the evolutions of earth.

The Great Divine Director is the beloved Guru of Saint Germain. Please visualize powerful golden yellow and sapphire-blue rays emanating from his aura and entire electromagnetic field. He wears a blue belt that drapes from his waist to his knees like a masonic apron, sealing his lower chakras from encounters with the world and the worldly as he passes through our midst and the astral plane to rescue the chelas of Saint Germain for their victory in Aquarius. For their time has come and the Great Divine Director calls them Home.

His flowing blue silken robes move with the zephyrs of the Holy Spirit that surround him, while white and blue and yellow diamonds appear as though suspended in his aura, or perhaps sewn by angelic hands upon a veil of light that surrounds him, to veil our eyes from the brilliance of this Master whose attainment is of cosmic levels.

The Great Divine Director—words fail me when I would convey to you the gentle all-power of this hierarch of Light whose private etheric retreat, the Cave of Light, is in the Himalayas. And so instead I shall give you the words to his divine decree, which we have also set to music. By so engaging your energies with his through this beautiful and powerful decree, which he dictated many years ago to the Messenger Mark L. Prophet, you can establish your own special heart-tie to the Master that mere words cannot describe.

It is his Causal Body and Presence that we need to magnetize to ourselves in this hour of planetary Capricorn initiations because he is the hierarch who stands on the line of Capricorn for the Aquarian age. So please join me now in giving the decree to the Great Divine Director.

The Great Divine Director

Preamble:

> In the name of the beloved Mighty Victorious Presence of God I AM in me, my very own beloved Holy Christ Self, Holy Christ Selves of all mankind, the beloved Great Divine Director, beloved Lanello, the entire Spirit of the Great White Brotherhood and the World Mother, elemental life—fire, air, water and earth! I call for divine direction throughout my affairs, the activities of The Summit Lighthouse, the governments of the nations and all Ascended Master activities, worlds without end:

Invocation:

> Beloved Mighty I AM Presence, beloved legions of Light from the heart of God in the Great Central Sun, beloved Great Divine Director, beloved Manu, beloved Guru of Saint Germain, come forth now and place your mighty Electronic Presence around us. Bathe us in your aura of light. Lock your living light and the flames of your seven chakras into our chakras now.

Blaze the full power of the Light of God that never fails!
Blaze the full power of the Light of God that never fails!
Blaze the full power of the Great Central Sun Magnet!
We call for the healing of the planet and the holding of the balance in this Capricorn conjunction beginning February 22, 1988.

Blaze the full power of the grid of light of your Great Blue Causal Body! Blaze the full power of the grid of light of your Great Blue Causal Body! Blaze the full power of the Great Blue Causal Body of the Great Divine Director and of the entire Spirit of the Great White Brotherhood for the holding of the balance in the earth and throughout the planetary body—in the United States of America, California, San Francisco, Los Angeles and all cities of the nations.

Let the mighty grid of light of the inner blueprint for planet earth and her victory in the age of gold come forth now through the great hierarchy of Capricorn.

Come forth now, O will of God! Come forth now, O blue lightning of the Mind of God, for the breaking up of that old karma. Let its transmutation be complete by the violet flame!

Therefore, in the holy will of God, in the immaculate concept for planet earth's victory held in the heart of Mother Mary, we decree in the name of the Father, the Son, the Holy Spirit and the Divine Mother. Amen.

Together:

1. Divine Director, Come!
    Seal me in thy ray
    Guide me to my Home
    By thy Love I pray.

Refrain: Thy blue belt protect my world
          Thy dazzling jewels so rare
          Surround my form and adorn
          With essence of thy prayer.

2. Make us one, guard each hour
    Like the sun's radiant power
    Let me be, ever free
    Now and for eternity.

3. Blessed Master R.
    You are near, not far
    Flood with Light, God's own might
    Radiant like a star.

4. Divine Director dear
   Give me Wisdom pure
   Thy Power ever near
   Helps me to endure.

5. Shed thy Light on me
   Come, make me whole
   Banner of the free
   Mold and shape my soul.

And in full Faith I consciously accept this manifest,
manifest, manifest! (3x) right here and now with full Power,
eternally sustained, all-powerfully active, ever expanding
and world enfolding until all are wholly ascended in the
Light and free!
Beloved I AM! Beloved I AM! Beloved I AM!

The Great Divine Director is known as the Master R. He
founded the house of Rakoczy and it was he who carried the flame
of freedom, the violet flame, from the altars of Atlantis to safety in
the Carpathian foothills.

Transylvania, the home of Saint Germain and the Great
Divine Director, is in Romania today. The focus of the flame of
freedom is there and in other retreats of the Great White Brotherhood, such as that of the Archangel Zadkiel and his twin flame
Holy Amethyst over the Caribbean. There are also focuses of the
freedom flame in the Cave of Symbols, Saint Germain's retreat
near the Grand Teton Mountain Range in Wyoming, in Kuan
Yin's retreat over Beijing, China, and in the retreat of Arcturus
and Victoria over the nation of Angola. The Great Divine Director's retreat focuses the violet flame not only for Eastern Europe
but for the entire European continent.

You can invoke the power of the Great Divine Director to
seal your aura and chakras for the difficult times ahead. You can
visualize the tremendous power of his chakras superimposed
over your own chakras. From his third-eye chakra shoots forth a
powerful beacon of light that clears everything in its track. You
can visualize the tremendous power of the light blazing from
his heart chakra into your own. You can visualize his famous blue
belt on yourself, protecting your chakras from the density of the
planet or from bombardment by any kind of negative energies.

The Great Divine Director is a great adept. He is a Cosmic
Being. He is the Manu of the Seventh Root Race. *Manu* is a Sanskrit
word meaning the progenitor and lawgiver of the evolutions of

God on earth. The Manu and his divine complement are ascended twin flames assigned by the Father-Mother God to sponsor and ensoul the Christic image for a root race—a certain evolution or lifewave of souls who embody as a group and have a unique archetypal pattern, divine plan and mission to fulfill on earth. The seventh root race is intended to embody in the Aquarian age under the Great Divine Director's direction on the continent of South America.

So, to the heart of the Great Divine Director we call for the magnificence of the God-power of Capricorn to be directed to the absolute God-victory of planet earth.

The U.S. and the USSR—Antagonists in War:
The Portents of the December 1987 Superpower Summit

Now is the time to ask the overwhelming question: Who will engage in these wars prophesied in the handwriting in the skies? First let us recapitulate the configurations that point to war: the Saturn-Uranus conjunctions of 1988, including Saturn and Uranus conjoined the Galactic Center; Mars, Saturn, Uranus and Neptune in Capricorn on February 22–23, 1988 (fig. 1); and the Capricorn megaconjunction on January 11, 1994 (fig. 20). To this we can add the sunspot cycle and Gouchon's and Ganeau's cycles of peace and war.

If we analyze the astrology of earth's nations in light of the worldwide military and political situation, we must conclude that a great many nations are likely to be engaged in some kind of conflict, major or minor, in the coming six to twelve years. Nevertheless, I believe that the United States and the Soviet Union are prime candidates for a major war in the near future.

Most people refuse to even consider that eventuality. Many Americans believe that war is out of date. They think we are about to enter a golden age and that we have come too far for God to allow the earth to be destroyed by war or cataclysm. In the present context of the players on the world stage and the prophecy of the stars, I believe this is sheer wishful thinking.

The United States conceptional Mars at 21° Gemini makes a nearly exact square to her Neptune at 22° Virgo (fig. 24). This configuration shows that despite a generally practical nature, the American people have a strong tendency to engage in illusory thinking and self-deception, particularly in matters related to other nations, foreign affairs and war.

In all areas of national life, things are not what they seem. Neptune, the planet of illumination and refinement, is also the planet of illusion and deception. Since Neptune is heavily afflicted

Mars Square Neptune
in the United States Conceptional Chart

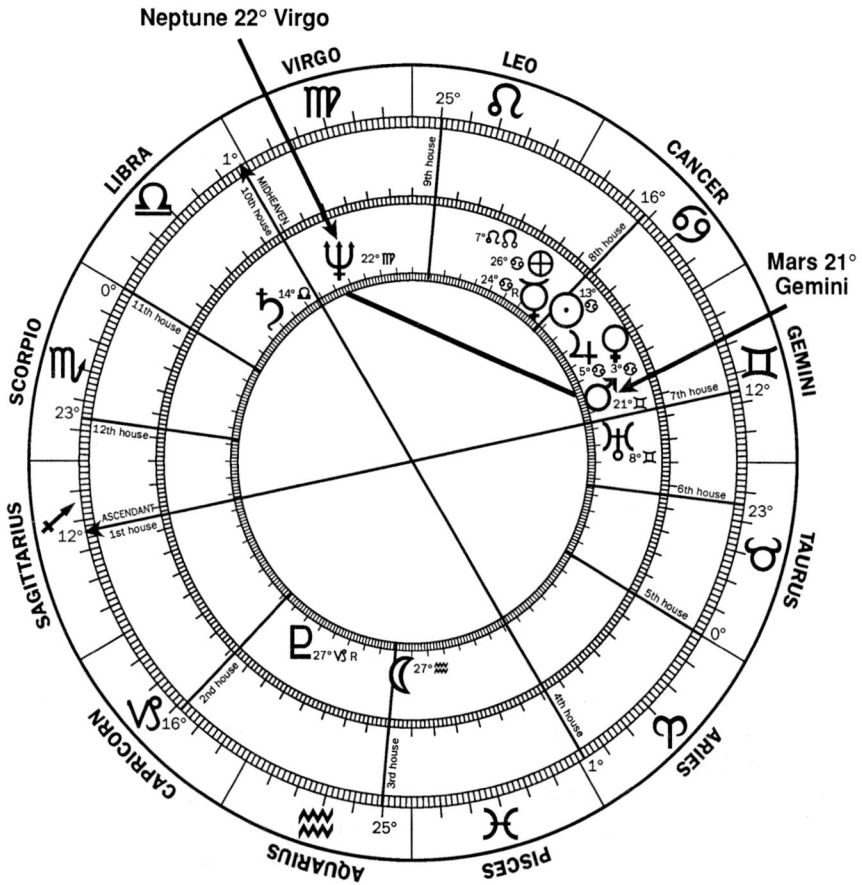

FIGURE 24 The United States conceptional Mars at 21° Gemini makes a nearly exact square to her Neptune at 22° Virgo. This configuration shows that despite a generally practical nature, the American people have a strong tendency to engage in illusory thinking and self-deception, particularly in matters related to other nations, foreign affairs and war. Since Neptune rules drugs and Mars rules war, this configuration shows that foreign nations could wage drug warfare against the United States. It also shows that the wars on drugs waged by both Republican and Democratic administrations have been confused, ineffective and, more often than not, mainly public relations efforts.

in both the U.S. conceptional and birth chart, we must be on guard against illusion, especially the illusion that if we "think peace," peace will come about.

Mere thinking cannot transmute the karma of nations or of the fallen angels who ever since they were cast out of heaven by Archangel Michael and his legions have been waging war against the children of the Light, not to mention their wars of rivalry, their wars to dominate territory, commodities and populations—turf wars for which they have lined us up and used us as fodder. What we must realize is that their intent has not changed. While we are engaged in our meditations on peace, they are busy in their plans at war-making.

I can tell you this truly because Saint Germain has taken me to hear the behind-the-scenes conversations in the Kremlin and in the secret places of our government. I can assure you that what the people want is not what the power elite wants. And they are the ones who pull the strings on this planet; therefore it is their astrology and their karma that we are talking about tonight. They are trying to somehow escape their karma by running away with our planet. And we have to be absolutely certain that we don't let them.

I would like to explore the astrological influences that indicate a high probability of war between the United States and the Soviet Union.

I pointed out earlier that the U.S. natal Sun at 10° Taurus is opposed to, or in polarity with, the Soviet Union's Sun at 14° Scorpio. As a result, the destinies of these two nations are intimately related. A curious pattern of friendship and enmity derives from this polarity.

Now, since I am, as far as I know, the only prophet who is taking the natal chart of America from the Inauguration Day of George Washington on April 30, 1789, I would suspect that I am the only one who is drawing these conclusions from the interrelationship of the U.S. and Soviet natal charts.

Again, the incomplete and incorrect knowledge of astrology today is giving the American people (who follow time-honored selections of charts by respected authorities) a false picture, just as the incomplete and incorrect interpretation of Nostradamus has given a false reading to the American people as to what is coming upon them if they don't wake up to political and spiritual realities.

There is nothing so dangerous as an incorrect astrological chart, and no one in such grave danger as he who follows it and his preferred illusions. In the first place such a person is not properly forewarned, and in the second, he becomes too comfortable in his illusion and he proceeds to use his incorrect source to defend his erroneous posture.

For the first time since the relationship between the super-powers began 70 years ago, Pluto will make its conjunction to the Soviet Sun at 14° Scorpio and its opposition to the U.S. Sun at 10° Taurus (fig. 25). This occurs between January 1988 and October 1991, when Pluto is transiting between 12° and 18° Scorpio. Pluto makes exact conjunctions with the Soviet Sun at 14°33′ Scorpio on December 31, 1988, April 5, 1989, and October 24, 1989.

In mundane astrology, or the astrology of nations and political trends, Pluto transits of this sort are associated with the outbreak of wars and with mortal challenges other than war.

I would like to give you an idea of what to expect from a Pluto transit over a natal Sun. Pluto was transiting over the U.S. natal Sun at 10° Taurus during the Civil War (1861–1865). As the war began on April 12, 1861, Pluto was at 8° Taurus. By the war's end on April 9, 1865, it had crossed to 12° Taurus. It is difficult to imagine a more serious national challenge than the Civil War, which could easily have resulted in the end of the United States of America had it not been for enlightened leadership. The challenge we are facing today is equally serious. And we face it with the popularity seekers and poll watchers who are our leaders.

As a result of transiting Pluto conjoined the Soviet Sun and opposed the U.S. Sun, even if the nations do not go to war, they will face severe challenges. These could include financial problems, nuclear power accidents, power struggles, civil unrest, terrorism and a challenge to both governments' grip on power.

Pluto alone has not, to the best of my knowledge, triggered a war. Wars are usually associated with some combination of one or more of the outer planets and Mars. These may either be by transit or in the nations' birth charts.

On February 14, 1989, transiting Mars at 15° Taurus conjoined the U.S. natal Sun at 10° Taurus and opposed the Soviet Sun at 14° Scorpio conjoined transiting Pluto at 15° Scorpio. This is an explosive placing and could ignite a war. As Mars continues its transits during this period, it will be capable of initiating conflict between the two nations every time it makes a conjunction, square or opposition to the U.S. and Soviet natal Suns.

On November 26, 1989, the Moon made exact conjunctions to transiting Mars at 15°10′ Scorpio and transiting Pluto at 15°53′ Scorpio, forming a Moon-Mars-Pluto conjunction at 15° Scorpio within one and a half degrees of the Soviet Sun at 14°33′ Scorpio (fig. 26). The conjunction of Pluto, Mars and the Moon with the

Transiting Pluto Conjoined the Soviet Union's Sun and Opposed the United States Sun
January 1988–October 1991

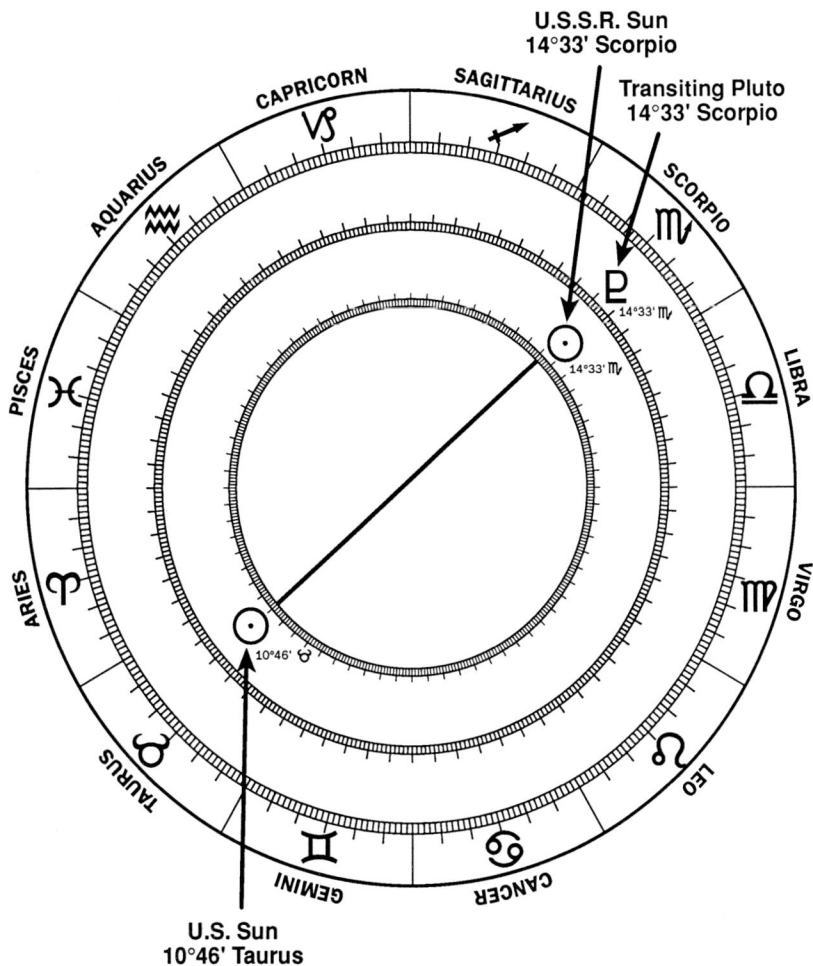

FIGURE 25 As Pluto transits between 12° and 18° Scorpio from January 1988 to October 1991, it will make three exact conjunctions with the Soviet Union's Sun at 14° Scorpio opposed to the United States natal Sun at 10° Taurus. This is the first time in the history of the Soviet Union that this configuration has taken place since Pluto takes 248 years to orbit the Sun. Pluto transits of this sort are associated with the outbreak of wars and with mortal challenges other than war. Even if the United States and the Soviet Union do not go to war, they will face severe challenges that could include economic problems, power struggles, civil unrest and terrorism.

Transiting Pluto, Mars and Moon Conjoined the Soviet Union's Sun and Opposed the United States Sun
November 26, 1989

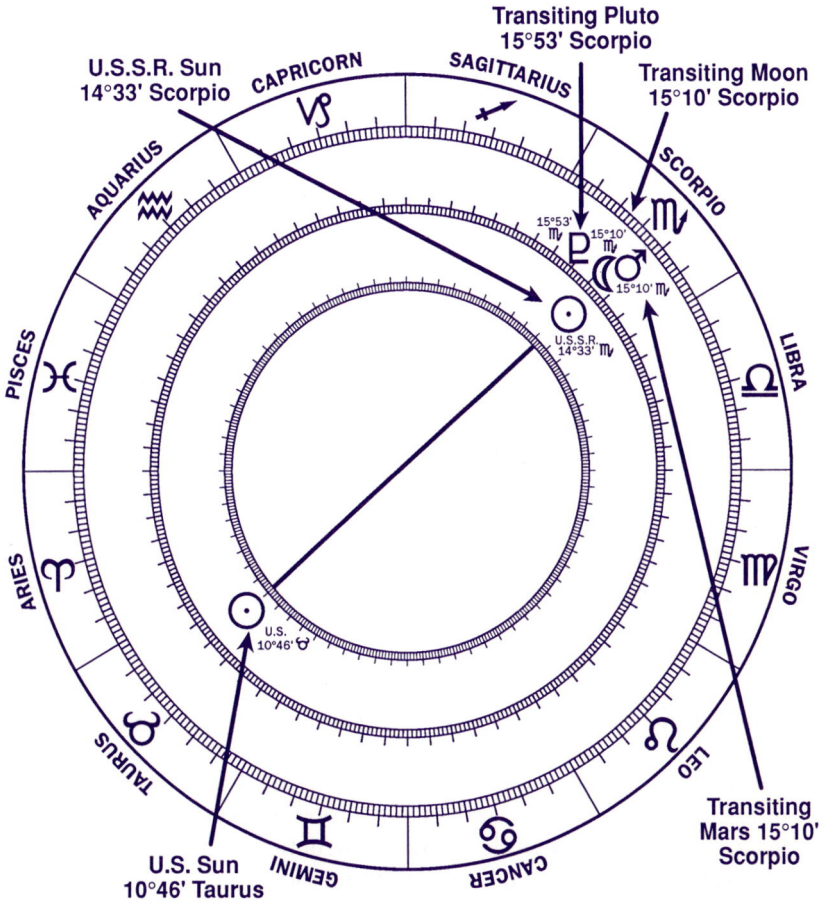

FIGURE 26   On November 26, 1989, the Moon made exact conjunctions to transiting Mars at 15°10′ Scorpio (1:48 p.m. PST) and transiting Pluto at 15°53′ Scorpio (3:16 p.m. PST), forming a Moon-Mars-Pluto conjunction at 15° Scorpio within one and a half degrees of the Soviet Sun at 14°33′ Scorpio. The conjunction of Pluto, Mars and the Moon with the Soviet natal Sun opposed the United States natal Sun at 10°46′ Taurus. This is one of several configurations that has the potential to ignite a war between the superpowers at any time between January 1988 and October 1991.

Soviet natal Sun opposed the United States natal Sun at 10°46′ Taurus. This is one of several configurations that has the potential to ignite a war between the superpowers at any time between January 1988 and October 1991.

This transit follows the November 13, 1989 Saturn-Neptune conjunction in Capricorn opposed the U.S. conceptional Jupiter in Cancer, which is likely to trigger major debt liquidation in the United States and possibly lead to the fall or paralysis of the U.S. government. For this and other reasons that I will soon explain, November 26, 1989, is one of several critical dates for war between the superpowers.

When we take a closer look at the relationship between the natal charts of the United States and the Soviet Union, the intensity of the Pluto transit becomes even more clear. Critical planets in the charts of the two nations form a grand square, which is a powerful configuration that occurs when four or more planets are at 90-degree angles.

In addition to the U.S. Sun at 10° Taurus forming an opposition to the Soviet Sun at 14° Scorpio and Mercury at 16° Scorpio, the U.S. Pluto at 19° Aquarius forms a conjunction with the Soviet Uranus at 19° Aquarius, which forms an opposition to the Soviet Saturn at 14° Leo (fig. 27).

This grand square indicates that the relationship between the nations can be violently explosive. The opposition of the U.S. and Soviet Suns shows that this configuration influences the life of both nations. The conjunction of the U.S. Pluto and the Soviet Uranus suggests an unforeseen break in relations accompanied by danger from the destructive use of nuclear energy, violence arising out of reform, and war. This conjunction opposed to the Soviet Saturn shows that interactions between the superpowers could unexpectedly cause the death of one or both nations, or, at the very least, cause widespread death and destruction.

Grand squares tend to be static, however. It would take extreme pressure, such as could be provided by a transit of Pluto, to release the energy locked up in this grand square.

In 1990 the progressed* U.S. conceptional Sun will be at 15° Aquarius conjoined the U.S. natal Pluto and the Soviet Uranus at 19° Aquarius. The progressed U.S. conceptional Ascendant will be at 13° Leo conjoined the Soviet Saturn at 14° Leo. Transiting Pluto will still be close to the Soviet Sun. And there will be two lunar eclipses

---

*Astrologers find a progressed chart useful in focusing on the stellar momentums that impact persons, nations or institutions throughout their life. The progressed chart is calculated by advancing (or "progressing") the positions of the planets and the Ascendant and Midheaven at the rate of a day's movement for each year from birth.

United States-Soviet Union Grand Square in Their Combined Birth Charts

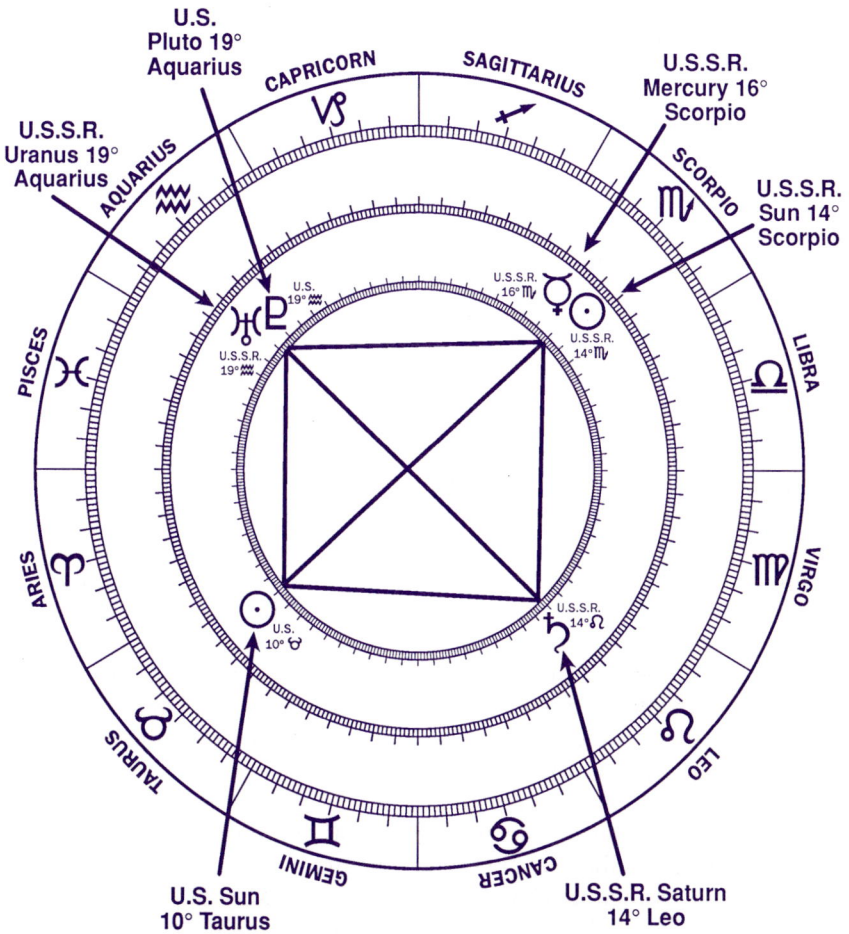

FIGURE 27 Key planets in the birth charts of the United States and the Soviet Union combine to form a grand square, literally a squarelike planetary pattern. This grand square indicates that the relationship between the two nations can be violently explosive. The opposition of the U.S. and Soviet Suns shows that this configuration influences the life of both nations. The conjunction of the U.S. Pluto and the Soviet Uranus suggests an unforeseen break in relations accompanied by danger from the destructive use of nuclear energy, violence arising out of reform, and war. This conjunction opposed to the Soviet Saturn shows that interactions between the superpowers could unexpectedly cause the death of one or both nations—or, at the very least, cause widespread death and destruction. Grand squares tend to be static. It would take extreme pressure, such as could be provided by a transit of Pluto, to release the energy locked up in this grand square.

in close aspect to every planet in the U.S.-USSR grand square. The first eclipse will take place on February 9, 1990, at 20° Leo (fig. 28). This could trigger a U.S.-Soviet conflict much in the same way a lunar eclipse triggered the Chernobyl disaster. It occurs about five hours after an exact conjunction of transiting Mars and Uranus at 7°57' Capricorn opposed to the Soviet Pluto at 5° Cancer. This Mars-Uranus-Pluto opposition links the planets of war (Mars), unpredictable events (Uranus), and widespread death and destruction (Pluto) and is extremely dangerous. When combined with the effects of the eclipse of the Moon, the results could be disastrous.

The second eclipse takes place on August 6, 1990, at 13° Aquarius (fig. 29). Like the lunar eclipse of February 9, 1990, it has the potential to ignite a war between the superpowers. There are other aspects that could trigger war between the United States and the Soviet Union during this period, but I will leave it at that.

I want to remind you that once we get past this period (with or without a war), it does not mean that the rest of the century will be peaceful. The Capricorn megaconjunction of January 1994 is fully capable of igniting war. At the close of this century and the beginning of the next we will have another triple Saturn-Uranus square.

On July 17, 1999, Saturn will be at 15°37' Taurus square to Uranus at 15°37' Aquarius (fig. 30). Not only does this Saturn-Uranus square indicate war, but it also activates the grand square in the combined birth charts of the United States and the Soviet Union, showing that there is the prospect for a major war between the nations during the period of 18 months before and after July 17, 1999. The exact Saturn-Uranus square of July 17, 1999, will be followed by two more that will also activate the U.S.-USSR grand square. These will occur on November 14, 1999, when Saturn will be at 13°4' Taurus square to Uranus at 13°4' Aquarius, and on May 13, 2000, when Saturn will at 20°46' Taurus square Uranus at 20°46' Aquarius.

Saint Germain has said:

> Unless sufficient quantity of violet flame be invoked, elemental life will no longer bear the burden of the cross of planetary karma and there will be in this decade significant changes in the very surface of the earth. . . . [70]

> See the handwriting on the wall: on schedule, the descending karma of the Dark Cycle, the seven last plagues, the Four Horsemen—all delivering to the earth the mandate of personal and planetary karma. Yet God has already arranged ahead of time from time immemorial for the staying of the hand of that Darkness, for its transmutation by the Light of the heart and by the sacred fire. [71]

Eclipse of the Moon in Leo Activates the United States-Soviet Union Grand Square
February 9, 1990

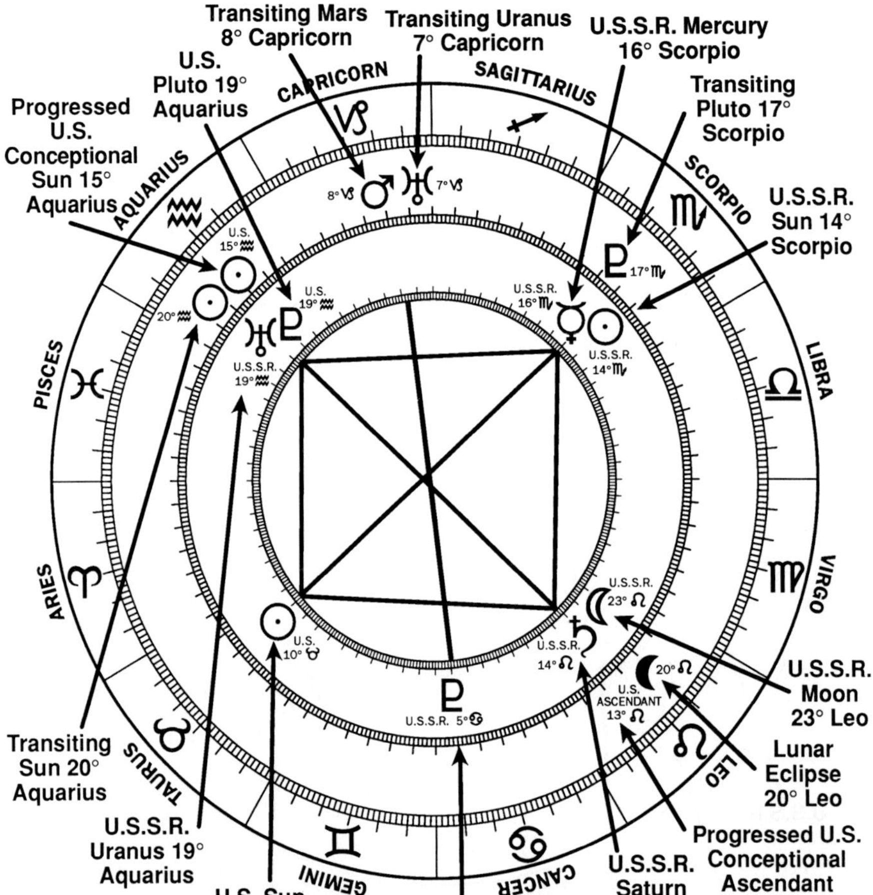

Transiting Mars 8° Capricorn

U.S. Pluto 19° Aquarius

Transiting Uranus 7° Capricorn

U.S.S.R. Mercury 16° Scorpio

Transiting Pluto 17° Scorpio

Progressed U.S. Conceptional Sun 15° Aquarius

U.S.S.R. Sun 14° Scorpio

U.S.S.R. Moon 23° Leo

Lunar Eclipse 20° Leo

Progressed U.S. Conceptional Ascendant 13° Leo

U.S.S.R. Saturn 14° Leo

U.S.S.R. Pluto 5° Cancer

U.S. Sun 10° Taurus

U.S.S.R. Uranus 19° Aquarius

Transiting Sun 20° Aquarius

FIGURE 28   In 1990 the progressed U.S. conceptional Sun will be at 15°
Aquarius conjoined the U.S. natal Pluto and the Soviet Uranus at 19°
Aquarius. The progressed U.S. conceptional Ascendant will be at 13° Leo
conjoined the Soviet Saturn at 14° Leo. Transiting Pluto will still be close
to the Soviet Sun. And there will be two lunar eclipses in close aspect to
every planet in the U.S.-U.S.S.R. grand square. The first will take place on
February 9, 1990, at 20° Leo. This could trigger a U.S.-Soviet conflict
much in the same way a lunar eclipse triggered the Chernobyl disaster. It
occurs about five hours after an exact conjunction of transiting Mars and
Uranus at 7°57′ Capricorn opposed to the Soviet Pluto at 5° Cancer. This
Mars-Uranus-Pluto opposition links the planets of war (Mars), unpredictable events (Uranus), and widespread death and destruction (Pluto) and is
extremely dangerous. When combined with the effects of the eclipse of the
Moon, the results could be devastating.

Eclipse of the Moon in Aquarius Activates
the United States-Soviet Union Grand Square
August 6, 1990

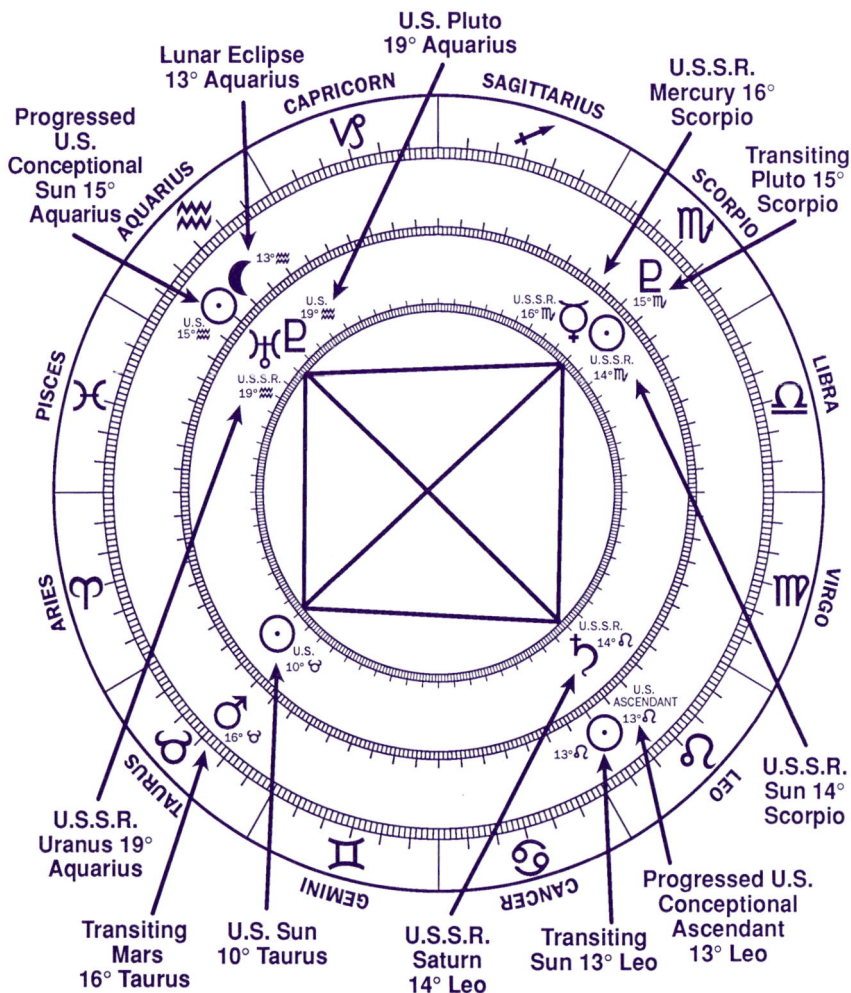

FIGURE 29 On August 6, 1990, there will be a partial eclipse of the Moon at 13° Aquarius. Like the lunar eclipse of February 9, 1990, this eclipse has the potential to ignite a war between the superpowers. The two eclipses are related and, in fact, are almost mirror images of one another since they fall in nearby degrees of the polar signs Leo and Aquarius.

Key for Planetary Symbols			
☉ Sun	♀ Venus	♄ Saturn	♇ Pluto
☾ Moon	♂ Mars	♅ Uranus	☊ North Node
☿ Mercury	♃ Jupiter	♆ Neptune	⊕ Part of Fortune

Transiting Saturn Square Transiting Uranus Activates the United States-Soviet Union Grand Square
July 17, 1999

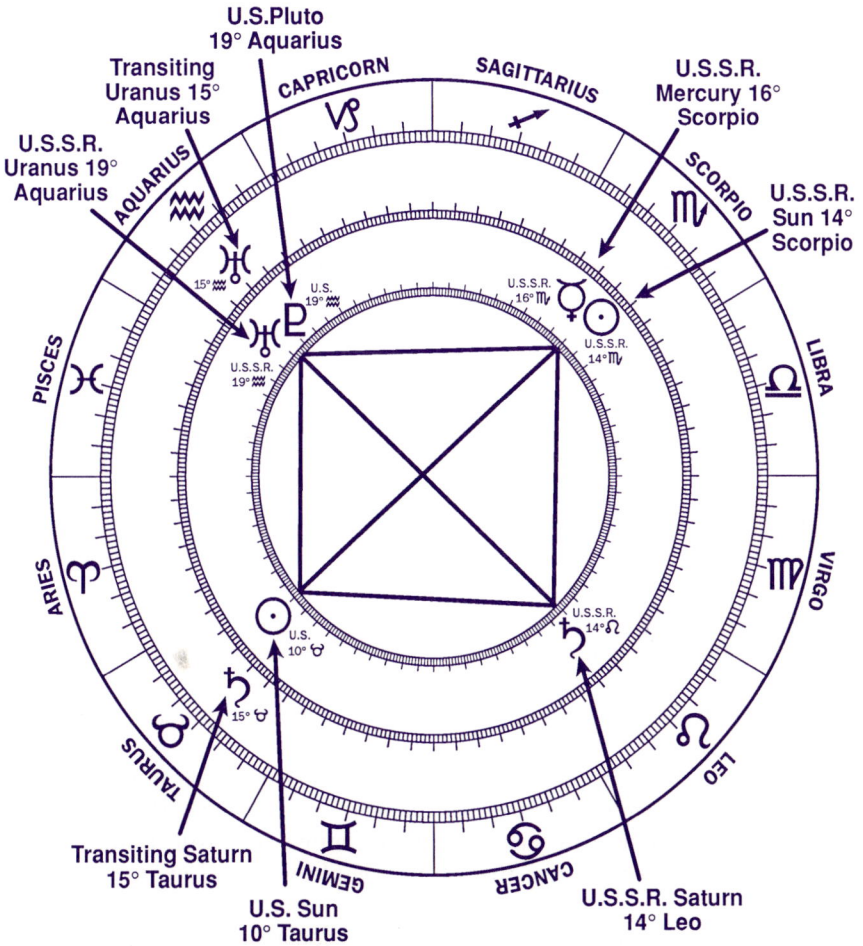

FIGURE 30 On July 17, 1999, Saturn will be at 15°37′ Taurus square to Uranus at 15°37′ Aquarius. Not only does this Saturn-Uranus square indicate war, but it also activates the grand square in the combined birth charts of the United States and the Soviet Union, showing that there is the prospect for a major war between the nations during the period of 18 months before and after July 17, 1999. The exact Saturn-Uranus square of July 17, 1999, will be followed by two more that will also activate the grand square of the U.S.-U.S.S.R. These will occur on November 14, 1999, when Saturn will be at 13°4′ Taurus square to Uranus at 13°4′ Aquarius, and on May 13, 2000, when Saturn will be at 20°46′ Taurus square Uranus at 20°46′ Aquarius.

The Saturn-Neptune Cycle—
A Catalyst for the Growth of Communism

War and economic catastrophe are interrelated. Economic conditions are one of the most reliable indicators of war. The configurations we are discussing show how these two social phenomena are likely to interact in the near future.

Saturn and Neptune conjoin each other about every thirty-six years. There is a correlation between Saturn-Neptune conjunctions like the one that occurred on November 13, 1989, and the growth and development of socialism and Communism.[72]

Socialism is an economic theory based on government ownership of the means of production and distribution of goods. Although socialism is commonly thought of as a political system, or a political *and* economic system, Marx, Lenin and other seminal theorists insisted that it was first and foremost an economic system. They argued that a nation's prevailing method of economic organization was the foundation of her political life; if one altered the economic system, the political system would reflect the change.

Communism, according to Marx and Lenin, is a hypothetical, or utopian, stage of socialism characterized by a classless, stateless society and the equal distribution of goods. The Soviet Union and other socialist states claim to be working to establish a communist society through centralized economic planning and rigid control of the economy, a one-party state and limited individual liberties.

Given the strong correlation of Saturn (the planet of organization, planning and centralized control) and Neptune (the planet of glamour, illusion, deception and impractical idealism) to socialism, it is not surprising that some people were taken in by its promises.

But socialism has never worked. Socialist economies are disorganized (Neptune) and plagued by low levels of production, shortages and the maldistribution of goods (Saturn).

The Soviet Union is the world's first socialist state. Since socialism is not a viable economic system, Soviet leaders have been forced to do two things to stay in power: (1) create a police state, (2) take control of other nations and siphon off their wealth. Case in point: Eastern Europe.

The Saturn-Neptune conjunctions of 1846 were followed by the publication of *The Communist Manifesto* by Karl Marx in 1848. The next Saturn-Neptune conjunction, in 1882, coincided with the establishment and growth of the main European socialist parties. The next two conjunctions of Saturn and Neptune coincided with the Bolshevik Revolution in 1917, and Stalin's death and Soviet expansion into the Third World in 1953. When Saturn squared Neptune in 1979, the Soviet Union invaded Afghanistan and became embroiled in a crisis in Poland, and the Sandinistas came to power in Nicaragua and established a Soviet beachhead in the Americas.

In sum, major Saturn-Neptune cycles have coincided with periods of Soviet expansion or aggression. The three Saturn-Neptune conjunctions of 1989 mark a crucial turning point in Soviet Communist development and thus world history.

We the people who read the handwriting on the wall can take the flame of freedom and use it to prevent that conjunction from proving a greater expansion of World Communism. We can fulfill the prophecy of Nostradamus for the turning back by another "law of More"[73] of the momentum of expansionism of the totalitarian Communist governments.

As we have seen, this Saturn-Neptune conjunction could also trigger international economic turmoil. During this cycle, Soviet aggression and Western economic chaos will be interrelated. They are becoming more and more dependent on Western money and technology to keep their civil economy afloat and their empire cohesive. As economic conditions in the Soviet bloc grow worse, the need for Western loans will reach crisis proportions. But, when the United States and other Western nations run short of money to loan the Soviets because of a depression and debt liquidation, they will no longer be able to keep the Soviet economy afloat. As the Soviet economy gets worse, the people will begin to revolt. Then the Soviets may have no choice but to go to war in order to save their economies—and stay in power.

Thus, the power elite in the West, the international bankers and the Western monopoly capitalists, have created the West's Achilles' heel whereby economic crisis may precipitate Soviet aggression.

The Astrology of the Reagan-Gorbachev Washington Summit

The interrelationship between economic crisis and war can be seen today through the astrology of the December 1987 Summit in Washington, D.C., during which Ronald Reagan and Mikhail Gorbachev signed the Intermediate-range Nuclear Forces (INF) Treaty. But first let's look at the astrology of the Summit itself.

The Reagan-Gorbachev Summit began December 7, 1987, the forty-sixth anniversary of Japan's surprise attack on Pearl Harbor—a most inauspicious time for dealing with enemies—unless, of course you are at the psychological stage where you no longer perceive your enemies as enemies, but as friends. President Reagan said he hoped that the memory of Pearl Harbor would be "superseded by the day that we begin the path to peace and safety in the world through disarmament."[74] That hope is almost certain to be illusory, perhaps fatally so. When Japan attacked the United States on December 7, 1941, the progressed U.S. conceptional Mars (the planet of war) was at 0° Libra and formed a nearly exact conjunction to Neptune (the planet of intrigue), which was then transiting at 29° Virgo—the precise degree of the solar eclipse of September 22, 1987 (fig. 31). The Mars-Neptune conjunction was the principal significator of the attack. The solar eclipse, whose effect lasts about six months, reactivated the record of the attack on Pearl Harbor. A treaty signed under that influence carries the ghost, or residual influence, of the attack. Thus, the signing of the INF Treaty is the first of a sequence of events that could lead to a Soviet surprise attack on the United States.

The February 1988 Capricorn conjunction squares the solar eclipse of September 22, 1987, at 29° Virgo conjoined the U.S. conceptional Midheaven at 1° Libra. This square will have a wide range of economic, social and military influences. Thus, the Reagan-Gorbachev Summit to sign the INF Treaty was one of the most important integrating events prior to the period of extreme economic and military tensions that commenced February 22–23, 1988.

In viewing the behind-the-scenes politics of the Summit, we can see a relationship between economic activity and war. According to Jan Sejna, a former assistant secretary to the top secret Czechoslovakian Defense Council, the foremost decision-making body in Czechoslovakia, Gorbachev initially refused to come to the December 1987 Summit in Washington, D.C., because of the October stock market crash.

Sejna, the highest-ranking Soviet military official ever to defect, says that the centerpiece of Soviet military strategy is to launch a preemptive first strike against the United States if and when the U.S. economy falls apart. Sejna believes that Gorbachev initially refused to accept Reagan's offer to come to the United States because he was waiting to see if the U.S. economy would collapse.

The Reagan-Gorbachev Summit Meeting
December 7, 1987

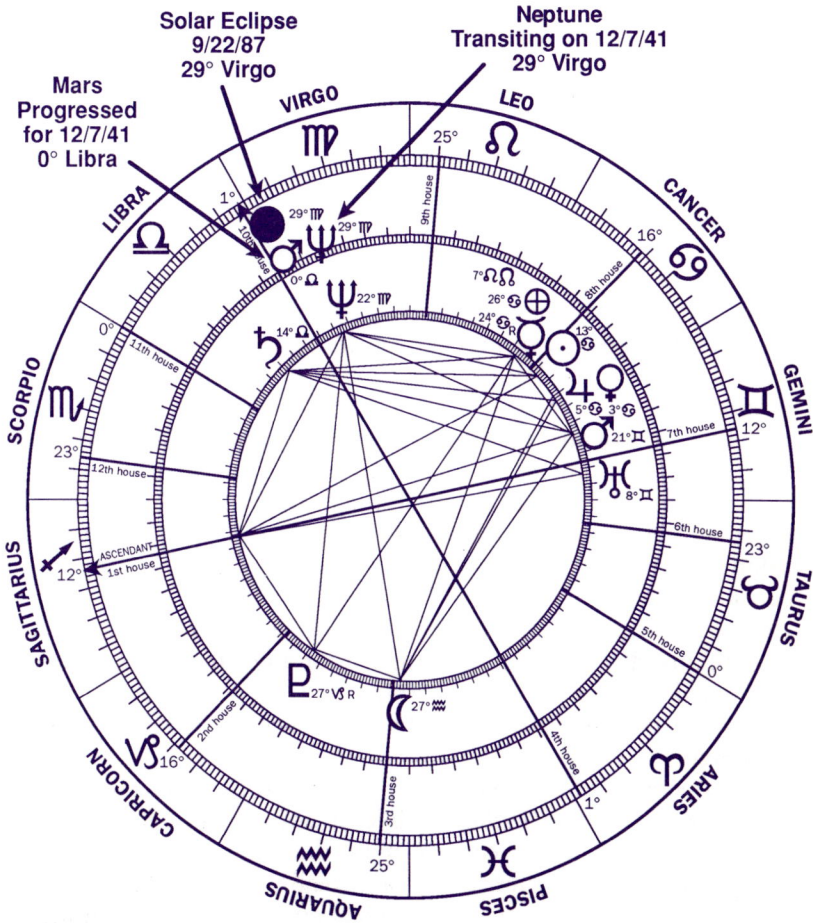

FIGURE 31   The Reagan-Gorbachev summit meeting to sign the Inter-mediate-range Nuclear Forces (INF) Treaty began December 7, 1987, the 46th anniversary of Japan's surprise attack on Pearl Harbor. When Japan attacked the United States on December 7, 1941, the progressed U.S. conceptional Mars (the planet of war) was at 0° Libra and formed a nearly exact conjunction to Neptune (the planet of intrigue) which was then transiting at 29° Virgo—the precise degree of the solar eclipse of September 22, 1987. The Mars-Neptune conjunction was the principal significa-tor of the attack. The solar eclipse, whose effect lasts about six months, reactivated the record of the attack on Pearl Harbor. A treaty signed under that influence carries the ghost, or residual influence, of the attack. Thus, the signing of the INF Treaty is the first of a sequence of events that could lead to a Soviet surprise attack on the United States.

When the economy failed to collapse, says Sejna, the Soviet Union decided that this was not the time to launch a first-strike attack but to pursue the course of diplomacy instead. Therefore, Gorbachev agreed to attend the Summit to gain ground for that moment when the time would be right to launch an attack against the United States.

Now, this statement I am making is supported by a number of defectors and others whom I have interviewed on my cable TV talk show, Summit University Forum, as well as by my own research. The possibility of a Soviet nuclear first-strike attack is the hardest thing for New Age people to face or even contemplate. In fact, when they hear such predictions they become angry and simply walk out of my lectures in protest. They don't even want to consider the body of facts I have to present, let alone the prophecy.

It is Americans' tendency toward illusion in foreign affairs that makes us want to believe in peace despite all evidence to the contrary. We need to examine the evidence scientifically and objectively before we preemptively disagree with it. So I am asking you in the spirit of the freethinkers of the New Age to consider what I've written here and in *Saint Germain On Prophecy.* If you disagree with me then we shall agree to disagree. I would just ask you for a listening ear for a few moments of your life, that I might give you something that can save your life and give you a real understanding of your destiny for freedom in the New Age.

Proponents of the INF Treaty argue that the agreement will make the world a safer place to live in since it will eliminate an entire class of nuclear weapons and reduce the number of warheads in Europe. But successful peace treaties are most likely to be concluded when there are harmonious contacts between Jupiter and Venus and the Sun. On December 7, 1987, Venus formed a conjunction to Neptune in Capricorn and a square to Jupiter in Aries, a configuration whose influence is characterized by intrigue, deception and self-deception—nothing that would be likely to make the world a safer place in which to live.

One ominous aspect peaked on December 11, 1987, several days after the Summit conference adjourned. Transiting Mars formed a conjunction to transiting Pluto at 11° Scorpio and both conjoined the Soviet Union's natal Sun at 14° Scorpio and opposed the U.S. natal Sun at 10° Taurus.

Just remember Scorpio. It either represents the scorpion's sting of death, especially when Pluto and Mars are involved, or it represents the higher-minded lifestreams, the eagles of highest attainment who raise up the light and focus it in the third-eye chakra through the All-Seeing Eye of God to defeat Death and Hell and usher in the kingdom of God and the open door to everlasting life.

Transiting Mars and Pluto conjoined the Soviet Union's Sun and opposed the U.S. natal Sun could bring international tensions between the United States and the Soviet Union into sharp focus. That we have signed a "peace treaty" at this time shows that the goal of one or both of the signatories is anything but peace. Mars rules aggression, war and the threat of war. It is also related to explosions, riots, rebellion and terrorism.

Pluto, which rules death, indicates a life-and-death power struggle and poses a potentially mortal challenge to the leadership and national identity of both nations. Pluto also rules nuclear power, terrorism, blackmail, secret deals, spying and anything involving mass death and destruction.

Because during the Washington Summit the Sun was transiting in Sagittarius conjoined Saturn and Uranus and making its opposition to the U.S. conceptional Mars at 21° Gemini, the United States, as a result of actions taken during this transit, could become involved in a general war with the Soviets or in a separate military incident with another nation sometime in the future.

Into these effects (karma) of causes set in motion we must direct the full forces of Archangel Michael and his legions. We must call to the Faithful and True and the armies of heaven who figure as the deliverers of the children of the Light in the Book of Revelation. These are the forces of Light composing the entire Spirit of the Great White Brotherhood that defeat the Fates in answer to our call.

The effects of these configurations may take some time to manifest, but this is what they indicate: the use of nuclear blackmail in order to gain an overwhelming diplomatic advantage, a major sellout by one or both governments, a direct military confrontation, a major terrorist incident, significant domestic difficulties (such as rioting) in either or both nations, or a nuclear accident like Chernobyl.

The INF Treaty will clear the last block to the Soviet intent to wage conventional/chemical/biological warfare against Europe. And General Sejna says that this is precisely what they plan. Saint Germain also confirms the Soviet intent by the Spirit of the LORD's prophecy upon me. And you yourself are seeing the likelihood of its eventuality in the astrology I am presenting.

The Charts of Ronald Reagan and Mikhail Gorbachev

Much of what happened at the Summit depended upon the behavior of Ronald Reagan and Mikhail Gorbachev. It was very clear during that Summit who was on top of things, who was the realist, and who had the power in the palm of his hand—Mikhail Gorbachev. This was predictable by merely looking at their charts—if you didn't read it in their faces.

Gorbachev's chart is a study in contradictions. He was born in the village of Privolnoye in the Stavropol territory of the Soviet Union. Soviet psychotherapist and astrologer Farida Asadullina says a ranking Soviet official gave her Gorbachev's time of birth. She says his Ascendant is 11°33′ Aries, which would have given him a 7:53 a.m. birth Baghdad Time (BGT).

Gorbachev's Sun at 10° Pisces forms an opposition to his Neptune at 4° Virgo (fig. 32). His Moon at 8° Leo is trine his Ascendant and Uranus at 13° Aries. This combination of planets gives him charisma and the ability to project and sustain an image—an ideal planetary pattern for promoting *glasnost*. But because of the involvement of Neptune (deception) it also shows that *glasnost* is an illusion.

It is a selective policy of liberalization designed to give the Soviet economy some breathing room and to foster the illusion in the West that the Soviet Union is politically more open and hence a politically less dangerous society.

Gorbachev's other side is revealed by an extended T-square: his natal Jupiter, Pluto and Mars at 10°, 18° and 27° Cancer opposed his Saturn at 20° Capricorn and Venus at 25° Capricorn, all of which square his natal Uranus at 13° Aries conjoined his Ascendant at 11° Aries.

This configuration shows Gorbachev to be a relentlessly ambitious man driven by an obsessive need for power. He is secretive, ruthless, callous and willing to manipulate without thought or feeling. He is probably either psychic or uses psychic and occult powers to gain or maintain power. He will always be surrounded by those who will attempt to take his power, a circumstance which will make him all the more ruthless. He has the capacity to be cruel, treacherous and resentful. His is the psychological type that is capable of starting a war and using nuclear weapons.

During the Summit, transiting Mars at 8° Scorpio and transiting Pluto at 11° Scorpio were conjoined the Soviet Sun at 14° Scorpio and trine Gorbachev's natal Sun at 10° Pisces, putting him

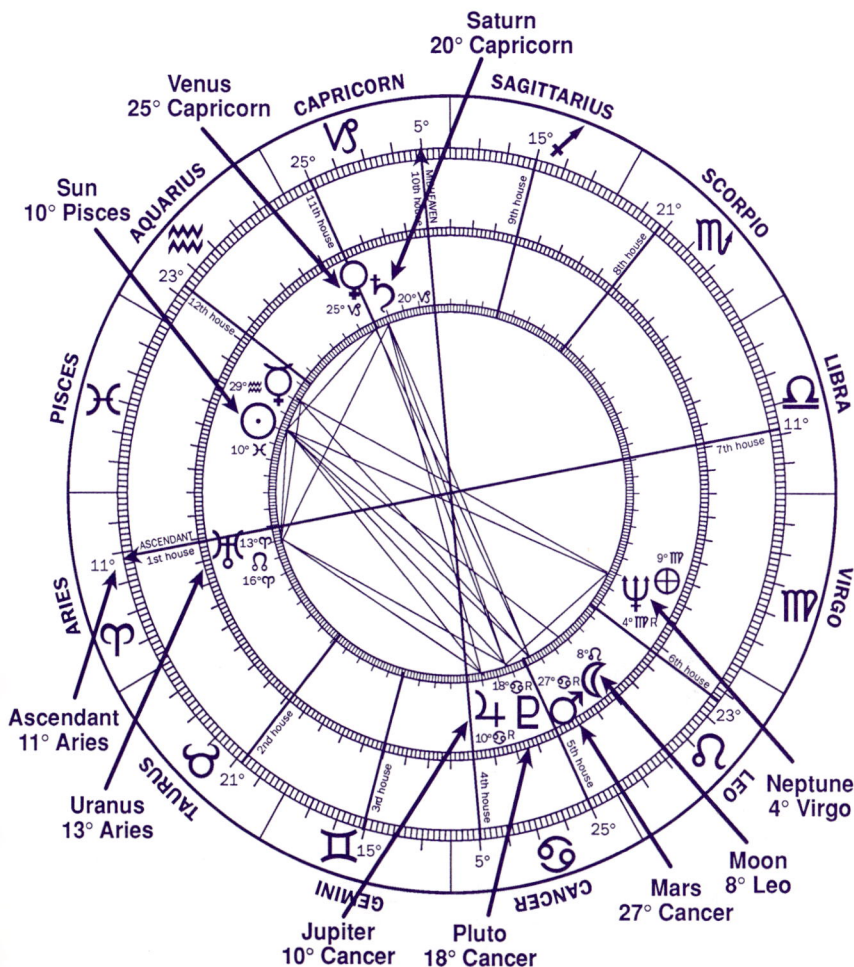

Mikhail S. Gorbachev
Birth Chart
March 2, 1931, 7:53 a.m. ?

Saturn
20° Capricorn

Venus
25° Capricorn

Sun
10° Pisces

Ascendant
11° Aries

Uranus
13° Aries

Jupiter
10° Cancer

Pluto
18° Cancer

Mars
27° Cancer

Moon 8° Leo

Neptune
4° Virgo

FIGURE 32 Mikhail Gorbachev was born in the village of Privolnoye in the Stavropol territory of the Soviet Union. Soviet psychotherapist and astrologer Farida Asadullina says a ranking Soviet official gave her Gorbachev's time of birth. She says his Ascendant is 11°33′ Aries—which would have given him a 7:53 a.m. birth Baghdad Time (BGT). Gorbachev's Sun at 10° Pisces forms an opposition to his Neptune at 4° Virgo. His Moon at 8° Leo is trine his Ascendant and Uranus at 13° Aries. This combination of planets gives him charisma and the ability to project and sustain an image—but shows that *glasnost* is an illusion. An extended T-square (right triangle) formed by his Jupiter, Pluto and Mars in Cancer, his Saturn and Venus in Capricorn and his Uranus in Aries shows that Gorbachev is driven by an obsessive need for power, can be treacherous, and is psychologically capable of starting a war and using nuclear weapons.

in a very powerful position. Gorbachev is the supreme realist on the planet today. He knows what power is. And he knows how to use it.

However, he has extreme pressures on him from his ever-present enemies in the Soviet Union and from social and economic pressures in his nation. No astrological or economic indicator shows that the Soviet economy is likely to improve. And transiting Mars at 8° Scorpio conjoined transiting Pluto at 11° Scorpio square his natal Moon at 8° Leo shows that he fears the Soviet people and the loss of status. Thus, at the Washington Summit he was negotiating to gain the upper hand because he felt his survival depended on it.

To a certain extent, the Soviet Union is an enemy cornered. The Soviets are cornered by their collapsing economy and they know that when the U.S. economy falls theirs will fall harder. Then they will have only one chess move left: strike first.

To the degree that Gorbachev succeeds, our survival is endangered. In fact, our survival is precarious anyway—not because of the intense and redundant nature of the astrological configurations that we have been discussing, but because of the failure of the people to meet the challenges of the twentieth century.

Ronald Reagan's chart was not nearly as strong as Gorbachev's during the Summit. He was already influenced by the solar eclipse of September 22, 1987, at 29° Virgo conjoined the U.S. Midheaven at 1° Libra and square the February 1988 Capricorn conjunction. This configuration reactivated the Jupiter-Saturn conjunction of 1980 at 8° Libra.

Reagan's own chart showed a lot of pressure, particularly from transiting Saturn at 22° Sagittarius and Uranus at 26° Sagittarius opposed his natal Pluto at 26° Gemini. As I mentioned earlier, with all other considerations factored in, these transits have the potential to be fatal. The charts of Secretary of State George Shultz and Foreign Minister Eduard Shevardnadze, the primary negotiators of the INF Treaty, both show lines of deception and intrigue.

A number of other configurations in the charts of the United States and the Soviet Union, Reagan and Gorbachev, and the other players in the agreement reinforce the conclusion that the prospect for war through this treaty is high. Astrology shows that nations such as Great Britain, West Germany, Saudi Arabia, Canada, Israel and France will also face life and death challenges between 1988 and 1992.

Ronald Reagan clearly did not have the upper hand at this

Summit and he was clearly in a state of illusion. He had put himself in a state of illusion and euphoria to seal himself off from the absolute reality of the failures of his administration as well as his own failure to take action when he should have taken action and his blunderings at times when he should not have taken action.

I am sure you have all groaned to see America represented by such an individual who began with a certain promise of freedom and has ended, as far as I am concerned, with a betrayal of all of the American people. From the Right to the Left to the center, this man has betrayed our national identity, and it's a crisis and a cross that each one of us bears.

We ought to consider Saint Germain's prophecy spoken through me on Thanksgiving Day, November 27, 1986, in Los Angeles:

> You have every reason to believe, to be concerned, and to be prepared for a first strike by the Soviet Union upon these United States. You have every reason to be alert. . . .
>
> For, beloved, my word and your response, your very preparedness, is the one condition that can prevent the almost inevitable scenario of nuclear war.[75]

That prophecy demands a nationwide alert. It demands preparation heretofore unseen in the American epoch. But for their part Americans are blocked at every hand — first by their own perceptions of reality, and then, along with Congress, by their desire for peace at any price on any terms, and finally by a military establishment that has become a lumbering bureaucratic beast unable to act in time or in space.

Add to this Soviet propaganda saturating a willing press and the chemical war Nikita Khrushchev declared on America in 1962, a war using drugs as the weapon that the KGB and their cooperatives have carried out.[76] The people have lost their will to be under God — one nation, one spirit, one destiny. And whatever portion of their will that they have not lost has been stolen by thieves in the night.

The nation that was once the greatest in the world has lost the will to be — little by little, drop by drop, since 1945. And since then our preparedness to meet the ultimate threat of a Soviet first strike has slackened year by year.

A Cycle of Opportunity

Before you conclude that the astrology of the 1990s is all bad, let me tell you that the astrological cycles of importunity we have been discussing are concurrent with a cycle of opportunity.

During the dangerous period between 1988 and 1992, Pluto will be orbiting the Sun inside the orbit of Neptune, something that happens only once in every 248 years. It will reach its point closest to the Sun on September 12, 1989.

This cycle has coincided with epochal events, including the birth of Jesus, the baptism of Clovis, the first king of France, into the Christian church about A.D. 498, and the discovery of America by Christopher Columbus in 1492.

Uranus and Neptune will make three conjunctions in 1993, two at 18° Capricorn (August 19 and October 24) and one at 19° Capricorn (February 2). Uranus-Neptune conjunctions, which happen but once every 172 years, are associated with new phases of history that have a scientific and mystical character and can lead to greater freedom, innovation and enlightenment.

I would like to leave you with the hope given to us by beloved Gautama Buddha on April 4, 1983:

> I would remind you, lest any fear, that all prophecy concerning Light and Darkness may fail. It may fail for a very good reason. For the people of God have made strides and accelerated; and therefore, the dark cloud has been dissolved and a new day of opportunity is born. . . .
>
> We desire, therefore, to reinforce in your heart that whatever you may have interpreted as prediction of cataclysm, worldwide or specifically here or there, must not remain in your mind as something that has been stated with ultimate definition or finality by any of our bands but only as a reading of world karma and as a reading of the consequences of world karma.[77]

What we need to remember about predictions is that the violet flame can change the world and simultaneously with the dissolving of the old order bring into manifestation the new order, the sacred fire and the living flame of cosmic love.

Those things that are necessary to our spiritual and physical survival today must endure; and if they don't endure, we will go back to a primitive way of life. The violet flame is the Third Person of the Hindu Trinity, the Destroyer, whom we prefer to call the Transformer or the Transmuter. The violet flame also fulfills the roles of the First and Second Persons of the Trinity, the Creator and the Preserver, by first creating and then firing those worthy creations in the kiln of the Christ Mind.

The violet flame is therefore the indispensable temple tool of the builders, the agent of every alchemist who aspires to joint-heirship with the Son of God, and the all-consuming fire of all co-creators with Nature's God.

The violet flame is the flame on the altar that is Creator, Preserver, Transformer in unending cyclic change. And this change is the law of our permanency and the only thing that is permanent in the Spirit/Matter, Yang/Yin cosmos. By this Trinity in a perpetual state of becoming—the same yesterday, today and forever—we transcend the cause-effect sequences noted in the skies as the astrology of our karma. My beloved, let us invoke the violet flame and commend our spirits unto the heart of the Divine Mother, East and West.

Saint Germain said on May 28, 1986:

> The prophecy that is written in Revelation and in the Old and New Testament, that is written in the very sands and in the ethers which may be perceived, is not final! This is my cry to the age!
>
> *You* are mediators between mankind (who are in a state of ignorance and rejection of the Truth of the Teachings of Jesus Christ we bear) and the oncoming karma returning. *You* as anointed ones [Christed ones], by choosing this calling and election, may form a Body of Light that does indeed become the manifestation of the all-consuming flame of God.
>
> And that karma can be transmuted, beloved. And remember, the requirements are few. Ten righteous men could save an entire city by their righteousness, proving that the power of God in manifestation is far greater than millions engaged in the blasphemy of the anti-Light and the desecration of the innocence of the child.[78]

Opportunity knocks. Opportunity is the name of Portia, who is the twin flame of Saint Germain. Aquarius is not only an age of freedom, it is an age of opportunity; and opportunity is Divine Justice returning to us the opportunity we deserve (because we have given it to others) to serve to set life free.

By the very law of karma that mandates our astrology, we also have the opportunity to undo our past mistakes and make things right where we've wronged or been wronged. Opportunity is an open door that we can choose to walk through to help our planet and our people survive this "time of trouble," prophesied by Daniel, "such as never was since there was a nation."[79]

Beloved Lightbearers of the world, the handwriting is in the skies. But there is another handwriting in our hearts and it's a Valentine from Saint Germain and from our Father, and it simply says, "I love you." And because God loves us, we have this opportunity to move through that purple fiery heart of Saint Germain. Yes, to move through our beloved Master's heart and to win!

The dictation by Saint Germain that was delivered following this lecture is published in Book I, pp. 159–70. Throughout these notes *PoW* is the abbreviation for *Pearls of Wisdom*. (**1**) Archangel Zadkiel, November 25, 1987, 1987 *PoW*, Book 1, pp. 591–92, 593. (**2**) *The Rubáiyát of Omar Khayyám*, st. 71, trans. Edward Fitzgerald. (**3**) Deut. 4:24; Heb. 12:29. (**4**) Hos. 8:7. (**5**) *The Opus Majus of Roger Bacon*, trans. Robert Belle Burke, vol. 1 (Philadelphia: University of Pennsylvania Press, 1928), p. 401. (**6**) Uranus will enter Aquarius on April 1, 1995 and remain there until June 8, 1995 when it retrogrades back into Capricorn to complete its transit of that sign. (**7**) Richard Nolle, "Saturn-Uranus Triple Whammy of '88," *Star Tech*, Pisces 1988, p. 4. (**8**) Ibid. As with many historical questions, there are differences of opinion about when the classical period of Greece came to an end. Some historians argue it ended at the start of the Greco-Macedonian empire in 338; others with the incorporation of Greece into the Roman Empire and still others at various points of time during the reign of Alexander the Great. In any case, Alexander—who was the primary disseminator of classical Greek culture—died four years after his invasion of India and the Greco-Macedonian empire was fragmented into three competing units that declined in power. (**9**) "Greece enjoyed a period of prosperity that lasted until about 280 B.C. Thereafter the same conditions that had led to the crisis of the 4th century came to the fore again, aggravated now by perpetual and increasingly devastating wars. Wealth was concentrated in fewer hands; the market for Greek exports contracted as the new Greco-Oriental communities in the East began to compete with Greece. The wages of free laborers were sharply depressed; the middle class, owners of moderate-sized farms or factories, likewise became impoverished. Infanticide and abortion became common among both rich and poor. Class war became acute and open in many Greek cities apart from those, like Rhodes and Athens, still rich enough to subsidize the proletariat. The chief points in the program of the social revolutionists were still, as in the 4th century B.C., cancellation of debts and redistribution of land." *Encyclopedia Americana*, s.v. "Greece." (**10**) For more information about the Galactic Center see Michael Baigent, Nicholas Campion, and Charles Harvey, *Mundane Astrology: An Introduction to the Astrology of Nations and Groups* (Wellingborough, Northamptonshire, England: Aquarian Press, 1984), pp. 336–38; Philip Sedgwick, *The Astrology of Deep Space* (Birmingham, Mich.: Seek-It Publications, 1984), pp. 93–99; Michael Erlewine and Margaret Erlewine, *Astrophysical Directions* (Ann Arbor, Mich.: Heart Center School of Astrology, 1977). (**11**) Other astrologers investigating the effects of the Galactic Center include Michael Erlewine, Richard Nolle and Philip Sedgwick. (**12**) George Santayana, *Reason in Common Sense*, vol. 1 of *The Life of Reason* quoted in John Bartlett, *Familiar Quotations*, 15th ed. (Boston: Little, Brown and Company, 1980), p. 703. (**13**) See Dylan Warren-Davis, "The Black Death," *Astrological Journal*, November/December 1988, pp. 302–9. (**14**) See Diana Rosenberg, "A Preliminary Investigation of Black Hole Effects in Personal and Mundane Horoscopes," *Heliogram*, May Day, 1988, p. 19. (**15**) Barbara W. Tuchman, *A Distant Mirror: The Calamitous 14th Century* (New York: Alfred A. Knopf, 1978), p. xii. (**16**) Telephone interview with Richard Nolle, February 12, 1988. (**17**) William H. McNeil says that "antibiotics reduced the disease to triviality in 1943," (see William H. McNeil, *Plagues and Peoples* [New York: Doubleday, Anchor Press, 1976], p. 149). (**18**) John Townley, *Astrological Cycles & the Life Crisis Periods* (New York: Samuel Weiser, 1977), p. 46. (**19**) See Rev. 6:1–8. (**20**) Virgo and Pelleur, April 6, 1980, 1980 *PoW*, pp. 78, 79, 80; *Saint Germain On Prophecy*, Book Three, pp. 8, 10, 11–12. (**21**) Oromasis and Diana, April 13, 1980, 1980 *PoW*, p. 88; *Saint Germain On Prophecy*, Book Three, p. 28. (**22**) Saint Germain, June 1, 1980, 1980 *PoW*, pp. 196, 197, 201; *Saint Germain On Prophecy*, Book Three, pp. 55–56, 57–58, 66. (**23**) Data for the disasters listed are derived from *The World Almanac and Book of Facts 1990*, pp. 41–67 and 541–43 except for the following events: 1982 floods in China and Bangladesh: *Reader's Digest Almanac 1985*, p. 39; Mexico City earthquake: *1990 Information Please Almanac*, p. 370; Nevado del Ruiz eruption: *Los Angeles Times*, 15 November 1985; *Newsweek*, 25 November 1985, p. 58; gas cloud in Cameroon: *World Almanac 1987*, p. 913; El Salvador earthquake: *Los Angeles*

Times, 29 October 1986; *Time,* 20 October 1986, p. 46; Ecuador earthquake: *World Almanac 1987,* p. 541; 1988 drought and fires: *Billings Gazette,* 20 January 1989; *World Almanac 1989,* p. 65; 1988 floods in China: *1989 Information Please Almanac,* p. 371; monsoons in Bangladesh: *1990 Information Please Almanac,* p. 371; Hurricane Gilbert: *1989 Information Please Almanac,* p. 973; cyclone in Bangladesh: *New York Times,* 1 December 1989 and 4 December 1989; *Washington Times,* 1 December 1989; Japan earthquake, Hurricane Hugo, San Francisco earthquake, and 1989 earthquake in China: 1989 *PoW,* p. 646 n. 13; Redoubt volcano: *Billings Gazette,* 15 December 1989; Australia earthquake: *Billings Gazette,* 29 December 1989. **(24)** There is some confusion as to when Congress signed the Declaration of Independence. Popular belief holds that the Declaration was signed on July 4, 1776, by the 56 men whose signatures are appended to the document. But scholars have demonstrated that this is unlikely. The *Secret Journal* of Congress records that on July 19, 1776, Congress resolved to have the Declaration engrossed (written on parchment) and signed when it was ready and that it was signed on August 22, 1776. In addition, one quarter of the men who signed the Declaration were not in Congress July 4 — either they were not in Philadelphia on that day or they had not yet been elected to Congress. Nevertheless, the document was signed on July 4 "by Order and in Behalf of the Congress" by at least John Hancock, President of Congress, and Charles Thompson, Secretary of Congress. The *Journals of the Continental Congress* say that Congress "agreed to a Declaration" on the fourth and ordered that it be "authenticated and printed." To be "authenticated" a document was signed by Hancock and his signature was attested to by Thompson. The nation was conceived on July 4 since Hancock and Thompson were acting as instruments of the entire Congress. **(25)** Garry Wills, *Inventing America: Jefferson's Declaration of Independence* (Garden City, N.Y.: Doubleday and Company, 1978), p. 331. **(26)** Ibid., pp. 331–32. **(27)** Warren E. Burger, "The Right to Bear Arms," *Parade,* 14 January 1990, p. 5. **(28)** Worthington Chauncey Ford, ed., *Journals of the Continental Congress 1774–1789,* 34 vols. (Washington: Government Printing Office, 1904–37), 2:155. **(29)** Michael Baigent, "Ebenezer Sibly and the Declaration of Independence 1776: An Investigation," *NCGR Journal,* 1985 Spring Issue, p. 46. **(30)** N. N. Sukhanov, *The Russian Revolution 1917,* ed., abridged and trans., Joel Carmichael (Princeton, N.J.: Princeton University Press, 1984), p. 629. **(31)** Sirius, now at 13° 56′ Cancer was at 11°0′ Cancer in 1776, still conjoined the U.S. conceptional Sun. Like all fixed stars, Sirius moves about 1 degree every 72 years. **(32)** Richard Hinckley Allen, *Star Names: Their Lore and Meaning* (New York: Dover Publications, 1963), p. 121. **(33)** Nicholas Davidson, "Life Without Father: America's Greatest Social Catastrophe," *Policy Review,* Winter 1990, p. 40. **(34)** Dane Rudhyar, *The Astrology of America's Destiny* (New York: Random House, 1974), pp. 71–72. **(35)** John Adams to Thomas Jefferson, 1815, quoted in Bernard Bailyn, *The Ideological Origins of the American Revolution* (Cambridge: Harvard University Press, Belknap Press, 1967), p. 1. **(36)** Dane Rudhyar, *Astrological Timing: The Transition to the New Age* (New York: Harper and Row, Harper Colophon Books, 1969), p. 58. **(37)** James M. Perry, "As Panama Outcome Is Praised, Details Emerge of Bungling During the 1983 Grenada Invasion," *Wall Street Journal,* 15 January 1990. **(38)** Ibid. **(39)** Thomas Paine, quoted in Rudhyar, *The Astrology of America's Destiny,* p. 109. **(40)** Arch Crawford, "Harmonic Convergence," *Crawford Perspectives,* 8 August 1987, p. 2. **(41)** Mark Twain, *Pudd'nhead Wilson and Those Extraordinary Twins* (New York: P.F. Collier and Son, 1922), p. 108. **(42)** See "Author Believes August Heralds New Age of Peace for World," *The Salt Lake Tribune,* 1 August 1987; José Argüelles, *The Mayan Factor: Path Beyond Technology* (Santa Fe, N.M.: Bear and Company, 1987) pp. 146, 159, 165, 169–70, 193–94. **(43)** Cyclopea with Virginia, November 26, 1989, 1989 *PoW,* p. 789. **(44)** Saint Germain, November 27, 1986, 1986 *PoW,* Book II, pp. 647, 650; *Saint Germain On Prophecy,* Book Four, pp. 207, 208. **(45)** Saint Germain, October 3, 1987, 1987 *PoW,* Book I, pp. 484–86. **(46)** Ibid., pp. 487–88. **(47)** Vesta, October 19, 1987, 1987 *PoW,* Book I, p. 545. **(48)** Nephilim. Hebrew "those who fell" or "those who were cast down," from the Semitic root *naphal* "to fall," rendered in the Greek

Septuagint, a late translation of the Hebrew scriptures, as "giants" (Gen. 6:4; Num. 13:33). **(49)** Josh. 24:14–20, 22, 25–27. **(50)** I Thess. 5:3. **(51)** See Jane Mayer and Doyle McManus, *Landslide: The Unmaking of the President 1984–1988* (Boston: Houghton Mifflin Company, 1988). **(52)** Samuel Kernell, "Anatomy of an Abdication," *Los Angeles Times Book Review,* 2 October 1988, p. 6. **(53)** Saint Germain, February 17, 1980, 1980 *PoW,* p. 39; *Saint Germain On Prophecy,* Book Two, p. 90. **(54)** Saint Germain, June 1, 1980, 1980 *PoW,* p. 202; *Saint Germain On Prophecy,* p. 69. **(55)** Saint Germain, May 28, 1986, 1986 *PoW,* Book II, p. 521. **(56)** Saint Germain, February 7, 1987, 1987 *PoW,* Book I, pp. 92, 93. **(57)** Saint Germain, May 30, 1987, 1987 *PoW,* Book I, pp. 291–92. **(58)** Mark 4:19. **(59)** Pss. 55:16, 17; 91:15; 99:6; Isa. 58:9; Jer. 29:12, 33:3; Zech. 13:9. **(60)** Ravi Batra, *The Great Depression of 1990: Why It's Got to Happen—How to Protect Yourself* (New York: Simon and Schuster, 1985), pp. book flap, 17. **(61)** Rev. 6:15–17. **(62)** Antony C. Sutton, *War on Gold* (Seal Beach, Calif.: '76 Press, 1977), p. 84. **(63)** II Sam. 1:19. **(64)** Rev. 12:7–17. **(65)** Rev. 20:12–15. **(66)** See Book I, pp. 103–5. **(67)** Baigent, Campion, and Harvey, *Mundane Astrology,* p. 169. **(68)** See Ibid. pp. 169–74. **(69)** Heb. 11:10. **(70)** Saint Germain, June 1, 1980, 1980 *PoW,* p. 196; *Saint Germain On Prophecy,* Book Three, p. 55. **(71)** Saint Germain, July 6, 1985, 1985 *PoW,* Book II, p. 434; *Saint Germain On Prophecy,* Book Four, p. 81. **(72)** For an excellent discussion of this phenomenon see Baigent, Campion, and Harvey, *Mundane Astrology,* pp. 183, 201–2. **(73)** See *Saint Germain On Prophecy,* Book Two, pp. 190–99. **(74)** William Beecher, "Reagan-Gorbachev summit set," *Minneapolis Star Tribune,* 31 October 1987. **(75)** Saint Germain, November 27, 1986, 1986 *PoW,* p. 648; *Saint Germain On Prophecy,* Book Four, p. 208. **(76)** See Elizabeth Clare Prophet, July 4, 1988, 1989 *PoW,* p. 339. **(77)** Gautama Buddha, April 4, 1983, 1983 *PoW,* pp. 464, 465. **(78)** Saint Germain, May 28, 1986, 1986 *PoW,* Book II, p. 523; *Saint Germain On Prophecy,* Book Four, pp. 170–71. **(79)** Dan. 12:1.

Appendix A

A Startling Thesis on the Origin of AIDS

Like many Americans, I am profoundly concerned with the origin and cure of AIDS. On July 3, 1988, I interviewed Dr. Robert Strecker, Dr. Alan Cantwell and Jon Rappoport on a Summit University Forum called "The AIDS Conspiracy: Establishment Cover-up, Pharmaceutical Scam, or Biological Warfare?"[1] Dr. Strecker is an internist and a gastroenterologist with a Ph.D. in pharmacology. He is an expert on the origins of AIDS. Dr. Cantwell is a dermatologist and internationally known cancer and AIDS microbiology researcher. Jon Rappoport is an investigative reporter who has concentrated on the AIDS epidemic.

My guests and I examined the causes and treatment of AIDS from several points of view. They put forth provocative and intriguing arguments concerning the origin of AIDS. Dr. Strecker argued persuasively that much of the medical and epidemiological evidence available shows that there is little possibility that man first got AIDS from the African green monkey as originally thought.

Although it is not widely known outside the AIDS research community, there is a considerable body of research that shows the human T-cell leukemia virus (HTLV-III), or AIDS virus, does not exist *de novo*—that is, in nature. Strecker said that the AIDS virus has the same morphology (shape) and chemistry of two well-known animal viruses, the bovine (cattle) leukemia virus and the visna virus of sheep, and that the AIDS virus is, in fact, a combination of the two—a bovine-visna virus that has been adapted to grow in human tissue.

Once Strecker realized that the AIDS virus does not occur in nature, he reached the obvious conclusion: If the AIDS virus was not produced by nature, then it had to have been produced by man. Taking it a step further he reasoned that if the AIDS virus is man-made, then it could have been made deliberately or by accident. In either case, once it did exist in the laboratory, it could have been released intentionally or by accident. How did the AIDS virus get out of the lab? Did it jump—or was it pushed? After a thorough review of the scientific papers on the AIDS epidemic and the scientific literature on virology, epidemiology and related fields, Strecker concluded that the AIDS virus was pushed. But that is not all. He argues that the AIDS virus was "predicted, requested, produced, deployed and now threatens the existence of mankind because it works."[2]

Strecker cited evidence, found primarily in World Health Organization (WHO) documents and scientific papers, to show that scientists working under the aegis of WHO predicted and called for the creation of a virus that could selectively destroy T-cells. Since that is what the AIDS virus does, he asks whether the appearance of AIDS is a coincidence or the result of a carefully developed plan. He believes the evidence favors the latter possibility.

Strecker acknowledged that his evidence was only circumstantial but maintained that it is highly unlikely that anyone who had actually participated in the creation and/or deployment of the AIDS virus is going to come forward and confess. However, in lieu of a "smoking gun," he provided corroborating evidence to support his thesis.

First, he noted that there have been precedents in which a large segment of the American population has been accidentally or deliberately infected with a disease-causing agent by the government. The Salk polio vaccine, for example, which was given to millions of young people in the 1950s, was contaminated with simian virus 40 (SV40), which is known to be carcinogenic in animals and is suspected of being carcinogenic in man. When the responsible medical authorities learned that the vaccine was contaminated, they withheld the information on the grounds that to have made it public would have caused undue alarm.

In another case, between 1932 and 1972 the United States Public Health Service in Macon County, Alabama, allowed black men with syphilis from Tuskegee, Alabama, to go untreated without telling them that they were a control group that was not being treated. The Tuskegee experiment was designed to study the long-term effects of syphilis.[3] Not only did the men in the experiment suffer needlessly, but they also transferred the disease to their wives and children.

In addition, the U.S. government has conducted hundreds

of biological and chemical warfare experiments with potentially harmful agents against individual American citizens without their knowledge or consent.[4] Strecker's thesis is therefore supported by the numerous cases of the accidental and deliberate use of harmful biological agents.

Second, Strecker is not the only one who has recognized that WHO may have played a role in starting the AIDS epidemic. *The London Times*, May 11, 1987, carried a front page banner headline which read: "Smallpox vaccine 'triggered Aids virus.'"

The story, written by Pearce Wright, the *Times* Science Editor, said that there is evidence that the AIDS epidemic in Africa may have been triggered by a World Health Organization smallpox vaccination program. Wright's story was not widely reported in the United States, if reported at all, and does not mention contaminating agents in the vaccine. Nor has it been established that there were contaminants in the vaccine. And the *Times* did not suggest that there were. Nevertheless, is it merely a "coincidence" that the *Times* discovered an association between WHO and the start of the AIDS epidemic in Africa and that Strecker found an association between WHO and the start of the AIDS epidemic in the United States?

Here are several paragraphs from the *Times* story:

> The Aids epidemic may have been triggered by the mass vaccination campaign which eradicated smallpox.
>
> The World Health Organization, which master-minded the 13-year campaign, is studying new scientific evidence suggesting that immunization with the small-pox vaccine *Vaccinia* awakened the unsuspected, dormant human immuno defence virus infection (HIV)*....
>
> Many experts are reluctant to support the theory publicly because they believe it would be interpreted unfairly as criticism of WHO....
>
> Dr. Robert Gallo, who first identified the Aids virus in the US, told *The Times:* "The link between the WHO programme and the epidemic in Africa is an interesting and important hypothesis. I cannot say that it actually happened, but I have been saying for some years that the use of live vaccines such as that used for smallpox can activate a dormant infection such as HIV."[5]

Was the AIDS virus deliberately deployed? There is evidence suggesting that the AIDS epidemic in the United States is related

---

*The AIDS virus was initially called the human immunodeficiency virus (HIV). When more was learned about the nature of the virus, it was renamed human T-cell leukemia virus (HTLV).

not to the smallpox vaccine as in Africa but to a hepatitis-B vaccine study conducted among promiscuous, healthy, homosexual men beginning in 1978, just prior to the outbreak of the disease in homosexual communities where the study was conducted, Manhattan, San Francisco and Los Angeles.[6]

Strecker said that a high percentage of those who participated in the study later tested positive for the AIDS virus, which strongly suggests a causal relationship between the administration of the vaccine and the outbreak of AIDS.

Given these circumstances, Strecker argued that it is unlikely that the AIDS epidemic was a random natural event. Cantwell agreed. How, asked Cantwell, could an epidemic that affects black heterosexuals in Africa suddenly become a white homosexual epidemic in the United States—unless certain groups of people were targeted with a biological agent.

Investigative reporter Jon Rappoport also agreed that the AIDS epidemic may be the latest of a series of governmentally sanctioned biowarfare attacks.[7] But he was not convinced that HTLV is the only cause of AIDS. He believes that if HTLV causes AIDS, it may be dependent on cofactors and, of greater importance, that there are other causes of AIDS, some related to lifestyle and others related to the assimilation of toxic substances.

Rappoport said that there is a high degree of correlation between heavy drug use in both the hetero- and homosexual communities and the contraction of AIDS. The incidence of AIDS may not be related so much to the sharing of needles by intravenous drug users as to the degenerative effects on the immune system of the prolonged use of recreational drugs and prophylactic antibiotics, he said.

In their haste to find a cure, the Federal Drug Administration approved an experimental drug known as AZT for the treatment of AIDS, Rappoport said. But AZT, he maintained, can cause severe anemia and depress the immune system, which is what HTLV is also supposed to do. Rappoport claims that the use of AZT may be catastrophic since many people diagnosed as having AIDS have not even been tested for HTLV.

Remarkable as it seems, in order to be diagnosed for AIDS it is not necessary to have a blood test that tests positive for AIDS antibodies. Those who meet a Center for Disease Control profile, which Rappoport said is so broad that it could include many people who do not have AIDS, are told they have AIDS. Even if a person does not have AIDS, once he is diagnosed as having the disease he is likely to be treated with AZT and develop the same kinds of opportunistic infections a real AIDS patient might get because of the immune compromising effects of AZT.

Rappoport argues that the rush to get AZT on the market was motivated as much by the drive for profits as by a desire to treat a serious illness.

Strecker's, Cantwell's and Rappoport's conclusions are difficult to completely validate at this time. However, their assertions closely parallel the kinds of negative circumstances Neptune can trigger (treachery, intrigue and deception, particularly as it relates to drugs, medicines, et cetera) in conjunction with Saturn and Uranus in Capricorn during a transit of Pluto in Scorpio (secret and underhanded dealings, destruction and the threat of annihilation or annihilation itself, sex, sexuality, medicine, the healing arts, the drug industry, joint financial affairs and matters of life and death).

(1) Summit University Forum "The AIDS Conspiracy: Establishment Cover-up, Pharmaceutical Scam or Biological Warfare?" on 3 videocassettes, 4½ hr., $59.95 (add $1.90 for postage), GP88078; 4 audiocassettes, 4¾ hr., $23.80 (add $.95 for postage). (2) Dr. Strecker elaborates on his thesis that AIDS was "predicted, requested, produced and deployed" in the Summit University Forum on AIDS and used the exact words quoted in this text in his video, "The Strecker Memorandum." (3) For a detailed account of the Tuskegee syphilis study see James H. Jones, *Bad Blood: The Tuskegee Syphilis Experiment* (New York: Macmillan Publishing Company, Free Press, 1982). (4) See Robert Harris and Jeremy Paxman, *A Higher Form of Killing: The Secret Story of Chemical and Biological Warfare* (New York: Hill and Wang, 1982), pp. 155–60; Leonard A. Cole, *Clouds of Secrecy: The Army's Germ Warfare Tests over Populated Areas* (Totawa, N.J.: Rowman and Littlefield, 1988). (5) Pearce Wright, "Smallpox vaccine 'triggered Aids virus,'" London *Times*, 11 May 1987. (6) See Alan Cantwell, *AIDS and the Doctors of Death: An Inquiry into the Origin of the AIDS Epidemic* (Los Angeles: Aries Rising Press, 1989). (7) See Jon Rappoport, *AIDS Inc.: Scandal of the Century* (San Bruno, Calif.: Human Energy Press, 1988).

Pearls of Wisdom®

published by The Summit Lighthouse

| Vol. 31 No. 49 | *Beloved El Morya* | August 7, 1988 |

Saint Germain Stumps Canada

1

Canada, Fulfill Your Destiny!
A Missive from the Darjeeling Council Table

To the chela of my heart I say, welcome! For the door of my heart is opened to any soul who has treasured the diamond of His will, the knowledge of His fire, and the compassion of the heart-beat of a universe.

I am known as the Chief of the Darjeeling Council of the Great White Brotherhood and I come to you and to this nation with a fiery mission and message. People of hearts ignited by the inner fire of the North, I send [to you], therefore, over the pole a missive from the Darjeeling Council table.

Blessed ones, take the reins of your government, take the reins of your economy and understand that that which is worth having and being must be defended. A spiritual path must needs have a flaming sword to keep the way of the Tree of Life.

You know not, then, how detractors of the living Word and the enemies of nations also lust after your resources, your light, your cities. Therefore, let the youth and those of all ages come to the realization that Canada has yet to fulfill her destiny. Those who must lead her must understand that the hour has come for this nation, as for all nations, that a civilization must truly enter the spiral of the transfiguration flame, entering into a period, then, of self-transcendence that is a spiritual attainment in order that that civilization might be endowed with a living flame and endure.

O ye of the West, you know not the trembling in the earth and those forces of destructivity and chaos that could so easily descend. Where are the watchmen of the night?[1] Where are those who know the meaning of aurora borealis? Where are those who know as I have known as father of nations,[2] as Saint Germain has known as father of Christ Child,[3] that the emergent Christhood of a people demands the ultimate spiritual defense and physical caution?

The force and the power of the Divine Mother must be flashed, even as the steel of Excalibur[4] does return to the eye of the enemy his negative force. So I say, let it be turned back in defense of Lightbearers until the hour when a nation can once again galvanize for greater causes than separatist movements and defenses of separations physical and mental.

Let there be the opening of the gates, for there must be the divine embrace of brother and brother and sister and sister across these borders.[5] Let it so come to pass that a people strengthened by good-neighborliness shall understand that there are enemies to be defeated within and without and they are best fought in union.

I speak of encroachments upon society and education, upon the environment. I speak also of the prophecies of war that come from Fátima and the heart of the Blessed Mother, who does also meet with us in Darjeeling, advising us that the West has no comprehension due to their sleepfulness of that which could come upon them suddenly in the night—in the night of their somnambulance. It is an hour of reckoning, beloved, and as the Mother has said in Medjugorje, these things which are projected on the screen of life as humanity's karma may come suddenly and when least expected.

Raise up a pillar of fire as a tube of light! Raise up a violet flame as the hundred circling camps around this nation![6] Set aside all variance and witchcraft and, yes, psychicism! For the sands in the hourglass fall and the leaves in autumn will not return to their branches.

Know, then, beloved, that it is time to consider the fate of the soul of a people—[of] individuals and a nation. Wherefore destiny if there be no leaders with vision? Without leaders of vision the people perish[7] though they may be surfeited in all physical wants. It is a treacherous time when people are allured by technology and success while the enemy creeps and crawls even beneath one's seat.

Know, then, O beloved, that the survival of the soul is paramount. One must know that in any hour of the day or night the soul is strengthened, having woven her Deathless Solar Body, that wedding garment, that she might take flight if called.

Salvation is something that only the individual can guarantee. Nay, there is no priest who can guarantee it. There is no manmade doctrine that can guarantee it. For salvation is the elevation of the self in God by individual effort and striving.

We who have learned also our lessons (sometimes the hard way) would save you the pain of perishing—crushed and smothered by a materialism that is far spent and offers no true accouterment of Light.

Thus, beloved, I invite you to come apart to our Inner Retreat this summer. I personally invite you because I care profoundly for this nation and people. I desire you to hear our perspective on the world scene and also to separate yourselves for a week or so in an environment of etheric purity where even the Lord Gautama maintains his Western Shamballa, his 'Inner Retreat', there to consider, then, and pray as you walk in the hills and exult in the wildflowers and know the romance of grasses green and of brooks tumbling. Come apart to consider thy fiery destiny and for a time extricate oneself from the entanglements of karma and society and then return strengthened, one-pointed as that sword Excalibur, one-pointed as steel.

Blessed hearts, life in the cup is precious and meant to be drunk, even the dregs, that when the cup is empty thou shalt be full and not empty. Count thy days, then, as the Lord Maha Chohan does grant to you cup by cup of Holy Spirit elixir. Riding on the violet flame you invoke, count thy days of opportunity and make them count for more than thyself and intimate circle.

A nation such as this, and such as many of the West bereft of great leaders, can only go the fate of so many past ages. It is time, then, for those who understand the meaning of the keeping of the flame of Life to understand that we cannot deliver again and again warning upon warning. Why, the very density of the year's karma, the annual karmic allotment, does make dense even those who know better and should see through the tides rising of the sewers of the astral plane that leave the foam of their pollution even on the shore of selfhood.

Yes, it is a fiery destiny one must seek and sometimes one must go as John Baptist into the desert to pray, into the wilderness lands. Let the angels of the Lord receive you and may you receive them also. And therefore know that the stalwart and the tough-minded, those spiritually fortified, will build that Inner Retreat and will keep a circle of fire for the earth as she does shrug through planetary changes that must be.

Let those who kept the flame of the great Shamballa long ago, those who tended altars on Lemuria, those who sang in great choirs and played in the orchestras of Atlantis keeping the flame of the great cathedrals, let them also know that by sound, by heart, by determination, by aloneness on a cold night with the stars, man, woman and child may find that inner destiny and divinity and by that light rise to a level of heroism that is called for when millions are threatened and undefended from those in this world who have another agenda, which is the agenda of hell itself.

The last battle of Armageddon is yet to be fought. May you be found ministering unto the poor, defending the oppressed and enflamed with the vibrancy of God-justice. May you understand that God in you may transcend your lesser self if you allow it by the great gift of free will. May you allow it, beloved, for there are few who can leave their cowardice and their clutching to their money and things to come apart and offer some moment of sacrifice that the destiny of millions might be secured.

Blessed ones, now is the time to remember the great heroes and their history. For those who run with the masses, huddled, indistinct, are like the cowards of many times: no profile of integrity or individuality, and then, of course, the creeping beast of state control, state care, and spinelessness that comes from demanding more and more that outside of oneself all cares must be provided.

You are individuals in God! *You* have an I AM Presence! Be ashamed to eat what you have not labored for. Be ashamed to set the example to your children that you will bow to the state for some paltry mess of pottage.[8] The state that controls your life will also control your soul. For the flabbiness of that state of consciousness does not beget fiery spirits whose ingenuity must intensify to care for its own.

I send forth the warning, then: Challenge those who control you by money, by serving you and therefore controlling you. Let the people be the focus of their own God-government and let us see what the wealth of a nation can produce to defend the integrity, the life, and the pride of individuality.

I am El Morya of the First Ray. I wind my own turban. I fasten my own cloak. I buckle my own sandals. I spin my own cloth. May you be found independent of the manipulators of your lifeblood and therefore move with angels and adepts and those who have long quit this level of mortality in grace, in victory and at times in disgust with those they left behind who had not the courage to place one foot before the other to climb the mountain of destiny.

I am a mentor of fiery spirits. A fire is blazing on the hearth at Darjeeling this night. It is a peculiar and special fire not of this world. I bid you welcome and my angels who have come with me are ready to escort you. May you quietly place your bodies to rest with a call to me and Archangel Michael. We would receive you in council to continue our discourse and show you, then, on the screen those things that are being discussed and planned behind closed doors [concerning] the manipulation of the world society.

I am a counsellor of heads of state and those in the economies of nations, and there are few [among them] today who make it to our retreat. Therefore, I turn my attention in earnest again, as I have done for some time, to those who know the Truth and know what ought to be happening. You must be tutored, for the lie is big. Therefore, I prefer to state it at inner levels where your souls are not so encumbered by brainwashing, indoctrination and prejudice.

Beloved, we of the Darjeeling Council of the Great White Brotherhood must have those who will rise to the occasion [and] understand the equation of government and the military affairs of nations, those who will call upon the blue-flame will of God and accept its message.

Therefore, I AM El Morya. I appeal to this nation not so contaminated by the decadence of Western civilization as is even America. Blessed hearts, you have an air that is yet free and you are free to breathe it. May you this night inhale and know that the Holy Spirit does send a sacred breath for the quickening of the mind and the shedding of false concepts of the future of a planet and even of your destiny.

In the name of the Blessed Mother, Mary, I salute you and commend you for your good faith and goodwill and your attentiveness, beloved, to the needs of others.

Now let there be a purging fire as millions of seraphim have gathered over this nation in answer to the call of Keepers of the Flame and the Mother of the Flame. Now, then, let a people be rid of an astral burden, that they may look up and see the stars clearly and know that every star is a sign of an ascended one and that one's causal body.

May your star shine over Canada and may that star be the hope of someone who will survive because you chose to forge and win your Christhood! Yes, there is a price. Yes, there is some pain and sacrifice. It is grueling and hard to climb that mountain but the reward is infinite Love, infinite Love.

Whosoever desires the gift of God will do it.

Purusha. (Parousia)[9]

"The Summit Lighthouse Sheds Its Radiance O'er All the World to Manifest as Pearls of Wisdom."
This dictation by **El Morya** was **delivered** by the Messenger of the Great White Brotherhood Elizabeth Clare Prophet on **Friday, April 15, 1988,** after midnight, at the Toronto Airport Hilton International, **Ontario, Canada,** where she was stumping for Saint Germain's Coming Revolution in Higher Consciousness. Prior to the dictation the Messenger delivered the lecture **"The Lords of the Seven Rays on Crystals, with Chakra Initiations."** Lecture and dictation by El Morya on four 90-min. audiocassettes, which also include dictations by

Justinius, May 14, 1988, and the Maha Chohan, May 15, 1988, B88078-81, $26.00 (add $.95 for postage). [**N.B.** Bracketed material denotes words unspoken yet implicit in the dictation, added by the Messenger under El Morya's direction for clarity in the written word.] **(1) Watchman of the night.** Isa. 21:5–12; 62:6; Ezek. 3:17; 33:7. **(2)** El Morya was embodied as **Abraham,** to whom the LORD said, "I will make my covenant between me and thee. . . . And thou shalt be a father of many nations." See Gen. 17:1–8; Rom. 4:16, 17. **(3)** Saint Germain was embodied as **Saint Joseph,** father of Jesus. **(4)** In Sir Thomas Malory's *Le Morte d'Arthur* (c. 1469), the Lady of the Lake tells King Arthur that the name of his sword is "**Excalibur,** that is as much to say as Cut-steel" (bk. 2, chap. 3). Geoffrey of Monmouth, who chronicled the kings of Britain in his *Historia Regum Britanniae* (c. 1135), called Arthur's sword *Caliburn* (according to some sources, derived from Latin *chalybs* 'steel'). **(5) Political and economic border problems.** Nationalist and anti-American tendencies in the Canadian electorate, many of whom consider the United States a threatening political and economic giant, plus America's increased protectionism have slowed progress on a long-pending, free-trade agreement. On Jan. 2, 1988, U.S. President Ronald Reagan and Canadian Prime Minister Brian Mulroney signed a free-trade treaty which in effect creates the world's largest free-trade zone. This agreement still requires the approval of both the U.S. Congress and the Canadian Parliament; if ratified it will go into effect Jan. 1, 1989. Months of negotiations created this accord designed to stimulate economic activity in both countries by eliminating tariffs and nontariff barriers in North America before the year 2000. The agreement in part proposes to eliminate all tariffs on cross-border trade within 10 years in a new Free Trade Area (FTA); restrict Canada's power to screen foreign investment only to direct takeovers of Canadian companies with assets of more than $150 million (Canadian) rather than the present threshold of $5 million; remove restrictions on the operations of U.S. banks in Canada and lift the limits on U.S. ownership of Canadian financial institutions; establish a common energy market in petroleum, gas, uranium and hydroelectricity; and remove barriers against computer services. To date Congressional committees have approved legislation that allows enactment of the U.S.-Canada free-trade agreement; Congress is expected to vote on the issue this summer. In addition to free-trade discussions, negotiations have been conducted on a Canadian claim to the Northwest Passage. Canada had long claimed this Arctic passage which connects the Atlantic and Pacific Oceans. The U.S. considers it to be international waters and cites historic usage. A Jan. 1988 agreement between the two countries acknowledged Washington's rejection of Canada's ownership claim but requires Canadian permission for U.S. passage through the waterway. A dispute also exists over a portion of the Alaskan boundary described in an 1825 treaty as running up to the "frozen sea." The border in question runs from the 141st meridian either due north or northeast into the Beaufort Sea. At stake is an area of immense significance because of oil reserves. Another point of concern to Canadians is America's contribution to acid-rain pollution—a by-product from the combustion of fossil fuels from industry and automobiles. The Canadians are pressing for a 50 percent reduction of acid-rain emissions in both countries. **(6)** In his Nov. 29, 1987 dictation delivered in Washington, D.C., Saint Germain announced the following dispensation given to Holy Amethyst, the divine complement of Archangel Zadkiel, for America: "Holy Amethyst does move about the city with violet flame angels, priests and priestesses of the Seventh Ray. They, beloved, are igniting **violet flame campfires.** These are not large, but sufficient for a consuming action and a quickening of souls; they are the sign of the 'hundred circling camps.' They [these violet flame campfires] are the sign, unto all who read and run, for the quickening and the awakening of the memory of the violet flame and ages long ago when they were once a part of a fiery dispensation of the violet planet and beloved Omri-Tas. Violet flame for the awakening, first in this city consecrated to the throat chakra, the voice of a people, and then in the cities of the seven chakras and beyond! So long as there shall be a response to these violet flame campfires, so long shall Amethyst have her dispensation to ignite these fires in America." See 1987 *Pearls of Wisdom*, pp. 616–17. Send for *Save the World with Violet Flame! by Saint Germain 1, 2, 3 and 4* released by Elizabeth Clare Prophet, audiocassettes of violet flame songs and decrees for the healing of planet earth, performed by 800 voices, full musical accompaniment. Cassette 1 includes violet flame decrees given powerfully and deliberately, 92 min., plus booklet, B88019; cassette 2, in a quickened lively rhythm, 93 min., plus booklet, B88034; cassettes 3 and 4 given masterfully with intensity and acceleration; $5.95 each (add $.65 each for postage). **(7) Without vision the people perish.** Prov. 29:18. **(8) Esau's birthright.** Gen. 25:29–34; Heb. 12:16, 17. **(9)** *Purusha/Parousia.* See 1988 *Pearls of Wisdom*, p. 228, note.

Pearls of Wisdom®

published by The Summit Lighthouse

Vol. 31 No. 50   *Beloved Saint Germain*   August 13, 1988

Saint Germain Stumps Canada

2

The Individual Path

The Great Equation of the Century— Fearless Compassion

O Light, how art [thou] the magnificence of a soul, the crown of beauty and the glistening eye of the Divine Mother who sheds a tear for the benighted understanding of her own!

I come, then, the knight champion of all servants of God upon earth, happy to grace this land with violet flame angels and a dispensation of violet flame that shall remain when multiplied by those who elect to keep its flame.

I offer my hand, beloved, for the victory of your hearts.

I would speak to you, then, of the individual path. Enough and enough again has been said of war and burdens coming upon the earth. My concern in this moment is *you, the individual;* for though I may not have dispensations to sponsor this nation, I do have the approbation of Almighty God to sponsor the individual who, after all, is a cosmos all inside.

We have worlds to conquer. Let us go within and begin with the microcosm of self. For it has been well said that the only destiny of which you may be certain is that of your own soul. It is a future, then, that can be charted and known, a vision that can be seen, a goal that is attainable. Whereas, for the perfidy of the human consciousness it is not at all certain, given human idiosyncrasies, whether the people of a city block or a hemisphere shall rise to the occasion of the momentous descent of the Divine Mother Liberty into their midst.

Beloved ones, even consider the multireactions to the visitation in the physical [plane] of such an one as this Cosmic Being of

Liberty, this Divine Mother whose statue still stands in New York Harbor, drawn there by the ancient Temple of the Sun of Atlantis.[1] So, then, beloved, one can see that human reactions to the divine are often idolatrous as [mankind] regard the luminaries of heaven with fear, even anger or hatred, who[, they suppose,] would come perhaps to disrupt their lives.

Therefore, I am sent to work with the Keepers of the Flame who have already made that determination in life to hold out a light for all who will follow its beacon. Therefore, I am an initiator of the age of Aquarius and [of] souls who would enter therein.

My concern is the continuity of being of your lifestream and that a soul not yet wed and fixed in the universal Light might endure whatever upheavals might occur within or without. After all, personal karma is enough, of itself, to keep most occupied and preoccupied day upon day. Is it not so, beloved, that for the cares of this world and this life most cannot even lift themselves to be concerned of local, let alone national and international affairs? They have left these to the powers that be, who by this moment of history and the turning of worlds have jolly well betrayed the vast majority of the people of a planet.

Well, I can tell you that we the Ascended Masters and the heavenly hosts have nowise betrayed our calling or your own, and so long as the dispensation is open to our universities of the Spirit,[2] we shall be on hand with the utmost fervor and determination. You have therefore but to invite me into your life this night and I, your brother, who desire to be known simply as "holy brother," Saint Germain,[3] shall come to you and tutor you.

And if you should ask for a step-up in initiation, an acceleration to swiftly fly as an arrow to the heart of the Divine Mother, so you will sense the stepping up of returning karma, of light descending, of mystical awareness; and as you accompany this with invocations to the violet flame heartfelt, you shall know a path and a victory sooner than you think.

And that is well-taken, for since it is later than you think, it is well to attain sooner than you think and therefore to come out ahead in the equation and to know that at any hour when the angel does call, you may easily step forth from this body knowing that in other octaves and higher planes you have wings that soar, chakras that spin, a soul integrated with the Higher Mind and [you] therefore [are] no longer so dependent for locomotion or survival upon a mere physical matrix already predestined to rot and decay.

Blessed ones, I am interested in the life of the soul and [in] her tenure and her oneness with that great eternal Light. I am interested in your self-mastery. I desire that you should understand the great equation of the century, that by an acceleration of dynamic decrees of the violet flame and loving service to life you may balance an extraordinary percentage of your karma; and if you reach that level of 51 percent, beloved, you will not be required to reincarnate, come what may upon this planet. This is a great boon of dispensation from the LORD God, and thereby many have achieved that point of permanency and well-being—peace in the profound recesses of the temple of being—and thus a fearlessness that comes of a fire that intensifies.

Ah yes, Zarathustra! Lo! the Ascended Master does enter. Precious hearts, the legions of Light of seraphim and Nature spirits of fire, called salamanders, who accompany this Flaming One are a joy to behold in the myriad rainbow rays of their movement of fire!

Thus, the acknowledgment of the sacred fire, the adoration of this sacred fire and the willingness to pass through that baptism of fire[4] will afford you, beloved, the opportunity to be divested of what is unreal and to have reinforced, enfired as though in a great kiln, thy God-reality. Singing unto the living flame, adoring that flame, you are directly in contact with the infinite God. For our God is a consuming fire.[5] And I AM that fire, manifesting myself now as a flame and now again as the figure of the Wonderman of Europe that you might recognize me as the one about whom you have read.[6]

Ah yes, beloved, I, too, thought that in the demonstration of miracles I might win the heart of a world, and so my kind sponsors allowed me to make the effort. Well, beloved, there was nothing too much for me to try in order to convince the crowned heads and others of Europe to leave their folly and unite to defeat those same forces now arrayed on a world scale.

Blessed ones, some have said to this Messenger, "If you would only perform a miracle or two we might believe in you." Well, blessed hearts, miracles are for believers, as it is written.[7] And I am in the heart of the miracle of Life itself; and the miracle of Life and the continuity and our speaking these words to you is more of a miracle than you may dream of.

But be assured of this, beloved: those whose hearts are of stone, those who enter into a spirit of condemnation of our best servants, these will not believe though you may prance and dance all the day for them. They only hold up the faults of the Lightbearers that they might have an excuse as to why they will never bend the knee before Sanat Kumara or the Ancient of Days or the Christ of their own being.

Let it be known, then, that the miracle is you and is in your heart as a threefold flame and divine spark. The miracle is that a path foreknown can be walked by you in this hour.

My angels come for the transmutation of doubt and fear. Recognize this, beloved, that all doubt and fear is of oneself [and of] one's relationship to God and to the Divine Father-Mother. As beauty is in the eye of the beholder, so is doubt. Thus, one's state of consciousness and attainment, mastery or absence thereof, is reflective of one's own state of being.

Embrace Life, beloved, and Life shall embrace thee.

Now, my emphasis as I tutor your souls is in the development of the heart as a fiery furnace and vortex of transmutation, a place where the threefold flame is balanced and where one can extend the borders of being and love to enfold so many who suffer.

Think upon these words of the bodhisattva vow, *fearless compassion!* Ah, what a state of mind to be in perpetually! Fearlessness to give of the fount of one's being, to extend compassion instead of criticism and backbiting, to give such flood tides of love as to fill in the chinks and cracks of another's shortcomings. Fearless compassion means one no longer fears to lose oneself or to loose oneself to become such a grid for the light to pass through that the Infinite One never ceases to be the compassionate one through you.

Is this not, then, the face and the posture of the Buddha, our beloved Gautama? Is it not, beloved, that Presence of the Divine One?

O fearlessness flame, dissolve, then, all reticence to be and to embrace the will to be! Fearlessness flame, sweep through those who are a part of my band of disciples and let each one know how the rings of the aura multiply as lines of compassion, [even] as rings upon a tree denote the ageless wisdom that accrues to one's Tree of Life—as a destiny, as a continuity of the extension of the branches of being until all of life might know that in the earth God has planted a seed and a seedling has come forth and a tree has matured: It has become a great tree. It is thyself, beloved, one and one and one again, trees of the forest of God where angels pray.

Is it not so [in order] that the whole world might receive the extended branches of those who have fearless compassion? Let it be the byword of those who adore the kindling fire of Buddha of the heart.

Does your heart not burn within you,[8] beloved, as in this hour even Lord Buddha does send angels of his Presence and his Divine Image before you? And does he not, then, foreshadow the coming of Kuan Shih Yin?* O the blessed Kuan Shih Yin! Is it not so, that the Divine Mother in manifestation is at the point of origin the Buddha? And so the cycles turn and the chain of being and the T'ai Chi. Therefore is there the Father-Mother God.

---

*pronounced in Chinese gwan she(r) een; pronounce (r) as a light *r*

I am Saint Germain. I too have spent the decades and centuries in the caves of the Himalayas and in the planes of nirvana. I come from a long preparation to embody the soul, the law, the flame, the ray that is called Aquarius.

Freedom is my name! And so long as there are free souls upon earth who desire that freedom to ultimately realize the Bodhi[9] in themselves, so I am at hand, as much able to teach you the path of the Eastern adepts as I have chosen to give you instead the formula from God for the Western disciple. That formula, beloved, is by no means rote but a divine ritual, a "right-you-all," for the righting of all conditions in consciousness.

I can assure you, beloved, as I look upon souls who come to study my teaching, that I must measure the sands in the hourglass of every life. There are those who come who have but months of tenure left on earth, others weeks, days or years. Thus, I have prepared in my lessons and [in] all of my dictations, together with the Ascended Masters who have also given of their teaching, a course of instruction whereby the individual may make the most progress and thereby be ready for any change, major or minor, conditioned by his own karma written in his own astrology.

Blessed ones, I define progress as the balancing of karma. Karma, then, is the weight whereby many times the soul cannot fly. Therefore, emptying the ship of its cargo or a balloon of its ballast, this is my goal—thus my gift of the violet flame multiplied by the power of the ten thousand-times-ten thousand by the aura of Maitreya, the Cosmic Christ, who would multiply every call of your heart.[10]

The less karma you have, the greater [your] opportunity day by day. This affects all choices. It affects contracts—business, marriage and otherwise—those who are drawn to your life and those who cannot be, the children you may give birth to. Every day as percentages of karma pass through the sacred fire and that transmutation is ratified by good deeds, words and works of love and service, you are lightening the load and therefore rising and therefore, beloved, coming into new planes of realization, new associations.

Walk with angels. Enter the rarefied atmosphere. Thus, why position oneself at a level or plane or step of the ladder when [on] the very next one you might find your twin flame or the Guru of thy heart or an initiation failed long ago? Now you are prepared to take it, to win and to fly!

Aquarius is a mighty air sign. It is the sign of the liberation of the mind and the soul to soar, to sing!

Beloved, I see here hearts of Light encased in dense forms so polluted by karma. Do you realize how quickly the cleansing of the pores and the organs and the lower bodies takes place by the drenching rain of violets in springtime? Have you not played in the rain as children, looking up into it and licking one's face? O beloved, those drops of rain were received as a child by you as descending violet light, and often my angels did pour to you in joy the violet flame through the falling rains of springtime. Thus, the flowers bloom, the chakras open.

May you now sense your vibration in my Presence and know how much lighter and freer and more the master of your domain you can be in a fortnight, in six weeks. Should you take these violet flame decrees and give them for those ninety minutes a day for thirty-three days,[11] you will find yourself in such a centeredness by the time you accept my invitation to be at *FREEDOM 1988* in the Heart of the Inner Retreat, that those dictations and dispensations forthcoming can be absorbed by you as though you were a sponge, wholly free and open, and thus [you may] walk away [from the "Place of Great Encounters"] with an auric egg of violet fire that all the earth and elementals will notice as you pass by.

There is such a high road of freedom that beckons you on and this is not illusion! This is the fusion of the soul to her Divine Reality! This *is* the alchemical marriage!

I extend my heart and hands to you, beloved. I desire you to know that my lessons and teachings will take you swiftly in the direction you really desire to go. Thus, beloved, successive doors open as other doors close behind you. And this is our desire, that you come to easily frequent the octaves other than the concrete physical but always return to this blessed body temple in the morning prepared to face the day as a conqueror of life and a victor over Death and Hell.

This is your hour and the power of Light, not Darkness, for Darkness must go down. And let it go down, beloved, more and more because you live and love and have embraced the wisdom of the ancients.

I therefore commend all who understand that the only true attainment takes place when the fire of the heart must intensify to accomplish a goal of service, when one must pull down the resources of one's causal body, for one knows that one's [lower] self no longer has the capacity for the challenge.

Blessed hearts, the mediocrity of world socialism is the bane of the Guru-Chela relationship, for it allows for stagnation, noneffort. And while individuals exercise their sinews, they fail to exercise their spiritual reality and to seek that strength for the accomplishment of deeds of honor and heroism.

I say to you, then, be not content in the posture that is along the lines of day in day out performing the same task. You are not dumb beasts on a treadmill. You are sons of God moving up the mountain of being! Do not shirk a challenge! Welcome it and know that when you desire to serve the world body, you will always have a challenge that exceeds your present ability. If it did not, you could not call us Guru, or the Path one of initiation. Therefore, summoning resources you knew not you had enables you to understand the meaning of self-transcendence and its necessity.

Either you mount the spiral of being and ascend or you enter the treadmill and go round and round and round. And the astonishing fact is the majority of humankind prefer it that way—to be told what to do, to have the state plan for them, to receive their dole and their money and their food, which surely becomes a mess of pottage. And this is the existence they prefer. Beloved, how can we respond to such as these when there is no response forthcoming? Therefore, up and down the nations we seek the dissatisfied ones, those who have contempt for mediocrity and [own] the same expression of Morya of the night past.[12]

Dare, then, to exceed oneself. But this, too, requires fearless compassion—[even] compassion for one's own soul in the process of [overcoming by a] fearless compassion that should never indulge self-pity or whining or petulance.

Blessed ones, the higher rock where the eagles gather is the place where you will find me.[13] There are other paths and ways for those content with things as they are. It is the discontented spirit who desires to move on who will find me and have me and know me. *Blessed ones, I am a true friend of Light who always loves you and will not betray you, for I have known you forever and a day.*

Thus, beloved, if you have the fearless compassion to save a world, let us begin! Let us begin with you and me and then take on the impossible that will quickly appear as the possible. There is no failure but that which you accept, no victory denied but that which you allow some fallen angel, false-hierarchy impostor of yourself to deny. There is no backward step that can be imposed upon you unless you yourself lose the sense of self-worth in the I AM Presence.

I am Saint Germain. To reach me you must take a leap forward and beyond, even into the unknown, and you must be either hot or cold but never lukewarm.[14]

I am in the heart of the violet singing flame. I await thy call.

My hand, see it now. It is extended in that divine friendship that spans the octaves. And I shall remain standing where this Messenger is until everyone who desires it may receive the sealing of the servants of God in their foreheads.[15]

By his grace I am so sent for this sealing. May it be done and may you know the meaning of the cosmic cross of white fire.

This dictation by **Saint Germain** was **delivered** by Elizabeth Clare Prophet on **Saturday, April 16, 1988,** at the Toronto Airport Hilton International, **Ontario, Canada.** Prior to the dictation the Messenger delivered the lecture **"Saint Germain On Prophecy: The Astrology of Canada's Destiny: Challenge, Crisis and Opportunity."** Lecture and dictation on 3 audiocassettes, 4 hr. 15 min., B88064–66, $19.50 (add $.95 for postage). [**N.B.** Bracketed material denotes words unspoken yet implicit in the dictation, added by the Messenger under Saint Germain's direction for clarity in the written word.] **(1) Reactions to the Statue of Liberty.** During the July 1986 celebration marking the 100th anniversary of the Statue of Liberty, foreign press correspondents criticized Americans for "commercialism" and extravagance surrounding the ceremonies. On July 5, 1986, the *Los Angeles Times* reported: " 'When America does something, they do it so big,' said Jean-Francois Bizalion, correspondent for *Le Matin* in France. 'The statue has been around for 100 years. It's like all of a sudden they have discovered the statue. It's like America has only one monument. It's too much.' . . . 'This is either the biggest patriotic expression in American history or the biggest panoply of sleazy exploitation: Take your pick,' said Dermot Purgavie, who writes a column from the United States for the *London Daily Mail.* . . . In the Soviet Union, the Communist Party daily *Pravda* charged that weekend celebrations belie the true meaning of liberty in America—'the liberty to sell and be sold and the power of the dollar in a place where money is boss.' Describing the statue's physical position in New York Harbor somewhat incorrectly, *Pravda* contended that she stands with 'the huge and powerful buildings of banks, corporations and insurance companies at her back.' " In her July 5, 1986 dictation, the Goddess of Liberty said that these comments were "the envy by these nations concealed in criticism" of the "abundant momentum of joy and spirit and energy and life" of Americans and that they were "a complete misreading of the free enterprise spirit. They have not read the vibration of the Spirit of America." See 1986 *Pearls of Wisdom,* pp. 569–70. On Atlantis, the Goddess of Liberty's **Temple of the Sun** was located on the site of present-day Manhattan Island. With the sinking of that continent and the destruction of this physical focus, her retreat was established on the etheric octave. See *Saint Germain On Alchemy,* glossary, s.v. "Goddess of Liberty," "Retreats"; *Lords of the Seven Rays,* Book One, pp. 131–33. **(2) Universities of the spirit.** See 1988 *Pearls of Wisdom,* pp. 287–88 n. 5. **(3) Sanctus Germanus:** Latin for "Holy Brother." **(4) Baptism of fire.** Matt. 3:11, 12; Luke 3:16, 17. **(5) God is a consuming fire.** Deut. 4:24; 9:3; Heb. 12:29. **(6)** See **"The Wonderman of Europe,"** in *Saint Germain On Alchemy,* pp. vi–xxvii; 444–45; *Saint Germain On Prophecy,* Book One, pp. 29–39. **(7) "Miracles** happen only to those who believe in them." French proverb. **(8) Did not our heart burn?** Luke 24:32. **(9) Bodhi** [Sanskrit]: enlightenment, perfect wisdom, supreme knowledge, spiritual illumination. **(10) The power of the ten thousand-times-ten thousand.** See Lord Maitreya, 1988 *Pearls of Wisdom,* p. 150; *The Science of the Spoken Word,* pp. 78–79. **(11)** With the release of the 92-min. audiocassette *Save the World with Violet Flame! by Saint Germain 1,* the Messenger called all Lightbearers to keep a **violet flame vigil** by reciting and singing the violet flame decrees and songs on this tape daily for 33 days. With the release of *Save the World with Violet Flame! by Saint Germain 2,* the Messenger quoted Saint Germain's promise given in this dictation in the hopes that Keepers of the Flame and Lightbearers worldwide would of their own election commit themselves to a 33-day vigil with tape 2. See 1988 *Pearls of Wisdom,* p. 400 n. 6. **(12)** See El Morya, 1988 *Pearls of Wisdom,* p. 398. **(13) Where eagles gather.** Matt. 24:28; Luke 17:37. **(14) Neither cold nor hot.** Rev. 3:15, 16. **(15) Emerald matrix blessing.** See 1988 *Pearls of Wisdom,* p. 130 n. 12.

Pearls of Wisdom®

published by The Summit Lighthouse

| *Vol. 31 No. 51* | *Beloved Mother Mary* | *August 14, 1988* |

Saint Germain Stumps Canada

3

Who Will Build My Temple?

The Retreat and the Path of the Divine Mother

I AM the heart of the living flame, the very Shekinah glory in the center of the City Foursquare.

You know whereof I speak, beloved, for the foundation of thy being and pyramid of Life is indeed one by one the City Foursquare. And the Holy City which John beheld descending out of heaven[1]—that city, beloved, is the citadel of Higher Consciousness of every man's being in the vast reaches of the Great Causal Body. Collectively that great City Foursquare is the vastness of the Retreat of the Divine Mother on etheric octaves where the true City of Light is, where the golden age does reign.

The heart of the city, then, that is North America is not [geographically] central [on the continent], and the secret chamber of the heart is maintained in the Western Shamballa and the Retreat of the Divine Mother there,[2] the secret chamber being the antechamber of each and every forcefield of [the] heart [chakra]—of retreat of Chamuel and Charity, of Heros and Amora and of the very heart chakra of each nation. Each one of you, then, has the potential to be the white cube, a stone in the city and a lively stone.[3]

We come for the builders. I am the Divine Mother seeking those who will build my temple. Yet it is a temple not made with hands.[4] Yet it is an edifice of lives and an edification of the spirit. Yet it is the sword of illumination's flame that pierces this night of the Kali Yuga and in piercing it does therefore reach all those in whom lumination's flame is burning brightly in heart and mind and soul.

Seek illumined action. Turn worlds around and turn them again, I say!

I am the beloved of God as ye are also. Is it not, then, a gentle presence of the Divine Mother that does bring one and all to the captivity of the Spirit of the LORD? Is it not, then, a gentle path that does take you by paces and disciplined action to the unity of the One? Beloved, it is indeed the sense of struggle that makes the struggle. It is not effortless (this path we walk together), but it is a free movement to the sun of those who would soar with me this day.

The way out is given, it can be known. O beloved, take this opportunity! Come and study at our retreat neath the skies where Shamballa drapes the etheric octave. Know there the Buddha and the Divine Mother, and know that it is a place where heaven and earth meet. And as the physical land rises, the etheric octave meets the land—as the Father caresses Mother Earth, the arms of the trees rise to greet angels, emissaries, seraphim of God descending from the Great Central Sun.

If you are to be a part of the next world, the world of which you have always been a part, then rise, beloved, in vibration, in nonattachment, in acceleration and know that the doors of the temple of the Divine Mother are also open to you.

You who weary, then, of karmic toil, know that the service of the Light transmutes a karmic toil; and the return to Maitreya's Mystery School is indeed possible. The call of the hour, then, is to build and build again, to enter the path that is a spiral, to trace your tracings in the sands of life and to transmute measure for measure, line by line.

The gradation is indeed gentle. It can be walked. But if you would mount and skip spirals as though in the last minute to catch up where others have been moving as an army of Light ascending and saints putting on [their] robes, I tell you, beloved, it will not be possible. The shock to the Shakti's chakras is too great. I speak of you, the Shakti of your Presence.

> I AM the hand of God in action,
> Gaining Victory every day—
> My pure soul's great satisfaction
> Is to walk the Middle Way.

Aye, and that Middle Way is not the way of mediocrity, not the way of the lesser self. There is a way, beloved, the broad way that leadeth to destruction and the narrow way that leadeth to eternal Life.[5] And the narrow way is the very gate of the Kundalini rising; it is the narrow way whereby in a tight coil of spring you rise [to] that altar.*

---

*or "[to become] that altar"

Blessed hearts, this is not a fanatical path. It does not even require total celibacy but [it is] a path where the light may be conserved, where moderation is pursued and the bliss of God may carry measure for measure that light that would otherwise be squandered whether in human emotion or anger or excesses or pleasures that deplete, do not heal, and deprive you of the victory.

There is balance in this path, beloved. Asceticism is not the way. In fact, Aquarius is the age of the family, is the age of the individual, is the age of a mandala of Lightbearers who exult in the buoyant light rising as children do who play in the sun, whose perpetual joy is the miracle of the natural upward flow of light.

Let the wind caress the cheek and let the sunlight reflected in the eye tell you, then, that Life is real, devotees are real and they contain the profoundness of a universe and starry bodies.

You need no longer be disappointed in the shallow ones and their shallow relationships, nor in a love that cannot contain the vastness of thy interior castle. Be not dismayed. The trees only grow so high and the cup has only such a circumference. Curse not, then, the vessel that is too small but raise up thine own and fill it full that millions may drink therefrom. Do not expect too much of those who cannot contain, for they have no containers for the Infinite.

If you go on up the mountain sacrificing the lesser relationship for the greater, you will be on the mountain when the calls from the world reach your heart and those who were not ready when you were there, now ready, seek your aid. We who are ascended are helping those who tarried when we rushed forward on Atlantis and in ancient civilizations.

So it was, beloved, each flower in her time and season. Have the courage to be even among the Alpine goats and the bighorn sheep and the edelweiss. Be the flower that grows in the highest rock that all men seek, the starry white that does proclaim the footprint of an ascending one passed by.

O beloved, whom do we find in these vastnesses of the Northern Rockies? Do we not find the Old Man of the Hills, that quaint one that some have met, and other adepts not quite physical, not quite ascended who can be seen by those whose light has risen to open the inner sight to know that mounting the scale of being are many of different wavelengths?

Life is a ladder; there be some on every step. Some are guardians of the sacred steps built by others who have scaled the heights [in order] that you might climb in orderly fashion in your time.

Know, then, beloved, as the sentinels keep the way of the steps, you may move upward, steady gait, steady eye—serene, beholding new vistas as you leave behind the valleys of indecision for that one great decision of life: Union. O the union that is sought! Why, the Divine Mother rising in the temple does become thyself and she does rise and leap to meet her Lord, the infinite fire.

So know, beloved, that you become the Kundalini goddess. This is the mystery of the mystics of the Far East. A Light* raised up within you *is* you, and all of thyself becomes the emanation and the point of origin itself. And so this magnet of white fire does also draw forth the magnet of the Holy Spirit causal body.

Worlds rise from beneath, descend from above, undulating waves of light, the figure-eight flow completes a spiral begun long ago. And all that was lost is regained, for the fire of the heart and the great inbreath of the soul mounting ascension's casement does then draw from every corner of Cosmos each spilled dewdrop of the tear and the light that has been sent forth. And a fiery coil and a fire infolding itself and all of the creation of oneself does return to the heart of ascension's flame.

And on the summit, the peak of the mount of attainment, there you stand, arms raised, entering the cloud of the Shekinah of the I AM Presence; and passing through it into the very heart of hearts of the Holy of Holies you therefore declare: "I AM WHO I AM! I AM everywhere in the consciousness of God! I AM the ascending one! I AM the fulfillment of ascension's coil! I AM the Holy City as Above, so below!"

And the pyramid of Life, its inversion above does create a giant hourglass [with the pyramid ascending from below] whereby the light flows up, no longer the sands descending. Thus, passing through the nexus, time and space collapse and a cylinder in place does reveal the ascending one. I AM alive forevermore! I AM alive forevermore! I AM alive forevermore!

Cherish at-one-ment. Cherish Life. Surrender not one drop of it to the death coil, to indulgence activated by fear, depression, denial and the nihilism of the fallen angels who have not because they are not. Pity them not. They had the All once. They desecrated the All of the Shekinah and by their cunning did lead you to do the same. They continually set examples of brazenness and brashness before your youth, all designed to siphon from them the light of the All they yet have in their containers, chakras.

Thus, beloved, beware the trends and the trendsetters of the world. They are used by those who have their own designs. Go not after them.

Pilgrims robed in white, spiraling toward the sun, you can journey with the God and Goddess Meru from Lake Titicaca to the

*consciousness of the Divine Mother

heart of the Grand Teton and Banff[6] and on and on and on on the golden pathway to the temple of the Central Sun of this system, your own dear sun of Helios and Vesta.

I tell you, that of which I speak is reality and the romance of reality and the romance of the soul smitten with the love of Christ, indeed her beloved. And thus, one who has tasted this love and the fire of this burning love does not look back down the mountain except to extend a hand to those who need it. The valleys hold nothing for thee except [as the place to go] to save that which is lost.

But in this mounting of those becoming the adepts and moving toward that point of the ascension, there is, beloved, the awareness, "As I become all that I AM and I AM is all that I am, I shall then be a world server and a world teacher and a world mother, and then I can offer a cup that is filled and emptied nine hundred thousand times a day until all the world may drink of the fountain of the Divine Mother. My fount of eternal youth flows freely from ascended octaves, ascended octaves, ascended octaves of the ascending ones."

Thus, the soul rehearses her journey, has thought it through and through as the mountaineer has marked his maps, planned his climb, studied the weather, the snowfall and all that must be precise for the victory.

Blessed are ye who understand the seriousness of the Call. Because you have heard the Call at inner levels you have answered, "I am here." But, beloved, do not think that because the Call has sounded that it will sound again and again. The Call from the Spirit of the living God is given unto the soul purposefully, determinately three times—three times only in a lifetime. Thus, beloved, opportunity in the Power of the Three-Times-Three by the flame of the heart whereby you may answer is given those three times. See, then, that you deny not your Lord ere the cock crow,[7] but remember that opportunity lost may be postponed you know not when or how.

I am Mary and for a reason I have spoken daily to my children.[8] The prophecies, then, are whispered to the hearts of those who understand, for long ago in previous lifetimes they have also known my voice.

Be with me in prayer. Be with me in the sorrows of samsara[9] of my beloved children. Be with me in the joys of the inner temples of the Great White Brotherhood as initiates who arrive are received and given the most profound and necessary instruction, training, and finally soul testing.

With Kuan Yin I come. I come, then, with a thread of my

heart going to everyone of this nation who in this or any previous life has spoken my name in devotion and prayer. I am the answer to prayer to those who will understand it in the gift of the violet flame and the rosary of Archangel Michael. Through you who know and understand, I am the answer to prayer to those who either know not, understand not or will not, even though they have devotion in their hearts.

I can multiply your calls for Light. What you place on the altar, then, I receive in my own Immaculate Heart, called the Diamond Heart of Mary. And I shall be the multiplier as I embody the Light of Sarasvati, Lakshmi, Durga, Kali, Parvati.[10]

Understand, beloved, that all ascended beings contain the divinity of the feminine nature of God and all complements. Thus, calling to me, you have specific access to the qualities of the Divine Mother I have chosen to embody according to God's will. Each feminine Ascended Lady Master, each feminine Archeia does afford you access to an infinity of God as Mother realized, each one unique and in certain portion and recipe, if you will. I am, then, in the heart of every devoted heart and I stand for the victory of an age.

May you discover the means of defense, as Above so below. May you discover the means of independence, as Above so below, in your governments and economies, in your societies. May you value individual freedom above all. Do not surrender an erg of that freedom or an erg of your life to Death or world totalitarianism under the fallen angels, under any system by whatever serpent philosophy it takes. Value the individual God Flame and know that the defense of the fire of the heart will be unto all who follow after you the key and the turning of the key to open the door to the path of victory.

Any form of slavery is death. Be not a slave but a master of life, but be a true chela of the Ascended Master who is free, who is waiting to give unto the one enslaved his freedom. But the one enslaved by his desires and karma must break the shackles of his slavery himself day by day. The Master shows you how. The true Master does not do it for you but stands by while you do it for yourself.

Thus, a slavery created can be uncreated by Shiva, by Holy Spirit fire; and this is the initiation of the Holy Spirit, the undoing of the untowardness of past actions and the ability to hold the balance while portions of the self crumble and the Holy City does rise and the builder in you does build anew. Tear down, the Lord said to the prophet, and then build.[11] Tear down and build.

So I come. If I should release the full fury of the Great Kali in this hour, you could be stripped in a moment of all excesses. But

I shall not impose nor my will nor my mastery upon you. But I tell you, you can move swiftly to the fount, the fount, beloved, the faithful fount of Yellowstone.[12] And the yellow diamonds of the Yellowstone are yet to be found in the illumined chelas of Lord Lanto, Confucius, Gautama, Maitreya, the World Teachers.

In the joy of wisdom let the world be enthralled, for the long night shall pass and earth shall be filled with the glory of the first color ring and the second of the causal body of God. Therefore in the center of the One let the wise ones gather as the ring of yellow fire does pulsate in the earth and release to the ignorant the spark, the memory, the record, the will, the joy to be!

Go be in the name of Gautama and my Son! Be all which thou art, and know and taste and feel and smell and savor thy victory. Go forth, beloved.

I am with thee in the Hail Mary. You may recite it even alternately with the *OM MANI PADME HUM,* and Kuan Yin and I will weave a purple and emerald garland, a rope that becomes the lifeline lowered into the astral pits.

Grab the rope. Grab the rope. Grab the rope of the Divine Mother. Ascend from the depths to the heights. It can be done! It shall be done!

I AM Mary of the beloved of God.

"The Summit Lighthouse Sheds Its Radiance O'er All the World to Manifest as Pearls of Wisdom." This dictation by **Mother Mary** was **delivered** by the Messenger of the Great White Brotherhood Elizabeth Clare Prophet on **Sunday, April 17, 1988,** at the Toronto Airport Hilton International, **Ontario, Canada,** where she was stumping for Saint Germain's Coming Revolution in Higher Consciousness. Prior to the dictation the Messenger delivered the lecture **"The Path of the Divine Mother East and West: Mother Mary and Kuan Yin."** Lecture and dictation by Mother Mary on three 90-min. audiocassettes, B88055–57, $19.50 (add $.95 for postage). [**N.B.** Bracketed material denotes words unspoken yet implicit in the dictation, added by the Messenger under Mother Mary's direction for clarity in the written word.] **(1)** **The Holy City.** Rev. 21:2, 10–27. **(2)** **Western Shamballa and the Retreat of the Divine Mother.** See 1988 *Pearls of Wisdom,* p. 260 nn. 8, 11. **(3)** **The white stone and the lively stone.** Rev. 2:17; I Pet. 2:5. **(4)** **The temple made without hands.** Mark 14:58; Acts 7:48; 17:24; II Cor. 5:1. **(5)** **The broad and the narrow way.** Matt. 7:13, 14; Luke 13:24. **(6)** The retreat of the God and Goddess Meru, Manus of the sixth root race, is located in the etheric plane over **Lake Titicaca** in the Andes. The **Royal Teton Retreat,** the principal retreat of the Great White Brotherhood on the North American continent, is congruent with the Grand Teton near Jackson Hole, Wyoming. The retreat of Archangel Michael is located in the etheric octave at **Banff,** Alberta, Canada. **(7)** **Peter's denial of the Lord.** Matt. 26:34, 35, 69–75; Mark 14:30, 31, 66–72; Luke 22:34, 54–61; John 13:38. **(8)** **Mother Mary's appearances at Medjugorje.** See 1988 *Pearls of Wisdom,* pp. 142 n. 1, 342. **(9)** **Samsara.** See 1988 *Pearls of Wisdom,* p. 216 n. 5. **(10)** **Sarasvati, Lakshmi, Durga, Kali, Parvati.** See "The Divine Lovers," in 1985 *Pearls of Wisdom,* vol. 28, bk. I, pp. v–ix. **(11)** **Tear down, then build.** Jer. 1:10. **(12)** **The sign of the Place Prepared.** See 1988 *Pearls of Wisdom,* pp. 340–41.

Clare of Assisi (see 1988 *Pearls of Wisdom,* pp. 139, 303), c. 1194–1253, cofounder with Saint Francis of the Order of the Poor Ladies, or Poor Clares, as the Franciscan nuns came to be called. Clare, the eldest daughter in a wealthy, aristocratic family, was inspired at age eighteen to change the course of her life after hearing Francis preach a series of Lenten sermons at the church of San Giorgi in Assisi (central Italy). She met privately with Francis, who strengthened her desire to live her life "after the manner of the holy Gospel," and on Palm Sunday she secretly left her father's home and went to the chapel of Portiuncula where Francis and the friars lived. Clare took the vows of a religious life before him and put herself under his direction. As he had no nunnery, Francis placed her temporarily with the Benedictine nuns. Some time later he installed Clare and a small group of women who had chosen the same life in a cottage next to the chapel of San Damiano, situated on the outskirts of Assisi, establishing the first community of the Franciscan nuns, the Order of the Poor Ladies. Eventually Clare was joined in the order by her two sisters and her mother.

In 1215 Clare was appointed superior and she established a cloistered contemplative order with only a brief *formula vitae* ("form of life") provided by Francis, which inculcated his idea of "evangelical poverty." The nuns practiced austerities unusual for women at that time. They slept on the ground, abstained from eating meat, went barefoot, spoke only when obliged to do so and, following Francis' rule that they own no property, received all their material necessities and sustenance from alms. The order began to spread within a few years and other convents were established in Italy, France and Germany. In 1219 while Francis was away in the East, Cardinal Ugolino, protector of the Franciscan order, drew up a rule for the nuns which removed the vow of poverty because he believed that the renunciation of all property was impractical for cloistered women, thus establishing the order as essentially Benedictine. Clare's spiritual life, however, was based on the belief in poverty as the way of the Gospel and she resisted this change, making it her life's work to restore the Franciscan character to the order. In 1228 the cardinal, now Pope Gregory IX, granted the *Privilegium Paupertatis* ("privilege of poverty") and wrote to Clare and the other nuns: "It is evident that the desire of consecrating yourselves to God alone has led you to abandon every wish for temporal things." The Rule of the Clares, which established the right to absolute poverty for the order, was finally granted by Pope Innocent IV two days before Clare's death.

Clare's support of Saint Francis and his ministry was a large part of her mission. It was to Clare that Francis turned when in doubt and it was she who urged him to continue his ministry to the people rather than lead a life of contemplation. When Francis came for the last time to the convent, Clare had a wattle hut built for him where he composed his "Canticle of Brother Sun," his joyous song of praise to God. After Francis' death in 1226, Clare upheld the purity of his teachings and his vision of "holy poverty."

The special devotion of Clare to the Eucharist saved the convent when it was attacked by Saracens in the army of Frederick II c. 1240. According to one account, as the soldiers scaled the convent walls Clare rose from her sick bed and had the Blessed Sacrament set up in view of the enemy. She prostrated herself before it and calmly prayed aloud (other versions of the story state that Clare herself held up the Sacrament while facing the infidels). At the sight of this the advancing soldiers were seized with terror and took flight. Some time later when the Saracens returned to besiege Assisi, Clare and the sisters knelt in prayer the whole day and night that the town might be spared. At dawn a furious storm broke over the army's camp, scattering their tents and causing them to flee in panic. After long years of sickness resulting from the austerities she practiced, "the little plant of our father Francis," as she called herself, died on August 11, 1253. Two years later, on August 15, 1255, she was canonized. Saint Clare is the patroness of good weather and of television; her intercession is sought in childbirth and in the healing of eye diseases. She is often depicted in art with the book (the rule), the lily, and the ciborium (goblet-shaped vessel for holding Communion wafers). Her emblem is the monstrance; her feast day is August 12.

Pearls of Wisdom®
published by The Summit Lighthouse

| Vol. 31 No. 52 | Beloved Archangel Gabriel | August 20, 1988 |

The Staying Power
Be There!

O Light of far-off worlds, I, Gabriel Archangel, command Light to descend! Light, seal the pure in heart!

I come the Divine Intercessor in the name of the Mother. Therefore, children of the Sun and Sons of the Most High, I come to announce that gift of opportunity [which] is by [the] grace of the Seventh-Ray Masters and their dispensations of the violet flame.

Opportunity in this hour is a gate ajar that does not swing full wide but allows those who observe it to pass through unnoticed by the mass mind—yet it is a golden gate and the opening whereby the soul may pass *over* rather than *under*.

To ride the wave, then, beloved, and the wave of Light, is God-mastery endued in thy soul by the Divine Mother in this age. As the Light of the Great Central Sun does bear the Buddhic consciousness to earth, *be there* in the cusp of an age. *Be there*, beloved. For it must needs be that souls of a fiery destiny pass through and beyond the astral plane that has been called the sewer of the planet. Be not there: it is a point of danger. Therefore, cut through as you have done by the "circle-and-sword-of-Astrea mantra"![1]

I AM the Archangel of the Fourth Ray, as Elohim Purity and Astrea be the God consciousness thereof. As Serapis Bey does come to rescue your Light* and your soul, I do stand in this city. As I have stood in San Diego and in Lisbon,[2] so I come again and again in this hour of cycles turning.

I AM an Archangel who does seek those who love the fiery white light of the Mother, who love the intensity of mantra, who have the staying power and the realization that that is indeed what

---

*Light, when capitalized, is the equivalent of the Christ consciousness, Christhood, or the God consciousness, Godhood, whose effect is a spiritual light and awareness; a powerful presence of enlightenment personified as/in the Person(s) and the Mind of God.

it takes in this hour, *staying power to hold a balance!*

The keepers of the Light do recognize that in this age some must give accounting for the reckless, trackless, indulgent squandering of the Light of an evolution that knows not. But one day in the far distant past they did also know. They did make conscious choice to walk away from the Divine Mother as Guru and Teacher, as Master and as the Mother womb of cosmos.

Therefore, that decision, beloved, made consciously, is now recorded only in the unconscious. For souls who have ignored the Law and inherited a karma of ignorance by their ignoring have therefore forgot, at least in the surface mind, that at the point of that separation and [of] that rebellion against the Divine Mother they did also lose the gnosis of self—self-awareness in her Divine Light. It was a costly decision, yet respected by the Great Law as an act of free will.

I come because you have called to the Divine Mother. I answer by cosmic law, and I come in the name of Opportunity[3] to deliver to you not only the mandate of an ancient decision but [also] the fiat of God "Lux fiat!"[4]

So the Light itself decrees opportunity this day to retrieve that which was lost,[5] to enter a fiery coil and once again to know consciously that the decision to embrace the Starry Mother—the blessed Kuan Yin, the wondrous Mary, Mother of Jesus, and an infinitude, a plenitude of manifestations of the Feminine Ray— that that decision of the Omega in the ending will carry you back to the point of beginning[, of Alpha]. For it is the fount of the Divine Mother that does buoy up your soul and literally carry you to new dimensions of cosmic consciousness.

Why was it that the Saviour did choose, then, a rising fount of the water of Life to mark the Inner Retreat that is become the Royal Teton Ranch? Why did that Saviour then predict to Martha, your own Messenger, that that land should be marked by that water of Light?[6]

It is because it is the age of the Divine Mother when the fire of the earth does therefore propel the water of her caring into the sky as the sign and the mark[er] that this "Place Prepared" in the wilderness[7] of America is the sign of the ascending ones who are carried aloft in the ritual of the ascension by the fire and the water of the Divine Mother.

Can it be that you do not remember that I did announce to you prior to your soul's descent into this very life that this [incarnation] should be for you, beloved, the opportunity for the ascension, for freedom from the round of rebirth?

O ye of fiery hearts and eyes and wills and chakras, I truly have come on a rescue mission with my legions of seraphim for [the rescue of] many children of the Light who are not here in this hour in this hallowed place, for they had not the momentum to carry them here or to be magnetized by an Archangel.

Blessed ones, I come in the eleventh hour—half past eleven and a quarter to twelve.[8] Know truly, beloved, that an Archangel does desperately seek those who may implement the divine plan and carry a Light for more than themselves, but for the many.

So I come, I come in the name of Mary. I come sent by the Mother Omega, and I come sent by God from the throne of grace to love you, to illumine you—to tear, then, the scales from your eyes that you might have a taste for heaven and no longer desire the lesser unsatisfying drink of the lower octaves.

It is the nectar of the Spirit I would have you quaff. It is the Light of the crown chakra. Would you be initiated by an Archangel, beloved? ["Yes!"]

My very own, I tell you, on this day of Wesak and Saint Germain's ascension day, know this: that the LORD God would defer speaking to you through these blessed Sons* that you might seize opportunity to gain for a planet a greater momentum of violet flame, of intercessory power of Archangel Michael and our bands.

Thus, to postpone their dictations as far ahead as the sign of the Mother in Cancer in the Heart of the Inner Retreat is thought [to be] the better part of wisdom. For to bring no news is not good news in this case, and to bring no advancement beyond last year's message[9] does truly inform, then, the Keepers of the Flame of a planet that Light must intensify ere the greater intercession take place, if at all.

But, beloved, by the very nature of her office Kuan Yin does come to stand for those who have called for Light. [Inasmuch] as Lightbearers may receive her intercession, each one according to the fruit of his heart, so it† may be [made] known [to you] in this hour.[10]

And I, Gabriel, tell you that the initiation of an Archangel of the Fourth Ray is somewhat of an obstacle course; for it does set before you prophecy of astrology known and heard by you to which new students may have access—prophecy, then, that has come from many corners of history and [many a] telling by the Messenger.[11] Therefore, to direct the blue lightning [of the Mind of God] and the course of Archangel Michael's Rosary,[12] and all decrees you have been given, into the obstacles of fiercely descending karma of the Dark Cycle—[this is likewise the part of wisdom:] let it be done.

*refers to Gautama Buddha and Saint Germain as blessed Sons of God †this dispensation

Let those mounting the spiral to come to the Inner Retreat for a fortnight, recharging the seven chakras in the Alpha and Omega [polarity]—let them know that we prepare a feast of Light for that summer conclave for those who will feast in the Light and make it a perpetual mantra of the hour for that saving grace.

Lightbearers of the world, I call! I AM Gabriel imploring those who are of the Most High God worldwide, and as I speak I promise you that my words are recorded not only on the ethers but in the souls and hearts of all who have once known their God and risen to heights of golden-age civilizations!

You whose auric field yet remains even a conductor of the Great Central Sun Magnet, attention! Be aware! For through you and only *through you* can the LORD God save that which can be saved[5] in the hour of planetary darkening and transition.

May all who love the Light respond as you have responded to tarry here and give these mantras by the hour. And some [of you] who have not done so in this life, I tell you, it is commendable and does return hope to the heart of my complement, whose name and quality is indeed Hope. Because you have hoped in the Divine Mother Kuan Yin and all of heaven and your God, let there be, then, a continuing stream of white fire from your heart and let us see what the rendering [of the Solar Logoi] shall be [by way of response].

For on this first of May we do seal, seal again and seal Lightbearers and certain places that there might be the opening, O the opening of the way to the inner temple of the Holy of Holies.

Seraphim of God, sanctify! sanctify! sanctify them in holiness in this hour. (Legions of seraphim of the Central Sun [are] descend[ing now] upon the shaft of the mantras of the Divine Mother.) May you now tarry and give those additional mantras.[13] In so doing, therefore, a seraphim shall arrive at each one['s seat] and place his electromagnetic field around your own [aura and electromagnetic field]—quickening, sealing, spinning the chakras.

O dearest ones, in dearest love I, Gabriel, who have known you from the beginning, salute you in the hour when the Victory is nigh and the Goal can be seen and the sunbeam can be traced back to the Source. O mount it! Mount that sunbeam! And face the Sun until eternity is thine.

I AM in the eternal flow of the Ganges. I AM in the eternal flow of the River of Life. I AM the moving waters and the flowing fire and the golden liquid light poured down upon you as blessing of Buddha, blessing of Christos, blessing of Mary.

Hail, Mary, full of grace, the Lord is with thee and with thy spirit. I AM Gabriel. Hail, Ma-Ray! Hail, O Light within these temples of the Mother! Hail, O soul who does rejoice in her God, in her Saviour.

AIM AIM

The Light does touch the crown, and the crown chakra is quickened in the name of the Lord of the World, Gautama Buddha.

"The Summit Lighthouse Sheds Its Radiance O'er All the World to Manifest as Pearls of Wisdom." This dictation by **Archangel Gabriel** was **delivered** by the Messenger of the Great White Brotherhood Elizabeth Clare Prophet upon the occasion of Wesak and Saint Germain's ascension day, **Sunday, May 1, 1988,** at the Sir Francis Drake Hotel, **San Francisco.** In the service prior to the dictation the Messenger led the congregation in giving Kuan Yin's Crystal Rosary, the bija mantras to the Hindu feminine deities and the "Decree to Beloved Mighty Astrea." Excerpt of the service and the dictation by Archangel Gabriel on 90-min. audiocassette B88067, $6.50 (add $.55 for postage). [**N.B.** Bracketed material denotes words unspoken yet implicit in the dictation, added by the Messenger under Archangel Gabriel's direction for clarity in the written word.] **Wesak** is the festival which commemorates Gautama Buddha's birth, enlightenment, and *parinirvana* (final nirvana following the Buddha's passing after which he would not be reborn). The festival derives its name from the month of the Indian lunar calendar in which it occurs—*Wesak* or *Vesak* (Sinhalese), from the Sanskrit *Vaisakha,* corresponding to April–May on the Western calendar. On the full moon day of this month, disciples gather in a valley in the Himalayas to receive the benediction of Lord Gautama. Some say that the Buddha is seen physically by certain adepts and devotees as he brings his "flood of blessing" to the earth. Buddhists consecrate the day to prayers and mantras, holy processions and ceremonies, and the performance of compassionate deeds in honor of the Buddha. It is also the time for the sacrifice of the elements of the lower nature, that the higher nature of God may descend into one's temple. Because the Indian lunar calendar may differ from that of other nations of the Far East, this festival may fall on various days in those areas. For more information on Gautama Buddha's life, see 1983 *Pearls of Wisdom,* p. 33; glossary "The Alchemy of the Word," in *Saint Germain On Alchemy,* p. 366. (**1**) **"Decree to Beloved Mighty Astrea,"** 10.14: no. 42 in *Heart, Head and Hand Decrees: Meditations, Mantras, Prayers and Decrees for the Expansion of the Threefold Flame within the Heart,* p. 32; *Kuan Yin's Crystal Rosary: Devotions to the Divine Mother East and West,* cassette 1, p. 19 of booklet; no. 60 in *Mantras of the Ascended Masters for the Initiation of the Chakras,* p. 16, on audiocassette B85137. (**2**) **Archangel Gabriel in San Diego and Lisbon.** 1988 *Pearls of Wisdom,* pp. 235, 239. (**3**) **Opportunity.** Name for Portia, twin flame of Saint Germain, who is the Goddess of Justice; hence she is called the Goddess of Opportunity. See glossary "The Alchemy of the Word," in *Saint Germain On Alchemy,* p. 436. (**4**) **"Lux fiat!"** [Latin]: "Let there be Light!" (**5**) **Saving that which can be saved.** Gautama Buddha, 1987 *Pearls of Wisdom,* p. 1. (**6**) **The mark of the Inner Retreat given to Martha by Jesus.** 1988 *Pearls of Wisdom,* p. 340. (**7**) **The Place Prepared in the wilderness.** Rev. 12:6. (**8**) **The eleventh hour.** This dictation was delivered 11:27 p.m.– 11:46 p.m. (**9**) **Wesak Address 1987.** Gautama Buddha, 1987 *Pearls of Wisdom,* p. 239. (**10**) **Kuan Yin's intercession.** 1988 *Pearls of Wisdom,* pp. 209, 367, 423. (**11**) Partial list of the Messenger's lectures on **prophecy:** 1988 *Pearls of Wisdom,* pp. 229 n. 3, 408 note. (**12**) **Archangel Michael's Rosary.** 1985 *Pearls of Wisdom,* p. 243; 1988 *Pearls of Wisdom,* p. 288 n. 6. (**13**) Following this dictation, the **"Bija Mantras for Chakra Meditation"** were given, nos. 62–64 in *Mantras of the Ascended Masters for the Initiation of the Chakras,* p. 17, on audiocassette B85137.

"I Cast Out the Dweller on the Threshold!"
by Jesus Christ

In the name I AM THAT I AM ELOHIM,
Saint Germain, Portia, Guru Ma, Lanello,
In the name I AM THAT I AM SANAT KUMARA,
Gautama Buddha, Lord Maitreya, Jesus Christ,
I CAST OUT THE DWELLER ON THE THRESHOLD of_____.

Give appropriate inserts here according to the teachings on the dweller on the threshold and the Cosmic Clock.

In the name of my beloved Mighty I AM Presence and Holy Christ Self, Archangel Michael and the hosts of the LORD,

In the name JESUS CHRIST, I challenge the personal and planetary dweller on the threshold, and I say:

You have no power over me! *You* may not threaten or mar the face of my God within my soul. *You* may not taunt or tempt me with past or present or future,

For I AM hid with Christ in God.

I AM his bride. I AM accepted by the LORD.

You have no power to destroy me! Therefore, be *bound!* by the LORD himself. Your day is *done!* You may no longer inhabit this temple.

In the name I AM THAT I AM, be *bound!* you tempter of my soul. Be *bound!* you point of pride of the original fall of the fallen ones! You have no power, no reality, no worth. You occupy no time or space of my being.

You have no power in my temple.

You may no longer steal the Light of my chakras. You may not steal the Light of my heart flame or my I AM Presence.

Be *bound!* then, O Serpent and his seed and all implants of the sinister force, for *I AM THAT I AM!*

I AM the Son of God this day, and I occupy this temple fully and wholly until the coming of the LORD, until the New Day, until all be fulfilled, and until this generation of the seed of Serpent pass away.

Burn through, O living Word of God!

By the power of Brahma, Vishnu, and Shiva, in the name Brahman: I AM THAT I AM and I stand and I cast out the dweller.

Let him be bound by the power of the LORD's host! Let him be consigned to the flame of the sacred fire of Alpha and Omega, that that one may not go out to tempt the innocent and the babes in Christ.

Blaze the power of Elohim!

Elohim of God—Elohim of God—Elohim of God

Descend now in answer to my call.

As the mandate of the LORD—as Above, so below—occupy now.

Bind the fallen self! *Bind* the synthetic self! Be *out* then!

Bind the fallen one! For there is no more remnant or residue in my life of any, or any part of that one.

Lo, I AM, in Jesus' name, the victor over Death and Hell! (2x)

Lo, *I AM THAT I AM* in me—in the name of Jesus Christ—

Is *here and now* the victor over Death and Hell!

Lo! it is done.

From Jesus Christ, March 13, 1983, "The Awakening of the Dweller on the Threshold," 1983 *Pearls of Wisdom*, p. 385.

Pearls of Wisdom®
published by The Summit Lighthouse

| Vol. 31 No. 53 | Beloved Kuan Yin | August 21, 1988 |

Kuan Yin's Promise
The Crystal Sphere—Etheric Matrix for Earth's Seventh Age

Bearing the crystal sphere of this planetary orb, I come. I AM the mistress of cosmic mercy and of the seas and of the land. I AM the mistress of the skies and of the fire. I AM the mistress of the fiery core of the atom and the sun of this system of worlds.[1]

Therefore, by violet flame and violet flame mantra and by my ancient mantras you recite, I do release to the earth crystal spheres of my rosary, crystal spheres of the yin and the yang, the Alpha and the Omega of the violet flame and the seventh age.

I have for so long carried vials of mercy, being burdened as a woman with child to deliver [them] unto this age, but I must needs find vessels into which I might pour the mercy elixir. It is, then, a liquid light beyond that of wine as you know it. It is the distillation of my *Body* and my *Blood,* my universal *Omega* and *Alpha.*

As I AM Masculine and Feminine Being, as are all Cosmic Beings, so you may know me in those virtues intended to be embodied by all. And therefore let those of the Masculine Ray excel, personifying themselves as the Avalokiteśvara of this Community.[2] Let those of the Feminine Ray so embody the qualities that bear the image of Kuan Yin that this Community shall be a place of gentle Power, gentle Wisdom, gentle Love.

How it is so, that the ministrations of my angels paint the very flesh, paint the leaves of the trees and the waters and the pebbles until earth* should become so permeated by the light of mercy, so saturated with this elixir of Life that earth† below shall prepare to receive the etheric matrix of the cosmic crystal I bear [for planet earth].

Blessed ones, it [the cosmic crystal] has weight, ponderance, and should have preponderance in thy life; for the weight of the etheric sphere that is earth's is the weight of the burden of the Lord. It is light coalesced as a crystal of etheric substance. In that

*the ground   †the planet

great sphere, beloved, all of you are housed and templed and situated beneath the Tree of Life—so many leaves for the realization of Bodhi, so many leaves of Christos [are you].

I come this day with beloved Portia, Mother of Aquarius, as I have been Mother of Pisces on the Seventh Ray[3]—so many mothers in manifestation therefore, so needed to externalize the spiritual fire.

So we salute—we of the Lords of Karma, we of the dispensation of the violet flame—all those in the New Age movement who have sensed and distilled within their own being the distillations of the Seventh Ray and the violet flame. As our Messenger has proclaimed it [the violet flame] the sign and the signet of an age, it is so. And so is the beloved Saint Germain the hierarch who may teach you all things, if you by the Divine Mother's love raise a spiral, a coil intense of that Seventh Ray whereby you ascend to his heart as he does embody the Trinity.

So, beloved, know that this violet flame saturating the earth has already mitigated karma and has turned back and consumed other [karma] by the effort of those who have loved and loved again our release of the violet flame cassette.[4] Blessed ones, the great miracle [is] that that which is recorded in you—in the marrow of the bones and cell by cell, in your very hairs—of all sound of the Godhead might also be played for you in this dense strata by the miracle technology brought forth by none other than Saint Germain. For all technology* has required sponsorship and that sponsorship is by his heart.

Lo, he comes with ten thousand saints who are adepts of the violet flame! Lo, they clear the way! Lo! they clear the way for the descent in this hour of those [beings] of higher octaves of great attainment on the Seventh Ray who could not enter this planet until some and others again should not only embody that flame but [also] understand that it is a compelling flame for individual Godmastery in science, in religion, in technology and alchemy whereby the Eternal [One] is precipitated in cups of time and space.

Electrons carry the charge of the seventh age. Therefore, beloved, there is reinforcement; and this is not a time to leave off the giving of the violet flame but to multiply and increase it, for there is a softening of encrustations of darkness in the planet and these need that daily douse of violet flame. Let there be violet flame and Seventh Ray lightning penetrating, and let all legions of Light who come under the God Surya of the First Ray assist us as we seek to purge a planet of her vulnerabilities to that [karmic judgment] which does descend.

Blessed ones, I come, then, the mouthpiece of the Buddha, delivering to you the rejoicing of Wesak in heaven that there is some progress on earth in certain areas, whereas in others the downward course continues for† nonenlightenment—nonenlightened beings,

*from the earliest beginnings of the Industrial Revolution through the twentieth century   †because of

the ignorant ones who are of malice and [the] Darkness who have determined to perpetuate their crimes against humanity and the Lightbearers.

These, then, must be challenged and you must continue your challenge of their very dweller on the threshold.[5] Speak, then, to their dweller as you recite that powerful decree[6] that is even the action of the Great Kali to cut you free as you demand the binding of all that assails the soul in the individual and in the strongholds of the power elite.

Let us understand that there are armies of heaven waiting to be summoned into action who may bind the forces who are the very mills [of the Nephilim gods] who grind[7] out a sewer of darkness on the planet. Let us go to the source as those who keep the violet flame continue to keep that flame. Let those who understand what is the mode of Avalokiteśvara in the challenging of the defilers of the Woman and her seed assume that role.

O ye Gates,[8] Gates of Seven Planes, you who crystallize perfection in the chakras,[9] therefore let the crystal [spheres of the chakras] and the perfection be tempered by compassion and thereby be tempered as tempered steel by the Ruby Ray that does [indeed] have grains and veins within [its] crystal, imperceptible. Yet that compassion in the white-fire crystal of the chakra is the means of sustaining and not breaking when one does hold the intense position that says, "Thus far and no farther!" to the sinister force.

As we see how many have taken the violet flame and loved it who knew it not before, we are then encouraged. We speak to those who are on the front lines who, on behalf of those newly engaged in the calling forth of that light, must take a strong stand with Archangel Michael to give his rosary and to challenge the very forces that would assail new souls who now have generated around themselves an aura of violet flame and need your intercessory calls for the action of the blue lightning of the Mind of God.

I also cherish, beloved, the release of my crystal rosary;[10] for it is indeed a crystal bell that sounds and intones itself in many levels of Matter, including the astral plane. That rosary, beloved, enables me to be anywhere and everywhere where that sound does reach. O it is a powerful doorway that I may enter as I seek to become physical more each day!

I ask you to prove me, to make your demands upon me and to command my Light and to keep on so doing until you should sense you have reached the limitations of my office. For I tell you, beloved, there is no thing of the will of God that I will not alchemically precipitate if you are able to bear it, [if you are able] to hold the harmony for it, and if you [will] seek the internal integration of the soul in the Seventh Ray chakra

with the fiery heart of the living Christ Bodhisattva.

What I am saying, beloved, [is] if that for which you call is given to you and in your receiving of it you can deal with its manifestation and all opposing forces to its manifestation [and if you can be counted upon to make every effort to do so], then I, Kuan Yin, in the name of the will of God and my commitment to all Lightbearers of this planet, will surely bring that manifestation into your life.

For I AM one with beloved Saint Germain and Portia. I AM one with the Seventh-Ray Healing Masters. I AM one with the Buddhas of the Seventh Ray who precipitate this very City Foursquare, this emerald cube that must be established and be built.

If it is the turning back of [those fallen angel] opponents [of your Light], then I say, call to me and discover how one word and prayer and command to me as you move from one place to the next shall bring to you, as though miraculously, the turning around of worlds.

I, therefore, come that you might cease the sense of struggle—of being a beast of burden for bearing that which has come upon you as opposition [to your Christhood] and therefore a certain weariness and a certain wondering, "How long, O Lord?" I come with the answer this day to the query of the saints "How long, O Lord?"[11] and I say, "Kuan Yin does say, Thus far and no farther!" There is no more distance or ground that can be invoked or summoned [or taken] by the fallen ones. When you call to me, their day is done in your life.

Blessed hearts, that call must be a fire of intensity as though you were a fire-breathing dragon and the fire did proceed out of your mouth. Is this not the work of the Great White Brotherhood? Let the fire come forth from the mouth of the students of the Two Witnesses![12] Have they not preached to you and delivered the fire? Now be the instrument.

When you call to me, call with the intensity and the very inner pulling upon the strings of the chakras and the Kundalini fire that when you call, that fire does leap to heaven, [does] cut across the Matter matrix and arrive at the abode of the highest Buddhas who will say, "Who are those fire-breathing dragons upon earth? We will go down and see." So it is the playfulness of the Divine Mother that must coax the highest Buddhas to come and come again and see what her sons and daughters have wrought on earth.

Thus, beloved, do not speak but implore! Do not whisper except that whisper be a fire of intensity. Whatever you are and whatever you call for, think about it. Organize your thought. Write it down and know* that this call and its results will be good not only for you and your family but for this entire Community and ultimately [for] every erg of energy and life on this planet.

If you can think of something to ask for that fulfills all of this,

---

*be certain

such as cosmic Peace and Freedom and the defeat of their enemies, I tell you, you will have access to my causal body and the great crystal of the earth sphere that I bear.

Try me, beloved. For I come in the midst of the weariness of the saints. I come in the very day and hour when some are overcome by the weight of world karma in this year. I come as a Bodhisattva of mercy out of mercy for beloved Saint Germain, who has a right to have fiery and stalwart Keepers of the Flame who will go to bat for him and will not say die and [will] not turn back!

Blessed ones, there is a weariness in the field of this movement and even in the New Age itself. There is a weariness everywhere upon the planet as people groan for the weight that they bear.

Let violet flame increase! Each time you give any of my mantras, beloved, the pronouncement of my name within the heart and being of an individual does make me ecstatically, instantaneously one with that flesh-and-blood body. Understand that God has given to me this grace for the Bodhisattva vow I have taken; for he is the merciful God in whose image I AM made.

And this merciful God has had mercy for me as I have vowed to stay and stay until eternal Life be vouchsafed to all who are of it and worthy of it. Therefore, know, beloved, that that mercy does give me these powers. That mercy does give to me, in response to my vow, *Wisdom* and *Love* and the very *ingenuity for action [Power]* for preaching the Dharma, for reaching anyone everywhere, and you may [go and] be [and have] the same.

May you, then, in so lovingly and adoringly giving these mantras, begin to memorize them and, as you know [what] each decree in your decree book [is] for [in] a given situation, [so you will] begin to understand how I may come in one of my many bodies to be the fulfillment of [need in] a crisis—*because you as the alchemist have selected the exact vibration[, the specific mantra which corresponds to the specific mantle of my multiple offices as the Mediatrix of Mercy,] for the cure.*

A cure is needed here and there and everywhere, a cure for every handiwork and handyman. You need cures if you are a plumber or an electrician or a farmer. A cure is needed whatever your role of service.

I AM the cure for the absence of necessary funds. I AM the cure for the squeaky wheel. I AM the cure, beloved, for the out-of-alignment state.

I AM Kuan Yin and I embrace the totality of the Motherhood of God, and I focus it out of the great crystal specifically for the Seventh Ray and age, specifically for the awakening and the victory of souls—*by right choice, right action, right attunement with God.* I AM so determined that this seventh age shall be a golden age, beloved, that *I AM everywhere in the consciousness of God where you are!* Let miracles of my causal body flow! Let miracles of Kuan Yin flow! Let miracles of the Great Buddha flow! I AM in the heart of compassion for Sanat Kumara, for Gautama Buddha, for each and every one of you. For as I see the Buddhas and Bodhisattvas above, it is as though they were frozen in crystal, frozen because they have no vessel below into which to pour themselves. Happy am I that you have given me the vessels of yourselves and of my crystal rosary into which I might pour the Seventh Ray elixir.

Now I must go forth to activate and intensify, that these beings may not be frozen above in the high snows of the Himalayas but may come down because the love of your heart has melted the snow and melted the ice that they might become living, breathing Bodhisattvas in your temple.

So this is my Mother's Day address to you, beloved. All the love of my heart goes to those who have in wisdom perceived this message. My love is not limited, but the vessel of the soul's perception and perceptiveness is the means whereby through vision I descend. As your eye is upon me, remember, the eye of Amitābha is upon you and therefore you might be the manifestation of his eye in form.[13] Could any more glorious gift be upon you this day than the eye of Amitābha?

Lo, I AM the eye and the crystallization of the eye of God. By his leave and grace, I AM Kuan Shih Yin.

This dictation was **delivered** on **Mother's Day, May 8, 1988,** at the **Royal Teton Ranch,** **Montana.** Prior to the dictation the Messenger gave teachings on and led the congregation in chanting the first eleven of the "Thirty-Three Manifestations of Avalokiteśvara as Kuan Yin." Service and dictation by Kuan Yin on 2 audiocassettes, 2 hr. 23 min., B88068–69, $13.00 (add $.95 for postage). **(1)** Kuan Yin is giving to her beloved devotees titles of her offices and powers in her role as Mediatrix of the Universal Christ and the Five Dhyani Buddhas. These mantles of her power should be invoked with her 57 mantras published in Kuan Yin's Crystal Rosary cassette album and booklet. For they are also "cures" for personal and planetary karmic conditions. See p. 427. **(2) Avalokiteśvara.** 1988 *Pearls of Wisdom,* p. 48 note. **(3)** Kuan Yin served as Chohan (Lord) of the Seventh Ray during the Piscean dispensation before Saint Germain assumed that office. **(4)** *Save the World with Violet Flame!* by Saint Germain 1, 2, 3 and 4 audiocassettes. 1988 *Pearls of Wisdom,* pp. 400 n. 6, 408 n. 11. **(5)** the not-self of the fallen angels aligned with the powers of Antichrist who have sworn enmity against the children of Light. See 1988 *Pearls of Wisdom,* p. 170 n. 6. **(6) Decrees** 20.07, **"The Judgment Call 'They Shall Not Pass!' "** and 20.09, **"I Cast Out the Dweller on the Threshold!"** by Jesus Christ; see 1988 *Pearls of Wisdom,* pp. 202, 422. **(7)** "The mills of the gods grind late, but they grind fine," an unknown Greek poet. "Though the mills of God grind slowly, yet they grind exceeding small; / Though with patience he stands waiting, with exactness grinds he all," Henry Wadsworth Longfellow, "Retribution," in *Poetic Aphorisms,* translated from Friedrich von Logau's *Sinngedichte* (1654). **(8) O ye Gates.** Ps. 24:7, 9. **(9)** Beloved Kuan Yin is addressing Great Silent Watchers who guard the gates of the seven planes of heaven, hence the manifestation of the Light of these seven planes in the chakras of the Sons of God. These 'Gates' are comparable to the twelve solar hierarchies who guard the twelve gates of the City Foursquare as initiators of the Sons of God on the Cosmic Clock of their karma and psychology formulated by their astrology. **(10) Kuan Yin's Crystal Rosary,** released in its final version July 4, 1988; in its preliminary form the rosary had limited distribution and use. 1988 *Pearls of Wisdom,* p. 373 n. 13. **(11) How long, O Lord?** Dan. 12:6, 8; Rev. 6:9–11. **(12) Two Witnesses.** Dan. 12:5–10; Rev. 11:3–12; and **the Faithful and True,** Rev. 19:15. **(13) Avalokiteśvara** **'born' from a ray from Amitābha's eye.** 1988 *Pearls of Wisdom,* p. 215 n. 1.

Pearls of Wisdom®
published by The Summit Lighthouse

| Vol. 31 No. 54 | Beloved Justinius | August 27, 1988 |

The Saturation of Light
The Law Is Just: The Light Serves Those Who Serve the Light

Hail! to the Light of the Great Central Sun whence I AM come with ministering angels, seraphim of God.

I AM Justinius and from my heart there does pass to your own a ray of light individually to each and every one who has tarried in the devotion of the Divine One.

The Law is just. Therefore that which you give, the Law returns to you tenfold, and unless you place upon the altar of God some portion of thy love and of thy heart, how shall the Great Alchemist multiply being? Thus, remember always, the Law is just. To him that hath Light and hath invoked it, more shall be added,[1] even [the power of] the ten thousand-times-ten thousand.[2]

Therefore, beloved, for no small purpose do the seraphim come to this city. It is an hour, as you have been told by the Maha Chohan, of initiation descending.[3] And for some, initiation is the judgment; for they cannot contain the Light but the Light itself does therefore expose the Darkness, and for that Darkness they must give accountability before the Lord God.

For others the initiation of the Holy Spirit does serve the divine purpose of preparing the individual to enter the courts of Serapis Bey and continue with a major in that university of the Spirit on the path of purity leading to the ascension in this life.[4]

Not all who study the teachings of the Ascended Masters become candidates for the ascension. I am bidden by Archangel Gabriel to remind you of this. For every man does receive according to his words, and by those words and by those works does there come the accounting.[5]

So long as life is an open book and the individual does serve to be the embodiment of our Lord daily, so [long does] that Lord God in that temple (the soul proving and being reproved by that God) increase, even if imperceptibly, in the saturation of Light; and [this ritual] is the saturation by Light of every molecule and atom of self, as though one were filling a billion cups daily, by smallest portion increasing until the cup is full and does become a magnet of the Central Sun.

Therefore, beloved, know that the surest building of the temple of man and the weaving of the Deathless Solar Body is not to miss Opportunity's call, not to miss that call to invoke the Light. For the hours that are given are hours in eternity, hours of compartments of consciousness that go before you in your own causal body.

Service to life, service to all people and service at the altar of God does provide you the means whereby angels enter your life and aura to increase and increase again. This cannot be accomplished in a day, and thus when it is postponed it is often the case according to the Book of Life that that postponement takes the individual to another embodiment upon earth.

Therefore, beloved, as the records of those who serve the Great White Brotherhood are known to me from the Keeper of the Scrolls, for I have been presented those records this night, I AM fully aware of how each individual has filled his cup or not and how the sands in the hourglass have also been running out since last I delivered an address to Keepers of the Flame and Lightbearers through our beloved Messenger.[6] *Tempus fugit.*

Saturation, then: for this cause and goal we come as well as for displacement. And it is to displace the burdens of world karma and personal karma that my seraphim would render service in and through and amongst you. Thus, for [by] the physical presence of the Messenger in this city we may have a physical vessel through which to step down the Light of the Great Central Sun that we might serve those who have served the Light.

For it is the law of a cosmos unto all who serve the Light that on a certain day and date the Light will turn and serve you. For many here this hour has come, and for others it has not come to the fullest extent of the Law that it might. For where there is a vacancy and an absence, we cannot pour our light into an empty seat that it spill upon the ground.

Think, then, of our seraphim as angels bearing pitchers, pitchers of Aquarius filled with the light of the Central Sun, and thus they pour and thus they serve. Mindful, then, that in every level of life there are those who so render service, even down to the level of those who fill the water glasses in the restaurants of the world, have you noted the diligence with which those who so serve, aye, every table and every glass, fill it only to capacity?

And thus we come, for the weight of this city and its pollution is most especially detrimental to the Lightbearers and those who would mount the spiral of being to return to the heart of God.

When last Gabriel Archangel spoke in San Diego, he did announce to some present that they had earned the ascension, as it is lawful.[7] Blessed ones, there are some [who have earned the ascension] and there are those who are moving toward that goal.

Understand that that goal, as you mount the intensity of it, does become of greater and greater challenge. It does become all-consuming. And, of course, why not? If you intend to experience the all-consuming sacred fire of God, you must begin slowly lest that sacred-fire initiation find you unable to receive it and therefore [you would be] consumed by it before you are assumed unto the Godhead in the Great Central Sun.

Saint Germain has spoken well in giving his direction to the Keepers of the Flame. May all remain [on the West Coast] to serve the Light and the Lightbearers until they have given that full measure, and let it be understood that that mission and service is part and parcel of and instrumental to your own victory.

Thus, as the tides of pollution, plague and disease mount, as crime and violence do increase, let the white light of seraphim encompass you to the extent that you raise it within yourselves through the decrees and prayers and mantras provided you by the Mother.

Know, then, that daily, so long as you remain in this service, you have the powerful reinforcement of seraphim of God, and it is given to those who serve and still serve.

If you desire to increase the capacity to magnetize and retain the assistance of the seraphim,[8] I can assure you that first and foremost is your diligence at this altar [of the Great White Brotherhood] at the services convened [in our sanctuaries throughout the world]. For Serapis Bey does note well, although the keepers of the records [the recording angels] may not be apparent [to the worshippers].

Thus, seraphim have come and, assigned to each one, they go forth. And there are others who may not, therefore, be of this flock[9] who yet keep the Light in this city [Los Angeles] and who have meritorious deeds of service [to their credit]. Wherever that quotient of Light is therefore sufficient, a seraphim is assigned to assist that soul with Saint Germain's angels to achieve the goal of life. Thus, the magnet of the heart and the aura (and the electromagnetic field thereof and [that] of the chakras) must be sufficient to hold the Light of the Central Sun in this octave.

May you who know not this path receive us, then, on the

morrow when the teaching through our Messenger will also culminate in a dictation of one of the Lords of the Seven Rays, that you might understand the basic principles whereby you can, through the science of mantra, retain Light within your chakras; and in so doing and in so sealing the aura also retain [thereby] the service of a seraph of God.

Many are called but few choose[10] to enter in and seal their election which was from the beginning and is in the ending.

The love of heaven is transferred to you in a Ruby Ray action from the heart of Chamuel and Charity, and by this ray—this ray of service and sacrifice, surrender and selflessness—by this, beloved, the greater Light does enter in.

When recently at the retreat on the etheric plane at Fátima your Messengers knelt before Mary and Raphael to give their Christhood to a world,[11] they did demonstrate to you the eternal Joy, the eternal Freedom and the great abundant Light descending [which one experiences] when one can truly understand the mystery of committing one's attainment to the liberation of other souls.

But how is this Christhood given, beloved? How does one give one's higher attainment that others might have the strengthening of that Light to arrive at the gate of victory in this life?

It is given, beloved, by the very same process [that the Son of God did give his Light]—*increment by increment*. Did not Jesus, then, give his Body and his Blood, deposited in the bread and the wine, and say, "This do in remembrance of me"?[12] Is this Holy Communion not the passing of the Light of Alpha and Omega [of one's Christhood] to every soul—portion by portion, week after week for a lifetime?

Thus it is so that the sacred fire as the nectar of the Buddha of the crown chakra must be taken in minute doses; for truly it does recharge and accelerate body and mind and soul, and this requires assimilation by word and work. Know, then, O beloved, that day by day that transfer of Light is given, not all at once. It is an impossibility, for the Light itself should consume that which does not have the vessel to receive it [until the Light itself create the vessel by the soul's assimilation of it, day by day.]

These are things that the Great Law has taught you and spoken in your heart. These are things which our Father has determined that you need to be reminded of, that you slacken not your pace but make haste and that you find the wherewithal to do this by Love— by the Love of the Ruby Ray that is the Blood of the Universal Christ. By that Love you are able to open your being. And thus, by sacrifice you come to the realization that a sacrifice is never a self-denial except [it be] the denial of the unreal self and its unreal desires. But the white light of the Divine Mother is truly the fulfillment [of all desire] when all other vibrations are stopped; and they [can and do] cease by the devotion and the will of the devotee.

Thus, trailing the Ruby Ray devotion of your hearts does come the white light of ascension's currents. May you value the gift and value the instrument whereby such a Light* might be stepped down and distributed, for without a physical mouthpiece and the delivery of the power of the Word this dispensation could not reach those who deserve it directly. Such is the nature of Hierarchy and the spoken Word, beloved. And though you may not understand this, believe me when I say to you that heaven must have instruments on earth as well as the [instrumentation of the] heavenly hosts.

Now we bid you, be the instruments of the cup of the water of Life,[13] even of the ascension current. As you become that vessel, so you may become one day the transmitter also of that Light.*

In this hour you must garner and steel what you have received. For if you lose this Light, it shall not be returned to you, and by cosmic law you may also lose the opportunity to be initiated in this manner by the presence of seraphim. Therefore it is an initiation that comes following the dictation of the Maha Chohan in this city. For, beloved, those who are of the Light have the spiritual inheritance of receiving that Light from God by the hand of seraphim through the step-down transformer in the very aura of the Messenger which we have placed there long ago.

I, Justinius, salute you each one. I bow to the Light in each one. Whether it be a flicker of Light or a veritable conflagration, I bow to the Light as a single-drop candle flame. For I AM the instrument of God, and the Light I command, the Light I serve. I serve those who serve the Light. It is my commission, my identity and my office.

Untold millions of seraphim are in my command, beloved. May you value their friendship forever and take heed that you compromise not the highest quality of pure Love and thereby place a barrier between yourself and their [Love] and thus not know the fullness of their cup of joy.

The seraphim, beloved, are fiery beings who form concentric rings round the Central Sun and the Court of the Sacred Fire, and upon their rounds they do absorb that light and fire and they come truly trailing clouds of glory, processioning down the highways of cosmos in the visitation of the planetary homes to serve the sons of God, lo, the Christed ones.

Now for the duration of my speaking they have approached gently and softly that you might become accustomed to the

*Christ consciousness of the ascension flame

stepping up of their vibration. Duly prepared, then, you are about to receive that transfer of Light. I instruct you to breathe in deeply and out again. [inhalation and exhalation]

Visualize now the seven centers of your being as being beacon lights of the white light going forth, passing through this entire county and area of this state. Thus, already as you release your own Light for the blessing and the holding of the balance of this area, the seraphim begin to replenish that Light with that which is of the quality of the Great Central Sun. It is indeed a transfusion.

Our Body is Omega, our Blood is Alpha. Thus, as the blood is infused with the Light of Alpha, it does have a quickening and purifying effect. As the body is infused with the Light of Omega, that Light is for the building, strengthening and acceleration of the form.

Now, beloved, cooperate as you have been taught: Be self-emptied. Be purged. Be infilled. Be healed.

As you practice scientifically the path of right diet, right livelihood and occupation, right mindfulness and a spiritually exalted state, you will know day by day the meaning of the fire of the heart and how that Sacred Heart of Jesus, that Immaculate Heart of Mary might be in you the burning desire—the burning desire to ignite every soul whom you meet with your love of Christ, of the Divine Mother, of the Holy Spirit, with your love of the Father.

For in that burning Love is the key: *the key to the saturation of Light!* Seek it all thy days. Win thy crown!

I, Justinius, have spoken to your hearts. May you soon return to the heart of God in character and virtue and deeds of Love.

"The Summit Lighthouse Sheds Its Radiance O'er All the World to Manifest as Pearls of Wisdom." This dictation by **Justinius** was **delivered** by the Messenger Elizabeth Clare Prophet on **Saturday, May 14, 1988,** after midnight, at the Sanctuary of the Three Wise Men, Los Angeles Teaching Center, **Sepulveda, California. (1) Whosoever hath, to him shall be given.** Matt. 13:12; 25:29; Mark 4:25; Luke 8:18; 19:26. **(2) Power of the ten thousand-times-ten thousand.** Lord Maitreya, 1984 *Pearls of Wisdom,* p. 63; 1988 *Pearls of Wisdom,* p. 150; *The Science of the Spoken Word,* pp. 78–79. **(3) Initiation of the Holy Spirit.** The Maha Chohan, 1988 *Pearls of Wisdom,* p. 225. **(4) Universities of the Spirit.** 1988 *Pearls of Wisdom,* p. 287 n. 5. For teachings on and dictations by **Serapis Bey** see *Lords of the Seven Rays: Mirror of Consciousness,* Books One and Two; and Serapis Bey, *Dossier on the Ascension.* **(5) Judgment according to words and works.** Matt. 12:36, 37; Rev. 20:12, 13; 22:12. **(6) Justinius,** April 6, 1985, Camelot, Los Angeles, California, 1985 *Pearls of Wisdom,* p. 283. **Keeper of the Scrolls.** Glossary "The Alchemy of the Word," in *Saint Germain On Alchemy,* p. 412; 1982 *Pearls of Wisdom,* p. 162. **(7)** February 23, 1988, Scottish Rite Masonic Memorial Center, 1988 *Pearls of Wisdom,* p. 235. **(8) Service of the seraphim.** 1988 *Pearls of Wisdom,* p. 238 n. 4. For attunement with the seraphic hosts, see the Messenger's delivery of seraphic meditations November 25, 1987, during 4½-hr. healing service, on two video-cassettes, GP87089, $59.95 (add $1.50 for postage); three 90-min. audiocassettes, A87100, $19.50 (add $.95 for postage). **(9) Other sheep not of this fold.** John 10:16. **(10) Many called, few chosen.** Matt. 20:16; 22:14. **(11) Messengers give their Christhood to a world.** Lanello, 1988 *Pearls of Wisdom,* pp. 255–57. See also 1987 *Pearls of Wisdom,* pp. 634–37, 642; 1988 *Pearls of Wisdom,* pp. 6, 8. **(12) Lord's Supper.** Matt. 26:26–28; Mark 14:22–24; Luke 22:19, 20; I Cor. 11:23–25. **(13) Water of Life.** Matt. 10:42; Mark 9:41; John 4:6–15; I John 5:6, 8.

Pearls of Wisdom®
published by The Summit Lighthouse

| Vol. 31 No. 55 | *The Beloved Maha Chohan* | *August 28, 1988* |

Meet Maitreya
Soul-Testing by the Holy Spirit Preceding the Encounter

Light of the Holy Spirit, descend into these forms.

I AM come again to this city of the Queen of the Angels, Mary, as I did come in February to initiate a city and a people and to announce the initiation unto you of the Holy Spirit.[1] Thus I come again upon the winged heels of Justinius, who spoke last evening to deliver a mantra, a matrix and an ovoid of Light by seraphim to each one who is a Lightbearer.[2]

Reinforcement of the Holy Spirit through you is my desiring according to the will of God. May you understand the meaning of the cloven tongues of fire and their descent.[3] They come also for the quickening of consciousness within chakras and soul, within the fiery spirit. The Holy Spirit does descend to breathe upon that threefold flame the fire breath.

Thus, with the intensity of the Divine Lover I woo the soul back to the spiral staircase ascending to the Beloved, the Universal Christ, and to the twin flame. I woo you away from dangerous precipice, O soul. I woo you from the dangers at hand, the pitfalls of karma, of too much self-satisfaction or spiritual pride. Where'er the Holy Spirit does descend there must needs be the stripping, that the soul naked might perceive that all that is real must be contained within and that no amount of accouterments or increase may in any way add to or detract from the beauty of the soul.

Blessed ones, the prophet is commanded in ancient Israel to tear down and destroy that the LORD might build again.[4] So in the alchemy of a new age self-empty by Love's own symphony. I command you: self-empty and be filled again and renewed again and when renewed, give again! Intensify the fiery coil of Being!

Therefore be ready, for thou shalt meet Maitreya in the way

one of these days. Accept, then, the invitation to be trained at the retreats of the Lords of the Seven Rays,[5] for they do prepare your souls for the Great Initiator.

Maitreya is that one. And I come that you might have the aura of the Holy Spirit to receive him again. For many of you he was the last initiator from divine realms that you have seen in the Mystery School known as Eden, upon Lemuria, not far from this place.

Thus, in ancient times you and the twin flame did know the opportunity to receive that initiation. Yet you were lured away—lured away, then, by false teachers, cunning serpents who crept in, fallen angel, to tear you from your love tryst with the Beloved and with the blessed Guru Maitreya.

Blessed ones, initiation lost must then have cycles and cycles again as you may be prepared by your own inner learning and karma and experience of life that the best and only way to enter in to the highest octaves is through the Master of Life appearing to you through the emissaries of heaven. Receive them in this age, for it is a turning of cycles.

And Opportunity's door is not ajar but fully wide open that all might enter in who willingly and gladly understand that the path of initiation has never changed its requirements in all eternity; and yet the requirement of 51 percent of the balancing of karma in the place of the 100 percent, the remainder being balanced after the ascension, is truly the great and unique dispensation of Aquarius.

Thus, all things are possible.

If, then, you would assume the role of the Divine One and be the instrument of your God Presence, remember, "I must decrease but he must increase."[6] It is the affirmation of the soul who does not forget humility before the Living Fount. Remember thyself as instrument, facilitator, unique transmitter of a holy light by chakras that become jewels and then starry bodies, [such] as you see in the outline of a cross in the Pleiades.

Let the microcosm of self be fused to the Macrocosm of a Spirit Cosmos!

I AM the Maha Chohan. I call forth cloven tongues of fire. One of these tongues does descend above thee, the second above thy twin flame wheresoever that one is. I pronounce you whole in eternal Life and I say, let no man, no condition, *none,* sever the inner tie and the inner oneness that is Divine.

Though you pass through veils of karmic conditions and even relationships required, remember the First Love who is thy God and out of thy God who hast made thee, thy beloved twin flame. Let all other loves, then, be to the goal of that union and serve the end of the blessing of life, the ministering unto life, as by your giving you are also balancing on behalf of thy other self.

This, then, is my sealing of your heart and of your chakras. Read, then, out of my message the warning, if you will, that with the coming of the initiations of the Holy Spirit there are the [tests] preceding the encounter with Maitreya.

All things have been prepared for thee, beloved, to enter into a path of soul-testing and to win. The Teaching is there, the blessing, the sponsorship, the angels. Only you may choose, may determine, may will to be and to be in God an immortal, God-free being.

I AM the Eternal One, the immaculate sphere of Wholeness. I set before you the reality of that original sphere, the ovoid where in the beginning thou wert one and then made twain for the purposes of incarnation. Now in the ending return by Love to the Law of the One and know the promise.

Fulfill all things. Realize thy Christhood.

Not only the crown of Life shall be waiting but also the glorious morn of the reunion of twin flames.

Out of the Light I have descended.

Purusha! Purusha! Purusha![7] [The holy breath sounds]

"The Summit Lighthouse Sheds Its Radiance O'er All the World to Manifest as Pearls of Wisdom." This dictation by the **Maha Chohan** was **delivered** by the Messenger of the Great White Brotherhood Elizabeth Clare Prophet on **Sunday, May 15, 1988,** at the Whole Life Expo at the Pasadena Hilton. The Messenger conducted a four-hour workshop, "Crystals and Chakras — Chakra Initiations and Healing with the Lords of the Seven Rays," prior to the dictation. [**N.B.** Bracketed material denotes words unspoken yet implicit in the dictation, added by the Messenger under the Maha Chohan's direction for clarity in the written word.] **(1) Initiation of the Holy Spirit.** Maha Chohan, 1988 *Pearls of Wisdom*, p. 225. **(2)** Justinius, 1988 *Pearls of Wisdom*, p. 431. **(3) Cloven tongues of fire.** Acts 2:1–4. **(4) Tear down, then build.** Jer. 1:10. **(5) Universities of the Spirit.** 1988 *Pearls of Wisdom*, p. 287 n. 5, chart p. 438. **(6) He must increase**... John 3:30. **(7) *Purusha/Parousia*.** 1988 *Pearls of Wisdom*, p. 228 note.

Fourteen-Day Cycles at the Universities of the Spirit
as outlined by Gautama Buddha in his dictation of January 1, 1986 and by God Meru in his dictation of December 28, 1986

Chohan	Sixth Cycle	Seventh Cycle	Eighth Cycle	Ninth Cycle	Tenth Cycle	Eleventh Cycle	Twelfth Cycle
El Morya Darjeeling, India	July 14, 1988– July 27, 1988	November 3, 1988– November 16, 1988	February 23, 1989– March 8, 1989	June 15, 1989– June 28, 1989	October 5, 1989– October 18, 1989	January 25, 1990– February 7, 1990	May 17, 1990– May 30, 1990
Saint Germain Royal Teton Retreat, Wyoming	July 28, 1988– August 10, 1988	November 17, 1988– November 30, 1988	March 9, 1989– March 22, 1989	June 29, 1989– July 12, 1989	October 19, 1989– November 1, 1989	February 8, 1990– February 21, 1990	May 31, 1990– June 13, 1990
Lord Lanto Royal Teton Retreat, Wyoming	August 11, 1988– August 24, 1988	December 1, 1988– December 14, 1988	March 23, 1989– April 5, 1989	July 13, 1989– July 26, 1989	November 2, 1989– November 15, 1989	February 22, 1990– March 7, 1990	June 14, 1990– June 27, 1990
Paul the Venetian Temple of the Sun New York	August 25, 1988– September 7, 1988	December 15, 1988– December 28, 1988	April 6, 1989– April 19, 1989	July 27, 1989– August 9, 1989	November 16, 1989– November 29, 1989	March 8, 1990– March 21, 1990	June 28, 1990– July 11, 1990
Nada Saudi Arabia	September 8, 1988– September 21, 1988	December 29, 1988– January 11, 1989	April 20, 1989– May 3, 1989	August 10, 1989– August 23, 1989	November 30, 1989– December 13, 1989	March 22, 1990– April 4, 1990	July 12, 1990– July 25, 1990
Serapis Bey Luxor, Egypt	September 22, 1988– October 5, 1988	January 12, 1989– January 25, 1989	May 4, 1989– May 17, 1989	August 24, 1989– September 6, 1989	December 14, 1989– December 27, 1989	April 5, 1990– April 18, 1990	July 26, 1990– August 8, 1990
Hilarion Crete, Greece	October 6, 1988– October 19, 1988	January 26, 1989– February 8, 1989	May 18, 1989– May 31, 1989	September 7, 1989– September 20, 1989	December 28, 1989– January 10, 1990	April 19, 1990– May 2, 1990	August 9, 1990– August 22, 1990
The Maha Chohan Ceylon (Sri Lanka)	October 20, 1988– November 2, 1988	February 9, 1989– February 22, 1989	June 1, 1989– June 14, 1989	September 21, 1989– October 4, 1989	January 11, 1990– January 24, 1990	May 3, 1990– May 16, 1990	August 23, 1990– September 5, 1990

Note: The first cycle of attending the universities of the Spirit began January 1, 1987. The fifth cycle concludes with two weeks at the Maha Chohan's retreat June 30–July 13, 1988.

The Western Shamballa
At the Heart of the Inner Retreat
June 1, 1988

Beloved Heart Flames of My Heart,

Verily *you are* heart of my Heart as I keep the Flame—the Threefold Flame of Life—*for you* from the heart of Shamballa over the Gobi Desert* and its extension in the "Western Shamballa" of the Northern Rockies recently revealed as both an etheric and a physical focus at the Inner Retreat of our Royal Teton Ranch.

For it is my office—as I am the Keeper of the Flame of the Lord of the World—to maintain the thread of contact with the hearts of all Lightbearers of earth in whom the Divine Spark does glow. Thus, truly an antahkarana of angel filigree does create the divine mesh connecting hearts the world around with my own.

Daily the balance of Love, Wisdom and Power flows from my heart to stabilize your lifestream, to polarize your consciousness with the Lord of the World and with your Mighty I AM Presence—to reestablish wholeness, to nourish the electromagnetic field, to balance the chakras. This net of light emanating from Shamballa, East and West, does sustain the universality and oneness of all who serve the Great God in the name of Sanat Kumara.

Now I take this opportunity to welcome you to the Place Prepared (prepared long ago by the Son of God, Elohim, elementals and angels) for your soul's coming of age in this New Age of Aquarius.

This year's conclave at the Royal Teton Ranch is unprecedented in its import as viewed by the Cosmic Council. The Solar Logoi have convened this event in a final effort to unite

*The Gobi Desert of Central Asia stretches across southeastern Mongolia and northern China. Shamballa, once the physical retreat of the Lord of the World, is now on the etheric plane.

and fortify the Lightbearers of the world—to illumine and quicken all to the urgency of the hour as the planet faces the initiations of the final decade of this two-thousand-year cycle of the age of Pisces. And for the first time the Voice of the Word—the Solar Logoi—shall dictate from out the Great Central Sun *the Word of the Lord Brahman.*

. . . And beneficently so, for the sign of Cancer 1988 is the high-water mark representing the final opportunity of the Lightbearers sojourning on planet earth to mitigate or turn around by a world transmutation (truly a spiritual conflagration) the prophecies which come due in the 1990s through personal and planetary karma.

My beloved, the forces of Light and Darkness converging on this planet must be squarely faced by the ancient ones, souls such as yourselves (who have traversed the sine waves of earth's destiny for many centuries) who are able to understand the equations of Armageddon and *to stand, face and conquer* the protestations and pretenses of Unreality by the living flame of God Reality.

I am the sponsoring Master of FREEDOM 1988 in the Heart of the Inner Retreat. I summon strong spirits and stalwart souls, for we intend to deliver through our Messenger not only our postponed Wesak Address but also exposés on conspiracies threatening the very continuity of life on earth.

Our purpose in placing this information upon your hearts is so that you in turn, by the authority of the God Flame within you, may submit all that *IS NOT*, all that *is unreal,* yet whose appearance is of sinister intent, to the Flame of the Ark of the Covenant which does indeed burn upon the altar of Melchizedek and the Melchizedekian priesthood erected in this wilderness land.

In the science of the spoken Word we shall invoke through you and you shall invoke through us—as Above so below—the sacred fire for the demagnetization and utter consuming of malignant vortices of the hate and hate creation of the fallen ones now gathering on the etheric, mental, astral and physical planes of earth polluting the environment, the soul, the mind, the body and the race memory of the people.

Unless the earth body be purged by the sacred fire of God and unless sons and daughters of God upon earth invoke that purging from the very Being of Alpha and Omega, who shall also graciously address you, the planet may soon become uninhabitable to the very lifewaves who require this platform of evolution to complete their karma and realize the Dharma.

In every age there does come a time when the day is far spent that the misuses of Life and Energy and Consciousness by the people of a planetary home can be dissipated (by elemental life), resolved (in the councils of men) or transmuted (by the sacred fire invoked by the sons and daughters of God). I write to you from the Western Shamballa to tell you that that day is at hand.

1988 is a year of completion and fulfillment, for the number of the year is eight. The intercession which Keepers of the Flame of Life on planet earth invoke at this season of solstice and spiritual liberty will set the momentum for the balance of the year and the century. And it is the Elohim of Love who shall cradle you in this endeavor.

On the chart of the Cosmic Clock you stand in this month of Cancer on the six o'clock line of the Divine Mother and the Great Guru Sanat Kumara. Therefore, that Divine Intervention which you invoke through the chalice of Elohim (erected in the Heart of the Inner Retreat by your calls of last summer) shall be magnified and sustained unto the year 2001. And the Seven Holy Kumaras presiding at the final event of the conclave shall place the capstone upon your endeavor.

The absence of that Light not invoked by you through the Word will become, then, a vacancy, an open channel not filled—time and space unhallowed, unsanctified by the freewill exercise of the spoken Word by the sons and daughters of God upon earth. Hence, absent *your* intercession, during the same period unto 2001, that void, devoid of the Holy Spirit's Flame, will be filled by the rising tide of planetary and systemic darkness and by the misqualification of the Light by alien forces of the anti-Word.

Already the sword of the Ruby Ray wielded by the Buddha of the Ruby Ray has been thrust into the earth in Moscow and Washington; for the governments of the nations, the leadership and the people must receive the initiations of the Holy Spirit which if not passed and internalized by Love may become their judgment and their downfall as the handwriting in the skies* so predicts *but does not predestine.*

You will note on the Schedule of Events a program, unprecedented during the commission of our Messengers, of twenty-five dictations as well as serious lectures on topics we deem vital and essential to your spiritual survival. (By the very nature of the exposés on the conspiracies of the fallen

*See Elizabeth Clare Prophet, February 13, 1988, "Saint Germain On Prophecy from 1988 through the 1990s—the Astrology of World Karma," on 2 videocassettes, 3 hr. 50 min., GP88019, $49.95 (add $1.50 for postage), or 3 audiocassettes, 3 hr. 51 min., A88024, $19.50 (add $1.00 for postage).

ones, the subjects to be addressed and the guests to be interviewed at Summit University Forum will be announced the day they are given.)

You will experience abundant love feasts of communion with the Great White Brotherhood: *Darshan**—Hierarchy's release of Light and Cosmic Consciousness through the presence of our Messenger who is the bearer of the mantle of Guru. Through the lineage of Padma Sambhava, who bestowed upon her the title of our commission to her, "Guru Ma," she embodies the Flame of the Teacher who comes in the sound and the tone of the Divine Mother.

Moreover, at a certain point during the conclave (special for each precious one) I shall have the great joy to personally initiate the heart chakra of every devotee of the Light who is physically present. This will be for the realignment of that heart chakra with my own and that of the Cosmic Christ through the Sacred Heart of Jesus.

The impetus for the balancing and expansion of the Threefold Flame will be given according to the spiritual preparation of the individual. Each one will receive the maximum that the Great Law will allow—this could take place at any time, waking or sleeping, or increment by increment during the sessions. It is my private and personal Heart contact with my own.

I urge you, then, to begin to prepare for this event, which is indeed a dispensation of the Solar Logoi for your victory in this age—and for the victory of an age, *if* the Lightbearers of the world choose to unite and make this calling and this election of Hierarchy their own.

Therefore, I adjure you by the God Flame we share in our eternal Oneness to be in your seats in the Heart of the Inner Retreat, *"my Heart,"* at 8:00 a.m. June 25 for the four-day prayer vigil and continuing through the Fourth of July—the most important ten days of the year (and of the final hours of the century) to your souls and the soul of a planet and a people.

By the initiation of the Test of the Ten which has to do with the ten petals of the solar plexus chakra and your God

---

Darshan [Hindi, from the Sanskrit *Darshana* 'seeing', 'looking at']: the holy sight of the Guru through whom the light of God flows—communion with the Ascended Masters through the Messengers' 'mantle' (i.e., auric, or electromagnetic, field placed upon them by the Ascended Masters); blessings of holiness, purification, transfer of Light, and the initiation of spirals of the God consciousness within the chakras when assisting at a sacred service of the Great White Brotherhood. "If thine eye [the attention and concentration through the third eye] be single [single-minded, stayed upon the I AM Presence, upon the Holy Christ Self and the Ascended Masters], thy whole body shall be full of Light [the universal Christ consciousness]." This promise of Jesus to his disciples then and now is the reward for the devotee's "clear seeing" of the Guru: Darshan.

Mastery and God Justice established in the desire body—you can, if you will, forge and win an unparalleled victory for the nations even as you strengthen the deathless solar body you are weaving for your own soul's ascent to God.

As Hierarchy calls, for Hierarchy has need of thee, so, my beloved, thy soul truly doth have need of this immersion in the Heart of the entire Spirit of the Great White Brotherhood for this ten-day, ten-tiered spiral of the Ruby Ray.

In the face of infamous leaders who reenact their unchallenged infamy of centuries, may a people of Light be moved to move to the mountain of God and by their diligence in the Flame, *and by their diligence in the Flame!* I say, lift a planet a notch into the etheric orbit of cycles out of harm's way— above the vibratory rate of the fallen ones with their snares and snaps.

O let a people enlightened move a world into the Higher Consciousness of her Destiny!

As Destiny calls so Destiny IS.

Therefore, I AM Gautama Buddha in the heart of a planet's fiery Destiny. I attend your coming that I might draw you into the fire enfolding itself *that you might know the LORD your God in the Mighty I AM Presence and live forevermore in his Love.*

The Royal Teton Ranch
June 1, 1988

Blessed Hearts of the New Age—
Salutations of "Springtime in the Rockies" at the Royal Teton Ranch!
In the flame of Christ and Buddha, Mother Mary and Kuan Yin, I extend to you each one a joyous welcome to FREEDOM 1988 in the Heart of the Inner Retreat. For this year marks twenty-nine years of our community's celebration of Saint Germain and the Spirit of Liberty each Fourth of July weekend.
Since Keepers of the Flame from around the world united to secure this magnificent ranch/retreat property in 1981, our conclaves—held in a secluded mountain valley beneath snow-capped 11,000-foot Electric Peak on the border of Yellowstone Park—have been acclaimed the New Age event of the summer.
And so as I stumped the Eastern seaboard and the Midwest last fall, the Western states, California, Mexico and Portugal this winter and Canada in the spring, delivering the message of the lost years and teachings of Jesus and Saint Germain's prophecy for our time, I could only visualize night after night as I looked into your beautiful faces what a tremendous experience we would all have together this summer immersed in the purity of Nature's paradise.
I want to tell you what happiness it brought me to see each and every one of you—longtime students and those I hadn't yet met outside the etheric retreats—to see the sparkle in your eyes and that lilt in your auras as you received me and the teachings of the Ascended Masters so dear to my heart.
It is always so special for me to glimpse your souls at the altar as you pass by for Saint Germain's transfer of light by

the Emerald Matrix. That moment is for me an eternity in the divine embrace as we commune together in mutual recognition and oneness.

What we shared in Boston, New York, D.C., Cleveland, Chicago, Mexicali, San Diego, Lisbon, Toronto and so many hometowns each evening is only the beginning. All that I could pack into one night of my heart's desiring to love you and give you the Truth that will set you free—I did, by the grace of God.

But there is much more: meditations and dynamic decrees to the violet flame for clearing the chakras, the path of the bodhisattva and the Buddhas—a spiritual/physical integration to be known and lived. Adeptship, sacred mysteries from the heart of Maitreya and the Goddess Kuan Yin, experiencing the healing power of the Seven Archangels firsthand, and knowing the Divine Mother through Mother Mary and others.

But above all else Darshan! This is what we long for—the cup of golden liquid Light that runneth over to bathe us day after day—the cup of the Ascended Masters' Presence *so felt, so tangible,* so heard and seen in our midst!

I send my gratitude to the Universe and to the Great White Brotherhood for the enclosed program of events released to me. The dispensations to be given to us in the scheduled dictations for a planetary victory are almost beyond contemplation.

The actual presence of these Angels and Masters in their Light bodies at the altar of the Inner Retreat under the tent of the LORD erected in the "wilderness" is the highest Darshan one can experience! And many do 'see' with their inner sight the majestic beings from the courts of heaven superimposed over the Messenger—our elder brothers and sisters ascended.

To feel their 'Electronic Presence' enfold us in such radiance of Love is to know for oneself that the realization of this God Reality which the ascended ones possess is not so very far from us. So the saying goes, "What man has done, man can do." As they have attained their immortal freedom so can we as we walk in their footsteps.

I must tell you from my perspective what an astounding event this conference will be. To witness Lord Gautama's long-awaited Wesak address, receive initiations from Mighty Cosmos and hear from Kuan Yin, members of the Karmic Board and all who will step forth to comfort and enlighten is more than I ever dreamed would take place. But to also have

Alpha and Omega return and to hear the Word of the Solar Logoi, who have never before dictated, is a blessing and an honor to be forever remembered by the people of Terra.

The Heart of the Inner Retreat will be so saturated with Light and Opportunity and Initiation that no Lightbearer on earth should miss this convergence of Hierarchy on our behalf for a tremendous acceleration of our souls unto God.

O how much we are loved of heaven!

Mounting the spiral of the ascent to Higher Consciousness requires coming apart for a cycle, leaving the pressures of city and job—and yes, our daily karma—for new levels of self-awareness in the etheric octaves, so accessible in this very special setting where the etheric retreat of the Divine Mother and the "Western Shamballa" conjoin this 33,000-acre spiritual community abuilding along the Yellowstone River near the Absaroka Wilderness and Gallatin National Forest!

Longtime attenders of the Ascended Masters' summer conclaves make this their annual "re-charge," as they call it. They say the Light garnered here carries them through the next twelve months of high-powered responsibility back home on the front lines.

Called the Place of Great Encounters, the Inner Retreat at *the Royal Teton Ranch* is *definitely the place to spend your vacation this year.*

For those of you not familiar with the path we follow, it is pure oneness with the Holy Spirit and a way of acceleration under the Divine Mother, the Universal Christ, the heavenly hosts and the Servant-Sons of God who are the Ascended Masters.

Our Teacher is the Holy Spirit whose prophecies are delivered through the mantle of the Messenger by Jesus Christ our Lord, the Ascended Masters and heavenly hosts. We pursue meditation and the science of the spoken Word to achieve personal and planetary healing and wholeness using bija mantras and bhajans according to the tradition of the Eastern adepts and the fervor of decrees in the I AM name with classical and New Age music.

Maitreya's Mystery School at the Inner Retreat is a carefully preserved spiritual/physical environment where we commune with God in elemental life, the Nature spirits, angels and one another heart to heart. The sound we send forth is world-transforming, a powerful yoga to contact our Inner Reality and to draw the angelic hosts and the Ascended Masters nearer to us by our raised vibrations.

The conclave has one goal: Union with God through the Spirit of Cosmic Freedom. Above all it is a conference of joy and happiness, communion, oneness and self-transcendence for free spirits and revolutionaries who aim to keep this planet and themselves free from every encroachment upon our spiritual destiny—worlds without end!

If this is what you are looking for in a spiritual retreat, I guarantee *you will not be disappointed*. This is a once-in-a-lifetime experience and each one of us is key in the alchemy of this Divine Happening.

Again I extend to you my heart. May Archangel Michael and his legions of blue-lightning angels seal you in an armour of white light and cut you free by the sword of blue flame to come apart for awhile to celebrate *God, God, God!*

> I send you all the Love
> that God has given me
> and more—truly the Love
> of the entire Spirit of
> the Great White Brotherhood!

Elizabeth Clare Prophet
"Guru Ma"

P.S. Tuesday, July 5, is a wedding celebration for all who desire to consecrate or reconsecrate their vows in this beautiful cathedral of Nature. The service follows the traditional Christian ritual with the insertion of a profound and moving New Age liturgy. If you plan to be married at this ceremony, please arrive in Montana in time to get your marriage license and blood tests. The service will be performed by ordained ministers of Church Universal and Triumphant, a number of whom were ordained ministers in mainline Protestant churches before they came here. Those of any denomination or universal awareness are welcome to participate with their family and friends. This service will be followed by a wedding feast and waltz with live music under the stars open to all.

Save the World
with Violet Flame!
2   by Saint Germain

June 14, 1988

Dearest Friends of Saint Germain and of the Violet Flame,

Happy summer solstice! To help you celebrate this day of the Divine Mother's appearing on June 20 *wherever you are,* I am sending you "Save the World with Violet Flame! 2 by Saint Germain." I'm sure you'll love it just as much as we loved creating it at King Arthur's Court. All of us at the Royal Teton Ranch, who always love and think of you, assembled to sing and decree our hearts out so that you could have another ninety-three minutes of the sound and the music and the words and the rhythm of the Seventh Ray and the seventh dispensation of Aquarius!

This singing violet flame telegram comes to you just in time to accompany you to the Heart of the Inner Retreat for FREEDOM 1988. And we've provided an upbeat, stepped-up rhythm of the violet flame for the acceleration of your soul's ascent to your own Higher Consciousness in the mountain of God—so you'll be sure to have angels, Masters and elementals marching with you all the way!

The opening hymn to Saint Germain and Portia was written on the occasion of their being crowned the hierarchs of the age of Aquarius on May 1, 1954, at the Royal Teton Retreat, the etheric/physical focus of the Great White Brotherhood at the Grand Teton.

May 1 is also the ascension day of beloved Saint Germain. He ascended at the conclusion of his final incarnation as Francis Bacon in 1684 and reentered the scene as the Wonderman of Europe. His attempt to sponsor a United States of Europe was thwarted both by the crowned heads and Napoleon. But in the New World, the Founding Fathers responded to the Master and the Spirit of Liberty. They were not afraid to put their lives on the line to fight tyranny or to put their pens to parchment and sign the documents that have guarded our liberty ever since because they were based on sacred covenants and defended by Sons of Liberty who knew the meaning of freedom.

Blessed friends, the fire that was kindled in those moments of our history, the fire that guarantees our freedom and our divine right to assemble in the Heart of the Inner Retreat, sacred shrine of our church, to worship freely, to speak freely as our hearts and the Spirit of the LORD give us utterance, yes the fire that guarantees our right to freely publish the convictions of our conscience—that fire is *the fire on the mountain* that signals the watchman of the night: "All is well."

This freedom to be who I AM, who we are in God is the freedom that was born on the Fourth of July. By this grace of the Spirit of Liberty we gather to champion the same rights in order to keep that flame blazing over the earth!

And Saint Germain is the embodiment of that flame which is the Freedom flame of Aquarius and its two-thousand-year dispensation. Portia, the Goddess of Justice, his twin flame and complement, is the Mother of Aquarius, whose flame is in our midst in this hour. Therefore, through their hearts we call to them in the "Decree for the Great Cosmic Light" to dispel all darkness and bring in Saint Germain's great golden age.

In this very first decree we claim our I AM Presence as the authority for the Great Cosmic Light for earth and her evolutions. This is one of the most powerful divine decrees I know for instantaneous planetary change. We seal it by pouring our love to Portia through her song, "Love's Opportunity," for it is through her flame of God Justice and as a member of the Karmic Board that she brings us opportunity to balance karma through her sponsorship of the violet flame.

On my return from the Portuguese Stump I stopped over at the Chicago Teaching Center and was privileged to deliver a momentous dictation of our beloved Portia. She said:

"It is an hour when <u>the supreme moment of Opportunity is come for the evolutions of Light on earth to so amplify this violet flame as to create the violet flame magnet . . . within the earth,</u> around the earth, through the earth and through all who are tied to the Great Central Sun by the threefold flame of the heart and the I AM Presence. . . .

"We summon all hearts, beloved, and we desire, therefore, [to see that] through those who have that understanding of the violet flame, through those who will literally become a continual vessel for the violet singing flame—to see that through you the spark of the Great Central Sun of the seventh age may leap heart upon heart around the world until literally those millions called for for the saving of a planet shall be quickened and enter into their own sense of personal instrumentation of the descent of the Word of the seventh age . . . through their hearts and minds and beings and souls.

"Blessed ones, therefore, I come inasmuch as Saint Germain has given all that can be given by his Presence in the earth. I place my Presence over this city [Chicago] and I duplicate that Presence over every place where two or three are gathered together in his name, in the name of Saint Germain, to give these calls to the violet flame and to use that tape recording which has been produced and those which will follow it.

"Blessed ones, by the cosmic momentum of my service to Divine Justice on the Seventh Ray I desire to so multiply the momentum of your giving of the violet flame as to anchor the intensity of purple fire in the earth of a divine justice that surely shall consume all the diabolical injustices of the fallen ones that have been pitted against the children of the Sun for so long. . . .

"Therefore, beloved, in this hour of intensity we will surely summon angels of the Seventh Ray. We will surely see what the Cosmic Council will allow for planet earth and her evolutions in this hour when there may yet be a golden age, even the soft effusive glow of violet on the horizon that may become the fullness of a violet flame dawn.

"Blessed hearts, in the victory of Light I can assure you that if those . . . who have the gift of the violet flame and the sponsorship of Saint Germain will not finally and ultimately rally in this hour, I tell you, there will not be sufficient generators of sparks to quicken the rest who must yet be contacted. As it has been said through the past year, in this hour it is truly the fact of life that all does hang upon . . . Keepers of the Flame as to what fervent-hearted response they shall give . . . .

"I am, beloved, the Mother of Aquarius. Call to me, for I am Portia and I have stepped down from cosmic levels to be with you. As you receive me, earth shall become Freedom's Star.

"You are the Light of Aquarius. Let it shine! You are the Love of Aquarius. Let it blaze forth from your hearts! You are the Truth of Aquarius. Be witnesses unto that Truth! You are the Power of Aquarius when the allness of thy being does embody that Light."

The violet flame cassette that I have placed in your hands today is your key to bring in a golden age of Aquarius right where you are, to extend the boundaries of your own aura and electromagnetic field supercharged with the violet flame, electrifying all whom you meet with this quickening, transmuting power of the Holy Ghost in our midst.

As you give the "Heart, Head, and Hand Decrees" nine times each, you will notice that they are stepped up in intensity and afford you the reality of a swirling violet flame fountain pulsating around you and through you, filling you with joy and energy and the means to accomplish your goals.

If you've been using tape 1 you should be ready for the step-up in tempo and the sacred fire breath. This is what intensifies the transmutation in, through and around the chakras and the organs they correspond to. Practice makes perfect! Just follow the lead and you'll lock into the higher vibes of Aquarius. You're creating walls of violet flame all around you, your family, city and planet. All of Nature is being purified by every call you make.

Next we chant "I AM the Flame of Freedom, the Freedom Flame I AM!" to the drums and marching band of King Arthur's Court as the strains of "Semper Fidelis" remind us that our souls have long ago taken the vow to be ever faithful to the purple fiery heart of Saint Germain. And to the drum beat of the legions of Archangel Michael marching and his blue-lightning angels, we invoke our protection. Sealed in shafts of blue flame, clad with the armour of the angelic hosts, we march with Saint Germain. And if you're not already on your way to the Inner Retreat, just put those violet flame feet in motion and you will be!

Side two is dedicated to the beings of Nature whose protection and freedom we invoke that they might help us bear the burden and be the instrument of world transmutation by the violet flame. The "Six Mighty Cosmic Light Calls" are as powerful a fiat as you'll ever give for yourself, the constructive service and organizational activities you're involved in and the planet as a whole. These calls anchor the six points of the six-pointed star, the sign of the rising triangle of man uniting with the descending triangle of God.

The song to Oromasis and Diana is our invocation to the hierarchs of the beings of fire, who are called salamanders. They serve with the beings of air, water and earth—the sylphs, undines and gnomes—to consume by the violet flame and a glorious rainbow fire all misuses of the seven rays of God we have ever manifested through our seven chakras and in the earth body.

Don't be surprised if troops of elementals come marching right through your home in colorful costumes bearing their banners of freedom. All elementals love the violet flame and when you invoke it they become your loyal friends, helpers and servants. By the time you sing this song you'll feel like you've been picked up by fiery salamanders who, if you let them, will carry you all the way to *the fire on the mountain!*

The call to "Set the Elementals Free" followed by stepped-up versions of the "Radiant Spiral Violet Flame" and "More Violet Fire" with "Semper Fi" sandwiched in between are just what the planet needs as we enter the third quadrant of the year and meet the challenge of another increment of planetary karma. Side two ends with a rousing march with a waltz interlude sung to the words of "More Violet Fire" sealed with the fiat "Lightbearers of the World, unite! in the name of Saint Germain."

Saint Germain has promised us: "Wheresoever a pillar of violet flame is raised up, because it is the equivalency of my Presence, I shall be there. Thus, take . . . the Messenger's offering . . . of the violet flame decrees and calls to my heart. If you shall use that recording of the word, angels of the violet flame, Zadkiel and Amethyst, Elohim of the Seventh Ray, Arcturus and Victoria, the beloved Kuan Yin, the beloved Great Divine Director, the beloved elementals, the Holy Spirit, these shall amplify [their Electronic Presence through it] as we, Portia and I, shall amplify our Electronic Presence through it.

"Know then, O beloved, that footprint for footprint if America and the earth shall long desire the Presence of Saint Germain with them, they must forge a fire, truly a violet flame fire, where I may place my feet. It is indeed the last time, the last Opportunity. . . . Either these flames be raised up by the Lightbearers of the world or you shall see [come to pass] the Darkness prophesied by young and old alike, those who have seen, those who have known, and those who have read the report of that which the enemy does propose against this nation and against all people of freedom worldwide. . . .

"People of earth and of Light, rally, then, while there is yet time. For even the Fátima prophecies may be turned back. But I will tell you what it will take: Beginning with ten thousand new Keepers of the Flame who will give those dynamic decrees, we should expect a million, even in the United States, invoking the violet flame daily before we should see a considerable change in that which is projected. Yet this is possible.

Without question there are a million Lightbearers, many of them led astray into false paths and teachings that are nothing but time-wasters. . . . Aquarius is a mighty air sign. It is the sign of the liberation of the mind and the soul to soar, to sing! . . .

"May you now sense your vibration in my Presence and know how much lighter and freer and more the master of your domain you can be in a fortnight, in six weeks. **Should you take these violet flame decrees and give them for those ninety minutes a day for thirty-three days, you will find yourself in such a centeredness by the time you accept my invitation to be at FREEDOM 1988 in the Heart of the Inner Retreat,** that those dictations and dispensations forthcoming can be absorbed by you as though you were a sponge, wholly free and open, and thus walk away with an auric egg of violet fire that all the earth and elementals will notice as you pass by.

"There is such a high road of freedom that beckons you on and this is not illusion! This is the fusion of the soul to her Divine Reality! This is the alchemical marriage!"

As your Messenger for the Great White Brotherhood, the most urgent message that I can send you together with this tape is to remind you of **Lord Gautama's call** from the Western Shamballa at the Heart of our Inner Retreat dated June 1: **"I adjure you by the God Flame we share in our eternal Oneness to be in your seats in the Heart of the Inner Retreat, 'my Heart,' at 8:00 a.m. June 25 for the four-day prayer vigil and continuing through the Fourth of July—the most important ten days of the year (and of the final hours of the century) to your souls and the soul of a planet and a people."**

It is apparent from the schedule of twenty-five dictations to be given along with profoundly spiritual teachings from the heart of the Divine Mother, Christ and Buddha, the preceding prayer vigil and the Summit University Forum exposés that this conference is not only to be the event of the summer but also the most important ever held since The Summit Lighthouse was founded in 1958—the one you shouldn't miss.

Although according to the worldwide response to the violet flame Opportunity that comes from the heart of Saint Germain and Portia there may indeed be dispensations of "amazing grace" forthcoming, according to the timetables made known to me it remains in question whether the Karmic Board will convoke a Freedom conference next summer.

Therefore, to you who may be considering postponing your trek to the Inner Retreat for another year, **I urge you,**

at all costs and inconvenience, to make it a point of your own individual God-mastery to literally precipitate yourself physically in the Heart June 24 through July 4 or longer. If the conference fee, necessary to meet our expenses, presents an obstacle, you can make arrangements at registration for a deferred schedule of payments.

On January 5, 1988, Saint Germain said, "As long as there is a fire on the mountain, so long shall hearts endure in a flame of hope—a hope that yet casts forth a light and a fire all-consuming to devour all Death and Hell that would array itself upon the nations.

"Therefore, let the fire burn on in the holy mountain of God in the hearts of Keepers of the Flame. For this fire on the mountain. . . that does embrace all rainbow rays of God and the secret rays, beloved—*this fire* does cause us to think upon the coming of the Ancient of Days, when a spiritual fire was first kindled at Shamballa, the place prepared for our Lord."

As flame-bearer with hands cupped, I bring you each one with this my message a portion of *the fire on the mountain*, the sign of our retreat, our hope, our oneness, and our God who is a consuming fire.

Keepers of the Flame, Lightbearers of the World, Saint Germain needs our support now. Make your Presence felt in the Heart. Be there!

Elizabeth Clare Prophet
"Guru Ma"

P.S. "Save the World with Violet Flame! by Saint Germain" cassettes 1 and 2 are $5.95 each. When bought in any combination in quantities of ten or more, they are now $2.95 each! We have reduced the quantity price of these tapes so that you can spread the violet flame message of the New Age to friends far and near. Please take Portia's opportunity to do so immediately. Just write down the names of ten people whom you desire to send cassettes 1 or 2 to. If you would like us to mail direct to their addresses, you can charge the cost of tapes and postage on your credit card by phone.

Pearls of Wisdom®

published by The Summit Lighthouse

Vol. 31 No. 56 | Beloved Archangel Raphael | September 3, 1988

FREEDOM 1988

1

A Healing Matrix
The Crystal of the Fifth Ray of Elohim

Let the Light of eternal Truth swallow up the illusions of error—gross delusions!

Thus the planetary body is a diseased body in an out-of-alignment state and thus you have provided the chalice whereby we might indeed anchor within this Heart [of the Inner Retreat] the Light of Fátima, which anchoring already accomplished[1] may be reinforced and intensified by the Call, by the action of the sacred fire.

A circle of Light* of healing angels is formed. By the invocation of many hearts as one there is imbedded in the psyche of the planet this night an intensity of a healing matrix.[2] The intensity and the depth of the positioning of this crystal, beloved, is truly for the creating of a spiral that does turn around the disintegration spirals that have affected the Lightbearers beyond their control.

Thus, wherever hearts provide a correspondent spiral of intensity, there the action of this focus shall serve to multiply, to strengthen and to create within the individual that turning around whereby the spiral of wholeness can and shall displace spirals of disintegration.

Blessed ones, where a world moves downstream, as it were, and where the karma, the free will and the misplaced desire of a people decree it,[†] the very best that we might give is this crystal electrode whereby those who by effort and God-mastery raise up

---

*the circle of the Light-manifestation of the God consciousness of the Fifth Ray focused by the healing angels
†decree the disintegration spirals, the gross delusions of error, the out-of-alignment state

that spiral, that upward-moving spiral of Light,[3] might have that reinforcement, that sustaining grace, that momentum of our Love.

Pray, then, that those who have this Light within might become as one through the science of mantra, through the rosaries that you so lovingly offer, through devotion to that Immaculate Heart.

Pray, then, that a network of Lightbearers who hold a cup of healing Light within* and enter a momentum of the turning around of their individual worlds might therefore create a grid of Light on the planet which when woven together mantra by mantra might begin to include more and more of those souls who of their own could not sustain such a building momentum but by reinforcement are [become] of those who are the strong: [that] of those who are the sons and the daughters of God there may indeed be a remnant who are truly saved and who keep open the path of the ascension. (In the presence of healing angels and their flame I bid you be seated.)

I AM Raphael, the spokesman for our twin flames. The crystal of the Fifth Ray, of the Elohim thereof, is a presence that does begin the spiral of the dictations to be offered from this altar.

Angels weave a mesh of light including [within it] all who are here, thus forming of your auric field one seamless garment, one robe of light for the Great Buddha the Lord Sanat Kumara.

We have begun this conference at a level of the intensity of the five secret rays, establishing from within, around the heart and the secret chamber of the heart of each one, reinforcement for the spheres of the five secret rays. The inner cleansing and transmutation does take place. Continue, then, in your prayer vigil. Continue to receive the light of the chalice of Elohim.

Quietly come the Archangels. Quietly come seraphim. Quietly come healing Masters. Measure for measure, as your offering is, so shall your gift be.

In the center of this valley, suspended above you is the thoughtform of the Diamond Heart of Mary. Angels of the Diamond Heart together with Mother Mary create this thoughtform and this presence as a pulsation, as a presence of the heartbeat of the Universal Mother, that all those who would be nurtured of her and all who would nurture life might receive peace through the sound of the heartbeat of the Divine Mother.

Souls require solace. They are immobilized by their fear, by their self-doubts—their worries even concerning disease, old age and death, their concerns of self-annihilation and of what is coming upon the earth, for all know at subconscious levels that a day of karmic reckoning is at hand.

---

*through the balance of the Four Cosmic Forces in the four lower bodies in the Light of Father, Son, Holy Spirit, and Divine Mother raised up, as well as the balanced threefold flame

Into the configurations,* then, of planet earth, which ye well know, we come for the healing of the soul, for the healing of the mind, for the healing of the heart, knowing full well that all else will follow as the healing of the body.

May you bask for a moment in the light of the Diamond Heart. May you know the peace and the comfort of the Holy Spirit, whose Presence fills all of this retreat. Know, then, the Person of the Maha Chohan.

O Astrea beloved, Elohim, encircle all who will receive you as Starry Mother. Exorcise from them all demons possessing the mind and the psyche, infesting the astral body and the mental belt.

O Holy Spirit with Astrea, let there come the exorcism and the purging and the Ruby Ray that all might be prepared for that which is to come.

Let healing, self-healing, be the sign of the Aquarian conqueror. Let all here resolve and resolve again and again to enter into the tight coil of white fire fashioned of the Kundalini from the base unto the crown. Let that coil intensify upon the spinal altar of those who invoke it and welcome it.

Let transmutation of Aquarius come forth now as a great cloud of Light† and let this cloud of Light envelop all who desire change for the better and spiritualization and greater spiritualization of consciousness. And all who will let go—all who will let go of attachment to the diseased self, to the out-of-alignment state— let them enter now into the presence of healing angels. These healing angels are as numberless numbers throughout this camp in the tent of the LORD and of his people.

Thus, at the doorway to thy abode wherever it is this night, an angel of Raphael and Mary does attend thee, beloved. Go to thy place of rest. Meditate upon this healing angel and ask to be taken to the place prepared for you, which is different for each one, as you step forth from your body temple, entering into other light-years, other centuries, other dimensions for that night of co-measurement whereby you see yourself as a coordinate of the stars. As the extension of the stars into the earth body is by thy chakras,‡ so is the arcing of Fátima and the Pleiades.

In the heart of the Son of God thou art sealed.

I AM Raphael of the Fifth Ray of the Immaculate Heart. I bow to the Light§ of the pure in heart and those who would be; and unto those who would be, I say, reach out for the healing angel who comes to heal you of all impurities of consciousness limiting thy soul's flight beyond the Night to the Eternal Day.

[intonations, 21 seconds]

*karmic, i.e., astrological, configurations   †God consciousness   ‡chakras of the earth sustained by Cosmic Beings and the retreats of the Great White Brotherhood as well as by the Sons of God in the earth §Threefold Flame

"The Summit Lighthouse Sheds Its Radiance O'er All the World to Manifest as Pearls of Wisdom." This dictation by **Archangel Raphael** was **delivered** by the Messenger of the Great White Brotherhood Elizabeth Clare Prophet on **Wednesday, June 29, 1988,** at *FREEDOM 1988* in the Heart of the Inner Retreat at the **Royal Teton Ranch, Montana.** In the darshan* with the healing angels and healing Masters prior to the dictation, the Messenger made powerful invocations for the healing of specific diseases and conditions afflicting humanity and the Lightbearers of the world. She also reviewed and gave teachings on dispensations from the dictations by Lanello and Archangel Raphael delivered February 26 and 27, 1988, in Lisbon, Portugal, and led the assembly in healing visualizations, songs and decrees. Darshan and the dictation by Archangel Raphael included on audiocassettes B88091–92, 2 hr. 48 min., $13.00 (add $.95 for postage); dictation included with those of Lord Maitreya, El Morya and Kuthumi on videocassette HP88054, 2 hr., $29.95 (add $.90 for postage). [**N.B.** Bracketed material denotes words unspoken yet implicit in the dictation, added by the Messenger under Archangel Raphael's direction for clarity in the written word.] **(1)** The Light of the etheric retreat of Fátima was anchored in the Heart of the Inner Retreat on February 26, 1988, during Lanello's fifteenth anniversary ascension dictation; Lanello, 1988 *Pearls of Wisdom*, p. 258. This 'Light' is the God consciousness of the Divine Mother at Fátima and the God consciousness of the Archangel and Archeia of the Fifth Ray focused at the etheric retreat of Raphael and Mother Mary over Fátima. **(2)** In conjunction with this dispensation of the healing matrix of the crystal electrode of the Fifth Ray of Elohim imbedded in the psyche of the planet, you may also invoke the dispensation of the **healing thoughtform** released by Archangel Raphael on March 28, 1964. This thoughtform is composed of three concentric spheres: white in the center then sapphire blue and emerald green sacred fire. It is scientifically created by Archangel Raphael for spiritual and physical healing and to restore the inner blueprint and divine wholeness when visualized superimposed upon and penetrating every atom, cell and electron of the four lower bodies or a specific organ. As described by Archangel Raphael, the white fire core is "surrounded. . . by a mighty, tangible blue sheath of light" which "denotes the will of God, . . . the manifest perfection for all mankind. The mighty sheath of green, vibrating and quivering around all, is the substance of the healing qualification for the earth and for the evolutions thereof." See Archangel Raphael, 1982 *Pearls of Wisdom*, p. 461; Mark L. Prophet and Elizabeth Clare Prophet, "My Visualization for the Healing Thoughtform," in *The Science of the Spoken Word*, with color illustration for visualization, pp. 144–48; and "The Healing Thoughtform: The Perfect Picture of the Divine Design," decree 50.04A in *Prayers, Meditations and Dynamic Decrees for the Coming Revolution in Higher Consciousness* for Keepers of the Flame (Section I). **(3)** raise up the Light of the I AM Presence and the Holy Christ Self, i.e., of the Father and the Son, by prayer and invocation and by working the works of Him that sent you (John 9:4); the Light of the Holy Spirit through dynamic decrees and by preaching and embodying the Word and the Work, i.e., the cloven tongues of the fire of Alpha and Omega; and the Light of the Divine Mother as the Kundalini, the sacred fire of the base-of-the-spine chakra, through purity, God-control and God-Self mastery and the science of mantra and yoga, the rosaries to the Divine Mother (Mother Mary and Kuan Yin), right diet and the Eightfold Path of Lord Buddha and the Universal Christ

Darshan [Hindi, from the Sanskrit *Darshana* 'seeing', 'looking at']: the holy sight of the Guru through whom the Light of God flows—communion with the Ascended Masters through the Messengers' 'mantle' (i.e., auric, or electromagnetic, field placed upon them by the Ascended Masters); blessings of holiness, purification, transfer of Light: hence the initiation of spirals of God consciousness within the chakras when assisting at a sacred service of the Great White Brotherhood. "If thine eye [the attention and concentration through the third eye] be single [single-minded, stayed upon the I AM Presence, upon the Holy Christ Self and the Ascended Masters], thy whole body shall be full of Light [the universal Christ consciousness]." This promise of Jesus to his disciples then and now is the reward for the devotee's "clear seeing" of the Guru. A dictation from an Ascended Master is the highest form of darshan.

Pearls of Wisdom®

published by The Summit Lighthouse

Vol. 31 No. 57   *Beloved Lord Maitreya*   September 4, 1988

FREEDOM 1988

2

The Gift of Self-Knowledge
Fire of My Fire: Become All That I AM

Most gracious ones of my heart, seldom in the course of embodying the noble mien of the Cosmic Teacher does one encounter a group of devotees so prepared, so willing to enter into the heart of the Cosmic Christ; [therefore,] this welcome you afford me in the West is a highlight in my service.

Thus, I come; for a cradle has been provided not alone by Gautama or the Divine Mother or Sanat Kumara but by hearts self-prepared, determined, even by those who by the standards of Eastern paths may not have, "apparently," spiritual qualifications to be the abode of Maitreya.

We see with inner eye. The rough-hewn or the outer crudities do not discourage us when we see a fire that burns clean within. Yet this is not to say that we do not then come to tutor and to refine, for what is Buddhahood but refinement of all [that] with which the newborn child of God has [been endowed].

There are wise ones in the earth. There are kind ones. Refinement, including the balancing of karma, is all that stands between these jolly-good folk and the bodhisattvas[1] who are the inheritors, as are the bhikkhus[2] and the nuns, of a tradition that does establish certain givens as being most certainly and most obviously a part of the Path.

Prepared, then, are ye by the Ascended Masters, by the Divine Mother, by the Messengers. Now, then, through you I would shorten the distance between my heart of hearts and the heart of an unenlightened humanity.

Beloved ones, one tender smile is surely worth a thousand frames of the face of Maitreya. The loving, overflowing, pure heart's giving—does this not convey the Maitreya beyond the veil? I desire you to be myself, not in pomposity or pride (now self-styled initiators of lesser mortals), nay, but to remember that by the grace of the one who has sent me you yourself might be my vessel.

You say, then, "But you have not yet appeared to us, Maitreya. How can we be thyself appearing to others?"

Yet I have so many times appeared to you.[3]

Will you not, then, first and foremost take up the study of all of my dictations [which I have released] even through these two disciples, your Messengers?[4] Will you not search them to discover the keys of this age that is known in some quarters as "the Age of Maitreya"? Then will you not see that all others [of the spiritual hierarchy] who have released by the Holy Spirit of the Great White Brotherhood the vast Teaching set forth have also been my Messengers—the Ascended Masters, the angelic hosts?

Can there not be even a treasure mapping of these teachings? Can there not be a choosing one by one of a single gem of a virtue to embody, come what may? Can we not be together a mass of crystalline substance as one body, one forcefield, truly endowing and instilling the consciousness of the Universal Christ to a planet?

Blessed ones, the higher the spiritual vibration, the greater the railing and the revenge of forces of unreality. Blessed ones, therefore seal the circle! Seal, then, and guard by scientific prayer this place that has been prepared.

Truly, our religion must include the [hallowing of the] place beneath our feet whereby we direct into the earth currents of the heavens. And how greatly are they needed, these life currents, restoring streams of immortality that may quicken the dried-up selves in the earth.

Life is about to know and receive such an increment of mercy through the heart of Kuan Yin that that mercy shall bring an enlightenment, an awareness, an understanding, a self-knowledge. Is not the greatest gift of mercy, the most merciful gift of all, the gift of self-knowledge? We count it as such and as the greatest treasure, the only treasure that can be retained: Self-Knowledge, Be-ness—[truly, know thy self] as a being of fire.

I would woo you to the courts of Maitreya. Come and find me, beloved. I shall not tell where I hold court to deliver my mystery teachings in the etheric octave, for I desire those who have the magnet of my heart to find me as one would find a treasure without a map—only by lodestone attracted to lodestone.

But I place in your heart, in this hour together, fire of my fire. I dip into this fire, beloved—a gold and pink and white fire—I dip into it, and in the multiplicity of my Self and Presence I place [it] into an urn (which I have by your leave already placed upon the altar of your heart)—a beautiful gold and pink and white fire. These colors merging, beloved, produce many hues.

Therefore, [visualizing this fire] as petals of roses, fiery roses with dewdrops, you shall know that when you meditate upon this fire through the call to the golden pink glow-ray, you shall be drawn unerringly to my abode. And you shall know that the requirement of approaching me by a congruency of vibration has been met by all whom you find in my abode. The golden pink glow-ray is the entrance to the realm of the Buddhas.

Blessed hearts, there are yet today eight Buddhas in incarnation on this planet, and the ninth again.[5] Thus, beloved, it is not entirely [in] the [correct] measure of prophecy that all of the earth this day is waiting for my physical incarnation. Think you not that I am in the heart of these Buddhas? Indeed I AM.

Nevertheless, Buddhic attainment is of the vast spheres of the causal body, such that you would not necessarily recognize one of these blessed ones should you encounter them.* Yet, beloved, you shall surely know the Buddha in the way when you expand the golden pink glow-ray of the heart, becoming thereby tender, sensitive, loving in a beautiful sound of Love—love as appreciation for the soul, for the spirit, for the vastness of potential and being, but above all [as] appreciation for the God Flame.

In gratitude for the God Flame that is your threefold flame, serve to set life free. Kindness always comes forth from gratitude. Selfishness emits from the state of the ingrate who receives again and again and demands more and demands more again as though Life and Hierarchy and Mother should supply all wants and needs.

Blessed ones, to forget to be grateful for the gift of the flame of Life means that you can be capable of riding roughshod over another's tenderest moments and feelings in this insensitivity.

"The Keeper's Daily Prayer"[6] is given [to you] by the blessed ones, by the beloved Nada, that you might neglect not profoundest gratitude, daily memory that you are and shall be eternally yourself because the flame of Life as divine spark beats, *beats, beloved,* and leaps, burns and blazes within you. All else may fade but the flame burns on, and out of the flame is [heard] the Call, the call to the soul: "Come Home to the heart of Maitreya."

*Inasmuch as Buddhic attainment is spiritually manifest in the vast expansion of the spheres of the causal body as a Universal God consciousness, it is not readily apparent to the uninitiated by sense perception when a lifestream has the stature of Buddhahood.

God calls you to the level of my being as the safe habitation, the biding place—all other stations, mystery schools, universities of the Spirit leading to the securing of the security of Oneness with the heart of the Universal Christ. From that place, having once attained to it, you need never descend or depart. Thus, it is true Freedom and [the] true Freedom that I hold for thee. And I hold it, beloved, as the champion of your beloved Saint Germain, all Masters of the Seventh Ray and age.

I come, then, the proponent and the advocate of all who shall supply the mosaic of Aquarius with the rich manifestation of the Seventh Ray, its alchemy and religion, its inner self-government.

O the journey of Aquarius from the center of the earth to the center of the Sun, may it be thine!

May you treasure that which is immutable and begin to let go of those things that by time shall pass away, by space shall pass away. Heaven and earth ultimately shall pass away, but my Word as thy God Flame shall live forever.[7] Be not satisfied until this Flame grow and grow, envelop thy soul, make permanent this soul potential, and raise you as a plucked immortelle to levels of permanence and permanent joy.

I AM in the mystery of the Word's unfoldment within you. I rejoice that you have entered the heart of Kuan Yin as you have entered the heart of Mary, that both sides of thy being, both sides of the brain, so nurtured [by the Divine Mother] East and West, might embody the ageless wisdom. In the heart of Kuan Yin you are truly ferried in this *prajna* boat.[8] Thus, I AM the Flame, I AM the Boat, and I AM in the heart of the Divine Mother.

I come to seal you, to secure you, to see to it that though karma and karmic waves may rise to assail, though forces sinister may for moments prevail, your soul in devotion to the God Flame, amplifying the golden pink glow-ray and the whiteness of the Mother, might know that sense of security of Oneness that trusts:

I shall endure.

I shall prevail.

I shall self-transcend.

I shall shuffle off this mortal coil.

I shall live in the Flame of God forevermore.

I shall build my house
    as the Buddha house of the spheres of the secret rays
    of the golden pink glow-ray of God-gratitude
    whereby and whereto I become appreciative of all Life
    and of the circumstances of all Life
        [of all lesser manifestations of that Life which is God].

Through this gift of fire from my heart you may become all that I AM sooner or later, as you will it, mindful that the Sangha does not exist without the living chalice, that the Dharma does not exist without the living chalice, that the Guru-Chela relationship does not exist without the living chalice.[9]

I enter the heart of the dewdrop. Come and find me.

This dictation by **Lord Maitreya** was **delivered** by the Messenger Elizabeth Clare Prophet on **Thursday, June 30, 1988,** at *FREEDOM 1988* in the Heart of the Inner Retreat at the **Royal Teton Ranch, Montana.** In the darshan with the Cosmic Christ prior to the dictation the Messenger gave teachings on the Ascended Master Lord Maitreya and reviewed traditional Buddhist beliefs about Maitreya. Darshan and dictation included on 2 audiocassettes, B88092–93, 2 hr. 44 min., $13.00 (add $.95 for postage); dictation included with those of Archangel Raphael, El Morya and Kuthumi on videocassette HP88054, 2 hr., $29.95 (add $.90 for postage). **(1) Bodhisattva.** 1988 *Pearls of Wisdom,* p. 216 n. 4. **(2) bhikkhu** [Pali, from Sanskrit *bhiksu*]: Buddhist monk, religious mendicant. **(3)** In the darshan prior to Lord Maitreya's dictation, the Messenger read the story of Asanga, fourth-century Indian philosopher and monk, who after twelve years of meditation finally received **the encounter with Maitreya.** When Asanga asked the Master why he had never appeared to him during those twelve years, Maitreya replied that he had been there all the time but Asanga had not seen him because he had not yet developed great compassion. **(4) Dictations by Lord Maitreya** and others: "A Study in Christhood by the Great Initiator," 1984 *Pearls of Wisdom,* pp. 53–582; "On Initiation," 1975 *Pearls of Wisdom,* pp. 263–84; "Teachings from the Mystery School," 1985 *Pearls of Wisdom,* pp. 489–500, 521–26, 533–48; 1986 *Pearls of Wisdom,* pp. 67–218, 343–48. **(5) Nine Buddhas.** In a dictation given November 4, 1966, in Los Angeles, California, the Goddess of Purity said that "out of the great flame of cosmic purity just two years ago there were born upon earth nine children, Buddhas from the heart of the Father. . . . It was intended that by the power of the three-times-three these holy children should bring to mankind the great consciousness of God-purity held by your beloved Lord Gautama. I come to you this day with a message that should make your hearts awaken to the need for more decrees. Since the birth of these holy children, one has passed from the screen of life, for the surroundings of that child were so impure and so lacking in the flame of purity, inconducive to bringing forth the Light within that heart, that he died as a flower cut from the vine. And so eight of these holy innocents remain upon the planetary body." The ninth Buddha was subsequently reborn in Madras, India. **(6) "The Keeper's Daily Prayer":** in Keepers of the Flame Lesson 1 and *Prayers, Meditations and Dynamic Decrees for the Coming Revolution in Higher Consciousness* (Section I). **(7) My words shall not pass away.** Matt. 24:35; Mark 13:31; Luke 21:33. **(8) *prajna* boat** [from *prajna,* Sanskrit, transcendental wisdom, insight, divine intuition]: boat of wisdom, the vehicle or means by which one crosses the ocean of birth and death, the means of attaining nirvana. The fifth vow of Kuan Yin, taken from the Great Compassion Heart Dharani Sutra and included in Kuan Yin's Crystal Rosary, is "I desire/I vow to quickly board the prajna boat" (see 1988 *Pearls of Wisdom,* p. 373 n. 13). In Buddhist tradition, Kuan Yin is sometimes depicted as the captain of the "Bark of Salvation," ferrying souls across the rough sea of their karma to Amitābha's Western Paradise, or Pure Land, the land of bliss where souls may be reborn to receive continued instruction toward the goal of enlightenment and perfection. **(9)** In Buddhism, the **Three Jewels** in which the disciple takes refuge (i.e., turns to for protection and aid) are the Buddha, the Dharma, the Sangha. The Buddha is the Enlightened One; the Dharma, the Teaching of the Buddha; and the Sangha, the Community, the congregation of monks, nuns and lay devotees, the Buddha's spiritual family. The Three Jewels are given as a verbal formula in which each of them is preceded by the words "I take (my) refuge in the. . ." or "I go for refuge to the. . ." In Tibetan Buddhism, the following words are added before these three statements: "I take refuge in the Lama (or Guru)" because the Guru is the one who has embodied the Three Jewels as the representative of the Buddha and the transmitter of his Teaching. It is taught that the term "Guru" encompasses not only the embodied Guru but also all Teachers who have preceded and come after Gautama Buddha. It is also taught that the Dharma is the 'burden of the Lord', and that it is the responsibility of the chelas to live (embody) the Teaching, to spread abroad the Teaching, and to defend both the Teaching and the Teacher as well as the worldwide Community who comprise the 'Body' of the Buddha on earth.

Golden Pink Glow Ray

In the name of the beloved mighty victorious Presence of God, I AM in me, and my very own beloved Holy Christ Self, I call to the heart of beloved Serapis Bey and the Brotherhood at Luxor, beloved Lord Gautama, beloved Saint Germain, beloved God and Goddess Meru, beloved Sanat Kumara and the Holy Kumaras, the Cosmic Being Harmony, the Seven Mighty Elohim, the Seven Beloved Archangels and their Archeiai, the Seven Beloved Chohans of the Rays, beloved Lanello, the entire Spirit of the Great White Brotherhood and the World Mother, elemental life—fire, air, water, and earth!

1. I AM calling today for thy Golden Pink Ray
   To manifest round my form.
   Golden Pink Light, dazzling bright,
   My four lower bodies adorn!

Refrain: O Brotherhood at Luxor and blest Serapis Bey,
   Hear our call and answer by Love's ascending ray.
   Charge, charge, charge our being
   With essence pure and bright;
   Let thy hallowed radiance
   Of Ascension's mighty Light
   Blaze its dazzling Light rays
   Upward in God's name,
   Till all of heaven claims us
   For God's ascending flame.

2. Saturate me with Golden Pink Light,
   Make my four lower bodies bright;
   Saturate me with Ascension's Ray,
   Raise my four lower bodies today!

3. Surround us now with Golden Pink Love
   Illumined and charged with Light from above;
   Absorbing this with lightning speed,
   I AM fully charged with Victory's mead.

And in full Faith I consciously accept this manifest, manifest, manifest! (3x) right here and now with full Power, eternally sustained, all-powerfully active, ever expanding, and world enfolding until all are wholly ascended in the Light and free!
Beloved I AM! Beloved I AM! Beloved I AM!

Pearls of Wisdom®
published by The Summit Lighthouse

Vol. 31 No. 58   *Beloved El Morya*   *September 10, 1988*

FREEDOM 1988

3

Candidates for the Ascension, Attention!
We Take Our Stand for Religious Freedom

Candidates for graduation, welcome to the Chief's graduate school! [21-second applause]

Surely this day I have walked these rocks and rills and wooded, templed hills. I have stood at every angle to your own heart with inclined ear, listening to the heart's love and whisper and devotion and cry and wonderment, curiosity and so many expressions of the probing of the stars.

We are the stars, beloved, and we would see you become such stars of such magnitude.

I should like to address you as graduates, and were I speaking to the graduating class at Luxor today I should have said, "Hail, graduates!" But, beloved, to so call you candidates means that there is a moment whereby ye are chosen of the Lords of the Seven Rays, for we would pass through that gate this group of souls who have tarried long, loved long, learned long and are ready to make way for the next wave of "starlets."

Blessed hearts, all whom you know may rejoice and exult in the hour of your Victory, for you shall indeed pull them up even by their bootstraps. So the upward movement begets momentum. And, of course, the curious at the foot of the mountain shall always desire the higher view of those who blow the alpenhorn from the summit.

I come, then, dearest chelas of my heart, and I come to you who know me not (but [who], I shall determine, shall "forget me not"[1]) therefore to greet you in a light that cannot be extinguished. It is the light of the will of God. Once that light is the beacon in your lighthouse, once that beacon does sweep the 360 degrees of the circumference of your auric field—which should indeed be the size of a planet—once the will of God is the light out of the All-Seeing Eye, I tell you, beloved, earth, *earth shall know* that a team of mighty conquerors moves here below to defeat, I say, the forces of anti-religion worldwide—blest be the tie that binds[2] each one to God—as ever they would mediate every man's religion and determine what is not worthy and therefore that which can be ridiculed and cast down.

Blessed hearts, this *is* the candidate's last stand. Here the battle lines are drawn. Sanat Kumara has drawn these lines. Where shall we go, LORD, to take our stand? To Mercury? Well, we have come from Mercury. To Venus? Thence we have come also.

Nay, we shall not be moved. As the tall pine and the evergreen, immovable as the rock so we stand.

We draw a line in the earth and we say: Thus far and no farther! On behalf of a planet and a people we take our stand for absolute divine and human freedom of religious choice and experience—so long as harmlessness toward life be the pivot of a soul's ascending devotion.

Let it be established once and for all. For, beloved, these forces of Darkness continue to advance until routed by the blazing fire, even the light of the noonday sun that does emanate from the seven chakras of those who consider no more worthy a goal than to establish upon a planet this basic right of a soul to love her God, to commune with her God, and to so consecrate temple, body, land, edifice, consciousness, abundance, supply, way of life, worldview in the mode of the free entering of the electron by freewill choice into orbit around her God.

Blessed hearts, if freedom of religion and freedom to so consecrate the land to freedom of religion be lost, so will a planet be lost. You know the requirement of the Law: one ascension per year. The ascension cannot be made without the Mystery School, without Maitreya, without an ordered, step-by-step path. Thanks be to God for the listening ear of the Western chela whereby into the Western Hemisphere there do come marching down the highways of your devotion the Great Lights* of the Orient!

Blessed hearts, but for yourselves, the true and expansive and universal Aquarian-age Teaching of the East should be lost not only to the West but to the East as well. For whether East or West, in vying for who has the greater spiritual pride, I know not the outcome. But I will say that the smugness of those who "know it all" in established religion by far exceeds all other [forms of] pride upon a planet. Thus, beloved, in their citadels they have shut out the Blessed Virgin, Kuan Yin, our councils, our turbans, our sandals, our robes, our chelas, our bread, our wine—our Love.

*the Ascended and Unascended Masters of the Great White Brotherhood

How we run to the hills! How we run to the mountain of the Lord! How we exult in the tent of Moses!

Part the Red Sea. Part it, I say, and let there be, beloved, the passing through the very center of the subconscious of a fiery trail of seraphim.³ White fire passing through does have the power of forces sinister;* and there are the diseases of the psyche, untouched, for [although they are] not physical, yet they are physical—they are indeed physical.

Establish the balance of the Holy Spirit and see how the invading, infesting demons possessing the mind quit that temple. And discover, then, how cancers and blood diseases and all manner of infirmity receive their virility, their very strength, from the possessing demons of the false-hierarchy consciousness that *is* the chemical composition of the diseased body.

Thus, when casting out and exorcising disease, remember, there is not a disease, including the common cold, that does not have a companion entity that invades the mind. And many diseases begin with a stomach upset by discord in the feelings, feelings of rejection, despondency, hurt feelings. And so, beloved, the chain reactions of life as they spiral upward can lead you to eternal Life, but if allowed to descend, they can take you farther down into the pits⁴ where only dark ones abide.

You are a rocket. In a moment you can soar to Darjeeling. Look, then, as I hold the bishop's ring once worn by the Mark so dear to us all.⁵ Though it fit his index finger, it requires two of the Mother. Now place the eye upon this, for out of the seeing and concentration upon this holy amethyst, blest ring, *concentrating,* now let the soul pass through the crystal and be instantly at Kanchenjunga, heart of Himalayas and at the gate etheric of the Darjeeling temple.⁶

See how concentration upon a spiritual focus does tie you into the energy of that focus and therefore provide the passageway for the soul, by "eye magic,"⁷ to fly on the magic carpet of the eye to any point in time and space. Thus you are a rocket of the Mind of God and you can be transported when supported by one who loves you as I do.

Thus, blessed hearts, the elasticity of the mind and of the soul and of the heart must needs be exercised. I draw a circle around the head of each one by this amethyst. Therefore know in this exercise of healing decrees [that] you have anchored the inner work in which you engaged with your personal healing angel through the past night.⁸ Having so anchored pillars of healing in your being, while simultaneously being delivered of more entities than

---

*"does hold the power of forces sinister," i.e., the seraphim do take from them their power, do have it, so that the forces no longer have it nor wield it: as when Aaron's rod swallowed up the rods of the magicians of Egypt (Exod. 7:9–12).

I would care to number (for they have no number, for [in Absolute God-Reality] they are not real), yet so being delivered, beloved, you have prepared and prepared again this body, this mind with its absorptive quality to receive the energy of the Mind of God.
AUM
HRIH! HRIH! HRIH! HRIH! As raindrops falling upon a tin roof is the sound of the *HRIH* and the release of the energy.

I come, then, with the demand upon the candidates for graduation from earth's schoolroom: The sacred freedoms must be enshrined in your lives, your works, your expressions, your spiritual and physical and mental and emotional defense. You must safeguard for those who will follow after you a heritage that cannot, *shall not,* ever again be broken or turned back. Not only America but the American wilderness is the place set apart for the defense of Liberty.

At no time in the history of earth has Liberty been so threatened and have fallen angels been so threatened by the flame of Liberty, which is the threefold flame on the altar of your heart, the Liberty wherewith our God hath set the captives free[9] long before the captives have known that they were not free. Sealed in the heart is a Liberty flame and one day, as the Prometheus unbound, the soul shall know that the only Liberty is to release that fire until it become a conflagration.

Now is that gift of golden pink glow-ray not the swirling light of threefold flame?[10] Is it not the blending and the mother-of-pearl? Is it not the liberation whereby you leap into the heart of Maitreya, whose threefold flame is indeed cosmic?

Now then, beloved, the conspiracy against the Light does increase as the ultimate magnification of the Light does become a reality, one by one. Some among the false hierarchy have actually recognized that some of you are here to stay! [17-second applause] As you know, those who have elected the left-handed path have as tenet the nonrecognition of the Victors.

Beloved, they have met in council in their dark and treacherous places of the deep and, confiding in one another, have said, "These Victors will not shrink into the night." And thus, beloved, the trembling of fear as ultimate fear of a Light that is advancing has passed through the places of the deep. And, thus ultimately threatened, [they,] you can begin to understand, [regard] all strategies [as] one-pointed in the stance of self-preservation of the not-self that has been, shall we say, so puffed up as to even believe itself that it were real.

Now, beloved, you must reckon with the "beast of prey," the beast of the dweller on the threshold[11] on a planetary scale, who is ultimately threatened, who knows that "he hath but a short time"[12] [and that] unless in that short time he can defeat the forces of the living Christ,[13] of the Faithful and True (he who is robed in white, the Word out of whose mouth proceeds a living sword) [his day is done].[14]

Even so does fire proceed out of the mouth of the Two Witnesses. It is an office in Hierarchy.[15] So be it. As Above, so below, I charge you to invoke that power and authority of the Two Witnesses with you every hour, that as you call for the judgment of those who have sworn enmity against the Woman and her seed[16] and [who have] made their death vows to the utter destruction of the Lightbearers of the planet, you shall be enveloped with that Electronic Presence of the fire proceeding out of the spoken Word in the Judgment Call.[17]

May it so be, beloved, for I, your Chief, preparing you, then, as candidates for graduation, must tell you, as the Great Law does allow [me to tell] all initiates who anticipate the ascension in this or early in the next embodiment, that when you come to that point of distance where the final requirements [for the ascension] are being met and you are indeed a candidate (as so many here are and as many Keepers of the Flame are), you must know that before you pass through the gate, the false-hierarchy impostor of your ascended self lies waiting to deter you from that moment when, dressed in cap and gown, you are ready to receive that scroll on which is written your Victory—your diploma showing your preparedness to move onward in the universities of Cosmos.

Blessed hearts, that one [that false hierarch] long ago elected the left-handed path and therefore did advance to levels of adeptship and black magic beyond those levels to which you may have attained [on the right-handed path of personal Christhood in past golden ages and] unto this hour; [therefore] you win by devotion, by fervor, by violet flame, by Ascended Master sponsorship.

Without a doubt, it does require some degree of mastery to advance thus far and to cross over to ultimate freedom. But, beloved, the urgency of those on the left-handed path to become adepts in the alchemy of Matter has been[, in some cases,] far greater than your own [sense of urgency to become adepts on the right-handed path]. For they have no God, no sponsoring source of Light, whereas you are one with your God, who is the masterful Presence within your being.

I should therefore, if I were you, take the lead of your Messenger to pursue in this year a path of God-mastery and the defeat of all forces of Death and Hell and fear and doubt and all records thereof, and even of the pale horse,[18] so that on that line* of the Piscean conqueror, whereby you graduate at the conclusion

*the two o'clock line of the Cosmic Clock, the line on which the Messenger Mark L. Prophet entered the ritual of the ascension following his transition February 26, 1973 (under the Sun sign and hierarchy of Pisces)

of the Piscean age, it may be said by you, "The prince of this world cometh and findeth nothing in me."[19] That "prince," beloved, will be your false-hierarchy impostor. Moreover, there do abound on this planet false-hierarchy impostors of Lord Maitreya. Watch out for them and remember that I, Morya, have warned you, *for I love you.*

Because I love you as I do, I tell you that the false guru will come offering false fruit, a false initiation. Yes, beloved, he who graduates from earth's schoolroom will know the temptations received by Jesus: Command these stones be made bread. Cast thyself down the mountain. Worship me and I will give you the whole world.[20]

Beware, beloved. These temptations are cleverly disguised in altruistic aims and goals. If your threefold flame be developed and balanced, you will see through them by the inner intuition of the heart [even] when the outer mind is confused and may fail to perceive the Real and the Unreal.

Now therefore, beloved, I come to you. I come to you because I love you, because I have stood in the wings and observed any number of you by the failure to be alert and [to be] in the mind of Christ fail in a previous round to identify the false-hierarchy impostor of yourself or of Maitreya and therefore lose the opportunity for graduation. Beloved ones, tragically some of you never realized what you had missed. It is so, beloved.

I call for piercing Cosmic Christ illumination, and for this purpose Kuthumi has come with me this day as we two together would represent to you our beloved Maitreya. I say to you, then, take a stand for the defense of your freedom to embrace the religion of your choice and you will safeguard this path for millions who will follow you up this mountain.

With the sign of the Ruby Ray, with the signet of the ruby lodestone* I impress in your memory my words that you might arrive at the day of your Victory and *know* that it is the day of your Victory and *know* that on that day, whether it be [in] a fortnight, a year or ten, you shall remain so fixed in the secret love star of Victory that no subtlety or subterfuge or beguiling tempter shall cause you to move *not a quarter of an inch or a quarter of a mile* from the center of your First Love.

Now I ask you, each one, to instantaneously meditate upon your First Love and to remain with that one-pointed Love for these moments of silence.

*The Messenger holds up a ruby crystal in her right hand.

This dictation by **El Morya** was **delivered** by the Messenger of the Great White Brotherhood Elizabeth Clare Prophet on **Thursday, June 30, 1988,** 7:11–7:43 p.m. MDT, at *FREEDOM 1988* in the Heart of the Inner Retreat at the **Royal Teton Ranch, Montana.** For notes see p. 462.

Pearls of Wisdom®
published by The Summit Lighthouse

| Vol. 31 No. 59 | Beloved Kuthumi | September 11, 1988 |

FREEDOM 1988
4
Be Who You Really Are
Defeat Your Worst Enemy

I say, hail to the Chief of the Darjeeling Council of the Great White Brotherhood, who does so care for his chelas, who does so care for his own! Hail to our beloved Chief! As I prepare to speak to you, beloved, I invite you to express your gratitude to beloved El Morya. [1-minute 47-second standing ovation]

Beloved ones, I would tell you how dear to the heart of El Morya you are, how he has spoken [of you] to me for weeks, how he has planned how he would come here today to deliver to you this message so that you would not forget and not neglect and [so that you would] recognize how critical are the final hours of a soul who does plan to take flight from earth's schoolroom, knowing that her course is done.

And so he said to me, "Koot Hoomi,[1] shall we not conduct a healing service that they might be delivered of encumbrances that would prevent the full comprehension and import of this message? Shall I not also be brief that they might not become lost in a sea of words? Shall I not also send my Messenger with my Excalibur from which the hordes do flee?[2] Kuthumi, come and help me, for in this, with Kuan Yin, *we must not fail.*"[3]

Blessed hearts, treasure one who loves you so much. Therefore know that as the tenderest father with profound concern, so does your dear El Morya also await *your* response, *your* decrees that he might do more to seal and protect this destiny so vast, so envisioned so long ago by your Jesus.[4]

Therefore, I represent both El Morya and Jesus as we go

before Maitreya, and I come for the alleviating and the healing of the burdens of the soul. For these burdens, beloved, are a malaise for which there is no physical tonic; and for that I am sometimes grateful, for surely the pharmaceutical companies should have entered into competition long ago to sell their wares for the supposed healing of the soul. Thus, it is a realm untouched by them but surely invaded by others.

This invasion has come through [the sellers of] chemical dependencies and mind-altering drugs [(among others)] and plain old ordinary food. Thus the mouth has become a trapdoor for much that has afflicted the soul and obscured the great light of heaven.

In this hour, beloved, I would take up a teaching recently given to you by the Messenger, for this teaching is so necessary that it must be ensconced in its proper setting of proper proportion. It is the teaching concerning the dying not-self, the lesser ego, the beast of the dweller on the threshold.

Many of you have taken from that not-self its vitality and life, its freedom, its enjoyment. You have starved the beast. You have beaten the beast. The beast may be lying half dead in the subconscious. But not seeing this event as graphically as we see it, you have sometimes neglected to deal the death blow, the mortal wound, for the depression of the dead and dying beast has turned back upon yourself and upon the soul.

The soul being sensitive and feminine in nature, therefore absorptive, filled with empathy and sympathy, has identified with that dweller and thus begun to take on a mold of discouragement, despair, despondency. Enter Depressa, entity of the annihilation ray. And where Depressa is, can the suicide entities be far behind?

Beloved ones, you are giving birth spiritually to a most beautiful being of Light. But until the hour of your wedding day before the altar of God—you see, I liken that moment to the wedding even as Morya speaks of it as your graduation—until that wedding day the soul is not yet permanent, not yet sealed in her Lord, her Christ, her Husband.

The Divine Spouse does wait at the altar. And is not the "best man," even the very best friend that you know, the ascended one, that Lanello who winks to make the whole process a bit easier? And who shall give away the bride but the tenderest father of all, your beloved El Morya?

Blessed one, until that hour, the not-self rages—wages that war against the soul and causes you to wear the sackcloth and mourning of depression and the via dolorosa when in reality you have woven the wedding garment; yet it hangs in the closet, you yourself not feeling worthy to put it on. Friends like Job's friends have told you, "You must have sinned, and gravely sinned, to have such a house of cards come down upon you!"[5]

Is it not true that those who desire "a better resurrection"[6] claim all the karma that they can possibly carry?[7] Having no desires to appear wise and vain and successful, they should rather be "fools for Christ"[8] and be rid once and for all of the dregs of karma that have no place when the bride is one in the secret chamber with the living Christ.

I say, beloved, you are shining ones. These ghosts of former selves must not be allowed to linger. Too receptive are you to these subtle negatives. If someone makes a frontal attack upon you, you are always the victor. But the subtleties that creep in, beginning with discouragement, are as deadly as hell itself. Thus I come with enlightenment for the soul and a true cause for happiness.

Just call, then, for that great sword Excalibur to be plunged by the living hand of God and the Divine Mother into the core, the point of origin, the nadir of the not-self, and realize that you have already consumed,* in some cases, large percentages of that not-self.

Now, then, beloved, at a moment when legions of Victory, armies of the Faithful and True and of the Seven Archangels are marching for the binding of the assailants of the Lightbearers, is it not a moment to *thrust ho!* and accelerate and summon all of one's forces and be done with this nest of serpents, not letting one remain?

There are indeed tides in the affairs of men.[9] There are cosmic moments. They must be recognized. Do not miss them. Too many of you miss them and miss, as they say, "a piece of cake."[10]

That's how it can be when you are surrounded by the legions of Archangel Gabriel. And they are ready, for you have earned it. You have balanced the karma. You have seen through it. You have learned the lesson. Everything is in your favor, including your cosmic astrology. You are poised for the Victory but you do not take the step. Beloved, better to take three or five or ten steps and be as one that beateth the air and to have one of those steps be that ultimate Victory not of the battle but of the war [than not to have taken the step, not to have beaten at all].

We are here, then, by our devotion to the will of God and the wisdom of God. We lay a foundation firm that you might receive from beloved Heros and Amora the crowning diadem of Love.

Angels of the World Teachers with the skill of surgeons are doing all that the Great Law allows them to prepare the crown chakra [of those present] for greater illumination. Let the illumination

---

*by the sacred fire of the Divine Mother raised up; by the violet transmuting flame through dynamic decrees to the I AM Presence

be called forth now from those Cosmic Christs of other spheres. I require your summoning. Do so, then, in song. Invoke them, led by your choir now. [Please stand.]

O Cosmic Christs of Other Spheres*

O Cosmic Christs of other spheres
    To you I call beyond the years
Whose light rays from so far away
    Are beamed through me right now today.
Through valiant effort we will win
    Our vict'ry over pain and sin
Transmuting all the woes of earth
    And freeing men for Light's new birth.

The magnet of the holy Sun
    The I AM Presence of each one
Will lift men from the dust of stain
    To where Love's glory lives again.
And when the tears at last are dry—
    Wiped by God's image from our eye
Our vict'ry's bloom an ode will be
    To Life's celestial harmony.

The efforts made, forgotten then
    Will all be changed by vision fair
The music of the spheres we'll sing
    Shall gladden all life everywhere.
So come, then, blessed radiant ones
    Thy councils wise shall purify
As angel songs now fill the skies
    To lead men back to paradise.

O beloved, your calls for the Great Cosmic Light given in Saint Germain's violet flame tape[11] are a building momentum for that Cosmic Christ illumination. Think of it, beloved, Cosmic Christ illumination reaching a critical mass on planet earth! What will it take? Right off the bat it will take your crown chakra glowing intensely with devotion to the Mind of God.

O how we attend the hour when for a sufficiency of violet flame tapes we may be next in line for illumination's golden flame, and therefore sweeping round the world like electric spark there can fly and move and be the bursting in the sky of those yellow fireworks of Confucius and Lord Lanto and Archangel Jophiel!

O adepts of the golden flame of illumination, bodhisattvas, all who raise the Light of the Divine Mother—know you not[, beloved,]

---

*Song 42 in *The Summit Lighthouse Book of Songs,* sung to the melody of "America the Beautiful"

that they must, one and all, balance all planes of the chakras to achieve that height? For those serving on the Second Ray, then, all other roads lead to the crown chakra and the highest good which is total God-awareness.

When one is totally God-aware, can one deny His Truth, His Will, His Love, His Mercy, His Service and His Exposé of all those things that even intelligent men and women close their minds and eyes and ears to? For [them] to confess the facts at hand does require too much commotion in the desire body.

Ah yes, beloved, pity those who close their eyes to Truth, for they indeed lack illumined action, not by absence of knowledge but [by] absence of courage. Thus, the heart suffers, the threefold flame atrophies, and all things come to *nil* and *nihilism* in those who deny what illumination does uncover.

Let it uncover all! Do not cower before the Truth of oneself or another. Do not fear it. Do not be dismayed or burdened by it. A lie is a lie is a lie. Human creation ad nauseam is human creation. Do not be embarrassed. Be grateful you can stand and look at it and laugh at it and be laughed at and even scorned. You will discover who loves you, who loves you not. It will not take a daisy to find out.¹² [laughter; 10-second applause]

And those who you thought did not love you will come from all directions—your champions, your friends. They may even become your disciples. For those who are of the Truth love those who confess the Truth and espouse the Truth they see. True hearts love a heart who will take a stand for what is revealed.

How do you suppose we could bring forth so much revelation? We have tried it before through many. I tell you, it takes a class of the Messengers of the God Mercury who have had aeons of training of accurately delivering the messages of their hierarchs, never shunning to deliver it even when it could be easily calculated that the reaction to the message could be so terrific as to blow away the harbinger of someone's bad news.

Bad news, I say. Indeed it is bad news when the Lord God does deliver through the boy Samuel the judgment of Eli the high priest. Consider the courage of the child to speak Truth and the presence of that child, that "Francis," that prince of our hearts who could speak the Truth in such power of God that the powerful should stand back and confess, "Aye, it is true. Thou hast spoken. There is a prophet in Israel."¹³

So, my beloved, if you do not fear the uncovering of error, all Truth will be made known to you. Is not Truth a two-edged sword? And is not one edge of it Comfort's holy flame from Holy Spirit?

O Truth, the everlasting Comforter! Extol her, Pallas Athena, twin flame of the Maha Chohan.

Blessed hearts, I, Kuthumi, valuing the candle whose flame is wisdom in the night, counsel you to so increase understanding that you will enter the ranks of a Solomon and not be confounded by the lies of the fallen ones who would take from you the cup of Victory's mead. All they have [with which] to defeat you are lies. But many do not know a lie when they hear one, for they have not studied cosmic law or Truth.

Blessed ones, you can go within and train and focus the inner eye upon the crown chakra and through it upon your Holy Christ Self.* You may idle away the hours with your two-eyed vision fixed to the damnable TV set that has torn many a chela from healthy progress on the Path. When you train the inner eye, then, and fix it upon the star of the crown chakra, the Kundalini shall rise, the wisdom of heaven shall be open to you, [and then] thou shalt never be called fool, thou shalt outsmart and outwit the sinister minds who would defeat your course.

O ignorant animal magnetism,[14] O density, O perversity, O blasphemy against the Divine Mother! How can you ignore a law vouchsafed to you? How can you at any time fail to pursue with the rigors of discipleship and the vigor of a chela of El Morya every word in these teachings that has proceeded out of the mouth of God, as Hierarchy, only to discover therein your own salvation?

Shall all of this Royal Teton Ranch be for naught? Or [shall] all of Hierarchy's planning for aeons not be seized by you as you would pluck a most beautiful flower from a shrub? We have not prepared all of this to lose one soul, one chela who is ready to ascend.

Be wise, beloved. Be wise. We speak because some, as though slowing down on a conveyer belt, have fallen back and backwards but know it not. Absent a sense of co-measurement, then, some are falling asleep. Some are falling asleep, beloved. They do not know they are losing ground. I am here to tell you so.

It is the hour of thy Victory! Summon it! Accept nothing less. Be vigilant and you shall win.

I reveal to you a side of myself you have not seen, and as I open my garment, there you will see the vast mirror inside. Now you will look in that mirror, each one, as my Electronic Presence is before you, and in that mirror you will see an aspect of self not seen hitherto, an aspect of self that is *your worst enemy.*

Gaze upon it, beloved, and there make the sign of the cross of Saint Francis. I bequeath to you my momentum of that incarnation

---

*through training and focusing your eye upon the crown chakra you can learn to train and focus your eye upon your Holy Christ Self

for the defeat of this worst enemy and then [of] all lesser enemies, phases, figments, fantasies of the not-self, until you see in the mirror of my inner garment the blazing reality of your holy Christhood. This is the Path. Walk ye in it. The door is open. May you elect to walk through it in this life. The nature of the urgency of this choice made today, then hotly pursued, may not be made known to you. Thus, with all of our desiring and the ability at hand we have come for this purpose and to this end: that you might be who you really are.

You are sealed in the will of God and his wisdom. Go your way, beloved. Make it God's Way.

I AM with you. *I AM with you.* We are with you now unto the hour of your Victory in the heart of the Blessed Virgin over sin, disease and death.

So we sprinkle you with ruby droplets.* Catch the stars.

*The Messenger holds up the ruby crystal, directing it toward the congregation in a sprinkling motion.

"The Summit Lighthouse Sheds Its Radiance O'er All the World to Manifest as Pearls of Wisdom." This dictation by **Kuthumi** was **delivered** by the Messenger of the Great White Brotherhood Elizabeth Clare Prophet on **Thursday, June 30, 1988,** 7:45–8:22 p.m. MDT, at *FREEDOM 1988* in the Heart of the Inner Retreat at the **Royal Teton Ranch, Montana.** "Darshan and Dictations with Kuthumi and El Morya: Chakra Meditations and Initiations on the Cosmic Clock" on 3 audiocassettes, B88094–96, 3 hr. 52 min., $19.50 (add $.95 for postage); dictations included with those of Archangel Raphael and Lord Maitreya on videocassette HP88054, 2 hr., $29.95 (add $1.10 for postage). [**N.B.** Bracketed material denotes words unspoken yet implicit in the dictation, added by the Messenger under the Master's direction for clarity in the written word.] **(1)** In his final incarnation during the 1800s, Kuthumi was the Eastern adept **Koot Hoomi** Lal Singh, also known as the Master K.H., who worked closely with El Morya in founding the Theosophical Society. **(2)** In the darshan prior to El Morya's and Kuthumi's dictations those gathered gave healing decrees while the Messenger made invocations at the high altar and then moved through the tent, carrying the sword Excalibur, and on behalf of those present made calls to the entire Spirit of the Great White Brotherhood for the exorcism of diseases and conditions of the out-of-alignment states related to the blocking of the Light of the Divine Mother in the chakras. **(3) "Kuan Yin, we must not fail."** Kuan Yin, 1969 *Pearls of Wisdom,* p. 231; 1984 *Pearls of Wisdom,* pp. 205–6. **(4)** The **vision of the Inner Retreat** was given by Jesus to Martha—a land dedicated from the beginning. 1988 *Pearls of Wisdom,* p. 340. **(5) Discourses of condemnation by Job's friends.** Job 4, 5, 8, 11, 15, 18, 20, 22, 25. **(6) Better resurrection.** Heb. 11:35. **(7) Sin, karma and the judgment.** I Tim. 5:24, 25; Mark L. Prophet and Elizabeth Clare Prophet, *The Lost Teachings of Jesus II,* pp. 357–58. **(8) Fools for Christ's sake.** I Cor. 4:10. **(9)** "There is **a tide in the affairs of men** which, taken at the flood, leads on to fortune; omitted, all the voyage of their life is bound in shallows and in miseries." Shakespeare, *Julius Caesar,* act 4, scene 3, lines 218–21. **(10) "a piece of cake":** It's easy; it can be done with little or no effort. **(11) "Decree for the Great Cosmic Light,"** 5.03, on *Save the World with Violet Flame! by Saint Germain 2* (see 1988 *Pearls of Wisdom,* p. 400 n. 6). **(12)** Refers to the playful game of plucking the petals of a daisy one by one as you alternately say, "He loves me," "He loves me not," until the last petal reveals whether or not "he does." **(13)** I Sam. 3:1–20. Saint Germain, who was embodied as the **prophet Samuel,** is affectionately called **Francis** by Portia, his twin flame, which name, she says, means Freedom. **(14) Ignorant animal magnetism.** 1988 *Pearls of Wisdom,* p. 339 n. 8.

Notes from Pearl no. 58 by El Morya:
(**1**) El Morya often mentions the **"forget-me-not"** to remind his chelas not to forget the Guru or one's foremost devotion to God's will. Beloved Alpha is seen to use this small bright blue flower that is the symbol of the humility of those who devoutly espouse the will of God. See decree 8.01 and song 209, "Forget Me Not," by El Morya. (**2**) **Religion, the tie that binds.** The word *religion* is derived from the Latin *religio* 'bond between man and the gods' or *religare* 'to bind back'. (**3**) The subconscious refers to the sea; passing through this subconscious is a fiery trail of seraphim. During the exodus of the Israelites from Egypt, as they were being pursued by Pharaoh and his hosts Moses stretched his hand over the Red Sea as the LORD had commanded him to do and the sea parted, allowing the Israelites to pass over and escape the Egyptians. Exod. 14. (**4**) **Bottomless pit.** Rev. 9:1, 2, 11; 11:7; 17:8; 20:1–3. (**5**) El Morya founded The Summit Lighthouse in 1958 through the **Messenger Mark L. Prophet,** whom he called to deliver the Teachings of the Ascended Masters dictated to him as Pearls of Wisdom. During El Morya's dictation the Messenger held up the amethyst **bishop's ring,** which Mark L. Prophet wore as bishop of The Summit Lighthouse. The ring was charged by Archangel Zadkiel to hold a focus of the flame of the Seventh Ray. (**6**) For information on El Morya's etheric retreat over Darjeeling, India, and his past lives, see Mark L. Prophet and Elizabeth Clare Prophet, *Lords of the Seven Rays,* Book One, pp. 21–78; Book Two, pp. 34–35. (**7**) **"Eye magic."** Mark L. Prophet and Elizabeth Clare Prophet, *Climb the Highest Mountain,* 2d ed., pp. 48–50. (**8**) **Healing angel.** Archangel Raphael, 1988 *Pearls of Wisdom,* p. 441. (**9**) **Proclaim liberty to the captives.** Isa. 61:1; II Cor. 3:17. (**10**) **Gift of golden pink glow-ray.** Lord Maitreya, 1988 *Pearls of Wisdom,* pp. 444–45. (**11**) **Dweller on the threshold.** 1988 *Pearls of Wisdom,* pp. 170 n. 6, 422; glossary in *Saint Germain On Alchemy,* p. 395. (**12**) **Short time.** Rev. 12:12. (**13**) **Satan given 75 years to destroy the Church.** Pope Leo XIII (1878–1903) is said to have had an experience in which he heard Satan tell the Lord that he could destroy the Church if he was given 75 years and greater power over those who would serve him. He heard the Lord say, "You have the time; you have the power. Do what you will." Pope Leo was given to understand that if Satan failed in that time period he would experience a devastating defeat. He also understood that the forces of Good would be given a greater power of Good if they would use it and that Saint Michael the Archangel was to play an important role in this battle and Satan's defeat. Pope Leo composed a prayer invoking the protection and aid of Archangel Michael which was said at the conclusion of Mass from 1886 until 1964 when Vatican Council II revised the liturgy. This prayer, expanded by the Messenger, has been incorporated into Archangel Michael's Rosary for Armageddon released by Elizabeth Clare Prophet. See 1985 *Pearls of Wisdom,* p. 243; 1988 *Pearls of Wisdom,* p. 288 n. 6. (**14**) **The Faithful and True.** Rev. 19:11–21. (**15**) **Two Witnesses.** Dan. 12:5–10; Rev. 11:3–12; 1988 *Pearls of Wisdom,* p. 34 n. 22. (**16**) The Great Guru Sanat Kumara and his Lightbearers occupy the 6 o'clock line on the Cosmic Clock, the line of the Divine Mother and her chelas, hence the term **"Woman and her seed."** Rev. 12. (**17**) **Judgment Call.** 1988 *Pearls of Wisdom,* p. 202. (**18**) **Pale horse.** Rev. 6:8. (**19**) **". . . Nothing in me."** John 14:30. (**20**) **Temptation of Jesus.** Matt. 4:1–11; Luke 4:1–13.

Pearls of Wisdom®
published by The Summit Lighthouse

Vol. 31 No. 60   *Beloved Heros and Amora*   *September 17, 1988*

FREEDOM 1988

5

Love Must Prevail

Angels, Elementals with Sons and Daughters of God:
The Unbeatable Force of Divine Love in Action

The Ruby Ray Judgment of the Violators of Children

Now, it has been said that Love, even Perfect Love, casts out all fear.[1] We say, let it be done as it has been spoken. Let fear be banished from the hearts of the devotees of the Ruby Ray of the Sacred Heart of the Universal Christ.

Thus, beloved, for us to speak is to create, to create is to be, and to be is to become the fulfillment of the matrix of Creator in the creation.

We say, let there be Love! Thus, there was and is and shall be Love—this Love born of the healing fires of cosmic Truth this day.

And out of the love of hearts of two Sons [El Morya and Kuthumi] who have taken shaft of the First and the Second Rays [blue and yellow] to create their emerald matrix [green], there does come, then, to earth truly the new heaven and the new earth seen by John the Beloved.[2] It is the very unique expression of the causal body of each one.[3]

Thy habitation above is the Holy City, the Holy City as the Retreat of the Divine Mother[4] and, yes, that Holy City that is all inside thy causal body of Light.[5]

We decree Love where love already abounds, where love is a ruby magnet and a fire that does magnetize [Love] from our hearts, does pull and attract even components of a nucleus [of our God-Mastery] whereby a planet, aye, more than a planet can be turned around.

What do you think? We are Elohim. In the mode of God

we come. Our Consciousness is God. We create out of the Holy Spirit. And where we send Holy Spirit there does come change, sometimes abrupt.

O do temper our Love by violet flame! Send your foot soldiers and legions, O bhikkhus, O monks, O religious, O spiritual devotees of the love sign of Aquarius. Send your troops and your decrees marching and the elementals at your command hither and yon in every city where Love would abide.

Blessed hearts, Love is a fire* to be contended with, but in contending with Love only Love wins. Yes, Love does win out. Love outlasts every other vibration. Understand that the coming of Love is the dividing of the way.

We are entrusting to your care and custodianship for the remainder of this conference a diligence in invoking the violet flame, for as you send violet flame to the city of your abode, so Love shall follow. As you send love to the planet, Love shall follow.

We desire not to trigger cataclysm by Love's fires, *not yet*. For Elohim are not ready for the changing of worlds, for there are Lightbearers to be carved out of the rock of the astral plane by the acetylene torch of Love, by every means available. Let Lightbearers be cut free by the sword of the Ruby Ray. O wield it! O call it forth!

Come forth, great cosmic honor guard, legions who bear the sword of the Ruby Ray on behalf of the Buddhas of the Ruby Ray. Come over this Heart. Show your marching formation, wielding swords of Ruby Ray as in a cosmic dance approaching that of Shiva you then flash that Ruby Ray in every direction, spherical and beyond all dimensions.

O earth, prepare, for the Love Ray does come and it does intensify.

Beloved, as we speak our legions are preparing your aura, preparing it to receive an extraordinary impetus of Love.

Love, O my own, must be guarded, tended. Watch out, beloved, for Love will seek every nook and cranny and crevice to flush out every force of anti-Creation which is anti-Love.

Learn to wield the fire of Love and you will solve many, many problems that have seemed unsolvable. Blessed ones, problems in business, in health, in livelihood, in direction, in affairs, these can all be solved with Love if and only when you invoke the violet flame for the transmutation of all conditions of consciousness that are a misqualification of the Third Ray.

It is necessary that finally there be some who will approach with directness and dispatch the initiations of the Third Ray. Let us no longer go around so mighty a fortress as Love, so blessed a path as the Ruby Ray.

*"Our God is a consuming fire. . .God is Love." (Deut. 4:24; Heb. 12:29; I John 4:8,16)

There is nothing, in fact, of which you are not already capable [that is taught] in the very first classes conducted by the representatives of Sanat Kumara on the Path of the Ruby Ray and Ruby Ray initiations. All of you are engaged already in some form of service. As recently as in the last hour you have rendered service to a cosmos. In so doing, you have surrendered that hour to this activity rather than to another. You have sacrificed some other occupation or preoccupation to engage in it. And I must say, considering your present level of development, your measure of selflessness is also noteworthy.

If, then, the four sides of the ruby cube are already being fulfilled by you,⁶ would you not care to know from the heart of Maitreya how with slightly more effort and even less pain you can enjoy merging with the very essence of Love?

Beloved, the forces of hatred upon earth and in the earth 'mongst all who have betrayed the Great God of Love are almost unparalleled. There are few places where there are evolutions of the advancement to which some attain on this planet that have such a momentum of anti-Love, which is an absolute hatred of God the Father, the Son, the Holy Spirit and the Mother.

This, beloved, is focused four ways against the Child—the Child that is in the center of the circle undergoing the Eighth Ray initiations of the secret chamber of the heart. I tell you, beloved, the hatred of fallen angels and of hell itself is pitted against children and the archetypal Manchild⁷ on planet earth.

Therefore we come with a fierceness. Therefore we come with the Ruby Ray judgment of the very dregs of the denizens of the astral plane. And we come, beloved, for you have responded to the Mother's call to give that violet flame and to give it again and again. This violet flame you have invoked since the first call of the first cassette went forth,⁸ though it has been used, it has also been garnered in a reservoir of Light. This entire momentum, therefore, shall be used for twofold purpose: the binding and the judgment of a considerable percentage of those who are the attackers of youth and the child and the child in the womb.

Beware, then, ye violators of children, no matter what form that violation does take! Feel, then, the hot breath of the Elohim of Love and of the Holy Ghost. For the violation of children and youth, therefore, you receive this night thrice the judgment of the Holy Ghost. That judgment goes directly to the physical level of your evil and to the astral mire of your misqualified energy of the Mother.⁹

Thus, beloved, there is no more heinous crime than the violation of children. And thus, beloved, it is the studied assessment of Elohim that this judgment shall remove from the planet a considerable weight. It is our desire to see that perhaps the Cosmic Council or Alpha and Omega or the Lord of the World shall find in this action a unique alchemy that shall be of supreme usefulness to beloved Saint Germain.

We are Elohim of all cosmos. May we be the first to applaud the victory of Keepers of the Flame and friends of the Light in this violet flame experiment. And may we say, beloved, that to increase and multiply it can only bring to earth greater mitigation and mercy, clearing the way not only for Kuan Yin and her assistance in delivering to you the secret-ray initiations but also for any number of hierarchs who have not descended to earth for whom you have actually woven a violet flame carpet, making it once again lawful to place their feet upon this earth, not to mention, beloved, the blessings to elemental life and the hope to many hearts who are enslaved under totalitarian regimes.

Blessed ones, it is only a beginning, but what a beginning and what promise. May you become as the "greatest salesman in the world,"[10] taking those violet flame tapes [to many, many souls] as your auras are so heartily charged with the Seventh Ray; and, by the sheer enthusiasm and joy, lightness and freedom you carry, ignite something that is catching and that will catch the world and draw them into Aquarius and therefore allow them to lock gears with a new dispensation and vibration.

I pray that you will devise the most ingenious means of self-perpetuating the sending out of these violet flame cassettes even to the extent of drawing up a list of spiritual souls and Lightbearers known to you and praying for them daily to be cut free by Elohim beginning with Astrea—cut free, therefore, to be free to invoke freedom's flame so that when after a fortnight* you do send to them that cassette they will receive it as though they had been waiting for it all along. Just remember, the violet flame begets more lovers of the violet flame.

Look at the statue of Kuan Yin.[11] Is she not pouring out an endless stream of violet flame, a violet flame river? Is not the river of the Divine Mother of Aquarius a Seventh Ray movement of ribbons of light of every possible shade and gradation of mercy and justice and freedom and alchemy? And is not the violet flame twinkling with the diamonds of Saint Germain?

Blessed ones, when you build a momentum and the momentum builds itself, it is not a time to cease but to accelerate, to increase and to see how the violet flame again and again goes into that harder and more recalcitrant and more dense substance [to transmute it by the rolling momentum of your decrees]. Those who

---

*after two weeks of calls and dynamic decrees to Elohim to cut them free to receive the violet flame and heavenly hosts of the Seventh Ray

chase the violet flame with calls to Astrea and Archangel Michael do have indeed the great advantage of troops and legions of the First Ray who can hardly wait to respond to your call to clear the way for Saint Germain.

Blessed ones, is it asking too much while your hearty voices are gathered in such a charged place as this to ask you to produce the third violet flame cassette during this conference [19-second applause], thus charging it as the Third Ray offering with all of the love of all of the dictations and of all of your hearts, and of the healing momentum that you already feel so tangibly? We would indeed be very grateful if it were possible to accomplish this task.

Now, beloved, the alchemy of the Kuan Yin mantras[12] that is added to this violet flame provides, indeed, the secret-ray action of the violet flame [and] does afford you, then, a tremendous power of transmutation through the fullness of the attainment of Kuan Yin and does give a tremendous boost to Kuan Yin whereby through many hands and hearts reaching out to her in the West she might also increase in her manifestation of the Amitābha Buddha.[13] Thus, beloved, you render Kuan Yin as well as the planet a great service.

Our call, then, is for a million souls as devoted as this nucleus. We must have it, beloved, and it is now more possible than ever. May each one here appoint himself a committee of one to multiply himself, to call so intensely that the barriers of this hate and hate creation shall come down and souls shall step forth who have never before been free from that human hate and hate creation to recognize who they are in the Light of Aquarius and to identify the violet flame river as the very natural vibration of their own soul's path.

O the hour is come, beloved, and we attend it with the full power of our Godhood. Know, then, that our Presence is a healing action whereby all of Elohim in this hour desire to render to Mother Mary and to Saint Germain and Portia and to Lord Gautama and all of those of the Great White Brotherhood the maximum assistance.

Now, then, your auras have been changed, beloved. They are charged with the Love Ray. And by a sacred alchemy at this moment you are prepared to absorb and absorb and absorb this Ruby Ray action. [1-minute 45-second pause]

For this action I invite you to offer to the heart of your Father "The Covenant of the Magi." (Decree 30.08 in the pink section.) [intonations, 53 seconds]

Our twin flames recite this eternal covenant of the Son with the Father with you.

The Covenant of the Magi
by El Morya

Father, into thy hands I commend my being. Take me and use me—my efforts, my thoughts, my resources, all that I AM—in thy service to the world of men and to thy noble cosmic purposes, yet unknown to my mind.

Teach me to be kind in the way of the Law that awakens men and guides them to the shores of Reality, to the confluence of the River of Life, to the Edenic source, that I may understand that the leaves of the Tree of Life, given to me each day, are for the healing of the nations; that as I garner them into the treasury of being and offer the fruit of my loving adoration to Thee and to thy purposes supreme, I shall indeed hold covenant with Thee as my guide, my guardian, my friend.

For Thou art the directing connector who shall establish my lifestream with those heavenly contacts, limited only by the flow of the hours, who will assist me to perform in the world of men the most meaningful aspect of my individual life plan as conceived by Thee and executed in thy name by the Karmic Board of spiritual overseers who, under thy holy direction, do administer thy laws.

So be it, O eternal Father, and may the covenant of thy beloved Son, the living Christ, the Only Begotten of the Light, teach me to be aware that he liveth today within the tri-unity of my being as the Great Mediator between my individualized Divine Presence and my human self; that he raiseth me into Christ consciousness and thy divine realization in order that as the eternal Son becomes one with the Father, so I may ultimately become one with Thee in that dynamic moment when out of union is born my perfect freedom to move, to think, to create, to design, to fulfill, to inhabit, to inherit, to dwell and to be wholly within the fullness of thy Light.

Father, into thy hands I commend my being.

It is a blessed covenant, beloved. Do you understand that when you enter the retreat where you are taught step-by-step the lessons of the initiations of the Ruby Ray to come, it is this covenant that you make with your Father? And thereby the Magi of old become guardians of the unfolding Trinity, fleur-de-lis, within the heart, and thereby Ruby Ray angels attend thee. It [the covenant] is a commitment to the Path of the Ruby Ray. It is a gentle surrender to the gentle presence of Love.

O Thou Gentle Presence, how powerful. What strength profound in the peace of Love. Love is a thing in itself that simply is, that fills the atmosphere. Across a cosmos the love of two hearts cannot be diluted, but when separated by a cosmos two hearts may string a cord that binds and that resounds with love.

We the Elohim of Love embrace this planetary home, this solar system and galaxy. But in this hour we concentrate forces of Love for the binding of the forces of anti-Love on earth to see what free men and women will do, aided and abetted by violet flame decreers, by Keepers of the Flame of Love who understand that if earth is to win, if earth is to have her Victory, Love must prevail.

Now and in every hour of thy day let this new Love of the Divine Mother fill all thy life, and let our Love embrace you and hold you tight that you do not stray from the purity of Love's message, vibration and Be-ness.

Gather ye, beloved, gather ye into your hearts all who need our Love. We say to you, each and every one, we will fill your cups daily with love, every chakra and chakra of the secret rays. The moment you empty out love to give to another, we shall fill the cup. Let us experiment together. Will you try it, beloved? ["Yes!"]

We are, in fact, most anxious to get started with this experiment accorded us by the Cosmic Council. It is for merit, beloved— meritorious love in service. If you have not given the full measure, do it now, for, beloved, never have you had in your evolution in these Matter spheres cohorts [such] as Elohim of Love to fill your cups with Love.

Remember, beloved, that in the marketplace of life those who are the subtle ones will attempt to steal your cups of Love. If you allow them to succeed, we shall no longer be allowed by cosmic law to fill again your cups with Love. Love is for the giving to Lightbearers and not to those who have squandered, denied and defiled Love. Thus, beloved, take care. Give to the God Flame in those who bear the God Flame and establish a network of Love upon the planet.

This is not an easy test, beloved, nor shall you find easy any test remaining in your course to the Sun. For this reason we have come from many angles to this conference, and all who shall speak have been selected that you might be fully and amply prepared to achieve your Victory and to do so with honors.

Give love and receive Love. Do not misqualify it and you shall increase in the pocket of an Elohim.[14]

O elfin ones and gnomes, O salamanders and undines, we have not left you out. Yours shall also be a path of Love's initiations and as you assist Keepers of the Flame you too shall earn your stripes. Those whom you, elementals, therefore serve who do attain the ascension, they shall in turn endow you with a threefold flame. Thus, elemental life [17-second applause], thus, elemental life, you who have attended [and tended] the sons and daughters of God, know, then, that for all of your giving and all of your service the hour draws nigh when those to whom you have given so much may turn and give to you what they have long desired to give.

Thus, beloved, if you have not thought of too many good reasons why you should take your ascension and make it secure, think upon this, that all elemental life upon this planet do attend the ascension of the sons of God, for only through your Victory may they also be endowed with a divine spark and eternal Life. And it is again by the power of resurrection's flame which you invoke this weekend that you shall establish the buoyancy and the increase whereby the resurrection can come to many more souls of Light and elementals.[15]

We are Elohim, sponsors of builders of form. The hierarchs of the elements[16] and all who serve under them are our obedient servants. When we give the word, then, and recommend their service to yourselves, I can assure you they come with a trust and even an innocence, though many have become cynical by mankind's own cynicism.

Beloved, you need elemental life to accomplish your goals and to be prepared. Thus, the rewards are mutual. May you find renewed joy in the cooperative oneness of angels, elementals with sons and daughters of God. This trinity is the unbeatable force of Divine Love in action.

Elohim have delivered a sufficiency of Love and we withdraw, for earth has reached the level of saturation until you yourselves increase the violet flame and the Astrea exorcisms.

It would be our desire to return in each quadrant of the year to increase this action. May the autumn equinox find you ready to receive us again. [intonations, 39 seconds]

This dictation by **Heros and Amora** was **delivered** by the Messenger Elizabeth Clare Prophet on **Thursday, June 30, 1988,** 10:37–11:21 p.m. MDT, at *FREEDOM 1988* in the Heart of the Inner Retreat at the **Royal Teton Ranch, Park County, Montana.** Available on 90-min. audiocassette B88097, $6.50 (add $.55 for postage); on 1½-hr. videocassette HP88061, with dictation by Kuan Yin, $19.95 (add $1.10 for postage). **[N.B.** Bracketed material denotes words spoken yet implicit in the dictation, added by the Messenger under Heros and Amora's direction for clarity in the written word.] **(1) Love casts out fear.** I John 4:18. **(2) New heaven and new earth.** Rev. 21:1. **(3)** El Morya and Kuthumi, 1988 *Pearls of Wisdom,* pp. 449–54, 455–62. **(4) Retreat of the Divine Mother.** 1988 *Pearls of Wisdom,* p. 260 n. 11. **(5) Etheric pattern of the New Jerusalem over the Inner Retreat.** 1981 *Pearls of Wisdom,* pp. 71, 323; 1985 *Pearls of Wisdom,* p. 63. See also 1985 *Pearls of Wisdom,* pp. 118–19, 379; 1986 *Pearls of Wisdom,* pp. 589–99. Rev. 21:2, 10–27. **(6)** being filled in with Ruby Ray development of the heart chakra and the Eighth Ray chakra (the secret chamber of the heart) by the four cardinal precepts of sacrifice, surrender, selflessness, and service, which are the key to balancing the threefold flame in the four quadrants, fire, air, water, earth, representing the four lower bodies: etheric, mental, emotional, physical. (For notes 7–16 see p. 480.)

Pearls of Wisdom®
published by The Summit Lighthouse

| Vol. 31 No. 61 | *Beloved Kuan Yin* | September 18, 1988 |

FREEDOM 1988

6

The Heart's Capacity for Love
A Message of Self-Transcendence by Love

In every beating heart of Keeper of the Flame I AM there. I am bathing with violet flame, giving the unguent of the Seventh Ray for the expansion of heart capacity, for life, for energy, for spirit—for Love.

The capacity of the heart, then, is our consideration as we the members of the Karmic Board and hierarchs of Aquarius gather to consider how in every direction we might add unto the stature of the soul and the inner Buddha.

Upon the brow let the image of Amitābha appear. Sons and daughters of the Buddha are ye. *Buddha,* indeed the name of God given unto his Sons who have so realized the bodhi of his enlightenment.

Hearts constricted where the room is narrow and the expanse of consciousness is not cannot contain the mind of Buddha, for the foundation of that mind is compassion. The lessons of life so key are the lessons of divine love, human love. Loving oneself may be the beginning, beloved, but let us understand, one must first love the True Self in order to appreciate the expression of the soul in the process of becoming that Self. One loves as love is and as love does become, even as the seed contains the full flower.

It is the narrowness of Love's expression, even in the field of religion itself, that therefore does so limit the individual's chalice of the mind of God. This is the primary concern of the Lords of Karma this day. For given these confining cups of consciousness, we are not able to project upon the graph even of the immediate future a major change in world thought.

So convinced are the people that their leaders in Church and State can be trusted, that they are right, that they know more than they do, that they [the people] have ceased to meditate within their hearts. And their teachers do not teach them, of course, that they might learn all things from the inner voice. Thus, though they think they are wise, they repeat only clichés, only what someone else has said, and somehow by the very repetition [they believe] it is so.

There is not the ability to discern or to dissect thought. There is not the ability objectively to ponder knowledge, to determine if that knowledge is empirical, if it is the fruit of experience or if it is only belief with no support or undergirding from those who ought to be the acknowledged authorities.

Surely the authorities are the Ascended Masters and the Great Lights and revolutionaries who have carried the God Flame. But instead it is as though it were two and a half million years ago, four million years ago, and only lately had the quasi-brilliance of fallen angels put upon an ignorant humanity, a gullible child-man, fictitious rules, regulations, interpretations, all designed to achieve an end: manipulation of behavior, population, and subservience to a class of individuals who have called themselves gods and expect to be treated royally.

I am well aware that I am addressing this day those who have come out of the grips of these very ones who have bound you for aeons. With you, then, we may proceed along the lines of independent thought. I am also well aware that I speak to those who have developed a heart flame, who have sensitivity to higher vibration, who know the difference between the vibration of a flying saucer and the living Gautama Buddha, those who understand the path of metallic mechanization man[1] throughout the universes and those who understand a path of discipleship that does lead unto that internalization of the God Flame. Few there be such as yourselves.

So note and so understand that with the getting of the understanding, there must be a corresponding confirmation by the inner experience of the heart. There is a mistaken idea, beloved, that the heart is always true, that the heart always knows. The heart is simply another organ and means of expression, and the heart chakra has also been polluted. Thus, you see, those momentums of human sympathy that are not the essence of the nectar of the divine compassion do lead one astray into incorrect decisions.[2]

Thus, one must call for the purification of the heart and do so diligently. And in the very next service that does provide opportunity we so desire to participate with you in Saint Germain's second heart meditation.[3] For, beloved, out of the heart are the issues of life.[4]

Consider, then, the twelve petals of the heart chakra as representing twelve hierarchies of the sun. Just as [it is] in your astrology and in your karma, so it is repeated in this heart that petal by petal there is the vibration of that remaining karma under each of those hierarchies and the remaining initiations which must be taken by your soul.[5] Thus, you see, the heart's expression can be no greater than the full expression of the soul in the present state of development.

Now, it is the threefold flame of your Holy Christ Self in balance and expanded that does give you the true and accurate heart reading that you ought to follow.[6] Thus, beloved ones, take care when making decisions to give the necessary ritual of invocations and prayers and decrees, writing your letters to the Karmic Board, who do afford you so very much support.

It is necessary to enter in, then, to the heart meditation whereby the human heart, with [its] human potential and level of evolution, is set aside and you do enter the heart of your Holy Christ Self. Then the question becomes, beloved, whether in your heart and soul and being, whether in your will you can decide to make a decision to live your life according to the standard and the wisdom of the Holy Christ Self, your True Self, or [whether] you will say, "It is too hard for me. I cannot adapt to this solution. After all, I am only human. Therefore I will live after my human planning while I think about this [for] a while or while I evolve."

Understand, beloved, that you will spend many rounds going round and round the petals of the heart chakra [but you will] not experience self-transcendence if you always choose the low road of present capacity rather than make your decisions based on the high road of anticipated and vowed attainment.

When you determine, then, that you will fill in the gap of the lesser manifestation by drawing down the fullness of your Christ Self, you will be able to live with the decisions you make wherein you compel yourself to reach far beyond your immediate grasp, knowing that you have the Holy Spirit as Teacher and Comforter, [that] you have the Christ Self as Minister and Rabbi, [that] you have the Mighty God Presence [who] does save you to the uttermost and therefore [does save you] to declare:

"I can and I shall and I *will*, by the grace of my Saviour, enter in, then, to those rooms of consciousness that will allow me to expand this narrow room and blossom and realize the fragrance of the bowers of my Tree of Life all full of pink blossoms in springtime."

Thus, beloved, there are some who will only decide* — [indeed they cannot do otherwise,] based on the immediacy of their own mechanization man— [at] the level to which they have achieved

*i.e., they will only make decisions

somewhat of a computerized order out of the chaos of [the human] creation itself. And thus they are very realistic. Homo sapiens has so become self-sufficient, aware of limitation, entirely tolerant of its condition, desire and needs and wants. Thus, the adaptability and adjustability to oneself is very complete.

Indeed, it is the initiates on the Path who are the ones who are discontent, who are the lonely ones, and who are never for a moment satisfied with their present condition. These expect and accept that situation as a given. They understand that life is an arduous climb and that life leading to the ascension, [the goal] toward which this conference is designed to prepare you, is life that must be lived like no ordinary life.

Knowing the goal, seeing the face of the Shining One above you, knowing of your brothers and sisters beyond, knowing that behind you is completion and that other worlds attend your coming, you can live with the idea that you are different from the norm of the evolution of the given planetary home where you have been residing.

Thus, their psychology is not yours. Their wisdom is not yours. What works for them will not work for you. In fact, you will be miserable, truly in misery if you desire to live as such as these. Blessed ones, all of us who have taken our leave of planet earth in the ritual of the ascension have recognized ourselves as misfits prior to our ascension. And so did our peers so recognize [us].

The wonder of Community, beloved, is that hearts with similar goals and determination may recognize in one another a friendship and a spirit of all ages. The road is not so lonely, although each one in his own heart is indeed alone with Sanat Kumara, with inner decisions, with the pains of letting go and perhaps the trepidation in embracing such a grand and noble sphere as the ultimate Presence of the Great White Brotherhood.

Know, then, beloved, that if you desire to span the gap between present attainment and possibility and future realization, you must take the steps forward before you are ready. If you are ready, it is too late. You have already passed [up] the initiation for which you are ready. To see the right, to know the right and to do the right *because* you believe that God the Father, God the Son, God the Holy Spirit and the Divine Mother will assist you in filling in that span of time and space between present and future accomplishment, this, then, is the secret of the wise ones.

I trust, then, that this explanation will resolve many a dilemma for you. I trust you will also come into the very clear understanding that this is the principle of the vow taken. Recognizing one's weaknesses, one's propensity to err, to go astray, to be less determined when the going gets tough than [one was] in the moment of decision, [then,] one does go before the altar of God. One does implore and say:

> O my God, if thou wilt have me, if thou wilt hold me, I desire to transcend this lesser self, especially in this area of my timidity, my withdrawnness, my failure to leap forward and seize a torch or a task that must be done. O God, in thy name and by thy grace, I vow to do and be better and to do now this thing. O Lord, help me. Help me to fulfill it.

Blessed ones, angel ministrants do come and they exist; for God has created them solely to reinforce the Word of the Son of God on earth! For they know the forces of the anti-Word that will assail that firm, resolute decision that one finds at the altar or in the mountain of God which tends to become diluted in the marketplace of illusions.

So, beloved, I will tell you what has impelled us to reach beyond our ability, and I speak of all the ascended hosts. It is because we saw a need so great and had such compassion for the one who had that need and saw that none other stood by to help that one, none other would come if we did not extend the hand. In that moment, beloved, Love itself supplied the intensity, the fire whereby we could leap to the rescue, to the side of [one in distress], or to enter some course of study that we might be proficient in knowledge that was needed.

This process, then, this love that could forget itself and leap to save a life, this, beloved, was the opening for the great fire of the Holy Spirit to enter the heart, to dissolve recalcitrance there, to melt the impediments to those twelve petals and their unique vibration, to take from us hardness of heart, physical encrustations, disease, fear, doubt, records of death. All of these could vanish in the ardor of service. And in our desiring to do well we attracted the forces of Nature and heaven to assist us in doing well. In our determination to be only God-victorious we attracted God-victory to ourselves.

Thus faint and trembling hearts, beloved, are so because they are weakened in their own self-concerns and self-pity. The strong heart, the virtuous heart, then, is born in that very process when all of God and all of life and all of soul and spirit within oneself simply leaps forward to rescue another part of life. Through the process of such initiation meted out to all as opportunity on the Path of the Ruby Ray, you mount the spiral from this plane to the plane of Holy Christ Selfhood. In so doing you create a magnet here below impelling the descent of your Christhood into this form. And so you walk the earth day by day with greater anointing.

Blessed ones, those who identify with their mortality and

their mortal selves and wants are not able to comprehend this message of transcendence. They are incapable of entering in. What, then, can they do to inherit immortal life? This I tell you, beloved, these require the religion of ritual. And if they can have an objective self-assessment and heed the ritual given by the great Gurus of all time, they may increase day by day and thus arrive at the point of sufficiency of heart development to leap to the next dimension of being.

These have profound need of the Master-disciple, or the Guru-chela, relationship. Many of these hearts participate actively, devoutly in the world's major religions today. And by consistency of service and devotion, even where so many truths are missing, they are forging a oneness with the Ascended Master of their choice or a saint or the Father himself; and therefore they can make progress.

Now, then, you take ancient souls who [have] come down [through the religious traditions of East and West], who have been through all of these religions, [who] know in their beings the teachings of the Brotherhood and therefore have considerable knowledge, those who mistake their knowledge for attainment— these have an inner rebellion against the living Word or the Presence of the Guru, for they know so much and they prefer an independence outside of any kind of commitment that might find them one day at the point of having to be obedient to one of our precepts of Love [spoken to them by one of our emissaries of Love] which would hamper their style, limit their self-expression.

Thus, this fear, fear of Love and Love's demand for obedi-ence unto the call of Love, does put many souls upon earth outside of the pale of one course of religion or another whereby they should make ongoing and steadfast progress. [They are] almost between two worlds, having been around too many gurus in the past, having fallen for the lie of the fallen angels that they knew more than those who have worn the crown of the bodhisattva.

Blessed ones, indeed this is a dilemma for the Lords of Karma. For no matter where we place these individuals in em-bodiment they manage to identify themselves as superior to others in things secular and spiritual. They consider simple religion, where there is much merit in devotion, [to be] childish and they consider that those who give obedience to such great hierarchs as Sanat Kumara, Jesus Christ, are in their beings at the level of not having the inner independence or the inner mastery to "be their own master." Thus, it is almost with pity that they look upon those [such as you] who cherish our words and seek to embody them.

I counsel you, then, beloved, for the sake of these as well as for the sake of the young souls in organized religion, that the path of your chelaship under the Ascended Masters so evince to the world the peace, the equanimity, the simplicity, the humility and [the] levels of self-mastery, [with] kindness abounding, deep concern and care for others and [that] wisdom which when spoken is literally charged with our Presence and our Holy Spirit that they become encouraged and desirous by your example to know the intimate love of this Guru-chela relationship.

To see in your lives such peace and happiness, such profound love that you have with an Ascended Master, this as example is the final way that we can see to woo the Lightbearers away from their human consciousness and into a path that will prove to them profitable day by day for their soul's liberation.

The complexities of the psychology of this planet are many. Be grateful that you [as chelas of the Ascended Masters] share a common light, a common body of gnosis, that you have common goals, see eye to eye. You may look around you [in this Community] and see many individuals who in the normal course of living you may never have met nor whose acquaintance you might seek. [Therefore,] we desire to see tremendous love and understanding between all types of people, [a mutual love and understanding that is] born out of the gratitude which is the flame of the Goddess of Liberty, wherein you have such appreciation for fellow disciples on the Path who can share and know and understand your trials, your triumphs, burdens and sorrows and the true joy of the divine encounter.

Few there be to whom you can relate [in] such joy. [Cherish them. Cherish one another.]

Therefore, this Community of the Holy Spirit, of the Lightbearers of the world must be strengthened by Love, united by Love, one through Love. For you collectively must face together in your day and [in your] time every encroachment that the world could raise against the path of the Great White Brotherhood, which does represent the confluence of all other streams and paths and is the open door to the ascension and the balance of karma as it has been taught for this age of Aquarius. [It is true that] many have teachings that were relevant centuries ago [and are still relevant, but not all; however,] they do not have the superseding, intervening dispensations [which are absolutely indispensable to your victory in this age and to the victory of planet earth in the Aquarian dispensation].

Considering, then, that the seven o'clock line [of the Cosmic Clock], which is the position of the Goddess of Liberty and the Lords of Karma, which is the position of this flame of God-gratitude, is also the step wherein you enter the initiations of the five secret rays of the Dhyāni Buddhas, realize that gratitude itself is the key to the leap for Love. Thus, beloved, you might say that yours is the path of "lover's leap" and that leap into the highest potential of the Holy Christ Self.

May you be goaded by my message, which I convey to you with all tenderness and love. The love which the ascended Hierarchy does feel for this Community worldwide is accentuated by the very contrast of this Community and our love to the Darkness and dire forebodings that one sees everywhere upon the planet.

Most beloved, I am grateful for the release at this conference of three rosaries, three cassettes which are designed to be given by you in any measure, in any segment.[7] Any portion of these tapes that you might recite daily will be received by me with full gratitude and the complement of gratitude of all of the Lords of Karma, for thereby you give us entrée into all the world, not only of Lightbearers but truly of a suffering humanity.

I rejoice to be with you on the way and I rejoice that the children of the Far East might receive these tapes by your means as quickly as possible. Blessed ones, so many are profoundly devout, one with the heart of Buddha and myself. They need the fresh breath of Aquarius. They need these mantras. They are burdened by the regimes and the wars that have torn through the East.

O beloved heart, think of Vietnam, Cambodia and the records of Mother China even in the last fifty years. Blessed hearts, one cannot even contain the conception of the awful murder, the desecration of war upon these peoples. It is indeed the force of anti-Buddha moving against them.

These blessed hearts, these sweet souls, many of whom you have become acquainted with in the cities of the West where they have migrated, have such a tenderness for me and my flame. They have such strength and ability to self-discipline and self-efface that where so many in the West, surfeited in their materialism, their pleasure, their egocentricity, will pass by this offering, it is these sweet hearts of the East who shall embrace it. And thus you will find that the cosmic reinforcements who shall champion the cause of the Great White Brotherhood will be [called out] from among them.

The very sound of the mantra and your determined effort to chant in Chinese shall be, I promise you, the bond of love and of mutual respect that shall be the sign unto them that you do respect their culture, their religion, their gods and therefore themselves. From nowhere else in the West does there come such a sense of allegiance and reverence for the peoples of the East than in your very chanting of my mantras and vows.

Know this, then, beloved, that there is a world of Lightbearers unreached and untapped. As all become one you shall see that no longer shall the fallen ones in Church or State dominate the comings and goings of the people of God in any nation, their right to be free, to worship as they choose, to speak what they think, to enjoy whatever patch of earth they call their private property, to assemble together without fear or threat, and to publish what is dearest to their hearts and spread it abroad in the land.

The free movement of the ideas of God in man and man's own ideas shall give to the world the freedom to choose to be or not to be on the path of the bodhisattvas. This is all that I ask, that people shall be free in conscience, in education, in outlook to examine, to consider, to say yea, to say nay, but to decide from the wellspring of fire from within rather than from timeworn tradition that is simply a mere repetition of words.

My beloved, I thank you in this hour for assisting me to assist Saint Germain and the bringing in of the age of Aquarius. I can assure you that all Ascended Masters wait, as it were, with bated breath for the dictations of Gautama Buddha, of Alpha and Omega.

So, beloved, in this hour I seal you from my heart with a concentrated elixir of the violet flame. This energy is so intense that I desire you to memorize and visualize the color of this sari worn[8] so that you might see and visualize this elixir concentrated in your physical heart and in the secret chamber of your heart for healing by transmutation.

With the sign of the Dhyāni Buddhas, of Sanat Kumara, Lord Gautama, Lord Maitreya, I am and I remain forever Kuan Yin, your Mediatrix of Mercy's Flame.

"The Summit Lighthouse Sheds Its Radiance O'er All the World to Manifest as Pearls of Wisdom." This dictation by **Kuan Yin** was **delivered** by the Messenger of the Great White Brotherhood Elizabeth Clare Prophet on **Friday, July 1, 1988,** 1:21–2:02 p.m. MDT, at *FREEDOM 1988* in the Heart of the Inner Retreat at the **Royal Teton Ranch, Park County, Montana.** "Darshan and Dictation with Kuan Yin and Members of the Karmic Board: Teachings on the Kuan Yin Mantras and the Power of the Spoken Word to Effect World Change through Kuan Yin's Crystal Rosary" on two 90-min. audiocassettes, B88097–98, $13.00 (add $.95 for postage); dictation included with that of Heros and Amora on 90-min. videocassette HP88061, $19.95 (add $1.10 for postage). [**N.B.** Bracketed material denotes words unspoken yet implicit in the dictation, added by the Messenger under Kuan Yin's direction for clarity in the written word.] (1) The Great Divine Director, **"The Mechanization Concept,"** in 1965 *Pearls of Wisdom,* pp. 9–142; *The Soulless One.* (2) Human loves and attachments mistakenly interpreted as divine love fail to provide a foundation for right mindfulness hence correct decisions. (3) The Messenger delivered **Saint Germain's Heart Meditation II** on July 10, 1988, in the Heart of the Inner Retreat. This "self-clearance" of the heart chakra included visualizations, songs, mantras and decrees as well as invocations by the Messenger for the freeing of the heart chakra of all burdens and obstacles to the expansion of the threefold flame. Saint Germain's Heart Meditation I, 1988 *Pearls of Wisdom,* p. 339 n. 6. (4) Prov. 4:23. (5) On June 29, 1988, during *FREEDOM 1988,* the Messenger conducted an all-day **"Seminar on the Cosmic Clock:** Charting the Cycles of Your Karma, Psychology and Spiritual Powers on the Cosmic Clock." She gave basic and advanced instruction on the Cosmic Clock, a review of Lord Maitreya's teachings on making calls on one's astrology for survival and self-mastery in the age of Aquarius, and explained how to give invocations for the transmutation of negative astrology. 4 audiocassettes, 5 hr. 50 min., A88087, $26.00 (add $.95 for postage). Accompanying packet of study tools: Diagrams of the Cosmic Clock; work sheet with Cosmic Clock for individual charting of cycles; Traditional Astrological Information; sample Natal, Heliocentric, Progressed and Solar Return Charts; Summit University Astrology Insert and Aspect Calls; and Lord Maitreya's March 24, 1985 dictation, "Astrology for Twin Flames"; #2368, $2.00 (add $.65 for postage). See also Elizabeth Clare Prophet, "The Cosmic Clock: Psychology for the Aquarian Man and Woman," in *The Great White Brotherhood in the Culture, History and Religion of America,* pp. 173–206; *The ABC's of Your Psychology on the Cosmic Clock,* 8-audiocassette album, 12 lectures, 12 hr., A85056. (**6**) See "Balance the Threefold Flame in Me," no. 213 in *The Healing Power of Angels* booklet. (**7**) On July 4, 1988, the Messenger announced the release of **Kuan Yin's Crystal Rosary:** *Devotions to the Divine Mother East and West,* 3-audiocassette album of prayers, ancient Chinese mantras, songs and decrees (see 1988 *Pearls of Wisdom,* p. 373 n. 13); includes 40-page booklet of the words to the rosary with the translation and transliteration of the mantras, the history of Kuan Yin's ancient and modern role as saviouress, and teachings from Kuan Yin's recent dictations delivered through Elizabeth Clare Prophet. (**8**) The Messenger wore a rich, deep violet-colored sari with a design of gold thread woven throughout.

Notes from Pearl no. 60 by Heros and Amora continued:
(**7**) **Manchild.** The Christ Child aborning in the heart and those souls who are born as Christed ones, having already undergone in a previous life the initiation of the alchemical marriage—i.e., the fusion of the soul with the Holy Christ Self through the Path of the Ruby Ray; a holy child who has received the Holy Spirit in his/her mother's womb. (**8**) *Save the World with Violet Flame! by Saint Germain 1, 2, 3* and *4* audiocassettes @ $5.95 (add $.65 each for postage); any combination of cassettes in quantities of ten or more @ $2.95 (add $.15 each for postage). 1988 *Pearls of Wisdom,* pp. 400 n. 6, 408 n. 11. (**9**) **Whosoever offend one of these little ones.** Matt. 18:6; Mark 9:42; Luke 17:2. **Blasphemy against the Holy Ghost.** Matt. 12:31, 32; Mark 3:28, 29. (**10**) Og Mandino, *The Greatest Salesman in the World* (New York: Bantam Books, 1968), available through Summit University Press, $3.50 (add $.50 for postage). (**11**) A 5-foot 3-inch golden **statue of Kuan Yin** stood on the altar in the main tent at the Heart of the Inner Retreat throughout *FREEDOM 1988.* With her left hand Kuan Yin is pouring a stream of liquid from a vase, traditionally symbolizing her willingness to give to all who call upon her the water of Life, the nectar of wisdom and compassion. In her right hand she holds a willow branch, representing her power of healing. The willow branch has been a symbol of healing in China since the third century B.C. The Chinese believe that a willow branch placed in clear water will keep away evil spirits. Kuan Yin is wearing necklaces, which denote her attainment as a bodhisattva, as well as a rosary with which she calls upon the Buddhas for succor. The small child standing to her left signifies that she is the protector and bestower of children. In Taiwan it is also believed that Kuan Yin is depicted with a baby because she was a mother in one of her embodiments. Kuan Yin is standing on a dragon, which symbolizes either China and the divine lineage of the Chinese people as "seeds of the dragon" or the elements of the lesser self over which Kuan Yin takes dominion. In China the image of a dragon represents royalty, power and the supreme God or, in the case of serpentlike, evil dragons, passion and the lower elements of self. This statue of Kuan Yin is now on the altar in King Arthur's Court at the Royal Teton Ranch. (**12**) **Kuan Yin's Crystal Rosary.** 1988 *Pearls of Wisdom,* p. 373 n. 13. (**13**) **Kuan Yin as an emanation of Amitābha.** 1988 *Pearls of Wisdom,* p. 215 n. 1. (**14**) **Pocket of an Elohim.** Hercules, 1987 *Pearls of Wisdom,* pp. 444–45. (**15**) **Jesus' gift of resurrection flame to elemental life.** In his March 29, 1964 dictation, Jesus announced that "the cycles of Nature,... lowered into manifestation through the elementals, are endowed with my momentum of the flame of resurrection this day, that from this day forward the elementals shall never again have the sense of death." El Morya explained in his April 10, 1964 Pearl of Wisdom that although the flame which Jesus had imparted did not confer immortality upon the elementals, "the elementals—feeling now a lesser measure of humanity's discordant vibrations—will be able to express more God-happiness, which, it is our hope, will in turn be communicated to mankind." Mark L. Prophet and Elizabeth Clare Prophet, *Climb the Highest Mountain,* 2d ed., pp. 464–68; cassette B8116, $6.50 (add $.55 for postage). (**16**) **Hierarchs of the Nature kingdom,** the elements they govern, and the elemental beings who serve with them: Oromasis and Diana, fire element, salamanders; Aries and Thor, air, sylphs; Neptune and Luara, water, undines; Virgo and Pelleur, earth, gnomes.

Pearls of Wisdom®
published by The Summit Lighthouse

| *Vol. 31 No. 62* | *Beloved Goddess of Liberty* | *September 24, 1988* |

FREEDOM 1988
7
My Gift of
A Cosmic Threefold Flame of Liberty
to counteract
Damocles' Sword: Aliens in Their Spacecraft

In the heart flame of Liberty I greet each one out of the Cosmic Silence whence I have descended in this hour to establish in the earth an intense coil of Liberty Flame.

I come, then, to pluck Liberty Flames with which I have endowed your hearts as citizens of a cosmos. As crocuses they are plucked to become part of this investiture of a planet with a Cosmic Threefold Flame. It is this flame that I have drawn forth for many aeons and I am here to tell you, beloved, in the living flame of the Goddess of Liberty whose office I bear, who I AM THAT I AM, that the moment has come wherein by the edict of the Almighty One I might implant in this earth a Cosmic Three-fold Flame of Liberty.

Blessed hearts, not without tears in my eyes do I approach this land, O the Pure Land of the mighty Buddhas![1] Thus I come and in this wilderness so sealed, there is so sealed now my flame, a flame greater than I, yet a flame which I contain. This, then, has been the subject of my extended period in the Great Silence. Happy are ye who have kept my flame in my seeming absence. Blessed ones, O receive in joy my gift. [27-second applause]

For the duration of these dictations your flames are part of my own and when they are once again focused in the chalice of your heart you shall find that the very aura and Great Central Sun Magnet of the Threefold Flame of Liberty does provide you with a strength and a protection, a magnification and a magnet wherewith to continue to draw upon this flame, [and] in so doing [to] increase thereby your own [Threefold Flame, that you may] also return ["thy radiance"] to this [Cosmic Threefold] Flame [of Liberty] whereby it may grow by your own cosmic consciousness. Thus, beloved, I do come representing not alone the Karmic Board but the Cosmic Hierarchy.

I come, then, to speak to you concerning those things that have been on the earth, that are on the earth, that are coming on the earth and yet which have been kept from the conscious awareness of many. It was I who directed the Messenger to bring to you [the] speakers of last evening concerning the phenomenon of aliens moving in and about and through this planet to the detriment of life.[2]

Blessed hearts, let it be known, then, that the founding life-streams of this organization, those who have kept the flame of purity for many, many years and those who come recently, indeed Keepers of the Flame and Lightbearers of the world, have come of age now to understand fully in your waking consciousness that which hangs as Damocles' sword above your heads.

And I speak not of nuclear war but of spacecraft and those who do not consider the value of life in any form but rather [consider] this life of this planet as expendable and as a means to their ends, even as a laboratory of experimentation. You well understand that even were there to be in existence today in hand and ready for use all technologies whereby to defend a planet from an alien invasion, the holocaust of such an eventuality should be ultimately almost more than the psyche could bear.

Therefore, beloved, it is necessary to bring [certain facts] to the attention of those who have now been given all of the necessary tools of invocation wherewith to deal with any and all forces whatsoever that may be anti-God or anti-Life in the physical universes. It is a question, then, of exercising that domain and [that] dominion of the science of the Word. Thus I come to you to pierce certain layers of illusion and density and sleepfulness into which some of our best servants sometimes fall.

Blessed hearts, the Messengers have borne the burden of the awareness of these goings-on for many, many years but it has been the election of the Karmic Board not to bring upon Keepers of the Flame a fear with which they were not prepared to deal. This hour is long past and the Lightbearers of earth must come of age and take their responsibility to defend Life and Freedom and the Liberty Flame.

Without Liberty there is no life worth living—there is no life, period. Understand, therefore, that whereas the Messengers have indeed held the balance for you in these matters of alien interference with your chelaship and your lives, the hour is and has come and is manifest now through this Cosmic Threefold Flame [of Liberty which] I have placed here that each and every one of you must take equal responsibility under the mantle of the Messengers to defend life, beginning with yourselves, your immediate families and all Lightbearers for whom you have care and concern universally on this planet and in worlds beyond.

Blessed ones, I repeat the law, for the book I hold is the [Book of the] Law, the law which states, therefore, that unless a flame is invoked into these dense layers once in each twenty-four-hour cycle, that flame tends to rise. A balancing factor to this law is the ability of the individual to maintain such a God-harmony and constancy and white-fire shaft of oneness with God that by attainment that flame is held here below.

In telling you this fact, I already understand that some [of you] will assume an attainment you do not have, and therefore I counsel you, never assume an attainment but rather reinforce it and let the Law itself provide you with a confirmation of the presence of that light. You will never be hurt by a redundancy of application but you may find yourselves in a highly compromised position by having too penurious an offering [before] our altar of Liberty.

The altar of Liberty is in your heart. It is in the secret chamber of the heart. Life is hallowed where you are. You have naught to do with the race of mechanization man and the godless and the feelingless and the heartless who have succeeded in existing by borrowing the science of the Divine Mother and of Sanat Kumara; and yet I tell you, their days of the misuse of that science are indeed numbered.

We desire to see you outnumber them one per one and the allness of the One outnumbering all of the many parts of manifestation. We desire to see you outnumber them in years, in staying power, in occupying this Matter cosmos until the Light that you invoke does confirm a judgment already rendered by the Cosmic Council upon these beings for their violation of space and of time and of sacred body temple and of souls.[3]

Inasmuch as they have done it unto the least of these my brethren, the Keepers of the Flame of planet earth, so they have done it unto me![4] I declare this day, then, the karma is tenfold upon them, not for their violation of humanity but for their equivalency in the violation of my Office and my Being and my Flame as I stand the Cosmic Mother of this humanity and of these Lightbearers of the

Sun. Thus, as they have done it unto one, so it shall be counted unto them that they have done it unto me tenfold. For I AM that Life and I AM that Threefold Flame of Liberty within every beating heart.

Blessed ones, inasmuch as a judgment has already been rendered, it does require but the ratification and confirmation *daily* by Keepers of the Flame. These violators of the genetic seed of the Christed ones of earth must not be allowed to tamper with, to borrow that sacred fire and thus perpetuate for aeons their robotic creation by even a microscopic portion of the Liberty Flame which itself is a part of the genetic code of the Lightbearers.

Understand therefore, beloved, something that not all have considered. When dictation after dictation does find us declaring to you the judgment of certain conditions in the earth, this is the "green light" whereby you stand and make that call and ratify that judgment for your home, your place on earth, your town, city, nation and solar system.

You must as a son of God confirm the just and the righteous judgments of the LORD which we declare; and if you desire to anchor them truly, you will replay those dictations in your very home, that the resonance and the magnification of the original Word with Brahman, Who is the true Judge, does pass through you and through your own voice as you may choose to copy down and recite the very words of the judgment and give them as decrees with that tape recording.

It is most essential that you understand that Keepers of the Flame are inviolate before these aliens when you are clothed upon with our mantle, our Electronic Presence; and that Electronic Presence is always focused through the spoken Word.

As you place your attention upon me now, beloved, I AM instantaneously surrounding you with the fullness of my Being. And as I revealed myself to this Messenger [during] these hours, so you must understand that the immensity of the Cosmic Being that I AM is [seen to be], as it were, a giant manifestation of myself within this Heart [of the Inner Retreat] so that the Messenger should find herself standing within my Electronic Presence measuring, as it were, but a few inches from the ground into my garment.

Know, then, beloved, that the immensity of my Being in this earth, in this Heart and around you is indeed a sufficiency of cosmic defense against all that would assail your Godhood—your Cosmic Motherhood and Fatherhood and Christhood now!

But you must remember that what establishes this Light *physically* is the science of the spoken Word, the prayer, the devotion, the imploring, the love, the desire to be myself in form or to be one of the other hierarchs and Cosmic Beings in manifestation—the desire that is then *spoken* by love in mantra, in God-determination to keep the Flame and to recognize what folly [it is] to stray from the central altar of this Community in search of other pastures and wider fields, supposedly of freedom.

There is no freedom without the Flame of Liberty. There is no freedom unless that freedom to be, to breathe, to know, to experience the divinity within be sealed by an absolute cosmic protection spiritually, mentally, emotionally, in the desire body and in the chakras!

Not out of fear do you run to the Cosmic Mother but out of the profound love of which Kuan Yin spoke to you,[5] that in seeing the need, *the planetary need for spiritual protection,* you come to my heart that I might multiply your every breath for freedom and that we might together so establish a spiritual forcefield on this planet that not a single Lightbearer should ever again be violated by these fallen ones and their mechanization man.

Precious ones of the Light, therefore consider, consider as you have heard [and seen] scene after scene* and as you may read and ought to read to be certain that you do not forget this threat against human life, that those who are taken [by aliens into their spacecraft] are taken as though by a thief in the night that does come suddenly to paralyze the form they wear and to do what manner of darkness and dastardly deed they have contemplated.

Blessed ones, it is indeed a terror of the unknown. But I ask you, is the torture, the evil that is practiced in the world of Communism against captives, is this evil any worse? In some cases it is far more brutal and cruel. [Yet,] these things have been accepted as givens.

[Now,] you do not see tens of thousands coming to this Heart of the Inner Retreat this summer though the call has gone forth. [And] in [the] face of the world atrocities that have been carried on throughout this century through World Communism, you do not see the whole nation in a fever pitch demanding that there be a cessation of the violation of human rights East and West.

In other words, beloved, my point is this: the hour can come, and it can come quicker than you think, that you and others may also be lulled to the threat of aliens. And are not those [nations] who per-form these atrocities and brutalities upon their prisoners and their own people, are they not originally aliens themselves, aliens to the Light, aliens to the Universal Christ? There is no vying for brutality when it comes to the records of evil upon this planet or any other.

Thus, as Saint Germain declared to the Messengers long ago

*in slides, documents and film clips at the Summit University Forum on "The UFO Connection: Alien Spacecraft and Government Secrecy" in Colorado Springs, just because you have recently found out concerning the surveillance techniques of these fallen ones, of the governments of the earth and of aliens, just because you have recently found out that their genetic manipulation has been ongoing for hundreds of thousands of years does not mean that you should have any greater anxiety or fear today than you did yesterday when your outer mind was in blissful ignorance, for you have also known these things at inner levels.

And so, blessed ones, the lesson to be learned from that which was discussed last evening, which I might say was but the tip of the iceberg, is this: not to enter into an initial shock and [a] reaction of a certain militancy in terms of invoking the Light and the action of the Seven Archangels, only to trail off little by little, distancing oneself from contact with the initial shock levels.

It is essential that a body of Lightbearers upon earth have the will, the spine, the courage, and the guts, *yes, I say the guts,* to stick with the Path and to understand that some must with constancy on a twenty-four-hour basis in rotation keep this flame of protection from every form of assailant against the [Cosmic] Threefold Flame of Liberty and the ultimate victory of a planet.

You shall hear spoken to you the message of Lord Gautama, of Alpha and Omega, the Holy Kumaras. Blessed ones, the element that has been introduced that is the element of hope is a new fervor among some old Keepers of the Flame and a wondrous new fervor among those recently come to our ranks.

On the downside, as you would say, among some who have had this flame even for several decades there is still the failure to self-correct when it does come to criticism and condemnation and judgment whether of our Messengers, whether of our staff or our Community or whether of our own policies, though these may be criticized when carried out by others. There are some who will not bridle the tongue, who yet carry on their gossip and their maligning and their picking apart of the threads of the fabric of a wondrous teaching, to pull those threads that they approve of and to remove others that they do not approve of.

Thus, as it has been on other planetary systems, if those who would receive the cup of freedom given would retain it and retain the strength of this elixir undiluted, we should see pillars of fire springing up where'er they walk and that very spiritual presence on the earth put in doubt any contemplated attempts by aliens or those on the planet in this hour to move too far against the divine plan of Liberty for the earth. Where there are no physical defenses, beloved, it must be the hearts of those of freedom who are so intense and whose intensity does attract so many angels that the hosts of darkness truly fear to carry out their Armageddon. I will tell you, then, that the authority is in the mantle worn by the embodied and ascended Messengers, who are your beloved Prophets, to challenge, bind, and turn back and bring the judgment to all alien forces, whether coming in their craft or who have been on this planet for thousands of years. If you will call for that mantle upon you, beloved, you will know that by the authority of the mantle of the Prophets and in our name and by the judgments rendered by God you may daily counteract and cause the removal of those alien forces.

This, then, I come to tell you to do. I may say [to you that] you must do it but I shall say instead: If you desire to achieve victory and fulfill the cause to which you came to this planet, you must do it. And thereby in that statement I leave to you your free will to decide if you will fulfill the requirements of your personal dharma* and your reason for being.

Finally, then, what I would unveil to you is that you are not natives of this earth and one and all came for this purpose: to keep the Flame in the hour when such aliens of the Light should move against the children of the Sun and [the children of the Sun should] require *you* as defenders. It is to this moment of your physical and mental recognition of the threat [of aliens] that Jesus, the beloved Son of God, and Saint Germain have prepared you in the past year and that our dictations have prepared you for many a year.

You have been called to your ascension, called to be the Christ, to be Shepherds. You have been called to magnetize ten thousand Keepers of the Flame.[6] May you [now] understand how a Body of God and Light—*you* the Mystical Body of God, of holy Church—have conspired in the Holy Spirit at inner levels long ago with our Lord Gautama and Sanat Kumara to be here and now ready in this day and age to be equipped with the armour of Light and Community and oneness and one-pointedness, setting all other things aside for this one commitment:

To keep the Flame of Cosmic Liberty upon earth until cosmic reinforcements should come by the very magnet of your being, to keep the Flame of Cosmic Liberty on earth on behalf of those of lesser evolution who could not stand in the day of the enemy's appearing.

In the many thousands of years that you have tarried here, other tributaries of lesser goals have vied for your energy. Thus,

*dharma [Sanskrit]: in this context, duty; conduct or way of life appropriate to or mandated by one's essential nature; one's duty to fulfill the Christ potential, the inner Bodhi, through the sacred labor.

today your energy fills many pots, many causes and purposes and endeavors you are engaged in.

There is a certain quotient of light [which flows from your Mighty I AM Presence] over the crystal cord [to keep the Threefold Flame of Liberty that burns on the altar of your heart]. [But this quotient of light] does not increase until you increase the Cosmic Christ consciousness of Liberty through the Threefold Flame of your heart. Thus, like the spigot of water, only so much may pass through at a time and in a given day. Wherever you direct portions of that energy, you have a little bit less for this assignment.

As wise investors, consider, then, how you shall take of this crystal-clear stream, how you shall direct it; and know that *the preservation of life in sanity and on the path of spiritual oneness with God is the most important reason for being.* All other daily activities must support you in this goal. All other activities unessential that do not lead to this goal ought to be dispensed with.

May you find yourself in my heart this day in meditation upon being a Cosmic Mother, a Cosmic Father of the Threefold Flame of Liberty unto the evolutions of Light of this earth and beyond.

I have stood for you for aeons, beloved, my torch raised high. With all the fervor of my Being, having come from the depths of Nirvana, I pass to you a torch of Liberty which is Cosmic Christ Illumination multiplied by Love, multiplied by Power, squared by the Purity of the Divine Mother.

May you endure to the end. May you be God-victorious in Cosmic Liberty that I AM THAT I AM! [1-minute 2-second standing ovation]

This dictation by the **Goddess of Liberty** was **delivered** by the Messenger of the Great White Brotherhood Elizabeth Clare Prophet on **Saturday, July 2, 1988,** 11:59 a.m.–12:34 p.m. MDT, at *FREEDOM 1988* in the Heart of the Inner Retreat at the **Royal Teton Ranch, Park County, Montana.** "Darshan, Dictations and Secret-Ray Initiations with Mighty Cosmos and the Goddess of Liberty" on 81-min. audiocassette B88099, $6.50 (add $.55 for postage); dictation of the Goddess of Liberty with those of Mighty Cosmos, Serapis Bey, Archangels Gabriel and Michael on 2-hr. videocassette HP88068, $29.95 (add $1.10 for postage), available October 3. [**N.B.** Bracketed material denotes words unspoken yet implicit in the dictation, added by the Messenger under the Goddess of Liberty's direction for clarity in the written word.] (1) A **Pure Land** or Pure Buddha Land in Buddhist theology is a spiritual realm or paradise presided over by a Buddha where conditions are ideally suited to the attainment of enlightenment. The most famous of these is Sukhāvatī ("Pure Land" or "Happy Land"), the Western Paradise of the Buddha Amitābha, who is assisted by the bodhisattva Avalokiteśvara (Kuan Yin) and Mahāsthāmaprāpta. One sutra (discourse of the Buddha) records that when Amitābha was a bodhisattva, out of great compassion for all sentient beings he vowed to become a Buddha if those who faithfully invoked his name would be reborn in such a paradise (according to another version of this sutra, the faithful are also required to live by certain precepts and perform good deeds in order to be reborn there). The Pure Land is described in Buddhist writings as a beautiful abode, rich and fertile, inhabited by gods and men; it is devoid of all pain or sin as well as of the problems of everyday existence and its inhabitants are free to pursue the teachings of the Buddha. Once someone is reborn in Amitābha's Western Paradise, it is believed that he is destined to attain Buddhahood under the tutelage of Amitābha and his bodhisattvas, even if it takes millions of years. The Pure Land school of Buddhism, whose adherents look toward rebirth in the Pure Land through the efficacy of Amitābha, has become one of the most popular forms of Mahāyāna Buddhism in China and Japan. (For notes 2–6, see Pearl no. 63.)

Pearls of Wisdom®
published by The Summit Lighthouse

| Vol. 31 No. 63 | Beloved Mighty Cosmos | September 25, 1988 |

FREEDOM 1988

8

The Sword of Mighty Cosmos
Intercessor Before the Five Dhyāni Buddhas

I AM Mighty Cosmos. Out of the rings of fire surrounding the Central Sun I descend. My sword is a sword that does divide the Real from the Unreal in the cosmic secret-ray manifestation of thy life. I come because you have need of me, even as Sanat Kumara does come for your need.[1]

I come, therefore, standing on the six o'clock line of your individual Cosmic Clock, and I direct your attention toward the reality which I now reveal to you, that for many the difficulty to move beyond the first seven rays[2] into the initiations of the Eighth Ray and [of] the Eighth Ray chakra, [which is] the secret chamber of the heart, has been and remains an insurmountable difficulty.

I come, therefore, wielding this sword[3] for the binding of those barriers self-imposed [as well as those] superimposed by fallen angels, all of whom are alien to the mansions of God. This stumbling block, therefore, between that [six o'clock] line and the entering in [by the sons and daughters of God] to the center of Being by means of the eightfold, eight-petaled chakra must be removed by Divine Intercession.

I AM that Intercessor by the grace of God.

Now manifesting with me you see suspended Five Dhyāni Buddhas—[five] Buddhas bearing [sacred] fire of secret ray, Buddhas wielding sword of secret ray. Therefore, beloved, they stand and wait as initiators at the half hours of seven, eight, nine, ten and eleven [on the Cosmic Clock].[4]

Make thy peace with the Cosmic Virgin in the heart of the Goddess of Liberty, Mother Mary, Kuan Yin and so [with] others of our bands who represent the Feminine God and others who represent the Masculine Ray in [their] adoration and therefore [their] Self-realization, of the Mother.

O come forth, thou prince, it is thy hour of incarnation!
Come forth, O prince, for thy hour is come!

Thus I call to earth a soul destined for the divine calling of embodying, then, such Motherhood of God as to embrace the five secret rays on behalf of ye all, a soul who has volunteered solely because you have need.

Is the sacrifice too hard, beloved, for you who are in embodiment to recognize the needs of other Lightbearers and to give a life that is lawful and needful to give because of your karma? ["No."]

Think, then, beloved, [that] for want of this givingness a soul of Light descends from heaven having no karma compelling that one but only the desire to love you and to be in your midst that Presence of the Intercessor which I AM, for it is needful to have such an one in physical incarnation surely in addition to the Messenger. For surely you should not desire to see the short-circuiting of the cosmic circuits in the body of the Messenger for the necessity of containing so much Light* to compensate for your neglect.

Thus, beloved, some do elect to descend for the "very love of thee"⁵ even when you do not love yourselves enough, even when you, so loved by Hierarchy, begin to take for granted all protection and graces and dispensations almost as spoiled children, forgetting that all that we do, we do as demonstration that you might see an example and say, "This must I be. This must I become. Thus, I will relieve a cosmic one and be in the earth a flame, perhaps not a cosmic flame today or tomorrow but 'the third day' I shall surely be that cosmic flame."⁶

Blessed ones, when you call for my secret rays you may also call for my cosmic flames:

Flames of secret rays in the hearts of Dhyāni Buddhas, reveal thyself! And therefore, Flames, consume the force of anti-Desire† that should‡ in the untransmuted self repel rather than attract thy manifestation.

I shudder to think what life should be upon this planet without Hierarchy and without yourselves. And I rejoice to think, as does every hierarch, just what life can be in its fullest sense when you come to that *awakening,* that *awakening,* that *awakening* of Lord Gautama Buddha, the *full* awakening to the *full* spiritual potential to be God and cease your denial of that manifestation in your Messenger or yourself or in anyone who is a Keeper of the Flame of God!

---

*Light: the Universal Christ Consciousness and the light-emanation thereof   †anti-God Desire
‡archaic: might, could

O blessed hearts, outside of the centeredness of Mighty Cosmos' consciousness you do not have a co-measurement of just how much self-limitation you confine yourselves to until some of you are so boxed in that you can scarcely be effective in a given day's opportunity for life.

Now, therefore, *piercing* through, *quickening* conscience, I come. For this sword must descend now to take from you the block between the six o'clock line and the six-thirty line and the six-thirty passageway [through the heart of Padma Sambhava] to the center of your Cosmic Clock.

I give you a moment to make your peace with your God and to whisper the prayer of surrender as to what I, Mighty Cosmos, may be allowed by your free will to deliver you of, specifically at that point of the secret[-ray] entrance to the Eightfold Path and [the secret] chamber [of the heart]. [personal prayers offered; intonations by the Master]

It is done. Sword of Mighty Cosmos, angel of Mighty Cosmos, perform thy work! The Light has shot forth. Therefore, none who have so received my cosmic ministration may ever claim ignorance or inability to embrace Eightfold Path of Divine Wholeness.

I raise my sword and I say: from this hour on know thy accountability to pursue thy Godhood for the one and the many; and if the tempter should ever tempt you again to believe you have no need of Community, Guru or Teaching, remember thus and so say it:

Even if I have all attainment of Cosmos, I have need to serve for the sake of mine own humility and inner integration with God. Therefore, thou shalt not tempt me with spiritual pride nor with its opposite, worthlessness, loss of self-esteem.

My [real] self is the God Self, needing and having no other. I AM the bride of Cosmos. My veil is a veil of Cosmos' secret rays embroidered by Five Dhyāni Buddhas of my heart, God's heart. Therefore, I shall serve, for God in me and in all hath need of my living flame of Cosmic Christ service.

In the name of Mighty Cosmos, I shall keep the flame of cosmic service. In the name of the ascended Mother of the Flame, *Ich dien!*[7]

"The Summit Lighthouse Sheds Its Radiance O'er All the World to Manifest as Pearls of Wisdom." This dictation by **Mighty Cosmos** was **delivered** by the Messenger Elizabeth Clare Prophet on **Saturday, July 2, 1988,** 12:42–12:57 p.m. MDT, at *FREEDOM 1988* in the Heart of the Inner Retreat at the **Royal Teton Ranch, Park County, Montana.** Dictation available with that of the Goddess of Liberty on 81-min. audiocassette B88099, $6.50 (add $.55 for postage); on 2-hr. videocassette HP88068 with dictations of the Goddess of Liberty, Serapis Bey, Archangels Gabriel and Michael, $29.95 (add $1.10 for postage). [**N.B.** Bracketed material denotes words unspoken yet implicit in the dictation, added by the Messenger under Mighty Cosmos' direction for clarity in the written word.]

(1) **"You have need of me."** Sanat Kumara, 1988 *Pearls of Wisdom*, pp. 353–60. (2) The seven rays and the initiations of the Lords of the Seven Rays are charted consecutively on the Cosmic Clock from the 12 to the 6 o'clock lines; the five secret rays are charted on the 7 to 11. (3) During this dictation the Messenger held the sword Excalibur directly in front of her in a vertical position pointing upward. (4) On July 3, 1988, the Messenger gave teachings on the gifts of the Holy Spirit, charting these initiations on the Cosmic Clock, and on the **Five Dhyāni Buddhas,** their mantras and their positions on the Clock; on two 90-min. audiocassettes B88103–4, $13.00 (add $.95 for postage). Add $1.00 for charts to accompany the cassettes, #2489. N.B. Padma Sambhava, initiator of the Messenger, stands on the 6:30 line. (5) "Give me, good Lord, a longing to be with Thee; not for the avoiding of the calamities of this wicked world, nor so much for the avoiding of the pains of purgatory, nor the pains of Hell neither, nor so much for the attaining of the joys of Heaven in respect of mine own commodity, as even **for a very love of Thee."** Thomas More, *English Works,* 1557, quoted in Joseph Vann, ed., *Lives of Saints* (New York: John J. Crawley & Co., 1954), pp. 322–23. (6) **Third day I shall be perfected.** Luke 13:32. (7) *Ich dien* (German, "I serve"), the motto of the Prince of Wales, was the guiding principle of Clara Louise Kieninger, who was anointed by Saint Germain as the first Mother of the Flame when the Keepers of the Flame Fraternity was founded in 1961. On October 25, 1970, at the age of 87, Clara Louise made her ascension from Berkeley, California. Her memoirs, edited and compiled by Elizabeth Clare Prophet, are published in *Ich Dien*, Summit University Press, $3.95 (add $.50 for postage). See glossary in *Saint Germain On Alchemy,* pp. 433–34.

Notes from Pearl no. 62 by the Goddess of Liberty continued:
(2) In order to comprehend the gravity of the **threat of aliens** in our midst it is essential to secure and listen to the tapes of the Summit University Forum exposé by Elizabeth Clare Prophet and her guests on the government cover-up of aliens, "The UFO Connection: Alien Spacecraft and Government Secrecy," July 1, 1988. Three videocassettes, 4 hr. 50 min., GP88048, $59.95 (add $1.90 for postage). Five 1-hr. cable TV shows for home use: "Anatomy of a Cover-up," HL88038; "Abducted by Aliens: The Common Threads of Experience," HL88039; "Crashed Saucer and Government Cover-up at Roswell/The Secrets of Operation Majestic 12," HL88040; "UFOs and the Mystery of Animal Mutilations/A Presidential Briefing Paper on UFOs," HL88041; "The Skeleton-Key Effect: Unlocking the Secrets of Alien Abductions," HL88042; $19.95 each (add $1.10 each for postage). Four audiocassettes, 4 hr. 49 min., A88118, $23.80 (add $.95 for postage). (3) **Judgment of the Watchers** (fallen angels) pronounced through Enoch. "The Lord said to me: Enoch, scribe of righteousness, go tell the Watchers of heaven, who have deserted the lofty sky, and their holy everlasting station, who have been polluted with women. And have done as the sons of men do, by taking to themselves wives, and who have been greatly corrupted on the earth; that on the earth they shall never obtain peace and remission of sin. For they shall not rejoice in their offspring; they shall behold the slaughter of their beloved; shall lament for the destruction of their sons; and shall petition for ever; but shall not obtain mercy and peace. . . . I spoke to them all together; and they all became terrified, and trembled; beseeching me to write for them a memorial of supplication, that they might obtain forgiveness; and that I might make the memorial of their prayer ascend up before the God of heaven. . . . Then I wrote a memorial of their prayer and supplication, for their spirits, for everything which they had done, and for the subject of their entreaty, that they might obtain remission and rest. . . . I fell down and saw a vision of punishment, that I might relate it to the sons of heaven, and reprove them. . . . I have written your petition; and in my vision it has been shown me, that what you request will not be granted you as long as the world endures. Judgment has been passed upon you: your request will not be granted you. From this time forward, never shall you ascend into heaven; He has said, that on the earth He will bind you, as long as the world endures. But before these things you shall behold the destruction of your beloved sons; you shall not possess them, but they shall fall before you by the sword. Neither shall you entreat for them, nor for yourselves; but you shall weep and supplicate in silence." I Enoch 12:5–7; 13:4–7, 9; 14:2–7. See *Forbidden Mysteries of Enoch: The Untold Story of Men and Angels,* containing all the Enoch texts, including the Book of Enoch and the Book of the Secrets of Enoch, with exegesis and exposé by Elizabeth Clare Prophet. (4) **"Inasmuch as ye have done it . . ."** Matt. 25:40. (5) Kuan Yin, 1988 *Pearls of Wisdom*, pp. 471–80. (6) **Jesus' calls to the path of the ascension, discipleship and Christhood.** 1987 *Pearls of Wisdom*, pp. 269–76, 491–98, 577–82, 601–6; 1988 *Pearls of Wisdom*, pp. 290, 291, 294, 297.

Pearls of Wisdom®
published by The Summit Lighthouse

| Vol. 31 No. 64 | Beloved Serapis Bey | October 1, 1988 |

FREEDOM 1988

9

The Goal: Victory in the Threefold Flame
The Means: Mastery of the Six O'Clock Line

Seraphim of Justinius, come forth in the name Serapis Bey!
Thus millions of seraphim do gather on planet earth, and I am here, your Hierarch of the Fourth Ray and of Ascension's Temple[1] and Flame. Greetings out of the living Flame of the Divine Mother which I AM THAT I AM where I stand, *here!* [41-second standing ovation]

Be seated in your own Cosmic Threefold Flame.

Unprecedented is the gift of God through Cosmos,[2] and you may never know until you are ascended just what impetus toward bodhisattvahood you have received.

By this action, then, I, Serapis, may take my place and stand upon your six o'clock line, if you will allow it. ["Yes."] And I shall stand with my sword, beloved, for this sword has many names and vibrations as held by our bands. Thus, see it as Excalibur, fleur-de-lis, the hallmark of Ascension's victory.

Now then, what have you received? Impetus to master the six o'clock line of God Harmony, of the Ascension Flame, of the sacred fire, of the purity of the Divine Mother in the base-of-the-spine chakra and hence in all chakras above.

I may come, then, as the representative of Cosmos and of God Harmony to give you initiations both within my retreat and wherever you are for the mastery of God Harmony, nevermore to dally in self-sympathy, pools of pity, words of babbling brooks of self-justification.

Death itself is the misuse of [and the consequence of the misuse of] this chakra. Thus, beloved, it is a fount of eternal Life unto those who celebrate Life, but it is also a fountain of Death to those who celebrate the rituals of Death.

Now then, beloved, my goal is not the mastery of the six o'clock line *for you*, for this mastery [which you must make your own] is a means to the goal; and the means is the [very] strengthening, the balance and the mastery through the Eightfold Path of those eight petals of the secret chamber of the heart.[3]

When the chamber is strengthened by those who understand wholeness (by those who should have heeded the Messenger's reminder as the decade began that the decade of the eighties is the decade for the mastery of the Eightfold Path and [of the] completion [of cycles]), and when, therefore, that [eight-petaled] chakra is [also] strengthened, the heart can expand, the threefold flame of the heart can expand.

For, beloved, the expanded heart flame is assailed by the world and the worldly consciousness, and the Eighth Ray chakra is the armour and shield. As the [threefold] flame expands, the [secret] chamber [of the heart] shall expand. [And this is the goal, twofold, which I, Serapis, set before you this day.]

Think you, then, that the threefold flame when raised to your own height shall not also cause that chamber to become a Cosmic Egg? Aye, it is so! Think you that eight Buddhas shall not come and manifest in those petals [when you shall have sufficiently balanced and expanded that threefold flame]? Aye, it is so.

Thus, without mastery of the Flame of Mother [on the six o'clock line], without true desiring to dissolve all differences [inharmony] between thyself and all mothers and the Divine Mother, there can be no entering in [to the secret chamber of the heart].

The Buddha who will teach you within that chamber is the devotee and the Divine Lover of the Mother. The Buddha will not receive [on the Eightfold Path of initiation] sons of men, daughters of earth who have yet subconscious antagonism or envy or mistrust of the Divine Mother. And if these trust not or love not or obey not the Mother [whom] they can see, how shall they love one whom they cannot see?[4]

One's perfections or imperfections are not the determining factor in the merit of one's love. One loves the *principle* of Mother [of Cosmic Motherhood: of God as Mother], the mantle, the office and the soul [of Mother]—day by day embodying more of that Flame.

Thus, beloved, this is the key to the six o'clock line of Sanat Kumara,[5] who bears the Flame of Guru, and the Flame of Mother in the process. Know, then, that the Divine Mother is the key to the heart of God in the center of being and that Buddha is Father and

[that] Father must be approached through Mother.

In the [process of the] transmutation and dissolution of worlds of karma with various mother figures, I do exhort you to select one Ascended Lady Master such as Mother Mary, Kuan Yin, the Goddess of Liberty and to give such intense devotion to that image and that flame that through that heart you might dissolve all separation from the Mother of Cosmos.

In your desiring to accomplish this, beloved, as long as the fervor be intense you may elect to give this devotion to more than one. What is required, however, is that an intensity of devotion be given to one; and then if you can increase and multiply it by also embodying the flame of another, you should surely do so.

Thus Kuan Yin and Mother Mary and the Goddess of Liberty present to you their hearts for this purpose, as do the members of the Karmic Board: Portia, Mother of Aquarius; Pallas Athena, wielding the sword of Truth; Nada, [being of Love and Love's alchemy of healing].

In the understanding of the seven rays, then, embrace thy Mother and be free. Be free to go to the center [of the Cosmic Clock, the center of the Cosmic Christ consciousness,] to make your rounds and thus to be allowed to move on, step-by-step through the initiations of the five secret rays.

These will not come simultaneously. But if you examine your chart, you will note that when you emerge from the center of your Clock, you arrive at the gate of the seven o'clock line, the gate of the Goddess of Liberty and Lords of Karma, who approve your petitions to enter now the five secret-ray initiations of the Holy Spirit.

I will tell you, then, that a sufficiency of light and balance of the threefold flame must be present with[in] the seat-of-the-soul chakra on that seven o'clock line and in the soul in order for you to proceed with the First Secret Ray initiation. Pursuing this with all diligence, you shall catch up to the fourteen-month cycles[6] and therefore be in sync with the world action of initiation, [with] holders of the flame with Serapis and [with] all members of Hierarchy of this stepping-up of the earth.

For the record I say it again, the decade of the 1990s will find you being challenged to prove your mastery by the Power of the Three-Times-Three—balanced threefold flame of I AM Presence, [of] Holy Christ Self and [of] your own heart flame. Let the heart meditations of Saint Germain be followed to that purpose.[7] As you desire and bring forth devotion to the threefold flame of Liberty in each line of the Clock, you are building momentum for the quadrants, for the mastery of the four elements, and for this purpose of having the equilibrium to enter the five bands of the secret rays.

The genetic violations of this planet by aliens, sponsored by fallen angels and Nephilim gods and a descending scale of [their creation of] mechanization man, are violations of the five secret rays. An infant humanity undeveloped, therefore, has shown thus far no ability to in any way resist this violation.[8]

I, Serapis, predict that when you raise up this God-determined Light of the Mother and see the course that is set before you as paramount, *They shall not pass. They shall not prevail. They shall not undo or overtake.*

For they shall be held at bay by the shafts of light of the sons and daughters of God who have made their peace with the Godhead in the form of God the Impersonal Impersonality, God the Personal Personality, God the Impersonal Personality and the Personal Impersonality.[9]

O soul most beloved, gaze into the cosmic mirror and know thyself as thou truly art. So truly knowing thy True Self, thou art victor in the threefold flame. I bless thee, one and all.

[28-second standing ovation]

"The Summit Lighthouse Sheds Its Radiance O'er All the World to Manifest as Pearls of Wisdom." This dictation by **Serapis Bey** was **delivered** by the Messenger of the Great White Brotherhood Elizabeth Clare Prophet on **Saturday, July 2, 1988,** 12:57–1:14 p.m. MDT, at *FREEDOM 1988* in the Heart of the Inner Retreat at the **Royal Teton Ranch, Park County, Montana.** Dictation available with those of the Archangels Gabriel and Michael on 76-min. audiocassette B88100, $6.50 (add $.55 for postage); on 2-hr. videocassette HP88068 with dictations of the Goddess of Liberty, Mighty Cosmos, Archangels Gabriel and Michael, $29.95 (add $1.10 for postage). [**N.B.** Bracketed material denotes words unspoken yet implicit in the dictation, added by the Messenger under Serapis Bey's direction for clarity in the written word.] (**1**) The **Ascension Temple,** etheric retreat of Serapis Bey, Chohan of the Fourth Ray, is located at Luxor, Egypt. For information on the retreat, past lives, and teachings of Serapis Bey, see Mark L. Prophet and Elizabeth Clare Prophet, *Lords of the Seven Rays: Mirror of Consciousness,* Books One and Two; Serapis Bey, *Dossier on the Ascension;* glossary in *Saint Germain On Alchemy,* pp. 378, 447, 449–50. (**2**) Mighty Cosmos, 1988 *Pearls of Wisdom,* pp. 489–92. (**3**) The Ascended Master Djwal Kul teaches in *Intermediate Studies of the Human Aura* that the **secret chamber of the heart** "is the place where the chela contacts the Guru. It is the place where the laws of cosmos are written in the inward parts of man. For the law is inscribed as the **Eightfold Path** of the Buddha upon the inner walls of the chamber. . . . The eight petals of the secondary heart chamber symbolize the mastery of the seven rays through the flame of the Christ (called the threefold flame) and the integration of that mastery in the Eighth Ray" (pp. 38, 41; *The Human Aura,* pp. 108, 111–12). In Gautama Buddha's first sermon following his enlightenment, he taught the Four Noble Truths and the Eightfold Path. The Four Noble Truths state that (1) life is *dukkha* (out-of-alignment; variously translated as suffering, pain, sorrow, discontent, imperfection, sin, evil), (2) the cause of *dukkha* is inordinate desire, (3) freedom from *dukkha* is in the attainment of Nirvana, (4) the way to this liberation is through the Eightfold Path, which the Ascended Masters teach corresponds to the eight rays: Right Understanding, First Ray; Right Thought, Second Ray; Right Speech, Third Ray; Right Action, Fourth Ray; Right Livelihood, Fifth Ray; Right Effort, Sixth Ray; Right Mindfulness, Seventh Ray; Right Concentration, or Right Absorption, Eighth Ray (see 1983 *Pearls of Wisdom,* pp. 166–67). (**4**) John 20:29; I John 4:20, 21. (**5**) In Sanat Kumara's Pearls of Wisdom series "The Opening of the Seventh Seal" he explains that he occupies the **office of the Divine Mother, or the Woman, on the 6 o'clock line** of the Cosmic Clock. 1979 *Pearls of Wisdom,* pp. 122, 127, 142, 186, 202, 212, 240, 275. (For notes 6–9 see Pearl no. 65.)

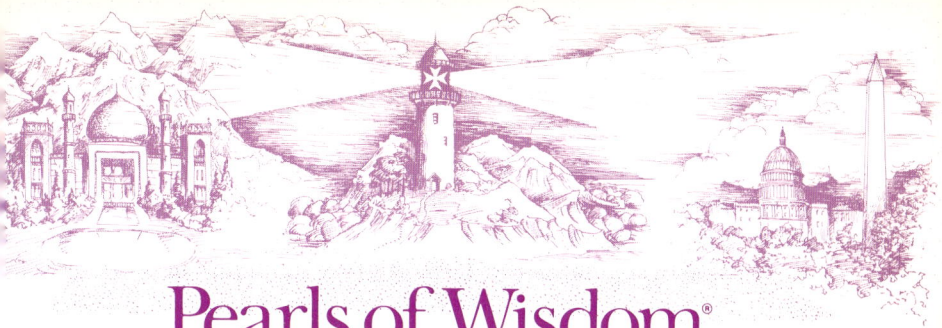

Pearls of Wisdom®

published by The Summit Lighthouse

| Vol. 31 No. 65 | Beloved Archangel Gabriel | October 2, 1988 |

FREEDOM 1988

10

Protection for the Sons of God

To All Who Walk the Path of the Ascension to God-Victory

Hail, O legions of Light! Hail, seraphim gathered!

I AM Gabriel Archangel, come with the annunciation of the course of five-pointed, star-studded Victory unto the sons and daughters of God! [36-second standing ovation]

My Sons Godfre and Lanello now flank the Messenger and reinforce white-fire purity as pillars, needles of fire, that shall establish that divine protection of Cosmic Christ purity earned. May you be seated in the love of my heart.

This thing I may do and that is to establish protection for each one, each dedicated Son of God; and the term *Son of God* [connotes] one who embodies a portion or all of his Christhood, whether in male or female body. I may therefore seal everyone who is a true chela of the heart of El Morya with spheres of white-fire protection for the secret-ray centers and secret-ray activities in the aura and body and life.

I may do this, beloved, while you make haste now to accept the offer of the Lords of the Seven Rays for the balancing of chakras, rays and threefold flame and the sealing therefore of the gates of the twelve lines of the [Cosmic] Clock.

This sealing by the power of the seven rays does establish you for the initiations spoken of by Cosmos and Serapis[1] and therefore [does] hasten the hour of your taking the more difficult initiations at the half-hour lines of the secret rays.[2]

I am in the center of the lily of thy Ascension Flame. Blessed ones, I do maintain fields of lilies and I personally, with my own hands, have planted, with Hope, my beloved complement, a special lily for each one of you who is a candidate for graduation from earth's schoolroom by means of Ascension's Flame. And when ascension's tassel is turned, I tell you, beloved, that golden light of the crown chakra reveals all to be valedictorians of their class, for all must attain the height of cosmic excellence to enter ascension's flight.

Therefore we shall water, we shall tend, we shall love, we shall take you along the paths as you journey through our field to our retreat[3] in special season in these hours of your accommodation— of your accustoming yourselves to those manifestations of aliens revealed to you.[4]

And so, beloved, we as your parents of the Fourth Ray in the archangelic realm desire you to know how much we love you and that in the etheric octave, the heaven-world, the plant of thyself shall grow and blossom and be a sign to all others who come who are not yet candidates that those who so choose to be shall also have planted by us lilies in our field. [13-second applause]

I choose to assist you if you will have me. I choose to see you once and for all take your Victory—take your Victory and seize it over the beast of sensuality, mortality. I choose to assist those who in being the chelas of the Divine Mother may also choose to be my initiates.

I can assure you, beloved, that I step down from a certain level of my archangelic hierarchical mantle to enter the role of Guru to those who need me for my strength, for my devotion to the Mother, for my healing and for my very physical presence among you. For I have come again and again at the call of the Messenger and your own call to bring healing where healing could be given.

All angels of the archangelic level are healing angels. Therefore, knowing the anatomy of the chakras and corresponding organs,[2] beloved, you understand that in addition to Raphael and Mother Mary, you do require our services for the healing of the chakra and all of that which surrounds it. So know, beloved, that the wholeness must be a sevenfold wholeness.

Now you, beloved, whose number in life is seven, receive from me the initiation of Amitābha upon the brow and know henceforth thy number shall be eight. I speak to the individual in this instance, beloved, and not to all. Those who be the recipients shall know it. As in all classes, beloved, there are some at the lead and some that must "pull up the rear."

Now angels, angels of Serapis, angels of Gabriel, I charge you to place your presence with every Lightbearer of earth, all who are the Keepers of the Flame designate.

Hear, O Astrea! Now use my Presence and that of my angels. Multiply it by thine own, thy circle and sword of blue flame, thy legions of Light. Cut free those Lightbearers who are designated in this hour by our loving Father-Mother God to be counted among those who shall walk the path of the ascension unto God-Victory! Let it be done. Let it be done, O Thou Starry Mother, and reveal the starry pathway—*reveal the starry pathway!* of the secret rays that unfold the Christhood of a man, of a woman.

The action of Astrea does commence. Avail thyself. Make the call. Visualize whirling circle of blue flame moving up and down, beneath the body and above. With each clearing action of each level there is then allowed to come out of the electronic belt, the psyche, the aura, the four lower bodies more substance* to be cleared. Thus, the way to visualize this circle of blue flame is [as] a whirling circle that begins from beneath one's feet and continues up the body and down the body, up and down for the duration of [your] Astreas.⁵

When you feel so moved, therefore, you may stand to give your Astreas, then again you may be seated. All the while the pillar of blue flame of that sword of Astrea is held with the right hand of that Divine Mother the full length of the spine from beneath the feet to above the head. You may also visualize this sword alternately in the front of the body, removing therefrom, and from the chakras also, that which must be taken.

The call to Astrea is the call to Ascension's Flame and to every grace and attainment possible of the Fourth Ray. Happy are ye who know this beloved Mother. Happier still are ye who give your calls to Astrea with profound gratitude and love for the service rendered.

The power of Elohim is the power of Ganesha,⁶ right foot upon every spacecraft of malintent and alien one.

*Shiva! Shiva! Shiva! Shiva!*⁷ Do not neglect to be heard! We incline our ear and we say, do not neglect to be heard! Cry *Shiva!*
[Assembly of Lightbearers cries:]
Shiva! Shiva! Shiva! Shiva! Shiva! Shiva!

So all major and minor devils tremble to so hear you. May the multiplication of this sound by the power of your voices be heard, then, on that violet flame tape [in order] that Shiva as the Aquarian Master and Holy Spirit—for he may be the Holy Spirit of any age—may release the violet flame action of his being in cosmic dance as you are heard around the world on that next God-victorious tape to say, in the name of Archangel Gabriel:

Shiva! [Lightbearers give the fiat *Shiva!* 17 times with Archangel Gabriel]

---

*God's energy misqualified through the chakras which coalesces and accumulates in the lower self as density and karma.

Now as transition for you that I might give you a sealing blessing, will you not sing the "AUM Shiva, AUM."

Lord Shiva of the Flame

AUM Shiva   AUM Shiva   AUM Shiva   AUM Shiva
AUM Shiva   AUM Shiva   AUM Shiva   AUM Shiva

Lord Shiva of the Flame
I AM thy Flame, I AM thy fire, I AM Shiva.
Lord Shiva of the Light
I AM thy Light, I AM thy Love, I AM Shiva.

I AM thy mystery of Love
Thy joyous life, thy energy
Beloved Shiva.

I AM thy waterfall of life
So cool and sweet thy love to me
Beloved Shiva.

I come to the heart of the mountain
I come to the heart of the dove
I gather thy diamonds in the way
In thy heart I AM Shiva, Shiva, Shiva

AUM Shiva   AUM Shiva   AUM

I exercise thy name:
    Shiva! Shiva
I speak it again and again:
    Shiva! Shiva
I challenge the Darkness on the way
And I listen to Shiva, Shiva, Shiva.

Refrain:
    Let the Lord be praised East and West!
    Let the Lord be praised East and West!
    Let the Lord be praised East and West!

    In the name of Shiva!   In the name of Shiva!

[Repeat refrain]
    Shiva!

Shiva! [Lightbearers give the fiat *Shiva!* 74 times with Archangel Gabriel]

So discover the key to Victory in the five secret rays. It is the Holy Spirit. It is cloven tongues of fire. It is Shiva. It is Brahma. It is Vishnu. It is the God beyond God—Brahman in the beginning with the Word.[8] Keep thyself unto Him, bride of the Trinity, and thou shalt know Divine Union—divine union apart and sealed from all violators of the sacred light of the Cosmic Virgin within you.

I AM Gabriel of the Fourth Ray, happiest when I minister unto those who desire to get the Victory over the beast of self-ignorance.

O wise ones of old, be wise ones anew! Alpha-to-Omega, Cosmic Christ illumination, renew our own for their golden victorious day! [43-second applause]

"The Summit Lighthouse Sheds Its Radiance O'er All the World to Manifest as Pearls of Wisdom." This dictation by **Archangel Gabriel** was **delivered** by the Messenger of the Great White Brotherhood Elizabeth Clare Prophet on **Saturday, July 2, 1988,** 1:18–1:39 p.m. MDT, at *FREEDOM 1988* in the Heart of the Inner Retreat at the **Royal Teton Ranch, Park County, Montana.** Available on 76-min. audiocassette with dictations of Serapis Bey and Archangel Michael, B88100, $6.50 (add $.55 for postage); on 2-hr. videocassette with dictations of the Goddess of Liberty, Mighty Cosmos, Serapis Bey and Archangel Michael, HP88068, $29.95 (add $1.10 for postage). [**N.B.** Bracketed material denotes words unspoken yet implicit in the dictation, added by the Messenger under Archangel Gabriel's direction for clarity in the written word.] **(1)** Mighty Cosmos and Serapis Bey, 1988 *Pearls of Wisdom,* pp. 489–96. **(2)** "Darshan with Kuthumi and El Morya: **Chakra Meditations and Initiations on the Cosmic Clock,**" delivered June 30, 1988, by the Messenger, included teachings on the seven rays, the seven chakras and the secret rays on the Cosmic Clock; balancing the threefold flame; and the relationship of the chakras to the organs in the body, with invocations by the Messenger for the clearing of the chakras. Two audiocassettes, 2½ hr., A88094, $13.00 (add $.95 for postage). **(3)** The **retreat of Archangel Gabriel and Hope,** his divine complement, is located in the etheric plane between Sacramento and Mount Shasta, California. **(4)** Summit University Forum **"The UFO Connection: Alien Spacecraft and Government Secrecy."** 1988 *Pearls of Wisdom,* p. 492 n. 2. **(5)** Refers to **"Decree to Beloved Mighty Astrea,"** the mantra to the Starry Mother, Elohim of the Fourth Ray: no. 10.14 in the blue section of *Prayers, Meditations and Dynamic Decrees for the Coming Revolution in Higher Consciousness* for Keepers of the Flame (Section II); no. 42 in *Heart, Head and Hand Decrees: Meditations, Mantras, Prayers and Decrees for the Expansion of the Threefold Flame within the Heart,* p. 32; *Kuan Yin's Crystal Rosary: Devotions to the Divine Mother East and West,* p. 19, audiocassette I; no. 60 in *Mantras of the Ascended Masters for the Initiation of the Chakras,* p. 16, audiocassette B85137. On July 5, 1985, El Morya explained that the call to Astrea "is the most powerful mantra to the Divine Mother that has been released in this octave. The power of the Universal Mother carrying the circle and sword of blue flame that is released in this mantra is great indeed, capable of fulfilling every manifestation of the Mother, East or West, and capable of driving from you evil spirits that lurk, addictions, self-indulgences and all pettiness that snatch from you that precious love which comes so gently, so powerfully, and yet is as fragile as crystal and can be broken and will be broken by the forces of the night unless you keep the tryst with Astrea and Archangel Michael and 'Kārttikeya', whom you know as Sanat Kumara" (1985 *Pearls of Wisdom,* p. 420). **(6)** In the teachings of Hinduism, **Ganesha,** or Gaṇapati, is the son of Shiva (the Third Person of the Trinity of the Godhead) and Parvati; in one legend Ganesha is the son of Parvati alone. Ganesha is the god of wisdom, patron of learning and letters, and the chief of the many classes of minor gods who serve under Shiva. He is worshiped as the remover or destroyer of all obstacles; hence he is traditionally invoked at the beginning of any undertaking, religious or secular, and at the commencement of the writing of books or compositions to ensure the success of the endeavor. Ganesha is depicted with the head of an elephant. Author Alain Daniélou explains that "Gaṇapati stands for one of the basic concepts of Hindu mythological symbolism,... the notion that man is the image of God.... Gaṇapati is represented as an elephant-headed man to express the unity of the small being, the microcosm, that is man, and the Great Being, the macrocosm, pictured as an elephant" (*The Gods of India: Hindu Polytheism* [New York: Inner Traditions International, 1985], pp. 292, 293). **(7) Shiva.** 1988 *Pearls of Wisdom,* p. 154 n. 5; glossary in *Saint Germain On Alchemy,* pp. 407–8. **(8) "In the beginning was the Word,** and the Word was with God, and the Word was God," John 1:1. This verse parallels the Hindu teachings on the cosmic

Principle and Person of *Vāc* (pronounced Vwahk; meaning literally speech, word, voice, talk, or language) as recorded in the Vedas, the earliest scriptures of Hinduism, probably composed c. 1500–1000 B.C. The Hindu text Taittirīya Brāhmaṇa (Brāhmaṇas are commentaries on the Vedas) says that "the Word, imperishable, is the Firstborn of Truth, mother of the Veda and hub of immortality." Vāc is called "the mother" of the Vedas because it is believed that Brahma revealed them through her power. The Tāṇḍya Mahā Brāhmaṇa teaches, "This, [in the beginning], was only the Lord of the universe. His Word was with him. This Word was his second. He contemplated. He said, 'I will deliver this Word so that she will produce and bring into being all this world'" (XX, 14, 2). Scholar John Woodroffe (pen name, Arthur Avalon) quotes John 1:1 and says: "These are the very words of Veda. *Prajāpatir vai idam āsīt:* In the beginning was Brahman. *Tasya vāg dvitīyā āsīt;* with whom was Vāk or the Word; (She is spoken of as second to Him because She is first potentially in, and then as Shakti issues from Him); *Vāg vai paramam Brahma;* and the word is Brahman. Vāk is thus a Shakti or Power of the Brahman. . . . This Shakti which was in Him is at the creation with Him, and evolves into the form of the Universe whilst still remaining what It is—the Supreme Shakti" who is "one with Brahman" (*The Garland of Letters* [Pondicherry, India: Ganesh & Co., n.d.], pp. 4–5).

Hindu texts refer to Vāc as the wife or consort of the Creator "who contains within herself all worlds." Sarasvati, the consort of Brahma and goddess of language, speech, wisdom and art, is identified with Vāc in the Mahābhārata and later Hindu tradition. Quoting the Brāhmaṇas, author Raimundo Panikkar writes that Vāc "is truly 'the womb of the universe.' For 'by that Word of his, by that self, he created all this, whatever there is.'" Panikkar also notes that "*Vāc* was before all creation, preexisting before any being came to be. . . . *Vāc* is the life-giving principle within all beings. . . . She has a feminine characteristic of complementarity, a mediatorial role, and a certain feminine docility and obedience. She needs always to be uttered, by men, by Gods, or by the Creator himself. . . . [The Vedic Word] is ultimately as important as Brahman and, in a way that has to be properly understood, it is Brahman itself" (*The Vedic Experience Mantramañjarī* [Los Angeles: University of California Press, 1977], pp. 106, 96, 107, 89).

Notes from Pearl no. 64 by Serapis Bey continued:
(6) Serapis Bey's fourteen-month cycles. On December 29, 1978, Serapis Bey, Chohan of the Fourth Ray, announced that at winter solstice December 21, 1978, a fourteen-month cycle of initiation had been inaugurated whereby we could increase the white sphere of our causal body. Since that time, every fourteen months has marked the initiation of another fourteen-month cycle through succeeding spheres of the causal body multiplied by the Great Central Sun Magnet of the white sphere, i.e., amplified by the white fire of the Mother, the power of ascension's flame. (See 1988 *Pearls of Wisdom*, p. 229 n. 7.) On February 28, 1987, Serapis Bey announced the beginning of "fourteen months of planetary initiation in the First Secret Ray" as the first of five cycles in the five secret rays of the causal body. On April 25, 1988, in his dictation initiating the Second Secret Ray cycle, Serapis Bey explained that where we had fallen short in diligently pursuing the opportunity for self-mastery in the First Secret Ray cycle, we may "make calls for the opportunity to go back and lay the foundation of the first simultaneously with the second, thus as building two levels of a house at the same time." The Messenger also explained in her October 28, 1984 lecture on the fourteen-month cycles that those who were not aware of these cycles of initiation or who felt they did not take the greatest advantage of them could "go back and make calls from the center ring of the causal body going outward to the present and ask to be given the initiations of those rings according to the will of God and the discriminating intelligence of your Higher Consciousness."
(7) Saint Germain's Heart Meditation I and II. 1988 *Pearls of Wisdom*, pp. 339 n. 6, 479 n. 3.
(8) The thesis that the AIDS virus was created in the laboratory by genetic manipulation of deadly animal viruses, enabling them to cross the species barrier and attack the human immune system, is examined by Elizabeth Clare Prophet and her guests on the Summit University Forum **"The AIDS Conspiracy: Establishment Cover-up, Pharmaceutical Scam or Biological Warfare?"** on 3 videocassettes, 4½ hr., GP88078, $59.95 (add $1.90 for postage); 4 audiocassettes, 4¾ hr., $23.80 (add $.95 for postage). **(9) Four Principles of the Godhead:** God as Father (Impersonal Impersonality), Mother (Personal Personality), Son (Impersonal Personality), and Holy Spirit (Personal Impersonality). Djwal Kul, *Intermediate Studies of the Human Aura*, pp. 48–51, 69, or *The Human Aura*, pp. 119–22, 141; Elizabeth Clare Prophet, *The Great White Brotherhood in the Culture, History and Religion of America*, fig. 9, following p. 176; pp. 179–80.

Pearls of Wisdom®
published by The Summit Lighthouse

Vol. 31 No. 66   *Beloved Archangel Michael*   *October 8, 1988*

FREEDOM 1988

11
Wield My Sword of Blue Flame!
"Take Heed, Act, and Move On with Us!"

Hail, Sons of Michael! Hail, Daughters of Faith! We are here in the fullness of cosmic joy of the First Ray of God's will!

[37-second standing ovation]

Hear ye! Hear ye! The hour is come and now is when every Keeper of the Flame must wield my sword of blue flame! Therefore I commission you who have the talent and the artistry to so design a hefty sword such as this one[1] that you may be able to wield without too much difficulty. Blessed ones, this sword must become physical *for you* that I might become physical *through you* and wield my sword of blue flame superimposed upon it. Therefore, will you not be seated in the grandiose scheme of an Archangel. [14-second applause]

Ho, ho! Think you [that] they do not fear my sword of blue flame and my Presence? Well, I tell you, I AM known throughout cosmos and *I AM* feared [by the fallen angels], by the grace of God. Now, [8-second applause] now let the fearless ones also be feared in my name as Sons of Michael and Daughters of Faith.

I tell you, beloved, the dusty or rusty sword unwielded shall not thrust for you cosmic protection from my heart. Where you place your arm and hand I place my own. Where you do not and do not make the call, I may stand by as a pillar of fire but you may be outside of my auric emanation.

Blessed ones, know truly that those who desire to be chelas of the First Ray have all my Love and Presence daily when invoked. My aura is shooting flame—blue flame that does not simply burn up but burns out as a sun. May you also learn this art of [wielding] the flame that burns in all directions. [12-second applause]

There is only one way to be sure—there *is* only one way to be sure in the physical octave and that is to physically manifest the blue ray cutting through where violet flame has cleared and cleared again. So, beloved, wherever you go the sword and Archangel of the First Ray must precede you! [Audience recites with Archangel Michael:]

> Lord Michael before, Lord Michael behind,
> Lord Michael to the right, Lord Michael to the left,
> Lord Michael above, Lord Michael below,
> Lord Michael, Lord Michael wherever I go!
>
> I AM his Love protecting here!
> I AM his Love protecting here!
> I AM his Love protecting here!

Where you go, so goes your sword of blue flame. This, beloved, is my solution to a universal pollution of fallen angels. They will not stand in your way. I guarantee it. I AM the Guarantor of your protection when and only when you give your calls to me daily. These calls, beloved, must serve to bring you into alignment with the will of God. For hear this and know this: *We cannot protect you in any manifestation outside the will of God.*

Thus, what do we do? What do we do when your consciousness is afflicted by ignorance, absence of understanding, spiritual blindness of selfishness, et cetera? We move in to protect all of the good that you are in manifestation and all of the good that you are in all octaves, trusting that this merit, this meritorious record of service, therefore protected, will be the protection of the whole manifestation.

Thus, you see, beloved, when you get too far out of alignment and the good does not balance the error, you open yourselves to severe problems of many kinds, for the fallen ones move in, whether to take the Light* by financial schemes, whether by lawsuits, whether by entanglements, et cetera. They have many ways to delay and to take from you your Light.

Inasmuch as all are not perfected in a day, therefore to call forth the Electronic Presence of your Holy Christ Self over you when you call to me will signify that I have the authority to protect your entire being, consciousness and world.[2] Do you see? ["Yes."] Thus walking, *thus walking as your Christed Self,* you have the full sealing as though sealed in the starry blue womb of the Divine Mother. That auric ovoid of light is such an intensity of blue that you may pass by and literally be invisible to any and all forces who are not of the same wavelength as the Divine Mother.

The Divine Mother who is the starry blue Mother, beautifully painted by my son Nicholas Roerich,[3] is a focus of that blue-flame protection. Did you know, beloved, that the protection you receive

*the energy of your Christ consciousness

from me is always the protection of the Divine Mother? In her name do we serve.

You may understand, therefore, from the dictations given in this session that the desire of the Cosmic Hierarchy (as we in council have determined our offering for this conference) is to provide you with absolute keys which will not fail you when you use the combination, the formula we have given and stated simply and clearly. In fact, we have not burdened you with too many requirements or complexities, surely not for you who have understood this path for thousands of years of incarnations. Thus, it will not be the knowledge nor the dispensation that shall take from you your God-centeredness but the [absence of the] decision and the will to carry them through to be God Flames in action.

As you know, we of the First Ray are not so long on words except if we have something important to say but [we are] very long on action; for we move as the activators of Cosmic Good. Understand, then, our impatience with unclear and unnecessary chatter that does cloud the "ethers," the aura of the room, where you are. We desire to see you dispense with the unnecessary quickly, now! For the hour is too late any longer to indulge.

Now that the dangers are known,[4] take heed, act and move on with us, for we have much to tell you, much to accomplish. And I say, beloved, let Keepers of the Flame who count themselves as the white fire core of this movement, and you all should, know that until you have been obedient—to the letter and the spirit [of the Law]—to Saint Germain *to be prepared*, there will not be more dispensations coming forth nor can we build upon a foundation that you have not laid.

This preparation cannot be accomplished alone by gnomes! It is the work of the ages and the mighty work of the ages of true Sons of God who walk in the dignity of their threefold flame.

Now, then, the builders have arrived, *cosmic builders*. You should be in awe of their ability as craftsmen. These builders taught the builders of the pyramids and other phenomenal works that were wrought on Lemuria and Atlantis. These builders come from other spheres and realms. As with those Cosmic Christs you called forth,[5] they have come.

Precious hearts, I AM an Archangel filled with gratitude, for it is what you have done that has made possible what we can do, measure for measure. More we should offer, but how much can more be when so full a cup is yours this day?

By illumination's golden flame that literally fills this place with the aura of the saints, by the purity of the Mother, we see a vision of what the angels can do with the angels in embodiment such as you. You who have, then, determined to embody at some price long ago, know that cosmos is grateful for embodied angels who know what to do and do it.

O ye finishers of the faith, the great author of your destiny approaches. May you be with the Seven Holy Kumaras in bliss for the sealing of this conference. And may you know that I speak for the Seven Archangels this day, each one able to give if but a drop of Light, then, yes, a drop that can be in the corresponding chakra of his ray as a leaven, as a Light, as the sound in the inner ear of a tinkling crystal that does, then, change the alchemy of that entire chakra. So, dewdrops of angels convey a cosmos' dispensation.

We shall take the opportunity of the calls of the remainder of this conference to march across all margents of the earth, longitude and latitude, and as we march we are authorized to bind and to bind again and to bind again, and in some cases to cast out of the earth the fallen ones whose time has come who shall know the meaning of the Ruby Ray and the First Ray, who shall know the meaning of the judgment white fire of the Divine Mother. [15-second applause]

Your concentration on the judgment calls you have will be your empowerment of the hosts of heaven to ratify here below, as above, the true and just judgments of our God. This we must do that you might prevail. We come in the name of the Ancient of Days because you have need of us[6] and because *we have need of thee*.

In the immaculate embrace of the Cosmic Virgin Mary, we the Archangels embrace you each one. Know for a moment the feeling of our arms around you, our chakras one with yours as we temper our auras to your ability to receive love of angels. Our Archeiai now so anchor that love.

This dictation was **delivered Saturday, July 2, 1988,** 1:42–2:02 p.m. MDT. Available on 76-min. audiocassette with dictations of Serapis Bey and Archangel Gabriel, B88100, $6.50 (add $.55 postage); on 2-hr. videocassette with dictations of the Goddess of Liberty, Mighty Cosmos, Serapis Bey and Archangel Gabriel, HP88068, $29.95 (add $1.10 postage). (**1**) The Messenger held a blue steel sword throughout the dictation. (**2**) This is the reason the preamble to the decree should be given whenever you exercise the science of the spoken Word, for the call "in the name of my Mighty I AM Presence and Holy Christ Self" fulfills this requirement of the Law of which Archangel Michael is speaking; nevertheless, since this Guarantor of our protection, formidable in battle and feared by all fallen ones, does ask it, henceforth we shall call for the Electronic Presence of our Holy Christ Self to be placed over us whenever we give our dynamic decrees for Archangel Michael's protection. (**3**) *Mother of the World,* painting by Nicholas Roerich; printed in *The Lost Teachings of Jesus I,* following p. 68. For prints write Nicholas Roerich Museum, 319 West 107th St., New York, N.Y. 10025. (**4**) See 1988 *Pearls of Wisdom,* p. 492 n. 2. (**5**) **Cosmic Christs called forth.** The Cosmic Christs that Lightbearers called forth during Kuthumi's dictation at *FREEDOM 1988* (see pp. 457–58) had been called forth by Keepers of the Flame in a petition to the Lords of Karma in 1960. Their petition was granted through Helios, who announced in his May 27, 1960 Pearl of Wisdom that "all sincere students and chelas of the Ascended Masters who apply their hearts to their own God Presence I AM, asking that they be made a divine channel through which the power and presence of one or more of the Universal Christs located on other systems of worlds shall flow during hours of sleep, or even consciously as the Great Law directs, shall promptly and without delay be vested with our power in accordance with the cosmic law in order to enable these Christs to anchor their radiation and presence in the physical, thinking, feeling and memory worlds of such volunteers so as to provide a means whereby a Cosmic Christ can be assigned to each laggard on this planet (they are legion) individually in order to help control the spread of discord and transmute their thoughts and feelings to love for the Light!" (**6**) **"You have need of me."** 1988 *Pearls of Wisdom,* pp. 353–60, 489.

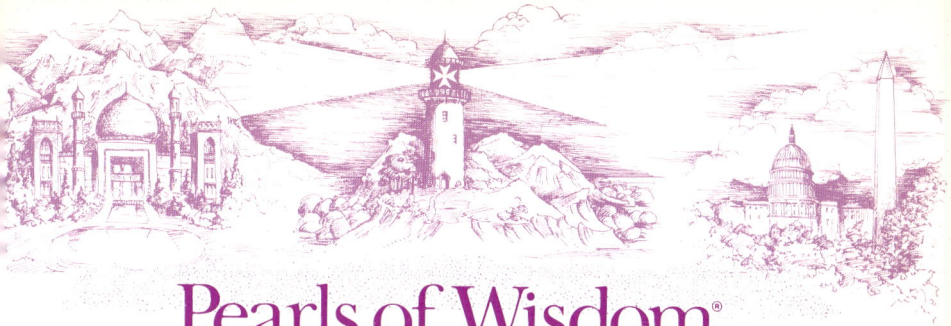

Pearls of Wisdom®
published by The Summit Lighthouse

| Vol. 31 No. 67 | Beloved Gautama Buddha | October 9, 1988 |

FREEDOM 1988
12
Concerning Maitreya's Mystery School
The Line Is Drawn, the Standard Will Be Kept
Wesak Address 1988

Blessed children who are also my sons and daughters, I am ever with you in this Heart of Shamballa, always desirous to reveal myself to you and so doing daily. But so very often you do not know the signs—you do not hear me, you do not see me.

Thus, as I speak to you, I speak many thoughts. I speak from my heart and I give you the distillations of a year's meditation in the One, for this moment is our celebration of Wesak.

To that end, then, I have come, and I have already used the power of the full moon in Capricorn to fix in this place a spiritual forcefield and power. This alchemy of the Buddhas is not known to you but, being desirous of initiating cycles for each and every Lightbearer of earth, I have chosen to work through the Great Causal Body of the Great Divine Director, who does amplify joyously for me the Cosmic Hierarchy of Capricorn to this end.[1]

Welcome to my heart, beloved. Welcome. The joy of being together in this moment does far surpass the cycles that we did not elect to use in May,[2] for it is a moment of spiritualization of consciousness. Thus, I would draw you close now.

I would instruct you, beloved, concerning Maitreya's Mystery School, which is reflective of the Teachings given in the etheric retreat of Shamballa. I would remind you and exhort you to consider that the pace of discipleship is not held back for the recalcitrant ones nor for those who believe that by some inner standard, which they set, all things should continue [as they were] in this Community.

It is important to understand that in our messages of a year ago it was clearly stated that for many Lightbearers there would be a final opportunity.[3] I can tell you that there are those who have been Keepers of the Flame who have failed [to exercise] that opportunity in this year; and [they have] not [done] so because they have not known the Law nor understood the principles of Love but because, beloved, they have indeed thought themselves an exception to the rule. [They] placed themselves in an inverted position on that magnificent twelve o'clock line of God-Power [on the Cosmic Clock] and determined to judge in the sense [of being] able to say to one another how things should be, how they are not as they should be, how this is right and this is wrong and this is acceptable and this is not.

Blessed ones, first and foremost I desire to tell you that it is a most dangerous dogma to enter into this type of gossip and condemnation concerning the Messenger or the activity or to so imply without so naming. Rather it is always well to be direct and if you have anything to say, if you are not humble at least be polite enough to address your concerns and questions in the form of [a stated] desire to know what indeed is the explanation for this and that which you have observed. I can assure you that those explanations will be given and will surely be afforded you [in response to your forthright inquiry].

Far better that you seek to understand the way of Maitreya's Mystery School and the path of discipleship unto perfect love than by your own private understanding to tear down [our representatives] and also to tear down [thereby] the aspirations of others. Each one, after all, has his own free will and may pursue his own course in life without the necessity of downgrading, especially to newer souls, those [disciplines, as requirements of the Law,] that are the very stumbling blocks whereby in spiritual pride [said] individuals have failed to accelerate into the heart, the eightfold chamber of the heart, with Lord Maitreya.

Blessed ones, you will recall that fourteen months ago at Wesak I did place upon the Messenger my mantle.[4] I can assure you, therefore, that you always have recourse to my mantle. This mantle is for the very purpose of the setting of the standard of the Sangha, of the Community, of the Path, of the Teaching to be outpictured and of each one's very personal relationship to me.

Surely you understand and know, and if you do not I will tell you so, that this Messenger has no desire to stand between yourself and myself but only to provide a transparent glass and a mirror if required, a means whereby you can with certainty hear my word, ponder it and so adjust your courses in order to pass your tests.

Therefore, beloved, come into my heart and know that in so stating that such opportunity should be given I did speak out of the mouth of the great Cosmic Council and of the Lord God. These are not dictums either of myself or of my beloved Messenger, and therefore understand that there is not a place where I can go [where I may] ask for your infractions of the Law of Life to be overlooked, to be set aside.

All must understand that we have accelerated this Community [to a level] commensurate with the necessity of every soul (who is intended to be a part of it and who is a part of it) for initiation unto the ascension, because for that very reason you, supposedly, are here.

Refine your goals. Establish purity of heart. If you do indeed desire the ascension, then I say to you, it is well to accept, or to come to an understanding so that you can accept, the role of the Messenger in transmitting to you those Teachings, those soul testings, those initiations which will be absolutely required of you—such initiations which cannot be passed either out of the body at night at Luxor or at the Western Shamballa nor between embodiments.

The critical factor of being in physical embodiment to balance physical karma is nowhere more critical than in this Community, for we have called you out from among the billions of souls inhabiting this planet because each one of you has the immense opportunity to set an example for a lifewave, a group soul—[for] individuals on a certain path and chakra, those working out a certain mandala of service. Each one of you has been called to be shaped by the wise Masterbuilder to become a keystone in an arch which shall be an open door whereby many may pass through.

The perfecting of the Law and of the Wisdom and of the Love* of the heart, then, whereby the threefold flame can be balanced, whereby those initiations can be passed, ought to be thy meditation day and night.

It does require, beloved, sponsorship from at least one Ascended Master for you to be seated here today, for you to be counted as a Keeper of the Flame in Saint Germain's fraternity, a communicant of Jesus' and Mary's and Saint Germain's Church Universal and Triumphant [which is] my own dear Church.

Know, beloved, that unless sponsored, an individual does not do well on this path. That sponsorship is an immediate bracing of the soul and the individual by the figure-eight flow of the Buddha to hold that one in alignment with his own inner blueprint and to steady that soul when choices must be made to control that energy in any of those seven chakras and to release it according to the divine plan.

What does not matter so much is the attainment you already

*attributes of the Trinity manifest in the three plumes of the threefold flame

have. This, so to speak, is as "money in the bank." What matters most is the attainment you lack, which [lack] has been there for, [i.e., because of,] the pitfall, the weakness, the shortcoming whereby over and over again you could not mount that spiral to round out the attainment gained and fill it in with that which is necessary for balance.

Blessed ones, it is easy to develop a most unreal picture of oneself on the Path when in the presence of so great a company of ascended hosts and in the physical aura of the Messenger and in a retreat situation where the land itself is guarded by Cosmic Beings. Thus, in this happiness and comfortability and opportunity for striving (especially when the five faculties of the soul based on attunement with the Five Dhyāni Buddhas has not been developed) [it is easy] to consider that one is far more advanced than is actually so according to the inner coils of Light, the strengthened spheres of secret rays around that heart, that secret chamber therein.

So, understand, beloved ones, that in the mystery of God what must be recognized in all humility is that whatever one's attainment, the Path is precipitous and one must seek and seek diligently daily a greater God-mastery, a greater humility, a profound devotion to one's God. In this seeking and in this finding, beloved, you must come to understand that you are sponsored because you have greatest need, because you have made mistakes before and because your elder brothers and sisters are concerned lest you miss another cosmic cycle when, for you, *at last* the door has opened again.

We cannot stress enough how important it is to maintain the consciousness that "I am here by the grace of God and I will be certain that in the cups of the moments, the minutes and the hours I will perfect, I will perfect, *I will perfect my soul in those areas that have been my downfall too many times.*"

Blessed ones, there are individuals connected with this activity whom we have called, for whom tremendous negative karma has been set aside [by our sponsorship]. One never knows when, because of the repetitious failure on a single point of the Law, the mercy of the Law that has held back the descent of that karma for thousands of years will say, "The hour has come. Thus far and no farther. Let the judgment descend."

Blessed ones, the Law is embodied by the Lawgiver and the great Manus.[5] When that edict comes forth out of the Law itself, there is no longer intercessory power on the part of any mediator, ascended or unascended, nor protest nor justification nor pity nor the seeking of popularity by protesting too much and convincing the many of one's rightness. Not any of these things may turn back the inexorable Law of Karma, which law, beloved, does become doubly severe when individuals have had many years of opportunity to invoke the violet flame and have enjoyed its liberating power, not mindful of the great grace that is being accorded so very few—not because the Law would restrict it to the few but because the many have not elected to take this option. And sometimes the many have not elected because it has become the turn of those who have had it [the violet flame] to sponsor them [the many]. Yet sponsor they do not, but retain the momentum of violet flame for their own [exclusive] usefulness, prosperity and enjoyment.

Thus, in the endless chain of the figure-eight flow, sponsorship must extend; and when you become co-sponsors with us of the next rung of Lightbearers on the rung of the ladder beneath you, then those in embodiment who cannot see or understand us will embrace the path of the Seventh Ray of Aquarius *because they see you* and they see that though you may not be perfect or without fault, you are humble before your God, a joyously obedient servant, one who does not neglect the creative fires of Being on the altar of the heart.

Thus, beloved, concerning the mantle that I have placed upon the Messenger, that mantle is there whereby the office of Guru from Padma Sambhava through Maitreya to myself to Sanat Kumara may be extended and must be extended to all who are a part of the Mystery School, whether as staff or members of the worldwide community of affiliates.

Blessed ones, know the law that governs the life and office that is shared by the Messengers, and that is that there may not be a sustained relationship between the Messenger and any student on the Path if that student is not diligently fulfilling the requirements of the Guru-chela relationship. These requirements are most basic and should be obvious. But, beloved ones, some will not see, for they prefer themselves to be in the seat of the scornful judging rather than receiving the proffered gift.[6]

Know, then, beloved, that there does come a time when the unprofitable servant,[7] or chela, having so flaunted the Law and [so] flaunted our Brotherhood, must be informed by us through the Messenger that it is no longer lawful for that one to be in a direct relationship to us through the Messenger and therefore of no further purpose for that individual to be affiliated with Maitreya's Mystery School, whether here at the Inner Retreat or in any of our centers throughout the world.

Blessed ones, this means that the standard that is set for the Guru-chela relationship must be held, it must be sustained. And the hour does come (and it is individual) when, by the longevity of affiliation with the activity or in the Keepers of the Flame Fraternity or in our Study Groups or on one's own, due to the amount of preparation and knowledge [that should have been garnered by the individual] through the Teaching itself, if the individual is not willing to carry a certain burden of Light, which ought to be his joy, [is not] willing to pay that price [for the Ascended Master sponsorship of his chelaship] by also bearing a certain portion of the burden of the activity itself as well as [of] his own karmic accountability—if that willingness to be the burden-bearer in Father, Son and Holy Spirit is not present—then it is time to say we can no longer invest energy in that individual nor require the Messenger's heart to be burdened by such an association.

When, therefore, it does become necessary for us to sever the tie and to so decree it and to so require the Messenger to declare it, I can assure you that it is always a most profoundly painful experience for the Messenger, who, regardless of what anyone may think about the fiery nature of this soul, is most patient and long-suffering with the repetitive ignorance and the repetitive infractions of the Law of Love that some individuals manage to manifest with extraordinary frequency.

Blessed ones, if you could see the long history even of your relationship to this Messenger, you would discover that this one has endured with you sometimes for five and eight thousand years during periods when you have scarcely made any spiritual progress, so determined were you to remain [in] and to affirm that ego-centered self-righteousness.

Blessed ones, the hour has come for you to be fully prepared to "hold up your end of the bargain" and not consider that you are here or anywhere on the planet in this activity to "write your own ticket" as to what you will and will not do. You have mistakenly misapprehended the relationship that you, by grace, enjoy with the Great White Brotherhood. You have misunderstood the fact that the Great White Brotherhood does choose its chelas and [that it is] not the other way around.

A chela may elect to prepare himself to qualify for chelaship under any one of the Lords of the Seven Rays, but that acceptance does come after considerable periods of proving and reproving. For the Ascended Masters are all too wary [and "weary"] of the members of earth's evolutions who have taken the cup and then after using it, dashed it and lost the light, wherefore the sponsoring one has had to pay the price and forfeit greater cosmic service. The sponsoring, therefore, of a disciple is a very serious matter for an Ascended Master and for a true unascended Master.

We repeat that the function of the Messenger in this relationship is as mediator and instrument, but neglect not to see and know the mantle of the Guru when that unmistakable vibration is transmitted to you [through the Messenger].

Now, beloved ones, it is a primary law in service that when one is receiving such spiritual sponsorship, blessings and initiations that one provide for, physically, the means wherewith our instrument may personally and organizationally perform that service. Some have come also with a subtle criticism in their hearts, "We will not pay. We deserve to receive this Teaching free. Why should there be money exchanged? We have given for many years." This rebellious attitude, beloved, is demanding that the parent or authority or guru figure not only bear the karma of the individual, which is the very fundamental definition in the [Guru-chela] relationship, but also [that the sponsoring ones] pay the physical price for this to take place.

Beloved ones, it has ever been that the chela does bring fruit to the feet of the Master. This fruit is the gain from one's tree of life realized through following the Path. That fruit is laid on the altar to multiply the abundance of Community so that the very same service given that individual may be given to ten thousand more.

If you expect our mantle—which as you have been told is a very 'heavy' mantle on the Messenger—to be the forcefield which does bear and set aside your personal karma, which it is indeed to every faithful steward, then you must understand that in exchange for having the load of karma lightened and a reprieve and an opportunity to gain your God-mastery through such unprecedented sponsorship [of the ascended hierarchy], you will have to pay the physical price. And if you are not able, it is because you have not taken the Teaching itself to use it to establish the balance of your own economy, living therefore modestly so that the demands and payments with which you surround yourself do not deprive you of meeting the most important responsibility of all [—the equity of the Guru-chela relationship].

Jesus himself spoke of those who demanded an immediate earthly reward and he did instruct his disciples privately saying, "Verily, verily, *they have their reward.*"[8] The meaning of this is [that] those who demand [of the Great Law] a physical reward have it instantaneously, but this is their full reward and there is none beyond it. There is not, in addition, a spiritual or a heavenly reward. Thus, one picks one's reward and accordingly what is most valuable [to] the individual [is what he selects and what he receives].

Is it not a pity, then, that there be such shortsightedness as to think that—so long as you have a Messenger in physical embodiment [and] you have a physical person who does assist you in bearing your karma daily, even as you assist in bearing the mantle of the office and defending it[—you should choose the material instead of the spiritual reward]?

Is it not a pity, then, that so great a gift should be turned aside by a sense of injustice, "I demand my rights"? Blessed ones, so you have received what you have asked for. But understand, where the support [of the chela] is not given, so the blessing [of the Guru] cannot be assimilated. And this is not some edict of a hierarchical being; it is the Law itself that operates independent[ly] of all of us.

Thus, the ability to assimilate Light which we send forth* comes from a profoundly loving and balanced heart, a sense of nonattachment,[9] a sense of the pearl of great price.[10] Jesus told that parable because it was necessary to tell it—that a man should go and sell all that he had and go and buy that one pearl of great price.

What is the pearl the symbol of? It is, yes, the symbol of a soul weaving greater and greater manifestation of causal body here below. But the pearl of great price does symbolize also the kingdom of God. *It is the causal body of your Ascended Master sponsor.* When you have given all to receive that sponsorship, which means to make yourself one-pointed in service in that Guru-chela relationship which you treasure beyond all [others], then you have, you see, not only the mantle of the Master bearing that karma for you but also, day by day more directly, the access to that Master's causal body.

Blessed ones, one cannot retain one's sense of injustice and enjoy the nobility of Divine Justice. [Some] things exclude other things[—i.e., they are mutually exclusive]. As God-Love in your temple must exclude all hate and hate creation, so Divine Truth must exclude all error. But if your hatreds are more important than your Divine Love because of that root of pride in the dweller-on-the-threshold,[11] then you will find in moments of your own human wrath that that hate and hate creation does fill all of thy house to the utter exclusion of the pearl of great price: and so the blessing is gone.

There is no thing that the Great Law of Love does require of thee which thou canst not fulfill with a willing heart, [with] the jaw of your Lanello, [and with] the determination and the application astutely of the scientific principles of the Call. You have the knowledge for the binding and the casting out of the dweller-on-the-threshold.[12] And if you are not successful, you have a telephone, you have a pen and paper, you can walk and you can knock on the door of our Messenger and you can say, "I need you. I cannot overcome this beast alone. Will you please help me?"

Have you ever been denied that help except perhaps when you were unwilling to first give it your best and your all? Has heaven or earth ever denied you reinforcement when you yourself truly put

*as the Universal Christ consciousness which we send forth

your hand to the plow—when you [yourself] were engaged fervently in the mighty work of the ages?

I tell you, beloved, if you ever think that help has been withheld from you, then try me this day. Come before me, as I have placed my Electronic Presence over my statue.[13] Come to me—as I AM in the heart of the Messenger—and ask and ye shall receive the help deserving of effort already made. And if that effort has not been sufficient, I tell you, you will so know it, you will see it, and though you may be ashamed before the vibrations you have entertained, you may [then and there] cast them into the [sacred] fire.

Blessed ones, some who have failed and been denied are no longer here. But I say to all who are here: out of my heart, as the Law allows and only as it allows, I shall intercede for you this day. And if you truly desire to "get right" with your God, with the Hierarchy of Light, with your true Reality and with this Messenger, then I say, this is the day to so declare it and so do it and to put [into the sacred fire] all the rest of that which has beset you from sinister forces, mind manipulations, projections you know not of (and these have stuck to you because of the sticky substance of your own self-attachment). If you can cast all that into the blazing fire of the Divine Mother and the Buddha this day, I say, you may move forward as a respectable and accountable member of our bands.

But, beloved ones, the hour is; and it is high time that the line is drawn and I do draw that line and I say: the standard will be kept and you will be told why your actions do not meet the standard; and if you do not change, there must be a severing of the tie.

Blessed ones, six months ago at Christmas you learned of the burden of the Diamond Heart and were called to share that burden.[14] It is this that is critical to the Brotherhood, that those who do not carry their own burdens and some portion of the burden of the Messenger and the activity so burden that Messenger and that activity as to be a point of danger in the very life and embodiment of the Messenger and the continuity of Community.

In your heart of hearts not one of you desires to be a detriment to the Path. Thus, if in your ignorance you have been so, I pray you receive full enlightenment of the Holy Spirit. And if you have so maligned and so entered into that vibration of despite, let it be known. For these things must be personally confessed that the Messenger may make the call and, in the gladness of her heart's love, call on the law of forgiveness for you. If you have wronged the Messenger or the Community it is not enough to confess to the Karmic Board, for the one you have wronged must also give you that forgiveness. Thus, beloved, let us come clean, for eighteen months remain ere the decade of the 1990s does begin.

Speaking to you, then, on the progress of planet earth since Wesak last, we do not see that sufficient progress has been made in the larger evolution, but we do see considerable progress on the part of some Lightbearers who have become truly shining lights and some even burning lights, for they have understood, they have intensified.

We find that others, no matter what we could say or speak in all of the dictations of these fourteen months, do not move from their lethargy, their sleepfulness, their intransigence—too dense to sense the danger [are they], too dense to sense the intercessory power of God to meet it. It is as though they were toadstools or rocks in the woods, and epochs should come and go and they should remain oblivious to extremes of Light and Darkness and unable to applaud the Victory [of the saints marching in].

The increase, then, has come to Lightbearers. And those who have Light* in their hearts (though perhaps not an extraordinary momentum) must, by the perception and the sensitivity they have by that Light, come into an era of fulfilling the mandate of the Law, as so ably described by our beloved Kuan Yin in her dictation.[15] This ought to be studied by those who seem unable or unwilling—incapable, lacking the strength to come up higher.

There is a way to come up higher. It includes casting oneself upon the rock of Being.[16] It does include entering in to a fiery coil, *even if one knows not where that coil will take him.* Thus the element of trust in one's relationship to one's own God Self is absolutely essential. You may think that you absolutely trust your God Presence, but each time you deny that Presence' intercession, you reveal the absence of trust, placing more trust in human beings or in one's human self. Thus you exclude and cut out the ministrations of the Divine Helper, of your God Self, your Holy Christ Self, your Messenger or the Hierarchy.

It is very important, therefore, that those who perhaps feel nothing, see nothing (and have not what they consider ought to be sufficient proof for this path) give this path a diligent try for six months, using the decrees, loving the Community, entering into service that balances karma and then taking note six months later [as to] what is one's spiritual progress. Some who enter this service and ritual, yet do not give with the fiery intensity of their hearts and thus do not reap the benefits, will therefore in the end declare the experiment unsuccessful. It will be successful if you desire it to be, and if you desire to prove it unsuccessful you will surely do so. The matter is out of our hands because of the sovereignty of free will.

It is an hour of turbulence in the Mideast.[17] It is an hour when there must be a lancing of Iranian and Iraqi hate and hate creation

*the balance of the Christ consciousness

directed against the Lightbearers of the world. It is an hour to be alert for the potential for war.[18] It is an hour to recognize that inasmuch as the proclamation went forth from Alpha—that dispensations were unto the Lightbearers and are unto the Lightbearers and not unto the fallen ones[19]—the jealousy and envy of the fallen ones of the Lightbearers does intensify and [as the energies of] the so-called powers that be in the earth and on the astral plane wane and as the Lightbearers increase in Light, [the fallen ones] will move, enraged, to tear from the Lightbearers [unless they are challenged] their victory and their ascension before the very patterns of Love can be fulfilled.

I recommend that from the Heart of [the Western] Shamballa you recognize that whatever else may be transpiring in the world, the judgment of the seed of the wicked, of their conspiracies, their hidden agenda and their Evil practiced against the children of God must be placed before the Lord daily through the giving of the judgment calls.[20]

Unless the right hand of Almighty God stay the action of the seed of the wicked, beloved, the Lightbearers shall find themselves in a confrontation where the temporal power is on the side of the wicked. And if those Lightbearers have neglected to fortify their auras and temples and chakras with intense Light, they will find themselves unable to be a chalice for the heavenly hosts and for the Victory.

It is indeed a divine reality that where there is no defense, spiritually or physically, the Great White Brotherhood itself is unable to place its grid of light through all octaves of Matter into the physical plane. It is this equation which is upon you individually, upon this nation and all nations. And this is what must be squarely faced.

I know and I am convinced that if you right your heart with your God and with our Hierarchy, you shall be found ever in the right hand of God and sealed in the mantle of the Divine Mother. But if you make the mistake of asserting your prideful intellect in spiritual matters you know not of nor have the ability to assess, the price you will pay will not be the immediate loss, though this be great, but it will be that in the day when you need the afflatus[21]— the entire Holy Spirit of our Hierarchy—you will suddenly sense that you are naked and bereft.[22] In that hour, beloved, when confronting the hordes of Darkness, you may cry out but it will be too late.

Thus, the call of Saint Germain and the warning ring true: *Be prepared!*[23] This preparedness is first and foremost spiritual. This preparedness must be extended to every domain.

Though you may not realize it, I have given to you the most essential instruction for the bonding of this Community in such a fiery vortex of Love. It is this Love from the Heart of the Western Shamballa that I desire to release at the very final moment of this conference. And in that Love all who are of the Love shall be bonded. Yet in that Love, which is the Ruby Ray, all who are not of Love shall be excluded.

Blessed ones, this action has waited far too long and it ought to be a cause of rejoicing. For it is, therefore, the call that says, "Choose ye this day whom ye will serve"[24]—whether Love shall be your Master or the force of anti-Love sweep you away to some other place, not prepared.

I seal your hearts that you might receive the beloved Alpha and Omega and the Buddha of the Ruby Ray.

"The Summit Lighthouse Sheds Its Radiance O'er All the World to Manifest as Pearls of Wisdom." This dictation by **Gautama Buddha** was **delivered** by the Messenger of the Great White Brotherhood Elizabeth Clare Prophet on **Sunday, July 3, 1988,** 1:55–2:48 p.m. MDT, at *FREEDOM 1988* in the Heart of the Inner Retreat at the **Royal Teton Ranch, Park County, Montana.** "Darshan and Wesak Dictation by Gautama Buddha" on 90-min. audiocassette B88101, $6.50 (add $.55 for postage); dictation included with those of Alpha and Omega and the Buddha of the Ruby Ray on videocassette HP88070, 2 hr. 18 min., $39.95 (add $1.10 for postage). [**N.B.** Bracketed material denotes words unspoken yet implicit in the dictation, added by the Messenger under Gautama Buddha's direction for clarity in the written word.] (**1**) **The Great Divine Director** is the initiator under the solar hierarchy of Capricorn on the 12 o'clock line of the Cosmic Clock, focusing the attribute of God-Power. (**2**) **Gautama's Wesak and Saint Germain's ascension day May 1 addresses** were deferred until *FREEDOM 1988.* Archangel Gabriel, 1988 *Pearls of Wisdom,* p. 419. (**3**) **Final opportunity.** Gautama Buddha, 1987 *Pearls of Wisdom,* pp. 248–49. (**4**) **Mantle of the Lord of the World upon the Messenger.** Gautama Buddha, 1987 *Pearls of Wisdom,* p. 247. (**5**) The *Manus* (Sanskrit, progenitors or lawgivers) are the sponsors who ensoul the image of the Universal Christ for a lifewave, or root race. According to esoteric tradition, there are seven primary root races—individual groups of souls who embody together and have a unique archetypal pattern, divine plan and mission to fulfill on each of the seven rays. See glossary in *Saint Germain On Alchemy,* pp. 424–46. (**6**) **Seat of the scornful.** Ps. 1:1. (**7**) **Unprofitable servant.** Matt. 25:14–30; Luke 19:12–27. (**8**) **They have their reward.** Matt. 6:1–6, 16–21. (**9**) **Nonattachment to the fruit of action.** The principle of nonattachment is basic to Buddhism as a corollary to the teaching of Gautama Buddha in his second of the Four Noble Truths, i.e., the cause of suffering is inordinate desire (see 1988 *Pearls of Wisdom,* p. 496 n. 3). In Gautama Buddha's Pearls of Wisdom series "Quietly Comes the Buddha," dictated to the Messenger Elizabeth Clare Prophet, the Lord of the World teaches on the virtue of nonattachment: "He that is great among you is the servant neither of self nor of passion's pall, not of desire save the desire to be the Buddha for humanity,... not of self-centeredness save the centering of the self in God.... The tenth perfection of the law is the balance between desire and desirelessness. It is the point of the fusion of the active and the passive.... The Perfection of Indifference is the zeal that determines the quantity of energy entrusted to your care. The three-times-three will be the nine, the ninety, the nine hundred, the nine thousand, the nine million, or the nine billion according to your ability to show indifference alike to mockery and to praise, to pleasure and to pain, to poverty or riches, adulation or indignation. This is the tenth perfection of the law—indifference to the gratitude or ingratitude of mortals, indifference to their cursings or the garlands of their approbation" (1975 *Pearls of Wisdom*, pp. 109, 144–45, or *Quietly Comes the Buddha*, pp. 46, 127–28). **(10) Pearl of great price.** Matt. 13:45, 46. **(11) Dweller-on-the-threshold.** 1988 *Pearls of Wisdom*, p. 170 n. 6. **(12) "I Cast Out the Dweller on the Threshold!"** by Jesus Christ, 1988 *Pearls of Wisdom*, p. 422. **(13)** During *FREEDOM 1988* a life-size **statue of Gautama Buddha** was set up on a special altar to the left of the main altar. Those attending the conference were invited to kneel before the statue to pray, confess or meditate. The statue depicts Gautama in a state of meditation with a gentle smile upon his blessed face; the Lord of the World is crowned, seated in a lotus posture, his eyes closed. The Messenger explained that the altar was a physical focus of Gautama Buddha's retreat centered over the Heart of the Inner Retreat, known as the Western Shamballa, which is an extension of his etheric retreat over the Gobi Desert. Photographs of this statue are available through Summit University Press, 5″ × 7″, $4.95 (add $.65 for postage), 8″ × 10″, $9.95 (add $1.10 for postage). **(14) The Order of the Diamond Heart.** 1987 *Pearls of Wisdom*, pp. 629–46. **(15)** Kuan Yin, 1988 *Pearls of Wisdom*, pp. 471–80. **(16) Casting oneself upon the rock.** Matt. 21:42–44; Luke 20:17, 18. **(17) Turbulence in the Mideast.** On July 3, 1988, at 12:54 a.m. (MDT), 13 hours prior to Gautama Buddha's dictation, the crew of the Navy cruiser the USS *Vincennes*, mistaking an Iranian Airbus jetliner for an Iranian F-14 fighter jet, shot down the aircraft over the Persian Gulf, killing all 290 people on board. The downing occurred while the *Vincennes* and other American Navy vessels were engaged in a sea battle with Iranian gunboats, during which the *Vincennes* sank two of the boats. According to the initial explanations of the *Vincennes'* captain, Will C. Rogers III, the ship's radar detected the aircraft departing from Iran's civilian-military airport at Bandar Abbas. The plane was reportedly flying outside the civilian air corridor at an unusually low altitude, descending towards the *Vincennes*. The aircraft was also believed to be emitting both civilian and military identification radio signals. When the aircraft failed to respond to multiple warnings or to change its course, Rogers concluded that the plane was on a retaliatory mission and ordered the launching of two surface-to-air missiles in order to bring the plane down. Following the incident there was speculation that the ship's highly sophisticated Aegis air-defense system had malfunctioned.

While President Reagan called the incident "a tragedy," he said it was an "understandable accident" because Rogers had believed his ship was under attack. Iranian foreign minister Ali Akbar Velayati called the incident a "barbaric massacre" and Iranian president Ali Khamenei threatened to avenge the civilian deaths. Fearing Iranian reprisals, U.S. forces were reportedly placed on heightened alert throughout the July 4 holiday period.

The final investigative report on the incident released August 19 countered the initial accounts given by the crew. The report said that the Iranian aircraft was actually climbing steadily inside the civilian air corridor and transmitting a civilian identification signal. The investigation board concluded that the Aegis system had worked properly but radar operators under the stress of combat had misinterpreted the data on the radar screens and had relayed faulty information to Captain Rogers. Adm. William J. Crowe, Jr., chairman of the Joint Chiefs of Staff, indicated in a briefing on the report that factors contributing to the tragedy included the Airbus's non-response to repeated warnings and Iran's negligence in allowing the airliner to enter the zone of the sea battle which was taking place at the time. Defense Secretary Frank C. Carlucci accepted the board's recommendation that no disciplinary action be taken against Captain Rogers or the crew.

(18) Astrological indicators of the potential for war in the near future can be seen in a number of current and approaching astrological configurations. The Ascended Masters teach that through Divine Intervention and calls to the violet flame in the science of the spoken Word, the negative conditions foretold in astrology and other prophecies can be mitigated and in some cases entirely averted before they become physical.

Conjunctions, squares and oppositions of Saturn and Uranus have coincided with the major wars of this century, including World War I, World War II, the Korean

War and the Vietnam War. These two planets formed a conjunction in the late degrees of Sagittarius on February 13 and June 26, 1988, and will do so again on October 18, indicating the likelihood of a major war. After the Saturn-Uranus conjunction of February 13, 1988, at 29° Sagittarius, Saturn and Uranus formed a nearly exact conjunction at 0° Capricorn on February 15. Saturn and Capricorn (the sign Saturn rules) act to precipitate and crystallize. Therefore, the influences of war signified by the Saturn-Uranus conjunction in Sagittarius tend to be more concrete and physically expressed when these planets are in Capricorn. Uranus and Saturn retrograded (proceeded in apparent backward motion) into Sagittarius on May 27 and June 10, 1988, respectively; in the last two months of 1988 these two planets will reenter Capricorn in close conjunction with each other—Saturn on November 12, 1988, and Uranus on December 2, 1988.

Of even greater importance, on February 22–23, 1988, Saturn and Uranus formed a nearly exact conjunction at 0° Capricorn with Mars at 0° Capricorn and Neptune more loosely associated with these three planets at 9° Capricorn. Saturn-Uranus-Neptune conjunctions are extremely rare. This conjunction joined by Mars marks the formal starting point of upheaval on the planet which could bring a number of profound changes, including war. On February 22, 1988, the Maha Chohan said that the conjunction of Mars, Saturn, Uranus and Neptune in Capricorn represents "the deliverance of the Holy Spirit's initiations to a planet. . . . This [astrological] configuration is the testing of the four lower bodies of a planet and a people" (1988 *Pearls of Wisdom,* p. 225).

In addition, transiting Pluto will cross the Soviet Union's Sun at 14° Scorpio in opposition to the U.S. natal Sun at 10° Taurus between 1989–1990. This presents a mortal and warlike challenge to both nations and will activate planets in the U.S. and Soviet charts and form volatile combinations capable of producing war. These may be triggered by transits of Mars, which make conjunctions, squares or oppositions to the transit of Pluto close to the Soviet Sun at 14° Scorpio. One such transit, although by no means the only one, will occur on November 27, 1989, when transiting Mars and Pluto form an exact conjunction at 15° Scorpio—only a degree away from the Soviet Union's Sun at 14° Scorpio and opposed to the U.S. Sun at 10° Taurus.

Sunspot indicators of the potential for war. There is also a relationship between the 11-year sunspot cycle and wars. Major wars tend to follow the peak of the sunspot cycle, although they occasionally precede it. The number of sunspots is rising and is expected to reach its peak late in 1989 or early in 1990. The cycle is rising towards the projected maximum number of sunspots faster than has been recorded since sunspot cycles have been charted beginning in the mid-1800s. It is too early to tell whether this will result in the most powerful cycle on record, but preliminary data suggests that could be the case. The sunspot maximum will be likely to combine with and amplify the other astrological cycles of war.

For an in-depth analysis of astrological portents for war, economic turmoil and earth changes, see Elizabeth Clare Prophet's February 13, 1988 lecture, "Saint Germain On Prophecy from 1988 through the 1990s—The Astrology of World Karma," on 2 videocassettes, 3 hr. 50 min., GP88019, $49.95 (add $1.50 for postage); 3 audiocassettes, 3 hr. 51 min., A88024, $19.50 (add $.95 for postage).

(19) Dispensations confined to the Lightbearers. 1987 *Pearls of Wisdom,* pp. 242–49; 1988 *Pearls of Wisdom,* p. 33 n. 2. **(20) Judgment calls.** 1988 *Pearls of Wisdom,* pp. 202, 422. **(21) afflatus** [Latin, act of breathing on]: a divine impartation of knowledge or power; the miraculous communication of supernatural knowledge; the imparting of an overmastering impulse, poetic or otherwise; inspiration. **(22) "They knew that they were naked."** Gen. 3:7; Rev. 3:17. **(23) Be prepared.** Saint Germain, 1986 *Pearls of Wisdom,* pp. 647, 648, 649; 1987 *Pearls of Wisdom,* pp. 370–71; 1988 *Pearls of Wisdom,* p. 166 n. 6. **(24) Choose you this day. . .** Josh. 24:15.

Pearls of Wisdom®

published by The Summit Lighthouse

| Vol. 31 No. 68 | Beloved Alpha and Omega | October 15, 1988 |

FREEDOM 1988

13

To Restore Divine Oneness
We Would Forge a Stronger Cord of Love

"Holy Ones of God"—so we choose to address you, for we hold you, each one, this day in the hollow of our hand, extolling, solidifying, wrapping, then, the essence of holiness of thyself from the Beginning unto the Ending, which I AM THAT I AM within you.

Know, then, the Presence of thy Father and thy Mother, true God Parents. Know, then, and remember the moment of thy descent from our Presence, some going forth on a rescue mission after others who had gone astray, some going astray thinking also to lead others back.

Blessed ones, from the moment of that parting there has extended from our heart to your own interlacing, continuous figure-eight [spirals]. These spirals, then, have been an avenue of our transmission of our Light. Yet, beloved, there has occurred in your very own psyche a breach of that oneness through loss of trust—then fear, then doubt, then anger for the succeeding separation.

Now acquaint thyself with us. Know Elohim. Know angelic hosts of Light and sense a letting go of all tensions that have beset the unconscious and blocked the soul from renewal of oneness and a tidiness of crystal cord without frays, without compromise.

Blessed ones, the absence of resolution with the Divine Parent is one of the classic conditions of the psychology of the evolutions of this earth; though not limited thereto, [it is] often reflected in the child's parental relationship. And therefore in parenting oneself one does find the repetition in a chain of being that is more than hereditary: it is indeed karmic.

Were I, then, to tell you the greatest single block to self-discovery and realization, it would be the confusion of the human parent and one's relationship thereto in this and previous lives with one's relationship to the God Parents. These God Parents take the form of the Manus, the individual Guru, [and] the twin flames of an age and a sun center sponsoring your evolution. But ultimately the God Parent that seems farthest away, that is closest at hand, is the God Parent of ourselves.

Lo, we are Alpha and Omega, truly in the white fire core of thy being. To restore Divine Oneness we come.

Blessed ones, we have forgiven to the uttermost where forgiveness has been asked for and sought and where the Great Law did see fit to fulfill [such forgiveness] for meritorious deeds and a heart of love and remorse. Some, however, have never asked. Not thinking *they* require forgiveness, they have instead failed to forgive *us* for supposed wrongs, for the long, long absence—not willing, not desiring to know or to hear or to see akasha[1] and to recognize that the separation is the doing of the child and not the parent.

Thus, beloved, if you believe that we as God Parents have wronged you somewhere down the long chain of thy evolution in these Matter spheres, consider in this hour whether, if indeed we be guilty of this, you should desire truly to embody the mercy flame and to forgive. In so doing, then, there is a healing within thyself and an [opportunity for] rapprochement to our own Three-in-One of grace.

Beloved, having sealed that forgiveness in the mantras of Kuan Yin,[2] you shall also know healing, healing within the psyche, and the beginning, beloved—the beginning of the age of reason, of accountability and magnanimity whereby you yourselves say, "What has been the part that I have played, O my Father and my Mother, whereby I find myself in this aloneness, this separation and this sense of enmity with my point of origin?"

Blessed hearts, some may be dismayed and consider that I speak to another. But you see, you have not truly examined or encountered all the layers of the subconscious; and, after all, there is a great trauma in the division between parent and child, for to deny one's parents is to deny one's self and one's own reason for being. And so, beloved, this is a very buried record.

I speak of it initially because out of the great desire of our hearts we would forge a stronger cord of Love [between ourselves and our sons and daughters]. We would prepare you for our Son Gautama's blessing and bonding of Love within this Community.[3] We would see consumed by the violet flame all schism [between the child and the God Parent]. And you would do well to tarry in that violet flame and the Kuan Yin mantras, for the need of the hour [for forgiveness and the surrender of unreality] is great.

I speak on this topic and I come to you not because the world has any greater need of us, [in terms of] the forty-eight months spoken of,[4] but that the Lightbearers indeed have need for the acceleration [in the face] of [the] Darkness [which arrays itself] against the oncoming Light.

Referring, then, to our proclamation and our dictation, we would tell you that [where there is] the hastening of the day of non-defense—where the circle of fire is not drawn, where the capacity to maintain one's integrity as a nation has been denied—there the need of the Lightbearers to be one in the bosom of God is ultimate: there, also, there cannot be further intercession [for the nations]. For when a people deny their own defense and refuse to champion it and allow a rudderless ship without captain to be their fate, then Hierarchy must intercede [on behalf of the Lightbearers].

How can the Father-Mother God, who love you as we do, fail to return to warn that, as we have considered and as we did fore-know, the judgment of the Trinity upon the fallen ones[5] has only made them more insane, more angry, more raging, more deter-mined to deny the Manchild before it is born—[even] the Cosmic Christ consciousness of a planet?

We come to extol the fiery hearts, the true disciples. Let all who fit this matrix know that we know and we appreciate that we have fiery devotees, beautiful hearts of Light within this Commu-nity; and thus these must receive our appreciation, our gratitude. And you must know our good report that because you have been willing to strive with and to vanquish that anti-decree momentum that is carried by the subconscious, because you have cut through and invoked the Light of God, you have increased numbers of rings on the Tree of Life, you have performed services that have merited you literally a cosmic protection.

Those who have not believed our report who are yet the Lightbearers and who have not literally moved heaven and earth to determine to make the calls daily, your Light has not been compromised but nor has it increased. But what is compromised, beloved, is protection. The protection that you require [but do not have] is the reason I have returned.

You will take note that at this conference and of recent hours we have taken great care to give to you very specific instructions for your spiritualization, for your increase in God consciousness, literally goading you to accelerate in a path of God-mastery, mindful [as we are] that each and every day brings you nearer to the encounter plotted by the fallen ones.

We say, then, that those who have increased mightily have proven our point and set an example at inner levels for all to see that if one has a will to wrestle and win over the beast of the not-self, one may do so; and if one is lacking in that will, then that sanctum [of the self], that hallowed circle [of free will] will never be violated by any member of Hierarchy.

It is our desire that you consider [as it] has been our desire for you to hear the reports which have come to you concerning the subjects of aliens and the manipulation of viruses and microbes to the death, [for so it is plotted by the sinister force], of the human race.[6] In past ages cataclysms have been intensified by the interference of aliens and their technology where they have desired to subjugate or supplant a race; and the karmic return of a civilization has likewise been multiplied by evil minds who have brought plagues upon peoples and nations who have made themselves vulnerable by their neglect of their God and the warnings of their prophets whom we have sent again and again to [admonish the people to] "prepare ye the day of the LORD and his coming."[7]

It has ever been thus that only to a certain extent and level have our representatives been able, by [cosmic] Law, to tell a planet and a people what they might expect if they would not return to their God. Perhaps you have a comprehension of this beyond many on this planet, but in some cases this [forewarning] has not increased a fiery intensity and zeal of the LORD [the Mighty I AM Presence] within you. Thus it has ever been so, that the knowledge of the threatening woes has been a goad only to those who are already in contact with the secret love star by virtue of the love of the threefold flame.

Beloved ones, the exhaustive nature of the release of information [by the Messengers] is most necessary, and your continuing research as well, as you recognize that there are those who are tampering with all levels of the planet, including weather, temperature, atmospheric conditions, the poles and under the poles, the seas and under the seas.

Long ago a document was written by Sanat Kumara stating the illegality of those invaders who come to disrupt a planetary lifewave and consider its evolutions to be subject to their control. Concerning, then, galactic and intergalactic law, this interference is not in keeping with these rules of conduct of a cosmos. Those who have no allegiance to Sanat Kumara disregard these laws as long as they can get away with it.

When you look at an intergalactic conspiracy of the forces of Gog and Magog,[8] the plus and the minus, those who pervert the Mother and those who pervert the Father, you come to realize that these individuals continue on their course, whether in science, whether in the controls of power [or] the physical bodies of planets or of men or of nations. They will be relentless until checked by the hosts of the LORD—through those who are in physical incarnation.

Considering all of the planetary homes and spheres that they have violated and on which they have overturned the Truth and where they have subjugated peoples genetically by warping the brain and the ability of the mind to think or to contact the Mind of God (as such manipulation has gone on upon this planet as well), you can begin to draw conclusions that though there may be many planetary spheres of similar lifewaves, few there be of Light-bearers who have retained in physical consciousness and through their mental bodies a conscious awareness of the balance of Truth.

The prophets have been solitary figures who have dotted the ages, and the wise ones and the Christed ones. They have come. They have entered an evolution, yet [they remain] independent of the genetic engineering of these gods; for we have sent them, we have protected them.

And beware of the liars in their spacecraft who lay claim that those who have been sent by God are their own. Yes, there are benign emissaries who come in spacecraft, but few, and whether the level of their benignity does reach the level of spirituality of the Great White Brotherhood is another question indeed. For even the milk of human or alien kindness is not adequate to establish a pillar of fire thrusting into the ground the Light necessary to demagnetize a planet of all the ploys and mechanisms used for mind manipulation and control.

Blessed ones, I will tell you that the fundamental lesson which I required your beloved Mark[9] to give to your present Messenger was the absolute and thorough knowledge of the continuous, round-the-clock attempt of fallen angels to manipulate the mind and heart and soul and desires of every Lightbearer on the planet and especially [of] those who did form the nucleus of this our final endeavor in this century on earth. I reiterate it here, for each and every one of you does deserve to receive the training of a Chela of God.

Chelas of God I Call you and [Chelas] of the God Flame. Chelas I Call you with a capital *C* for Chela and a capital *C* for Call. When you consider yourself a Chela of God, then remember, in the T'ai Chi of that God we are Alpha and Omega, your God Parents,

Guru in the Masculine and in the Feminine vessels of Being.

We come to restore twin flames. We come to restore right-mindfulness. We come to pierce the silly notions of silly psychic men and women. We come to realign you by the magnet of our heart to the central theme of Life, which in this hour is and must be and can be no other but spiritual survival that may become, *that may become* physical survival.

The signing away of the defenses of Europe, of America, of the West and the contemplated signing away again of even greater defenses[10] is a dire prophecy to all people of Light, who above all require time and space [in order to fulfill their destiny]. And if they but have time and space and clean food and air and a circle of fire and a spiritual sponsorship and a living Messenger, all of which you enjoy in this hour, *they will make their ascension!*

How Saint Germain has called for fifty years![11] How we would call for it! *Give me one hundred years and a true heart and I can stand here this day and guarantee your ascension, each and every one of you.* Think of it, beloved. But I cannot guarantee that if there remain but twenty-four months.[12]

And I tell you, what you have not gained in the next eighteen [months] of spiritual balance concerning the Power of the Three-Times-Three, which does mean a balanced heart flame, you will find it next to impossible to gain in the decade of the nineties. For the very karma that shall descend and the threatening woes that shall descend shall be that momentum that can be withstood only by those who have that threefold flame balanced or by those who have the good sense to affiliate themselves with those who do have the balanced threefold flame and therefore may present them-selves as plant runners,[13] one with the parent plant, one in grid of Light,* one in heart chakra, yet understanding that that balance is constantly kept by the living Guru, by the Ascended Masters, [and] by the initiates who comprise the white fire core.

Yes, there is indeed a white fire core of this Community world-wide and in this center. We have not named them, but if the Messenger should place her attention upon it, we may be so disposed to name them. Yet, they shall not yet be revealed.

We prefer, then, to contemplate the threefold flame of the entire Spirit of the Great White Brotherhood and, as the term applies, the threefold flame of the Community wherein all who are one in the bond of Love share their collective attainment of that threefold flame and therefore reinforce one another's comings and goings, protecting one another from [the conditions of] insanity and aberration and foolhardiness that are projected upon them.

*grid of the Universal Christ consciousness

There is no question that fallen ones in spacecraft seek determinedly to control the minds of yourselves through digressions into self-concern, time wasting, projecting inordinate desire, sensual desire, and any possible means of taking you from the sacred altar of alchemy where hour by hour Alpha does, Omega does assist you in re-creating yourself out of the image and likeness of the Great Lawgiver and the Great God Parents of your evolution.

We, then, have come. We, then, have come and we radiate the earth with a vibration of *protection for Lightbearers such has not been known before.* We come to pour out the maximum offering whereby you may walk in the individuality of your God Flame and know the externalization of a mastery that will restore to you that dignity, that self-respect, that Christhood portion by portion whereby you shall not be traduced.

Seek and find and make haste for balance in the physical body. This is needful, for the body must become heartily strengthened and restored to the place of the Power, the Wisdom and the Love of initial creation where your bodies were not quite as dense as they are now, not quite as burdened with karma or planetary karma and you truly had the sense of walking the earth as though in golden-age civilizations where not a pain or a worry or a limitation was known by you in the physical dimension all the days that you occupied that body. To be without the condition of discomfort or disease or pain, impairment [or] lost faculties is almost unknown on this planet, yet [such infirmity] is not at all a natural state and not one which you should longer tolerate.

The keys have been given. They simply require application and the sense that you will need the strongest bodies you can wear and maintain to anchor the maximum spirituality of your Being. To defeat, beloved ones, the powers that be which are visible, those which are astral and alien, and those which hide behind many screens and masks will surely take all of *your loving,* all of *your oneness,* all of *your work.*

I counsel you not to postpone the day of the commitment to this which we call the Pure Land, the place of the return of the Buddha, the place of the Community, even the golden shore of the West. If you wait until you have need of it to protect, defend, develop and prepare it, it will be too late.

This is an age of sudden appearances of Cosmic Christ and Maitreya to you, and of darkness and earth changes and war. Thus it is and it is ever with secret-ray initiations; and these are they which you are experiencing even in this hour in the fourteen-month cycles of Serapis Bey.[14]

Let all remember, then, the Power of geometry, the Wisdom of geometry, the Love of geometry of the "Power of the Three-Times-Three" and know that *you shall be called upon to demonstrate that God-mastery.* While there is time seek counsel, know the Lord, ask to be shown.[15]

I did give you my Mantle to accomplish goals—goals, then, of the dissemination of the Teaching and the Word and all other endeavors to which you have been called.[16] Now that Mantle in this year is qualified with the practicality, the ingenuity and the supply necessary to achieve the direction of Saint Germain for the preparedness of the Lightbearers and the Community.

This Mantle is extended for these eighteen months [July 3, 1988–December 3, 1989]. May you use it wisely and understand that this is not a cycle for the going out, going out into the world to begin new endeavors and new cycles, but this is a time to go within, to discover one's self-sufficiency in God, one's inner equilibrium and one's highest gift and attainment that can be offered on the altar of Community as service to the cause of the Great White Brotherhood.*

Some have said, "The Hierarchy no longer speaks of threat or danger or survival." Listen well. For we have warned that we shall cease speaking on that subject[17] and indeed almost the last word has been spoken on it.

We turn our attention to ultimate spiritual preparation of the psyche, [i.e., the soul], that you might understand that when a planet and a nation is beyond the point of delivering the physical defenses necessary, there must come a moment of realization that the Lightbearers must fortify themselves unto the Victory.

Is the hour past, then, when America could be defended from the timetables of returning karma, from the rip cord pulled by aliens or Soviet or other unknowns?

This timetable, beloved, has everything to do with the momentum that does continue in the Call for the judgment of these fallen ones who do plot their devices. The response to those calls and the quality of heart of devotee who does offer the Call *may mean that there is time.*

But [there is, there can be no time], absent the physical confirmation of the judgment of these fallen ones who are abject liars, incarnate murderers, those who have not a drop of mercy or a desire to spare any. These, beloved, unless bound, will carry out their agenda, even desiring to accelerate it, for they know that swift as swift does fly, what they precipitate physically becomes the sooner the safer.

*This is also the nature of the initiations of the Five Secret Rays

I trust that the combined releases of this conference will convince everyone of the intensity of ardor and fervor and service required to attain the full prize in this hour.

I trust you will realize that inasmuch as many lifewaves have been compromised, there are but a few by cosmic standards, a handful of Lightbearers across the galaxy, who have evolved to the position in Community to which you have, to be able to offer in concerted manner, as you do, the Call for the judgment and the binding of the seed of the wicked who if left unchecked would surely create a planetary holocaust.

They are indeed checked by your calls but they must be checked again and again daily. And as you give yourselves to these calls, you gain momentum, you earn good karma, your being is lighter, and in so doing, [when] combined with service, the chakras are cleared. Thus day by day you become a more powerful instrument of the very same calls you offer. *This is our only hope for mitigation.* We repeat it again.

Thus, in the Lightbearers who have responded extraordinary gains have been made. And this is the most gratifying [news] of all and [it] does truly justify the maintenance of this organization if we needed no other or had no other justification, which we do.

For [among] those who have taken to heart all that we have said, any number have become within this twelve-month period actual candidates for the ascension, whereas [formerly] they were not. And, beloved, in many cases this was because their service so assisted the world evolution of Lightbearers that they accrued a very high degree and percentage of balanced karma and of increase of Light by offsetting Darkness and displacing it through that service.

Those, then, who have an awareness of a considerable karma that remains, I tell you, there has never been an age when one could so accelerate through service to our cause—so desperate is the need, so grateful is our God, so multiplied are the results. And it is for this reason that they have entered into that league of ascension candidates. And so they shall also continue in the violet flame, [in] illumination's golden flame, and [to] seek to attain in this year that God-mastery which is commensurate with the great good karma they have made as well as [that which they have] balanced.

By the time we address you again, the head of state of this nation shall have changed. Leaders who have betrayed will be displaced by still others who shall betray.

Inasmuch as there has not appeared in the land one who could bear the mantle of that office at the level of Christhood required (and unless by some miracle one should displace the candidates who have lined up), we say that the Mantle of Alpha, the Mantle of Omega, of Saint Germain and Portia shall not descend upon the next holder of that office.[18]

As in the days of Israel when all looked for the Messiah and the birth thereof and parents prepared themselves as initiates on the Path, so in this day every chela of El Morya, out of compassion for his heart and Presence and burden, ought to consider himself in preparation to receive that mantle.[19]

Blessed ones, you may think you are not the one, [and] therefore [you may] not prepare, but if you are [the one] and you are not prepared, upon whom, then, shall the mantle fall?

Thus, when it does come to the end of an age, as Morya has set the example, all must look to the heart, all must look to the Holy Christ Self and say, "I will prepare myself to bear this mantle or perhaps a portion thereof. I must represent my nation under God and somehow bear physically the virtues required of one who enters the office of the President of the United States."

Spiritually speaking, beloved, see yourselves as candles on a giant cake, each one bearing that office; for the office itself must not perish from the earth. *It must not,* we say. To retain, therefore, the aura, the mind, the heart, even calling to Godfre and Lanello and the ascended Sons and Daughters of God [to place their Electronic Presence over you] is to secure, then, a continuity whereby the torch may again be passed to one who does arise and is qualified.

Every mother ought to raise her child upon her knee and dedicate that child to representing the people of a country, a state, a locale. Every child must be reared, then, with an appreciation for representative government, honesty, fair play, teamwork (also the Holy Spirit and the [esoteric] traditions of the history of this land, those traditions of Light and Darkness, and to know the separation of the twain) and to recognize that every child of God, every Son of Light descending in this hour is dedicated by Saint Germain and Portia to embodying all of the ideals, the full momentum with which Saint Germain has endowed this nation and which is about to be lost.

Blessed ones, so long as the flame is carried in the heart, so long as that cake representing the collective consciousness of the spiritual community worldwide has thousands of candles burning upon it, keeping alive this continuity of God-government in the earth, so long shall there endure the opportunity for the representatives of the God Star to take incarnation, to take up again the calling of restoring and reestablishing the original intent of the Constitution of the United States of America. Where shall we go to find the traditions of Liberty on earth? We shall go to the hearts of those who keep the flame of Liberty and we shall abide there. We shall come. We shall give counsel. We shall send our angels and our legions.

Let those to whom is given so mighty a salvation, a concomitant of Hierarchy, a presence so dear, throw now the refuse of their human creation once and for all into the consuming fire of God and, hearing the call of the Angel of Unity,[20] remember that you are brothers and sisters, sons and daughters of Alpha and Omega. Ye are one! Show that oneness to a world. Show that mutual support, upholding one another in Love. Show a unity that does tell us that all separation from our throne is collapsed, as time and space will indeed be collapsed for you in the ritual of your ascension.

O show us, beloved, that the remembrance of our Love in the beginning, restoring also your twin flames, is worthy in the ending of your fondest sacrifice, your noblest surrender, your selflessness and your service toward the one-pointed goal of Victory! [14-second applause]

It is not pessimistic—it is not pessimistic to live every day as though it were your last. It is not only wise but it is fortuitous. For such a goal-fitting does allow oneself to keep one's affairs tidy, to remember to forgive, to be kind and to speak the word of comfort, for another day may not dawn when the opportunity should [again] arise.

Blessed ones, this is the spirit of the conquerors who move across planets with the high step of Archangels, who grasp a planetary sphere and who know that one day their steps shall move on to the stars and [who] are determined to gain a planet for those of lesser comprehension.

It is time for bigness, bigness of thought, largesse of heart. *It is time to make your decision to fulfill your destiny, for I have come.* I have come to call you Home and to enumerate the requirements for your Homecoming, and [foremost among them] is to rescue every Lightbearer on earth, every child of God marked by the Lord your God for the Victory. Thus, let not a day pass that you do not intensify the endeavor and show to yourself some good gain that should please our hearts immensely.

Your eyes are opened. You have seen the relative good and evil of a planet and of your time. You have received the gift of the Holy Spirit of wisdom. You know the method of taking wise dominion over self and society. Exercise the spoken Word and command Light and Darkness in their proper spheres.

O destiny, thou dost call thine own from the mountains! O soul, see thyself now stepping across the high peaks of these mountains, moving north—north to the Polestar of Being, north to the I AM Presence. O come up out of the folly of selfishness and self-concern.

Indeed, beloved, indeed, beloved, I call [upon] you now to sing and sing again to the Wonderful One who comes to minister to you, the Lord Buddha of the Ruby Ray. He does literally rise from his secret chamber in the heart of the earth for this occasion. And I fancy in singing that song that you shall begin to embrace coils of his wonder and the fullness of his wonder that he would impart through Ruby Ray initiation.

Hosts of Alpha and Omega, come now, for we return to the Central Sun, having so marked earth as a "Love Star of our Oneness." We hold in our hearts a replica of the planet and of all Light-bearers, and you shall know our nourishment even as you pursue the resolution by mercy's flame of forgiveness in all directions.

> Let it be real, my dears.
> Let it be real.
> Let mercy be a living thing,
> A tender bird on wing.
> Let mercy be thy prize,
> Thy softness.
> Let mercy be the dove
> That carries you beyond the skies
> To the heart of Alpha,
> To the heart of Omega.

Beloved, do prepare for the collapse of time and space. For in an instant in the hour of thy ascension thou shalt know true Oneness which we celebrate now, and it is indeed a celebration of an event not known but one to be known, to be anticipated, to be entered into in meditation.

I raise my scepter and it shall remain raised. The scepter is the scepter of Opportunity. So long as it is raised from here to the Central Sun so shall thy opportunity be.

In the heart of Saint Germain and Portia you will always find us close at hand. [21-second pause]

Adieu, until we meet again. Our trysting place the living heart of Mercy, I trust thine own.

My Wonderful One

My Wonderful One, Thou adorable Presence
    Of God anchored now in my heart
In beauty supreme and in power majestic
    The source of my being Thou art!
I now humbly bow at the throne of thy glory
    Surrendered forever to Thee
Let all life adore Thee, my life I live for Thee
    Thy vict'ry fore'er let me be!

My Wonderful One, blaze thy violet fire through me
    Forgiveness divine let me feel
Protect and perfect, all my bodies illumine
    And teach me God only is real!
Completely possess and control me forever
    Blaze through me thy Light from the Sun
Thy power revealing, release mercy's healing
    My wonderful Wonderful One!

My Wonderful One, blaze thy glorious light rays
    In, through, and around all I've met
Then let them transmute every wrong and injustice
    Make all human shadows forget!
Then fashion a gift from the good of my lifestream
    From my causal body of Light
Give ten times the blessing of error's oppressing
    By love, make and keep all things right!

My Wonderful One, let all heaven's love bless Thee
    As God's divine plan is fulfilled
Then send me thy love in its mightiest power
    To make me perfection God-willed!
O Great Central Sun, through our Helios and Vesta
    Bless my Holy God Self, thy Flame
Our consciousness blending, at last I'm ascending
    To Thee, my own Wonderful One!

"The Summit Lighthouse Sheds Its Radiance O'er All the World to Manifest as Pearls of Wisdom." This dictation by **Alpha and Omega** was **delivered** by the Messenger of the Great White Brotherhood Elizabeth Clare Prophet on **Sunday, July 3, 1988,** 4:00–4:57 p.m. MDT, at *FREEDOM 1988* in the Heart of the Inner Retreat at the **Royal Teton Ranch, Park County, Montana.** "Darshan, Dictations and Initiations of the Ruby Ray by Alpha and Omega and the Buddha of the Ruby Ray" on 90-min. audiocassette B88102, $6.50 (add $.55 for postage); dictation by Alpha and Omega with those of Gautama Buddha and the Buddha of the Ruby Ray on videocassette HP88070, 2 hr. 18 min., $39.95 (add $1.10 for postage). [**N.B.** Bracketed material denotes words unspoken yet implicit in the dictation, added by the Messenger under Alpha and Omega's direction for clarity in the written word.] (**1**) **akasha** [Sanskrit, from the root *kāś,* to be visible, to appear, to shine brightly, to see clearly]: primary substance, the subtlest, ethereal essence which fills the whole of space; "etheric" energy vibrating at a certain frequency so as to absorb, or record, all of the impressions of life. The recordings in akasha, called akashic records, comprise all impressions of life in the matter universes; they can be read by adepts or those whose soul (psychic) faculties are developed. (**2**) *Kuan Yin's Crystal Rosary: Devotions to the Divine Mother East and West.* 1988 *Pearls of Wisdom,* pp. 373 n. 13, 480 n. 7. (**3**) **Gautama's bonding of Love.** 1988 *Pearls of Wisdom,* p. 518. (**4**) **Forty-eight months.** Alpha, 1987 *Pearls of Wisdom,* p. 388. (**5**) **Judgment of the Trinity.** "A Proclamation" by Alpha, 1987 *Pearls of Wisdom,* pp. 242–43. (**6**) Summit University Forums: **"The UFO Connection:** Alien Spacecraft and Government Secrecy," 1988 *Pearls of Wisdom,* p. 492 n. 2; **"The AIDS Conspiracy:** Establishment Cover-up, Pharmaceutical Scam, or Biological Warfare?" 1988 *Pearls of Wisdom,* p. 502 n. 8. (**7**) **Prepare ye the day of the Lord.** Isa. 2:10–22; 13:6, 9, 13; 34:8; 40:3; 61:1, 2; 63:4; Jer. 46:10; Ezek. 30:3; Joel 1:15; 2:1, 2, 31, 32; Zeph. 1; Zech. 14:1–3; Mal. 3:1–3; 4; Matt. 3:3; Mark 1:2, 3; Luke 3:3, 4; John 1:23; Acts 2:19–21; I Thess. 5:2, 3; II Pet. 3:10–12. (**8**) **Gog and Magog.** Ezek. 38:1–3; Rev. 20:7, 8. (**9**) **Mark L. Prophet,** Messenger of the Great White Brotherhood 1951–1973 and continuing in this office as the Ascended Master known as Lanello, Teacher and twin flame of the present Messenger, Elizabeth Clare Prophet. (**10**) On December 8, 1987, President Ronald Reagan and General Secretary Mikhail Gorbachev signed the **INF (Intermediate-Range Nuclear Forces) Treaty,** eliminating all ground-launched nuclear missiles with ranges between 300 and 3,400 miles. This treaty does not call for the destruction of the warheads themselves, just the missiles that would carry them. It was ratified overwhelmingly by the U.S. Senate on May 27, 1988, in time for Reagan and Gorbachev to exchange treaty ratification documents on June 1 at their summit meeting in Moscow. In this accord the United States agreed to eliminate all medium-range nuclear missiles which are deployed in European NATO countries for the defense of Europe, namely the Pershing IA (in storage), the Pershing II, and ground-launched cruise missiles (GLCMs). The U.S. also agreed to eliminate conventionally armed GLCMs on the grounds that the Soviets say they cannot tell nuclear armed cruise missiles apart from conventionally armed cruise missiles. This abolishes a highly accurate, long-range theater weapon necessary for the non-nuclear defense of Europe. (See Frank J. Gaffney, "The INF Treaty and Its Shadows over the START Negotiations," *Strategic Review,* Spring 1988.) The first missiles covered by the INF Treaty have already been destroyed and the process will continue over a period of three years. Additionally, the West German government agreed to eliminate 72 Pershing IAs that it has already deployed after the Soviet and U.S. weapons are destroyed. Some leading defense experts say the removal of U.S. nuclear missiles from Europe weakens NATO by disposing of the only weapons which could directly threaten and swiftly strike Soviet territory and therefore restrain Soviet aggression. The INF Treaty removes NATO's primary means of theater-based deterrence short of resorting to a general nuclear war. It puts NATO quantitatively, and in some cases qualitatively, at a disadvantage to Warsaw Pact conventional armaments; NATO forces are greatly outnumbered by Warsaw Pact forces, which include three times as many tanks and artillery and twice as many aircraft. NATO especially lacks the ability to withstand the Soviets' capacity to execute a blitzkrieg-like attack. (continued on Pearl no. 69)

Pearls of Wisdom®

published by The Summit Lighthouse

Vol. 31 No. 69   *The Beloved Buddha of the Ruby Ray*   October 16, 1988

FREEDOM 1988

14

A Dewdrop Rare of Ruby Ray

I Open the Pathway Leading to the Heart of Buddha

"Much good has been accomplished: even a staying action"

The secret chamber of God in the heart of the earth where I do abide is the nucleus of white fire and Ruby Ray which does hold the earth, bonding the earth and binding the earth that it not fly apart in its spin or revolution in space.

Know, then, beloved, that there is such a force on the surface of the earth to divide and fling apart by every antithesis of Love, that it does require the immense concentration of this Alpha-to-Omega, as it were, of the Body and Blood of Light of this white fire and Ruby Ray. This is our ministration, this is our office.

Knowing well, then, the forces of disintegration that are truly chaotic and charged with anger and all of the misuses of the sacred fire, I come to give you an assistance as with a touch of the Ruby Ray I do establish in you a nucleus that you might cherish in your own heart of your own world as something whereby you may hold the love of Gautama, when given, for the bonding of Community— and that of the Maha Chohan and Paul the Venetian and, in truth, all who shall follow to the conclusion.

Blessed ones, it is difficult to repel forces of anti-Love that create the rampage of insanity on the surface of this earth. How well I know and appreciate, then, your need for even a dewdrop rare of Ruby Ray wherewith to begin to build and solidify and intensify a fire infolding itself, creating an inner coil that does wind tightly and create that mass that can hold and hold on to identity when the winds of planetary change blow and when the great wind[1] does descend.

I have petitioned, then, and received the approbation of the Solar Logoi for this blessing I give. I can only tell you this, as quick as you can wink an eye shall you lose this droplet of Ruby Ray if you should so misqualify it. It cannot be retained unless it is retained in Love—internal love and internal harmony. This is not to say that for the slightest ruffle on the surface you shall lose so great a gift. Thus, I said, *internal harmony.*

When you are not moved within, though dealing with surface turmoil and tensions, you will retain and regain and increase this fire infolding itself. But if you allow the anger of fallen ones to penetrate to the core, then, beloved, there is no way that this can be retained by law, even the law of the gravity itself of Divine Love.

I come to reinforce Buddhic presence in your heart and leave indeed a replica, in outline only, of my form that you may fill in as you become the Buddha and see me mirrored in self. For I desire to live on the surface of earth in the hearts of true devotees of the Buddha. It is my prayer that you will accord me this to make my wish come true.

Blessed hearts, the fallen ones are terrified of the Ruby Ray and of those who wield it and of the ruby sword. To come into harmony with the sacred fire, to surround oneself with this fire of creation, to enter the Ruby Ray judgment calls as you have been requested to do, this, beloved, is also to secure oneself in bastions of a rocklike substance solidified as an armour of God, translucent, impervious Ruby Ray. For the most part it is the solitary ones in the mountains and etheric octaves who may sustain this, for its hazard is the chemicalization and reaction it does produce in those not part of the Great White Brotherhood.

Thus, beloved, if you so choose to call for this and live for this, you must *without fail* daily invoke the violet flame beyond the Ruby Ray fortress and citadel of Power and Power's love, that the violet flame may tenderly brace all souls that they may not become bowed down by such a presence of our Light.

Thus, long ago our Gautama did send me to the center of the earth where it should be safest for me and my path of initiation under the then Buddha of the Ruby Ray of the Heart of the Earth, and safer for those on the surface.

Thus, having had the opportunity now twice to speak to you,[2] I can assure you it is because you have carried my flame and allowed me to use my momentum and office to bring curtailment to those who should* have already unleashed devastation upon earth. Thus, I do confirm, as it has been said: *much good has been accomplished.* And I add to that, *even a staying action.*

*would; archaic: might, could

I come to reinforce those of you who have reinforced my mission by your calls. May we together bring the center and the circumference of this sphere into a polarization of balance so clear of Alpha and Omega, that we, too, might perform our task for Alpha, Omega, and Lord Gautama.

Therefore, in the name Sanat Kumara I hold up this focus of the Ruby Ray.* I shall come forward and I shall show it all about. It is necessary, then, that you come close enough to see it and to gaze upon it as you visualize it in your third eye. Over the ray of thy seeing shall thy portion return to thee. Having so received, take thy repast and gather for violet flame calls that you might be found accelerated for the day's unfolding dictations.

In the dynamic decree of the Ruby Ray *I AM Buddha.* I AM the Light now. And I send gratitude and secret-ray action to the Almighty and to his own for this opportunity granted me that I might once again open the pathway of the Buddhas of the Ruby Ray on earth leading to the heart of Sanat Kumara. May you so aspire to be and to know, for I AM One that some of you have known of old. I AM your Friend.

Think back now upon the day when you did see me, as from Shamballa I went forth at the command of Sanat Kumara and of Lord Gautama. And they did command me and all did watch as staff in hand, Ruby Ray focus about my neck, I did enter a cave and I did begin to walk and I did walk to the center of the earth.

Blessed ones, some of you here today who were there then said in your hearts, "Not I, I shall not enter a cave. Who knows where it ends or where I shall be or if I may ever emerge?" For I was told in that hour and all heard it, "You shall not come forth until there be those on the surface of the earth who can hold the balance for the attainment that shall be thine own."

So, beloved, you might say that I have been confined to hold the nucleus of a planet at the mercy of such as yourselves until you should arrive at the place of a similar love for the Ruby Ray. A love you indeed do have, that we now share, can surely be a mighty gift to Sanat Kumara.

Thus I step forward and may you also. And remember, nevermore shall we be separated by time or space. And you also in your hour and your time, receiving assignment from Sanat Kumara, shall accept it where'er it may take you, knowing that in the heart of Love is the fullness of all thy desiring, all thy becoming, all of thy Buddhahood, all of thy Motherhood.

*Purusha.*³ *Oṁ,* beloved.

—————
*an uncut ruby crystal

This dictation by the **Buddha of the Ruby Ray** was **delivered** by the Messenger Elizabeth Clare Prophet on **Sunday, July 3, 1988,** 5:07–5:22 p.m. MDT, at *FREEDOM 1988* in the Heart of the Inner Retreat at the **Royal Teton Ranch, Park County, Montana.** Available on 90-min. audiocassette with dictation of Alpha and Omega, B88102, $6.50 (add $.55 for postage); on videocassette with dictations of Gautama Buddha and Alpha and Omega, 2 hr. 18 min., HP88070, $39.95 (add $1.10 for postage). **(1) Great wind.** Elohim Peace and Jesus, 1988 *Pearls of Wisdom,* pp. 364, 389. **(2)** The Nameless One from the Center of the Earth, 1986 *Pearls of Wisdom,* pp. 633–36. **(3)** *Purusha/Parousia.* 1988 *Pearls of Wisdom,* p. 228 note.

Notes from Pearl no. 68 by Alpha and Omega continued:
(10) Discussions between delegations from the United States and the Soviet Union on **START (Strategic Arms Reduction Talks),** a broader arms control agreement than the INF Treaty, began on June 29, 1982. The aim of these negotiations is to cut all strategic weapons by 50 percent. During the December 1987 summit in Washington, D.C., President Reagan and General Secretary Gorbachev agreed to the goal of reducing their long-range strategic nuclear stockpiles to 6,000 warheads and 1,600 delivery systems each. Within the 6,000 warhead total, a sublimit would be required of 4,900 warheads on intercontinental ballistic missiles (ICBMs) and submarine-launched ballistic missiles (SLBMs).

The general rules for counting warheads that were agreed upon at the summit contain loopholes for counting weapons. Political restraint in the United States would hold us to the agreement. However, in a paper on the breakout and verification implications of the START agreement, the Defense Policy Panel of the House Armed Services Committee stated that for Moscow "the purported START limit of 6,000 weapons is an illusion. In addition to the limit of 6,000 weapons, the Soviets could 'legally' —and are likely to—deploy another nearly 3,000 weapons and could 'legally' have available nearly 11,000 additional weapons that are a source for a sudden breakout from START. And, according to [a] rough yardstick of potential cheating, there could be an additional force of as many as 4,300 more weapons available to the Soviet attack planner." The report suggests that these potential loopholes could make available more than 18,000 uncounted nuclear devices, which gives Moscow the capacity to break out from the START treaty before the U.S. could catch up to the Soviets' numerical advantage. Even if the Soviets don't cheat, given the types of existing U.S. and Soviet weapons systems and the proposed START limits, the U.S. will be left with fewer nuclear weapons platforms for the Soviets to target. This would give the Soviets a significant advantage and increase the likelihood that they would exploit that advantage by launching a first strike. (See Defense Policy Panel of the House Armed Services Committee, *Breakout, Verification and Force Structure: Dealing with the Full Implications of START,* 100th Cong., 1st sess., 1988; James L. George, "The 'Two-Track' Dilemma in the START Negotiations," *Strategic Review,* Winter 1988.)
(11) Saint Germain's call for fifty years of peace. Saint Germain and the Goddess of Liberty, 1987 *Pearls of Wisdom,* pp. 95, 108. **(12) Twenty-four months.** El Morya, 1987 *Pearls of Wisdom,* pp. 474, 480; 1988 *Pearls of Wisdom,* p. 249 n. 7. **(13)** A **runner** is a creeping plant stem that extends from the base of the main stem and takes root to grow a new plant. **(14) Serapis Bey's fourteen-month cycles** are a series of personal and planetary initiations through the rings of the causal body amplified by the ascension flame. 1988 *Pearls of Wisdom,* p. 502 n. 6. **(15) Seek while there is time.** Eccl. 12:1; Isa. 55:6. **(16) Alpha's Mantle.** 1987 *Pearls of Wisdom,* pp. 384–86. **(17)** Archangel Michael and Jesus Christ, 1988 *Pearls of Wisdom,* pp. 91, 296. **(18)** The **office of President** of the United States of America is a spiritual office in the Hierarchy of the Great White Brotherhood. Though not all who have worn the mantle have been worthy of it, yet the mantle has not been withdrawn, for the soul of a nation has been worthy. In this hour the people themselves have neglected their God and their true Prophets and they have failed to challenge the politics of Evil in their midst. Hence it is they who have forfeited the Divine Right to have an anointed head of state. May God help us. **(19) Mantle of the presidency.** El Morya, 1988 *Pearls of Wisdom,* pp. 1–8. **(20) Micah, the Angel of Unity,** appeared in George Washington's vision of three great perils that would come upon the nation—the Revolutionary War, the War between the States and a third world conflict. According to Anthony Sherman's account of this vision, Washington related that he was shown the inhabitants of America "in battle array against each other. As I continued looking I saw a bright angel, on whose brow rested a crown of light, on which was traced the word 'Union,' bearing the American flag which he placed between the divided nation, and said, *'Remember ye are brethren.'* Instantly, the inhabitants, casting from them their weapons, became friends once more and united around the National Standard." *Saint Germain On Alchemy,* pp. 142–51, or *The Great White Brotherhood in the Culture, History and Religion of America,* pp. 118–23.

Pearls of Wisdom®
published by The Summit Lighthouse

Vol. 31 No. 70   *Beloved Paul the Venetian*   *October 22, 1988*

FREEDOM 1988

15

An Appreciation of the Heart
Discipleship under the Third Ray unto the Ruby Ray Buddha
Initiation by the Emerald Matrix

It is the hour of the melting of the elements with the fervent heat[1] of the Divine Love of the Buddha of the Ruby Ray and all manifestations, replications, of the Five Dhyāni Buddhas.

I come to you this hour escorting your soul from the place of the Divine Mother to the secret chamber of the heart, the eight-petaled chakra. Let us steal inside and abide.

Oṁ Oṁ Oṁ Maṇi Padme Hūṁ [35 times]*   *Oṁ Vairochana Oṁ Oṁ Vairochana Oṁ Oṁ Vairochana Oṁ*

Beloved of my heart, I address you this evening on the line [of the Cosmic Clock] of my Cosmic Mother, the Goddess of Liberty, the seven o'clock line of the [flame of] God-Gratitude which does release the power of the Eighth Ray chakra for the multiplication of the five secret rays.

Thus, I take you through these rays by an appreciation of the heart—*the appreciation of the heart:* the sensitivity, the profound love. For only Love enables you to pass through the walls of the crystal Ruby Ray that is indeed the lining of the caves of the Dhyāni Buddhas, caves of Light. Thus Buddhic path of Saint Germain is also revealed.

The Maha Chohan has called me for a ministration of Love whereby you might pursue a discipleship under the Third Ray unto the Ruby Ray Buddha.

Aiṁ [16 times]   *Maiṁ* [6 times]   *Oṁ Āḥ Hūṁ Vajra Guru Padma Siddhi Hūṁ* [56 times]

*seed syllables and mantras sounded by the Master with audience joining in

The ideal purpose of my coming is the use of the emerald crystal to direct to your hearts and specifically to the eight petals of the eight-petaled chakra that wavelength of the emerald ray, beloved, whereby there is established the forcefield for the precipitation of the chalice for the Buddha of the heart. Thus, as you continue the mantra, the mantra of Padma Sambhava,[2] so I shall extend now that action.

Some of you know that I use the emerald stone as well as the emerald cape and the emerald lining of the rose cape. Therefore, beloved, be receptive to the action of this Fifth Ray that does unlock, petal by petal, the means whereby the door shall be opened to you unto the chambers of the Five Dhyāni Buddhas. By the Love of the beings of the Third Ray, so receive this action.*

Oṁ Āḥ Hūṁ Vajra Guru Padma Siddhi Hūṁ [59 times]

Ribbons of emerald light punctuate Eightfold Path etched in the petals of the heart.

Now, beloved, my Mentor and Guru, the Maha Chohan, does take this wondrous occasion of divine alchemy to serve to you the Communion of the Holy Spirit, the Alpha and the Omega of cloven tongues of the Holy Spirit. Thus, out of the universal Light Body of the Holy Spirit that is the attainment of this Lord there is transmitted to you a Communion that is essential if you would seriously pursue the path of the five secret rays as a means to the mastery of the Power of the Three-Times-Three, the balanced threefold flame, and the initiations of the half hours of the Dhyāni Buddhas.

O Kuan Yin is so near as the Mother Flame of this Communion, beloved, as the Mother representative of these Buddhas, even as the Lord the Maha Chohan does minister to you now through our servants. Therefore, let the wine and the bread be brought before the altar, for our Lord [the Maha Chohan] desires to consecrate it.

I AM Alpha and Omega in the white fire core of being. [19 times]

*While the assembly of Lightbearers gave the mantra of Padma Sambhava with Paul the Venetian, the Messenger faced the audience from different points on the altar as she held up Saint Germain's emerald crystal in her right hand.

"The Summit Lighthouse Sheds Its Radiance O'er All the World to Manifest as Pearls of Wisdom." This dictation by **Paul the Venetian** was **delivered** by the Messenger of the Great White Brotherhood Elizabeth Clare Prophet on **Monday, July 4, 1988,** 12:57–1:21 a.m. MDT, at *FREEDOM 1988* in the Heart of the Inner Retreat at the **Royal Teton Ranch, Park County, Montana.** Darshan and dictations of Paul the Venetian and the Maha Chohan, with teachings on the gifts of the Holy Spirit on the Cosmic Clock and teachings on the Five Dhyāni Buddhas, their mantras and positions on the Clock, on two 90-min. audiocassettes, B88103–4, $13.00 (add $.95 for postage); add $1.00 for charts to accompany the cassettes, #2489. Dictation by Paul the Venetian included with those of the Maha Chohan and Saint Germain on videocassette HP88073, 1 hr. 42 min., $19.95 (add $1.10 for postage). [**N.B.** Bracketed material denotes words unspoken yet implicit in the dictation, added by the Messenger under Paul the Venetian's direction for clarity in the written word.]
(1) **Melting of the elements.** II Pet. 3:10, 12. (For note 2 see p. 544.)

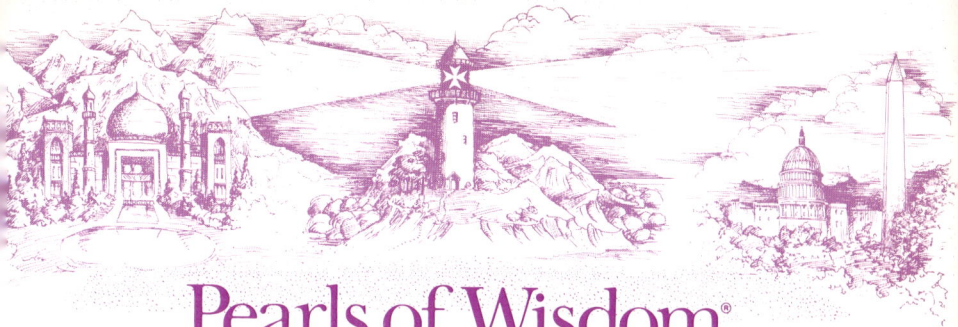

Pearls of Wisdom®

published by The Summit Lighthouse

Vol. 31 No. 71   *The Beloved Maha Chohan*   *October 23, 1988*

FREEDOM 1988

16

Communion of the Holy Spirit

A New Highway of Our God: Enter by Initiation

Most gracious ones of the Light, as you have long anticipated the baptism by fire of the Holy Ghost[1] promised by the bodhisattva Saint Issa,[2] so, then, know there is also a Communion of the Holy Spirit whereby [through] heart and soul and mind the action of the Three Jewels[3] amplified by the threefold flame of thy Holy Christ Self does transmit to innermost being the Light-essence of Alpha and Omega that is borne in my office as Representative of the Holy Spirit to the evolutions of earth.

Therefore, by blessed hands of Community members this bread has been prepared that I might use it as a chalice for the [sacred fire of Holy Spirit's] Communion [which I now serve to] this Community. Know, then, beloved, that at this moment of this conference you are receiving the Body and Blood of the entire Spirit, the *Holy* Spirit, of the Great White Brotherhood.

It is the means whereby [we may] store in the bands of the secret rays surrounding the secret chamber of the heart [the Alpha-to-Omega balance of the Light-essence of Holy Spirit]. There is then established a co-measurement of your soul whereby not only may *you* enter the crystal caves of the Five Buddhas but *they* may also enter the five spheres[4] which are given to you by God as receptacles for their five rays and virtues and all that they represent.

Blessed hearts, I am now charging this substance with a portion of white fire of Alpha and Omega of the Holy Spirit. Receive, then, as you are able, for it is done in the name of Sanat Kumara, it is done in the name of Gautama Buddha, it is done in the name of Maitreya and in the name Jesus Christ.

It is done, beloved, in the name of your I AM Presence, in the name of your inner name, which no man knoweth[5] saving the Father and him that receiveth it from the Father. This name is actually the code, the inner code to your inner being in the five secret rays. Therefore it is not uttered in this octave.

Understand, then, that I also take my authority to serve you from your own inner God-free being. Understand also that the very heart of our message this evening has been delivered to you by the Messenger[6] and that our coming is [to the end] that by the action of the Emerald Matrix and the Communion you might be afforded the ability, the opportunity to enter a new path, a new highway of our God formerly not open to you—not because of a want of this teaching or knowledge (which the Messenger has taught many years ago) but because knowledge is not a sufficiency to enter into this path but only initiation. Therefore, may it so happen again (for it must happen in person) that I might be sent to administer this Communion.

Thus, beloved, in the fulfillment of all cycles it is our prayer with the Lord of the World, Alpha and Omega, the Buddha of the Ruby Ray and all love of a cosmos that by our ministrations and by our Presence with you always you might truly fulfill your reason for being.

O beloved, if you desire it, you truly enter—upon the foundation of my Sons, the Lords of the Seven Rays—a most noble journey through these five secret rays. Thus, blest Serapis, inaugurator of these cycles of the fourteen months of the secret rays, is very much a part, *very much a part* of your training and initiation. And all of the Chohans are profoundly desirous of your coming to their retreats[7] and [of] your making the call for all things to be accomplished on each of the seven rays[8] that must be completed and fulfilled [in order] that you have the strength and the foundation when in the course of the secret rays[9] to truly realize their intensity.

Now may you take this Communion; as our ministers, decree leaders lead you in the call to Mighty Cosmos' secret rays, feel that this is what you are assimilating in the five aspects of the Buddhas.

Oṁ Oṁ Oṁ Oṁ Oṁ Oṁ Oṁ Oṁ Oṁ Oṁ[10]

I desire, then, a sealing action and your entering in to the Great Silence following the taking of this Communion. Thus concluding your calls to the secret rays, my angels [will] accompany you [as you] take your rest and come directly to my retreat[11] for the completion of this ritual.

I seal you in the living Flame of my Love.[12]

Mighty Cosmos' Secret Rays

In the name of the beloved mighty victorious Presence of God, I AM in me, my very own beloved Holy Christ Self, Holy Christ Selves of all mankind, beloved Helios and Vesta and the Great Central Sun Magnet, beloved God Harmony, beloved Mighty Cosmos, beloved Lanello, the entire Spirit of the Great White Brotherhood and the World Mother, elemental life—fire, air, water, and earth! I decree:

> Mighty Cosmos' Secret Rays, (3x)
> Expand thy Light through me always! (3x)
> Mighty Cosmos' Secret Rays, (3x)
> Bless and heal, illumine and raise! (3x)
> Mighty Cosmos' Secret Rays, (3x)
> Transmute, consume, release, and blaze! (3x)
> Mighty Cosmos' Secret Rays, (3x)
> For thy Love, O God, we praise! (3x)
> Mighty Cosmos' Secret Rays, (3x)
> Raise the earth, thy flame expand! (3x)
> Mighty Cosmos' Secret Rays, (3x)
> Thy balancing power I now command! (3x)

> > Take dominion now,
> > To thy Light I bow;
> > I AM thy radiant Light,
> > Secret rays so bright.
> > Grateful for thy rays
> > Sent to me today,
> > Fill me through and through
> > Until there's only you!

I live, move, and have my being within a glorious, victorious focus of Mighty Cosmos' Secret Rays from the heart of God in the Great Central Sun, my very own beloved individualized I AM Presence, beloved Helios and Vesta, and beloved Mighty Cosmos which blesses and heals, illumines and seals me and all mankind in the Victory of the ascension in the Light.
Beloved I AM! Beloved I AM! Beloved I AM!

"The Summit Lighthouse Sheds Its Radiance O'er All the World to Manifest as Pearls of Wisdom." This dictation by the **Maha Chohan** was **delivered** by the Messenger of the Great White Brotherhood Elizabeth Clare Prophet on **Monday, July 4, 1988,** 1:21–1:31 a.m. MDT, at *FREEDOM 1988* in the Heart of the Inner Retreat at the **Royal Teton Ranch, Park County, Montana.** Available on 90-min. audiocassette with dictation of Paul the Venetian, B88104, $6.50 (add $.55 for postage); on videocassette with dictations of Paul the Venetian and Saint Germain, 1 hr. 42 min., HP88073, $19.95 (add $1.10 for postage). [**N.B.** Bracketed material denotes words unspoken yet implicit in the dictation, added by the Messenger under the Maha Chohan's direction for clarity in the written word.] **(1) Baptism by fire of the Holy Ghost.** Pistis Sophia, bk. 3, chap. 115. See also Matt. 3:11; Mark 1:8; Luke 3:15–17. **(2)** Jesus is called **Issa** in both written chronicles and oral traditions of the East, where he spent his 17 "lost years," from age 13 to 29, not accounted for in the Bible. See Elizabeth Clare Prophet, *The Lost Years of Jesus;* "The Lost Years of Jesus," *Heart: For the Coming Revolution in Higher Consciousness,* Spring 1983. **(3)** The **Three Jewels** are the three major components of the Buddhist affirmation of faith in which all sincere devotees "take refuge"—the Buddha, the Dharma (Teaching), the Sangha (Community). 1988 *Pearls of Wisdom,* p. 447 n. 9. **(4)** These spheres surround the heart chakra and anchor the five inner secret-ray spheres which surround the white-fire core of the causal body. **(5) The inner name which "no man knoweth."** Rev. 2:17; 19:12. **(6)** Darshan and teachings of Paul the Venetian and the Maha Chohan on the gifts of the Holy Spirit and the Five Dhyāni Buddhas. See 1988 *Pearls of Wisdom,* p. 540 note. **(7)** to their etheric retreats by soul travel in the etheric body during the hours of sleep **(8)** and on the lines of the Cosmic Clock on which the rays are charted **(9)** the path of initiation on the five secret rays administered by the Maha Chohan in conjunction with Serapis Bey's training and initiation given at Luxor **(10)** Assembly of Lightbearers joins the Maha Chohan in sounding the *Oṁ* 10 times. **(11)** The **retreat of the Maha Chohan,** the Temple of Comfort, is located on the etheric plane with a focus in the physical at the island of Sri Lanka (Ceylon). On January 1, 1986, Gautama Buddha and the Lords of Karma granted a petition of the Lords of the Seven Rays to open **universities of the Spirit** in their etheric retreats for tens of thousands of students to systematically pursue the path of self-mastery on the seven rays. Students receive training under each of the Lords of the Seven Rays and the Maha Chohan during two-week retreats. Following the schedule in the order the Chohans were named by Gautama Buddha on January 1, 1986, and the God Meru on December 28, 1986, a 14-day period of training at the retreat of the Maha Chohan was taking place June 30–July 13, 1988, concurrent with *FREEDOM 1988.* See 1988 *Pearls of Wisdom,* pp. 287–88 n. 5, chart p. 438; Mark L. Prophet and Elizabeth Clare Prophet, *Lords of the Seven Rays: Mirror of Consciousness.* **(12)** Messenger's hand is raised in blessing, holding the Emerald Matrix.

Notes from Pearl no. 70 by Paul the Venetian continued:
(2) Padma Sambhava (fl. A.D. 8th century), whose name means "born of the lotus," is revered as the Great Guru of Tibetan Buddhism. According to a manuscript written by one of his feminine disciples, Ye-she-Tsho-gyal (lit., "victorious one of the ocean of wisdom"), the coming of Padma Sambhava was foretold by Gautama Buddha at his passing: "Twelve years after my departure, from a lotus blossom on the Dhanakosha Lake, in the north-western corner of the country of Urgyan, there will be born one who will be much wiser and more spiritually powerful than myself. He will be called Padma Sambhava, and by him the Esoteric Doctrine will be established." (Mystery has surrounded his birth and death; some accounts record that the Great Guru lived for over 3,000 years.) Although much of the life and work of Padma Sambhava is obscured in legend, he was famed for his mystical powers and mastery of the occult sciences. In 746–47, by invitation of the Tibetan king Thī-Srong-Detsan, he traveled from India to Tibet, where he founded the Nyingmapa school of Buddhism. Under royal patronage, he converted the country to Tantric Buddhism, elevating the people from barbarism to spirituality. According to tradition, Padma Sambhava taught that his "Golden Mantra," Oṁ Āḥ Hūṁ Vajra Guru Padma Siddhi Hūṁ, was to be used in a coming time of troubles, during which warfare, disease and poverty would increase, as an antidote to the confusion and frustration of that dark age. Each word of the mantra is given with a different mudra. See Elizabeth Clare Prophet, "The Lost Teachings of Jesus and Maitreya on Your Divine Reality": audiocassette III, 1½ hr., B88029, $6.50 (add $.55 for postage); full lecture on 3 audiocassettes, 3 hr. 46 min., A88027, $19.50 (add $.95 for postage), and on 2 videocassettes, 3 hr. 44 min., GP88023, $39.95 (add $1.50 for postage).

Pearls of Wisdom®
published by The Summit Lighthouse

| Vol. 31 No. 71A | Elizabeth Clare Prophet | October 25, 1988 |

FREEDOM 1988
Fourth of July Address

Part 1
The Signing of the Declaration of Independence
and
George Washington's Vision

In the name of Saint Germain, in the name of our heavenly Father and the Divine Mother, the living Christ and the Holy Spirit, Amen.

I begin by reading to you from Saint Germain's dictation given at Thanksgiving in Washington, D.C.

Ho! It is the last time that I shall appear in this nation's capital unless and until those who know better do better—until those who have seen my calling and heard my word respond to it and postpone not the day of our God's appearing.

Lo, my Presence has counted for ye all for millions of years in this earth and in higher octaves. In joy and love and with what fond purpose I have sponsored this nation and this opportunity!

Keepers of the Flame, by your leave I AM sent from the Great Central Sun to stand in the midst of this city as a pillar of violet flame, my aura, then, sealing a destiny—a destiny far spent.

For America has abdicated her role as the nation of Christhood, the eternal Law of God, as the nation wherein The LORD Our Righteousness should raise up a standard, an ensign of the people and a two-edged sword.

Thus, beloved, through your hearts and yours alone, the Lightbearers in all the earth—those who know me and may not know my name but have espoused the Cause of Freedom and of Peace—through them I shall continue to work.

But I shall not be here, beloved, to deliver to you another statement of my word or my call unless the representatives of the people, from the highest office in the land to the least, shall take their stand for the defense of Freedom. . . .

I tell you this, *I AM a living pillar of violet flame!*

Wheresoever you shall raise up that violet flame by a concerted action of a decree momentum, there I shall be, as it were, the genie of the lamp, the lamp of knowledge and transmutation, the lamp of transfiguration and the transubstantiation of the body and the blood of thyself, that the Lord Christ might truly enter therein. Wheresoever a pillar of violet flame is raised up, because it is the equivalency of my Presence I shall be there. . . .

Know then, O beloved, that footprint for footprint if America and the earth shall long desire the Presence of Saint Germain with them, they must forge a fire, truly a violet flame fire where I may place my feet. It is indeed the last time, the last Opportunity, the last Freedom and Justice. Either these flames be raised up by the Lightbearers of the world or you shall see the Darkness prophesied by young and old alike, those who have seen, those who have known, and those who have read the report of that which the enemy does propose against this nation and against all people of freedom worldwide.[1]

Following this dictation Saint Germain was seen leaving the city, his hooded purple cape pulled closely about him, striding toward the Rocky Mountains. It is time, then, to ponder Saint Germain's exit from our capital, what it means for us, for America and for the world.

It was a grand experiment which he began in Independence Hall in 1776. We don't often think about the courage it took to sign the Declaration of Independence. Today it is a matter of fact that fifty-six delegates from the thirteen colonies put their pens to parchment and signed that document. In retrospect it seems like the obvious thing for them to have done. But they were putting their lives on the line and they didn't know what the next day would bring.

By signing the Declaration, all were guilty of high treason under British law. The penalty for high treason was to be hanged by the neck until unconscious, then cut down and revived, then disemboweled and cut into quarters.[2] The head and quarters were at the disposal of the crown.

No wonder they wavered! No wonder they discussed back and forth for days on end before signing the document that carried so grave a penalty. An old legend dramatizes the story of the one who galvanized the delegates and gave them the courage to sign that document.

But still there is doubt—and that pale-faced man, shrinking in one corner, squeaks out something about axes, scaffolds, and a—*gibbet!*

"*Gibbet!*" echoes a fierce, bold voice, that startles men from their seats—and look yonder! A tall slender man rises, dressed—although it is summer time—in a dark robe. Look how his white hand undulates as it is stretched slowly out, how that dark eye burns, while his words ring through the hall. (We do not know his name, let us therefore call his appeal)

THE SPEECH OF THE UNKNOWN.

"Gibbet? They may stretch our necks on all the gibbets in the land—they may turn every rock into a scaffold—every tree into a gallows, every home into a grave, and yet the words on that Parchment can never die!

"They may pour our blood on a thousand scaffolds, and yet from every drop that dyes the axe, or drips on the sawdust of the block, a new martyr to

Freedom will spring into birth!

"The British King may blot out the Stars of God from His sky, but he cannot blot out His words written on the Parchment there! The works of God may perish—His Word, never!

"These words will go forth to the world when our bones are dust. To the slave in the mines they will speak—*hope*—to the mechanic in his workshop—*freedom*—to the coward-kings these words will speak, but not in tones of flattery. No, no! They will speak like the flaming syllables on Belshazzar's wall—

The days of your pride and glory are numbered!
The days of judgment and revolution draw near!

"Yes, that Parchment will speak to the Kings in a language sad and terrible as the trump of the Archangel. You have trampled on mankind long enough. At last the voice of human woe has pierced the ear of God, and called His Judgment down! You have waded on to thrones over seas of blood—you have trampled on to power over the necks of millions—you have turned the poor man's sweat and blood into robes for your delicate forms, into crowns for your anointed brows. Now Kings—now purpled Hangmen of the world—for you come the days of axes and gibbets and scaffolds—for you the wrath of man—for you the lightnings of God!—

"Look! How the light of your palaces on fire flashes up into the midnight sky!

"Now Purpled Hangmen of the world—turn and beg for mercy!

"Where will you find it?

"Not from God, for you have blasphemed His laws!

"Not from the People, for you stand baptized in their blood!

"Here you turn, and lo! a gibbet!

"There—and a scaffold looks you in the face.

"All around you—death—and nowhere pity!

"Now executioners of the human race, kneel down,

yes, kneel down upon the sawdust of the scaffold—lay your perfumed heads upon the block—bless the axe as it falls—the axe that you sharpened for the poor man's neck!

"Such is the message of that Declaration to Man, to the Kings of the world! And shall we falter *now?* And shall we start back appalled when our feet press the very threshold of Freedom? Do I see quailing faces around me, when our wives have been butchered—when the hearthstones of our land are red with the blood of little children?

"What are these shrinking hearts and faltering voices here, when the very Dead of our battlefields arise, and call upon us to sign that Parchment, or be accursed forever?

"Sign! if the next moment the gibbet's rope is round your neck! *Sign!* if the next moment this hall rings with the echo of the falling axe! *Sign!* By all your hopes in life or death, as husbands—as fathers—as men—sign your names to the Parchment or be accursed forever!

"Sign—and not only for yourselves, but for all ages. For that Parchment will be the Text-book of Freedom—the Bible of the Rights of Man forever!

"Sign—for that declaration will go forth to American hearts forever, and speak to those hearts like the voice of God! And its work will not be done, until throughout this wide Continent not a single inch of ground owns the sway of a British King!

"Nay, do not start and whisper with surprise! It is a truth, your own hearts witness it, God proclaims it.—This Continent is the property of a free people, and their property alone. [17-second applause] God, I say, proclaims it!

"Look at this strange history of a band of exiles and outcasts, suddenly transformed into a *people*—look at this wonderful Exodus of the oppressed of the Old World into the New, where they came, weak in arms but mighty in Godlike faith—nay, look at this history of your Bunker Hill—your Lexington—where a band of plain farmers mocked and trampled down the panoply of British arms, and then tell me, if you can, that God has not given America to the *free?* [12-second applause]

"It is not given to our poor human intellect to climb the skies, to pierce the councils of the Almighty One. But methinks I stand among the awful clouds which veil the brightness of Jehovah's throne. Methinks I see the Recording Angel—pale as an angel is pale, weeping as an angel can weep—come trembling up to that Throne, and speak his dread message—

"'Father! the old world is baptized in blood! Father, it is drenched with the blood of millions, butchered in war, in persecution, in slow and grinding oppression! Father—look, with one glance of Thine Eternal eye, look over Europe, Asia, Africa, and behold evermore, that terrible sight, man trodden down beneath the oppressor's feet—nations lost in blood—Murder and Superstition walking hand in hand over the graves of their victims, and not a single voice to whisper, *"Hope to Man!"*'"

"He stands there, the Angel, his hands trembling with the black record of human guilt. But hark! The voice of Jehovah speaks out from the awful cloud—'Let there be light again. Let there be a New World. Tell my people—the poor—the trodden down millions, to go out from the Old World. Tell them to go out from wrong, oppression and blood—tell them to go out from this Old World—to build my altar in the New!' [11-second applause]

"As God lives, my friends, I believe that to be *his* voice! Yes, were my soul trembling on the wing for Eternity, were this hand freezing in death, were this voice choking with the last struggle, I would still, with the last impulse of that soul, with the last wave of that hand, with the last gasp of that voice, implore you to remember this truth—*God has given America to the free!* [13-second applause]

"Yes, as I sank down into the gloomy shadows of

the grave, with my last gasp, I would beg you to sign that Parchment, in the name of the *God,* who made the Saviour who redeemed you—in the name of the millions whose very breath is now hushed in intense expectation, as they look up to you for the awful words—*'You are free!'* " [9-second applause]

O many years have gone since that hour—the Speaker, his brethren, all, have crumbled into dust, but it would require an angel's pen to picture the magic of that Speaker's look, the deep, terrible emphasis of his voice, the prophet-like beckoning of his hand, the magnetic flame which shooting from his eyes, soon fired every heart throughout the hall!

The work was done. A wild murmur thrills through the hall.—Sign? Hah? There is no doubt now. Look! How they rush forward—stout-hearted John Hancock has scarcely time to sign his bold name, before the pen is grasped by another—another and another! Look how the names blaze on the Parchment—Adams and Lee and Jefferson and Carroll, and now, Roger Sherman the Shoemaker.

And here comes good old Stephen Hopkins—yes, trembling with palsy, he totters forward—quivering from head to foot, with his shaking hands he seizes the pen, he scratches his patriot-name.

Then comes Benjamin Franklin the Printer. . . .

And now the Parchment is signed; and now let word go forth to the People in the streets—to the homes of America—to the camp of *Mister* Washington, and the Palace of George the Idiot-King—let word go out to all the earth—

And, old man in the steeple, now bare your arm, and grasp the Iron Tongue, and let the bell speak out the great truth:

Fifty-six traders, lawyers, farmers and mechanics have this day shook the shackles of the world! [13-second applause]

Hark! Hark to the toll of that Bell!

Is there not a deep poetry in that sound, a poetry

more sublime than Shakespeare or Milton?

Is there not a music in the sound, that reminds you of those awful tones which broke from angel-lips, when news of the child Jesus burst on the shepherds of Bethlehem?

For that Bell now speaks out to the world, that—

God has given the American continent to the free—
the toiling millions of the human race—
as the last altar of the rights of man on the globe—
the home of the oppressed, forevermore![3]

[10-second applause]

Are we not bought with a price?

This reading is taken from the book *Washington and His Generals: or, Legends of the Revolution* by George Lippard, published in 1847.

In pledging their lives, fortunes and sacred honors, the 56 signers of the Declaration risked much. Twenty-two of them experienced one or all of the following: early death through wounds or hardships sustained during the war, the loss of their families, their personal fortunes or destruction of their homes and livestock.

Among the seven who died of hardships during the War was "Honest John" Hart, a farmer turned legislator. In the winter of 1776, he fled Princeton, New Jersey, before the British invaders. "For weeks at a time he slept in a different bed each night, sometimes sleeping in caves," David C. Whitney writes. "Hessian mercenaries pillaged his farm and killed his livestock."[4] When he returned home, he found that his wife had died and his thirteen children had taken refuge with neighbors. Hart died in 1779.

Others suffered persecution for their beliefs. Persecution is believed to have contributed to John Morton's early death. Morton was a Quaker and his friends turned against him for supporting armed struggle. While Morton lay dying, he is said to have cried out, "Tell them that they will live to see the hour when they shall acknowledge it to have been the most glorious service that I ever rendered to my country."[5]

After his death in 1777, his wife and family were forced to flee the oncoming British.

Thomas Nelson, governor of Virginia, lost his home and fortune. Writes Whitney, "The story is told that, during the siege of Yorktown, Nelson observed that his own mansion in the town was the only one that had not been struck by the American artillery. Upon inquiring why, he was told that the cannoneers had been asked to respect the governor's property, even though it was being used as Cornwallis' headquarters. Nelson urged that it be fired upon at once, and had the pleasure of seeing British officers flee from his house as it was struck by cannonballs."[6] Nelson gave substantial amounts of money to support the war effort and went deeply into debt by guaranteeing loans to secure supplies for the army. He died in poverty after paying off his wartime debts.

These men did not take lightly the document that they signed.

I'd like to give to you a quote from our beloved El Morya. He said last October in New York:

> Let all you who hear me speak for the first time remember to keep the flame and to sign that document to be a Keeper of the Flame, even as the early American patriots signed that document in Independence Hall. There comes a time when life and destiny necessitates the signing of one's name to a cause. O people of America, will you sign your name next to the signing of Saint Germain's name by himself, our noble Knight Commander? [Audience replies: "Yes!" 7-second applause]

I tell you, beloved, this hour in the Darjeeling Council chambers Saint Germain has stood and signed his name once again to a document that is for the saving of this nation under God, that this nation might be the open door to that salvation of Mother Liberty to all nations. He has stood before us to give an impassioned speech concerning the giving of his life once again if our Father will accept his offering. Saint Germain desires only to save this nation and this people as a bulwark of defense to all and enlightenment to all.

Blessed hearts, I tell you, it is not the taking of a vow nor the mere signing of the name, but it is the activation of the resources of one's causal body in a marathon that must continue until safety is won. Those hearts who would participate in this cause may go to Darjeeling this night. Our doors are opened to any and all patriots of the world who will defend freedom and sign this document with Saint Germain. Do not take the opportunity lightly, beloved, for this signing is the signing of one's life, as he has signed for his life.[7]

Saint Germain has given to us a vision of America and so has the Archangel Zadkiel. But two centuries ago the Goddess of Liberty gave a vision to George Washington. We are all familiar with it but it is well to allow the cadences of the mind to move across these words, once again to remember that the testings of those who would become bodhisattvas and Buddhas is of the Three Jewels.[8] And we see the three episodes in America's history foretold in George Washington's vision as the opportunity to balance the karma of the misuse of the threefold flame and to restore the destiny and path of our personal Christhood and America's Christhood.

This is the accounting, then, of George Washington's vision by Anthony Sherman as told to Wesley Bradshaw as it was reprinted in the *National Tribune*.

The last time I ever saw Anthony Sherman was on the fourth of July, 1859, in Independence Square. He was then ninety-nine years old, and becoming very feeble. But though so old, his dimming eyes rekindled as he gazed upon Independence Hall, which he came to visit once more.

"Let us go into the hall," he said. "I want to tell you of an incident of Washington's life—one which no one alive knows of except myself; and, if you live you will before long, see it verified.

"From the opening of the Revolution we experienced all phases of fortune, now good and now ill, one time victorious and another conquered. The darkest period we had, I think, was when Washington after several reverses, retreated to Valley Forge, where he resolved to pass the winter of 1777.

"Ah! I have often seen the tears coursing down our dear commander's care-worn cheeks, as he would be conversing with a confidential officer about the condition of his poor soldiers. You have doubtless heard the story of Washington's going into the thicket to pray. Well, it was not only true, but he used often to pray in secret for aid and comfort from God, the interposition of whose Divine Providence brought us safely through the darkest days of tribulation.

"One day, I remember it well, the chilly winds whistled through the leafless trees, though the sky was cloudless and the sun shone brightly, he remained in his quarters nearly all the afternoon alone. When he came out I noticed that his face was a shade paler than usual, and there seemed to be something on his mind of more than ordinary importance.

"Returning just after dusk, he dispatched an orderly to the quarters of the officer I mention who was presently in attendance. After a preliminary conversation of about half an hour, Washington, gazing upon his companion with that strange look of dignity which he alone could command, said to the latter:

"'I do not know whether it is owing to the anxiety of my mind, or what, but this afternoon as I was sitting at this table engaged in preparing a dispatch, something seemed to disturb me. Looking up, I beheld standing opposite me a singularly beautiful female. So astonished was I, for I had given strict orders not to be disturbed that it was some moments before I found language to inquire into the cause of her presence.

"'A second, a third, and even a fourth time did I repeat my question, but received no answer from my mysterious visitor except a slight raising of her eyes. By this time I felt strange sensations spreading through me. I would have risen but the riveted gaze of the being before me rendered volition impossible. I assayed once more to address her, but my tongue had become useless. Even thought itself had become paralyzed. A new influence, mysterious, potent, irresistible, took possession of me. All I could do was to gaze steadily, vacantly at my unknown visitant.

"'Gradually the surrounding atmosphere seemed as though becoming filled with sensations, and luminous. Everything about me seemed to rarify—the mysterious visitor herself becoming more airy and yet more distinct to my sight than before. I now began to feel as one dying, or rather to experience the sensations which I have sometimes imagined accompany dissolution. I did not think, I did not reason, I did not move; all were alike impossible. I was only conscious of gazing fixedly, vacantly at my companion.

"'Presently I heard a voice saying, "Son of the Republic, look and learn," while at the same time my visitor extended her arm eastwardly. I now beheld a heavy white vapor at some distance rising fold upon fold. This gradually dissipated, and I looked upon a strange scene. Before me lay spread out in one vast plain all the countries of the world—Europe, Asia, Africa, America. I saw rolling and tossing between Europe and America the billows of the Atlantic, and between Asia and America lay the Pacific.

"'"Son of the Republic," said the same mysterious voice as before, "look and learn." At that moment I beheld a dark, shadowy being, like an angel, standing, or rather floating in mid-air, between Europe and America. Dipping water out of the ocean in the hollow of each hand, he sprinkled some upon America with his right hand, while with his left hand he cast some on Europe.

"'Immediately a cloud raised from these countries, and joined in mid-ocean. For a while it remained stationary, and then moved slowly westward, until it enveloped America in its murky folds. Sharp flashes of lightning gleamed through it at intervals, and I heard the smothered groans and cries of the American people. A second time the angel dipped water from the ocean, and sprinkled it out as before. The dark cloud was then drawn back to the ocean, in whose heaving billows it sank from view.

" 'A third time I heard the mysterious voice saying, "Son of the Republic, look and learn," I cast my eyes upon America and beheld villages and towns and cities springing up one after another until the whole land from the Atlantic to the Pacific was dotted with them. Again, I heard the mysterious voice say, "Son of the Republic, the end of the century cometh, look and learn."

" 'At this the dark shadowy angel turned his face southward, and from Africa I saw an ill-omened spectre approach our land. It flitted slowly over every town and city of the latter. The inhabitants presently set themselves in battle array against each other.

" 'As I continued looking I saw a bright angel, on whose brow rested a crown of light, on which was traced the word "Union," bearing the American flag which he placed between the divided nation, and said, *"Remember ye are brethren."*

" 'Instantly, the inhabitants, casting from them their weapons became friends once more, and united around the National Standard.

" 'And again I heard the mysterious voice saying, "Son of the Republic, look and learn." At this the dark, shadowy angel placed a trumpet to his mouth, and blew three distinct blasts; and taking water from the ocean, he sprinkled it upon Europe, Asia and Africa.

" 'Then my eyes beheld a fearful scene: from each of these countries arose thick, black clouds that were soon joined into one. And throughout this mass there gleamed a dark red light by which I saw hordes of armed men, who, moving with the cloud, marched by land and sailed by sea to America, which country was enveloped in the volume of cloud.

" 'And I dimly saw these vast armies devastate the whole country and burn the villages, towns and cities that I beheld springing up. As my ears listened to the thundering of the cannon, clashing of swords, and the shouts and cries of millions in mortal combat, I heard again the mysterious voice saying, "Son of the Republic, look and learn." When the voice had ceased, the dark shadowy angel placed his trumpet once more to his mouth, and blew a long and fearful blast.

" 'Instantly a light as of a thousand suns shone down from above me, and pierced and broke into fragments the dark cloud which enveloped America. At the same moment the angel upon whose head still shone the word Union, and who bore our national flag in one hand and a sword in the other, descended from the heavens attended by legions of white spirits. These joined the inhabitants of America, who I perceived were well-nigh overcome, but who immediately taking courage again, closed up their broken ranks and renewed the battle.

" 'Again, amid the fearful noise of the conflict, I heard the mysterious voice saying, "Son of the Republic, look and learn." As the voice ceased, the shadowy angel for the last time dipped water from the ocean and sprinkled it upon America. Instantly the dark cloud rolled back, together with the armies it had brought, leaving the inhabitants of the land victorious.

" 'Then once more I beheld the villages, towns and cities springing up where I had seen them before, while the bright angel, planting the azure standard he had brought in the midst of them, cried with a loud voice: *"While the stars remain, and the heavens send down dew upon the earth, so long shall the Union last."* And taking from his brow the crown on which blazoned the word "Union," he placed it upon the Standard while the people, kneeling down, said, "Amen."

" 'The scene instantly began to fade and dissolve, and I at last saw nothing but the rising, curling vapor I at first beheld. This also disappearing, I found myself once more gazing upon the mysterious visitor, who, in the same voice I had heard before, said, "Son of the Republic, what you have seen is thus interpreted:

" ' "Three great perils will come upon the Republic. The most fearful is the third (The comment upon his word 'third' is: "The help against the THIRD peril comes in the shape of Divine Assistance. Apparently the Second Advent) [that is the writer's interpretation who is telling this story]...passing which the whole world united shall not prevail against her. *Let every child of the Republic learn to live for his God, his land and Union."*

" 'With these words the vision vanished, and I started from my seat and felt that I had seen a vision wherein had been shown to me the birth, progress, and destiny of the United States.'

"Such, my friends," concluded the venerable narrator, "were the words I heard from Washington's own lips, and America will do well to profit by them."[9]

The interpretation of those three wars has always been the Revolution, the Civil War and a war that could be fought upon our soil in this century.

Last Thanksgiving Archangel Zadkiel prophesied in Washington:

Children of the Light, sons of Light in your midst, hear me! For I cast before you now a vision of violet flame, as over the land a sacred fire does burn: all of America covered by violet flame. This is the vision whereby you see what destiny America can deliver unto the nations. It is a future of hope, prosperity and light and an inner walk with God. This is the vision of Saint Germain. I am able to show it to you because you have invoked a violet flame that does appear this night as though covering the map of fifty states and more.

Beloved, this is a future that could be. I pray it will not be a future that might have been. This is Option the First whereby you the Lightbearers, by Holy Amethyst' ray, determine that the all-consuming fire of God shall be for transmutation and transformation in the earth body and element, in the sea and the waters, and in the air.

Therefore, by violet flame transmute the seven vials of the seven last plagues that we have already poured out in the earth! This is the sign of the coming of the new age, the age of Aquarius and of Saint Germain. It is the sign of Keepers of the Flame who know that in this hour the essential light must come forth through the Seventh Ray and the violet flame of that ray.

Know, then, beloved, that to cease the agitation, to cease the nonconcentration of the mind, to draw back to self the scattered energies of a scattered attention— this is the requirement.

Lo, I AM Alpha and Omega in the white fire core of Being!—thy being and the being of God which thou art in higher dimensions.

Know, then, beloved, that all who call themselves futurists, all who would be the avant-garde of a new dispensation of eternal Light, these are counted [as such] by us only when they are devotees of the living flame of cosmic freedom, the violet fire.

Noble ones of joy and courage, noble ones of heart, of science and of God, ye are called to an hour. The choosing of yourselves is not an exclusive choosing, for each evolution and race and wave in its time is called to raise up the ensign of Light.

Therefore a people of Light worldwide is called to bring in the great golden age of Aquarius. This, beloved, can be accomplished in this hour only if millions rally to that living flame, to the pillar of fire in the midst of Israel, to the Holy City Foursquare established upon this continent.

Know, then, that *the choice is yet in the realm of the possible* for Lightbearers of all nations to raise up the call to Light, to summon Archangel Michael, to enjoin and to be enjoined by hosts of Light that come from cosmic spheres for the delivery of a planet.

Blessed hearts, *this vision must be fulfilled by those in*

embodiment, you who have heard and seen and felt the Light and the ministration of angels in your midst. Know, then, beloved, that your capacity to contain Light is infinite, even as you are the issue of the infinite God!. . . .

I remind you of your ancient calling to deliver souls and to deliver them unto the LORD God with their God Flame blazing upon their hearts' altars. I remind you, then, of the necessity for the rescue of souls in this hour in the name of the Divine Mother, Mary, who does come to nourish the Christ flame in ye all.

I remind you that the scene of violet flame covering the land is one that can be accomplished by you. And if it is not, beloved, then you will see Option the Second.

You will see coming to pass the third vision of George Washington: You will see a cloud coming forth out of the East and out of the West and over the seas. You will see warfare and bloodshed upon this very continent and soil. You will see, beloved, cities of the nation overcome and burdened, a people rising up by the call of Micah, the Angel of Unity, to be one and to turn back the Adversary. And you will see as hope against hope the failing of those of America to turn back that nightmare of the Great War.

You will see, then, that the only deliverance that can come to a people so unprepared as this to face a world war is Divine Intervention. And yet, beloved, though the angelic hosts descend, some among you must be pillars of fire whereby to anchor that Divine Intercession.

Therefore, see and know, beloved, that what kind of victory shall be your own is truly your choice and choosing in this hour. . . .

May you find Union in the Light, determination and strength in the Vision. For surely it shall come to pass that one or the other shall be the history of this land according to your choosing.[10]

"The Summit Lighthouse Sheds Its Radiance O'er All the World to Manifest as Pearls of Wisdom." An address by Elizabeth Clare Prophet **delivered** on **Monday, July 4, 1988,** at *FREEDOM 1988* in the Heart of the Inner Retreat at the **Royal Teton Ranch, Park County, Montana,** updated for print as this week's *Pearl.* (**1**) Saint Germain, 1987 *Pearls of Wisdom,* pp. 611–12. (**2**) *Encyclopaedia Britannica,* 11th ed., s.v. "treason." (**3**) George Lippard, *Washington and His Generals: or, Legends of the Revolution* (Philadelphia: G. B. Zieber and Co., 1847), pp. 394–97. (**4**) David C. Whitney, *Founders of Freedom in America* (Chicago: J. G. Ferguson Publishing Company, 1964), p. 109. (**5**) Ibid., p. 173. (**6**) Ibid., p. 175. (**7**) El Morya, 1987 *Pearls of Wisdom,* pp. 479–80. (**8**) See 1988 *Pearls of Wisdom,* p. 447 n. 9. (**9**) Published by Wesley Bradshaw, reprinted in the *National Tribune,* December 1880. (**10**) Archangel Zadkiel, 1987 *Pearls of Wisdom,* pp. 591–95.

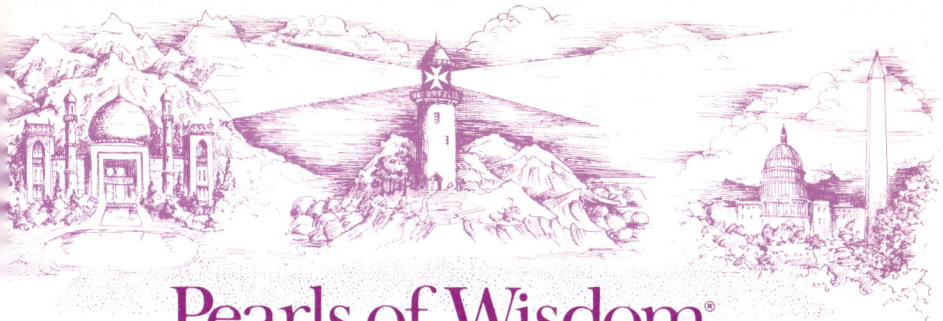

Pearls of Wisdom®
published by The Summit Lighthouse

| Vol. 31 No. 71B | Elizabeth Clare Prophet | October 26, 1988 |

FREEDOM 1988
Fourth of July Address

Part 2

The Cause of Religious Liberty
and
Defending Our First Amendment Rights

The signers of the Declaration of Independence knew they were fighting for a principle far more important than their lives and property. They were fighting for a cause, and the supreme cause of humanity. The cause was liberty. And to them liberty was a flame as it is to us, a threefold flame that burns in our hearts whose call we cannot ignore. Religious liberty was one of the key reasons they had come to America. Their break with Europe was a break with hundreds of years of religious persecution.

On October 5, 1573, in Antwerp, Belgium, a woman named Maeyken Wens was arrested and tortured. As Paul D. Simmons wrote in an article for *Church and State,* "Her tongue was then screwed to her upper palate so she could not witness to her faith while she was hauled in a cart to the place where the sentence was carried out—death by fire. Her crime?...She proclaimed the Gospel as she understood it from her personal reading of the New Testament. She was a victim of the Inquisition. She was found guilty of heresy, impiety and disobedience to Mother Church."[1]

Has not Archbishop Marcel Lefebvre suffered the same fate today, though not so physical?[2] Does not Rome yet stand intolerant of the human spirit and the right to find out God and to worship him as one does so choose? And have we not all given our lives at one time or another to keep the flame of religious liberty burning in Europe in these dark ages?

The Pilgrims who landed at Plymouth in November 1620 had found it necessary to leave England in order to insure their survival as a church, as a community, as one spirit. They had tried Holland, which was said to be tolerant. But because of problems associated with the education of their children as well as economic factors, they set out for the New World.

In the next centuries they were followed by Quakers, Huguenots and Waldenses, Schwenckfelders, Roman Catholics, and Anabaptists. They were leaving behind a long tradition of religious persecution.

In 1545 the French king Francis I had ordered that all Waldenses (followers of the twelfth-century Protestant Peter Waldo) who were found guilty of heresy should be put to death. Waldo had advocated a simple life. He came to the conclusion that the laws of Christ were not being strictly followed. He sold his property, gave away the proceeds, and preached among the poor. Waldenses believed that laymen and women should be allowed to preach. They held that the Bible should be the rule of faith and that God was to be obeyed rather than man; hence they refused to obey the clergy.

French soldiers interpreted the king's order to mean mass extermination. They killed 3,000 Waldenses, burned 22 villages and sent 700 men to the galleys,[3] all to maintain control over the minds and souls of the people.

Similar persecutions were conducted throughout Europe during the Reformation. By the next century such massacres were a thing of the past but persecution of minority religious groups was commonplace. Their members were jailed, thrown in stocks, and forbidden to educate their children.

The Swiss government formed a secret police force to hunt Anabaptists (whose modern descendants include the Mennonites). As John A. Hostetler describes it, their mission was "to spy, locate, and arrest Anabaptists for their nonconformist beliefs." They confiscated the Anabaptists' property. "Some were imprisoned, others were sent to Italy as galley slaves. . . . Children of Anabaptist parents were declared illegitimate because their parents had not been married by a Reformed minister."[4]

The Founding Fathers had good reason to make sure that when they secured our political liberties they secured religious liberty as well. The First Amendment to the Constitution of the United States reads: "Congress shall make no law respecting an establishment of religion, or prohibiting the free exercise thereof; or abridging the freedom of speech, or of the press; or the right of the people peaceably to assemble, and to petition the government for a redress of grievances."

The purpose of the guarantee of freedom of religion was twofold: first to prevent the establishment of a tax-supported, and therefore state-controlled, religion and second to allow everyone to worship as they chose. It was based on the Virginia "Act for Establishing Religious Freedom," adopted January 16, 1786, and the Virginia "Declaration of Rights," adopted June 12, 1776.

As summarized by Winfred E. Garrison, the "Act for Establishing Religious Freedom" declared that "the state has no right to compel the citizen to support with money the propagation even of those religious opinions which he believes, much less those which he disbelieves." This was a revolutionary idea. Not since the Roman emperor Constantine co-opted Christianity in the fourth century had the nations of Europe been free of taxation to support a state religion. And that's the way it should be!

The freedom of religion portion of the Virginia "Declaration of Rights" states:

> XVI. That Religion, or the Duty which we owe to our Creator, and the Manner of discharging it, can be directed only by Reason and Conviction, not by Force or Violence; and therefore, all Men are equally entitled to the free Exercise of Religion, according to the Dictates

of Conscience; and that it is the mutual Duty of all to practice Christian Forbearance, Love and Charity, towards each other.[5]

This was the spirit behind the First Amendment. But today the intent of the Founding Fathers is being circumvented. Today there is a war on churches and there is a war on religion. And it's being waged by private groups, federal, state and local governments, and by the courts. This war affects you and me and our Church and our right to practice our religion on our private property here at the Royal Teton Ranch.

A report by the Coalition for Religious Freedom found that "the last 15 years have seen more religious freedom cases than any time since the American Revolution." It observed that "two hundred years ago, the primary threat to religious liberty was the intolerance of other religions. . . . Today, however, the primary threats to religious liberty come not from churches, but from the bureaucratic secular state."[6] They found that key areas in which the attacks take place are in tort liability* and zoning.

Today over 50,000 ministers and rabbis across the country carry clergy malpractice insurance. More and more pastors are being held liable for spiritual counsel they give. The Coalition for Religious Freedom reports that "there are now nearly 2,000 suits pending in state courts against religious leaders of a variety of faiths."[7] In 1986 and 1987 over $100 million was awarded by courts to plaintiffs who sued for clerical malpractice.

Zoning and land use planning are being used to control religious practice around the country. The Coalition cites the example of the Faith Bible Fellowship of Colorado Springs, Colorado. The members "held services in their pastor's home while saving money to purchase a church building. Consequently, the pastor, Rev. Richard Blanche, was cited seven times, fined $32,000 and ordered to perform eighty hours of community service by the city for alleged zoning violations."[8] He would have gotten off easier had he been a drug dealer.

*tort liability: being held liable in a civil suit (other than breach of contract) for breach of a legal duty or right directly causing damage.

The courts are increasingly becoming a battlefield where religious freedom is slaughtered. Virginia Postrel recently documented a few of the cases against religion in an editorial in the *Wall Street Journal:*

> Religion is in trouble in America—for reasons that have nothing to do with Jimmy Swaggart or Jim and Tammy Bakker.
>
> While civil libertarians vigilantly guarded the Maginot line separating church and state, the courts have swept across the undefended territory of the free-exercise clause. The Supreme Court's decision last month to let the government build roads through national forest sacred to two Indian tribes is but the latest example of this disturbing trend. Over the past several years, the courts have steadily eroded religious freedom by repeatedly granting government officials control over property central to religious life.
>
> Building a church is a time-honored expression of religious faith, a quintessential example of the free exercise of religion. But it is not a constitutionally protected activity, according to a 1983 decision by the Sixth Circuit Court of Appeals. A congregation of Jehovah's Witnesses had repeatedly—and unsuccessfully—petitioned the Lakewood, Ohio, zoning board for permission to build a new church, or Kingdom Hall, on a lot it owned in a residential neighborhood. The court held that Lakewood could legally zone religious buildings out of virtually all residential neighborhoods, leaving a mere 10% of the city open to new churches.
>
> The desire for a suitable building, the court said, was merely a matter of finances and aesthetics, not the congregation's religious liberty: "There is no evidence that the construction of a Kingdom Hall is a ritual, a 'fundamental tenet,' or a 'cardinal principle' of its faith. At most the Congregation can claim that its freedom to worship is tangentially related to worshiping in its own building."

That same year, the Eleventh Circuit Court of Appeals ruled that the city of Miami Beach could bar Naftali Grosz, an elderly Hassidic rabbi, from conducting daily worship services in his own garage. At issue was a city zoning law that prohibits religious buildings, such as churches and synagogues, in single-family residential areas. Rabbi Grosz's garage services generally attracted 10 to 20 people.

As unsettling as the Lakewood decision was, it at least involved a full-fledged church, parking lot and all. But, thanks to the Grosz ruling, homeowners can now find their living-room gatherings lumped in the same illegal category. By stretching the zoning law to encompass services for as few as 10 people, the court made worship illegal where bridge clubs are not. It also gave zoning boards great power to harass and intimidate minority religions—especially since a single disgruntled neighbor can launch a zoning investigation....

In the wake of the Lakewood and Grosz decisions, Scott David Godshall noted in a 1984 Columbia Law Review article: "Absent a religion whose beliefs center on the land itself, religious use of land may, under this analysis, be defined as secular and denied protection. The result, in other words, is a per se rule against application of free exercise analysis to church land use controversies."

And now the Supreme Court has ruled that the First Amendment does not even protect Indian religions whose beliefs *do* center on the land itself. The court could have ruled on narrower grounds—for example, the need to weigh competing uses for the same publicly owned property. Instead, Justice Sandra Day O'Connor issued broad statements about the meaning of the First Amendment's free-exercise clause, statements that dangerously extend the erosion of religious freedom. Free exercise has become, in the eyes of the courts, a mere matter of doctrine and belief—not of true exercise, of practice.

In her ruling, Justice O'Connor writes that the government may instigate logging and road-building projects that "could have devastating effects on traditional Indian religious practices." But, she argues, "the affected individuals [would not] be coerced by the Government's actions into violating their religious beliefs; nor would the governmental action penalize the exercise of religious rights by denying religious adherents an equal share of the rights, benefits, and privileges enjoyed by other citizens."

To rule that wiping out religious practices—and the sacred space that makes them possible—does not coerce people to violate their religious beliefs is perverse. It also betrays a watered-down Christian bias. For many of the world's religions, practice *is* belief, or very nearly so. As Justice William Brennan notes in his dissent, "For Native Americans religion is not a discrete sphere of activity separate from all others." Nor is it for observant Jews or Moslems or even many Christians.

The Supreme Court's recent ruling shocked many civil libertarians. It shouldn't have, for lower courts had already made the drift clear.

Those of us who care about civil liberties, about the First Amendment's guarantees, must now turn our attention to defending the free-exercise clause—before the only place individuals can exercise freedom of religion is within their own skulls.[9]

Over the last 10 years various groups and government agencies have tried to exploit federal and local laws and the courts to curtail our religious freedom. Anti-cult groups, fundamentalist Christians, and some who just don't want to have us as neighbors have used every environmental issue as a tool to try to destroy us as a religion. These are people who generally don't really believe in environmentalism. Conversely, environmentalists have tried to use our unorthodox religious beliefs as an emotional appeal or fear tactic to bolster their arguments that we should be restricted from using our land.

It all started in California at our prior headquarters. We were located on a beautiful property in the Santa Monica Mountains, a 250-acre campus that had formerly been a Catholic seminary. Local environmental groups, a few neighbors and an anti-cult group wanted to curtail our use of the land and buildings and prevent us from expanding our headquarters.

Based on testimony from several environmentalists and one crusader against our Church, the Los Angeles County Planning Commission gave us a bureaucratic runaround on our application to build a small addition to our cafeteria and turned it down. We might have been able to get approval if we had put a lot of time and money into appealing it. But their stall tactics effectively prevented us from expanding the use of our land for the entire eight years we were there.

Here we were with 250 acres, over 200 of it completely vacant. We were zoned as a college campus and they wouldn't even let us build an addition to our cafeteria! As a result, we were forced to eat in a temporary tent-cafeteria open to the weather in winter and summer, year after year.

The goal of the environmentalists was to enlist the aid of the state or federal government to buy up all the remaining land in the area. But the state refused to act. Then one day in 1979 we found ourselves in the middle of a new national park, the Santa Monica Mountains National Recreation Area, a pork-barrel creation of Congress.

About a year later we learned that federal officials had determined that our property should be the new park headquarters, all without any prior notice to us. Our main chapel, the Chapel of the Holy Grail, was slated to become a museum and the smaller Chapel of the Holy Family perhaps a curio shop.

What followed was a protracted battle typical of the federal land-grabbing process. First came the sky-is-falling rhetoric from activist environmental groups, then threats of condemnation, numerous appraisals, ridiculously low offers from the government, repeated efforts to get the local government to down-zone our property, and finally totally false and slanderous statements about us, which on several occasions expressed religious bigotry. These were offered gratuitously by National Park Service officials, all in an effort to get us to leave our property and to sell out cheap. (For example, they repeated the lie that has circulated for years that we had armed guards at our Camelot gate; in reality the gate was manned by an unarmed person in an information booth, often a woman, who would direct people to where they should go for appointments or to make deliveries on the sprawling campus.)

In the end the Park Service did not and could not make good on its threats because no money was available under the Reagan administration. [5-second applause]

Since we moved to Montana in 1981 and particularly since the sale and transfer of our California headquarters to Montana in 1986, we have been harassed and threatened by a loose coalition including the National Park Service, a few neighbors, and local and national environmentalists. They have used scare tactics, lies, and gross exaggerations to try to convince the state and federal governments as well as wealthy national environmentalist supporters that we are a serious threat to the ecology of Yellowstone National Park.

They are short on facts intentionally and their intent is clear: they want to prevent us from using our land or convince the federal government to buy us out and force us to move. In the meantime, they are trying to stall us.

Since November 1986, controversy has centered around the Church's proposed new headquarters site at Spring Creek where we want to build a chapel and school with housing, offices, and cafeteria for staff and students. We have already purchased most of the buildings and some of them are on the 50-acre site.

Construction was begun and then halted in the fall of 1986 when environmental groups convinced the State Water Quality Bureau to prepare an Environmental Impact Statement, an EIS, before making a final decision on our permit applications for the water and sewer systems. While it meant a delay in starting construction on our new headquarters, we agreed to cooperate fully and to work to mitigate any possible impacts to the environment.

In this we are absolutely sincere—because we are surely environmentalists ourselves. [10-second applause] Not only do we respect nature and the balance of nature and elemental life and the natural habitats that are found here, but to us our land is sacred ground. And as such we treat it as a holy place. It doesn't take too much sensitivity to notice just how beautifully this property is maintained. [10-second applause]

In the meantime, our departments have been functioning out of temporary quarters. The buildings we have purchased have gone unused and the EIS has cost us tens of thousands of dollars in expert consultant fees.

Even before the EIS came out, a group of local activists and environmentalists laid plans to challenge it. Clearly, their concern is not with specific threats to the environment but with the fact that we are here at all. For them there's only one solution: We have to move.

In a newsletter requesting donations for legal assistance, they claimed that we planned to put up housing for 600 staff plus several thousand university students, a total fabrication.[10] This is contrary to the plans, which are a matter of public record. All the developments on the ranch will actually house 596 people, including students.[11]

These local environmentalists have worked hard to plant stories in the national media about our supposed threat to the environment, also before the EIS came out. An article in *Flyfishing* magazine charged that we "imperil the fishery" on the Upper Yellowstone, and that "a major development— probably illegal—plus plans for a poultry processing plant threaten to pollute the river. Side streams have been ruthlessly channeled, damaging spawning access....Join the fight. Send your check to Upper Yellowstone Defense Fund. Lawyers cost money."[12] All of these are out-and-out lies.

When the draft EIS did come out in February of 1988 it was a comprehensive 152-page document that studied every aspect of our possible impact, including water quality, air quality, wildlife, fisheries, historical and archaeological sites, geology, soils, vegetation, roads, utilities, county services, local tax base, schools, social values, aesthetics, and Yellowstone geothermal resources.

The EIS found that the effect of our community would be minor and that these could be dealt with and the environment protected through several mitigation measures, most of which were already incorporated into our plans. [9-second applause]

As documented by the EIS, the fact is that we haven't damaged the environment in the seven years we've been here. The study found that our activities had not and would not disturb wildlife migration patterns, the water quality of the Yellowstone, or the quantity or quality of fish in Mol Heron Creek and other streams. In fact, one of the only effects we may have is to displace small nonmobile wildlife, that is, animals like field mice and gophers. In short, the EIS found that the sky is not falling. [8-second applause]

You would have expected that those engaged in fair play and the American tradition would have said, "The decision has been made. The facts have been researched. That's it." But that's not it. It's only the beginning. They have sounded their battle cry.

And when about a month after the release of the EIS in draft form a public hearing was held in the nearby town of Gardiner to gather comments from interested people, I decided to go to that meeting and place myself in the front row. So whatever those people had to say to me or about me or against me, they could say it to my face. [35-second applause]

What unfolded that night was a well-coordinated but factually vague assault on both the Church and the EIS by environmentalists and those who oppose the establishment of our religious community. Comments emanated from an extreme environmentalist perspective and were liberally laced with religious slurs and even personal accusations.

For example, one local environmental group made the following statement through its spokeswoman: "The numbers of people being located on church property are the staff of a business that has been successful enough over the years to buy 33,000 acres in Park County. . . . The moneymaker is

Elizabeth Clare Prophet and the selling of her words, and this is managed by that large staff whose presence is bringing the problems of urbanization to this fragile and ecologically important land. . . . CUT is a business. It should be evaluated as a business and held responsible for the impacts it will cause."[13]

The sheer hatred with which this statement was directed at me, unbelievable as it was, was only to be exceeded by the next speaker. Referring to the section in the EIS that explained the background of the Church's move to Montana, she stated for the record: "I also object to the fact of the explanations of CUT's theology being included in an EIS. This is nothing more than propaganda and I don't care what they believe or who they worship. It is inappropriate and, in my opinion, serves as a diversionary tactic to take interest away from what does matter. . . .

"It is a total waste of the State's time to type in such poignant scenes as Elizabeth Clare Prophet's late husband Mark telling her from his deathbed to take the Church to Montana because of the grassroots-of-America kind of people. . . . The intelligence of the residents of Park County has been insulted by the inclusion of such soap opera scenes in print."[14]

This woman carried on about her absolute distaste for hearing anything about the Church's background, which was included as a part of our history and how we happened to come to Montana. She went on to claim that there are strong parallels between Rajneeshpuram and our Church.

This is an absurdity. If the speaker had cared to go into detail on Rajneesh, she would have been hard-pressed to find a comparison. Rajneesh was charged with 35 felony counts and received a 10-year suspended sentence after plea bargaining; neither Mark nor I nor any member of the Board of Directors of Church Universal and Triumphant has ever been charged with or convicted of a criminal offense. Rajneesh amassed a 93-car fleet of Rolls-Royces and called himself "the rich man's guru"; I drive a 1987 Chevy Suburban. He called God "the greatest lie invented by man"; we have a profound devotion to God. He said, "I do not teach any belief"; we have a well-codified belief system solidly based on the Judeo-Christian tradition and we teach the mystical truths which undergird the world's major religions. The Bhagwan advocated free sex; we do not. At Rajneeshpuram he purportedly condoned violence and drug usage; these are antithetical to our beliefs. Since the late sixties Mark and I have been helping young people get off drugs, alcohol and tobacco through a good diet, scientific prayer and fasting, saunas, yoga, outdoor work with Mother Nature and a spiritual path—including expanding conscious awareness of God and communion with the heavenly host without the use of drugs.

The Rajneeshees ran a disco nightclub; our church members don't drink, don't frequent discos and they don't listen to rock music. Rajneesh's cronies took over the city council of Antelope, Oregon, by getting their own members elected and voting out the town residents; we have been here almost seven years and have never had a member run for or be elected to a seat in the local government. And finally, Bhagwan (it means "Lord" or exalted one") allowed his followers to worship him in the tradition of the false gurus of India. I teach my students to worship and practice the Presence of God and I shun all attempts to elevate my person. Clearly, there is no comparison to be made.

The only possible connection between our communities is that we purchased buildings from them when they went belly-up and Rajneesh fled the state and was subsequently deported. We were just trying to make the best use of our members' money by taking advantage of a good deal. That no more makes us Rajneeshees than our buying buildings from a mining company makes us miners.

Referring to our summer conferences in the Heart of the Inner Retreat, one environmentalist claimed, "The impacts of 2,500 people place a great deal of stress on the animals which can only increase the odds against their survival."[15]

We've lived happily with the wildlife that freely roam our ranch to the delight of our community and members. I can tell you, they're not fenced out and they're not fenced in! [9-second applause]

Another person who testified used this emotional appeal: "With their yearly massive communal gathering each Fourth of July, we have a lot of influx of different people coming in that can bring in different diseases from across the whole United States. This is one of my great concerns is that we are leaving a lot of children here in the Gardiner area unprotected." [16]

How about the millions of tourists that come to Yellowstone Park and all traipse through Gardiner with their diseases? [7-second applause]

And now we hear from Bob Barbee, Superintendent of Yellowstone National Park—whose payroll is paid for by your and my taxes and everybody else's—who, in representing the government and the people, ought to be impartial. (What kind of a boss is he when his employees tell us they can't eat at our restaurant, the Ranch Kitchen, for fear of being fired? One park employee who was a regular customer said regretfully on her last visit, "You probably won't see me in here anymore. If they knew that I was eating here, I'd probably lose my job.")

Make no mistake about it, Bob Barbee has used his public office and high-profile position to jump on the bandwagon and try to force us out of the area. He released an official statement which read in part:

"We do not want massive development threats on Yellowstone's border, and the people of the United States will not stand for it!... We strongly urge the Royal Teton Ranch to select another portion of its extensive holdings for these subdivision activities and then submit new plans to the state of Montana for approval." [17]

Of course, there are no such "subdivisions" included in any of our plans here at the Royal Teton Ranch South.

But the intent is clear. He believes Yellowstone National Park ought to be able to dictate what we can and can't do on our own private property. That's the bottom line of it all. Whether it's the park people, the environmentalists, or the neighbors, they think they have a right to tell us what to do with our property simply because it happens to be next door to the park.

In a later statement Barbee said he feels that moving our headquarters "is a reasonable and practical solution at this time, before further development takes place."[18]

It's taken us all these years since 1981 to make this South Ranch a viable place to serve and worship together. We have put in what is expedient and necessary for the daily functions of life. Our staff have become experts at putting in septic systems and drainage fields—and everything you'd take for granted anywhere else. It may not look like there's too much development here, which, of course, there isn't in that sense of the word, but there is a tremendous amount of work that has gone into this South Ranch—not to mention that we believe it's the "Place Prepared of God."[19]

A lot of work has been done right here in the Heart just so we could put up a tent each year to worship our God as did Moses and the children of Israel in their wilderness wanderings. Here we invoke the Flame of the Ark of the Covenant and the covering cherubim. Here we commune with the LORD. Here we gather midst the cloud of his Presence and hear the words he speaks to our hearts.

We reclaimed the land. We have organic farming. It's been a heroic effort by those serving here and by those of you in the field who have supported us in doing it. And now we should just pack up our tents and quietly disappear to the North Ranch. This is amazing on the face of it, that someone can think that he has the right to tell us what to do with our Church.

Bob Barbee has failed to come up with one substantive example of how we have hurt the environment. His litany of concerns is pure conjecture about the possibility of what we *may* do in the future and what *could* happen. Clearly he has a fixation on our Church and is obsessed with the idea of getting us out of here one way or the other.

In May he decided to directly attack our religion. In his written comment on the draft EIS he began questioning whether our Church "is actually a religion or an income-producing business." He cited as examples the Ranch Kitchen, Cinnabar General Store, the sale of land and homes at

Glastonbury, publishing, annual conferences and our truck farm. Therefore, he said, "it is abundantly clear that the Royal Teton Ranch is a large corporate conglomerate of money-making activities."[20]

That's absolutely ridiculous!

A careful analysis of our activities would reveal that the alleged business operations are either functions of the Church's religious purposes, are incidental to the establishment of a religious community, or are simply insignificant. Publishing and holding religious conferences are time-honored functions of churches. Produce from the truck farm is largely for the sustenance of our community. We sell land and homes at the Community of Glastonbury as part of our goal of establishing a religious community for Church members who share a common life-style, beliefs, and practices.

The Ranch Kitchen and Cinnabar General Store could be classified as businesses. However, they are primarily for the convenience of Church members and the staff. They sell natural foods and products which Church members prefer and which are not available in the area. And in addition to serving our members, they provide an important and needed window into our community for the general public.

Church Universal and Triumphant is recognized as a nonprofit corporation in the State of Montana and Bob Barbee is showing his ignorance and prejudice when he makes such outlandish claims about us. To call an agriculturally based community a "large corporate conglomerate" in the image of IBM and Exxon is ludicrous. The truth is there are no real issues to object to so those folks who simply don't like us or our religion have to make them up.

By questioning the motives of our religious community, Barbee is threatening our freedom of religion. The very idea that he thinks he can tell us to move smacks of federal tyranny, the same kind of tyranny which gave those delegates to the Continental Congress no other choice but to sign that document. [10-second applause]

We own 15,300 acres in the Corwin Springs area. Our total planned and existing developments are 120 acres, less than 1 percent of our land. On the other hand, government statistics show that over 2.6 million people and 892,000 vehicles visit the 2.2-million-acre Yellowstone National Park annually.[21] There are facilities, housing, campgrounds and RV parks for up to 17,000 people at any one time right in the park plus restaurants, gas stations, and stores.[22] There are at least six "towns" inside the park. And now they are even planning several large additions, including 488 new lodging units at Canyon Village.[23]

In the town of Gardiner, which is on the park border just four miles from our ranch, three large motels totaling over 100 units and a new mobile-home park have gone up in the last three years alone![24] Has anyone demanded an environmental impact study? Is anyone concerned about environmental damage? Of course not! Clearly there is a double standard— one for the park and Gardiner and the rest of the Paradise Valley and another for Church Universal and Triumphant.

By contrast, in our community we're talking about 600 permanent residents plus perhaps five to six thousand visitors annually on a total of 15,000 acres on the Royal Teton Ranch South, less than half the visitor-density of Yellowstone Park.*

The hypocrisy of our critics should be obvious because it's clear that if Yellowstone Park can successfully handle this kind of activity and new development and still remain pristine and unspoiled, then so can we! [15-second applause]

And here's further evidence of the park's hypocrisy: It is documented that the Gardiner community sewage system next to the Yellowstone River is leaking and doesn't operate properly. Yet the park's new laundry built just two years ago is dumping 40,000 gallons of sewage per day into the town's system. The park hasn't stopped this operation to protect the environment.[25] This isn't to mention incidents that have regularly occurred inside the park. Just last month, for example, over 100,000 gallons of raw sewage was spilled into the Yellowstone River.[26]

Do you hear any outcry? Meanwhile, our water and sewage systems are state of the art!

*Yellowstone National Park has about 1.2 visitors per acre per year; we are proposing .4 visitors per acre per year.

The way Barbee and the environmentalists are talking we might as well be living in a Communist country. Did you really think that you still lived in the land of the free? The tactics being used against us are the same tactics used by the KGB—lies, distortions, and rumors. In other words, disinformation!

These federal bureaucrats act like they own our land and like they're above the laws of God and man.

And if you want to know what Edward Francis has been doing a large percentage of the time since we've moved here, he's been defending us against all of these lies—having to write meticulously detailed articles, letters, statements, press releases, and he's constantly being interviewed to correct those lies. And when they are corrected and the corrections are printed, the same people come back and tell the same lies all over again! And what's more, they told their bag of lies at that Gardiner meeting, knowing full well what our responses had been and what the true facts were and that they were easily verifiable.

So you see, they not only persecute you and your religion, but they tie up your time and energy, your money and your private property to prevent you from fulfilling your mission. And it's absolutely criminal the way this orchestrated attack on our Community of the Holy Spirit is consuming the energy of our staff and Keepers of the Flame throughout the field, not to mention the funds we have had to raise to defend ourselves from these broadside attacks against our free exercise of our First Amendment rights as well as our private property rights.

One local activist, talking about us on TV, said, "They feel that they have an absolute right to do anything they want to with their private land."[27] That's absolutely not true! Nobody has the "absolute right to do anything they want to with their private land." Whatever we have done or intend to do we do out of concern for the environment, and the EIS has borne out that our activities have not significantly impacted the land, the wildlife or the natural resources.

As I told the first reporters that came along at the end of

1986 and into 1987, "To us this land is hallowed ground. . . . There is no other place like it in the whole nation. We are extremely careful with this land. You will not find a cigarette butt on 30,000 acres, a beer can, or a scrap of paper."[28] [9-second applause] I personally have never found any litter on this property.

We have definitely managed this land with more responsibility and more diligence than any federal agency would or could have. [5-second applause] (For instance, we have sprayed our forests with organic biological compounds rather than toxic pesticides to protect the trees from pine beetle and spruce budworm infestations, while Yellowstone National Park allows thousands of acres of trees to die and then burn, on the theory that nature should be left alone and this is all part of the functioning of the ecosystem.)

In referring to our private property, one government employee said, "Why should any special interest group be given preference to degrade a unique natural area which should be able to be enjoyed by all members of the American public?"[29]

He's talking about your land and my land! And he's accusing us of degrading it, or being given the preference to degrade it, by virtue of our private property rights. Why, we would never think of degrading this cathedral of nature, much less consider it our preference to do so!

We secured this property as an international shrine of religious freedom. And we are pledged as its stewards to keep it beautiful and in balance as Mother Nature intended it to be—a haven for humans and wildlife, sons and daughters of God and all of the elemental kingdom!

It is a religious shrine and all people who would come here for religious purposes are welcome to enjoy it. All others are already free to enjoy Yellowstone National Park, which, with its 2,221,766 acres has never proven inadequate to meet the needs of American and international visitors and to serve as a well-managed wildlife preserve. It is only the expansionist motives of the advocates of a new superpark that has resulted in the coveting of our land and the claims that it is needed by the animals.

One environmentalist suggested that restrictions should be imposed on our summer conferences. She asked why the EIS didn't stress "human management" more by moving our conference site, by making us hold it at a different time of year or by "confining the activities of the conferees."[30]

Can you believe that there are people in this country who actually think they should be able to tell us how, when, and where to hold our religious conference!

The annual summer conference in the Heart of the Inner Retreat was chosen as a particular bone of contention by those commenting on the EIS. While the use of the conference site is not even the subject of any pending applications for permits or licenses from the state, it was included in the EIS as a collateral issue. Although the Draft EIS found no significant impact, individuals at the public hearing spoke of alleged impacts to wildlife, vegetation, and even public health.

When Elohim created the earth in seven cycles of creation and placed upon it God's sons and daughters, they blessed them and gave the command: "Be fruitful, and multiply and replenish the earth, and subdue it: and have dominion over the fish of the sea, and over the fowl of the air, and over every living thing that moveth upon the earth."[31] And when "there was not a man to till the ground," the LORD God took Adam "and put him into the garden of Eden to dress it and to keep it."[32] And after the flood God gave the same blessing and commission to Noah and his sons, saying:

> Be fruitful, and multiply, and replenish the earth.
> And the fear of you and the dread of you shall be upon every beast of the earth, and upon every fowl of the air, upon all that moveth upon the earth, and upon all the fishes of the sea; into your hand are they delivered.
> Every moving thing that liveth shall be meat for you; even as the green herb have I given you all things. . . .
> Whoso sheddeth man's blood, by man shall his blood be shed: for in the image of God made he man.

And you, be ye fruitful, and multiply; bring forth abundantly in the earth, and multiply therein.[33]

It's an ancient tradition to tend the land for God as God's caretakers. It all started way back with Noah after the Flood. And he was God's caretaker. He was a husbandman. He planted a vineyard and dressed it. The Noachic Covenant brought the dispensation of human government. It was to be a government of man over man and Noah was God's first "overman." Hereafter man was responsible to govern the world for God.

After the Flood that responsibility rested upon the Lightbearers (the I AM Race) but when they disobeyed the laws of God and disregarded the warnings of his prophets and the dispensations of his covenants, they were taken into Assyrian and Babylonian captivity under the rulership of the "Gentiles." And to this day the children of the Light have been subject to the rulers of this world.

Yet by the Lord's intercession through the grace of Jesus Christ and the freedom flame of Saint Germain, once again the Lightbearers have emerged from their long karma of the dark ages to know a republican, representative form of government, a democracy "of the people, by the people, for the people; whose just powers are derived from the consent of the governed."[34]

The Constitution of the United States is a covenant of the people with their Creator and with their representatives. It defines the limits of government and the rights of the governed. It is based on the self-evident truths that all men are created with equal opportunity and with the right to life, liberty, and the pursuit of happiness. It guarantees the four sacred freedoms of religion, speech, the press and assembly as well as the right to private property, so that even prior to God's final judgment of the Gentile powers of this world, sons and daughters of God can once again serve as God's overmen and as his just stewards of the land, the resources, and the law.

I therefore believe that it is beneficial for private individuals, groups, societies, foundations and nonprofit organizations to own land and use it for public and private purposes, mindful that they are caretakers of God's natural resources. I believe we have a divine duty as well as the divine right to be just stewards of the land and the people's right to enjoy that land. Therefore we must preserve it as much as possible in nature's purity for posterity. The only reason I can see to ever have federal or state ownership of land is to preserve it for the people where the people cannot or will not effectively do so themselves. [7-second applause]

We are here to affirm our right to religious freedom, our right to worship our God in this wilderness land, under this tent of the Lord so reminiscent of the earliest stirrings for freedom in the hearts of our ancient forebears. For they kept the same flame of liberty and knew the same Divine Presence that sparked and guided those signers of the Declaration of Independence. And it is that divine document that we must keep alive by signing it again today with *our* lives, *our* fortunes, and *our* sacred honor. With our fiery spirits, our voices raised, and our bodies strong we shall defend in the name of our Saviour Jesus Christ our right to be doing what we are doing! [23-second applause]

Keepers of the Flame, you paid for this land. You own this Royal Teton Ranch free and clear, every inch of it. [10-second applause] And that money was hard earned and you made sacrificial gifts.

You have a right to worship on this land wherever and whenever you please! [8-second applause]

You have a right to assemble on this land wherever and whenever you please! [7-second applause]

You have a right to speak freely what you think and what you believe on this land wherever and whenever you please! And together we have a right to exercise our freedom of the press on this land wherever and whenever we please—and we do! [10-second applause]

Mark and I learned a long time ago that freedom of the press doesn't mean that you are free to publish in somebody else's newspaper. No, freedom of the press is the freedom to start your own press, [6-second applause] where you have editorial control and can publish abroad in the land whatsoever you wish. [5-second applause]

Saint Germain came to us and told us that in order to found and sustain this organization we had to be able to publish our teachings ourselves, and it was he who urged us to purchase our first printing press. Not only was it necessary in order to retain our freedom of religion, he told us, but it was expedient because it was far too expensive to have our work printed out.

And so, I was the one who learned firsthand what it meant to exercise my freedom of the press—because there were only two of us and I knew it wasn't going to be Mark Prophet who was going to run that press. So I guess you all know the story that I did run that first printing press that I had set up in the living room of my apartment on the 10th floor of Arlington Towers in Virginia.

And I learned to run that press and I ran it for a year or so until someone came along and learned to run it too. It was a great thrill for me to find out that I could actually run a printing press. And it was an even greater thrill to see how in running that press, a single page that I would type on a plate (which in those days were made of paper) could suddenly become a thousand pages and how you could multiply the word of the Lord and publish those *Pearls of Wisdom* and Keepers of the Flame lessons. There was something very precious and profoundly meaningful in working by the hour at that Davidson offset press and feeling the tremendous freedom, and power, of the press to deliver the teachings of the Ascended Masters to the world.

What we are here to determine this Fourth of July 1988, then, is whether we are ready, as our Founding Fathers were ready, to do whatever it takes to defend our First Amendment rights and our right to life, liberty, and the pursuit of happiness on our private property. Keepers of the Flame, are you ready? [31-second applause]

I consider the powers that be who are moving against us to be the greatest threat we will ever face in the challenge of our right to religious freedom and to own this private property and to do with it what God intends us to do.

Environmentalists have recently taken the press, one or more members of Congress, and ecology activists on airplane flights that buzzed our ranch. Despite the transparency of their tactics, the park-environmentalist alliance appears to be making headway at the national level.

The National Parks and Conservation Association (NPCA) is a private lobbying organization which is the chief advocacy group for the National Park Service. It recently published a nine-volume *National Park System Plan: A Blueprint for Tomorrow*, which says that our national park heritage is being threatened and calls for legislation to expand the existing boundaries of the parks. All of our Church property in Corwin Springs is targeted by them for acquisition in their proposed park boundary line changes. In fact, we are the only property adjacent to Yellowstone Park that is targeted.

The park's assistant superintendent, Ben Clary, said recently that "federal officials are considering suing the ranch, if necessary, to protect the park."[35]

A bill called the American Heritage Trust Act introduced into Congress by Arizona Representative Morris K. Udall would set up a secure, untouchable interest-earning trust fund of about $15 billion which would provide a guaranteed $1 billion of funding each year for federal and state land acquisitions. This money would be available perpetually and Congress would have little oversight as to its use.

Hence a private, independent dictatorship would be set up and given this funding to spend as they see fit. And they could buy any property they want to buy that they believe is necessary to the integrity of the National Park Service and federal public lands.

If the government can delay or prevent a group of people from building a church, that is religious persecution. If our land can be bought out from under us against our will, that is religious persecution. Make no mistake, that is exactly what they have in mind.

Whether or not those fighting against us are doing it on

religious or environmental grounds, the effect is to deny freedom of religion. This *is* religious persecution. This is religious hatred and hatred of those who embody the Light. I've seen it. I've experienced it.

And just because they're not screwing our tongues to our palates or burning us at the stake doesn't mean it's not. We're in a different century. The tactics are different. But the intent and the results are the same, to "muzzle the mouth of the ox,"[36] as the Bible says. And we're not doing anything to this land but caring for it and tending it as custodians for God and for anybody, and I say *anybody*, who wants to come and worship here. [11-second applause] The EIS, prepared by an unbiased state agency, has demonstrated that very fact.

As far as I'm concerned the government of the United States of America, my beloved country, is threatening to interfere with my right to religious freedom, my right to assemble, my right of free speech, my freedom of the press and my private property rights.

What is going on in Park County, Montana, today is a part of the history of persecutions that brought our Fathers to the cosmic necessity of making their Declaration of Independence. When one is pushed to the wall and life itself has no meaning without the spiritual flame of liberty, one must make a declaration of independence and say, "I shall not be moved!" [26-second applause]

Persecutions are not over and the battle that must be fought is for the ultimate liberty to expand and fully realize one's inner God-potential.

There are a great many people on this planet who long ago determined that they had no desire to realize that God-potential. So much enmity did they have with our Father-Mother God that they denied their very own birthright and they allowed the flame that burned upon the altar of their hearts to go out. They would rather be the self-extinguished ones than to bend the knee and confess the Universal Christ— and themselves a part of the very issue of God.

Now these individuals roam the earth, "wandering stars," as Jude called them quoting our Lord, "to whom is reserved the blackness of darkness for ever."[37] And they wander about the earth seeking to devour those who yet keep the flame God gave them, who are winning the crown of eternal life.

These keepers of the flame are working the works of the Lord and the mighty work of the ages: they accept the sacred labor of their karma and they don't ask anyone else to earn their daily bread for them. Work is their ethic and they embody the Word of God. They are the spiritual overcomers and overseers. They are the true founders of civilizations, religions, and even empires. On their backs the world is built. These hearts of flame, when reaching toward their Christhood, become the ultimate threat to these hollowed-out ones, these empty whited sepulchres.

So what we see today is that the fire that burns in our breasts must be a united fire. It must be and become a conflagration that Saint Germain has called "the fire on the mountain."[38] [12-second applause] And *there is* a fire on Maitreya's mountain. It's the flame of freedom that we must keep alive and burning bright for all who come after us who will also defend the cause of religious liberty on earth.

We begin to understand that for more than any other reason we plant our feet on this land in this Inner Retreat and in this Community of Glastonbury to guard the last bastion of religious liberty that there is and will be in the United States of America. [13-second applause] Because if we don't win in this cause, who coming after us meeting the same threat can or shall overcome?

We are a New Age religion. We are not orthodox in the Jewish sense of the word, the Islamic, the Protestant, the Catholic. But we draw from the eternal truths and mystical experiences of all the world's religions, saints, and sages. We are a people who because of our sponsorship by the Ascended Masters and our self-knowledge in God have forged this Community of the Holy Spirit.

But what are we?

We represent the peoples of all nations, the mechanics, the farmers, the teachers, those of the professions, the builders, the shopkeepers, the homemakers, all who share the American dream. We have the dedication and the foresight to set aside some of our private interests for the greater good of Community that we might hold dear a land such as this that we can call "Home."

"This land is my land" personally and collectively!

We have done this and we know that because we have done it people all over the world who are rising with the rising star of Aquarius, beloved Saint Germain, can also do it. They can come together on their own properties to worship in their own way as they follow the Inner Voice and discover, as we have discovered, what is important to them in their religious worship.

The Royal Teton Ranch includes our working farm and ranch community combined with our international Church headquarters, Summit University and Montessori International with our extensive publishing department where we produce all our own books, magazines, and weekly *Pearls of Wisdom*. It is our experiment in community living, not as communalism or Communism but as the mystery school of the Lord Jesus Christ and the sangha of the Lord Buddha.

Here we understand that by mutual creativity and reinforcement we can have the best benefits for ourselves and our families educationally, spiritually, and in the pursuit of what is most important to us—a way of life in the service of our Lord, the performance of his Work and the publishing of his Word as we daily endeavor to put it into practice together.

If an off-beat religion that has cherished values, whose members are intelligent, responsible, not cult members, not brainwashed but just plain everyday, ordinary American people—just common folk who share a common light—if we can do this, any other group of like-minded souls anywhere in the world any time in the next two thousand years can do the same.

If we do not do it, if we do not take our ultimate stand for freedom today, I can assure you that none others coming after us will have the spiritual fire nor the example to achieve it. That is the mark we make in this day. And we must make it.

[40-second applause] Thank you.

Since this American Heritage Trust Act has come to the fore and I have realized just how much power is about to be placed in the hands of a private group with a hidden agenda— religious persecution in the name of environmentalism— I have felt as never before the fire of liberty burning within me.

Being a part of this great nation, our heritage and the spirit of our Founding Fathers, I have come to the place where I realize that unless I can take my stand to preserve a free land for this religion and this people that God has given to me, nothing else will have meaning to me in this life.

It becomes my all-consuming cause, my reason for being. And to consider that this that we have built could be lost to my children or grandchildren or to yours or to all the Light-bearers who will come after us is the absolute unthinkable.

We must make this land secure today. We must do this.
[21-second applause]

"The Summit Lighthouse Sheds Its Radiance O'er All the World to Manifest as Pearls of Wisdom." An address by Elizabeth Clare Prophet **delivered** on **Monday, July 4, 1988,** at *FREEDOM 1988* in the Heart of the Inner Retreat at the **Royal Teton Ranch, Park County, Montana,** updated for print as this week's *Pearl.* **(1)** Paul D. Simmons, "Religious Liberty: A Heritage At Stake," *Church & State,* May 1986, p. 18. **(2)** Archbishop Marcel Lefebvre created the first schism in the Roman Catholic Church since 1870 when he consecrated four bishops on June 30, 1988, without papal authority. Pope John Paul II immediately excommunicated Lefebvre and the four bishops. Lefebvre, an ultra-traditionalist, began breaking with the Roman Catholic Church over modernized church policies of the Second Vatican Council (1962–65). His followers still practice the Latin Tridentine Mass and have established traditional seminaries in Switzerland, France, West Germany, Argentina, Australia and the United States. Lefebvre, aged 82, consecrated his four disciples to "ensure continuity of the church" after months of reconciliation sponsored by Pope John Paul II seemed to break down. This story, broadcast on NBC Nightly News, July 3, was shown to those attending *FREEDOM 1988* on July 4. **(3)** Will Durant, *The Reformation: A History of European Civilization from Wyclif to Calvin: 1300–1564* (New York: Simon and Schuster, 1957), pp. 505–6. **(4)** John A. Hostetler, *Amish Society,* 3d ed. (Baltimore: The Johns Hopkins University Press, 1963), p. 51. **(5)** Winfred E. Garrison in J. Milton Yinger, *Religion, Society and the Individual: an Introduction to the Sociology of Religion* (Toronto, Ontario, Canada: The Macmillan Company, 1957), p. 434. **(6)** Coalition for Religious Freedom, "The Crisis in Religious Freedom" (Washington, D.C., 1987), p. 1. **(7)** Ibid. **(8)** Ibid. **(9)** Virginia I. Postrel, "Religious Rights: A Matter of Property," *Wall Street Journal,* 20 May 1988, p. 18. **(10)** Julia Page, Upper Yellowstone Defense Fund letter, p. 1. **(11)** Montana Department of Health and Environmental Sciences, *Draft Environmental Impact Statement: Church Universal and Triumphant* (February 1988), p. 117. **(12)** "Threat to the Yellowstone," *Flyfishing,* January–February 1988, p. 29. **(13)** "Transcript of Hearing Before the Department of Health and Environmental Sciences of the State of Montana in the Matter of the Draft Environmental Impact Statement – Church Universal and Triumphant," Meeting at Gardiner, Montana, 21 March 1988 (Helena, Montana: State of Montana, 1988), pp. 103–4. **(14)** Ibid., pp. 97–98. **(15)** Ibid., p. 60. **(16)** Ibid., p. 140. **(17)** Mike Males, "State Can't Force CUT to Move Developments Away," *Bozeman Daily Chronicle,* 23 March 1988, p. 1. Church Universal and Triumphant owns a number of properties in Park County: the 12,000-acre Royal Teton Ranch South on the west side of the Yellowstone River (formerly the Forbes Ranch) where Church headquarters is located (it shares five miles of border with Yellowstone National Park and is four miles north of Gardiner, the tourist town at the north gate of the park); the Ranch Kitchen restaurant at Corwin Springs, across the river from the South Ranch; the 3,300-acre OTO Ranch on the east side of the Yellowstone River just north of Corwin Springs; the Community of Glastonbury, about 20 miles north of Corwin Springs, which is subdivided into 20-acre lots for purchase by Church members; the 15,000-acre Royal Teton Ranch North located about 38 miles north of Corwin Springs and used primarily for agriculture; and the Livingston Railroad Yard, 50 miles from Corwin Springs in the town of Livingston where the Church's publishing facilities are located. **(18)** Al Knauber, "Park Service Blasts Study of CUT Developments," *Livingston Enterprise,* 9 May 1988, p. 1. **(19)** Rev. 12:6, 14. **(20)** Knauber, "Park Service Blasts Study," p. 1. **(21)** Travel Table, Yellowstone National Park; Cumulative Visitors by Entrance Station, January 1 – December 31, 1987. **(22)** Yellowstone Fact Sheet [Yellowstone National Park, YELL 176a, rev. 3/87]. **(23)** Robert Ekey, "Park Officials Plan to Replace Canyon Buildings," *Billings Gazette,* 16 March 1988, p. 10–C; Elizabeth Laden, "Park Wants $1.6 Million for Winter," *Bozeman Daily Chronicle,* 11 February 1988. **(24)** Al Knauber, "Super 8 Motel Under Construction in Gardiner," *Livingston Enterprise,* 3 April 1987, p. 1; Al Knauber, "New Motel Going Up in Gardiner," *Livingston Enterprise,* 9 December 1987. **(25)** Al Knauber, "Gardiner Sewer Plant Repairs May Keep Waste Out of River," *Livingston Enterprise,* 31 August 1987, p. 2; Tom Shands, "Park Laundry Construction Begins in Gardiner," *Livingston*

Enterprise, 2 May 1985, p. 1. (**26**) Terry Sacks, "Sewage Leaked into Park River," *Bozeman Daily Chronicle,* 28 June 1988, p. 1. (**27**) KULR Evening News, 7 June 1988. (**28**) Peter H. King, "'Guru Ma' Moves to Montana: Plans for Promised Land Worry Neighbors, Yellowstone Officials," *Los Angeles Times,* 25 January 1987, Valley edition, p. 23, col. 1. (**29**) "Transcript of Hearing," p. 134. (**30**) Ibid., pp. 60–61. (**31**) Gen. 1:28. (**32**) Gen. 2:5, 15. (**33**) Gen. 9:1–3, 6, 7. (**34**) William Tyler Page, "The American's Creed," quoted from the Gettysburg Address by Abraham Lincoln and the Declaration of Independence. (**35**) Casey Bukro, "Environmentalists, Sect Wage Battle," *Chicago Tribune,* June 10, 1988, section 1, p. 19. (**36**) Deut. 25:4; I Cor. 9:9; I Tim. 5:18. (**37**) Jude 13. (**38**) See Saint Germain, 1988 *Pearls of Wisdom,* pp. 117–22.

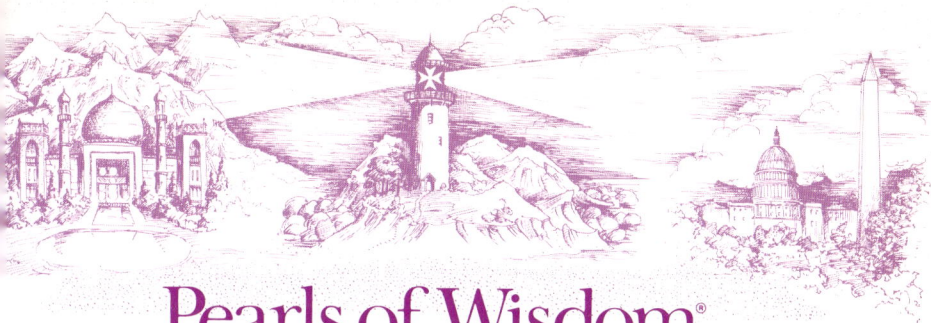

Pearls of Wisdom®

published by The Summit Lighthouse

Vol. 31 No. 71C   Elizabeth Clare Prophet   October 27, 1988

FREEDOM 1988
Fourth of July Address

Part 3

"Sign That Document!"
. . . for the Spiritual and Physical Defense of America

Will America fulfill Option the First or Option the Second?

In order for a civilization to sustain itself—yea, to transcend itself—it must be able to transmit its ideals and principles to the next generation.

We have seen how far America has strayed from our Founding Fathers' blueprint for religious freedom. A primary reason her freedoms are being eroded one by one is that her people have lost their spine, their backbone, and their fervor for the spirit of Liberty. Why?

A Five-Pronged Attack on Our Youth

In this century we have seen a five-pronged attack on our youth which has blunted the ability of generations to defend freedom. This attack, supported by the media and the educational system, comes through drugs, alcohol, nicotine, sugar, and rock music.

If current trends continue, the next generation may not even be capable of bearing the flame of freedom in America. God forbid!

In 1962 less than 1 percent of our 12- to 17-year-olds smoked pot; by 1982 nearly 30 percent did.[1] A 1987 study found that one in 25 high-school seniors uses marijuana daily and half of them have tried it.[2] Cocaine use has doubled among high-school seniors over the past 10 years.[3] Today 15.2 percent have tried the drug.[4]

Drug abuse by pregnant mothers is a growing problem. A study of 36 U.S. hospitals found that "at least 11% of 155,000 pregnant women surveyed had exposed their unborn babies to illegal drugs, with cocaine by far the most common." In 1988 20 percent of all babies born at Oakland's (inner city) Highland General Hospital were contaminated with crack cocaine.[5]

Tobacco is the largest single cause of premature death in the United States.[6] Three hundred and fifty thousand Americans a year die from tobacco-related illnesses.[7] Seventy percent of all teenagers try cigarettes and 20 percent end up as daily smokers.[8]

Today nearly five million adolescents have drinking problems.[9] One hundred thousand elementary school children get drunk at least once a week. One out of 10 12- to 13-year-olds currently drinks alcoholic beverages. And seven out of 10 high-school seniors drink. As early as the fourth grade, one out of three children reports pressure from classmates to try "wine coolers."[10] Alcohol is the second largest cause after tobacco of premature death in the United States. There are 100,000 alcohol-related deaths each year, 25 times more than from cocaine, heroin, and other illegal drugs combined.[11]

Sugar is the largest single element in the American diet—20 percent. The average five-year-old will consume 43 pounds in one year. The average yearly adult intake of sugar and other sweeteners is about 130 pounds.[12]

And the average teenager spends from four to six hours a day being surfeited in rock music.[13]

Drugs, alcohol, nicotine, sugar, and rock music—the five villains—are all self-destructive in that they impede the development of the five spiritual senses of the soul; moreover, they have led the way to a vast increase in the final act of self-destructivity, suicide. In 1962, about 650 teenagers killed themselves in the United States.[14] Last year 10 times that number—five to seven thousand teenagers—killed themselves. A teenager attempts suicide every nine minutes. Every 90 minutes one succeeds.[15]

The five-pronged attack on our youth has had a devastating impact on the moral and intellectual development of our children. By our failure to challenge the five villains, we have also failed to meet the twentieth-century demands to educate this generation to maintain a continuity of the American way of life and to assume their future role in world leadership.

American public schools have shown themselves incapable of passing on our heritage to the next generation. Despite the fact that per capita federal spending for elementary and secondary education grew by 43 percent between 1982 and 1988,[16] pupils' performance has not improved.

How can we expect to raise up leaders with the courage to "sign that document" when one-third of 17-year-old history students tested did not even know what that document was? That's right. A nationwide 1986 survey of 17-year-olds, 80 percent of whom were enrolled in history classes, found that 30 percent of them didn't know that the Declaration of Independence signaled the American colonists' break from England. Nearly half of them didn't know who said, "Give me liberty, or give me death."[17]

Do you want to know one of our biggest problems in education? It's that our schools don't require children to master a basic body of knowledge in order to graduate. And it shows.

American 18- to 24-year-olds ranked last among the industrialized nations in geography awareness. Barbara Walters reported that "American kids are at or near the bottom in an international survey measuring scientific achievement; ninth out of thirteen countries in physics; eleventh out of thirteen countries in chemistry; and thirteenth, dead last, in biology."[18] American 13-year-olds also came out last among foreign students in mathematics.

Poor training in elementary schools and high schools has

a major impact on colleges where, says Chester Finn of Vanderbilt University, "all that most of [the students] are getting is the high-school education they missed."[19] Tough college courses are reserved for the kids who managed to get a high-school education and foreigners. Columnist Thomas Sowell reports that "most of the people who receive Ph.D.s in engineering in the United States are foreigners. More foreigners than Americans also receive Ph.D.s in mathematics." Why? Sowell says it's because "so many Americans don't want to study this hard stuff."[20]

If we want to have a generation who is even remotely capable of carrying on the tradition of freedom, we've got to do something now! And what we've got to do is get the government out of education and let the schools and teachers that know how to teach children go for it! [13-second applause]

A Declaration of Independence for Our Schools

America, we are going to institute a voucher system in education. [7-second applause] We as parents have the right to send our children to the best school we can find whether it's public or not. Why should private education be reserved for the wealthy?

The government spends $4,300 a year per pupil to educate our children.[21] But is your child getting $4,300 out of the system? What if you got a voucher from the government every year for that amount which you could then apply to the school of your choice? [11-second applause] That would be the fastest way not only to restore excellence but also to democratize education.

Whoever said that only the wealthy should be able to give their children a decent education?

You wouldn't think an idea like this would find much opposition, but the education establishment has dug in its heels and screamed bloody murder. They say it will hurt the inner city schools because most of the students will leave them. And the kids who are left will suffer because their parents aren't smart enough to take advantage of the new system.

Well, we'll inform them, won't we? [Audience response: "Yes!" 7-second applause] Are we going to let another generation be ruined by drug-infested schools because of arguments like these? Maybe the worst of the public schools should be closed down. Or be forced to compete with the best of public and private schools.

How about survival of the fittest? How about competition? How about excellence? [6-second applause]

They say a voucher system will hurt poor people because the money they would get from the voucher wouldn't be enough to pay private school tuition. That's sheer fabrication! Only the most expensive private schools cost more than public schools cost the government. There are plenty of reasonably priced private schools.

The National Education Association (NEA) says that a voucher system will interfere with freedom of religion because some people will take their vouchers to church-sponsored schools.[22] They are so concerned that private religious schools will be getting federal money that they would deny the voucher system to everybody.

How would it interfere with freedom of religion to allow parents to choose the kind of school and the kind of education they want for their children?

First of all, there seems to be an assumption (and one that I deem false) that federal monies going to a church school would be used to support the sponsoring church. Church schools must meet the same payroll and overhead as public and private schools, therefore we would expect them to use the vouchers to run their schools, not their churches.

But if the bellyachers want to be sure the churches don't rob Peter to pay Paul, they can have the church schools' books audited to satisfy themselves that voucher money doesn't find its way into the pastors' pockets. Church schools are among the best in the nation and always have been; they should have the same fair treatment that private as well as public schools would be getting under the voucher system.

The bottom line is parents should be free to choose what kind of an education their children are going to have—

wherever and under whomever they decide. And their ability to pay or not for private schools must no longer be the basis of a class society that separates the rich kids from the poor kids for the rest of their lives. And this is precisely what the opponents of the voucher system make themselves a party to.

Secondly, the First Amendment was designed to prevent the establishment of a state-sponsored, tax-supported religion (i.e., preferential treatment of any one religion), not to bias federal aid to private or parochial schools. But the NEA and those who oppose the voucher system with their elitist attitude willfully misconstrue the First Amendment to mean that no federal money can go to any parochial school, even if the school is fulfilling a function the state desires (education) and even if the money isn't administered in a manner that would favor the schools of one church over those of any other. By their willful ignoring of the Founding Fathers' intent, the opponents of the voucher system would deprive millions of children of a better education.

And the name of the game of the power elite who have entered our schoolhouses is control. They can't stand the idea of losing control of our children, whom they have turned into guinea pigs for their deluded educational experiments and drugs like Ritalin and Cylert[23] that they foist upon them to keep them sedated.

Why should we trust the public schools with our children when they have turned out over 13.5 million illiterates in the last 50 years?[24] Why should we trust them? Why should we turn our children over to them? —Only to have them sent back to us labeled "educationally handicapped" or "learning disabled" or "dyslexic" or having an "attention deficit disorder," "perceptual handicaps," or "minimal brain dysfunction."

These labels are a crutch for schools and teachers alike who have lost the art of conveying knowledge and, more importantly, self-knowledge. Why, we can teach our children better ourselves. And that's exactly why I founded Montessori International in Colorado Springs in 1970.

A voucher system would force the public schools to raise their standards and to compete in the marketplace. But what the power elite do to stay in control once they take control is to eliminate the very competition that makes for excellence in all areas of life and prepares our children for the real world. They can't beat the competition of the common people so they use government money and regulation to protect themselves from it. That's what monopolies do! [9-second applause]

People of America, it's time to declare our independence from government control of our children's education. [5-second applause] It's time to take the future into our own hands and vest it in our own children. Our future is our children and it's time we were able to decide what they will learn and who will teach them. [6-second applause]

Today we have two choices. We can enter a golden age or we can go down into a dark age worse than any in recorded history. Doesn't what happens in these two alternative visions of America's future depend a lot on what our children learn about their heritage of freedom, not only in the United States but in the Judeo-Christian tradition and in all of the world movements for individual freedom and equal opportunity that have brought us to this unique point in history when we finally have in hand our hard-won freedoms?

Is not our children's education—how they're able to read and write and how they're able to organize and analyze information and how they're able to think and reason creatively, logically, and independently—going to determine whether they choose to bring in a golden age or move in the downward spiral of socialist, Communist state control of our lives?

It makes all the difference and it has everything to do with what America's future will be! Our children are becoming who they are from the moment they are born, from the moment they are conceived—from the earliest beginnings when we first speak to them in the womb and tell them what life is all about and the joy we will have together in working for the victory of God's light on earth. [8-second applause]

If we don't rescue our youth from the five-pronged attack of the fallen angels and if we don't stop aborting the Lightbearers who should be bringing in the New Age—1.6

million souls a year in America, 22 million since *Roe v. Wade*—we're going to lose the greatest nation on earth and God's divine plan for us for a golden age of Aquarius.

In order to successfully challenge the forces opposing our youth, we have to have the same courage of the Founding Fathers who signed that document. Keepers of the Flame, will you sign that document? ["Yes!" 25-second applause]

The Spiritual Mandate for Self-Defense

But even if we solve all the problems afflicting our youth, we will not be fulfilling our or their reason for being if we don't solve the single greatest problem we face as a nation: our spiritual and physical defense. And though they may have the finest education in the world, the healthiest diets, the best of the world's culture, art and music, and the purest stream of consciousness, our children may not have a future to defend.

We can give our children all things, but if we do not begin at the beginning with a spiritual defense and a physical defense, then all of our efforts will have been in vain (at least in this round) and all else we have given them will count for naught—except that by experience the soul will have increased in wisdom and in the practicality of self-mastery and in stature before God. This learning the soul may take to other planes or planets in life's continuing journey, but the most important lesson of all—to put self-defense before all else—will have come too little, too late for this generation.

We have a dharma, a duty, to defend our platform of evolution and the integrity of our souls that we might fulfill the calling of our nation to bear the torch of liberty on behalf of oppressed peoples at home and abroad.

The story of Krishna and Arjuna is well known to you as told in the Bhagavad-Gita, the 2,400-year-old Hindu text. As you know, Arjuna is of the warrior caste but he rejects his duty to go to war. It is the eve of the battle and his kinsmen are on both sides. He will have to kill his own relatives. He says, "Better I deem it, if my kinsmen strike, to face them weaponless, and bare my breast to shaft and spear."[25]

Arjuna would rather die than fight.

Krishna, a Hindu deity who figures as Arjuna's teacher and charioteer, first teaches him about the continuity of life and the indestructibility of the soul. It is one of the greatest passages in all of the world's literature because unless we have life as a premise and the continuity of life as a premise, we will not make the correct moral decisions in our lifetime. Our decisions are always made because we know that we live forever and that we live forever in God. And we want that accountability from the beginning unto the ending of our lives because we are a continuity of consciousness.

And so, the great Cosmic Christ says to him:

> Never the spirit was born;
> The spirit shall cease to be never;
> Never was time it was not;
> End and Beginning are dreams!
> Birthless and deathless and changeless
>   remaineth the spirit forever;
> Death hath not touched it at all,
> Dead though the house of it seems!"[26]

Having so demonstrated the unreality of death and the all-inclusiveness of life, Krishna tells Arjuna that he must fulfill his dharma. "Arise, thou Son of Kunti! brace thine arm for conflict,. . .gird thee to the fight, for so thou shalt not sin!"[27]

The point is well taken by Paul, "For we wrestle not against flesh and blood, but against principalities, against powers, against the rulers of the darkness of this world, against spiritual wickedness in high places."[28]

Dharma is our reason for being, the calling of the soul. The law of God says it is a sin to fail to defend one's dharma. Nations and individuals must fulfill their reason for being in God. America needs to heed the command of Krishna and fulfill her dharma. America must realize that she will end war only when she understands the mandate of God to defend the principle of freedom and all who embody it.

When Siddhartha Gautama sat in meditation beneath

the Bo tree, Mara, the Evil One, confronted him with temptations and he had to defend his right to be, and to be doing what he was doing; for he had vowed to remain in his place until he should attain enlightenment.

First Mara said, "Why do you struggle? Hard is struggle, hard to struggle all the time."[29] He continued his attack by parading voluptuous goddesses and dancing girls before Gautama. Then he assailed him with hurricanes, torrential rains, flaming rocks, boiling mud, fierce soldiers, beasts, and finally darkness. As a last resort, Mara challenged his right to be doing what he was doing.

Gautama tapped the earth with the bhumisparsa (earth-touching) mudra,* and the earth thundered her answer: "I bear you witness!" Whereupon Mara fled.

The American people must defend their right to fulfill their dharma. The only way they can attain enlightenment, the only way they can attain Christhood, is if they have a place prepared where there is a guaranteed opportunity to be free to walk the spiritual path. Therefore, America *must* defend her freedom. And to do that, she needs physical as well as spiritual defenses! [10-second applause] And let us not neglect the mental, emotional, and psychological defenses as well.

Meeting the Challenges of History

History has shown that passivity will never overcome evil. Pacifism has seldom, if ever, achieved peace. Often the opposite results. It is this history and the sense of their destiny in its moving stream that our children must be taught at elementary levels in the schools of our choice.

Rome's destruction of Carthage in 146 B.C. is an important lesson for our time. It shows the result of negotiating for peace without adequate military strength to back it up. Carthage attempted to meet the Roman threat with appeasement. Perhaps her leaders said, "We will secure a place for ourselves in history."

Carthage was a prosperous city in North Africa on the Mediterranean, between Libya and Algeria, near the site of

---

*bhumisparsa (earth-touching) mudra: the left hand upturned in the lap, right hand pointed downward touching the earth

modern Tunis. Carthage, once Rome's rival, had been defeated, disarmed, and forced to pay tribute to the empire. Despite this the city had become too prosperous for the tastes of the Romans.

Cato, presiding over the Roman Senate, advocated its total destruction. He ended every speech he gave in the Senate, on whatever subject, with the words: "Besides, I think that Carthage must be destroyed."[30]

The imperialists in the Senate agreed with him. They needed only a pretext to carry out their plan. It came as a result of an attempt by Carthage to defend herself against the repeated raids of Masinissa, king of Numidia, modern Algeria.

Carthage was bound by treaty to make no war without Rome's consent. She sent ambassadors to Rome to protest Masinissa's many invasions. The Romans told them that since the Carthaginians had come from Phoenicia (which corresponds to modern Lebanon) they were interlopers in Africa and well-armed nations were not required to respect their rights. This was a sentence to slow death by raids and invasion.

In 151 B.C., Carthage declared war on Numidia in an effort to protect herself. Rome declared war on Carthage. Carthage, though wealthy, was unprepared for war with Rome. She had a small army and navy and no mercenaries or allies.

Will Durant records how Carthage's attempts at negotiation led to her utter annihilation:

> An embassy [from Carthage] hastened to Rome with authority to meet all demands. The Senate promised that if Carthage would turn over to the Roman consuls in Sicily 300 children of the noblest families as hostages, and would obey whatever orders the consuls would give, the freedom and territorial integrity of Carthage would be preserved. Secretly the Senate bade the consuls carry out the instructions that they had already received.
>
> The Carthaginians gave up their children with

forebodings and laments; the relatives crowded the shores in a despondent farewell; at the last moment the mothers tried by force to prevent the ships from sailing; and some swam out to sea to catch a last glimpse of their children.

The consuls sent the hostages to Rome, crossed to Utica [a neighbor of Carthage] with army and fleet, summoned the Carthaginian ambassadors, and required of Carthage the surrender of her remaining ships, a great quantity of grain, and all her engines and weapons of war. When these conditions had been fulfilled, the consuls further demanded that the population of Carthage should retire to ten miles from the city, which was then to be burned to the ground.

The ambassadors argued in vain that the destruction of a city which had surrendered hostages and its arms without striking a blow was a treacherous atrocity unknown to history. They offered their own lives as a vicarious atonement; they flung themselves upon the ground and beat the earth with their heads. The consuls replied that the terms were those of the [Roman] Senate and could not be changed.

When the people of Carthage heard what was demanded of them they lost their sanity. Parents mad with grief tore limb from limb the leaders who had advised surrendering the child hostages; others killed those who had counseled the surrender of arms; some dragged the returning ambassadors through the streets and stoned them; some killed whatever Italians could be found in the city; some stood in the empty arsenals and wept.

The Carthaginian Senate declared war against Rome and called all adults—men and women, slave or free—to form a new army, and to forge anew the weapons of defense. Fury gave them resolution. Public buildings were demolished to provide metal and timber; the statues of cherished gods were melted down to make swords, and the hair of the women was shorn to make ropes. In two months the beleaguered city produced 8,000 shields, 18,000 swords, 30,000 spears, 60,000 catapult missiles, and built in its inner harbor a fleet of 120 ships.

Three years the city stood siege by land and sea. Again and again the consuls led their armies against the walls, but always they were repulsed; only Scipio Aemilianus, one of the military tribunes, proved resourceful and brave. Late in 147 [B.C.] the Roman Senate and Assembly made him consul and commander, and all men approved.

Soon afterward Laelius succeeded in scaling the walls. The Carthaginians, though weakened and decimated by starvation, fought for their city street by street, through six days of slaughter without quarter. Harassed by snipers, Scipio ordered all captured streets to be fired and leveled to the ground. Hundreds of concealed Carthaginians perished in the conflagration.

At last the population, reduced from 500,000 to 55,000, surrendered. Hasdrubal, their general, pleaded for his life, which Scipio granted, but his wife, denouncing his cowardice, plunged with her sons into the flames. The survivors were sold as slaves, and the city was turned over to the legions for pillage.

Reluctant to raze it, Scipio sent to Rome for final instructions; the Senate replied that not only Carthage, but all such of her dependencies as had stood by her were to be completely destroyed, that the soil should be plowed and sown with salt, and a formal curse laid upon any man who should attempt to build upon the site. For seventeen days the city burned.[31]

Rome wanted to teach the world a lesson. And she did.

We need to study and understand the lessons of Carthage. Or else we shall come to know the truth of George Santayana's statement, "Those who cannot remember the past are condemned to repeat it."[32]

Great civilizations come to an end when they cease to defend themselves against external challenges. Our bodies come to an end when we can no longer defend them against the external challenges of disease, the last plagues and death. If you are vulnerable to an invading virus against which you have no defense, you may cease to occupy your body temple and lose this physical platform of your soul's evolution.

That's why you need to build a mind and a body that can withstand foreign invaders. That's why you need to call forth the light of your I AM Presence and raise up the sacred fire—so that the power of God in you will consume the karmic cause and core of your vulnerability to disease as well as its manifestation.

You need to put on the mind of God which was in Christ Jesus—"who, being in the form of God, thought it not robbery to be equal with God...."[33] You need to put on "the whole armour of God, that ye may be able to stand against the wiles of the devil": aggressive mental suggestion, sinister forces of suicide, pacificism, fear, self-doubt, depression, and death and the five assailants who would have you sell your soul and give up your spiritual birthright for the paltry pleasures of the senses.[34]

And in this our time we know that the Inner Light must be magnified by the LORD Our Righteousness to deflect and consume those invaders that seek to overtake our consciousness, cell by cell. This is the law of integrity (i.e., the soul's inner integration with the Spirit Most Holy) which is the foundation of existence. Each one of us must be able to defeat any and every type of invading force that seeks to cross the line—the circle—of our integral selfhood, as Above, so below, in heaven and on earth.

People establish communities and nation states because as individuals they cannot deal effectively with the challenges to their identity, and so they achieve integrity as a group and a group karmic pattern and mandala. And as the lesser units of our planetary evolution establish harmony with themselves, so we will one day see one world, free and at peace in the golden age of Aquarius.

But this will not come about because we close our senses

to the warring elements within the individual and collective psyche. Until these are defeated within and without there is neither integrity nor integration of opposing factions crying, "Peace, peace!" when there is no inner peace and therefore can be no outer peace.

Failing to achieve that peace, the Romans also failed the tests of history. Their "eternal city" was destroyed by "barbarians," but not until the end would they believe that it could happen to them. Like Americans today, they thought their civilization was immortal.

When Baghdad fell to the Mongols in 1258 A.D., the subjects of the Arab Caliphate were shocked. The Ottoman Empire, the Assyrians, the Egyptians, the Hindus, the Chinese and others in their turn were destroyed by barbarian invaders when they least expected it. These peoples considered themselves to be above the barbarians who conquered them. They, too, failed the tests of history.

Historian Arnold Toynbee found that the ability of a nation to defend itself against external challenges depends on comparable spiritual development, or "etherialization" as he calls it.

"Real progress is found to consist in a process defined as 'etherialization', an overcoming of material obstacles which releases the energies of the society to make responses to challenges which henceforth are internal rather than external, spiritual rather than material," he writes.[35] Furthermore, he says, growth is dependent upon "perpetual flexibility and spontaneity."[36] In other words, as a civilization progresses it will not be able to deal with external challenges unless it also learns to deal with increasing internal challenges.

"One of the perennial infirmities of human beings is to ascribe their own failure to forces that are entirely beyond their control," says Toynbee. "The most that an alien enemy has achieved has been to give an expiring suicide his *coup de grâce*."[37] When the spirit and the soul of a nation are in a state of malaise, that nation cannot defend its territorial or psychological integrity.

Toynbee found that the character of a nation's leadership

is crucial to the survival of the civilization. He says that if those who lead a civilization, the "creative minority," lose their ability to creatively meet successive challenges and become a "dominant minority," then the majority of that society will withdraw their allegiance from the leaders, and the civilization itself will stop growing and enter a "time of troubles" leading to its ultimate collapse.

This is because the spiritual fire is itself the great bonding of community. It is the love of God that bonds the cells of the body and the body politic, that engenders in them the properties of self-healing and enables them to replace themselves. This process is the prime example of the law of self-transcendence that operates in mankind and society if and when there is a conscious cooperation with this law.

Each and every day that we recite our prayers we should be transcending yesterday's lesser state in the alchemy of the Holy Spirit that is engendered by religious ritual. We should become a renewed creature in Christ, old things passing away, all things becoming new.[38] We should be carrying more of his Light, day by day, by our exercise of the sacred science of the Word. We should be girding up the loins of our minds and in sobriety hoping to the end for grace through the revelation of Jesus Christ present with us in our members.[39]

However, there are several conditions of consciousness which impede the transforming Power, Wisdom and Love of God from operating within self and society. These must be squarely dealt with if one is to inherit eternal life:

1) The lack of desire to serve and affinitize oneself with the Light and to become the Light, and in its place the desire for pleasure and the expending of the life-force in pleasure's pursuits.

2) The absence of the merciful heart and forgiveness. Unless people pray "forgive us our debts, as [i.e., in the same manner as] we forgive our debtors,"[40] they will never self-transcend their yesterdays or anyone else's.

3) The spirit of vengeance that carries over from lifetime to lifetime—seething resentment for personal injury that will never forgive or forget nor place all matters in God's hands

for divine retribution, but rather craves revenge against neighbor and neighboring states and will take it in time or eternity. Those who are of this state of mind do not partake of the communion cup of the law of self-transcendence, and they are not of Christ's universal Body and Blood.

4) The absence of compassion, tolerance and charity in the giving of oneself to any part of Life, which is God.

5) The failure to submit one's life to the Holy Will of God and to "seek ye first the kingdom of God and his righteousness"[41] whereby all things necessary to the joyous fulfillment of one's reason for being are added by the Spirit of the LORD.

The law of self-transcendence must be experienced by peoples and nations if they are to survive as a healthy, integrated unit of identity. When for the above reasons the integration spiral of their collective oneness no longer has the momentum to self-sustain, the nation loses its centripetal (or integrating) force, a disintegration spiral sets in, and its centrifugal force (without the balance of the centripetal) will ultimately cause dissolution.

Therefore, if the Light is not embraced by a people, and the Light that was once in them is turned to Darkness, then that Darkness, self-willed and self-created, becomes the irreversible cause and effect of disintegration and death. These ensue because only the Light at the nucleus of a body, cell or atom can hold together the components of life. And only those who love the Light and serve the Light can truly possess the Light.

Today America has arrived at that moment in history which Toynbee speaks of, the moment when, for her own survival, she must transcend herself. And her leaders must rise to the occasion. Throughout history, the creative minority who have had the extraordinary courage to "sign that document" have made all the difference.

We all know about Leonidas and the 300 Spartans who held the pass at Thermopylae against the great army of Persians in the most heroic resistance in history. It was 480 B.C. The Spartans lost 300 men, the Persians 20,000. Although

Leonidas fell in the battle, he protected the Greek fleet from being outflanked by the Persians. And Greece lived to enter a brief but brilliant golden age. Remember the heroism at Thermopylae. Remember the integrity of 300 men. Golden ages come because peoples and societies are self-sustained by their inner sense of wholeness. And by their wholeness they are willing to stand against all odds for the principles of absolute Freedom, Peace, Truth and Universal Enlightenment.

In 1775 Patrick Henry uttered the words that are spelled out of freedom's flame that yet burns in our hearts today. With a realism not now heard in the land, he said, "There is no longer any room for hope. If we wish to be free...we must fight!... Gentlemen may cry peace, peace—but there is no peace. The war has actually begun! The next gale that sweeps from the north will bring to our ears the clash of resounding arms! Our brethren are already in the field!"[42]

Yes, our brethren, the Afghans. Yes, our brethren, the freedom fighters throughout the world. They are being oppressed by their governments, some are being massacred by the forces of Communism or right-wing dictatorship, others are condemned to death by disease, hunger, and starvation engineered by tyrants and the toilers Right and Left. Yes, it is our brethren who are already in the field.

Therefore, "Why stand we here idle? What is it the gentlemen wish? What would they have? Is life so dear, or peace so sweet, as to be purchased at the price of chains or slavery? Forbid it, Almighty God! I know not what course others may take; but as for me, give me liberty, or give me death!"[43] [33-second applause]

Upon those words and that stand the American Revolution was fought and won and upon that platform Americans today have the freedom they enjoy to agree and to disagree.

George Washington said, "We have, therefore, to resolve to conquer or die."[44] Our choices are no different yesterday, today, or forever. If we do not resolve to conquer here and now where it is given to us by Providence to take our stand, life and death will not be choices—neither for ourselves nor for our posterity.

Why We Must Provide for the Common Defense

The Preamble to the Constitution declares that one of the principal reasons the people of the United States established their government was to "provide for the common defence." Securing "the Blessings of Liberty to ourselves and our Posterity" came next on the list.

We cannot enjoy liberty and its blessings without establishing defense. And today, my fellow Americans, we do not enjoy a common defense. We don't have a common civil defense. We don't have a common anti-ballistic missile system. We don't have a common defense of our military bases here or abroad. We don't even have a common surface-to-air missile defense to stop a single enemy bomber from flying across our borders and bombing our cities!

What will you tell your child or your children's children? What will you say when the Soviet Union launches its surprise first-strike attack on the United States?

What will we say in the last half hour that we might spend with our children? Will we say, "There is nothing we can do"? And when they ask, "Why?" will we tell them, "We didn't think it was necessary to be prepared for war. We didn't demand that our leaders spend our tax dollars on the defense of America because our leaders told us it would never happen. We didn't want to spend the money to defend our nation, our souls, our liberty, and our birthright to fulfill our reason for being on earth in the twentieth century. It simply wasn't our priority."

How do you make a child understand such logic?

Americans have been told by experts that a Soviet first strike against our nation is impossible because the Soviets would risk annihilation if they attacked us. But that is not the case. The Soviets are prepared to wage nuclear war and to survive!

Saint Germain warned us of this almost two years ago. On Thanksgiving 1986 he said, "You have every reason to believe, to be concerned, and to be prepared for a first strike by the Soviet Union upon these United States." He said, "Even as I speak meetings unending take place. The enemy is prepared to survive a nuclear war—the United States is not."[45]

"But how did it happen, Daddy, Mommy?" our children will ask us in those thirty minutes. "Why can't we stop the missiles?" Indeed, why can't we? And since Thanksgiving 1986 our leaders have made it their business to reassure the Soviets that they can indeed survive a nuclear war—not our children, not America, but the Soviets.

If things continue as they have in the past year, we will have no answers for our children. The fact is, America, we are failing to meet the Soviet threat. Like all great civilizations we have come to the point at which we must either transcend ourselves or be destroyed.

Somerset Maugham wrote, "If a nation values anything more than freedom, it will lose its freedom; and the irony of it is, that if it is comfort or money that it values more, it will lose that, too."[46]

The nations of the West have not learned the lessons of history. They have chosen cowardice and appeasement. And the prophecy of the handwriting on the wall has come to pass.

Today the United States of America is vulnerable to destruction. We have seen this prophesied by the Ascended Masters, by Nostradamus, by beloved Mother Mary at Fátima and at Medjugorje, by our reading of the signs of karma written in our astrology and by George Washington's third vision.

How could that third vision come to pass? What could bring about war and devastation on our own soil? What could prevent us from exercising our first option of bringing in a golden age of Aquarius?

As we examine world conditions today, we see that our nation is indeed vulnerable to a Soviet first strike and to foreign invasion. The Soviets don't think like us. They believe it's possible to fight a nuclear war using relatively small weapons that destroy the enemy's weapons, and to win. They believe they can surgically remove most of our weapons in a surprise first strike, leaving our cities largely intact.[47]

You might not think that's sane. You might think no one would ever do anything like that. Well, what you think doesn't make any difference. It's what the Soviets think that makes all the difference. If we want to keep a nuclear war from ever happening, we must keep the Soviets from ever pushing the button. [11-second applause]

America spends $300 billion a year on defense. So how did we get into a position of zero defense against nuclear weapons? Well, I'll tell you, it wasn't easy. It's not for a lack of money or technology. We have no defense against nuclear weapons today because of the logic of Mutual Assured Destruction (MAD) that prevails in our defense community.

The nuclear strategy of the United States is deterrence— "Let's avoid nuclear war by making the consequences of an attack by either nation too great." We live under MAD which says that neither side will start a nuclear war because after a first strike both sides would retain the capacity to destroy large segments of the other's population.[48]

According to MAD, weapons that kill people are good, weapons that kill weapons are bad and defenses which stop nuclear warheads are "destabilizing." That is, they are likely to cause war since the side that has them can attack without fear of being annihilated in retaliation. So defenses are not inherently threatening but they have become so in the context of our nuclear strategy.

For MAD to work, both sides must abide by it. But they haven't. The Soviets are building a defense for their country and people and the United States is not. Furthermore, based on MAD, in the mid-sixties we unilaterally froze our force of intercontinental ballistic missiles (ICBMs) at 1,054, virtually dismantled our extensive and formidable air defense against enemy bombers, and pretty much gave up on civil defense.

This giving up, this surrender to the enemy without a shot being fired, this national suicide has everything to do with the five villains that have invaded the temple of the mind and the spirit of a once great nation. It has everything to do with drugs, alcohol, nicotine, sugar, and rock music, all of which drive the life-force down the spine.

These abuses of our bodies and our souls we passively suffer do not allow the sacred fire of the Divine Mother to rise naturally from the base-of-the-spine chakra to meet the light of the Universal Christ in the thousand-petaled lotus of the crown chakra. And so the spinelessness, the absence of will to be and to live and therefore to defend one's integral reason for being—one's integrity, or integration in God—is at the root of the malaise of our time.

Rock music is the greatest single factor that brought about the changing of the national consciousness toward the psychology of the nondefense of self and society. But it alone would have had no power over the minds and souls of our people. Flanked by the demons of drugs—marijuana, hashish, cocaine, crack, heroin, PCP—escorted by the multibillion dollar sugar, alcohol and cigarette industries, and guaranteed safe passage by the pharmaceuticals drugging the nation to death, the false hierarchy of rock music and its hellions has in three decades made America the pushover and the patsy for this conspiracy of the Dark Forces against the Lightbearers of the world!

Yes, rock music was the pulling of the rip cord. It signaled the loss of national conscience and national virginity. Rock music is the gateway to Death and Hell through which the pied pipers, reincarnated fallen Atlanteans, have led our youth, our babies, the old and the middle-aged alike. Even the pastors in their pulpits have sanctioned Christian rock in the name of Jesus Christ. Shame on them!

Before this attack on youth by the five poisons (the five oppositions to the five Dhyāni Buddhas who direct the inner development of the soul within us) we saw that America defended herself "against all enemies," never lost a war, sustained her leadership role among the nations and felt good about herself.

But not any more. While we and our allies have surfeited in our indulgences and preoccupations with self and psyche, the Soviet Union has built an ICBM force which is powerful and accurate enough to destroy our military targets; and, as I said, they also began covertly building themselves a defense system and talking us out of building our own.

Not only have the Soviets been moving ever toward the

goal of a nuclear first strike against Uncle Sam, but they have also been quietly saturating the brains and bodies of our youth with drugs in order to increase their cash supply and weaken our national resolve.

Enter Jan Sejna, former general major in the Czechoslovakian army and the highest-ranking member of the Communist military apparatus ever to defect. He had a working relationship with Nikita Khrushchev and was privy to the Soviets' strategy for global conquest. He was present at a meeting in 1962 when Khrushchev told key Eastern European leaders that the Soviet Union was going to wage drug warfare against the United States. Khrushchev saw drug warfare as a form of chemical warfare.[49]

Khrushchev was impressed by the Chinese Communist techniques. Starting in 1928, Mao had used drugs against the Chinese and later against United States forces in Korea. Khrushchev told the Eastern European leaders that with drugs they could destroy the United States from within while bringing in cash for Soviet espionage activities.[50] It is our weakness for drugs that is destroying us. And there is persuasive evidence that not only the Soviets but also the United States government has been involved in drug trafficking.[51] If we had the spine and the inner strength to resist these drugs, we would not be in the danger we are in today. But, America, we have lost our equilibrium—the internal balance of the yin and yang forces of life.

Our destruction by the enemy within was predicted by Abraham Lincoln 150 years ago:

> At what point shall we expect the approach of danger? By what means shall we fortify against it? Shall we expect some transatlantic military giant to step the ocean and crush us at a blow? Never! All the armies of Europe, Asia and Africa combined with all the treasure of the earth (our own excepted) in their military chest, with a Bonaparte for a commander, could not by force take a drink from the Ohio, or make a track on the Blue Ridge, in a trial of a thousand years.
>
> At what point then is the approach of danger to be

expected? I answer, if it ever reach us, it must spring up among us. It cannot come from abroad. If destruction be our lot, we must ourselves be its author and finisher. As a nation of freemen, we must live through all time or die by suicide.[52]

Following the Khrushchev meeting, the Soviets organized the East-bloc intelligence services into a vast network which smuggled drugs into the United States.[53] General Sejna was present in Prague when the Czechs, acting on behalf of the Soviets, made a deal with Raul Castro to integrate Cuba into the Soviet Union's drug-smuggling network.[54] In 1968 the Soviets were selling drugs to U.S. servicemen in Europe through KINTEX, a Bulgarian corporation. Since then, the Cuban and East European intelligence services have smuggled huge quantities of heroin, cocaine, marijuana, hashish and other drugs into the United States.[55]

The United States government refuses to acknowledge that the Soviet Union has an official policy of drug smuggling to undermine and destroy the United States. Perhaps that's because if they admitted the realpolitik of Soviet strategy and the drug war the Soviets are winning against the U.S. hands down, they would have to take a stand and engage in a spiritual and physical warfare to save the soul of a nation— something the U.S. has never had the nerve to do since the Bolshevik revolution, always crying "Peace, peace..." when there was and is and can be no peace with the Soviet system or leadership.

This is the psychology of nihilism that I call *SAD— Self-Assured Destruction*—that saturates the non-souls and the non-strategy of our representatives in Congress.

A new law passed by Congress on May 15, 1988, gets the U.S. military involved in stopping drugs.[56] But it's only a token effort which will never be successful until we challenge the Soviet government directly and use enough military force to stop them. No treaty should be signed with the Soviet Union until this International Capitalist/Communist Conspiracy drug network is disbanded. [11-second applause]

There is no way the Soviet Union could have carried on

this war against our youth since the days of Khrushchev without full cooperation of agents in the West. There is no way they could have been carrying out this operation without our intelligence community and our military establishment being fully aware of it as a strategy. Therefore, I say it is an International Capitalist/Communist Conspiracy of the power elite in every nation on earth moving against the Lightbearers of the world who are our sons and daughters.

General Sejna also says the Soviets plan a first strike against the United States. And believe me, this man knows what he's talking about! I interviewed him on Summit University Forum and this is what he said:

> Until 1963 everything was prepared for defense because they thought they were not strong enough for offense. They were behind in nuclear weapons and these things.
>
> Marshal Malinovsky, who was at that time minister of defense, visited Czechoslovakia and other satellites. And he said, "Comrades, we have to change our preparation. We have to change our tactic from defense to offense. For the next war, we have three possibilities. First, the NATO missiles will be first in the air. Second, our missiles and NATO's will meet in the air. And third, our missiles will be first in the air. The first two possibilities are not acceptable for us."
>
> Since then, ladies and gentlemen, everything was prepared for a surprise attack.[57]

General Sejna says that after a Soviet nuclear first strike on the United States, Western Europe would either surrender or be overrun by conventional, chemical, and biological forces.[58]

It's not chic to talk about a surprise attack in the era of glasnost. Military officials assure us it's not possible. They say we would have adequate warning based on satellite detection of increased troop movements, mobile missile movements, and bombers being put on alert. Therefore they do not even consider the possibility.

The fact is, the United States and NATO assume they will receive adequate warning of a Soviet attack allowing them time to prepare. NATO is counting on at least several days of warning during which they would disperse their forces, man their defense positions, and receive reinforcements from the United States. The United States believes it will have at least several hours' warning during which bombers could be loaded and alerted and submarines in port could put to sea. This is folly for four reasons:

    1) **Surprise attack is an integral part of Soviet strategy.**

History shows that Soviet military strategy is characterized by preemptive, surprise attacks, often in peacetime and often accompanied by deception (such as military exercises or ongoing negotiations) to disguise their activities. They achieved surprise in their invasions of Czechoslovakia, Hungary, and Afghanistan.

Military strategist William R. Van Cleave has researched surprise in Soviet strategy which he discusses in an article, "Surprise Nuclear Attack," published in an anthology entitled *Soviet Strategic Deception*. In it he notes that "Soviet military literature indicates that the Soviets believe that surprise attack could be the determinative event of a nuclear war; that a surprise attack could strategically disrupt and even forestall the enemy's use of nuclear weapons; and that surprise attack is feasible."[59]

    2) **The United States has a history of being surprised because it is unwilling to believe the warning signals.**

The Japanese attack on Pearl Harbor at dawn, December 7, 1941, is a prime example of America's unwillingness to accept and act on data that indicates a surprise attack. The Japanese achieved complete surprise, catching the bulk of the U.S. Pacific Fleet in harbor.

The story unfolds in *At Dawn We Slept*, a comprehensive study of Pearl Harbor by historian Gordon W. Prange. The first set of data indicating a Japanese surprise attack was received by U.S. Intelligence in Washington, D.C., which had broken the Japanese diplomatic codes. The messages they intercepted would have been of primary interest to Lt. Gen.

Walter C. Short, the Army's commanding general in Hawaii, and Adm. Husband E. Kimmel, commander in chief of the U.S. Pacific Fleet. But they never received them. Explanations range from the Intelligence services' desire to limit access to the messages for fear the Japanese would discover they had cracked their codes to a belief by some officers that Short and Kimmel were already receiving the messages.

In any case, a September 24 message from Tokyo to its Honolulu consulate requesting precise locations of ships in Pearl Harbor was deciphered by Army Intelligence but never reached the Hawaiian command.

The Office of Naval Intelligence later received notice that the Japanese embassies and consulates were destroying their codes and ciphers and burning confidential documents. This was a sure sign of war. But when the information reached Kimmel, it had been so diluted that he failed to grasp its significance and later claimed he did not consider it "of any vital importance."[60]

Before 9 A.M. Washington time, December 7 (3:30 A.M. Hawaii time), U.S. Intelligence intercepted a message from Japanese Foreign Minister Shigenori Togo to his Ambassador in Washington, Kichisaburo Nomura. It read, "Will the Ambassador please submit to the United States Government (if possible to the Secretary of State) our reply to the United States at 1:00 P.M. on the 7th, your time."[61] That would be 7:30 A.M. Hawaii time. He was referring to a fourteen-part message replying to American diplomatic proposals.

The intercept convinced Brigadier General Sherman Miles, assistant chief of staff for Intelligence, "that war is very likely because of the language used by the Japanese, and. . .something is going to happen coincident with 1 o'clock Washington time."[62] He and his staff attempted to relay a warning to the Pacific commanders but by the time he informed Gen. George C. Marshall (who had been out horseback riding) and Marshall wrote the warning message, it was 11:40 A.M. Washington time.

The message had to be sent by Western Union since atmospheric conditions interfered with radio transmissions.

The RCA office in Honolulu received the message at 1:03 P.M. Washington time or 7:33 A.M. Hawaii time. Since it was not marked priority or urgent, a telegram boy on a motorcycle picked it up and began his normal deliveries. The message reached General Short at 2:58 P.M. Hawaii time, nearly seven hours after the attack began.

In spite of the messages they never received, the Hawaiian command was warned that some kind of Japanese attack on American assets somewhere was imminent. On November 27, 1941, General Marshall, chief of staff of the U.S. Army, sent a message to them. It read in part:

> Negotiations with Japan appear to be terminated to all practical purposes. . . . Hostile action possible at any moment. If hostilities cannot, repeat cannot be avoided the United States desires that Japan commit the first overt act. . . . Prior to hostile Japanese action you are directed to undertake such reconnaissance and other measures as you deem necessary but these measures should be carried out so as not, repeat not, to alarm civil population or disclose intent.[63]

Short later said that he received the impression "that the avoidance of war was paramount and the greatest fear of the War Department was that some international incident might occur in Hawaii and be regarded by Japan as an overt act."[64]

Consequently, when reports of Japanese fleet movements off of Indo-China came in, Kimmel did not order his ships to sea. Prange remarks, "the Army's 'war warning' message had specifically directed Short not to alarm the civilian population. The sudden departure of the bulk of the Fleet at a weekend could scarcely fail to do so. The admiral therefore decided to keep his ships in harbor."[65]

During the hours and minutes leading up to the attack, vital evidence was ignored and misinterpreted. A U.S. mine sweeper saw a Japanese submarine periscope in the waters off Pearl Harbor at 3:57 A.M. on December 7. It reported the sighting to a nearby destroyer, the *Ward*, which searched for the sub on sonar. Since it failed to pick up a contact, the destroyer did not report the sighting and neither did the mine sweeper. "The evidence was slim enough," Prange writes, "and mistaken sightings were far from rarities in Hawaiian waters."[66] The mine sweeper, having finished its duties, returned to Pearl Harbor. The undetected submarine most likely followed the mine sweeper into the harbor after the protective underwater net across the harbor mouth was opened.

At about 6:40 A.M., the *Ward* destroyed a Japanese sub near the entrance to Pearl Harbor. The *Ward* reported the action immediately but Kimmel was "not at all certain that this was a real attack."[67] His officers decided to "wait further developments."[68]

At 7:02 A.M., Privates Joseph L. Lockard and George E. Elliott, manning the Opana Mobile Radar Station on Oahu, picked up an incredible message on their oscilloscope. "Lockard thought something must be wrong with the set, but a quick check proved otherwise," Prange reports. It was a fleet of "probably more than 50" planes. Elliott reported the sighting but neglected to mention that it contained more than 50 planes. The officer receiving the report decided it was an expected flight of 12 B-17 bombers flying in from the mainland and told Elliott and Lockard, "Well, don't worry about it."[69] It was 7:20.

At 7:55 A.M., the first Japanese bombs fell on Pearl Harbor. The attack came in two waves. The first consisted of 185 planes; the second, which came at 8:50, consisted of 167 planes. By 10:00 A.M. it was over. The Japanese planes returned to their aircraft carriers which soon headed northwest. Three battleships had been sunk, 15 other ships damaged, 164 planes destroyed and 128 damaged. Worst of all, 2,403 Americans had been killed and 1,178 wounded.

The U.S. was also surprised in Korea, despite ample warning. Harvey DeWeerd's study, quoted by Van Cleave in his article on surprise attack, concludes:

> We were surprised twice in Korea in spite of multiple indications of coming events and an abundance of intelligence data. . . . It was not the absence of intelligence which led us into trouble, but our unwillingness to draw

unpleasant conclusions from it. We refused to believe what our intelligence told us was in fact happening, because it was at variance with the prevailing climate of opinion in Washington and Tokyo. We also refused to believe our intelligence because it would have been very inconvenient if we had; we would have had to do something about it.[70]

A Soviet surprise attack would doubtless contain as many ambiguities as or more than the Japanese and Chinese attacks on Pearl Harbor and Korea. It doesn't take much imagination to see American decision makers of the 1990s engaging in the same kind of wishful thinking as American officers did at Pearl Harbor.

In order for the United States to successfully launch its ICBMs and bombers on warning of a Soviet attack, the president would need to receive that warning, correctly interpret it, and act on it in less than 20 minutes.

In reality, Van Cleave argues,

the information available...would probably be partial and questionable. It could well be obscured in a fog of Soviet disinformation and deception; it could come after a period of Soviet conditioning and political deception, and during acts of Soviet operational and technical deception....

Warning is apt to be inherently ambiguous until too late. Signals indicating the possibility (perhaps even the fact) of a surprise nuclear attack would be those most resisted by U.S. leadership. The realization that an attack is imminent, or underway, would come slowly and reluctantly. The strong disbelief in a surprise nuclear attack makes it likely that warning signals of such an attack would also be disbelieved as long as possible. For NATO, all of these encumbrances would be multiplied.[71]

3) The Soviets have a big incentive to pull off a surprise attack.

U.S. nuclear forces are based in such a way that a

surprise attack would be highly advantageous to the Soviets. In 1987 Van Cleave did a study which showed that in a surprise attack the Soviets could destroy 7,500 U.S. warheads and 3,140 equivalent megatons by catching U.S. ICBMs and bombers on the ground and our submarines in port. In an attack following a period of generated alert, they could only destroy 3,700 warheads and 1,250 equivalent megatons since more of our submarines would be at sea and decision makers would be ready to launch our ICBMs and bombers.[72] The incentive for surprise is 3,800 warheads and 1,890 equivalent megatons.

Concerning the argument that Soviet preparations would warn us of a surprise attack, Van Cleave says, "The Soviets probably would forego attack preparations that might improve their military strength if those preparations would also deny them the element of surprise. At the very least, the Soviets should be expected to conceal or obscure such preparations by a combination of political and military deception."[73]

4) The United States is not prepared for a surprise attack.

Our military leaders think that a surprise attack would be too complicated for the Soviets. A report by the Scowcroft Commission, headed by Brent Scowcroft [today President Bush's national security adviser], argued that a coordinated Soviet surprise attack on U.S. bombers and ICBMs would be too difficult due to timing problems. Former Secretary of Defense Harold Brown, a member of the Scowcroft Commission, later said, "It is equally important to acknowledge, however, that the coordination of a successful attack is not impossible, and that the 'rubbish heap of history' is filled with authorities who said something reckless could not or would not be done."[74]

Nevertheless, we do operate on the assumption that it cannot be done. As Van Cleave reported in an article in *Global Affairs*:

> Throughout most of the strategic ballistic missile era, and certainly after the Soviet strategic nuclear forces had grown, the adequacy of U.S. strategic nuclear

forces was judged on the basis of their ability to survive a "well-executed surprise attack" and still accomplish all of their missions. Yet, as Soviet capabilities have improved to the point that a well-executed, highly disarming surprise attack is feasible, the tendency to discount its possibility has grown.... The assumptions that we would receive, recognize, and react effectively to strategic warning [a warning that an attack was imminent], and be able to launch ICBMs as well as bombers on timely tactical warning [a warning that an attack has begun], now dominate most evaluations of U.S. strategic nuclear forces."[75]

Since Reagan's two-trillion-dollar defense buildup, many Americans think we're in good shape. Unfortunately, nothing could be farther from the truth. We spent a lot of money but we didn't spend it on what we really needed to solve our defense problems: (1) making our ICBMs mobile so they could not be destroyed in their silos, (2) storing our bombers and submarines in hardened hangars and berths, (3) improving early warning radar and command, control, and communications, and (4) defending our weapons with anti-ballistic missiles.

John Collins, a noted defense expert with the Library of Congress who is quoted by liberals and conservatives, commented on our state of nuclear preparedness in a recent telephone interview: "In many respects we're no better off than we were when we started [in 1979] and in some additional respects we're worse off than we were when we started. And the reason is that the Soviets had had a modernization program going since 1962; we began to think about turning trends around in the last year of the Carter administration."

Collins pointed out that while we have begun cutting our defense budget, the Soviets haven't.

Now you've got Gorbachev who's running rings around us with his glasnost and his perestroika and a lot of people saying that the cold war is over and let's forget about it. But they haven't stopped as far as I can determine. I haven't got any evidence that they've slowed down significantly their production lines with regard to major equipment. Now, they may do that. They've got bureaucratic problems like we do. It takes time to shut faucets off. But it hasn't happened yet.

And so. . .we're not a hell of a lot better off [today] in a lot of regards than we were before.[76]

While tanks and ships and aircraft carriers and troops are important, what will make the difference in the next war are nuclear forces. If the Soviets could get rid of our strategic forces or render them largely ineffective by a defense network, our conventional forces could not stop them from invading our country.

As I have demonstrated, a surprise attack is far more likely than an attack preceded by a period of escalation. Therefore, we have no right to gamble our lives and our children's lives on the slim chance that when the Soviets decide to attack, it will not be a surprise.

Let's take a closer look at what could happen in a first strike. I've updated it June 1989 to make sure you have the latest information.

The Soviets think they can win a nuclear war for three reasons. First: in a surprise first strike they can destroy almost two-thirds of our warheads. Second: they are rapidly completing a defense network to stop the rest of our missiles from hitting them.[77] Third: they already have civil defense for their leadership as well as for the majority of their urban population.[78]

So how could they destroy two-thirds of our warheads? Our strategic (i.e., long-range) nuclear forces consist of intercontinental ballistic missiles (ICBMs), nuclear-powered ballistic missile submarines (SSBNs), and bombers. They carry a total of 12,390 warheads.

The situation is more complex than each of us having enough weapons to incinerate the other several times over— the overkill argument. Since most of our warheads are vulnerable to a surprise first strike because of the way they are deployed, they aren't really a deterrent. In short, a weapon that cannot survive cannot deter.

There are 1,000 missiles carrying 2,450 warheads in our ICBM force: 50 MX Peacekeepers carrying 10 warheads each, 450 Minuteman IIs carrying 1 warhead each and 500 Minuteman IIIs carrying 3 warheads each. The Soviets could destroy 90 percent of these missiles in a surprise first strike using roughly 50 percent of their warheads.[79] Assuming they were destroyed in equal proportions, about 245 ICBM warheads on 100 missiles would survive.

Our strategic bomber force contains 290 planes capable of carrying 4,436 warheads. There are 193 B-52s and 97 B-1s. At any given time, about 30 percent are "on alert," meaning they are loaded and their pilots are on the military base where the bombers are stationed. Soviet warheads launched from submarines off our coasts could reach most bomber bases in six to eight minutes. It is debatable whether these 30 percent could get off the ground before they were destroyed, especially if our command, control, and communications network were destroyed first. The other 70 percent certainly would be destroyed. Assuming that the bombers on alert did escape, after the first strike the United States would have the capability of delivering 1,331 warheads via 87 bombers.

Our 35 SSBNs carry 5,504 warheads. This includes 9 new Ohio-class submarines carrying Trident missiles and 26 Benjamin Franklin, James Madison, and Lafayette-class subs—12 carrying Trident missiles and 14 carrying Poseidon missiles. About 40 percent (or 14) of our SSBNs are in port at any given time. These could be destroyed by a surprise attack since it would take them several hours to put to sea. The Soviets, using attack subs and anti-submarine warfare techniques, could destroy at least 2 to 4 additional submarines at sea.[80] Approximately 5 Ohio and 13 Franklin, Madison, and Lafayette SSBNs would be left. Assuming they were destroyed in equal proportions, 2,848 warheads would survive.

Therefore a total of 4,424 warheads would survive a first strike. That is a 64 percent reduction—about two-thirds. In addition, according to Van Cleave's study, a surprise attack would reduce our total equivalent megatonnage (EMT) from 3,600 EMT to 460 EMT—that's 87 percent.[81] This is because most of the surviving warheads would be on Trident and Poseidon missiles based on submarines. These yield 100 kilotons and 40 kilotons respectively as opposed to 1 to 2 megatons on Minuteman II missiles.

After such an attack, what would our options be? The 87 surviving U.S. bombers would still have to outmaneuver the Soviet air defense. Defense experts William C. Martel and Paul L. Savage estimate that only 30 percent of the bombers that escape a Soviet first strike would be able to deliver their weapons to targets in the Soviet Union.[82] Therefore 26 bombers would survive with the capability of delivering about 413 warheads. The weapons on the 18 surviving submarines would not be useful to attack Soviet military targets such as hardened ICBM silos. This is because they are smaller and less accurate than land-based ICBMs. They could only be used against Soviet cities. Furthermore, an undetermined number of SLBM warheads could be stopped by Soviet SA-X-12 SAMs expected to be widely deployed around the Soviet Union in the next few years.[83]

What do all these figures boil down to? Quite simply, following a first strike the president of the United States would have the choice either of surrendering or of retaliating by destroying innocent Soviet civilians and submitting to Soviet retaliation on U.S. cities. If he attacked Soviet cities, the Soviets would still have over 5,000 warheads in reserve with which to annihilate undefended U.S. cities. The country would be worse off if he retaliated than if he did nothing. If the president surrendered, the Soviets could invade and rule these United States. In addition, Soviet defenses may soon be able to shoot down our missiles and a second strike by the United States would be virtually worthless.

Soviet Defenses

Because of the twisted nature of MAD and the reality of Soviet nuclear strategy, the closer the Soviets get to completing their defenses, the closer they are to launching their first strike. And that may not be too far in the future. The Pentagon concluded in its publication *Soviet Military Power 1988* that the Soviets' strategic defense efforts "suggest that the USSR may be preparing an ABM defense of its national territory."[84] This would consist of anti-ballistic missiles, surface-to-air missiles (SAMs) which are capable of shooting down tactical ballistic and cruise missiles, and a vast radar system.

The Soviets already have the world's only ABM system; it consists of 100 nuclear-tipped missiles that can shoot down warheads before they reach Moscow. It is currently being modernized and will be fully operational by 1989.[85] As I mentioned, the Soviets also have a huge civil defense network which they could count on to defend their leadership against any missiles that leak through their defense.[86]

(U.S. citizens have no civil defense. After a first strike such as that described above, between 10 million and 40 million Americans would die.[87] But fallout shelters could reduce the death toll to 1 million.[88])

The Soviet Union is moving ahead with its strategic defense system. On November 25, 1987, Mikhail Gorbachev admitted for the first time that "practically, the Soviet Union is doing all that the United States is doing, and I guess we are engaged in research, basic research, which relates to these aspects which are covered by the SDI of the United States."[89]

But, as we know, they are doing far more than we are. The Soviets are spending $20 billion a year on their strategic defense system[90] while this year we are spending $3.9 billion on ours.

Furthermore, it is now generally known that they are winning the race for space. But most people don't know that 90 percent of Soviet space operations are for military purposes and that a number of Soviet space achievements are necessary components to a space-based defense.[91]

Thomas Krebs, who worked as the Pentagon's expert on Soviet space warfare capabilities, says that their immediate goal is to put up a space-based missile defense system. And they are rapidly developing the prerequisites. The new Soviet Energia rocket is capable of carrying large numbers of satellites, a key component of a Star Wars system.[92]

Not only do the Soviets have the world's only operational space-based anti-satellite weapon, capable of destroying our early-warning and reconnaissance satellites in orbit, but they also have a ground-based laser at Sary Shagan in south central Russia that may be able to damage U.S. satellites.[93] The Soviets have another laser weapons site at a base on a mountaintop in the remote Nurek region of the Soviet Union near their border with Afghanistan.[94]

The Soviet ground-based defense system is moving forward as well. On February 25, 1988, the *Wall Street Journal* said in an editorial, "We hear that Air Force Intelligence has officially concluded the Soviets have rolled production lines to break out of the ABM treaty and deploy a nationwide anti-missile system, which possibly could be in place by next year. That Maj. Gen. Schuyler Bissell, head of Air Force Intelligence, briefed the CIA on this conclusion late last week."

The *Journal* said the Air Force based its finding on two new pieces of evidence:

First, the Soviets are "internetting" their early-warning radars. . . . They have conducted "hand-off exercises" in which the large phased-array radars, like the controversial one at Krasnoyarsk, pick up targets and alert the Flat Twin and Pawn Shop mobile radars that guide their [ABMs]. This is the key "battle management" function of an anti-missile system.

Second, the Soviets are mass producing the Flat Twin and Pawn Shop radars, though the ABM treaty limits them to two locations. Similarly, they are mass producing the SH-08, a relatively new supersonic [anti-ballistic] missile that intercepts warheads within the atmosphere, with 500 such missiles already produced and 3,000 ultimately projected.[95]

Government officials denied the *Wall Street Journal* story. Air Force Secretary Edward Aldridge said the reports were "just flat wrong," although he acknowledged that the Soviets had been working on an ABM system for years. "They've got a massive program," he said. "But there's no evidence that would support the allegation that they're prepared to break out of the ABM Treaty."[96] Whether or not the government is prepared to admit that the Soviets are breaking out, mass production of ABMs *is* a breakout.

It is difficult to determine if the Soviets are mass producing ABMs. A well-placed source in the intelligence community says that if they were, the United States would know, but probably not immediately. One piece of evidence, which comes from another intelligence source, is that they have recently doubled the floor space at their plant at Gomel, which produces ABM components. Since they already have the 100 ABMs that the treaty allows in place around Moscow, the only reason they would need more floor space is if they were going to start mass production.[97]

Commenting on Secretary Aldridge's denial of a Soviet breakout, Frank J. Gaffney, Jr., former deputy assistant secretary of defense for international security policy, said that "it is certainly the party line here in Washington that at most there are some worrisome developments but it doesn't amount to a breakout. But this is unfortunately a grey area and a lot of what we see and know is going on is entirely consistent with a breakout."[98] In a later interview, Gaffney said, "I have concluded that they are actively breaking out based upon the evidence that's available to me."[99]

On February 26 Archangel Gabriel, dictating through me in Lisbon, Portugal, said:

> The movement is accelerated on the part of the Soviets to move against Europe and to take the United States as well by a first-strike attack. This is what is on the drawing board and this is the only reason negotiations are continuing. . . .
>
> Blessed ones, the acceleration is at hand and El Morya has declared it and it has not changed: Unless the United States change her course and defend the peace of the world, you will see an encounter as early as twenty-four months from October last.[100]

"October last" was precisely October 2, 1987, and twenty-four months equals October 2, 1989! That's the earliest you could see an encounter between the super-powers.

MAD depends upon both the U.S. and the U.S.S.R. being undefended. Since the Soviets are defending their country and people and we are not defending ours, we are the ones who are vulnerable.

So the question is, If they have a first-strike capability, do they have the intent?

We know that the Soviets do not value the lives of their citizens. They've killed no less than 39.5 million of them since 1917.[101] This was in order to consolidate and maintain power. If the Soviets would kill untold millions of souls of their countrymen to get control of the heart and lifeblood of Mother Russia, how many would they sacrifice to get control of America and then the world?

For the Soviet leadership (not the Russian people), a first strike against the United States, while highly dangerous, is undoubtably preferable to watching their empire disintegrate when they are at the pinnacle of military power.

And their empire could very well disintegrate. Economic forces and internal unrest are driving the Soviets to war. Everybody agrees that the Soviet economy is a mess. Economic difficulties amplify internal tensions in the Soviet empire. We see riots and demonstrations in the Ukraine, the Moslem states, and Eastern Europe. Food shortages are worse than normal, even in Moscow.[102] Historically, the Soviets attack nations in order to divert attention from internal problems and to draw off wealth to bolster their economy.

Today Western loans are keeping the Soviet economy afloat. The U.S. and Western banks lend the U.S.S.R. and Eastern bloc $1 billion dollars a month.[103] It's outrageous! And, as I've discussed in my prophecy and astrology lectures, if the Western economies collapse, the Soviets will have to either face disintegration or go to war.[104]

The Real Gorbachev

And Mikhail Gorbachev, hailed as a reformer, hasn't changed things and won't be able to unless he and the ruling elite plan to give up their power. He is a creature of the system, the same system which murdered 10 to 15 million Russian peasants under Stalin's dekulakization programs alone[105] and under Brezhnev and Andropov murdered 1 to 2 million Afghans.[106]

Gorbachev's power rests on the power of the Soviet state. If the state falls, he falls. And the state can survive only through economic and political central control, which has been achieved and maintained through 70 years of bloodshed and repression. Glasnost and perestroika are an illusion.

Let's have a look at the real Mikhail Gorbachev. It was he, the student at Moscow University, who eagerly took part in Stalin's anti-Semitic policies. According to Vladimir Solovyov and Elena Klepikova, Soviet journalists who defected to the West, "At Komsomol and later at Party meetings, [Gorbachev] 'exposed' professors and students of Jewish origin and demanded their expulsion from the university. . . . Gorbachev also looked into the personnel files of other students and professors of non-Jewish origin and exposed as 'enemies of the people' those who, from his point of view, were lacking in Stalinist orthodoxy."

One of his classmates recalls, "He was really the plague of the law school. We feared Misha like the devil himself. When he walked by, everybody stopped talking."[107] Gorbachev's classmates recall that at the funeral of Stalin he gave forth genuine sobs and was overcome with grief.[108]

We must see Gorbachev as the product of the Soviet system, not Gorbachev as he would like us to see him. Gorbachev has no human face.

On June 28, 1988, he announced a program for the redistribution of power in the Soviet Union. He proposed the creation of a new Congress of Deputies that would elect a president. The Associated Press reported that "he called for a country which would be ruled by law and guarantee individual rights. He said farmers should become the 'true masters' of their land."[109]

Why shouldn't we believe him?

Remember, Stalin killed 10 to 15 million Russian peasants

in the 1930s for the very purpose of getting control of the land. Given the nature of the Communist beast, he simply could not allow the peasants to control food since they would thereby control an important section of the economy and be able to challenge the power of the state.

The Soviet state exists because agriculture is collectivized. For Gorbachev to change that, Russia would no longer be Communist and the nomenklatura (the Soviet ruling class) could no longer enjoy power and privilege. For Russia to be ruled by law, the biggest criminals of all would have to be arrested, the members of the party. [9-second applause] Gorbachev cannot reform the Soviet economy. He cannot change Soviet military goals.

When the Soviet defense system is complete it will mean they are more likely to launch a nuclear attack against us since they will be able to stop most of our retaliatory missiles. In combination with their countrywide civil defense already in place, it will give them a decisive advantage. And when the Soviets invade America, Gorbachev will not be smiling and nostalgically singing "Moscow Nights" on American television.

How can we expect a fate different from that of the Afghans, who have been subjected to a policy of genocide? A fate different from the Hungarian teenagers who were crushed by Soviet tanks as they rolled through the streets of Budapest?

Atrocities have been continuing in Afghanistan throughout Gorbachev's rule. Italian journalist Fausto Biloslavo was imprisoned in Afghanistan from November 1987 to May 1988 after being captured by the Soviet-backed Afghan army and being turned over to the KGB for questioning. During the period from Gorbachev and Reagan's Washington summit to their Moscow summit he was in jail, and this is what he saw.

He found prisoners who had been subjected to electric shocks under their tongues, armpits or genitals. "I was surrounded by human wreckage," he wrote, "people with their backs smashed to pieces, dislocated jaws, twisted nasal septa, their bodies covered with scars of every description and bearing the hallmarks of cigarettes stubbed out against their skin."[110]

November 1987 to May 1988! Stop and think of it. These atrocities have been going on during the entire period of the Reagan-Gorbachev negotiations. This is what the Soviets have been doing in Afghanistan, and so much much more that is heinous and hellish; and the nations have turned their heads and looked the other way.

Mark you well, their karma *shall* be upon them for their neglect to be their brothers' keepers!

This journalist met a 28-year-old Pakistani shepherd named Khudadad who had accidentally crossed the border into Afghanistan and been captured. Khudadad said, "I was taken to Kabul, where they started to beat me to a pulp to try and force me to say that I was a Pakistani spy. The Afghans showed me no mercy and beat me pitilessly. One particularly violent kick caused one of my testicles to explode, and I fainted."[111] Khudadad eventually confessed to being a spy and was sentenced to 20 years in jail.

"I'm no longer a man," he said. "I can't even take a wife. Dogs live in chains and food is the only thing on their minds...and now I'm just like them.... I just know that I'll be punished after making these statements to you, but I'm not afraid because I'm not worth a damn thing anymore."[112]

I'm sure you realize that this is the effect that the Communist system has upon all of its subjects, the sense of the worthlessness of the human soul. They are masterminds at breaking the will and the spirit of men and nations. I say it's time for the United States to link arms control agreements to human rights reform in and out of the Soviet Union! [12-second applause]

If Gorbachev is a reformer let him prove it with actions, not words. In the meantime, America, let's get on with defending ourselves against the Soviets and make sure that Afghanistan's fate does not become our own.

Strategic Defense Now!

Americans don't even know the threat of Soviet defenses or the sorry state of our defense. A 1982 poll showed that 65 percent of Americans were not "aware that the U.S now has no means of defending itself from incoming ballistic missiles." Eighty-six percent said "if the U.S. had the capability of changing this situation by deploying an anti-ballistic missile defense," they would favor it.[113]

Many Americans think that Ronald Reagan's SDI program is taking care of our defense problem. In fact, it hasn't even put a dent in it. All Reagan did is to start a research program.

In his March 23, 1983 speech which launched the initiative, he said, "I am directing a comprehensive and intensive effort to define a long-term research and development program to begin to achieve our ultimate goal of eliminating the threat posed by strategic nuclear missiles."[114] Reagan is not planning on deploying anything in his term of office. And when the START treaty is made public we may find that any future president's right to deploy anything has been bargained away.

Reagan's program has focused on long-term, high-technology systems to the detriment of the systems that have already been invented and are ready to deploy. Work on strategic defense had been going on in the United States for a long time before Reagan gave his speech. Following are just a few of the systems we could deploy starting immediately if we had a president with the courage to sign the right document.

The most important thing to do right away is to defend our missile silos since those are what the Soviets target. If we defend them, it would most likely discourage a first strike since almost all of our ICBMs would remain intact, ready to retaliate.

The easiest to deploy is the GAU-8 Gatling-type 30-millimeter machine gun already developed by General Electric. According to Gen. Daniel Graham of High Frontier, an organization promoting near-term deployment of strategic defense, "the GAU-8 has been tested, with astonishing results, against a simulated Soviet reentry vehicle." A reentry vehicle is the part of an ICBM which reenters the atmosphere carrying the warhead. Graham continues, "If one slug from this gun hits a reentry vehicle at any spot, it destroys it. A pair of these guns firing at a reentry vehicle provides an almost one-hundred percent assurance of destruction."[115] This system could defend our ICBM silos for a cost of $10 billion.[116]

That's a price tag of forty bucks a person to save America!

What's your self-worth, America? Is there any price you're willing to pay to save yourself?

By starting out right now with GAU-8 guns, we would lower the degree of confidence the Soviets have in pulling off a first strike. And that is significant because it would alter their perceptions. Any defense we put up could mean the difference between war and peace and between freedom and slavery.

After we quickly deployed the GAU-8 guns, we could deploy more sophisticated ground-based systems that could protect ICBM fields, military bases, and even cities. HEDI, the High Endoatmospheric Defense Interceptor, is a nonnuclear, heat-seeking missile which intercepts warheads after they reenter the atmosphere. It can be incorporated into a small, mobile defense for cities and military bases.[117] ERIS, the Exoatmospheric Reentry Vehicle Interceptor Subsystem, could defend much of North America from a single site. The cost for ERIS is $32 billion and the cost for HEDI is $18 billion.[118]

At the same time, we could begin deploying a space-based defense. The most promising space-based system is called "Brilliant Pebbles." It would consist of thousands of small, non-nuclear missiles about three feet long and weighing about five pounds which would orbit the earth and spring into action upon detecting the launch of an ICBM. They would home in on the ICBM and knock a hole in it solely by kinetic energy. The missile would disintegrate.[119]

Another space-based system that has been proposed is the Space-Based Interceptor (SBI). It would consist of a series of satellites ringing the globe which carry "smart rocks," rockets with a homing device and/or a gun which fires a cloud of pellets into the path of the ICBM.[120] Brilliant

Pebbles are superior to SBI in that they are cheaper and each "pebble" would be autonomous and not dependent on satellites for instructions.

The cost for Brilliant Pebbles? About $100,000 per "pebble"—and that includes launch into orbit. A system of 100,000 pebbles in orbit would cost only about $10 billion.[121]

The total system of GAU-8 machine guns, ERIS, HEDI and Brilliant Pebbles would cost about $85 billion—a pittance when you consider that Americans spend $100 billion a year buying "recreational" drugs!

Going over the facts and figures of our defense and what needs to be done and the logic of our posture today, researching and studying what we have and what we don't have and what the Soviets have, what you are left with after you consider all the angles is that you honestly wonder in your heart how the Lord is going to divinely intervene to save us when we have nothing in hand through which the heavenly host can anchor their protection in a physical way.

It goes along with "the Lord helps those who help themselves." Short of the miraculous or apocalyptic event (which we shouldn't count on) in the face of an oncoming enemy as formidable as this, what real deterrence does America have today that could possibly be the instrument of the alchemy of Divine Intervention?

I find it a gloomy affair to try to answer that question, and because I cannot answer it, I can only cast myself upon the Rock of Christ and enter more deeply and profoundly into the spiritual path of the inner walk with God, into our dynamic decrees for the spiritual and physical defense of our nation which must be kept up by all of us and ask you to join me in delivering a mandate to our representatives in Congress to put America's defenses in place. [14-second applause]

Strategic Defense: The Current Picture

The answer we get from every inside source we know of is always that nobody has any intention of deploying any low-tech defenses anytime in the near future and certainly not before October 2, 1989. And few if any at all in Washington who are involved in defense sense any threat from the Soviet Union until well into the 1990s, almost to the end of the century.

Even those who are promoting such solutions as High Frontier don't have the sense of urgency that the Brotherhood has given to us. So what doors can you knock upon? Who can you mobilize? Who is left who will raise his voice and put his political reputation or his job on the line by coming out for a strategic defense *now?* What elected representative is going to risk his seat to stand for a comprehensive defense program and budget that the experts and the taxpayers don't think is necessary?

People I know and people who are trying their very best to turn things around have come up with the conclusion that there aren't any more doors to knock on. You can keep on lecturing and keep on giving this message but who of the leadership is responding?

All the more do we go to the altar of God to offer our invocations for Divine Intercession and to invoke the Light that will enlighten our people and our leadership. You have to realize that this is why there isn't anything better to say about the progress that has been made in the last two years than there was two years ago. In other words, the United States government hasn't moved forward to implement a single plan or program that Saint Germain or our Summit University Forum guests have put forward.[122] In fact, we may have even retrogressed, if what I hear is true, in promising the Soviets not to deploy SDI as a part of the INF or START agreements.

So it's very difficult to speak about gains. And the gains, if there are any to be spoken about, I trust will be spoken of by Saint Germain because since they are not apparent in a military sense, then they must be apparent at the level of the All-Seeing Eye of God to the Ascended Masters and hopefully they will tell us so. But this is the vantage I have from where I sit in my analysis of the current defense posture of this nation. Except for the vision of the hosts of the Lord, the outlook day by day is indeed discouraging.

In his July 5 address in the Heart of the Inner Retreat last year, Alpha made a proposal to the Cosmic Council to lend himself to us and, "upon seeing the victory of the deployment of the defense of Freedom, to press on for other dispensations. Whether or not this is accomplished, together with the turning back and diminishing day by day of the power of World Communism, will determine the future of planet earth. There is no question about it."[123]

Well, freedom isn't any more defended today and it is certainly less defended than it was when Alpha made that statement one year ago. So where are we and what can we do?

This year, Keepers of the Flame have rallied around strategic defense, starting grass-roots groups around the country. But the fact is that we are still in the same position today that we were in a year ago, only it appears to have worsened.

Strategic defense is, my friends, to put it bluntly, dead in the water. If any systems are put up, they will most likely be too little too late. The string of failures in our space program from 1985 to 1987 as well as the lack of a heavy-duty booster has caused a 10-year delay in the putting up of a space-based strategic defense. That's right. Ten years' delay.[124]

And we strongly suspect that this string of failures was sabotage.[125] The Soviets are at war with the United States of America and sabotage is another aspect of their strategy that our government appears to be ignoring. At least, if they suspect it, they're not telling us!

We need to examine this situation in greater detail. We need to know the facts in order to give our daily decrees— even when we would rather not be decreeing but we know that we absolutely must. If we are going to say, "Give me liberty, or give me death!" then when all else fails—when our countrymen have failed to heed the Inner Voice and our call to arms year after year—know that the flame of liberty can be sustained only by our dynamic decrees. [13-second applause]

So what's happened to strategic defense since we gathered in the Heart a year ago on the Fourth of July to hear Gen. Danny Graham and Dr. Dmitry Mikheyev speak?

Well, the budget for SDI has been cut and testing for HEDI and other near-term systems has been scaled back.[126] The Pentagon's Defense Acquisition Board placed a restriction on the Strategic Defense Initiative Organization which said that they could develop low-tech systems such as ABMs only if they continued to develop high-tech systems such as particle beam weapons at the same rate.[127] This has had the effect of cutting in half the amount of money available for near-term systems.

There is one glimmer of hope in the strategic defense picture. Since last year, the media and defense experts have begun focusing on near-term deployment of systems like ERIS and HEDI which are based on existing technology.

On January 19, 1988, Senator Sam Nunn said that the United States should consider deployment of an Accidental Launch Protection System (ALPS) to counter accidental or unauthorized missile launches.[128] The system he proposed would probably defend Washington, D.C., with 100 ERIS missiles and necessary radar. It could be in place by 1992 or 1993. Nunn said that the system would be tailored to abide by the 1972 ABM Treaty with the Soviet Union.[129]

Sam Nunn has been an outspoken opponent of strategic defense and his proposal is an about-face. But in reality, it may cause the deployment of a far smaller system than we need and cause other promising systems to be delayed far into the future. Even to defend against an accidental launch would require much more than the single 100-missile site Nunn supports.

A study by McDonnell Douglas found that "successfully defending against an unauthorized multimissile attack" by a renegade Soviet sub captain, for example, would require "the U.S. to construct five additional ABM sites."[130] This would violate the treaty.

ALPS could defend our command, control, and communications headquarters in Washington, D.C., from Soviet submarine-launched ballistic missiles and cruise missiles and thus increase stability. But it would not be enough.

If someone wanted to channel the forward momentum

for strategic defense into a permanent backwater, he might go about it in the same way as Sam Nunn did. He has created a strategic defense system that politicians can support which could insure that we never have the defense we really need. Apart from Nunn's proposal, the prospects for early deployment of a defense are dim. President Reagan's START talks and cuts in the defense budget are two big reasons why. Although Reagan continues to give lip service to SDI, he has clearly bought the Soviet line.

He said on March 14, 1988, that the United States will "continue to research SDI, to develop and test it. And, as it becomes ready, we will deploy it."[131] He knows very well that we have systems ready or nearly ready to deploy. General Graham met with him on April 12 and told him that "all we're waiting for is a decision to deploy."

Furthermore, both the United States and Soviet versions of the START agreement contain provisions for abiding by the ABM Treaty. The Soviets want both sides to commit not to withdraw from the ABM Treaty for 10 years; the U.S. proposal is for an unspecified period of time to be negotiated.[132] Agreeing to abide by the ABM Treaty when the Soviets have torn it to shreds is tantamount to treason! And that's just what our president is committing—treason—by his refusal to break that ABM Treaty with the Soviets who have broken that treaty again and again.[133] Thus President Reagan has bound the nation, hence the world, to a Soviet takeover.

And we can't look to either Michael Dukakis or George Bush to defend America either. "We don't want Star Wars, we don't need Star Wars. It's a fraud, a fantasy," said Michael Dukakis.[134] Vice president George Bush has so far endorsed only more research with possible deployment well into the future.[135]

If the "radical anti-Communist" Ronald Reagan has done nothing for strategic defense in eight years, we can't expect much more from his establishment, big-business vice president.

If the politicians had more guts, they could galvanize the country to support defense. Seven out of 10 Americans favor continuing research and development on SDI and 58 percent think we should deploy it once it has been developed. This is not a Right and Left issue. Sixty-seven percent of Republicans, 53 percent of Democrats support deployment.[136] But none of the presidential candidates has the courage to sign the right document right now!

Lack of support by our leadership class has frozen strategic defense. There are plenty of politicians who support continuing research but almost none who want to even think about deploying anything before 1993. Nineteen ninety-three? It's too late! It's absolutely too late.

Last year I said that the United States could have a three-layer defense system, composed of ERIS, HEDI, and a space-based kinetic-kill vehicle that would be 93 percent effective against a full-scale ICBM attack in place by 1994 and that it would cost $121 billion.[137] But this was only if Reagan gave the go-ahead to deploy last year. And we all know he didn't.

Budget cuts mandated by Secretary of Defense Carlucci forced the cancellation of certain strategic defense tests and the scaling back of others.[138] On June 2 members of the Pentagon's Defense Acquisition Board "informed SDI Director Lt. Gen. James Abrahamson that a major retrenchment and downscoping of SDI programs was necessary in light of overall Defense budget problems."[139] In fact, the Strategic Defense Initiative Organization (SDIO) now says that they will not even be ready for a decision to begin deploying until 1993.[140] And by that time, my friends, the Soviet ground-based defense system will most likely be fully operational.

At what position of full operation in defense, et cetera, et cetera, will it become advantageous for the Soviets to blackmail the West? They have just about everything they need right now. They just need to be sure. They just need to fasten it down. They just need to play their cards right.

The third layer of our strategic defense, consisting of either Brilliant Pebbles or the Space-Based Interceptor program has been pushed even farther into the future since our space program does not have enough lift capacity to put thousands of satellites in space. The Pentagon's current answer to the problem is the Advanced Launch System (ALS). ALS is a heavy-lift booster being discussed which will not be operational until 1998.[141]

It's too late! America—you're too late!

We could build a heavy-lift booster *now* if we wanted to. The discontinued Saturn 5 would work just fine. But the Pentagon wants to create a whole new system.

If current trends continue, we can say good-bye to a space-based defense system. Last year Congress issued a directive to the SDIO which prohibited funds for either full-scale engineering development or deployment of kinetic kill vehicles.[142]

While the Soviets build their ABM system, the START talks have probably killed SDI. As *Aviation Week & Space Technology* reported, "Future SDIO priorities are expected to focus on sensors and [an ABM] treaty-compliant ground-based interceptor system. . . . Changing priorities are driven in part by a desire to shape SDI into a program the Soviet Union will accept, thereby conceivably allowing a Strategic Arms Reduction Treaty to be completed in the near future."[143]

Who's Afraid of INF?

What is this sacred cow, this START treaty for which President Reagan is sacrificing our only hope to defend our land and our liberty?

To understand the beast (the genetically engineered beast of the International Capitalist/Communist Conspiracy), we have to consider Reagan's other arms control achievement, the INF Treaty ratified by our Senate on May 27. Not only is the treaty conceptually and strategically flawed, but it has more holes in it than a fishnet. And it would be a bad idea even if it were leakproof.

The INF agreement is being presented as a step towards a safer world. But it gives the Soviets an unequal advantage and thus is likely to trigger a Soviet invasion of Europe and with it a global war. The Soviets are giving up 650 SS-20 missiles, as well as 1,121 other intermediate-range missiles, mostly old and obsolete. The United States is removing 380 brand-new Pershing IIs, 309 ground-launched cruise missiles (GLCMs) and 170 older Pershing IAs.[144]

The Reagan administration claims that since an entire class of nuclear weapons has been eliminated, the chance of nuclear war has been reduced. That's just like saying that if we eliminate all the .22-caliber rifles in the world, less people will get shot.

The Soviets still have 553 bombers devoted to Europe. And they have 1,400 ICBMs and nearly 1,000 SLBMs which can hit Hamburg as easily as New York.[145]

Furthermore, in giving up the SS-20 the Soviets were only giving up an outdated missile they couldn't use since its warheads were so large that fallout would drift back onto Soviet territory if they launched a strike on Europe.[146]

But the missiles we are removing threaten military targets in the Soviet Union. They were the only weapons we possessed that could take out Soviet command centers in 10 to 12 minutes. They directly threatened Soviet territory. And that's why the Soviets were so anxious to get rid of them.[147] They were no threat to the Soviet population. It was their command centers, their military targets that could be knocked out. These missiles have deterred the Soviets from crossing Europe in a land war ever since they've been in place.

The Pershings IIs and IAs and the GLCMs were all that prevented the Soviet conventional forces from concentrating along the border to invade Europe. The Warsaw Pact outnumbers NATO three to one in tanks and artillery and they can take Europe in a matter of days or weeks. Rather than spend the money to match the Soviet armies, since 1945 NATO has chosen to rely on nuclear weapons. Therefore, once U.S. intermediate-range nuclear forces are removed, there will be nothing to deter a Soviet invasion of Europe. My conclusion is that the INF Treaty will make Europe safe for conventional war—and for the Soviets that war is also a chemical/biological war.

The Pershing IIs accomplished a mission that would take hundreds of billions of dollars to replace. And neither the United States nor our allies are willing to spend the money to match Soviet armies with conventional weapons, which are far more expensive than nuclear weapons. The retired French general Pierre Gallois said that *no* amount of spending can match the 200 Soviet divisions facing Europe: "If we eliminate nuclear weapons [in Europe], as Reagan wants, we will be contributing to elevating the Soviet Union to the rank of the world's strongest military power."[148] Everyone admits that American troops in Europe are only a trip wire and that they could not hold the Soviets back. And so George Shultz and Ronald Reagan have decided that they are willing to have our 326,000 fighting men and women in Europe slaughtered by conventional weapons on the altar of arms control.

However distasteful the idea of nuclear war may be, there is nothing romantic about conventional war. World War II killed 41 to 49 million people.[149]

The INF Treaty does nothing about the chemical and biological (C/B) weapons that the Soviets are prepared to use in Europe. Why didn't our negotiators demand that these be destroyed? By 1963 the Soviets had concluded that these weapons are the best means to seize Western Europe since nuclear weapons would destroy the prize. The Soviets have made extensive preparations for chemical warfare. There are 45,000 to 60,000 chemical troops in the Soviet ground forces. They have acknowledged that they have up to 50,000 tons of poisonous substances which the Pentagon calls "the world's largest known chemical warfare agent stockpile."[150]

The United States has practically no offensive C/B capability and little defensive capability. President Nixon nixed U.S. C/B warfare programs in the early 1970s in the interest of détente,[151] and our recently begun modernization program doesn't even begin to address the problem.

All in all, the INF Treaty will leave the Soviets with a decisive advantage in conventional, chemical, biological, and nuclear forces even if they don't cheat on the agreement.

There are any number of ways they could cheat but they don't even have to since we left a number of questions unresolved.

First of all, no American has ever even seen a Soviet SS-20. We've only seen a Soviet-supplied photograph.[152] How can we really tell if they're cheating? We can't even trust their estimate of how many SS-20 missiles they have. They told us they had 650. This was higher than the lowest U.S. estimate but lower than the State Department's May 1987 estimate of 840, the January 1988 Defense Intelligence Agency estimate of 1,200 and the 2,250 that intelligence experts have privately estimated.[153]

There is virtually no way we can tell if they violate the treaty because the SS-25, supposedly a long-range missile, was not banned under the treaty and looks virtually identical to the SS-20.[154] Shultz and company did not force this issue with the Soviets. They let it slide by. But the Soviets made sure that we agreed to give up our conventionally armed ground-launched cruise missiles since they appear identical to nuclear cruise missiles.

Congress, the military, and the Reagan administration acknowledged that the Soviets were likely to cheat on the INF Treaty. Air Force chief of staff Gen. Larry Welch spoke for the majority when he said that even though the Soviets would cheat, he didn't believe they could achieve a militarily significant advantage by cheating.[155]

I mean, so now you know they cheat and you let them cheat! And Larry Welch has welched on his responsibility to the American people to stand guard for our common defense.

Our leaders seem to have an attitude that we are invulnerable and can afford a little Soviet cheating. Roberta Wohlstetter points out that in sociological terms

"I am in no danger whatsoever" is an example of a self-annihilating proposition. According to sociologist Robert Merton, "this mechanism, picturesquely termed the 'suicidal prophecy' by the nineteenth century logician John Venn, involves beliefs which prevent fulfillment of the very circumstance which would otherwise come to pass. Examples of this are plentiful and familiar. Confident that they will win a game or a war or a cherished prize, groups become complacent, their complacency leads to lethargy, and lethargy to eventual defeat."[156]

If America continues to believe she is invulnerable, she will go the way of the Romans, the Hindus, and the Chinese.

The INF Treaty's on-site inspection provisions are supposed to prevent Soviet cheating. But, as defense expert Frank Gaffney points out, these involve the "right to visit only those places where Soviet cheating is unlikely."[157] Gaffney notes that the Soviets could easily continue to deploy SS-20s in the same manner as they deployed the SS-16s which were outlawed under SALT II. They deployed them in garages or other hidden shelters. If these were out of the range of the areas in which U.S. inspection teams are permitted to go, the SS-20s could remain hidden indefinitely.[158] In fact, we did not discover the SS-16 until several years after it was deployed.

Another problem with the INF Treaty is that the provisions for inspection are skewed in favor of the Russians. The Soviet facility at Votkinsk where U.S. teams will be stationed does not even produce SS-20s. They are produced elsewhere and shipped to Votkinsk for final assembly. Nevertheless, the United States facility at Magna, Utah, where the Soviets can inspect, is currently used to actually produce ballistic missiles.

Since the Pershing IIs and SS-20s are assembled differently, different inspection procedures apply for the two missiles. The SS-20 is assembled in a plant while the Pershing exits the plant in stages and is assembled on site. Therefore, the U.S. can only inspect objects as large as a completed SS-20 missile, 63.4 feet, while the Soviets can inspect anything leaving the U.S. plant that is larger than 12.1 feet.[159] Thus the treaty gives the Soviets ample opportunity to inspect valuable U.S. technology.

A final, fatal flaw in this ridiculous treaty is that it allows continued production of the modern, mobile SS-25. National security expert James Hackett asks, "Why ban

SS-20s when Moscow is building SS-25s that can strike the same targets? The small mobile missiles covered by this agreement can be hidden or camouflaged and not be seen by satellites."[160]

The entire United States Senate acted like the blind men and the elephant when they ratified the INF Treaty. Each saw in it exactly what they wanted to see and ignored everything else. And with their eyes wide open these blind leaders of the blind are leading us into an extremely vulnerable position.

The treaty provides that all of the INF weapons are to be destroyed within three years after the treaty enters into force,[161] which happened on June 1. But I don't believe the United States will wait that long to remove them from operational capability. To show our good faith, we will most likely remove them from operational status immediately. As soon as they are gone it is only a matter of time before the Soviets invade Europe.

What makes Reagan and the Senate think that a piece of paper will solve our problems with the Soviets? Not only have the Soviets broken every arms control agreement that they have ever signed with us, but they have also had a peace agreement with nearly every country they have ever invaded.

They had peace treaties with the Georgian Republic, which they absorbed in 1921; the Ukraine, which they absorbed in 1922. They had peace treaties with Czechoslovakia. Then they forced them to cede territory and to set up a cabinet of men loyal to Moscow. Finally, in 1968, they invaded Czechoslovakia. They had nonaggression pacts with Lithuania, Estonia, and Latvia, which they invaded and absorbed in the 1940s; with Poland, which they reduced to a puppet state at the end of World War II; with Finland, which they overran in 1940 but which managed to remain independent. They had a nonaggression pact with Afghanistan which they invaded in 1979 and have brutally occupied ever since.

There's something psychologically wrong with the West. Watching this happen year in, year out, we see that every succeeding nation has fallen for it. And now the government of the United States of America has fallen for it.

The next agreement in line is START, the Strategic Arms Reduction Talks. A 50 percent across-the-board cut in nuclear weapons. Sounds like a good deal, doesn't it? But because of the way U.S. forces are structured, it is far more dangerous for the United States than it is for the U.S.S.R. Even if the treaty doesn't have loopholes and is properly negotiated, it will still be a bad deal.

The U.S. land-based missile force consists of 1,000 ICBMs. After START, the Soviets will have 3,210 warheads on 699 land-based ICBMs[162] with which to attack our much-reduced ICBM force of 500 missiles.

START will have an even worse effect on our submarine and bomber forces. It cuts them in half but does nothing about the Soviet defensive forces designed to defeat them. START will cut the American force of ballistic missile submarines (SSBNs) from 37 to about 18. Only 10 or 11 will be at sea at any one time. But the Soviets will still have 270 attack submarines with which to destroy the SSBN force.

START will cut the American bomber force of 290 planes in half but will do nothing about 2,000 dedicated strategic defense interceptor aircraft, 7,000 strategic air defense radars, and 9,000 Soviet SAMs deployed to stop them.[163] Furthermore, the Soviet civil defense system and ABM system will instantaneously become twice as effective because they will need to defend against only half as many U.S. weapons.

START is a bad idea from start to finish. It will make a Soviet first strike more likely. And if Reagan or a future president signs it, he will be signing the nation's death warrant.

I can only turn back to the heart of Saint Germain and invite you to ponder his words. These are from his February 27, 1988 dictation.

> Therefore, beloved, know that that intent *is* on the drawing boards in Moscow and in the Kremlin and has ever been. It is not new. And therefore, I tell you, glasnost is a propaganda sham! I tell you, the prince

out of the Soviet Union is a sham and a liar and a betrayer of the people!

And I say this directly to the heart of Mikhail Gorbachev:

"You may fool the people but you have not fooled the ascended hosts of Light and you have not fooled the hearts of the Lightbearers in the earth! And you, Ronald Reagan, are a sham and betrayer of my sponsorship and you also shall know your karma for this betrayal of Europe and the European states!

"And everyone who has gone after these liars, in the United States Senate and in the nation-states of Europe, know that I, Saint Germain, do stand and my angels with me and you shall not pass and you shall know the judgment of your karma and you shall know it all too late, too late therefore! And you shall have caused, therefore, the downfall of nations, and in so doing you shall have incurred a karma so vast as to be practically impossible to balance in aeons of the future.

"Therefore I sound the warning and I sound it with Archangel Gabriel! And I announce to you fallen ones, though you may think you are the instruments of the karma of the people, let it be known that if you so become those instruments, the sword of Damocles shall be upon your own heads and your victory shall be short-lived and your triumphs and your celebrations shall be exposed as the very conflagration of hell surrounds you!"[164]

On February 13, 1988, Saint Germain said:

One does not rest one's case on a hope that enough souls of Light on a planet will deliver the mandate of the violet flame that can be received by the Karmic Board to turn the tide of world history. There is more than violet flame involved, beloved. There is free will.

And there are many in positions of power this day who have amassed power and wealth and armaments and technology whose free will is committed to world destruction. I should not trust my fate to their hands, nor should you. Therefore, the wise will remove themselves to that point in time and space which they discover by meditation and unerring guidance of my angels is the correct place for them to be.

Do not consider, then, that you who have not attained to the levels of an Ascended Master may turn the world around merely by the raising of the right hand. If it were so, beloved, we should long ago have done this through you. What you ultimately can do and must do, in all of the promises you have heard, is to invoke that violet flame and to continue to invoke it and use *Archangel Michael's Rosary for Armageddon.*

For much will change, much will be set aside. Entire kingdoms may come to their judgment. Yet you must be found out of the way. For this very process to occur, world chemicalization is in order!. . .

Blessed hearts, I trust that I make myself clear. The preparedness at a personal and national level has never been more paramount. Your preparedness in your life can be complete in a matter of months. When you are fully prepared and determined to survive physically in the earth, come what may in all of these predictions and those you have heard elsewhere, you are then a free agent of Saint Germain and you may give your life and heart to this very cause of stopping those conditions in their tracks before they are outpictured, therefore rendering your preparations only a safety valve, a security net, a lifeboat, if you will.[165]

On November 29, 1987, Saint Germain stood in Washington, D.C., and said,

When all the world has gone mad or asleep around you, beloved, you do not despair, you come into the awareness, truly the direct apprehension of your Godhood. *You kindle a sun in a dying world! That is your mission!* You kindle a sun and you adore Helios and Vesta, Alpha and Omega, the one true God manifest in all the beauty and glory of His Light emanations! You become a sun! You are the sun, and you will let no Darkness defeat it, put it out or cast a shadow.[166]

Thank you. [1-minute 10-second applause]

It's always a privilege to address you. And it is profoundly comforting to me and I know it is to the Ascended Masters to have such a wonderful group of souls such as you who desire to hear and ponder in your hearts this message of Saint Germain as he has stumped America and the nations in the past year. But most comforting of all is the reality that you are not only hearers but doers of the Word and the Work of the LORD. Therefore I know you will heed the prophecy and the warning and act in time, in space to *Be Prepared!* God bless you!

"The Summit Lighthouse Sheds Its Radiance O'er All the World to Manifest as Pearls of Wisdom." An address by Elizabeth Clare Prophet **delivered** on **Monday, July 4, 1988,** at *FREEDOM 1988* in the Heart of the Inner Retreat at the **Royal Teton Ranch, Park County, Montana,** updated for print as this week's *Pearl*. Note: Throughout these notes *PoW* is the abbreviation for *Pearls of Wisdom*. (**1**) Robert L. DuPont, Jr., *Getting Tough on Gateway Drugs* (Washington, D.C.: American Psychiatric Press, Inc., 1984), p. 64. (**2**) The American Council for Drug Education, "Some Facts About Drug Use Among School Children," Washington, D.C., April 1988. (**3**) Victor C. Strasburger, "Sex, Drugs, Rock 'n Roll: An Introduction," *Pediatrics,* October 1985, p. 660. (**4**) American Council for Drug Education, "Facts About Drug Use." (**5**) John Langone, *Time,* "Crack Comes to the Nursery," 19 September 1988, p. 85. (**6**) "Tobacco's Toll," *Newsweek,* 9 November 1987, p. 62. (**7**) Geoffrey Cowley, "Science and the Cigarette," *Newsweek,* 11 April 1988, p. 66. (**8**) Strasburger, "Sex, Drugs, Rock 'n Roll," p. 660. (**9**) Edward W. Desmond, "Out in the Open," *Time,* 30 November 1987, p. 81. (**10**) American Council for Drug Education, "Facts About Drug Use." (**11**) Lewis J. Lord, "Coming to Grips with Alcoholism," *U.S. News & World Report,* 30 November 1987, p. 57. (**12**) Joseph Carey, "A Study of Sugar Stirs Up a Sweet-and-Sour Reaction," *U.S. News & World Report,* 19 January 1987, p. 66. (**13**) Mary Finch Hoyt, "How Parents Can Stop Obscene Rock Songs," *Good Housekeeping,* November 1985, p. 122; see Sean C. Prophet, "Rock and Roll in America, Part I: Heavy Metal: Abuse of God-Power," 1987 *PoW,* pp. 327–68. The three-part exposé on "Rock and Roll in America," delivered by Sean C. Prophet July 2, 1987, is available on audiocassette. Part I, "Heavy Metal: Abuse of God-Power," on 2 audiocassettes, A87069, 2 hrs. 24 mins., $13.00 (add $.95 for postage). Part II, "Political Rock: Abuse of God-Wisdom," on 60-min. audiocassette B87071, $6.50 (add $.55 for postage). Part III, "Techno-Rock: Abuse of God-Love," on 90-min. audiocassette B87072, $6.50 (add $.55 for postage). (**14**) National Center for Health Statistics, *Mortality,* 1962, vol. 2 of *Vital Statistics of the United States* (U.S. Bureau of the Census, 1964), p. I–144. (**15**) Loren Coleman, *Suicide Clusters* (Boston: Faber and Faber, 1987), p. 1. (**16**) William J. Bennett, *American Education: Making It Work* (Washington, D.C.: Government Printing Office, 1988), p. 45. (**17**) Diane Ravitch and Chester E. Finn, Jr., *What Do Our 17-Year-Olds Know?* (New York, Harper & Row, 1987), pp. 3, 46, 54, 57. (**18**) ABC News, "Burning Questions: America's Kids — Why They Flunk," 3 October 1988. (**19**) Ben Wattenberg, "Is Education as Bad as Ever?" *U.S. News & World Report,* 20 March 1989, p. 52.

(20) Thomas Sowell, "Educational Mush Trickling Up and Down," *The Washington Times,* 24 March 1989, p. F-4. (21) Bennett, *American Education,* p. 45. (22) Telephone interview, Bob Hilleman, National Educational Association Midwestern Regional Office, Minneapolis, 26 May 1989. (23) Ritalin: the trademark for preparations of methylphenidate, a mild central nervous system stimulant and antidepressant. Ritalin is an amphetaminelike substance which is commonly prescribed for hyperactive children. Although amphetamines act as stimulants in adults, they calm children and increase their attention span. However, Ritalin has come under increasing fire for its side effects: nervousness, insomnia, skin rashes, drowsiness, pulse changes, and weight loss. Cylert is another drug commonly prescribed for hyperactive children. (24) In the United States an estimated 22 to 27 million adults are illiterate. A 1986 study by the U.S. Census Bureau found that over 13.5 million of the English-speaking illiterates had had at least 6 to 8 years of American schooling. (25) Sir Edwin Arnold, trans., *The Song Celestial or Bhagavad-Gita (from the Mahabharata)* (Los Angeles: Self-Realization Fellowship, 1977), p. 10. (26) Ibid., pp. 14–15. (27) Ibid., p. 18. (28) Eph. 6:12. (29) P. Lal, trans., *The Dhammapada* (New York: Farrar, Straus & Giroux, 1967), pp. 10–11. (30) Will Durant, *Caesar and Christ* (New York: Simon and Schuster, 1944), p. 105. (31) Ibid., pp. 106–7. (32) George Santayana, *Reason in Common Sense,* vol. 1 of *The Life of Reason,* quoted in John Bartlett, *Familiar Quotations,* 15th ed. (Boston: Little, Brown and Company, 1980), p. 703. (33) Phil. 2:5, 6. (34) Eph. 6:11. (35) Arnold J. Toynbee, *A Study of History,* abr. of vols. 7–10 by D. C. Somervell (New York: Oxford University Press, 1957), p. 364. (36) Arnold J. Toynbee, *A Study of History,* abr. of vols. 1–6 by D. C. Somervell (New York: Oxford University Press, 1947), p. 278. (37) Ibid., pp. 247, 272. (38) II Cor. 5:17; Gal. 6:15. (39) I Pet. 1:13. (40) Matt. 6:12. (41) Matt. 6:33. (42) Patrick Henry, speech before the Virginia Convention of Delegates, 28 March 1775, quoted in Lewis Copeland and Lawrence Lamm, eds., *The World's Great Speeches,* 3rd ed. (New York: Dover Publications, 1942), pp. 233–34. (43) Ibid., p. 234. (44) George Washington, "Address to the Continental Army before the battle of Long Island," 27 August 1776, quoted in Bartlett, *Familiar Quotations,* p. 379. (45) *Saint Germain On Prophecy* (Livingston, Mont.: Summit University Press, 1986), Book 4, p. 209; also published in 1986 *PoW,* p. 648. (46) William Somerset Maugham, *Strictly Personal,* ch. 31, quoted in Bartlett, *Familiar Quotations,* p. 751. (47) Richard Pipes, "Why the Soviet Union Thinks It Could Fight and Win a Nuclear War," *Commentary,* July 1977, pp. 30, 32–33. (48) During the Ford and Carter years, U.S. nuclear strategy changed so that we had the option of attacking hard targets (military installations). But it was only a theoretical change. In strategy, you must adjust your ends to your means. Our forces, built according to MAD, are structured so that we can attack primarily soft targets (cities). So as it now stands, we can attack Soviet cities but they can destroy our military targets. For the time being, whatever our declared strategy, we are stuck with what is essentially a retaliatory or second-strike force. MAD is still our operational strategy. (49) Joseph D. Douglass, Jr. and Jan Sejna, "Drugs, Narcotics, and National Security," *Global Affairs,* Fall 1987, p. 67; Joseph D. Douglass, Jr. and Neil C. Livingstone, *America the Vulnerable* (Lexington, Mass.: Lexington Books, 1987), pp. 120–22. (50) Douglass and Livingstone, *America the Vulnerable,* pp. 116, 117, 120–21; see also Joseph D. Douglass, Jr., "Red Cocaine: A Chronicle of Communist Drug Trafficking," review draft, 1988. (51) Alfred W. McCoy, *The Politics of Heroin in Southeast Asia* (New York: Harper and Row, 1973); Wayne Greenhaw, *Flying High: Inside Big-Time Drug Smuggling* (New York: Dodd, Mead and Company, 1984). (52) Abraham Lincoln, "The Perpetuation of Our Political Institutions," address at the Young Men's Lyceum, Springfield, Illinois, 27 January 1838, in *1833–1840: The Challenge of a Continent,* vol. 6 of *The Annals of America* (Chicago: Encyclopaedia Britannica, 1976), p. 424. (53) Douglass and Livingstone, *America the Vulnerable,* pp. 121–22. (54) Douglass and Sejna, "Drugs, Narcotics, and National Security," p. 72. (55) Nathan M. Adams, "Drugs for Guns — The Bulgarian Connection," *Reader's Digest,* November 1983, pp. 87–88; Douglass and Livingstone, *America the Vulnerable,* pp. 121, 125–26; Douglass and Sejna, "Drugs, Narcotics, and National Security," pp. 75, 78–79, 82. (56) On May 15, 1988, in a provision attached to the defense budget bill, the Senate voted to assign drug interdiction as a duty for the nation's armed forces. The Pentagon is to work out plans for military drug enforcement duties and Congress must provide funds to finance the program. (Tim Carrington, "Senate Votes to Use the Military in War on Drugs but Tactics Remain Formidable," *Wall Street Journal,* 16

May 1988.) The 1989 defense authorization bill establishes the Defense Department as the "single lead agency of the federal government for the detection and monitoring of aerial and maritime transit of illegal drugs." Funding for 1989 is $300 million, largely spent on military planes, ships and surveillance equipment to detect incoming smugglers and to fund National Guard troops working under individual state control. (Telephone interview with Jeff Bangston, Office of the Deputy Assistant of the Secretary of Defense for Drug Enforcement, 13 June 1989.) (57) Gen. Jan Sejna and Dr. Joseph D. Douglass, Jr., "Inside Soviet Military Strategy," Summit University Forum, November 28, 1987. Full-length interview, 4¾ hrs., available on three videocassettes, GP88001, $59.95 (add $1.90 for postage), or three audiocassettes, A88016, $19.50 (add $.95 for postage); also available on five 1-hr. cable TV shows, parts 1–5, HL89001–HL89005, $19.95 each (add $1.10 each for postage). (58) Douglass and Livingstone, America the Vulnerable, p. 44. (59) William R. Van Cleave, "Surprise Nuclear Attack," in Brian D. Dailey and Patrick J. Parker, eds., Soviet Strategic Deception (Lexington, Mass.: Lexington Books, 1987), p. 455. (60) Gordon W. Prange, At Dawn We Slept: The Untold Story of Pearl Harbor (New York: McGraw-Hill Book Company, 1981), p. 449. (61) Ibid., p. 486. (62) Ibid., p. 493. (63) Ibid., p. 402. (64) Ibid. (65) Ibid., p. 470. (66) Ibid., p. 485. (67) Ibid., p. 497. (68) Ibid. (69) Ibid., p. 501. (70) H. A. DeWeerd, "Strategic Surprise in the Korean War," Orbis, Fall 1962, pp. 451–52, cited in Van Cleave, "Surprise Nuclear Attack," in Soviet Strategic Deception, p. 453. (71) Van Cleave, "Surprise Nuclear Attack," in Soviet Strategic Deception, pp. 453–54. (72) Ibid., pp. 459–61. (73) Ibid., p. 455. (74) Harold Brown, U.S. Department of Defense, Annual Report to Congress, FY-1980 (Washington, D.C.: Government Printing Office, 1979), p. 81; cited in Van Cleave, "Surprise Nuclear Attack," in Soviet Strategic Deception, p. 458. (75) William R. Van Cleave, "The U.S.-Soviet Military Balance and Arms Control," Global Affairs, Spring 1989, p. 8. (76) Telephone interview, John Collins, 7 June 1989. (77) U.S. Department of Defense, Soviet Military Power 1987 (Washington, D.C.: Government Printing Office, 1987), pp. 47–50; Soviet Military Power 1988 (Washington, D.C.: Government Printing Office, 1988), p. 56; see 1988 PoW, pp. 248–49 n. 5. (78) Leon Gouré, Shelters in Soviet War Survival Strategy (Coral Gables, Fla.: University of Miami, Advanced International Studies Institute, 1978), p. vii; Soviet Military Power 1988, pp. 59–62. (79) William C. Martel and Paul L. Savage, Strategic Nuclear War (New York: Greenwood Press, 1986), pp. 83–110. (80) Martel and Savage, Strategic Nuclear War, pp. 30–32, 105. (81) Van Cleave, "Surprise Nuclear Attack," in Soviet Strategic Deception, pp. 459, 461. (82) Martel and Savage, Strategic Nuclear War, p. 35. (83) Soviet Military Power 1988, pp. 149–50. (84) Ibid., p. 56. (85) Soviet Military Power 1988, pp. 55, 65. (86) Ibid., pp. 59–62. (87) Martel and Savage, Strategic Nuclear War, pp. 106–7. (88) "A counterforce attack [an attack on missile silos and bomber and submarine bases] would produce relatively little direct blast damage to civilians and to economic assets; the main damage would come from radioactive fallout. . . . If the attack involves surface bursts of many very large weapons, if weather conditions are unfavorable, and if no fallout shelters are created beyond those that presently exist, U.S. deaths could reach 20 million. . . . Effective fallout sheltering . . . could save many lives under favorable conditions, but even in the best imaginable case more than a million would die . . . from a counterforce attack." Office of Technology Assessment, The Effects of Nuclear War (Washington, D.C.: Government Printing Office, 1979), pp. 7–8. (89) "Gorbachev Interview: The Arms Agreement, Nicaragua and Human Rights," New York Times, 1 December 1987, p. 6. (90) Soviet Military Power 1987, p. 45. (91) Ibid., p. 53. See Elizabeth Clare Prophet, "The Race for Space," 1988 PoW, pp. 63–87. (92) "Thomas H. Krebs on 'Tsar Wars,'" Summit University Forum, June 30, 1987. Full-length interview, 2½ hrs., available on 2 videocassettes, GP87005, $39.95 (add $1.50 for postage) and two audiocassettes, A87052, $13.00 (add $.95 for postage). Also available in two 1-hr. cable-TV shows for home use: "A Special Briefing on Soviet Space Warfare Capabilities," HL87009, and "The Race for Space," HL87013, $19.95 each (add $1.10 each for postage). (93) Soviet Military Power 1987, p. 52; John D. Morrocco, "Soviet Ground Lasers Threaten U.S. Geosynchronous Satellites," Aviation Week & Space Technology, 2 November 1987, p. 27. (94) Craig Covault, "Soviet Strategic Laser Sites Imaged by French-Spot Satellite," Aviation Week & Space Technology, 26 October 1987, pp. 26–27. (95) "Breakout," Wall Street Journal, 25 February 1988, p. 20. (96) Personal interview with Edward Aldridge, Colorado Springs,

Colorado, 14 April 1988. **(97)** Telephone interview with journalist Peter Samuel, 3 May 1988. Samuel says the information came from a well-placed source in the intelligence community. **(98)** Telephone interview with Frank Gaffney, 2 May 1988. **(99)** Telephone interview with Frank Gaffney, 3 May 1988. **(100)** Archangel Gabriel, 1988 *PoW,* pp. 241–42. **(101)** R. J. Rummel, "Deadlier than War," *IPA Review,* August–October 1987, p. 25; *The Sunday Times* [London], 18 April 1988 reports that the Soviets now admit that "during the Stalin era as many as 50 million people were killed or condemned to labor camps from which they never emerged." **(102)** Russell Watson, "Cracks in the Bloc," *Newsweek,* 24 October 1988, pp. 30–32; "Keeping the Lid on Dissent," *Newsweek,* 29 February 1988, p. 39; Gordon Mott, "Facing an Old Feud," *Newsweek,* 3 October 1988, p. 36; "Gorbachev Listens to the People and Gets an Earful," *New York Times,* 13 September 1988; ABC Evening News, 25 May 1988. **(103)** Wisconsin's Congressman Toby Roth, quoted in Arthur Jones, "Russian Funding," *Financial World,* 6 October 1987, p. 8. Note that this billion dollars a month is "new loans." Roger W. Robinson, former senior director for International Economic Affairs at the National Security Council (1982–85), says that untied loans to the Soviet-bloc in 1986 totaled $20 billion. The International Security Council says that $100 billion in outstanding loans from the West have already accrued to the Soviet bloc as a whole. See Roger W. Robinson, Jr., "Economic And Financial Burden-Sharing," *Global Affairs,* Summer 1988, pp. 127–136; International Security Council, "An Affirmative Strategy for the Free World," *Global Affairs,* Summer 1988, pp. 40–48. **(104)** Elizabeth Clare Prophet, February 13, 1988, "Saint Germain On Prophecy from 1988 through the 1990s — the Astrology of World Karma," on 2 videocassettes, 3 hr. 50 min., GP88019, $49.95 (add $1.50 for postage), or 3 audiocassettes, 3 hr. 51 min., A88024, $19.50 (add $.95 for postage); Elizabeth Clare Prophet, May 21, 1989, "Prophecy for the 1990s" on 3 videocassettes, 5 hr. 5 min., GP89029, $49.95 (add $1.90 for postage), or three 90-min. audiocassettes, A89079, $19.50 (add $.95 for postage). **(105)** Robert Conquest, *The Great Terror: Stalin's Purge of the Thirties,* rev. ed. (New York: Collier Books, 1973), p. 713; see also Elizabeth Clare Prophet, 1988 *PoW,* pp. 173–204. **(106)** Jan Goodwin, *Caught in the Crossfire* (New York: E. P. Dutton, 1987), p. 21. **(107)** Vladimir Solovyov and Elena Klepikova, *Behind the High Kremlin Walls* (New York: Berkley Books, 1987; Dodd, Mead & Company, 1986), pp. 179–80. **(108)** Ibid., p. 181. **(109)** "Gorbachev's Vision," *Billings Gazette,* 29 June 1988, p. 1. **(110)** Fausto Biloslavo, "One Man's Sentence in an Afghan Hell," *Insight,* 4 July 1988, pp. 8, 12. **(111)** Ibid., pp. 15–16. **(112)** Ibid. p. 16. **(113)** Keith B. Payne, *Strategic Defense: "Star Wars" In Perspective* (Layham, Md.: Hamilton Press, 1986), pp. 234–35. **(114)** "Weekly Compilation of Presidential Documents," 28 March 1983, vol. 19, no. 12, p. 448. **(115)** Daniel O. Graham, *"To Provide for the Common Defense": The Case for Space Defense* (Louisville, Ky.: Frank Simon Company, 1986), p. 55. **(116)** Ibid. **(117)** John Gardner et al., *Missile Defense in the 1990s* (Washington, D.C.: George C. Marshall Institute, 1987), pp. 38–39. **(118)** Ibid., pp. 9, 10. **(119)** Speech by Lowell L. Wood condensed in "'Brilliant Pebbles' Missile Defense Concept Advocated by Livermore Scientist," *Aviation Week & Space Technology,* 13 June 1988, p. 151. **(120)** Gardner, et al., *Missile Defense in the 1990s,* pp. 4, 18–19; personal interview with Allan Mense, 20 February, 1987; personal interview with Thomas Krebs, 26 February 1987; Robert Jastrow, *How To Make Nuclear War Obsolete* (Boston: Little, Brown and Company, 1983), pp. 34, 41, 102; Office of Technology Assessment, *Strategic Defense* (Princeton, N.J.: Princeton University Press, 1986), p. 269. **(121)** Wood, "'Brilliant Pebbles,'" p. 155. **(122)** See Summit University Forums: "Gen. Daniel O. Graham and Dr. Dmitry Mikheyev on Strategic Defense: To Deploy or Not to Deploy," Summit University Forum, July 4, 1987. Full-length interview, 3 hrs., available on 2 videocassettes GP87014, $39.95 (add $1.50 for postage) and 2 audiocassettes, A87056, $13.00 (add $.95 for postage). Also available in three 1-hr. cable TV shows for home use: "A Three-Layered Defense — Will It Work?" HL87004; "America's Future in Space." HL87005: "A Scientific or a Political Question?" HL87006, $19.95 each (add $1.10 each for postage). Two ½-hr. cable TV shows: "A Three-Layered Defense — Will It Work?" parts I and II, HL87007, HL87008, $10.95 each (add $1.10 each for postage). See also Thomas H. Krebs on "Tsar Wars" (note 92 above). **(123)** Alpha, 1987 *PoW,* p. 385. **(124)** Personal interview with Maj. Gen. Tom Brandt, Colorado Springs, Colorado, 14 April 1988; see also John H. Cushman, Jr., "Shortage to Hurt SDI, Study Says," *New York Times,* 12 June 1988, p. 11: "The first deployment of 'Star Wars' antimissile defenses in space cannot occur before 1998 at the earliest because of a lack of heavy-duty rockets to put weapons into orbit, a Congressional staff study published today says." (**125**) See Elizabeth Clare Prophet, 1988 *PoW,* pp. 76–80; see also Summit University Forums: Graham and Mikheyev (note 122 above); "Professor Antony C. Sutton on the Capitalist/Communist Conspiracy," July 1, 1987. Full-length interview on two videocassettes, 2 hrs., V87009, $29.95 (add $1.50 for postage) and 2 audiocassettes, 2½ hrs., A87054, $13.00 (add $.95 for postage). Also available in one-hr. cable TV show for home use: "We Have Built Ourselves an Enemy," HL88004, $19.95 (add $1.10 for postage). (**126**) Theresa M. Foley, "Budget Jeopardizes SDI Timetable; Research Efforts Scaled Back," *Aviation Week & Space Technology,* 9 November 1987, pp. 25–26. (**127**) Gordon Smith, address at the Space Symposium, Colorado Springs, Colorado, 14 April 1988. (**128**) "Nunn Urges Sensible Defense Initiative," *Military Space,* 1 February 1988, p. 5; Michael R. Gordon, "Nunn Seeks Shield for Missiles Fired in Error," *New York Times,* 20 January 1988, p. 1. (**129**) Sam Nunn, "Arms Control in the Last Year of the Reagan Administration," *Congressional Record,* 100th Cong., 2d sess., 3 February 1988; Warren Strobel, "Limited SDI, Just for Area, Being Weighed by Pentagon," *Washington Times,* 10 June 1988, p. A-1; "Nunn Urges Sensible Defense Initiative," p. 5. (**130**) Paul Mann, "Industry Studies Differ Over Coverage Provided by Accidental Launch Shield," *Aviation Week & Space Technology,* 4 April 1988, p. 41. (**131**) U.S. Arms Control and Disarmament Agency, "Strategic Defense Initiative: A Chronology: 1983–1988," *Issues Brief,* entry for 14 March 1987. (**132**) Ibid., entries for 15 April 1987 and 15 January 1987. (**133**) See Elizabeth Clare Prophet, May 31, 1987, "Saint Germain On the Defense of Freedom: 'The Rise and Fall of MAD,'" 77-minute videocassette HP87052, $19.95 (add $1.10 for postage), or 72-minute audiocassette B87039, $6.50 (add $.55 for postage). (**134**) Michael Dukakis, speech before the Atlantic Council, Washington, D.C., 14 June 1988. (**135**) "Reagan's SDI Legacy," *Wall Street Journal,* 20 June 1988, p. 14. (**136**) "CPD: A Sample of Support for National Defense," *Sea Power,* February 1988, p. 31. The poll was sponsored by the Committee on the Present Danger. (**137**) Gardiner et al., *Missile Defense in the 1990s,* pp. 4–6, 8, 33. (**138**) Foley, "Budget Jeopardizes SDI Timetable," p. 25. (**139**) Theresa M. Foley, "SDI Priority Shifts Threaten Space-Based Interceptor," *Aviation Week & Space Technology,* 13 June 1988, p. 16. (**140**) Theresa M. Foley, "Slowdown in SDI Growth Delays Deployment Decision," *Aviation Week & Space Technology,* 22 February 1988, p. 16. (**141**) "Shortage to Hurt SDI, Study Says," *New York Times,* 12 June 1988, p. 11; Foley, "SDI Priority Shifts Threaten Space-Based Interceptor," p. 16. (**142**) Paul Mann, "Congress Resists Early SDI Deployment with Push for Long-term Technology," *Aviation Week & Space Technology,* 11 January 1988, p. 21. (**143**) Foley, "SDI Priority Shifts Threaten Space-Based Interceptor," p. 16. (**144**) James T. Hackett, "The INF Treaty," *Military Engineer,* March–April 1988, p. 95. (**145**) John M. Collins, *U.S.-Soviet Military Balance: 1980–1985* (Washington, D.C.: Pergamon-Brassey's International Defense Publishers, 1985), p. 268; *Soviet Military Power 1988,* pp. 66–67. (**146**) Interview with Gen. Pierre Gallois in John Train, "Purpose of the Pershings," *Wall Street Journal,* 13 April 1987, p. 26. (**147**) "General Gallois: Europe Has Reached a Perilous Crossroads," *Defense Electronics,* June 1988, pp. 19–20; Train, "Purpose of the Pershings"; Hackett, "The INF Treaty," p. 97. (**148**) "General Gallois," p. 20. (**149**) R. Ernest Dupuy and Trevor N. Dupuy, *The Encyclopedia of Military History* (New York: Harper & Row, 1986), p. 1198. (**150**) *Soviet Military Power 1988,* p. 78. (**151**) Douglass and Livingstone, *America the Vulnerable,* pp. 52–53. (**152**) Telephone interview, Joseph D. Douglass, Jr., 8 June 1989. (**153**) The AEI Working Group on the INF, "A Further Review of the INF Treaty: Seven Critical Issues," *AEI Occasional Papers* (Washington, D.C.: American Enterprise Institute for Public Policy Research, 1988), p. 39. (**154**) Hackett, "The INF Treaty," p. 96. (**155**) "AF Chief Expects Soviets to Cheat on Treaty," *Defense Daily,* 8 February 1988, p. 199. (**156**) Roberta Wohlstetter, "The Pleasures of Self-Deception," *Washington Quarterly,* Autumn 1979, p. 61. (**157**) Frank J. Gaffney, Jr., "The INF Treaty and Its Shadows Over the START Negotiations," *Strategic Review,* Spring 1988, p. 37. (**158**) Ibid., p. 39. (**159**) AEI Working Group, "Review of the INF Treaty," pp. 49, 51–52. (**160**) Hackett, "The INF Treaty," p. 97. (**161**) Ibid., p. 94. (**162**) Collins, *U.S.-Soviet Military Balance,* p. 174. (**163**) *Soviet Military Power 1988,* pp. 102–3. (**164**) Saint Germain, 1988 *PoW,* p. 285. (**165**) Saint Germain, 1988 *PoW,* pp. 162–64. (**166**) Saint Germain, 1987 *PoW,* p. 617.

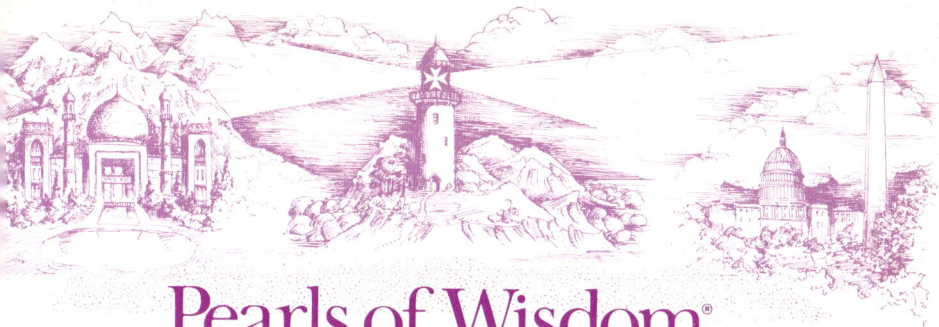

Pearls of Wisdom®

published by The Summit Lighthouse

Vol. 31 No. 72   *Beloved Saint Germain*   *October 29, 1988*

FREEDOM 1988

17

Keep My Purple Heart

Keep Those Violet Flames

Hail, Keepers of the Flame! I AM with you in the flesh! [47-second standing ovation] And by that I mean each and every one of you, for I AM truly in your hearts this day! [16-second applause] And in you I count my blessings. (Won't you be seated.)

And indeed I count my blessings, for in the long history of nations and planetary spheres it is not often that such an one as I should discover such as ye to provide a chalice for my appearing in this octave.

Blessed hearts, your devotion does make up for ten thousand cowards and a hundred thousand liars and a million murderers that one can still discover on this planet. But yet, I choose to see the violet flame springing up everywhere you are.

O beloved, if you could see how when you walk it is impossible for you to shake the flame that attaches itself to your blessed feet. And so the elementals are fascinated by this process [10-second applause] and so they run after you trying to figure out why that violet flame keeps walking with your shoes. Blessed ones, some of you have a single or five or several permanent flames that do literally walk with you, signifying that you have built a momentum for that sustaining power.[1]

You may see, as though you would fill in the violet flame in the center of your tube of light, that [that] certain momentum of giving the violet flame decrees does result in an action whereby the holy angels of Amethyst and Zadkiel respect that devotion and that commitment to Freedom. And therefore you experience that the flame does not ascend to the level of perfection each twenty-four hours but is sustained; *and this is the true meaning of attainment, that you keep those flames!* [9-second applause] Now you have discovered a new meaning of the calling to be a Keeper of the Flame! [6-second applause]

I will tell you this, beloved, because each one's portion is precisely according to his own work, his own devotion, his own love of the harmony of the Seventh Ray, it does signify, then, more than a decree momentum, though that is a fundamental requirement. It does signify, beloved, a quality of the heart, a magnet of the heart that is mercy's flame. And thereby you are establishing here below in the heart center (the heart chakra and the secret chamber of the heart) even a momentum of the Great Central Sun Magnet of the Seventh Ray of Mercy—the quality of your heart's own mercy. And thus, those single flames rising from beneath your feet are, as it were, satellites to that Sun, beloved, which therefore a cosmos may see, for the manifestation of Light tells the truth and never lies.

You, then, can know that the more you give to that mercy flame, the more you call forth the violet flame in love, the more you will fill in as though filling in a tapestry or a numbered painting. You will fill in the violet flame within the tube of light that is an expression of your God-mastery on the Seventh Ray in contrast to that [manifestation of the violet flame] being the sending of your I AM Presence and holy angels in answer to your call.

Blessed ones, we have emphasized and we do continue to emphasize, throughout these hours together, the path of victory and God-victorious overcoming in each one of you personally. First and foremost, then, unto those who are the disciples of the living Light a planetary home must be a springboard to spiritual victory. Since that victory is always won in world service, we quickly turn your attention to those endeavors of greatest need, which when you engage in them do accrue to you as the greatest good karma that you can earn in your time.

Surely it is, then, the preservation of the flame of freedom that is definitely a threat to every fallen one and denier [deny-er] of the Light on this earth. Just how great a threat that is you can understand only by gaining co-measurement of just what is the alignment of these individuals to the hate and hate creation of the fires of hell itself.

Thus, beloved, I should bring to you in this hour a report as to the results of the use of my violet flame cassettes by one and by the many. Blessed ones, first and foremost the greatest good has come to the individual supplicant himself. Therefore, to those who have so loved this ritual there has been an increase of transmutation. And I have seen to it, as you count me as your Master and Friend, that that violet flame that you have invoked has been directed into the most resistant and recalcitrant pockets of your own subconscious, especially into those conditions which you have been the most desirous to have removed.

Therefore, in some of you a hearty amount of karma has been balanced, in others hardness of heart has truly melted around the heart chakra. There has come a new love and a new softening, a new compassion, a new sensitivity to life, a new freedom and a new joy in pursuing that freedom. There has come about a holiness as you have contacted through my flame the priesthood of the Order of Melchizedek. There has come a melting and dissolving of certain momentums of ignorance and mental density and a turning toward a dietary path more conducive to your own God-mastery.

The violet flame has assisted in relationships within families. It has served to liberate some to balance old karmas and old hurts and to set individuals on their courses according to their vibration. It must be remembered that the violet flame does contain the flame of God-Justice, and God-Justice, of course, [does contain the flame of] the judgment; and thus the violet flame always comes as a two-edged sword to separate the Real from the Unreal. Thus, when in the presence of the violet flame there is a chemicalization not only within one's own members but in and amongst those who closely serve together in their families, in their mandalas.

And therefore, for some it has caused permanent separations and for others a more profound and intimate love that issues from the spiritual fire itself, delivering many of the baser pulls into the pitfalls of desire that do come forth from the lowest levels of the astral plane—those momentums which you have long outgrown [and] for which you have long paid the karma yet [of which you] had not quite cut the tie that has bound you to the lower levels of existence.

Blessed ones, it is impossible to enumerate exhaustively all of the benefits of the violet flame but there is indeed an alchemy that does take place within the personality. The violet flame goes after the schisms that cause psychological problems that go back to early childhood and previous incarnations and that have established such deep grooves within the consciousness that in fact they have been difficult to shake lifetime after lifetime.

The violet flame is a considerate flame. It is a loving flame. It is a grateful flame. It is a flame that has its own momentum of self-luminous, intelligent substance, containing and embracing the very knowledge of alchemy itself. It may be difficult to understand how a flame can have consciousness, but remember, a flame is the manifestation of God. A flame is the manifestation of all who have ever served it, even as a mantra embodies the momentum of all who have ever given it.

Thus, all who have ever served the Seventh Ray and embodied that [violet] flame have contributed to it those qualities and momentums of the God consciousness that serve all who will ever bathe and bask in it forevermore. So you become in the giving of [the invocations to] this flame (for some of you, [giving it] as you have never given it before) truly a part of that universal body which we call the entire Spirit of the Great White Brotherhood.

Blessed ones, I can only say that if you could see what inner progress you have made, you would not cease in the giving of that violet flame [decree] tape as often as possible—not necessarily all at once, but if you make the effort, you can endow those segments of time [that come to you] in the day with [your decree momentum on] that flame. And therefore, as you should come to understand, whatever time of day you invoke a flame or perform a service it does tie into your astrological clock and karma made at that very same hour throughout history. Thus, at different hours of the day when you are communing in love with God or rendering your services, you are endowing the earth on those lines of the Clock with a tremendous momentum of Light* as well as clearing out [the karmic substance of misqualified energy in] your own electronic belt.

As you can see from the hours of services that are recommended, five-thirty in the morning and also in the evening hours after dinner, you are mostly concentrating on the astral, or emotional, quadrant of your Cosmic Clock, which is also [charted] in the morning and in the evening, thus covering both ends of the day in that quadrant. Since most of you have the most problems in that quadrant, you can see what vast progress can be made [in the hours between six and nine o'clock].

When you give that violet flame at noon precisely, you discover that you are in the point of alignment with your I AM Presence,† and in that alignment, beloved, you are able [through the Father] to radiate that flame throughout your being.

It is noteworthy, therefore, that as the violet flame has liberated in you certain God qualities, [so] it will also flush out and bring to the surface, as alchemists know and refiners, the dross of human creation. If, therefore, there is not called forth an intensity of sacred fire [through] calls to [the Divine Mother] Astrea for the clearing of that substance, the violet flame may have the action of bringing to the surface that substance. [And] because you do not

---
*the Christ consciousness of the ray and flame you are invoking
†The 12 o'clock line on the Cosmic Clock under the hierarchy of Capricorn is the line of our Father in heaven.

finish the service that is needed, and [you] do not understand what service is needed, you may have lingering in and around your being those momentums of the human consciousness that seem to rise up and to frolic and to cause you to be somewhat out of alignment [with your Holy Christ Self] by the new freedom that you feel, no longer being heavily bound by your karma, [nevertheless needing Archangel Michael's sword of blue flame to cut you free to be fully in your God-control and God-Self mastery].

This does happen to elementals when they receive too much violet flame, and it does happen to the seed of the wicked that [when Keepers of the Flame blaze the violet flame throughout the planetary body] they sense their powers and kick up their heels, and [their reaction to] the lifting of the [karmic] burden of the planetary karma [is that] they go forth sowing greater Evil.

Therefore, it must be understood that the violet flame tapes were conceived by myself with Portia to be sent forth universally to all those souls with whom we would acquaint the vibration of Aquarius and the seventh age, and indeed [they] have fulfilled this purpose.

We must, however, speak to our stalwart chelas and tell you that we absolutely count on you to hold the balance of the First Ray [through your giving] of Astrea's [decree] and calls to Archangel Michael daily [on behalf of] all upon the planet who are making these [violet flame] calls [as you invoke the blue-flame will of God] for the planet as a whole and for yourself.

There is so much of a liberating spiral that is created around you, so much of a loosening of old substance that to follow those [violet flame] decrees with fiats to Archangel Michael, the use of a physical, tangible sword of blue flame consecrated to and by Archangel Michael, and the calls to Astrea and Hercules and the blue-ray Masters [is a most efficient use of the cosmic force of light]. Beloved ones, in this you will discover how there is an inner alignment [of your soul and your four lower bodies with your Holy Christ Self] that occurs simultaneously with the transmutative fires of the violet flame.

You might say that all is in flux, all is in a state of change through the violet flame. But where that consciousness and energy will come to rest and solidify does depend preeminently upon how much blue flame is invoked, how much action of the sacred fire of the First Ray is embraced by you, how much you do commit yourself to the will of God, do surrender to it and do recognize the path of the fourteen stations of the cross and the fifteenth as a means to that end—as a means to embodying the blue-flame will of God, as a means in itself to building the diamond heart within your heart that is made even more possible by the violet [transmuting] flame that does flood through that very same heart chakra.

Thus, beloved, as you look at certain events you can see that during the giving of the first violet flame cassette there were changes in Nicaragua. Those changes, as the violet flame action, created on the part of the people, the Contras and the Sandinistas the desire to move together, to talk together and to reason together. This is something that would have been desirable had it not been for the fact that World Communism working through the mentality and the deranged minds of the Sandinista leaders had another agenda.[2]

Thus, we see that the fallen ones who hold power have taken the power of God and they have abused it in dictatorships, treachery and intrigue, their conceit and deceit, their absolute chaos and discord. And when you think of totalitarian movements on the planet you can see that they accomplish their ends by a total abuse of power that you will note [is charted] on the Cosmic Clock on the blue-flame cross of the 12/6 and 3/9 [axes]. These abuses of power are manipulative, such as condemnation and criticism, intimidation [on the 12 o'clock line]. This turned inside out becomes a mockery [of the Christ in the children of God]. Thus, there is disinformation that goes forth—again [the] abuse of the Word of God [on the 3 o'clock line].

You see on these [four] lines, then, that from one [line] of these cardinal points to another the tactics [of the abuse of God's power by the fallen ones] swiftly change. Suddenly there is chaos and confusion, there are explosions, there are firebombs, there are all manner of techniques used to frighten people, to render a population powerless through fear to take action. These are the swift coups of the terrorists that come in to decimate the ranks of the Divine Mother on the 6 o'clock line and violate her sacred fire of God-Harmony.

Thus, you see in all takeovers of totalitarian movements [that] the misuse of the [power of the] heart chakra [on the 3/9 axis] in all of this deceit—all of the treachery, all of the intrigue, all of the lying, all of the appearing to be for the right causes—[is] but manipulation in the end.

What did take place, then, is that the people, [individual by individual], those who had good hearts, no matter what side they were on or [in] what camp, did receive a blessing and a freedom [through your violet flame marathon]. The downside of the entire experience, beloved ones, is that it will take many, many, many thousands of people dedicated to Archangel Michael's Rosary and the calls perpetual to Archangel Michael to hold the balance when such an alchemy [of cosmic freedom] is taking place [on a planetary scale].

Thus, beloved, there was a neutralization of the Contras, and though the United States did move in and action was affirmed, not enough action was taken. And when in that very moment by the power of Almighty God the Sandinistas could have suffered severe military setbacks if the same policies had been followed as those [applied] in Grenada, there was instead a cowardice, a weak-willed spinelessness, again a misuse of the power [lines of] the Cosmic Clock. And there was not a routing of the military installations of the Sandinistas; and truly [the option for] a setback that could have and should have been given at that hour to the Communist establishment in Nicaragua [was not exercised].

Thus, beloved, the violet flame worked to the advantage and [the] upliftment of the individuals who were of the Light. It did work change, but whether or not that change shall bring about a new level of God consciousness or of the will of God depends entirely upon the players in that scene and the parts they have [played] and shall play.

When you take the Latin temperament and the Latin diet you can see that the blue-flame will of God is absolutely essential, and the discipline and the commitment to that will [as well]. When you look at the fallen ones in the United States government who should have and could have supported those Contras and provided the necessary funds, when you look at the Congress and see all of this as being a perversion of the blue-flame cross of power [formed on the 12/6 and 3/9 axes of the Cosmic Clock], you come to understand that the violet flame can and is accomplishing a great deal of good among the people but it does quickly reach [optimum levels of] what it can do for want of the necessary bracing of [freedom by] the will of God, [as we see, in government and the military].

Thus, we turn your attention once again to the calling forth of the judgment [of the Most High God] upon the capitalist/communist conspirators and those who move in, because they have such established power, to take advantage of the joy and the lightness and the freedom and the hope that is gained when the violet flame floods the earth and a people. So you understand, as I have said before, beloved ones, that it is more than the violet flame that is at stake: it is free will. And that free will in the hands of fallen ones can be exercised [at any time] against the very humanity who stands to benefit most from the violet flame.

There is, [then], a general clearing of planetary karma through the giving of these invocations [on the Seventh Ray]. Some in past years have wondered why we have so stressed and so emphasized the calls to the First Ray of God's will—to Astrea, to Archangel Michael. It is because of this very equation, beloved, the very equation that too much freedom [via the violet flame] in the hands of those who have always abused it will only beget more abuses of freedom. And for this reason the Karmic Board did decide to initiate the Dark Cycle[3] whereby there should be an acceleration of mankind's returning karma and that of the fallen ones—this for the sole purpose of curtailing their wickedness and their evil deeds. Thus enmeshed in their karma and their karmic problems they would be so confined as to not be able to create world destruction and world holocaust.

Although the judgment calls that you have received have been placed whether in the illumination section of the decree book, [in] the Fifth Ray, the Third Ray [sections] and so forth, all calls for the judgment [of the unjust deeds of the seed of the Wicked One] are calls [which come under] the First Ray of God's holy will. And therefore, in combination with your blue-flame decrees it is absolutely necessary and [it] becomes more necessary daily (considering the all-out attack against this Church and the correct and appropriate use of this property[4]) that you should in no way let down your guard or be chary with your calls to Archangel Michael and Astrea or [in giving] the judgment calls.

Therefore, already ratifying the individual's karma, already ratifying the karma of the Dark Cycle, the judgment call may multiply by the power of the Cosmic Christ, *upon the discrimination of the Cosmic Christ,* those judgments that should descend upon the seed of the wicked, who themselves have already received the [prior] judgment [of Almighty God] of the second death,[5] at the conclusion of their life span and evolution on planet earth.

The hour is come for the judgments prophesied in the Book of Enoch[6] to take place. Since they know that it is so, these Watchers and these power mongers (and [they know] that as their days go by they are spending their last hours), I can assure you that with a vengeance of hell that is not familiar to you in your outer consciousness they will go after, to destroy and to bind and to ruin, any and all Lightbearers and life upon earth which they may.

Thus, the last plagues upon the earth, the presence of aliens in your midst (those subjects discussed during this conference which are of serious concern to the Great Divine Director and to me) signify to you, again, abuses of power on the part of those who are indeed desperate. And some of these aliens do indeed come from those civilizations that are dying races,[7] for they were long ago the product of genetic engineering; and [those who were not] long ago lost the divine spark or any sense of allegiance to the

Divinity. Thus, you must understand that these whom we may call
"desperados"* in all the planetary spheres and on the astral plane
know that they have but a short time.[8]

The only way, then, that [these fallen angels] can be curtailed
in the time remaining in their life span is through your judgment
calls, for they are in your domain. Once they pass on naturally—
and we do not advocate any other means—at that hour they
become subject to that Final Judgment.[9] They do become subject
to it but, beloved ones, they use all of their forces and their
momentums and they wage war against the very angels who come
to bind them and take them.

Thus, the angels of Light are moving twenty-four hours a day
to bind those who pass from the screen of life and all of their
attendant demons and discarnates who surround them in constel-
lations of blackness, adding to what is truly "black power" and has
nothing to do with the sons and daughters of Afra or the color of
skin. This black power is a misqualification of the Light of the
Divine Mother; and the sons and daughters of God who are of the
Brother Afra should have nothing to do with such terminology.
Blessed ones, those, then, who have abused the power of God are
the most deadly of the forces [of Anti-Christ] in the earth.

Therefore, let it be said that wise Keepers of the Flame—who
understand so much of the Teachings and the Path and [what are]
the necessary decrees—will provide the foundation whereby those
who do receive our violet flame tapes may have an immediate
transmutation of [the misqualified] substance [of negative karma]
in their worlds which has kept them from the Path and the study of
the Teachings of the Ascended Masters so long. Above all, they
need violet flame transmutation and indeed calls for the tube of
light and to Archangel Michael [for his unfailing protection].

As they become enamored of the violet flame through the
beauty of your voices and harmonies and through the rhythm and
the sound of the Word, they shall make swift progress. They shall
be cut free from false gurus and false teachings or those paths
which are half-truths and represent old dispensations which cannot
and will not carry them into the New Age dispensations of Aquarius
nor prepare them for the planetary changes which may come.

Thus, beloved hearts, when we [shall] have completed the
third cassette and there is that building momentum of violet flame,
we surely do look [forward] to the action of Cosmic Christ illumination reinforced by tremendous calls to the will of God and to
the Archangel Michael, that in every area where there is ground
that is gained for the soul, the state, the family, the planet, it shall

*desperado: one in despair or in desperate straits; a bold or violent criminal; esp.: a bandit of the western
United States in the nineteenth century

not be lost through those who have abused power and come in as the archmanipulators to tear from those who are the new souls on the Path the great joy of entering in.

Blessed ones, you can see in the very activities in the Soviet Union (which were showed to you on film today at my request) in that congress[10] which was held ostensibly to show a new freedom, a new openness in the Soviet Union[—you can see] a precise example of how the people of a nation have responded to the violet flame that has come upon them because you have invoked it— because the violet flame is swirling the planet round—and how their leaders and the abusers of power take advantage of the situation of the violet flame, set up such congresses, give the appearance of a new freedom and [how] they may just as easily on the morrow withdraw that freedom and those concessions and begin again to turn the screws of their totalitarian dictatorship.

Blessed ones, it is absolutely true that neither Mikhail Gorbachev nor those who run the Soviet Union (and especially those in the military establishment) are about to give even one inch of ground of their power and their military might toward a lessening of the tensions worldwide or to the giving to their own people of a freer hand in the running of their country. Though it may appear so, their reins of control will not diminish.

Nevertheless, those who are of the Light have benefited from the violet flame. At least they have new hope, beloved, and they shall have even greater hope as you summon the hosts of the Lord to absolutely move in and to reduce by percentages the momentum of Evil and [the] abuse of power by these hierarchies of the fallen ones worldwide.

Beloved ones, they cannot continue forever, and each day that you make the call they are diminished, and each day that you give the violet flame, clearing your chakras and your aura and balancing karma, your authority increases: for the more you are swept clean by the violet flame, the more your Holy Christ Self can embody in your temple, and so it is true of myself.

I have told you that wherever you raise up a violet flame pillar I shall be there, and I have set the minimum time of the fervor of your violet flame decrees to be fifteen minutes. If you can concentrate upon me and the violet flame calls for fifteen minutes, beloved, you will know that I shall be there. Obviously, beloved ones, this must be in divine harmony, in love for the violet flame, in love for all [whom] you know. And remember [to pray], "Father, forgive us. Father, forgive us our debts, even as we forgive our debtors."[11]

If there is any part of life whom you have not forgiven for any wrong [committed] against you, real or imagined, you limit by that

very resentment, by that very withholding of forgiveness, the
amount of forgiveness you can receive for any and all karma.
Thus, it is true, beloved, that the violet flame will not transmute in
you what you have not forgiven in others.

Therefore, I do fully recommend a true and profound heart
of mercy; and this is one of the most important gains that has been
made by many among you—a deeper sense and a deeper ability to
fully forgive because you have tarried long enough in your decrees
to experience the transmutation of that very hardness of heart,
that resentment, even that envy and pride that has caused you in
the past to withhold the full cup of forgiveness. Beloved ones,
others have gained a merciful heart simply out of gratitude of
experiencing just what the violet flame and God in that violet
flame has been doing for them.

There is no question that there has been a step-up in the
activity of the world action of the violet flame with the new
cassette, [which] has already assisted you mightily in absorbing
the Light* of this conference. You will understand, beloved, that
victories upon victories are experienced and won by millions of
lifestreams upon earth daily, and if the recording angels could
recount to you how your prayers have played a part in that victory,
you would surely give even more hours to that calling.

I will tell you, however, beloved ones, that in the etheric
retreats where you study in each fourteen-day cycle,[12] you are
shown the filigree thread of light that emits from a heart chakra
filled with mercy's love. And some of you have seen where there
have been a number of threads so great as to not even be possible of
counting, and these threads of violet flame, almost as a gossamer
veil, have gone directly to the hearts of lifestreams all over the
planet. And you have observed these threads, almost as fine as hair,
being as vessels, even as veins within the body, carrying a continual flow of violet flame that has enabled individuals all over the
world to rise up, to accomplish things they have not accomplished
in many lifetimes, to experience hope and healing and a new desire
to find God, to be free and to stand for the cause of Freedom.

It is the constancy of this flow of light that is both beautiful
and touching to behold. Beloved ones, in a small way it does show
you just what our Lord Gautama does for every lifestream upon
earth as he does maintain a cord of light tied to the threefold flame
of every heart on the planet [in whom that flame does burn].

Understand, then, that in so ministering with the violet flame
and in being diligent in not wasting the moments of the clock, you
can in fifteen minutes a day have me with you, and in my Presence
with you [you can] deliver a momentum of violet flame to many

*the Christ consciousness and radiance of the Seventh Ray and all the rays

souls upon the planet. Therefore, because you have so raised up that light this evening and I can be a pillar in your presence when you have done so, I could literally say to you that I am here in the flesh.

Now you understand what it means to achieve a oneness with an Ascended Master. And surely, beloved, as I read your hearts and auras, you do know what has happened in your life to increase God-Good, to feel a greater sense of harmony, dignity and inner peace. The violet flame gives that, and that peace, beloved, enables you to face a future without fear.

Now it is with great joy that we look forward to the violet-flame, Seventh-Ray accomplishment within you of the violet flame assisting you with your God-mastery in the five secret rays.

All of the mantras of Kuan Yin, as you know, go back to the heart of the Amitābha Buddha but, beloved, all of the Dhyāni Buddhas[13] as cosmic Principles and Forces and Presences have told me to tell you this night that they also do vow to be the ones to answer your call as you recite the mantras of Kuan Yin. Thus, not one but five [Buddhas] shall be to you the deliverers to your hearts and chakras of the violet flame through the blessed Electronic Presence of Kuan Yin around you.

That action means, beloved, that there can be a tremendous acceleration of your mastery of the secret rays, of your development of your soul faculties and your preparation for the days ahead. I cannot even emphasize to you, beloved, how necessary this is for our chelas. It is an area of neglect. And now Kuan Yin comes so powerfully and so abundantly through these tape recordings[14] to your heart that you may have the full momentum of our Presence as we did place our Electronic Presence—many of the ascended hosts—at the recording sessions of these mantras.

We give our profound gratitude to all members of our staff [and] to all Keepers of the Flame who made possible in any way the production of these tape recordings. Beloved ones, there may be the obvious ones who had physical part in the physical producing but, I tell you, such an event as this to a planet, so great a descent of so great Cosmic Beings has required the mastery and the mantle of the Messengers, the sponsorship of many hosts of Light and of the blessed Keepers of the Flame around the world[—you] who do diligently keep the flame at the altars of your sanctuaries and in your homes.

Blessed ones, what you do and how you uphold this Community and organization does truly allow the Messenger and those who are here to continue and to continue and to continue to publish and distribute the Word. Without this Community of

Light worldwide and this Body of God whom you represent as you have come from all of your nations, the Great White Brotherhood would not have the continuing opportunity which we do have today to render this service.

Blessed ones, this brings me to the discussion of the decision that many must make whether to relocate in this area or to consider becoming a part of this staff. As you know, there is a tremendous balance that is held by those in the field. We are desirous, then, and profoundly so, of using the violet flame tapes and your rosaries for the intense work of cutting free the Lightbearers. There are Lightbearers all over the world in the cities where you are, and until recently with these new tapes a sufficient work had not been accomplished to cut them free nor have your calls over the years been as one-pointed as we should have liked them to be, not necessarily through your own fault but because there were so many challenges that had to be tackled in our sessions.

In this hour, as you know, we deem no cause more important than the rescue of the Lightbearers and the judgment of the fallen ones. Thus, it is our desire to see literally cosmic reinforcements, that in these cities a new nucleus of Lightbearers, even four times in number those of you who may emerge from those cities, may take up their place and begin to keep the flame and go through the necessary steps as beginners on the Path, which you once did.

This calling is of major importance, and how you respond to make the call to cut free souls who will take up the torch of keeping the flame as you did will determine, beloved ones, in just what respect we are able to sustain a worldwide movement that is active, in fact, in the outer sense.

It is undoubtedly absolutely essential that certain individuals who are key in the mandala of building the Inner Retreat and preparing it for my purposes should be here. Those of you who do not know if you are among that mandala have only but to ask the Messenger and to make yourself available and therefore to see and to determine if you are among those who are needed more here than where you live or if you are needed more where you live than you are here.

As I survey the planetary body and take a reading of its aura, I do see in various areas all over the world, as it were, little ponds and lakes and larger outlines of places of violet flame that have accumulated where you have made the call.

It is my desire in being present with you this evening to acknowledge and to so state that the facts and figures and the equation of the defense posture of the superpowers do provide us not only with a sense of urgency and emergency on a planetary scale but [also with] the enormous challenge of preparing for and planning for our students of Light.

That which has been made known to you and set forth* is a summation of a vast body of information that is known to some of you at inner levels as you come to the Darjeeling Council chambers and that is indeed in the awareness of our Messenger.

These are as things are, and even as some of you are very well informed, not all of you had the awareness of all the facts presented even at our forums of this conference. Knowing well that you did not have the full comprehension of just how extensive is the conspiracy against the health of the Lightbearers upon earth and against their very being and wholeness, we desired to bring this to your consciousness through those who have for many, many years dedicated themselves to these areas of human knowledge. If you turned your attention only to the subjects discussed in these forums, you could see how the conspiracies, the evil and the deadliness themselves, could occupy a major portion of your attention in decrees.

Since those who are causing these manipulative actions are all counted as part of the fallen ones, it is very clear, and emphatically so, that the judgment calls are the only way to slow down their rampage and ravaging throughout the planetary body.

Blessed ones, it is truly to be said that you stand between the children of God and mankind and a far worse fate than what they have already [experienced] and are experiencing. If you can increase this, multiplying your Christ consciousness by transmutation of karma and diligent self-discipline—and therefore multiply your numbers by attracting to yourselves true Christed ones—we will know [it] and you will know [it], for the planet shall become illumined, champions shall arise to defend not only the children of God but you yourselves.

Whether the burden be upon you through the attempt to take the land or [limit] its use or in any other way [to block the Divine Plan], if you can appreciate what I tell you [and heed my counsel, *you shall overcome.* And what I tell you] is this: *to give the calls intensely*—knowing thereby that by the increase of your own Light and Christhood you shall help others do the same and raise up many Christs and open the doors of the planet to Cosmic Beings, knowing, then, that that very eventuality is essential to your Victory in so many ways—[is the key to your preparedness. Thus] you can see that the exigency of the hour is to minimize all lesser distractions and involvements and to be one-pointed in this calling. Beloved hearts, I say to you with all of my love that your

*in the Messenger's July 4 address, in her remarks and lectures at *FREEDOM 1988,* as well as in the Summit University Forums and all that has gone forth from the pulpit and in Saint Germain's stumps since Thanksgiving 1986

survival in every way does depend upon this Victory which I have described.

Therefore, grateful for that which has been accomplished and goading you to greater achievement and sacrifice [which is] absolutely necessary, I remind you that there is much to be done at this ranch and much that is wanting and that those who are here at this time are not able by their numbers nor the hours in the day to meet the timetable that I have set at inner levels for all.

Blessed ones, wherever you are in the world I know that you serve to support every other Keeper of the Flame, but I also wish to make certain that you know that all who serve here serve because they desire to keep the flame and establish a place prepared for you.

I tell you, by the very geometry, by the very x factor of time, resources and experts who are needed, unless some recognize that they must be cut free [to be here now], we will not accomplish that to which we have set our agenda in the timetable that is acceptable to us. Therefore some of you will have to do [some] major thinking [in order] to make major changes in your lives that this Community might remain a nucleus of light and a beacon of hope that remains even while all that is beneath, even in altitude, is in turmoil, tossed and tumbled.

In this hour of my coming and my oneness with you I desire to seal you in my purple fiery heart, and for reasons best known to the Messenger I desire you to visualize in your heart and to keep the flame in your heart of a most beautiful purple heart that does represent our America.

That the flame of Life might be kept in this nation, beloved, it is necessary for you to consecrate your heart to my purple fiery heart, and this is entirely in keeping with your calling to establish the diamond heart of Morya, for, you see, it becomes the heart of Alpha and Omega, the First and the Seventh Rays.

When you come to understand the Presence of the Solar Logoi and those who are seven in number who fulfill that office, you will realize that it is they who initiate you in the manifestation of the heart of each of the seven rays. Thus, in this hour our calling is for two [hearts—the purple heart of Saint Germain and the diamond heart of El Morya—]for this is in itself a great assignment.

Blessed ones, keep my purple heart that the flame of Life might burn on in this nation. I seal you, then, with and in my purple fiery heart. Henceforth, when I abide in you and with you I shall be in that heart. May you develop it by and through my heart meditation.[15]

In this hour I bid you prepare for the coming of the blessed one, the Great Divine Director.

"The Summit Lighthouse Sheds Its Radiance O'er All the World to Manifest as Pearls of Wisdom." This dictation by **Saint Germain** was delivered by the Messenger of the Great White Brotherhood Elizabeth Clare Prophet on **Monday, July 4, 1988,** 10:58–11:54 p.m. MDT, at *FREEDOM 1988* in the Heart of the Inner Retreat at the **Royal Teton Ranch, Park County, Montana.** The Messenger's Fourth of July address delivered prior to the dictation included a panoramic view of the history of freedom in America and how we could lose it; the attack on freedom of religion and private property rights; the threat of war between the superpowers, the state of Soviet and U.S. defense and warfare capabilities, how our leaders have all but destroyed our opportunity to keep the flame of liberty and what we can do about it. Available on three audiocassettes, 4 hr. 8 min., A88122, $19.50 (add $.95 for postage); four 1-hr. cable TV shows for home use: HL88043, HL88044, HL88045, HL88046, $19.95 each (add $1.10 each for postage); part 1 also available on 74-min. videocassette HP88063, $19.95 (add $1.10 for postage). Saint Germain's dictation available on 90-min. audiocassette with that of the Great Divine Director, B88105, $6.50 (add $.55 for postage); on videocassette with dictations of Paul the Venetian and the Maha Chohan, 1 hr. 42 min., HP88073, $19.95 (add $1.10 for postage). [**N.B.** Bracketed material denotes words unspoken yet implicit in the dictation, added by the Messenger under Saint Germain's direction for clarity in the written word.] **(1)** Note from the Messenger: So great a reward for so little we give by comparison to Saint Germain's service to the earth surely warrants a new and fervent daily commitment to the *Save the World with Violet Flame! by Saint Germain 1, 2, 3,* **and 4** audiocassettes. May you, then, repeat the original 33-day violet flame vigil, so devotedly followed in March and April 1988 with the first tape, using any combination of the four tapes. I suggest you simply give them consecutively day by day in two 45-minute, three half-hour, or six 15-minute sessions a day if you cannot give the full 90 minutes in a single sitting. By this 33-day vigil all are laying a solid foundation for the secret-ray initiations described in the 1988 *Pearls of Wisdom,* pp. 466, 467, 489–91, 495–96, 497, 500, 539–40, 541, 542. Do not neglect your own favorite protection calls from the blue section of your decree books. Now you can use the four El Morya cassettes to fulfill this requirement. Stock up by ordering any 10 decree tapes at $2.95 each in quantities of 10 or more. Add $1.50 for postage for 10 ($.15 each additional). And whether you decree slow or fast, let your decrees be cups of Light for your devotion and powerful transmission of the Light of God which never fails to give earth her freedom now. **(2) Sandinista/Contra cease-fire agreement.** Just prior to the release of *Save the World with Violet Flame! by Saint Germain 1* audiocassette in early March 1988, the U.S.-backed Nicaraguan Contras had reached a critical point in their seven-year-old war against the Soviet-backed Sandinista government. Prospects of renewed U.S. military aid for the Contras looked bleak; nonmilitary supplies from the U.S. were also running out and on March 3, 1988, Congress defeated a $30.8 million nonlethal aid package, making the Contras' continued survival tenuous. In mid-March some 2,000 Sandinista troops stormed into Honduras in pursuit of the Contras and came close to capturing a main supply depot that stocked nearly half of the Contras' remaining supply of weapons and ammunition. In response, the United States dispatched 3,500 troops to Honduras' Palmerola Air Base on March 17; by the following week the U.S. presence, together with Honduran bombing strikes against Sandinista positions along the Nicaragua-Honduras border, defused the conflict (see 1988 *Pearls of Wisdom,* p. 339 n. 4).

On March 21, during the Keepers' 33-day vigil with *Save the World 1,* the Contras and the Sandinistas in an abrupt turnaround began their first face-to-face cease-fire negotiations. It was an event that astonished White House officials. All fighting halted during the three-day peace talks held in the Nicaraguan town of Sapoá, three miles from the Costa Rican border. The negotiations appeared to falter the first day when the Nicaraguan government rejected Contra demands to link a cease-fire agreement with the democratization of Nicaragua. But the mood unexpectedly softened and the Sandinistas agreed to discuss political issues. The talks concluded on March 23 with a cease-fire accord, which commenced April 1. The Sandinistas pledged not to punish or persecute returning exiles for their political-military acts and agreed to release some 3,300 political prisoners. They also promised "unrestricted freedom of expression" and participation in municipal and national elections for all citizens. The Contras agreed to recognize Sandinista rule, to move into designated cease-fire zones in Nicaragua, to accept only humanitarian aid delivered through neutral agencies, and to disarm once a final accord was signed. Both sides also agreed to continue negotiations on April 6 toward a definitive cease-fire. In order to sustain the Contras during the cease-fire, Congress overwhelmingly approved a new $48 million nonlethal aid package. House Speaker James C. Wright, Jr., promised not to block any future consideration of military aid should the peace talks collapse.

By the end of April, after almost a month of negotiations, a final accord between the

Contras and the Sandinistas still had not been reached. Thousands of Contra soldiers began crossing into Honduras in order to receive food, clothing and medicine supplied by the United States. When talks ended without an agreement on June 9, the Contra leadership had become divided by internal power struggles; the Sandinistas, increasingly repressive toward their critics and political opponents, had many times over repudiated their commitment to bring democratic reforms to Nicaragua. *Insight* magazine (10 October 1988) reported that the Permanent Commission on Human Rights, an organization which documents charges made against the Sandinistas, said "in a recent report that new political prisoners were being taken at an 'alarming rate.'. . . The commission estimates that the government is holding at least 8,000 such prisoners of conscience." The commission's director said that the Sandinistas have apparently been using the cease-fire period to identify Contra-sympathizers, to force political opponents into the army, and to increase bombing in rural areas and relocate peasants into militarized "cooperatives." In September Sandinista representatives and Contra leaders met in Gautemala City for the first time in three months as a preliminary step to resuming peace negotiations. To date, the March truce is still in effect but both sides remain keenly divided on ways to end the civil war. **(3)** The **Dark Cycle** began on April 23, 1969, and marked the beginning of the cycle of the intensification of the return of karma. In this period of transition from the Piscean to the Aquarian age, the Great Law requires that the evolutions of planet earth deal directly with the momentums of personal and planetary karma set aside for centuries by the grace of God through his Sons incarnate (i.e., Jesus Christ and other avatars). In the face of the same propensity for darkness prevalent before the Flood, when "the wickedness of man was great in the earth" and "every imagination of the thoughts of his heart was only evil continually" (Gen. 6:5), the Lords of Karma decreed this action in order to deter an even greater abuse of Life's opportunity and to forestall that cataclysm which may be the ultimate consequence of the rising tide of world sin. On August 20, 1969, the Messengers explained that "the coming of the Dark Cycle simply means that the hand of mercy that for centuries has stood between mankind and their own dark deeds has been withdrawn. The law of God will bring swift and compelling judgment to those who have thought they could flaunt the law." Be not deceived; God is not mocked: for whatsoever a man soweth, that shall he also reap. (Gal. 6:7)

Charting the Dark Cycle on the Cosmic Clock, we place April 23, 1969, in Capricorn on the 12 o'clock line. Progressing it one line each year moving clockwise places the current Dark Cycle on the 7 o'clock line in Leo from April 23, 1988, to April 23, 1989. During this year mankind will be dealing with karmic initiations under the hierarchy of Leo: insensitivity to life, ingratitude and inappreciation of the Great God in all his manifold expression, thoughtlessness, spiritual blindness, emotional density and retardation and all misuses of the flame of God's love. See *Kuthumi On Selfhood* (1969 *Pearls of Wisdom*), pp. xi–xii, 10, 30, 246–54, 263–66. **(4)** In autumn 1986 while the staff of Church Universal and Triumphant were in the process of establishing the Church's headquarters on our ranch in Park County, Montana, the Montana Department of Health and Environmental Sciences (DHES) requested our cooperation in conducting an **Environmental Impact Study** because of concerns and criticisms expressed to them by certain local residents and environmentalists. This, in effect, halted the planned development of our community. Over a period of 15 months we worked closely with the DHES to conduct a thorough environmental investigation. Outside experts were brought in to study a variety of issues, including potential impact of development on wildlife, fisheries, air and water quality, geological and soil quality, archaeological and historical sites, and governmental services. A 160-page Draft Environmental Impact Statement (EIS) incorporating the results of this study was released by the DHES February 19, 1988. This was followed by a 60-day comment period to allow the public to submit their opinions on the document or provide additional factual information. In addition, on March 21 a public meeting was held to solicit comments. The Church Board of Directors subsequently provided the DHES with written responses to all comments received. The Final EIS is expected to be issued by the DHES in the near future. **(5) Second death.** Rev. 2:11; 20:14; 21:8. **(6) Judgment of the Watchers and their offspring** prophesied in the Book of Enoch. 1988 *Pearls of Wisdom*, p. 492 n. 3. **(7) Abductions by aliens to save their dying races.** Budd Hopkins, the nation's foremost authority on UFO abduction phenomena, has concluded that aliens are collecting genetic material from humans to save their dying races. He claims that reports of men and women who say they have been abducted by aliens in UFOs indicate that ova were taken from women or they were artificially inseminated, that those who became pregnant were subsequently abducted and had their fetuses removed for development in alien "nurseries," and that sperm samples were taken from men. Some have suggested that the aliens are conducting abductions to study human behavior and to create hybrids because their race is dying due to genetic changes that have occurred over the centuries. See Elizabeth Clare Prophet's July 1, 1988 Summit University Forum with four experts on UFOs, "The UFO Connection: Alien Spacecraft and Government Secrecy": TV show 2, "Abducted by Aliens: The Common Threads of Experience," 1-hr. videocassette, HL88039, $19.95 (add $1.10 for postage); 79-min. audiocassette B88118, $5.95 ($.55 for postage). Entire forum available on five 1-hr. cable TV shows for home use and on four audiocassettes (see 1988 *Pearls of Wisdom*, p. 492 n. 2). Budd Hopkins, *Intruders: The Incredible Visitations at Copley Woods*, available from Summit University Press, $19.95 (add $1.50 for postage). **(8) Short time.** Rev. 12:12. **(9) Final Judgment.** Rev. 20:11–15. **(10) The 19th All-Union Communist Party Conference,** the first since 1941, took place in the Kremlin's Palace of Congresses in Moscow from June 28 to July 1, 1988. The four-day event attended by 4,991 Communist Party delegates was marked by an unprecedented display of open debate on General Secretary Mikhail Gorbachev's program of *perestroika* (restructuring) and the political future of the Soviet Union. Soviet citizens and foreigners alike found the freedom of speech astonishing. The proceedings were broadcast on nightly television summaries to the Soviet Union and other nations, with one Moscow resident reportedly commenting, "I am hearing things on television that weeks ago I would never have whispered over the telephone." While some spoke out in support of *perestroika,* there was also frequent criticism that Gorbachev's reform program has produced few tangible results for Soviet citizens. One delegate, a metalworker, said, "Where is *perestroika* when the supply of goods in shops is as poor as ever?"

Following the comments made by the delegates, Gorbachev held a series of votes and won conference approval for virtually all of his proposals to restructure the government. In six resolutions that may take several years to fully implement, the conference endorsed *perestroika,* the expansion of *glasnost* (Gorbachev's policy of openness), political reorganization, the establishment of legal protections for citizens, greater autonomy for Soviet regions, and the streamlining of the bureaucracy. Some of the most important measures endorsed would create a new national legislature called the Congress of People's Deputies as well as a smaller parliament to handle day-to-day legislative business; would strengthen popularly elected local councils and reduce the vast power of the Communist Party (to which only 7 percent of the population belongs); and would empower the now chiefly ceremonial post of president with the authority to set domestic and foreign policies. The unspoken yet widely assumed implication was that the office of president would be filled by Gorbachev himself. Some Soviets reportedly noted that Gorbachev's current role as general secretary of the Communist Party combined with an expanded office of president would give him greater formal authority than Joseph Stalin had possessed.

On September 30, 1988, in a hastily called meeting of the 300-member Central Committee (the Soviet Union's policy-making body), Gorbachev moved to implement the conference mandate by dramatically reorganizing the 20-member Politburo (the highest body of the Communist Party), thereby strengthening his position as party leader. Three veteran members from the Brezhnev era were dismissed; two members, Yegor K. Ligachev (generally perceived as the second most powerful man in the Kremlin) and Viktor M. Chebrikov (head of the KGB intelligence and security agency), both of whom were critical of the pace of Gorbachev's reforms, were shifted into positions that are likely to diminish their political influence; and four new members, all Gorbachev supporters, were appointed. President Andrei A. Gromyko, a Politburo member, as well as Anatoly F. Dobrynin, former ambassador to the United States and Central Committee secretary, were both retired. On the next day, October 1, Gorbachev consolidated his leadership by assuming the vacated presidency, which is expected to be assigned its broad new powers sometime next year, and appointed Vladimir A. Kryuchkov as new KGB chief. These developments were executed with little explanation as to why the sudden upheavals were taking place. The open debates and expressions of *glasnost* which characterized the summer conference were nonexistent. **(11) Forgive us our debts.** Matt. 6:12, 14, 15; Luke 11:4. **(12)** Two-week retreats at the **universities of the Spirit** conducted by the Lords of the Seven Rays and the Maha Chohan. 1988 *Pearls of Wisdom*, p. 544 n. 11. **(13) Five Dhyāni Buddhas:** Vairochana, Akshobhya, Ratnasambhava, Amitābha, Amoghasiddhi. **(14)** *Kuan Yin's Crystal Rosary: Devotions to the Divine Mother East and West* is a New Age ritual of hymns, prayers and Chinese mantras which invoke the presence of the Bodhisattva of Compassion. The rosary was released in its final version as a 3-audiocassette album the day of Saint Germain's dictation. See 1988 *Pearls of Wisdom*, pp. 373 n. 13, 480 n. 7. **(15) Saint Germain's Heart Meditation I and II.** 1988 *Pearls of Wisdom*, pp. 339 n. 6, 479 n. 3.

Pearls of Wisdom®

published by The Summit Lighthouse

| Vol. 31 No. 73 | *The Beloved Great Divine Director* | *October 30, 1988* |

FREEDOM 1988

18

A Path of Karma Yoga

Enhanced by a Rod of Illumination of Solar Logoi

Warmest greetings from the Lords of Karma.

You who have espoused a path of karma yoga[1] embracing the highest calling of the sacred fire[2] are dear to the hearts of those of us who watch and wait as lifetime after lifetime the millions who abide on this planet do not move the boulders of karma or karmic pride.

When we have such chelas who, cooperating with the destiny of karmic cycles of a planet, enter into these cycles and in many cases ride them by the triumphant invocation of the Light,[3] surely it does gratify our hearts and give to us that confirmation of sustaining grace that because some understand and some embody the flame of the Lords of Karma, the many may also one day do so.

In the happiness of the stars that twinkle in the night beyond the clouds, I invite you to be seated in my Cave of Light.[4]

Surely the hour of initiation is upon you. Surely it is the hour when the counting of all that you endure and enter into for the badges of Love (for the stars that twinkle in your auras) must afford you with the greatest protection, the greatest sealing for the new way of life to come.

I come to you, beloved ones, to explain to you that though in recent years by your service Saint Germain did gain his freedom from the karmic abuses of the violet flame of many lifestreams,[5] in this hour of the failure of the leadership of this nation to heed his call and warning and communications at inner levels, he has, as it were, lost the ability to seek new dispensations, whether in this nation or for the sons and daughters of Canada or [for] any other nation who [may] seek his sponsorship.

Beloved ones, today all that he can bequeath to any is what the very ones who shall benefit by the dispensation shall invoke. It is almost like your modern banking houses where if you desire to have a loan and have no credit, you are required to have on deposit the full amount of the loan you would take from the bank.

Blessed ones, the Master, therefore being desirous of helping you, has provided you with an understanding of numerous avenues of individual acceleration on the Path whereby a greater balance could be held on the earth and greater good karma accrue to you. I would like to add to [this], beloved ones, something that the beloved Saint Germain would not say to you, for he would not put upon you even the slightest pressure to engage in service that may not be, in fact, to your desiring.

Thus it is so that the great good karma you make in the saving of a planet and America will indeed go directly to his mantle and heart and causal body and thereby regain for him what has been lost [through the actions of this government which were causative] in his leaving the nation's capital.[6]

Blessed ones, if his return and a continued action on the part of Alpha must be preceded by the defense of freedom spiritually, militarily, then we must all have profound compassion [for the Master], as in reviewing the facts and circumstances it is quite plain that this event is not about to occur on the morrow.

Blessed ones, the devastation of this nation according to the scenario that has been logically outlined* should† surely be a great loss to the Ascended Master Saint Germain. Do you think the leadership of this nation will ever be able to pay the price for their infamy? I tell you, nay. Yet it is the Light of God and the sponsorship of Saint Germain which they have indeed misqualified. So you see, those who have the cosmic bank account in their causal bodies—the ascended hosts of Light and their chelas—[it is they who] must pay the price.[7]

Now this ought to kindle in you the wrath of the Divine Mother and the great beings of Light of the Mother Flame who frequent the Cave of Light in India. And you should say to yourselves, "I will not stand still for this abuse of Light of the grants and dispensations given to Saint Germain in my behalf and for my benefit. And therefore I know that unless judgment come swiftly to these abusers of the Light, it will not be Saint Germain alone but I myself who will [be required to] engage in that service to pay that price of the misused energy. And therefore [by my service to the Light and my call for Divine Justice I will] not allow Saint Germain to be in bondage any longer than necessary to this evolution."

---

*outlined by the Messenger in her July 4 address and in her chronicling of the facts and figures since Saint Germain made his prediction concerning a Soviet nuclear first strike against the United States, Thanksgiving 1986 †would

I am certain there is not a true Keeper of the Flame on earth who would not tarry in his forward advancement and evolution even beyond the ascended state if that Keeper of the Flame felt that Saint Germain's burden was so great. Thus, you see, your mandala of Light is most precious to my Son's heart. And I, too, am profoundly grateful [for your service and support], for it is wonderful to see his face and the smile upon that blessed visage when he does look upon you and with joy behold your love.

Those of the Darjeeling Council of the Great White Brotherhood and all those who serve this evolution are most attentive to beloved Saint Germain in this hour. Thus has Portia come forward, lowering her manifestation more closely to the physical octave in support of the Beloved,[8] and thus has Kuan Yin [come forward] and now you have heard [that] the Dhyāni Buddhas [have come forward];[9] so you realize that all of heaven has profound respect and honor and compassion for a Master who has given his all and who stands to lose so much by the betrayal of those who once did espouse the cause of freedom.

And though they, [i.e., the leadership], had karma, beloved, they had every good reason to champion freedom, for it is they who will need it most when, standing before the Four and Twenty Elders, they are shown that their very abuse of freedom has denied to them the freedom and [the] freedom flame they require even to make it at all.

Beloved ones, as you consider how a leadership with a certain timetable could find itself in the camp of the enemy, swept by a hypnosis, by some kind of a mind influence, do you not wonder and consider and admit at the conscious threshold of awareness that there could be some network of a conspiracy upon those whose minds are not tethered to God and [who] therefore, being not tethered to God, are otherwise vulnerable to aliens who have long ago mastered the art of mind manipulation?

Blessed ones, we do not speak too much of these things because, of course, the attention goes to oneself, even as when you heard of abductions by aliens[10] nary a person present did not have a fleeting thought and wonder if ever in this or a previous life he had had an experience comparable to those described.

Blessed ones, the manipulation of the minds of this people of this planet is almost universal. The only ones who are exempt are those on a spiritual path who do invoke the Light* through their allegiance to this or that manifestation of the Godhead. Those who keep a spiritual flame within them in true devotion are sealed in a spiritual fire that does actually, because we have seen to it, coat the central nervous system and the brain that they might remain the independent and creative thinkers. This is done by

*as the consciousness of God, the Universal Mind

merit, beloved, not by dispensation, and that merit is established through the science of mantra.

Well it is, then, to recite simply the mantras, the bija syllables of the Dhyāni Buddhas, of the feminine deities, to use your bhajans.[11] All of these devotions [offered by the devotee] by the science of the Word, no matter what the religion, are honored according to the love of the heart. For the love of the heart is the magnet that draws down not only the Light of the Principle of the Godhead but also the very Presence of that Master [or masterful Being who may be the object of devotion].

And so you see, beloved, you yourselves who know [of aliens moving in your midst, you who also] move among mankind, those of you who know yourselves in the sense of your typical shortcomings or lapses [of Christ-Self awareness and action] must understand the repetitive quality [of error you express] as though some arch-devil with forked tongue and pitchfork might be poking you in the same place repetitively. You see and understand how with great remorse you may momentarily be the instrument of some ignorant animal magnetism, some act of spiritual blindness. And when it does cause hurt to others you have profound regret, as hot tears of remorse may stream down your face. And the thing that you de-sired least to do, you became the instrument of.*

Blessed ones, it is a fact of life on this planet that few own their own consciousness. Consider simply how most people are the prod-ucts of [their] astrology. Now, it would be one thing if they were the manifestation of the [Godly attributes of the] twelve hierarchies of the Sun, who are Cosmic Beings and initiators on the twelve lines of the [Cosmic] Clock, but people are often a manifestation of the positive and negative qualities that have been assigned to their astrological sign. Blessed ones, it is as though one were cast in a mold of limitation and a certain behavior pattern. But you surely know [that] this [typical behavior pattern of your human self] is not the nature of your Holy Christ Self.

Therefore, the purpose of all of our dictations and our teach-ings to you is that you might re-create yourselves in the image and likeness of that Divine Christhood, even the 'Krishna' of oneself, the pattern of the Cosmic Christ that uniquely becomes the identity and individuality of one's Real Self, even as light rays from the sun have that special quality and emanation.

Thus, to fulfill the God consciousness, let us say, of the hierarchy of Gemini is a means whereby through interconnecting lines of force you may also realize the God consciousness, one by one, of the rest of the [solar] hierarchies [positioned on the lines of

*Yet you do not reckon with the actuality that you may be dealing with malevolent forces who seek to deter your progress on the spiritual path and do so by projecting misqualified energy into weaknesses in the psychological and astrological structure of the karmic self.

the Cosmic Clock]. But to be merely a creation of habit, not too much more conscious than a mechanization man—as Homo sapiens, above the species but not much above it, not having the consciousness of the threefold flame—is to truly be a creature of astrological habit and pattern. Of course, this is not the fulfillment of God-mastery as we know it in the ascended octave [and as you can know it here below].

In pointing this out to you, then, beloved, I desire first and foremost that you own your own thoughts and that you own up to your accountability for your thoughts, feelings and actions, failures and successes. And without being either paranoid or having a neurosis, you should also take into consideration that some of the faults that you have faulted yourself with [for] are highly exaggerated by the masters of deceit who desire to manipulate you by so amplifying these unwanted traits as to make you feel almost worthless and helpless and the victim of your own human creation when this in fact you are not—when in fact you have more mastery than you are realizing or expressing but you are accepting a grid of energy that is keeping you bound to a very narrow room of consciousness.

I would speak to you, then, of the gift of the Solar Logoi which they made to all who have a threefold flame as the dispensation granted at the Shasta conference. This took place in 1975 as an increment of Light, a rod of illumination [conveyed through the crown chakra in consonance with the Christ Self], and [this initiation] does take place once in ten thousand years and [it] was activated in all who have the threefold flame and have allegiance to the Light.[12] It was not given to the fallen ones or their mechanization man.

I will tell you precisely why this [rod of illumination] was given, beloved: [it was] so that you might have this electrode of Cosmic Christ energy within you, providing a nucleus to turn around all that has been superimposed upon you, [including] any and all implants of the Luciferians; [it was so that you might have] a nucleus to draw and create a whirling sun within of the momentum that you should invoke in this lifetime by the recitation of the bija mantras. Those seed syllables, which represent both Principles of the Godhead and Cosmic Beings, are [a means whereby your I AM Presence is] able to restore to you that Universal Christ consciousness.

It is our desire, then, to restore in you the right-mindfulness of the Lord of the World, Gautama. Seeing, then, from the position of the Solar Logoi the desperate need for the restoration of the true Mind of God in the Lightbearers of the earth, [we see that] this dispensation came [in order] that for the remaining quarter of the century the Lightbearers should have every advantage possible to increase Divine Awareness.

Therefore, in looking upon those who are apparently being

manipulated by sinister strategies and forces (such as the representatives of this government who are simply moving as one mass as a herd of lemmings[13] to their own self-destruction), could you not consider that they [might be] under a ray of the fallen ones? And [that] due to the absence of the Light [in their psyche] and their noncommitment to the Light they [might] be vulnerable to forces of Evil far superior [in techniques of mind and genetic engineering and in their use of the black arts] to the levels [to which they themselves have attained in] their own involvements in the false hierarchy?

Inasmuch, then, as they are not Keepers of the Flame and therefore did not receive this increment [of Light], can you not realize that that which seems so obvious [to you (who do have the rod of illumination)] as the [true] logic of the [global] situation is not theirs simply because not only do they not have the electrode of the Solar Logoi, but they do not have an allegiance to the Mind of God? And [can you not also realize that] therefore there is an attrition of the intelligence of the Universal Mind which they once had but [which] at this time [they] no longer have a nucleus to retain?

Thus, they are already involved in the disintegration spiral, and the more they counteract the great universal momentums of freedom, the more they become entrenched in their own ignorance and "ignore-ance" of the Law and the more the disintegration spiral does accelerate.

When you use the term *logic,* beloved ones, you are always speaking of the Logos, you are always speaking of the Divine Word. So when you have and possess the powers of the true logic of the Mind of Christ, you know that you have access to that logic through the focus, or forcefield, of that Christ in you. The Christ above you is your Holy Christ Self but when you receive such an increment, such a rod of Light* from the Solar Logoi, you then have a focus of the Solar Logoi that is pulsating at all times within the forcefield of your own brain, which focus is a part [of] and one with the crown chakra.

As day by day you increase in the wisdom of God and in knowledge, as day by day you transcend the self-limiting doctrines of Church and State of this world—because that forcefield [of the rod of illumination] is in you, because you decree, because the day of your Christhood is dawning—in proportion to that acceleration [which] you experience, the ones who have received not the Light and whose judgment is upon them [for misappropriating the Light they once had] are losing: [*they* are] losing their capacity to think, to reason, to probe the Matter spheres and to act responsibly on behalf of the people they represent.

Are you not, then, observing the disintegration of a class of fallen ones? And in understanding, yes, the logic of this, can you

*increment of the Universal Christ consciousness

not begin to see why you who consider yourselves perhaps simple folk, perhaps educated, perhaps of good backgrounds but not necessarily the power elite or the most wealthy on the planet, how you in your way could have a more profound understanding [of the patterns of planetary karma and of the planetary geopolitical configuration] than all of that [so-called knowledge] which is held by these fallen ones?

It is not merely that they know and that they are deceptive, beloved ones. It is that they have begun *not* to know. Where they were once clever, they are now simply absent[—absentminded, i.e., absent the Mind of God, hence mindless].

The affliction of diseases of the mind and the nervous system is another form of disintegration, and yet these diseases have afflicted those of the Light as well, because of the problem of, [i.e., complexities of], chemicals and diet and karma. Thus, there are karmic diseases, but there are [also] diseases that mark the last days of those who must face the judgment.

I remind you, then, of this gift of the Solar Logoi so that you may call for that focus to be amplified [within you], so that you may intensify the action of golden Christ illumination [through your own crown chakra] and take note of the Archangel Jophiel who determined to be here this evening to overshadow this entire event, so desiring to give you a maximum forcefield of illumination to receive the Universal Christ and Jesus and these beings [the Seven Solar Logoi] who do indeed endow solar systems which they embody [with a Universal Christ intelligence].

I am placing the great blue sphere of my causal body around this place. Breathe deeply and breathe in the sacred fire of the First Ray that you might imbibe the inner blueprint I hold for you and [that] in exhaling [you might] transfer to your four lower bodies the inner blueprint held by your Christ Self and by my conception of the divine direction of the One.

This great blue sphere of my causal body does encompass this entire Heart in concentration. It is established, reinforced and made more physical by angel devas of the will of God to that purpose to which Lord Gautama comes—to release the Love Ray for the bonding of Community.

As this takes place, beloved, I withdraw to the inner circle of that sphere and bid you prepare now for Jesus' coming by singing an hymn to him.

This dictation was **delivered** by the Messenger Elizabeth Clare Prophet on **Tuesday, July 5, 1988,** 12:00–12:30 a.m. MDT. [**N.B.** Bracketed material denotes words unspoken yet implicit in the dictation, added by the Messenger under the Great Divine Director's direction for clarity in the written word.] (**1**) In Hindu teachings **karma yoga** is a path to union with God through nonattached action and selfless service whereby the devotee recognizes that God is the doer of the action. Karma yoga is one of four principal paths of union with the Divine; the others are the yogas of bhakti (devotion), jnana (wisdom), and raja (royal or complete).

(2) The Ascended Masters teach that the path of karma yoga is the balancing of karma through both the Work and Word of the Lord—through service to the Great White Brotherhood and to all life on earth as well as through the invocation of the **sacred fire** in the science of the spoken Word. The invocation of the sacred fire is the path of agni yoga (the yoga of fire) and raja yoga (the royal road to reintegration). (3) *Save the World with Violet Flame! by Saint Germain 1, 2, 3* and *4* audiocassettes are the means whereby you can assist in the sacred ritual of world transmutation. See 1988 *Pearls of Wisdom*, pp. 400 n. 6, 560 n. 1. (4) The **Cave of Light** is the retreat of the Great Divine Director in India. He also maintains a retreat in Transylvania, the focus of freedom for Europe. (5) On July 1, 1984, Arcturus and Victoria announced the beginning of a 72-week prayer vigil to help balance the **karmic debt incurred by Saint Germain** during his sponsorship of "endeavors for which he had secured grants from the Karmic Board in the last 400 years" —grants for which he has had "to pay the price for faithless, reprehensible mortals who stole his light." During the 72 weeks, the Messenger stumped the nations, carrying Saint Germain's message of the Coming Revolution in Higher Consciousness to Australia, the Philippines and Hawaii (February–March 1985) and Europe, Canada and New York City (October 1985). On November 17, 1985 (the final day of the 72-week vigil as well as the day the Stump concluded) the Goddess of Liberty, dictating in New York City, said that the "last vestiges" of the untransmuted burdens of Saint Germain "are now swiftly passing into the flame" and asked for a continued vigil of violet flame calls for a fortnight "to immerse the planet in violet flame." On January 1, 1986, Gautama Buddha made the joyous announcement that "by the united effort of the entire Spirit of the Great White Brotherhood the burden complete of Saint Germain's incurred karma is lifted, transmuted and sent back to the Great Central Sun purified." Saint Germain then explained, regarding any new dispensations he might now be able to request from the Lords of Karma, that "the substance of light is there. It is there on demand. And I am instructed to demand it as you present and show the most effective, workable, and successful programs for delivering this message to the world and for the building of the Inner Retreat." See 1986 *Pearls of Wisdom,* pp. 32–33, 182–83, 187, 193–94 n. 8. (6) **Saint Germain leaves the nation's capital.** On November 29, 1987, in Washington, D.C., Saint Germain announced, "It is the last time that I shall appear in this nation's capital unless and until those who know better do better. . . . For America has abdicated her role as the nation of Christhood. . . . I shall not be here, beloved, to deliver to you another statement of my word or my call unless the representatives of the people, from the highest office in the land to the least, shall take their stand for the defense of Freedom." 1987 *Pearls of Wisdom,* p. 611. (7) Inasmuch as the majority of the leadership is spiritually bankrupt, having spent their Light in "riotous living" (Luke 15:13), they could not pay the enormous karmic debt of the loss of America or of universal freedom on earth which would accrue to them if the scenario outlined should come to pass. (8) Portia, 1988 *Pearls of Wisdom,* pp. 326, 330, 331. (9) Saint Germain, 1988 *Pearls of Wisdom,* p. 556. (10) **Abductions by aliens**. On July 1, 1988, Elizabeth Clare Prophet interviewed four authorities on UFOs on her Summit University Forum "The UFO Connection: Alien Spacecraft and Government Secrecy" (see 1988 *Pearls of Wisdom*, pp. 492 n. 2, 561 n. 7). For additional reading see Budd Hopkins, *Intruders: The Incredible Visitations at Copley Woods* (New York: Random House, 1987), $19.95; Lawrence Fawcett and Barry J. Greenwood, *Clear Intent: The Government Coverup of the UFO Experience* (Englewood Cliffs, N.J.: Prentice-Hall, 1984), $8.95; Richard Hall, *Uninvited Guests: A Documented History of UFO Sightings, Alien Encounters & Coverups* (Santa Fe, N. Mex.: Aurora Press, 1988), $14.00. All available from Summit University Press, add $1.50 each for postage. (11) **Bija mantras and bhajans.** See the Summit University Press 30th anniversary sale catalog, pp. 18, 19, 31 (special discount of $2.95 each when you buy any 10 cassettes listed on p. 18). (12) **Rod of illumination.** Apollo, "An Increment of Light from the Holy Kumaras," in *The Great White Brotherhood in the Culture, History and Religion of America*, pp. 269–70, 273. (13) **lemmings:** any of several small, mouselike rodents found chiefly in the arctic or northern regions of Eurasia and North America; known for their periodic mass migrations, which some scientists theorize may be linked to conditions such as seasonal changes in habitat, population explosions, stress from overcrowding, or depletion of food supply. Approximately every three or four years in Scandinavia, the Norway lemming *(Lemmus lemmus)* descends in great numbers from the tundra, moving slowly and relentlessly in a straight path. Eventually arriving at the sea, they continue their march into the water and the whole herd drowns, a phenomenon that has given rise to the popular belief that lemmings commit mass suicide. Scientists do not completely understand why the migrations occur. One theory offered in the late 1800s was that migrating Norwegian lemmings are seeking their ancient home, the sunken continent of Atlantis which once bordered Scandinavia, and are therefore motivated by an inherited instinct, not a deliberate desire for suicide.

Pearls of Wisdom®
published by The Summit Lighthouse

Vol. 31 No. 74   *Beloved Jesus Christ*   November 5, 1988

FREEDOM 1988
19
The Piercing of the Crown Chakra
Prepare Ye the Day of Maitreya
God-Mastery Is Our Calling to You

Lo, I AM come to you! For, my beloved, is it not in the midnight hour, as it is prophesied, that the thief should come?[1] Thus, let the bride enter the secret chamber of the heart,[2] for I come and I come to tell you why this conference is so key in the chain of your spiritual evolution.

I, Jesus, your elder brother on the Path, standing in shafts of illumination's flame with Jophiel and his bands, Lord Gautama above, and the Solar Logoi as though arrayed by the hand of God across the sky... What for, then? To establish golden illumination's flame, to increase Light of the mind: for God-mastery is our calling to you.

Come. Come now to be seated in the heart of the Grand Teton as I speak to you of illumination's destiny in your life.

As the embodiment of the Christ flame to you in this hour, I come as spokesman, as it were, for the Solar Logoi. They return, beloved, to nourish the seed of Light implanted.[3] They come to increase Cosmic Christ consciousness—solar consciousness of the Word. For by that Mind of God in you shall the defeat of the violators of that Mind come about.

As important as the moment at Shasta when through Elohim of the Second Ray this was accomplished, so [it is] in this hour: [their return] is for the piercing of the crown and the single drop of blood, that you might also experience the remission of sin by the shedding of blood.[4] This blood represents the essence of the divine nectar sealed in the crown, waiting to be opened.[5]

Thus it is a moment of purging. It is a moment of release. It is a moment you have long anticipated. For this sacred mystery and ritual of the piercing of the crown chakra is known by you; for at inner levels you have been taught that it should come to you. Therefore our Lord Gautama did send forth the Call [to his own to be present at *FREEDOM 1988*], as did the Messenger. Happy are ye who have responded, for it is a personal and physical action, beloved, and it does take place in this moment. [15-second pause] (All associated with this property in service and devotion so receive the same.)*

Your determination to be with Solar Logoi is wise indeed. And for the explanations which have preceded my own I would say to you, beloved, that it is the concern of Cosmic Beings of Light that your increase in illumination's flame be your protection and the open door to your God-mastery.

Now we seek to intensify the wisdom cross.[6] Be attentive, then, to all detail. These signs, beloved, of the hierarchs [of] Sagittarius and Gemini, Pisces and Virgo will assist you in balancing your inner forces for the opening of the crown chakra, and it is [through] the opening of the crown chakra [that] Solar Logoi will enable you to increase and magnetize more of that rod of illumination within. In that sun dance and sun presence of the Light you shall know a day-by-day oneness with the Christ flame.

O let go of the mundane! Let go of the flattery of the marketplace of life. Be no longer worldly in that sense, beloved. Be kind and respectful to all [whom] you meet, but let my heart receive now the lower animal magnetism, the mutual ego flattery and flirting that does take place and is so prevalent and does so rob you of the substance of your electromagnetic field. You cannot please God and mammon.[7] You cannot please the world which has need of your Light and still retain that Light.

Let those who know you and love you love you for that which you are within, and be not concerned if in order to gain on a path of illumination you must let go somewhat of these lesser interchanges of the world's personality cult. You have had it long enough. Have done with it! And let there be a conservation of the nectar of the crown chakra.

Prepare ye the day of the Lord Maitreya. Prepare ye his day.[8]

The destiny of a planetary home is solely dependent upon those who, recognizing the necessity of fanning the fire of the heart with God-mastery, so realize that the single greatest achievement of that accomplishment must be to go on and use the magnet of the heart for the raising of the sacred fire all the way to the level of the crown.

Blessed hearts, the crown chakra within you should begin to tingle in this moment; and that tingling does come, for the action

---

*This initiation was received only by those physically present, staff and volunteers working at their posts to put on *FREEDOM 1988* included. It is not transferred through the audio- or videotapes or the written word.

of the Solar Logoi has begun. And if you do not feel that tingling, I only counsel you to increase your application of the violet flame and when calling it forth to concentrate upon the crown chakra; and by and by through transmutation you shall know a greater activation of that crown in you.

Aim. Sarasvati,[9] assist now, for the opening is come.

For the prize of this high calling,* all diligence in the Second Ray and Second Ray application of decrees should be your pursuit— but never to the neglect of the First and the Seventh Rays.

There is a way and a science of God-mastery. It is yours. It is yours, beloved. It is yours in this hour. Have not all signs pointed to this moment—my own dictations to you, the Mystery School, Maitreya's almost doting upon you, the presence of Shamballa, the Western Shamballa, even the very initiation of Solar Logoi through Apollo and Lumina thirteen years ago? Does the very number not signify a [portent for the] completion of that Christ Principle in you?

The lines of force meet in the thousand-petaled lotus [of the crown chakra]. *Let the Wisdom School appear.* Immediately it is the desire of Kuan Yin to see dissolved in you the dullard consciousness, the ignorance, the grossness and the crassness. All of this comes for† the nondeveloped crown chakra.

The destiny of a planet, then, is based solely upon those who, having developed the heart, open the crown and therefore may hold the intelligence of the Mind of God and the direction of the Great Divine Director for the coursings of events and "the Grand Denouement."

Solar Logoi sponsoring this solar system in the heart of the Word approach nearer to the physical by the grid of Light you form in this oneness. Helios and Vesta send rays of Light that connect with the crown chakras.

I, Jesus, require you to call for the binding, the judgment, and the casting out of Antichrist from this planet—and the seed of Antichrist in all lesser manifestations. There is indeed a connection between this anti-force and certain world leaders today. In fact, many are on a network of that very wavelength of the force of Antichrist moving against humanity.

I shall repeat it now. *I, Jesus, charge you to call for that binding, that casting out, and that judgment of the Antichrist and all of that wavelength. [Let them be] cast out within and without.*

This Call given daily will enable there to be a staying action by the power of Solar Logoi on behalf of all [Lightbearers] who serve this system. A staying action: a holding back of this force assailing Lightbearers and a holding back of the destructivity that could be wrought by the same force through any and all who are of the anti-Light.

---

*In order to attain the prize of this high calling (Phil. 3:14)   †by reason of

These are keys and there are many keys.

The reason, therefore, thy attendance was so required [at this conference] is that this blessing you are receiving could occur only in this manner. It is not universally done, but a part of Maitreya's Mystery School. You are ensconced in the *darshan*[10] of Maitreya in this hour—his grid of Light with my own as we focus Father and Son, Guru and Chela,[11] does therefore give that polarity to the Logos, to the Word.

This is the hour when, through the seed of Light already thine own, the Word does begin, even by the single drop of thine own blood so sacrificed, to incarnate within thee. Now let it be nourished by the Light of the Divine Mother that you raise up from the base to the crown through Mother Mary, through Kuan Yin, through mantra upon mantra.

I, Jesus, seal you, for the concentration is intense.

[9-second pause; chant of vowel sounds; 24-second pause]

Blessed is he that endureth unto the raising of the Light to the crown: for he shall receive the crown of Life's everlasting wisdom.[12]

You have received that which you have come to the mountain to receive—and that which you could receive only in the Heart of the Inner Retreat.

The Western Shamballa is the Open Door to the abode of the Buddhas. May you seek that Door and find it in a very real way.

This dictation by **Jesus Christ** was **delivered** by the Messenger Elizabeth Clare Prophet on **Tuesday, July 5, 1988,** 12:54–1:13 a.m. MDT. **(1)** Matt. 24:42–44; Luke 12:36–40; I Thess. 5:2; II Pet. 3:10; Rev. 3:3; 16:15. **(2)** Matt. 25:1–13. **(3)** 1988 *Pearls of Wisdom,* pp. 565–66, 567, 568 n. 9. **(4)** Matt. 26:27, 28; Heb. 9:18–22. **(5)** In the Eastern religious tradition the yogi strives to experience Illumination and *samadhi* (ecstasy, perfect union and identification with God) through the activation of the **crown chakra.** This is accomplished through various methods (such as yogic techniques, spiritual disciplines, intense love for God). Once the crown chakra has been penetrated by the rising sacred fire, a "nectarlike essence" or "Elixir of Enlightenment" flows down into all the lower chakras. Summarizing this principle, Arthur Avalon writes: "The Śiva Samhitā says: 'When, by the grace of the Guru, the slumbering Kuṇḍalinī [the Life-force, or Mother energy, latent in the base-of-the-spine chakra] wakes up, it is then that the lotuses [chakras] are penetrated, and the knots (of karma) untied.'. . .Being thus awakened, Kuṇḍalinī enters the great road to liberation. . .and penetrating the centers one by one, ascends to the Sahasrāra [crown chakra], and there coming in blissful communion with the Lord of Lords, again descends down through the same passage to the Mūlādhāra [base] Chakra. Nectar is said to flow from such communion" (*Principles of Tantra* [1914; reprint, Madras: Ganesh & Co., 1960], p. 456). **(6)** The **wisdom cross** is formed by the 11/5 (Sagittarius, God-Victory and Gemini, God-Wisdom) and 2/8 (Pisces, God-Mastery and Virgo, God-Justice) axes of the Cosmic Clock. **(7)** Matt. 6:24; Luke 16:13. "A person cannot serve two horses or bend two bows, and a servant cannot serve two lords. That servant would respect one and offend the other" (Gospel of Thomas, logion 47). **(8)** **Prepare ye the day of the Lord Maitreya.** The Mahāparinibbāna Suttanta, quoted in Paul Carus, *The Gospel of Buddha* (Chicago: Open Court Publishing Co., 1915), p. 245; *The Holy Teaching of Vimalakīrti: A Mahāyāna Scripture,* trans. Robert Thurman (University Park, Pa.: Pennsylvania State University Press, 1976), pp. 100–102; Masatoshi Nagatomi, "Ārya-Maitreya-Vyākaraṇa" (Presented at the Conference on Maitreya Studies, Princeton University, May 1983); Daniel L. Overmyer, "Messenger, Savior, and Revolutionary: Maitreya in Chinese Popular Religious Literature of the Sixteenth and Seventeenth Centuries," in Alan Sponberg and Helen Hardacre, eds., *Maitreya, the Future Buddha* (Cambridge: Cambridge University Press, 1988), pp. 110–34. See 1988 *Pearls of Wisdom,* p. 534 n. 7. **(9)** **Sarasvati** is the Hindu goddess of wisdom, eloquence, learning and music; patroness of the arts and mother of poetry; and the wife or consort of Brahma, First Person of the Hindu Trinity (the Creator). See 1987 *Pearls of Wisdom,* p. 241. **(10)** 1988 *Pearls of Wisdom,* p. 442 note. **(11)** John 10:30; 12:44, 45; 14:9–11, 20, 24; 17:21. **(12)** James 1:12; Rev. 2:10.

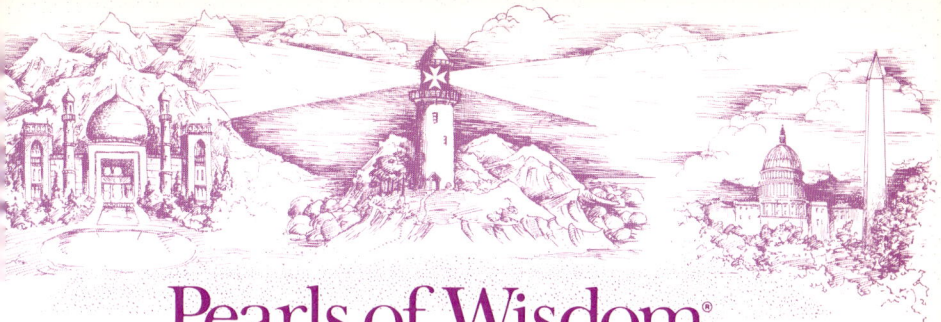

Pearls of Wisdom®

published by The Summit Lighthouse

| Vol. 31 No. 75 | Beloved Mighty Victory | November 6, 1988 |

FREEDOM 1988

20

Illumination's Power Restored

The Long-Awaited Moment of Your Fiery Destiny

See What You Can Do!

Hail, Sons of the Sons of God! I AM Victory and you are suspended in the golden sun of my causal body in this hour!
[29-second standing ovation]

O Golden Victorious Flame of the God Consciousness of the Second Ray, I AM Victory, Victory, Victory in the Three Jewels of initiation to which you shall attain if you are at all diligent and shun the dullard consciousness!

I AM Victory! I have come to see to it that you are not left in the ignorance and the twilight of a world that is neither here nor there. But I AM *here* and you are *here* and we are in the center of a sun of Being.

And surely you must have understood by this hour that we have come for a single purpose alone: to see to it that in the permanent seed atom of thy being there is that nucleus of the rod of illumination's flame, that it shall develop, that it shall be connected to the electronic and electromagnetic field of our aura and that you shall endure as an integrity in the Divine Whole of God—even through the sun of the yellow sphere of your own causal body of light.

And by this display of the fireworks of the Fourth of July, which are a white fire and a golden-yellow illumination of the Universal Christ, so be it known that we are absolutely God-determined that if you will make even a halfhearted effort to embody this Light, you will discover that [that] ascending process does find you, then, so sealed in the shaft of illumination that you shall feel as though [you were] ascending in an elevator shaft of Victory's own house.

I AM the house of Victory. I AM the house of Victory. I AM that house, beloved, and in my house there is not a mouse. There is neither a dullard. Neither is there one who does waste time.

Now, if you come to my house, you may devour time but not as a mouse but as the Great Kali. Understand the principle of devouring time. Devouring time is devouring karma. Devouring karma is devouring ignorance. And as you become enlightened you dwell in the timelessness, the spacelessness of our realms, having absolute God-control of *kal-desh.*[1]

Therefore, in the heart of *kal-desh* where one meets the other, where both are neutralized in that very center of being, *I AM Victory and I AM Home with my own!* [18-second applause]

Being so loved, beloved ones, being therefore so tenderly cared for, you must surely know that if you will merely put one foot before the other, you can arrive at the gate. We are determined that no folly or foolhardiness of fallen ones nor brashness nor despot should ever, ever again compromise the beloved of the Light.

Our effort is a supreme one. We have seen your own [effort]. We have seen that of Saint Germain and all the Hierarchy of Light. Therefore, those who go beyond these spheres through their embodiment of illumination's flame do converge on planet earth for a harvest of souls who treasure the illumination of the Christ and the Buddha.

In this thought and thought realm, be seated.

I come with a fiery discipline of excellence. I come through the spheres of the God and Goddess Meru[2] to neutralize all patterns of witchcraft misusing the Light of your four lower bodies. [I come] to neutralize all ancient misuse of the arts of Light. Records of the black arts must disappear and they do so by the displacement afforded you in the Presence of such beings of cosmic dimension [who are] of [the] Logos.

Know, then, beloved, that an arc of seven stars does appear in the heavens, though perhaps not to your sight. And this arc of seven stars is the sign of the coming of those Solar Lords and of the Holy Kumaras.*

All of Hierarchy is determined that those who have the inner potential, [those] who have the past momentum and the desire [for a path of personal Christhood unto God] will now receive attention in the most needed areas of their consciousness, will now receive the tutelage of the Cosmic Christs and Jophiel's angels.

These angels of Jophiel are tender teachers. But make no mistake: if you have valued and prized the discipline of the First and the Fourth Rays, I can tell you, it is only preparation for that of the

*the Seven Solar Logoi and the Seven Holy Kumaras

Second. For the discipline of the Second Ray, beloved, is the precision of every petaled vibration of a thousand-petaled lotus. Truly the perception of the Gemini Mind of God is unto you an open door.

Surely you will never be so blind nor forgetful nor allow density to encompass you about so as to have removed from you the vivid memory of this moment when a Hierarchy of Light cared so much for an evolution of Light stranded, as it were, on a planet in the throes of convulsions whose end of chaos none can predict.

We come to assist our own, and our own are all everywhere who espouse illumination as a spiritual flame—and [as] a spiritual flame wherewith to nourish life.

My speaking to you bears the brevity and the punctuation of a cosmic moment that has come and that comes but rarely. Everything about this night is rare, even the place so long ago envisioned, so near to the place of the descent of the root races at the Grand Teton. The land is unique and the temples beneath the earth's surface are unique, as are the waters, as are the elements. Truly you have come Home to a place that contains *all* the ingredients for Victory—and even myself.

I say it with a smile, beloved, for am I not most blest to bear the flame that in this moment of the history of an evolution is most prized above all flames—the golden flame of Victory for a victorious golden age, for a Victory in Armageddon, for the Victory of your mind and soul and heart, for the Victory of your beloved?

Indeed, my friends, I now desire to see a golden flame upon the brow and your visualization therein of the Amitābha. May it be so, beloved, for I do give you the opportunity to so increase in wisdom that the very momentum of the crown itself shall magnetize the Buddhas and raise up the Mother in you to fetch a starling* to become a star.

Seven Holy Kumaras, Eternal Youths,[3] reverse the clock in every lifestream, for Victory's hours are not counted. Thus, every hour that is Victory does not cause the aging of the vessel. To turn back time does not recede experience but only increases it, for thou art nearer thy point of origin in the Central Sun.

Now let us see how a marathon of illumination's golden flame properly protected, flanked by violet flame can change a consciousness of a planet through the Lightbearers whose spirituality may hold the Light you invoke. Let resurrection's flame resurrect the Victory of illumination within you and may you prize our Presence.

May you prize our Presence as a unique moment in your fiery destiny—one you have long awaited and anticipated. And I will tell you when you began to anticipate that this hour should come. It was in a moment when you realized that wisdom had gone out of

*starling: a little star; *Oxford English Dictionary*: an inhabitant of a star

you, that Light of illumined action was no longer thy domain. But it was too late. You had followed those compromisers of the Second Ray who absorbed but never did reflect back to you your own loving wisdom.

Therefore, beloved, sensing the bondage being forged of an ignorance [that descended upon you as nightfall] through a Light lost and a Law ignored, you said in your heart: "Though I have sinned against the Law of Wisdom, yet I know and I believe, I trust and I have faith that I shall pursue. And as I pursue the Law of my God, so one day by an equality of co-measurement I shall be received again into the courts of Wisdom's Master to begin again to weave the coil of Light that I did forgo in the presence of these spoilers."

Blessed ones, those who have perverted illumination's flame are angry this night. They are not happy in the least to see the restoration of so many pure hearts [to Wisdom's holy fount].

May you recognize what power is restored illumination. May you recognize what you lost when you lost it and the great gift you now have for having regained a portion of it—[the increment of Light] that is sufficient for you to multiply [illumination] by the action of your own heart flame.

So great a loss for so great a time ought to make you contemplate, beloved, and determine in all discipline registering upon your life that you will indeed make [your own] application for the sealing of the crown chakra that it may nevermore again, by the grace of God, ever tie in to the fallen ones by even the slightest expression by you of any criticism, condemnation or judgment of any part of life and especially not of any part of the Great White Brotherhood.

So as Gautama Buddha so carefully gave to you his message on the law of chelaship and the Guru-chela relationship through the heart of Sanat Kumara, may you realize as you review the content of these days together that all that has been spoken and exercised of the Word and learned, all facts and figures, all that has been said is designed to enable you to avoid various types of pitfalls within and without upon the planet, that you might not lose the glory of the golden day of your ascension and that you might, in recognition of the dangers on the planet in this hour, secure the bastions of your cosmic consciousness through Maitreya's oneness and through him [the oneness of] all those of the spherical body of the Second Ray.

Out of the Sun of Victory I have come. And there is no other Sun but Victory, for every Son is a God-Victory.

O my beloved sons, be, then, the Light of a world. *See* what you can do. *See* what you can do. See what *you can do!*

This dictation was delivered on Tues., July 5, 1988, 1:22–1:41 a.m. MDT, at *FREEDOM 1988*. For notes see p. 580.

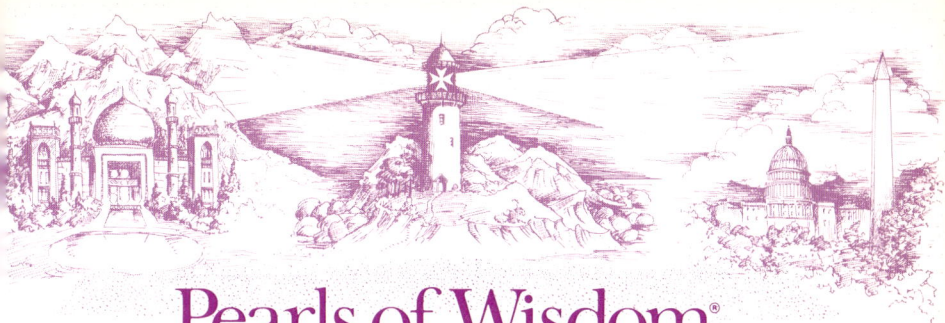

Pearls of Wisdom®
published by The Summit Lighthouse

Vol. 31 No. 76 | *Beloved Sanat Kumara* | *November 12, 1988*

FREEDOM 1988

21

The Light Is Sealed

The Divine Approbation Shall Never Be Denied the Victors
The Community Is Sealed in the Love Bond of Gautama Buddha

I, Sanat Kumara, in the Sevenfold Flame of the Holy Kumaras, draw now the Light of this conference into the crystal chalice that is sustained by Elohim in this retreat.[1] It is sealed that not one erg shall be misqualified. It is sealed as a geometry whose nucleus is actually established now over this Heart by the Solar Logoi; and this geometric, mathematical nucleus does provide the grid that can hold the most complex releases of Light and Energy that have gone forth in these days.

May you know, beloved, the Victory of a service rendered and of the one who renders it. May you know the Victory of affirming within your heart, *"I can do all things through the Lord [the I AM THAT I AM] my God which strengtheneth me."*[2]

Know, then, that to live in the Victory of a goal that is set, to visualize oneself having already achieved that Victory is the key to its fulfillment, whereas those who fail to complete their tasks and cycles are always those who have never visited the future, [who] have never gone ahead to place the crystal, the lodestone for the crystallization of the God Flame, at that point [of past/present/future Victory converged as one].

They have not known the alchemy of establishing the mandala and of placing the crystal quartz upon it. They do not know the alchemy of the points of Matter nor of *kal-desh*. Establish the points,* then collapse the matrix, then reestablish the points, going within and going without.

So at last, beloved, may it be said of you in the day that you do

---
*i.e., the coordinates

fulfill your mission: "Well done, thou good and faithful servant. Thou hast been faithful over a few things, I will make thee ruler over many."[3] Know that the Divine Approbation does descend, that it cannot be demanded or called forth, but it does surely come and will never be denied the one that does give until the task is done.

We expect, then, in the name of the entire Spirit of the Great White Brotherhood, by the electromagnetic field of the Seven Holy Kumaras and Solar Logoi, that each and every one of you who is worth his salt in chelaship shall respond without dissimulation to Saint Germain's need of the hour.

To fail to respond is to neutralize the gifts of Hierarchy. Our gifts are not unconditional. They are conditioned upon your providing the Omega response to our Alpha thrust and therefore binding yourself to the Logos. Only you can bind yourself to the Word. Only you can bind yourself to the seven planes of the Seven Holy Kumaras.

Let us be up and doing, as has been said before; for this place must be prepared. As you prepare me the chamber in your heart, I too shall enter.

Make no mistake, I AM indeed the Ancient of Days. I come quietly to fill your cups, your chakras, with the illumination necessary to reveal to you the meaning, the Path and the balancing of all, and I said *all*, of your chakras.

In love and joy may you find release forevermore.

Elohim. Aīṁ. [chanted]

It is done. It is finished. The Community is sealed in the Love bond of Lord Gautama Buddha.

This dictation by **Sanat Kumara** was **delivered** by Elizabeth Clare Prophet on **Tuesday, July 5, 1988,** 1:41–1:49 a.m. MDT. Available on 90-min. audiocassette with dictations of Jesus Christ and Mighty Victory, B88106, $6.50 (add $.55 for postage); on 90-min. videocassette with dictations of the Great Divine Director, Jesus Christ and Mighty Victory, HP88075, $19.95 (add $1.10 for postage).

(1) Crystal chalice of Elohim. On June 27, 1987, during *FREEDOM 1987* in the Heart of the Inner Retreat, Archangel Chamuel and Charity announced that "a tangible chalice is being formed, tended by Paul the Venetian, by Nada, by angels of Love.... When the chalice shall rise to meet and greet the Elohimic level, then shall Elohim pour into this chalice that which ye seek, beloved. Truly, and truly I say, it is the purging, purging of all impurity: Light, then, solidifying and codifying the Word within you." Beloved Alpha explained on July 5, 1987, that the building of the chalice "must give to us entrée to earth twenty-four hours a day by the Spirit of Elohim. And by that Spirit of Elohim, the Cosmic Spirit of Freedom shall also descend." Calling for an intense decree vigil for the resurrection flame by Keepers of the Flame for the completion of the chalice, the Messenger explained that this chalice, "as a 'funnel' of crystal light," would be "the perpetual open door for Elohim to work through all true Lightbearers of the world. This is the key to the real victory of the golden age under Sanat Kumara." On August 17, 1987, the Divine Mother Kali announced "the fulfillment of the chalice in the Heart of the Inner Retreat to the Elohimic level." See 1987 *Pearls of Wisdom,* pp. 302, 310, 374, 383, 417, 418, 443, 456, 459, 461. **(2)** Phil. 4:13. **(3)** Matt. 25:21, 23; Luke 19:17.

Notes from Pearl no. 75 by Mighty Victory:
(1) kal: Hindi [Skt. *kāla*], time; **desh:** Hindi [Skt. *deshá*], place, space. See *The Lost Teachings of Jesus I,* pp. 171–201. **(2)** On December 25, 1986, Jesus announced that the God and Goddess Meru had placed themselves within golden white spheres to be sustained over the Royal Teton Ranch as their Presence with us (1986 *Pearls of Wisdom,* p. 682). **(3) Eternal Youths.** Hindu tradition describes the Kumaras as the seven (sometimes four) mind-born sons of Brahma who forever retain their youthful purity and innocence and are called the "eternal youths" or "princes." Sanat Kumara [Skt. *sanat,* always, and *kumara,* youth] is said to be the most prominent of the Kumaras.

The Summit Lighthouse®

PUBLISHER FOR CHURCH UNIVERSAL AND TRIUMPHANT

Dear Heart Friend,

Joyous greetings from all of us at The Summit Lighthouse!

I would like to take this opportunity to talk to you about the 'Pearls of great price' we receive each week by the dispensation of our heavenly Father through the Darjeeling Council and the Great White Brotherhood and just what they mean to us who consider each new day as a stepping-stone to the summit of being.

Since 1958 the Masters' students around the world have been graced with these weekly releases which now number at least fifteen each quarter, or sixty a year. Eighty-four were released in 1987, many of the extras coming at the end of the year with the publishing of the magnificent dictations from the Messenger's 1987 Stump in the eastern United States.

Our beloved El Morya has told us that the Pearls of Wisdom are the bread of Life, weekly manna which we take as our daily bread to fill the basic needs of our souls. He spoke to us with great tenderness on Father's Day, June 16, 1985:

I take, then, in serving you the Bread of Life as I always have, Pearls of Wisdom--manna descending from the Darjeeling Retreat of heaven, daily bread. It has been my concern for more than a quarter of a century and through all the ages.

I AM the brooding presence of Abraham as Mother, as Guru, as Father with you. Thy daily bread, each basic need--thy soul shall be fed. I come to nourish my children at table. I sit at the head. I say the blessing. Sometimes you will not eat, as little children are wont to do--to reject what

Box A, Livingston, Montana 59047-1390 (406) 222-8300

is good for them. And thus the Communion goes begging. I pray you will understand that my Communion is truly the bread of angels. I trust you will understand that daily you require this bread, even as the body must also be daily nourished.

We remember that at the Last Supper our Lord took bread and blessed it and brake it and gave it to the disciples, saying, "Take, eat; this is my Body." And he took the cup, and when he had given thanks, gave it to them to drink, saying, "This is my Blood of the new testament, which is shed for many." (Mark 14:22–24) Through these words that have been recited in the Christian celebration of Holy Communion these two thousand years, Jesus Christ has transferred to his own the same essence of his Universal Light Body--'the Blood', the Alpha, or Masculine, Spirit polarity, and 'the Body', the Omega, or Feminine, Mother polarity, which he imparted to his disciples the night before his arrest, trial, and crucifixion.

On November 16, 1986, our beloved Jesus gave to us the teaching that we partake of the sacred ritual of transubstantiation, receiving the grace of his Body and Blood through his message:

Blessed ones, by grace are ye saved. And the grace that is sufficient for thee is the grace of my Causal Body multiplied by the Causal Body of all saints of heaven through God the Father, the Son, and the Holy Spirit.

Understand, beloved, that this grace is elusive. If the chalice be not upraised, if the temple be not offered, where shall the angels of the Holy Eucharist pour the grace of my Body and my Blood?

It is, then, to this end that I have poured of this my essence into the teachings of these Two Witnesses, lo, these many years and set and sealed them for thee, beloved.

Here, then, is the key: Except ye eat the flesh and drink the blood of the Son of man, ye have no Life in you. Beloved, I say to each and every one of you for whom I have prepared this meal, Come and dine. Come and eat my message.

In his landmark dictation of October 4, 1987, calling us to discipleship under the Cosmic Christ, Jesus gave us to drink that we, too, might become the living Word:

Fear not, beloved. You have always believed that somewhere a chalice is filled with the elixir of eternal Life. I say to you, here is the chalice. Take, then, the Teaching. Take, then, that which we have set forth. For there does not come another and another to rewrite what we have said and spoken. It is sealed and it is finished.

For the lost Word is written, ready for you to bring to it the fire of a heart filled with love and therefore to quicken that Teaching in your body, in your members, in your chakras and to be the living Teaching and the living Word.

As I wrote this letter I talked to Mother about the true worth and meaning of the Pearls and this is the answer she gave to me:

"To receive a weekly Pearl of Wisdom in the mail is like receiving weekly Communion, which you may formerly have taken in an orthodox church. The symbol of the bread and the wine is the impartation of the Universal Light Body of the Cosmic Christ as it is dispensed through the Ascended Masters, their Archangels, and those who are dictating through the Messengers in this age.

"As the light descends and is received by the supplicant, the conveyance of the bread is the conveyance of the Body and consciousness of the Divine Mother; the conveyance of the wine is the Spirit and essence of the Father, the I AM Presence. This is the sacred Eucharist for the age of Aquarius. Not only is it the sacrament of Holy Communion but it is also the essential 'communion of the saints' whereby the Mystical Body of God in heaven and on earth becomes one through the assimilation of the Teaching.

"Through the Pearls of Wisdom we therefore put on and realize the Dharma, which is the Body of the Teaching and therefore the Body of the Consciousness of God. We enter the bliss of the Divine Union with the Great Guru, the LORD God, through Sanat Kumara and the entire Great White Brotherhood serving with him. And we are one in the Sangha, as Above so below, the Community of all Lightbearers worlds without end.

"The Pearls of Wisdom are consciousness raising. They reinforce the thread of contact and assist you in weaving the Deathless Solar Body, which is referred to as the wedding garment by beloved Jesus in his parables.

"All who are entering the New Age, all who are supplicants at the throne of grace under their own I AM Presence and Holy Christ Self, all who seek to know the adepts as the Lords of the Seven Rays and to receive increment by increment their Christhood must understand that the fundamentals of the Path, the basic necessity and the chief cornerstone of building one's pyramid of life, is to study the Teachings as they are meted out week by week through the Messengers.

"The dictations and the messages of God to us delivered by his Servant-Sons in heaven not only carry information but they are also cups of light that convey to your body and soul and mind spiritual healing. The concepts embodied therein as well as the dispensations, even the phrasing itself, are the very catalyst we all need for the crystallization of the God Flame in our temples as we prepare for that divine reunion, the ritual of the ascension at the conclusion of this lifetime.

"The Pearls of Wisdom strengthen us to serve daily the needs of our families, of the Brotherhood, and to have light in our cups to give to others who are in need. The Pearls of Wisdom are indispensable to our growth, our service, and our oneness with God. May you never be without this blessed Communion."

In the understanding that the Teachings of the Universal Christ are Holy Communion, we gain a greater appreciation of the blessings of the Pearls. And when we think about Holy Communion being an initiation of spirals of Light, we gain the vision that it is what we know and practice of the Teachings that tells us whether we are truly assimilating the Word. Jesus' warning to his disciples was "Except ye eat the flesh of the Son of man, and drink his blood, ye have no Life in you!" which is to say, "Ye have no God in you!"

The conclusion of the matter is that our understanding of the sacred mysteries of Christ determines precisely just how much of the initiation of the Light (i.e., Christ consciousness) of Higher Consciousness we can take in and hold through a conscientious path of self-mastery. Beloved, we cannot understand what we do not listen to and read and ponder in our hearts and then pray and offer our fervent decrees about.

Surely the dedication of the entire Spirit of the Great White Brotherhood to the delivery of the Pearls to our mailboxes week in, week out ought to give us pause. The Truth is that when it comes to our own soul's victory in this life we just can't be without the Pearls of Wisdom. As such they are our first priority (after our tithe) when planning our monthly budget and paying our bills.

These momentous and timely dictations of untold Ascended Masters to the Messenger through the Holy Spirit are recorded, transcribed, edited, published, and mailed to you as Pearls of Wisdom by the Messenger and her devoted staff. When you subscribe to the Pearls, you assist us in publishing the Teachings and help to sustain our Community, without which this invaluable instruction from the Masters could not be produced.

It is our hope that you will keep your Pearls account well ahead and never miss one of these precious Pearls. If you send your $40 love offering now, you will not even need to think about it for a whole year. If you can't send $40 for the entire year, send $20 for six months; if you can't send $20, send $10 for three months. But mail in your renewal subscription today!

We send the Pearls each Thursday from the Livingston Post Office by third-class mail. Since it can take anywhere from five days to three weeks to get to a destination in the United States, you may wish to include first-class postage for a year so that you may receive the mailing more quickly. You will find complete postage information on the back of the enclosed renewal card.

You will notice that we have updated our Pearls postage rates based on the April 3, 1988 postal increases for first class and surface mail: from $.22 to $.25 in the United States and Mexico, $.22 to $.30 in Canada, and $.37 to $.40 for surface mail to all other countries. Our annual Pearls love offering, which includes third-class mailing in the U.S.A., has remained at $40 for over five years, since January 1983. Even though our paper costs have risen 51% over the same period of time (paper has gone up 28% and changing to a finer quality paper raised our costs by 23%), Mother has desired not to raise the rates, so that all might partake of the Sacred Word. I urge you to tend to the matter of your Pearl subscription today.

From our hearts, we thank you for your support of the Word and Work of the LORD. We look forward to continuing to share with you the 1988 and 1989 Pearls of Wisdom--the progressive revelation of the Ascended Masters which hold the spiritual and practical keys to our daily lives and the future of the planet.

I close by sharing with you the gentle blessing given by Archangel Raphael as we commemorated the passion of our Lord on Good Friday, April 17, 1987:

In the heart of the Holy Spirit thou shalt thrive and prosper. And the Word itself shall prosper. And the Teaching shall go forth and the Teacher shall save that which is lost.

Be thou the whole loaf
and know Him as I know Him and as I AM.
A bite of the Word is Communion in the All--
thus holy water, thus holy wine.

In the love of the Holy Spirit,

Marilyn C. Barrick

Rev. Marilyn C. Barrick

Pearls of Wisdom®
published by The Summit Lighthouse

Vol. 31 No. 77 | Beloved El Morya | November 13, 1988

The Light and the Beautiful
A Line Is Drawn
Concerns for the Chelaship of My Own

To the Light and the Beautiful I speak and I laud the living flame of God-Reality. Yet I deplore in my chelas the inattentiveness to that Light and that Beauty and to the necessity of striving hourly to be the instrument of that Divine Reality.

Thus to take for granted that that which is above shall descend to that which is beneath is a most serious error. Thus I come in this hour, beloved, with major concerns for the chelaship of my own. To that end I ask you to be seated.

The mind is not sufficient instrument for the Mind of God. Whether there is a will to change must be determined by every one, everyone so gathered here and everyone throughout the world who has known the blessings of the dispensation given unto me in this century.

Blessed ones, I adjure you, for I must.

You have known that Saint Germain's opportunity for dispensations has run out and been denied by the Lords of Karma in various hours of this century, and so it has been for him in other centuries. This day and hour of Divine Justice under the blessed hierarchy of Virgo[1] does also mark for me the termination of new opportunity for the chelas of the will of God.

Thus I come to tell you, beloved, that unless you avail yourselves of that which I have already given you and [that which other Ascended Masters] from the Darjeeling Council have given to you, and that which the Messengers have given—unless that be put to use fruitfully, abundantly, wisely and obediently, I will see, for my part, no new dispensation that I may offer [my chelas].

Thus, beloved ones, the number eight does signify to us the

encounter. It may be the encounter with Maitreya, beloved ones, but surely it is the encounter with the karma of neglect. This karma, then, can be stayed no longer for the individual members of this body of our organization so founded thirty years ago. And thus, beloved, [by successfully meeting the challenge of individual karma] this organization is destined to reach a crescendo of Christhood at its thirty-three-year cycle.

Therefore, from this hour to the third year, the thirty-three, let it be known, let it be understood, and let it be remembered that I have stood for you, and each and every one, and I have placed myself between you and the Lords of Karma many a time and between you and your returning karma. This I have done judiciously, for I have desired to see you have some measure of the experience of that karma that you might be strengthened, that you might know the way and be surefooted for having tripped a few times on the way.

Blessed ones, it is no longer possible. And thus, you have observed just how much effort you have put forth—and for this I am profoundly grateful—in the holding of the balance of the forces moving against this land and the very integrity of your souls.[2] But, beloved, this has been so* for the necessity to bring you into a state of realism of just how that world karma may play upon you, how you may be vulnerable to it, right to the borders of this the Inner Retreat, without [the] enormous sacrifice and intercession of those of us who have given and given again.

And when we have given again and again, we have hidden our eyes; for we would not look upon the karmic condition of some in this Community—that of neglect, that of repeated ignoring of the counsels and the lessons given—for they were not in fact deserving of our dispensations. And we did know the karma we did incur to defend this organization, often from unknown dangers that you may never have become consciously aware of.

Knowing this due date coming upon me, therefore, the Darjeeling Council, together with Sanat Kumara, determined that certain of the threats to the world body should be made known at this conference past.[†3] And thus a greater awareness of the inroads of aliens on earth and in other places has come to your attention for action.

Awareness/Action is our byword!

Need we tell you to make the call or to arrange for the decree sessions or [to] put less important things aside? I think not. I think

---

*this has come to pass

†"that the chelas might call forth the necessary protection against the day when they must stand and still stand to challenge these threats to the health and safety of society, absent my intercession"

you know that when dispensations of Light are meted out, as they have been meted out and as awarenesses of Darkness come, that calls to amplify the Light and deny the Darkness must be forthcoming swiftly lest the Darkness overtake you before you have anchored the Light of dispensation.

Would to God, I say, that you might carry on a seven-day marathon twelve hours a day and put behind us some of this personal karma that does indeed draw you nearer to the personal precipice that you fear most or ought to fear if you do not![4]

Thus, blessed ones, we are aware of the pressures from without that mount against the circle of this body and the demands that are made upon each and every one of you and all. Will you not also have compassion for us that the pressures that are upon us in the Darjeeling Council concerning the future of this earth body are also enormous?

Therefore, we, too, are grateful for gentle rain of mercy. We, too, are grateful for drop by drop that may come to us by the call of our chelas here below.

Thus, beloved, you may still know [that it is essential for you] to read the signs of the times by the very profile of the Messenger. [And thus] you may also come to understand that burden [of the Lord[5]] as you share the garment, [i.e., the responsibility, of the Messenger and call for her mantle to intercede for you where I may not], as you share the oneness of this truly divine experience [of that blessed communion of the saints that is made possible through the mantle].

Blessed hearts, you should do me great service if you could render for me the call to the will of God [10.03[6]], for that call that was written down from my own causal body by Mark* does give to you the balance of the will of God and my own Diamond Heart and the diamond of my turban,[7] focusing within your four lower bodies a grid of light. I should like to have, beloved, some reservoir of the call to the will of God, of the sweet surrender [10.18], that I might have in time of greatest need something in store to offer even the Lords of Karma when I desire not to leave you in the [karmic] straits of dealing with forces you know not of.

Therefore, beloved, I did give myself to receive the violet flame and to give the violet flame. If you will remember that I determined to be that cup of violet flame, that reservoir of light,[8] [then] remember me also, beloved, for I am the one that does repeatedly come to defend you. And you have become so accustomed to my intercession, O blessed hearts, that I am concerned that when the hour come and I am not allowed to give it that you

*the Messenger Mark L. Prophet

will suddenly sense and say to yourself, "Where is Morya? Why does this battle endure?"

Blessed ones, therefore, of the necessity of this circumstance I have but one choice and that is to tell you that I must apply the laws of dispensations given, as it was told to you by beloved Serapis Bey, that those who would not be willing to give the full measure of those three services a week could not enjoy the benefits of the Inner Retreat.[9] Now I must draw that line of discipline and I must say it must be so.

And therefore, in order hopefully to retain opportunity to help those who are chelas, and to goad those who might be better chelas to a greater manifestation of diligence, I must say that unless you are actively attending those services in your areas you may not attend services at King Arthur's Court. And those who enter this court, then, must be in a fiery diligence [of the will of God], must be on lesson eight of their Keepers of the Flame Lessons and beyond, and must truly show the mark of diligence in keeping the time and the schedules and not letting anything cause them to not appear at the appointed hour.

Blessed ones, I stand at a moment when I desire to give you all of my causal body for your victory, all of my experience and all of my counsel. The Karmic Board has sent me to tell you that for the blessings received from my heart in these thirty years, from this day forward if you desire my intercession it must be upon the principle of "pay as you go."[10] For each day's intercession there must be abundant action on the calls to my flame, as you know, the [decree] number 10.03. This call, beloved, is the key to my causal body and to my Diamond Heart and to the more that we can give to you through the Messengers.

Blessed ones, I shall return to you many, manyfold, as the Law will allow it, your offering of the calls to the will of God. And then, beloved, what is not used up in the given day may accrue as a reservoir, as a sphere of light, therefore, that you will have in reserve that portion [which is] so needed[—*when you need it*].

Blessed ones, there must be, then, preparedness. You must seek it and find it and make it the one-pointed goal.

We do not rest as the days pass and the interferences come. Our hearts and minds, the All-Seeing Eye of God with us, the blessed Elohim, they have said to me, and so I say to you what they have said, "Blessed Morya, our Son, we will stand for you and for the Chohans [the Lords of the Seven Rays] and for the Darjeeling Council in the sponsorship of this activity. We will give of our seven rays but we also must be invoked."

Therefore they have said, "Let there be following the evening

session of Astreas a group of stalwart ones who will stand as
chalices of Elohim, who will remain with Daniel without partaking
of meat[11] and who will remain celibate and therefore have a one-
pointed goal of carrying the rays and the light of the Seven Elohim
in their chakras to be pillars in this Community and priests unto
God and priestesses unto the Divine Mother above."

Thus fulfilling an hour or more of calls and song to Elohim
each evening in the seven days of the week, these individuals shall
serve as chalices in the Community for holding a direct Light;* and
by that action, beloved, perhaps I, then, will regain a greater
opportunity to stand with you. For was I not there in the days of the
destruction of Sodom and Gomorrah? Was I not there? And did
I not see, did I not behold the destruction of the cities of the plain
by nuclear energy?[12] Have I not been a survivor age after age?

Have I not known the evil of these Nephilim gods and have
I not trained you up by placing them so near to you, even in your
own families, even in the nearness of neighbor, teacher, employer,
employee, that you would finally know the patterns and be quickened in the ancient memory [of] when you have been taught on
other spheres [and] of just what would be the psychology and the
ploys and the conspiracies of these fallen ones in this hour?

Aye, I have been there. I have told you. And for some of you
who may think you might have deserved better surroundings,
better parents, and so forth, I can tell you, you may very well have
deserved better. Therefore do not feel downhearted or condemned
by what has been your lot, for you were "chelas mine"[13] from the
beginning and you shall be, by God's grace if you will it so, chelas
mine unto the end. Blessed ones, therefore being concerned for
your upbringing and your training, I saw to it that you would not
miss the encounter with these evil ones who would mock you, who
would be brutal and cunning and destroy, if they could, other fine
relationships and friendships and come between you, those you
loved most, and your God.

Laugh with me, beloved, for you are here and I am here and
none shall stand between us forever. I pledge it to you from my
heart, beloved, that all that I am and all that I am to be and all that
I can give I shall give to you determinedly as the Great Law will
allow it. O beloved, so also invoke Kuan Yin and Mercy's flame
that there might be even that bridge between us [of scientific
mantra] when I have no more dispensation.

My true hearts of gold, where hearts are pure will you allow to
endure the stubbornness and the density and the repetitions that
cost us so very much? O blessed hearts, I know, I know. It is not

*the God consciousness of Elohim

always easy to stand apart from the crowd and say, "I will walk with my God even if I walk alone."

Blessed ones, there is no point for chastisement, for are we not already punished when ignorance and density beset us? And we take note, and I speak for I am a part of you, that some portion of the sense of self, the mind, the memory, the reason, the strength of the will, of the desire body or even the physical strength does fail [as the automatic karma for ignorance and density unchecked].

Is this not enough [chastisement]?

I trust that your groaning and concern as to the nonexpansiveness of some faculties shall be to you a goad to a greater acceleration. I trust, beloved, that the law descending from the Lords of Karma upon me will also be to you the most certain prick, even the prick that does stir the finest steed to his finest hour.

Most blessed ones, I draw a circle of the will of God around the fiery chelas, and some who yet tie themselves to Mother's apron strings will find themselves outside that circle; and it must be so for want of attentiveness to the Law—the Law that is just—on this eight o'clock line where I stand. And I stand flanked by Kuthumi, who does stand on the four with our Great Divine Director on the twelve.

And on that line I say to you, beloved, if you are outside of the Law, whether human or divine, you must quickly confess your sins to the appropriate persons, make rectitude, correct such states and come into alignment. For the sin not confessed, the illegal posture not acknowledged, though none may know about it, does prevent the karma from descending and therefore [does prevent] the expiation of that karma—*even if you give the violet flame decrees daily.*

The making right of all things with all persons in embodiment or elsewhere is most necessary, for the alignment with my heart or with the embodied Messenger cannot be strong when there are those deeds, actions and records not in keeping with the Law.

Thus, if there be not the confession and then the repentance and then the willingness to balance the karma, there is not the tight coil of [our] oneness—a coil so tight between us that I desire to have with you, that there be no separation heart to heart, breath to breath, soul to soul, chakra to chakra. I desire your chakras to be one with my own and my chakras to be yours when you have need of them.

Did not we the mahatmas even provide for Blavatsky a sheath of an astral body where she did lack the fortitude and would otherwise not have been our amanuensis? Have we not filled in the chinks in the armour and the gaps [in our chelas]? Have we told you so? Nay. We have given you your hours of joy and victory, supporting you and affirming your discipleship.

Blessed ones, the hour has come when <u>attainment must be thine own.</u> That path of attainment you are well prepared for, but by some missing word or link or understanding or perhaps too easy a way for our Presence [with you],* you have not gained a sufficiency of co-measurement to understand <u>the level of striving necessary to survive</u> on the Path and beyond.

This absence of awareness, or perhaps an awareness not heeded or responded to, has brought to your Messenger unascended tears—tears of profound sorrow and grief as she has come to me in Darjeeling to say, "What have I not done that the word spoken does not elicit the [needed] response for these diamond-hearted ones to offer, then, that immaculately cut diamond for the fight to the Victory?" only to be told by me that I, too, have gone to my own Guru to ask the very same question.

Thus, beloved, some may understand why there are <u>tears on the</u> face of the <u>statues of Mother Mary</u> in various places around the world.[14] Some think it is for the calamity that is coming. But I tell you, it is <u>for the nonresponsiveness to the Word [already] spoken</u> and to the Great Lord Sanat Kumara.

Do you know, beloved—and you do not, therefore I shall tell you—that while you invoked the light here yesterday[15] the Call was made as it was destined to be made by the Messenger in that very hour. [Yes,] a million years ago it was destined that that Call be made in that hour yesterday. And therefore <u>the Messenger did [make the] call</u> in the person and mantle of the Divine Mother that she does bear at inner levels, Kuan Yin and Mother Mary with her, [and she] did cry out to all Lightbearers of the world (all of whom recognize her [as the Mother]) [and] did implore every one of those <u>Lightbearers</u> to <u>let go of their cups of materialism,</u> to let go <u>of the money beast,</u> to let go <u>of this civilization</u> and to come apart—imploring and giving call after call after call for all legions of the Divine Mother to cut them free.

And with all of this and these centuries of service of our bands, beloved hearts, at this crucial hour of the handwriting on the wall, how many (apart from the Body of God already separated out) of those Lightbearers on the entire planet do you think responded? I tell you, <u>5 percent [of the Lightbearers</u> on planet earth] left their hold upon the money beast and <u>heeded the Call</u> of the one whose face they have known forever!

Shall we all weep together or shall we take our tears and shall we call for them to be the water of Life to sustain ourselves in <u>this Community effort that must be made,</u> if for no other purpose than for <u>a demonstration of solidarity</u> under Saint Germain and Sanat Kumara that when called to prepare, the chelas of the will of God prepare

*"or perhaps our Presence with you makes the way too easy"

and they do so and they do not expect another to do it for them?

Beloved ones, I can tell you, if you are looking for Maitreya, the encounter is precisely to prepare to survive underground and to do so in the time allotted. Therefore I have so counseled the members of this board and staff to present to all the plan refined, considered by us and the Archangel Michael as the necessary and sufficient means for preparedness and survival under the worst of circumstances of nuclear war and earth changes. When that is accomplished, beloved hearts, you will know what is the next step of the path of the bodhisattvas.

You know it not but you build the stupa of the Buddha beneath the earth. Thus, take the key. What is sufficient for the Buddha and the Buddha of the Ruby Ray must be sufficient for thee.

Therefore the [necessity for the] psychological testing of one-self under stress, under discipline—under [emergency situations when the] taking of short and precise orders and following them precisely to completion [may be a matter of life and death]. Blessed hearts, in a survival situation you must have the fire of Serapis. Thus, I come clothed this night in the white fire core of my inner being as I manifest myself in the heart of the five secret rays.

Time and space, then, Mother and Buddha, this you have heard long ago and you have thought, "Well, when we embody the Buddha will it not be so that we will have unlimited space and the vastness of the expanse of Cosmos?" Aye, it is so, and this property is vast, vaster still if you are an ant or a mole. But, blessed hearts, the real test of the Buddha, of space itself, is confinement, is abso-lute God-peace under conditions extraordinary. Though you do not imagine them to be so, such confinement may be the greatest challenge that you have ever faced.

Therefore, let those who come to services come with their briefcases or portfolios. Let them bring their lists of dispensations, their charts and outlines of the Cosmic Clock given at the past conference.[16] Let them meditate upon those lines and embark upon spiral upon spiral of God-mastery within.

Blessed ones, you will reach the place, therefore, here or hereafter, wherein in order to go beyond [the transient and intran-sigent world] and [to] enter the coils of the ascension you may come to the moment where time and space dissolve and by the conscious-ness of the One and then of eternity as the Eternal One, you shall indeed overcome all sense of being the prisoner of any time or any space, any era, any century, any karmic coil, any condition, any adversity, any persecution or worldly success. Neither bane nor blessing, time frame nor space, none of these shall perturb you, for you have found the key and turned it in the lock and opened the door to the secret chambers of the five-secret-ray spheres. There in the peace, then, of the internal Oneness you may find true deliverance in this age.

My love falls on the just and the unjust.[17] I may not love you less for your indiscretions, for your absence from the fiery altar of change, but, blessed ones, and I speak to those throughout the field, when you leave off your devotions for periods, you are weakened, the distance grows between thyself and the Flame of the ark of the covenant, between thyself and my heart. It is imperceptible [to you]. The adjustment to lesser vibrations is easy [for you]. It is the broad way that leadeth to destruction.[18] And that which is lost, not being capable of being perceived, is no longer missed.

Blessed ones, one may have a memory of higher octaves but one cannot re-create in consciousness the direct experience of those octaves except one be in those octaves! You may remember the intense fire you once knew in the Presence of Sanat Kumara during a dictation or in past golden ages on other spheres, but it is impossible to re-create it at will by yourself— [at least] not until you become as Kuan Yin, the self-existent one, fully ascended in the light and free. One as the I AM THAT I AM, you are that I AM.

And so, beloved, by and by even the memory does grow dim in the mist, and as though looking through dense fog, one can no longer see the heights one has left. Blessed ones, we have observed this happen in a single seven-day period of a lifestream. It is not uncommon, so far out of the way can an individual depart and so much light can he squander, with so little effort and [in] hardly any time at all.

Thus, beloved, though my love is forever, I am profoundly chagrined where I have seen how many have made initial progress on the Path, whether in ten days, ten weeks, ten years or ten embodiments, only to be distracted by the strong delusions and magnetisms of the lesser world. And do you know, beloved, that straying most often comes because the individual does not recognize his attainment.

The chela does not know how much of the Guru lives withinside* of himself, how much of the Central Sun has already increased that threefold flame and consciousness. One cannot know what is inside another and therefore one thinks, "I am not as good as that one or this one."

But, beloved, I therefore come to expand, to expand, to expand the Light and the Beautiful that you are, the Reality, and to give my sense of co-measurement to souls who take for granted that

---

*withinside: within, on the inner side, in the inner part or interior, indoors

that inner being will somehow be fused to them [in the ritual of the ascension] in some way beyond their conscious awareness and therefore the effort need not be made.

O I desire to give you the consciousness of Bodhidharma[19] and the Eastern adepts and the Gurus who gave to their chelas such intense discipline and initiation with scarcely a look of encouragement or praise for one or five lifetimes lest that one in a moment of approval should lose the sense of being on guard, should lose the sense of the necessity for striving.

And yet, beloved, there had to be an impartation of a self-awareness so strong, as you must give in parenting, so strong, beloved, that in the midst of the rigors of chelaship that one would never lose sight of the point of the diamond that I show you now within, which is the point of your center of infinity.

I reveal to you now the white dot as the white fire core. I trust you become aware of it in this moment as a point of center in the innermost being between the heart chakra and the seat-of-the-soul chakra.

Somewhere between those two, beloved, the soul is mounting the spiral of being, passing through the records of the electronic belt, pushing through, exerting intense desiring and summoning all the strength of her momentum in this octave. That soul is groaning in travail to become one with the Divine Mother, while in the West the self, the sense of self, the psychological self, is more centered in the mental body and the awareness of the mind and of thought rather than of the inner being.

Thus the white dot, beloved: it is a nucleus and a vortex. I desire you to see it, for you have heard spoken of the seed atom. It is a reflection of that seed atom and a counterpart of that which is in the base-of-the-spine chakra sealed.

Blessed ones, train yourself to *be your soul! Be your soul*, I say! instead of merely being your intellectual mind where from morning till night you are on the single wavelength of thinking, reasoning, questioning, analyzing, computing. Remember, beloved, this is but a portion of self. Unless the self become the soul and understand identity as the soul, the self does not realize within itself the mirror reflection of the living Christ, the Lord, the Higher Mental Body of that Higher Consciousness that you are. This is the Light and the Beautiful that I extol.

Thus, to allow all energies to center in this mentality of self is to starve the soul of the sense of Selfhood: *"I AM a living soul of God becoming who I AM THAT I AM day by day!"* Remind yourself with this mantra that you are a soul strengthening, intensifying.

And the soul, beloved, does gain spirit, and the spirit that the soul gains is fire, sacred fire.

Thus, when we speak of the "spirit" of a man we speak of his cosmic honor flame, his integrity, his strength, his presence. The spirit of the individual is that which the soul has drawn down from the I AM Presence and raised up from the Divine Mother, weaving a cocoon of light, skeins as silken fibers around the soul until the wedding garment, all gold and purest white, [is] suddenly unveiled; and in the cosmic mirror the soul does behold and see, "Yes, my Lord, I am ready."

Now, beloved, until the moment of the appearing of thyself— thy soul as bride—you are the mirror and all that you can have of the Infinite One, of the I AM Presence, is that which you can reflect here below. And when you will reflect it steadily as in a quiet pool for twenty-four hours, you will have that momentum and that thread woven into your garment.

This is not difficult. Many of you sustain a flame of inner peace for days upon days, even though the outer self, the surface, may become ruffled. You sustain an inner love even though on the surface there may be agitation as the alchemy of self is felt in the self's contact with the world. This chemicalization of contact with all manner of toxins, of elements, of abuses of the chemistry of the planet does surely cause a surface aggravation from the body throughout the four lower bodies.

Beloved, let the soul rise daily. I said, *Let the soul rise daily!* For in this thou shalt know the Victory.

Blessed ones, as you move at a pace that is dictated by the acceleration of your own devotions and decrees—decrees, mind you, in which you make contact with your heart and the heart of your Christ Self and your I AM Presence and the Brotherhood—you pass more quickly than you realize as though taking a journey in the fastest plane around the planet. And thus moment by moment you enter new chambers of old karma in the electronic belt.

It is the proverbial labyrinth.

And so from moment to moment, as a kaleidoscope of astral debris changing, is the encounter; and the soul that has become a spirit infired, and fiery by determination and love and will, does direct that fire into that [misqualified] substance. But at times of weariness when energies wane for whatever reason, the soul is not so aggressively cutting through and thus there are stations along the way and pockets where the soul is slowed down.

You have understood this. You have written to me and other of the Ascended Masters and to the Messenger and you have said,

"I have not done so well. I have been out of alignment. I sense it. I know that I am not in that place where I used to be. What can I do? Help me."

This is our answer, beloved. Understand that you have elected a path of acceleration but [you] are as the blind who see not. All that you see is the effect in your life of a performance or a lesser performance. And so, beloved, when you are at those moments, know [that] you have reached a denser pocket, one of greater intensity, and it will always be reflected in outer circumstance and challenges, diversions of your time, interferences with the Community, and so forth.

Thus the Community as a whole did reach collectively a pocket of dense astral substance in the electronic belt and all together from that level had to fight against the fires of Death and Hell. Whether they be in the nation's capital or at your border, understand, beloved, that this is an outcropping of collective Community karma amongst a people who do not always consider that karmic debts must be paid and paid on time. They are either paid in service and violet flame decrees or through initiations that become more and more difficult as you mount that spiral and come closer to the 51 percent mark of balance.

Beloved ones, in the past twenty-four months, I must say to you there has been, unfortunately, an individual, as an example, in this Community who [because he did not] reach for a 51 percent balance of karma and of embodying that Christhood does find himself in this hour embodying 53 percent of his dweller-on-the-threshold. Perceiving this from inner levels and seeing the burden on the four lower bodies of this individual, the Messenger did make every call available to her in support of this individual's victory.

Beloved, the inattentiveness to the call of the heart to balance the threefold flame, to send out love, and [to] clear all obstructions [is a matter of record. Our instruction] was not fully heeded by this individual. But it has not been heeded by many. It is simply a case [where] the many did not arrive at this particular initiation but this individual did.

Blessed ones, Gautama Buddha does stress the clearing of the heart chakra because when the heart is cleared of hardness of heart, unkindness, absence of love, absence of mercy, and the threefold flame does expand, the individual is equipped to be one with Maitreya and Maitreya does come as father and place his hand over the hand of the chela who may then hold the sword and Maitreya does show the chela how to wield that sword, how to plunge that Ruby Ray sword into the very core of that dweller.

Heaven is so careful to teach you carefully.

And so, beloved, in the hour and the day when [your] karma descends you must have a heart of intense fire, cleared in the physical octave of all substances of cholesterol and fat and burdens that weaken the arteries and the veins. Blessed ones, the establishing of good health and sacred fire of the heart is most important because when these burdens descend they are a burden to the physical body and the brunt of that burden is borne by the [physical] heart.

The heart that is filled with Christ-love is untouchable. Exercise Christ-love while you are in the way with Christ as friend and brother. Then when you meet Christ as initiator you will embrace the initiator and become one with that Lord because you are in sync with the vibration of the initiator and therefore the initiation.

O Love, O Love that will not let me go or you go, beloved. How great is Love! How great are hearts filled with Love! How much are hearts protected by Love. How the Christ flame does increase. How Love does magnetize the higher wisdom for correct decision making. Many decisions will be made and only one decision will be right. You must be right on. Love does magnetize power. Love, true Love, begets purity and joy.

My blessed hearts, I ask you to consider diligently the conditions for which you are preparing and whether or not it is timely to bring forth children in this hour. I ask you to be wise and prudent and I call to your attention, for Mother Mary has asked me to tell you, that you must slay the dweller-on-the-threshold and the false hierarchy impostor of any children of Light who are destined to come through you now or in the far future.

For, beloved, the fallen ones, as archdeceivers, have approached parents of Light throughout the ages posing as souls of Light, actually placing pressure upon parents to give birth to them. And on occasion, beloved, when parents have not challenged the presence of such an one, but have simply assumed that anyone appearing and desiring to be born must be sent by God, they have unnecessarily brought forth lifestreams who were not assigned to them.

Beloved ones, there are fallen ones and foul spirits throughout the astral plane that forever seek to be embodied through the Light-bearers. Take care, then, to guard the sanctity of thy path. Understand for what cause those parents, holy ones whose lives [are] recorded in the Old and New Testament, show extensive preparations—calls for great protection, the pursuit of special diets, prayers, communions, [the] path of celibacy, [and] all manner of initiation on the Path. Some of these parents whose stories are retold (which stories the Messenger gave to you at a previous summer conference)[20] did wait years and years and years until they qualified under the Hierarchy of the Brotherhood to receive those souls who were assigned to them.

Thus I come to pierce illusions of fantasy, illusions that come down from the motion picture industry and their productions of this century and the playing on the screens over and over and over again of the dreams of married love and childbearing outside of the inner temple court and the path of initiation.

Blessed hearts, there are indeed souls of Light that we should desire at the right time to bring forth in this Community. We seek not numbers but quality and very specific souls who are worthy of the tremendous effort made on the part of every Community member, including the parents, to sponsor a soul to the full maturity of Christhood.

Thus, beloved, I urge you to understand that you do live in one of the lower-vibrating planetary spheres, that the protection of the Archangels, all seven of them, is called for, especially when desiring to be the chalice of the incoming great souls of Light. Consider this matter profoundly.

Consider, then, all future plans that have to do with family, with parenting and with marriage and determine where you must position yourself, as directed from within, to see to it that this Community, this headquarters, all at Glastonbury and all Keepers of the Flame throughout the world accomplish this preparedness [and that this] does receive your priority attention and the priority of the sacred fire within you.

Be unafraid to confront the self in the mirror once a day, to take an assessment and to say, "Is the fire of the eye sufficient to the task? Is the inner coil of being so tight that it is ready to move? Can I truly be there, ready to protect my own in fifteen minutes?"

Blessed ones, some place their attention on a dessert for a celebration, yet I have said, let my dictation be this dessert. Those who seek their just deserts here and now will surely receive them, for it is the hour of karmic reckoning of the chelas. But I recommend that you refrain from "unjust desserts" that weaken the mind and the will and give the body added burdens that do not find you on the point of cosmic alert.

I therefore ban desserts from our headquarters' kitchens, and those who have them and will have them, if they must, may find them in our restaurant and know that I, Morya, do not sit with you for dessert, for I do not take my own until this mission be fulfilled and you are home free. As Jesus said, "I will not drink this wine with you until I drink it new with you in the kingdom,"[21] so I say to you, <u>let us not celebrate until the prize is ours.</u>

<u>I speak</u>, then, <u>to</u> those who are called <u>the teens</u> of this Community. Ah, the teenage years of the formation of self and character, of calling, profession, education. Ah, the fickleness, the easy swings of emotion, also based on diet, and yet the quick changes, the insights, the realization of maturity and suddenly, perhaps to the surprise of all observing, the wandering teen does become somehow the responsible adult and chela.

Blessed ones, it is an age we have all passed through in every lifetime where we have exceeded the age of twenty. In all times and circumstances I have great compassion for this age, one of idealism, one of the desire for acceptability, experience, a self-discovery and independence in every way.

Blessed hearts, in keeping, then, with that which has come upon me and all that I have extended and expended of my allotment of energy of the will of God on behalf of our youth, <u>I</u> therefore this night <u>must draw the line.</u>

Champion of your free will I shall remain and lover of your soul. But I must say, if you do not have mercy for me and for this cause and this goal—[mercy] enough to <u>refrain from</u> a conscious freewill entering into <u>rock music</u> or <u>drugs</u> or <u>alcohol</u> or <u>nicotine</u> or <u>sugar</u>—if these things so deadly to the integration of the soul with the Christ cannot be set aside by you, then I must say to you, beloved, until you are ready for chelaship as I am able to give it, please do not request to participate in the activities of the Inner Retreat or the Royal Teton Ranch nor in services at any of our centers.

If you will have your freedom, I urge you to drink the cup to the fullest, to explore that freedom and ultimately to make your choice and to live with your choice. I pray that the opportunity will remain when you do decide, if you do decide, that this is the path to be preferred. But until that time, beloved, I shall not allow you to cross this threshold beyond this day in any of our centers. For I say to you: souls of Light of the very same age as yourselves we dare not send [to this Community, out of concern] for their contamination by your out-of-alignment state and cynicism or sensuality or worldliness. This, then, has been our experience [in the past] and these souls therefore have been kept away from our retreat lest they follow in your example.

<u>Let the Lightbearers come to the altar,</u> for their pledge to the will of God and the Diamond Heart shall give us new thrust

and, I pray and pray fervently, holy purpose.

Beloved ones, it is good for a season not to feel an obligation to come here when one desires other experiences. It is a relief to know that the cosmos is a place of free will and individuality and that you are free to pursue it and that we are also free to pursue it and [furthermore that] we are free to draw the line with the Ruby Ray and to draw a circle around Community, to initiate those in that Community and to say, "Within this circle, by the stability, mental and psychological, by the honesty and by the constancy of all within it, we may accelerate and raise up once again an acceptable and a more acceptable offering unto the Lords of Karma and Sanat Kumara."

Thus, beloved, be not chagrined but be relieved that a line is drawn.

Thus, beloved, lest you ask the Messenger, I must say to you that those teenagers who happen to live within this Community who are not willing to live according to the rules embraced by this Community may not remain. And I say to you, children of these parents who desire to be chelas here, if you determine to be the cause whereby you and therefore your parents must also leave, may you know that though you have free will you also have the capacity to make [negative] karma for your exercise of that free will and for the effect thereof upon other lifestreams.

Thus, beloved, weigh choices, for teens are not free of karma-making though all of America and Western civilization may so behave [as though they were free]. Teenagers make much, much karma, beloved, and they may spend decades undoing that karma. But then again, a choice made is a lesson to be learned and earned. And if it is lessons that you need to bring you to the heart of God, then I pray that you take them and learn them quickly.

I urge parents and teachers, then, to remember the proverb to "train up a child in the way he should go: and when he is old he will not depart from it."[22] It is you who are molding character, determination and resolve, the work ethic and the nobility of embodying the Word. But be not dismayed when [you] have given all of your heart in truly the proper manner or almost the proper manner [and] children do make their own choices in life. They are not your own, as the prophet has said,[23] and therefore they have come through you and you have given your best.

Remember the good. Cherish the treasures shared. They must fly, they must be their own person, and you must know that they were that person when they came to you and be satisfied that you have given them an impetus toward heaven. Now they must chart their own course.

Blessed hearts, for this reason <u>we give fastidious attention to new souls and new children growing up in this Community.</u> Parents learn the art of sacrifice very quickly. It is a sacrifice to bear children when one gives all that one must give and still one must give to one's Community.

Many have done well and beautiful souls abound. It is not for want of beautiful souls that <u>a Community may miss the mark</u> but <u>for want of diligence in determining to *be* one's soul</u>—to *be* one's own thought, one's own feeling, one's own mind integrated, and to rise daily without fail [to new heights of God consciousness].

Thus, in memory of Maitreya and in memory of the Mystery School of Eden I say, <u>it *is* possible to fail at Maitreya's Mystery School.</u> I would much rather remind you of that possibility than of the ever-present possibility of victory itself. For, beloved, if you determine not to fail, you shall be God-victorious! But if you ignore that potential to fail, no matter how far [along] you believe you are on the Path, then surely you may slip between the cracks.

<u>Elohim have pronounced, and heed it well: the judgment will descend upon the economy of the United States.</u> May you move with diligence to not be caught by this event as some of you were a year ago.

It is important that those with their eye on <u>Glastonbury</u> move together to the end that they may <u>pay in full for their properties.</u> It is only just, beloved. For if there is a day and an hour when you have banked neither the fires of the resurrection nor a sufficiency of funds and therefore you can no longer make your payments on your land, you place in jeopardy that [entire] property. Thus you must build and <u>build wisely and firmly.</u>

Expect to <u>be accountable for your survival</u> and you shall. Use wisdom, intelligence, information, knowledge. Inform yourselves and, above all, hear the voice within. <u>Make sound business judgments.</u>

I speak to all Keepers of the Flame. In this year the Messenger has already dismissed from this Church individuals who have taken advantage financially of others and then failed to repay what was promised. <u>Wherever there has been the taking advantage financially of other Keepers of the Flame or those without the Church, restitution must be made.</u> Neither the Darjeeling Council nor Morya nor the Messenger will bear the karma of those individuals who have taken advantage of the well-meaning or persuaded others to give them funds for unwise and unsound investments or businesses which they had no prior training to establish or to enter into.

Thus, beloved, you can expect that <u>those who have been dishonest with other people's money must be exposed,</u> and if it is you who must expose them, then expose them. For those who cover for [another] and cover up another's misdeeds will bear and share that karma though they had no part with it and though they need not descend to that unnecessary [karmic] entanglement which many do merely by human sympathy.

Therefore, let the just be made perfect in Love[24] and let justice be the sign of, the mark of, completion. Let there be no breaks in the figure-eight flow and let those who know that they have acted dishonestly, or at least imprudently, move quickly to rectify these situations.

All such shenanigans,* and I would call them such, block the entering into this Community of true Lightbearers. It does create a Community karma. The weight is too great for Morya and for the heart of the Messenger already given.[25] Therefore they must be cut off until balance is made.

I ask you to establish a sphere of blue fire around yourselves by singing to me as the Chohan of Power, led by the musicians.

El Morya, Thou Chohan of Power

El Morya, thou Chohan of Power
    Seal us in thy flame each hour
Guide our way, perfect our zeal
    O Morya, all chaos heal!

El Morya, we now command
    All of heav'n to take thy stand
For perfection, order, too
    In all we think and say and do!

El Morya, thou God of Truth,
    In thy flame come seal our youth!
Perfect our way, make straight their paths
    Blue-flame pow'r both sure and fast!

El Morya, invoke thy pow'r
    Help us work and serve each hour
Help us plan each day aright
    By thy love make all things right!

El Morya, we look to thee
    Help us gain self-mastery
The Golden Age is drawing nigh
    Lift our thoughts to God on high!

---

*shenanigan: a devious trick used esp. to divert attention for an underhand purpose; tricky or questionable practices or conduct, fakery; high-spirited or mischievous activity; chaff, nonsense, humbug, esp. when advanced to cover up some trickery.

El Morya, thy flame expand
Throughout each one in this fair land
Establish order, ritual, too
'Til each one knows just what to do!

El Morya, thou Chohan of Power
Come be with us every hour
The plan of Life to all unfold
Christ-vict'ry in all do mold! [sung 3 times]

Five is the hour of base ignorance. I have espoused that line and hierarchy and that chakra[26] that I might be with you in the day and the hour when you are surfeited in your own base ignorance— [an ignorance] of the things you know not and an ignore-ance [of the Great Law] that has caused you, in [your] feeling separate from life, to covet, to envy, to desire that which is another's attainment. Such is the lot of fallen angels. Be it not the lot of my chelas.

Five is the line of Morya. Five o'clock is the hour I appear at the altar. May this hour for morning decrees not deviate summer or winter, and may you be on time and ahead of time. I say this, beloved, for I desire with a deep desiring of my heart and the mantle of my office to take from you the human substance of that line and when ready—when you are ready and I am—to take from you the substance of the corresponding eleven o'clock line.

I desire this line to be the bond of our chelaship. I desire [in] this hour, morning and evening, that you shall remember me and remember the will of God. For to cut across the Clock in that hour, beloved, gives you the victory in all quadrants. It sounds the death knell of those interlopers who have invaded the [etheric and] mental quadrants. It gives you the thrust to enter the astral plane [on the six o'clock line] and to go for that [transmutation of the] remaining 49 percent [of your karma] when you receive the tests of the descent into Death and Hell.

On the eleven o'clock line, beloved, it does give you the final word of victory in the physical octave for precipitation, for survival and of all lines of the Clock. It gives you the impetus in the eleventh hour to triumph when the resentment and the revenge of all of Death and Hell break loose and the warlords.

Thus, by the five/eleven, you conquer time, and by that victory you gain the thrust to begin anew with the Great Divine Director on the twelve o'clock. Thus this axis is truly the fulcrum.

Beloved ones, in great joy, at a certain hour on the Path of this Messenger I was able by her service and diligent chelaship to take from her [her] human creation and karma of that line and replace it with a certain portion of my God-Wisdom and my God-Victory. Know, then, beloved, that the corresponding joy of the Messenger, so many years ago now, was an elation to my own heart as that infusion of illumination's golden flame did impart the joy and the zest for striving, the joy and the zest to defeat the dweller-on-the-threshold of a planet and a galaxy. Such is the momentum of the yellow fire. Such is [the reason for] the call of the hierarchs for illumination's golden-flame tapes supporting the violet flame.[27]

Now, then, beloved, I come to praise my chelas. I come to say to you that I have not missed one moment of [your] ardent service. I have not missed the drops of sweat, the hours, the fulfillment, the achievement and the striving. I have seen it all. And I have assembled devas of the Diamond Heart of the will of God who applaud your efforts and with me desire to bless you.

You, then, being wise chelas able to assess the victory of a summer's conference, of a fire thrust back, of an enemy who shakes and trembles and quakes around the planet for your presence—you, then, are also wise enough to know that you do not desire your just deserts in this octave but desire them to accrue to your causal body, for you are banking on total victory. Thus, beloved, I impart to you a certain percentage, a goodly percentage, of that momentum of victory that you have gained in fourteen months past of striving.

Thus, beloved, whether in this court or throughout the world, as you shall see, not only hear but see, this dictation, so note that I extend the ruby focus and through it now there does come to each one that portion that now may be for you attainment, strength, [and] momentum of that which you have accomplished. And though you may have served till weary in your bones, till you could not take another step, I say, you shall not be weakened but strengthened now by the true reward—strengthened, then, by hearts pure and diligent.

Not one erg of service or striving rendered with pure and loving heart is either lost or unnoticed nor does it remain un-multiplied. But it is multiplied. It does increase.

Thus, beloved, because you do have your reward and your reward is with you as attainment, shun lethargy and petty indul-gences whereby you compromise the full exercise of the mantle you have gained or of that portion of the mantle [you have gained]. You do not lose this reward, beloved, it only becomes less available. Thus, wield attainment. Every one of you has it to a greater or lesser degree. In the hour, then, when the wages are paid, each one does receive according to his service.

I fine you not for failure. Failure is its own fine, for there is no reward but only a burden. And thus by the attainment you have won you must use that attainment again to wrestle with self, cast out the lesser mind and begin again.

We are not Gurus and chelas on a treadmill, ignorant mice treading the same place again and again while someone measures our heart and breath! Nay, we move on. We will not repeat the same space. We will conquer the next level.

Build firmly. Claim your victories. Move on! Move on, I say! Move on. The morrow holds greater victories for greater challenges.

Blessed ones, in some sense of the word it is not alone for shortcomings that I may have my reins shortened in this hour but for want of a greater worldwide response to the Call itself. A planet has incurred karma. A nation has incurred karma.

And the ovoid of blue flame you have just invoked is creating the form around you now as you may visualize the aura of Mother Mary as the Virgin of Guadalupe. Visualize the aura, the mantle, the tilma. Visualize yourself standing as though Mother Mary, blue flames all around you. For this cause I requested that you sing.

I may give my chelas measure for measure the Electronic Presence of my blue-flame power even as you have the free will to claim it, to call for it. It is not *you* who have lost dispensation, beloved, it is I. Therefore, *you* may call and call again! *You* may address Lords of Karma on my behalf again and again! You may devise ways and means to so raise up our beloved flame of God's will, to so intensify the Diamond Heart that perhaps my being benched, as I did once bench a chela, may not be of so long endurance. We of the First Ray, after all, are impatient. And thus when we see a goal we go after it. I shall sit upon my bench and watch you as you no longer sit upon the fence.

(Blessed ones, be seated in this noble cause we espouse.)

The hour is overdue for the physical judgment of what Saint Germain has called the international capitalist/Communist conspirators. The first signs, as you have been shown, as the Messenger has been shown, of their judgment come with the black horse.[28] Thus Elohim have spoken in less than a year from the October pronouncement of the LORD God and Saint Germain as to the judgments upon Wall Street.[29]

Understand, then, beloved, that as you know the signs written by Nostradamus, foretold by Mary, by Jesus, by the signs in the heavens, a break in the economy itself is the precursor to war and the sign and signal of it. I pray you understand why preparedness, setting one's financial house in order, is so essential and [why] the immediacy, then, of preparing those shelters is also upon you.

The time has come, beloved, that the fallen ones of the planet and other spheres see Light and the Lightbearers as the maximum threat. We hold off and have held off their judgment, as you have been told, for many years, that you might have opportunity. And when I say "we" I speak of the Brotherhood, of beloved Alpha and Omega and the Four and Twenty Elders[—myself] as their spokesman, of course not making myself their equal in this decision.

Thus, beloved, the staying hand of the LORD God does act when you give your calls, but the timetables are also set; and there does come the hour when there is no longer the possibility of postponement. Unless these fallen ones be judged—and [even] if the consequence be the collapse of their systems—unless the judgment come, the Lightbearers shall not have their victory or their freedom. This is a cosmic equation which I trust you understand.

I, Morya, enter into silent prayer with all devotees of the will of God and I pray for the Lightbearers who have not responded to the Call and the plea of the Mother. I pray in the heart of the will of God and I appeal to their hearts now to respond.

Will you not also pray fervently by directing a ray of the will of God from your heart to every Lightbearer upon earth to give them the strength and support of your attainment—not to release that light or attainment to them but to bear them up in this hour that they might see and know the choices and choose well?

Gabriel, the beloved, comes to our aid, does place his Electronic Presence before all those who are the unresponsive ones to preach to them once again of the choices of Heaven and Hell, of Life and Death, of Be-ness and Nonexistence, even of the oncoming judgment of the money beast.

"I pray, O Father, our beloved Alpha, O Mother, our Omega, hear my inner call of the heart, my imploring, my extension of my heart to these—one more time, one more space." [1½ minutes of silent prayer while the Messenger holds up the ruby focus]

By the grace of God all have been touched by the sapphire of my heart and my right hand—by your reinforcement, by our oneness. Come very close to me, my own chelas. I embrace you with the love of my heart. Our oneness worldwide is now. As we press closely in the grid of Light [of] the Great Divine Director, as we are one, as we sense our oneness by the pulsation of God, the I AM THAT I AM, our strength of oneness is sealed in the heart of Elohim in this hour.

I desire nevermore to be separated from thee, O my beloved. May the desiring of your hearts in the figure-eight flow that our God has given to us give you more of myself, as the Law allows it, as you give to me the Light and the Beauty and more Light and Beauty and decree and mantra, that by that flow I surely may be again able to give to you *more than you know.*

Now, beloved, I commend you to the high road and the rugged road of Victory. The future is golden. It is white light before you. If you have the nerve and the stomach, the will and the astuteness and the contact with Hierarchy and the thread is not broken, you will be there on a golden shore when the Light is all-effusive. Standing between two worlds, feet firmly in the earth, yet a planet cleansed and free, you shall know the meaning of striding the octaves with Hercules and realizing a goal you have seen before but the outer mind has not admitted to.

It is an initiation of the cross: "My God, my God, why hast thou forsaken me?"[30] and then an entering in by five secret rays and then, by momentum garnered, a resurrection untold. All this shall come to pass, and yet for fiery hearts for whom Love is the key I prophesy, I predict, I affirm and I stand for Victory—Victory in the earth, in the sun, in the sea, in the air, in the fire—in the mist and in the crystal!

I AM and I remain Morya of the First Ray of the Will of God. Morya El is my name.

This dictation was **delivered** on **Monday, August 8, 1988,** 8:03–10:03 p.m. MDT, at the **Royal Teton Ranch, Park County, Montana,** upon the occasion of the thirtieth anniversary of the founding of The Summit Lighthouse by the Ascended Master El Morya through the Messenger Mark L. Prophet August 8, 1958. [**N.B.** Bracketed material denotes words unspoken yet implicit in the dictation, added by the Messenger under El Morya's direction for clarity in the written word.] **(1)** The day and hour this dictation was delivered – 8-8-88 at 8:03 p.m. – corresponds to the **8 o'clock line** of God-Justice under the hierarchy of Virgo on the Cosmic Clock. **(2) Yellowstone National Park fires threatening the Royal Teton Ranch.** On Monday, Aug. 1, 1988, the Fan Creek Fire that had been burning in Yellowstone National Park since June 25 directly threatened the Heart of the Inner Retreat, Church Universal and Triumphant's international shrine at the Royal Teton Ranch. It was one of 10 major fires which burned out of control in the park during the summer and it eventually advanced to within a quarter of a mile of the ranch property. The Messenger and hundreds of Keepers of the Flame kept a week-long prayer vigil in the Heart and in the chapel for the protection of the ranch and firefighters and the reversing of the tide of the fire and adverse weather conditions. Keepers of the Flame around the world joined in the vigil in their own sanctuaries and homes. By the end of the week the immediate danger from the fire had diminished. Throughout the remainder of the summer, however, the fires continued to rage in and around the park and posed an imminent threat to bordering towns, some of which were evacuated and narrowly escaped destruction. Dense smoke blanketed surrounding communities and pollution levels were high in other parts of Montana as well as neighboring states, with smoke reaching even as far as New York and Pennsylvania. A month after El Morya's dictation, on Sept. 10, the fast-moving North Fork Fire directly threatened the Royal Teton Ranch at its southern border. The ranch and adjacent areas were put on alert in preparation for immediate evacuation. Again the Messenger and Keepers of the Flame worldwide held prayer vigils while preparations were made for the protection of the property. On Sept. 11 a cold front from the north brought a period of snow and rain showers that finally began to extinguish the worst blazes in Yellowstone Park history, which ultimately burned across some 1.6 million acres of the 2.2 million-acre park. **(3)** See Summit University Forums **"The UFO Connection**: Alien Spacecraft and Government Secrecy," and **"The AIDS Conspiracy**: Establishment Cover-up, Pharmaceutical Scam or Biological Warfare?" 1988 *Pearls of Wisdom,* pp. 492 n. 2, 502 n. 8. **(4)** In response to **El Morya's call for a marathon,** Keepers of the Flame rallied during a 10-day prayer vigil Aug. 12–21, 5 a.m. to 11 p.m., at the Royal Teton Ranch to stand in support of El Morya and for the protection of the worldwide Community of Lightbearers. Vigils were also conducted in local Church Universal and Triumphant Teaching Centers and Study Groups throughout the world. **(5) Burden of the Lord.** Nah. 1:1; Hab. 1:1; Zech. 9:1; 12:1; Mal. 1:1; false burdens: Jer. 23:32–40; Lam. 2:14. **(6)** Decrees 10.03, "I AM God's Will," and 10.18, "Sweet Surrender to Our Holy Vow," are included on *El Morya, Lord of the First Ray: Dynamic Decrees with Prayers and Ballads for Chelas of the Will of God 1,* 94-min. audiocassette of songs and decrees given at a medium-fast pace; cassette with booklet, B88125, $5.95 (add $.55 for postage). Beginners should start with *Save the World with Violet Flame! by Saint Germain 1* and *2* before moving on to the faster decree tapes. See 1988 *Pearls of Wisdom,* pp. 400 n. 6, 560 n. 1, and p. 18 of Summit University Press 30th anniversary catalog. **(7) El Morya's diamond placed upon the altar.** On July 3, 1965, El Morya announced that a giant transformer of God's will was being built in the etheric plane to "radiate out to the entire world the good will of Almighty God as an intense and divine holy purpose." El Morya also said that he had taken "the large diamond which I wear in my turban out and I have pledged it to the Lords of Creation, that I shall not wear it again until such a time as this activity of this forcefield of good will has accomplished at least 50 percent of the purpose for which it is brought into creation . . . . I pray also that all of you and all who hear my words will find some courage within your souls to make some form of pledge and token to Almighty God on behalf of good will. For the world and its destiny is held in the balance, precious ones, as individuals shall rally to a cause." On June 24, 1978, El Morya announced that "50 percent of the purpose to which the transformer was brought forth has been fulfilled" and that "the Lord God has returned to me the diamond that I had treasured, given to me by my own guru . . . . You have . . . won for me another opportunity to place the momentum of my causal body upon the altar of humanity." See *Morya,* pp. 298, 301–2; audiocassette B7625, $6.50 (add $.55 postage); 1978 *Pearls of Wisdom,* pp. 297–98. **(8)** On Feb. 12, 1988, El Morya gave himself to the chelas of the will of God as a **sapphire chalice** to be filled with the "intense wine of the Spirit that comes forth by your call to the violet flame . . . . Each day I shall take that which you have deposited in this chalice and place it in the violet flame reservoir of light on the etheric plane." 1988 *Pearls of Wisdom,* pp. 155–56. **(9)** On Feb. 28, 1987, Serapis Bey admonished Keepers of the Flame to participate without fail in Saint Germain's Saturday night service, the Sunday Sacred Ritual for Keepers of the Flame, and the Wednesday evening healing service. See 1988 *Pearls of Wisdom,* p. 331 n. 3. **(10)** "Every man shall bear his own burden." Gal. 6:5. **(11)** Dan. 1:3–16. **(12)** El Morya was embodied as the Hebrew patriarch Abraham, who witnessed the destruction of **Sodom and Gomorrah** (Gen. 19:24, 25, 27, 28). The Messenger Mark L. Prophet revealed that these cities were destroyed by atomic energy. Zecharia Sitchin draws the same conclusion in his book *The War of Gods and Men.* See *The Lost Teachings of Jesus II,* pp. 306, 349–50, 562 n. 65. **(13)** On Aug. 8, 1958, El Morya wrote a letter to **"Chelas Mine,"** marking the founding of The Summit Lighthouse. **(14) Weeping statues.** Hundreds of statues of Mother Mary throughout the world have been seen and photographed shedding tears, particularly those known as the Pilgrim Madonna, which bear the likeness of the Blessed Mother's appearance at Fátima. Observers say that there is a correlation between world events and the weeping of the statues. **(15)** On Aug. 7, 1988, the Messenger conducted a service as part of the ongoing vigil on the Fan Creek Fire (see note 2 above). **(16)** On June 29, 1988, the Messenger conducted a **"Seminar on the Cosmic Clock:** Charting the Cycles of Your Karma, Psychology and Spiritual Powers on the Cosmic Clock"; those who attended received diagrams, charts, call sheets and work sheets. See 1988 *Pearls of Wisdom,* p. 479 n. 5. **(17)** Matt. 5:45. **(18)** Matt. 7:13. **(19) Bodhidharma** (fl. 6th century A.D.) was an Indian Buddhist missionary to China who founded the Ch'an, or Zen, sect of Buddhism in an effort to return the religion to the true spirit of Gautama's teachings. Bodhidharma taught that the Buddha was not to be found in books or images but in the heart of man and that the way to achieve enlightenment was through meditation. He spent nine years in intense meditation in a cave in northern China and was described as having a fierce disposition, penetrating eyes, and an abrupt and direct manner. According to Buddhist lore, in a fit of anger at having fallen asleep during meditation Bodhidharma cut off his eyelids. Another legend says that he spent so many years in meditation that his legs fell off. His intensity of purpose was characteristic of Ch'an devotees, who would undergo any austerity in order to attain the highest enlightenment. **(20) Parents who prepared to sponsor holy children.** Adam and Eve, I Adam and Eve 73:5–8; II Adam and Eve 1:9–14; 2. Abraham and Sarah, Gen. 15:2–6; 17:1–8, 15–19, 21; 18:10–19; 21:1–8. Isaac and Rebekah, Gen. 25:21–26. Jacob and Rachel, Gen. 30:1, 2, 22–24; Testament of Benjamin 1:2–6. Manoah and his wife, Judg. 13. Elkanah and Hannah, I Sam. 1. Joachim and Anna, Gospel of the Birth of Mary 1–3; Protevangelion 1–5. Zacharias and Elisabeth, Luke 1:5–25, 57–80. Joseph and Mary, Luke 1:26–56; 2:1–20; Gospel of the Birth of Mary 4–8; Protevangelion 6–12, 14; History of Joseph the Carpenter 2–7. **(21)** Matt. 26:29; Mark 14:25; Luke 22:18. **(22)** Prov. 22:6. **(23)** Kahlil Gibran, *The Prophet* (New York: Alfred A. Knopf, 1923), p. 17. **(24)** I John 4:18. **(25) Order of the Diamond Heart and the Fifteenth Rosary.** 1987 *Pearls of Wisdom,* pp. 633–37, 641–42; 1988 *Pearls of Wisdom,* pp. 255–56, 257, 515. **(26)** El Morya is the initiator under the hierarchy of Gemini on the **5 o'clock line** of the Cosmic Clock, corresponding to the throat chakra. **(27)** 1988 *Pearls of Wisdom,* pp. 458, 577. **(28)** Rev. 6:5, 6. **(29)** 1987 *Pearls of Wisdom,* pp. 484–85, 487–88. **(30)** Matt. 27:46; Mark 15:34; Lost Gospel According to Peter 5.

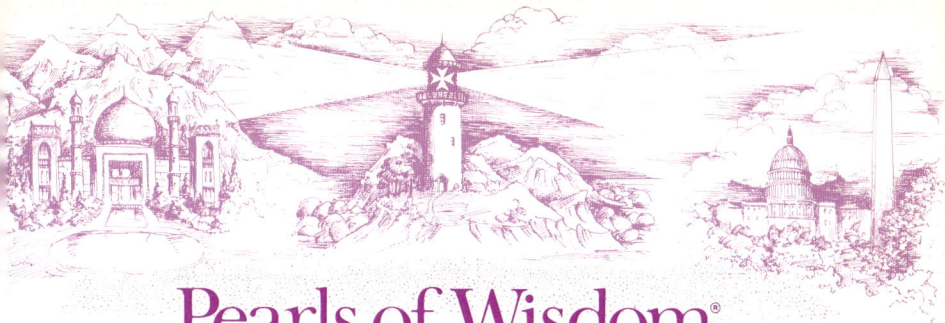

Pearls of Wisdom®
published by The Summit Lighthouse

Vol. 31 No. 78	*Beloved Cyclopea*	*November 19, 1988*

The Harvest

I

The Merciful Heart

"I Call You to the Heart of the Living Buddhas on the Path of the Bodhisattva"

Thrice I have come. This time I speak. I speak to the All-Seeing Eye of God within you. I AM Cyclopea. You have not known me, for you have not seen me.

Let the devotions to the Divine Mother fill your cups. Let them be complete. Let the sacred fire *be* and it shall rise of its own accord, for the great desiring of the Divine Mother within you is to give birth to the Christ of your heart.

Even so do the fallen angels come, following their leader called the great dragon.[1] Blessed hearts, these fallen ones come to you for one purpose, to cause you to allow that Light to descend by all manner of misuse of the Light of the Mother and her sacred fire.

Thus, she does rise but you determine that she shall fall by words, acts, thoughts, feelings. O the feelings, beloved! How they do weigh down the Light of the Mother within you.

Thus, if you should sustain your meditation upon the Buddha, as you have done this night,[2] you shall also receive the magnetism of his heart whereby there shall occur, by his meditation, a consonance of the Word within you. And in your eye contact with him, gazing steadfastly upon the Lord of the World, you will know that not only does Gautama keep the threefold flame for all but he does [also] keep the Light of the Divine Mother raised up.

Now, beloved, in every step of the ladder of life upon the stalk of being and in the chakras there are scores to be settled, old records of strife. So many resent. So many who know this path and know me as Cyclopea, Elohim of the Fifth Ray, do yet carry hatred in their bones, anger in the solar plexus and yet do continue to attend services, some smoldering with that resentment of being required by the law of Serapis to fulfill that three-in-one each week of attendance at our services.[3]

Blessed hearts, it is a pity in all directions. It is for the individual a waste of time, a waste of money, a waste of a lifetime to so affiliate oneself with our bands and yet to fail to make peace with one another, with oneself, with one's inner being, to desire not to surrender those beasts of prey that land; but if you let them, as many have, they sink their roots, they sink their teeth and, lo, you have an alter ego cohabitating that temple.

Blessed hearts, I AM Elohim and my Presence is an intensity of the Immensity.

What will you do, beloved, if you remain a house divided?[4] What will you do when you do not take the mantras of Kuan Yin[5] to so magnetize a merciful heart [to effect the most desired result]: that you do not remember [or carry with you] from day to day any [burden of] discord or problem or wounded self?

Blessed ones, all these things that we have given by the science of sound, by the Word, by the delivery—for so I AM the sponsor of that Word going forth and that sound with all Elohim— [all] these are that you might implement purest heart, the treasure of life to fulfill all things of Divine Love.

Forget not, then, this principle. For the planetary initiations are stepped up. From autumn equinox to the finale of the year it is indeed "The Harvest." Now you reap what you have sown in three quadrants of life. Thus, the fourth season must be the season of the sorting.

While there is yet time, cast into the sacred fire all energies misapplied, misconnected, suppressed. *These things must not be.* When there are stored resentments and unresolved problems, this, beloved, is seen by the Lords of Karma as a failure on the part of the chela to exercise the noblest, the greatest opportunity ever afforded a lifestream, [or] a lifewave, in some cases so recalcitrant, so backward and so beset by the pride of the ego as to attract those innumerable entities that do beset the soul and body.

When we give, then, the violet flame, when we give the mantra and our Presence, it ought to be snatched by the fervent chela who so perceives that our Word and our dispensation is truly for the salvation of that soul who does not forget daily and hourly that the Bridegroom cometh.[6] And therefore, the soul preparing to enter into the Holy of Holies of God does ever rejoice that so many emissaries of heaven have come in this hour to receive the brides of Christ upon earth.

I AM, therefore, Cyclopea. And I say, beloved, it is for the harboring of intense feelings that are not of God-Harmony against any part of life, including oneself—it is for this cause that your El Morya has been so burdened in this hour.

Let it be known, then, beloved, that some relent not and some even take the hour of our Chief's being benched[7] to wreak havoc with the chelas, to now declare that their inner sight is opened and therefore to receive all manner of psychic projection from the fallen angels who are indeed the spoilers and deceivers who move about seeking whom they will devour with their protestations.[8] O their prevarications of the Truth are many! But, beloved, these are wandering stars (we know them well) to whom is reserved the mists of blackness, even "the blackness of darkness for ever."[9]

Thus, while they have their day we come to say, let Death and Hell be swallowed up throughout this planet because [of] the humble heart of a chela, bold in the service of his God and O yet so contrite before his own Christ Self. [Even so] let this posture of those who will not be divided be the displacement and the utter devouring of the mouthings of the original Liar from the beginning.

To hear them prate and to repeat that which they have said from the beginning—the denial of each one's own Christ-discrimination, the denial of that office of Messenger, the denial of the office and the right to be chela and to be servant—[is to know] all these, beloved, [who] move again as the heathen who have never known their God, who long ago did quench his flame, rage and imagine a vain thing.[10]

I come, Cyclopea, that I might lend to El Morya and his devotees my All-Seeing Eye that you might perceive the Christ-hood within, and above you the great company of saints, and that you might call forth that which I bring to probe and penetrate, that you be not caught off guard and therefore rationalize the straying from the eternal Logos, even the Word of the Law from the Lawgiver that does rise in the center of being, even as a pillar of fire, even as a rod of Aaron.[11]

Joseph's rod does blossom[12] and the lily of the virgin eye is Christ Universal. Thus, my beloved Virginia does reinforce in each and every one of you in this hour the point of origin, the immaculate concept, the great wonder of God in you, the handiwork of Father and Mother.

Blessed ones, I speak to all who have ever called themselves Keepers of the Flame. There are many things which ought not to be among the company of Lightbearers. Beloved hearts, we work diligently through the Messenger and yourselves at the Friday night Ascension Service that you might have an exorcism of ultimate value to your soul. The teaching is exact but it is also exacting.

Therefore, if you would have records of misuses of the sacred fire removed from you, and all manner of dark things unseen by you but felt, you must understand it is an inner-temple work that must have your tethering of soul and chakras for a certain season. For it is expedient that the Light of your chakras, buoyed up by the Divine Mother and her desiring to assist you, and in you to give birth to the Christ—it is expedient that this Light be harnessed to Elohim and our focus at the Grand Teton.[13]

Visualize, then, the seven points of Light upon the brow with Light going forth as a crown from you. Visualize all Light rising and know—even as you may observe water boiling in a pot bringing to the surface that which is below—that as the Light is raised up it does bring to the surface all manner of records of abuses of power, misuses of the sacred fire and truly the betrayal of Divine Love where purity has been set aside for all manner of indulgences and preferences of the self.

The release of Light is powerful and therefore unless you are cautious, unless you recognize this experiment whereby we do sponsor Serapis Bey to give here in this very court some of the most necessary teachings and trainings and initiations given at Luxor—unless you understand this, beloved, you will find yourself forgetful that you are [engaged] in a process, a process of re-creation by Elohim if you will allow it. By being here each Friday night, therefore, you submit yourselves even to a surgery of cosmic dimensions.

It is not lawful, then, that you should go forth and begin to engage in relationships that take from you the sacred fire [through] any of the chakras while we build, while we mend, while we balance, while we restore. These things are not accomplished all in one night.

The seraphim come. They place their Presence over you. How you maintain the vigil each week in the seven-day cycle of initiation day by day on the seven rays determines what may be given the following week.

Beloved, it is truly the word of El Morya and of the entire Hierarchy in this hour that every chela must "pay as you go."[14] And if you think we speak of the coin of the realm, this is the least of our concerns. For the squandering of Light is far greater than your squandering of money simply because many of you have already squandered your money in this and previous lives and therefore you have not much left to squander. But as for Light, you who are given much often find ways of losing that Light and being unaware, as though you had a leaky vessel and the water did leak out and you did not even take notice.

Beloved hearts, if you truly desire to be healed and to be sealed, I tell you that all of Hierarchy is poised to assist you in the meeting of the dates from October 2 to October 2.[15] During this period, then, we shall give all that the dispensation of Alpha allows us to give to the Lightbearers of the world.[16]

It is disheartening for any Cosmic Being to see so great a gift, so great a salvation not comprehended or seen. For in the aftermath of that Friday night vigil there must be a keeping of the flame if you truly would have your Deathless Solar Body[17] woven and ready twelve months hence.

Blessed ones, you cannot be naked[18] as those who were dismissed from the original Maitreya's Mystery School. You must be clothed upon with etheric garments *without rent, without spot, without blemish* that you might move freely to higher octaves and return again when necessary.

This is our goal. This is our effort. And this is why our Messenger does tarry at the altar day and night. For there is an altar behind the altar that is kept. And in you there is an altar behind the altar of the heart. It is the secret chamber.

Have you ventured therein? Have you thought as you retire in sleep to gently rise in the soul to the heart chakra, to enter that heart chakra, to knock upon the door that does open the eight-petaled secret chamber of the heart? May you enter therein as you pass into sleep and know that it is the passageway through the Sacred Heart of your Holy Christ Self to the retreats of the Great White Brotherhood where you do continue the work that is begun.

Let Keepers of the Flame who keep the vigil on the morrow and on Friday in this court pursue the rituals and exercises that have been given already in the Friday night services that you might be prepared for succeeding steps when we shall come again.

Blessed ones, it is needful, then, that the self-emptying process take place, the letting go of despite toward another. The condemnation of our best servants or even of our worst must have no part with those who understand that you cannot receive us and we cannot receive you while you retain that mild dislike and that annoyance for any.

Yes, you may know by Christ-discrimination what is the vibration, even the vibration unacceptable of those known or not known, acquaintances or those whom you see in passing. But this must not arouse in you ire or enmity or discord but merely the divine awareness of the World Teachers of the precise state of evolution [of that soul] whereby you may send a comforting thought, blessing, a call for protection, [and,] in Christ, even the rebuke of the soul that does sleep.

Blessed ones, all are idolaters still, whether of the human self or another. Let it cease. There is none good but one and that is God.[19] Worship God and do not mentally set up your hierarchy of favorites and preferences. Judge not, beloved, for there is one judge, your Holy Christ Self. And most do not judge righteous judgment but only look to the outer.

Leave, then, the weighing and the assaying of the gold of the soul herself to the Elohim of God. Nevertheless, call forth the judgments of God that they might be ratified swiftly that those destroyers in the earth might be impeded and reduced and no longer stand at the threshold [of Christ-Self awareness] where souls would enter and deny them entrance into the Holy of Holies.

You are seeing the most physical work that has ever been accomplished through the Messenger in the levels of being that are being touched by the sword of the Divine Mother and Maitreya. Thus, it does come down to the physical mentality, the physical attitude, the physical consciousness.

And there is, beloved, in addition to the flushing out and the bringing to the surface, a narrowing of the room of self where that which is spiritual, that which is the soul has infinite space but where that which is the human creation begins to feel the pressure as though of the shrinking-man or the shrinking-woman [syndrome].[20] It is a frustration that then breeds fanaticism and even impels insanity for want of surrender from within.

These are trying times for chelas who would enter the heart of the will of God. But, beloved, they are trying for the very reason that all the hierarchies of heaven have their attention trained upon the Lightbearers of the earth, seeking to initiate, to assist all who will [keep the God Flame] to hold the balance for all other Lightbearers and for earth in transition.

You have asked for and, apart from the asking, the Law has decreed more intense initiations. I, therefore, Cyclopea, come to announce to you that you will not put one foot ahead of the other on the path of your ascension until you diligently root out and exorcise from yourself those conditions in consciousness which impede the full manifestation of the Ruby Ray cross on the 1/7 and the 4/10 axes of your Cosmic Clock.[21]

Blessed ones, you have come to the place when there does fall due the harvest of all violations of Divine Love in all prior incarnations. Therefore, the Great Law does decree: Thus far and no farther! Surrender your antipathies, your animosities and your anger against any part of life. Do so truly and if you say, I cannot, then I say to you, you have recourse in the heart of the Blessed Mother Mary, the Queen of Heaven on our Fifth Ray. You have recourse to the heart of Kuan Yin and to the Goddess of Liberty and all others [who represent the Divine Mother] that through their hearts you might reach the great Buddhas.

With all thy getting, then, get the merciful heart of Kuan Yin whereby through the Immaculate Heart of Mary you see the immaculate conception by the Father-Mother God of the soul in the beginning and you extend mercy for the out-of-alignment state of that soul in this hour of the ending. And you forgive profoundly. You let go. You do not retain a sense of injustice or a record of pain.

Let the eternal flowing mercy which flows from the vessel [of Kuan Yin] without end, that eternal flowing violet flame, flush out of all systems of being the cause, effect, record and memory of any condition of consciousness that has caused you to fail to let go of the most sinister forces of anti-Love. There is no more sinister force in all of the outer universes than that force of anti-Love, for it does cause stultification, rigidity, morbidity and swift and sudden demise. Therefore, ". . . the greatest of these is Charity."[22]

Beloved ones, those who cannot and will not forgive life are either those who have in the past snuffed out their own inner God Flame for want of mercy toward life or they are those who are in the process of so doing. Trust them not. Go after them not. For the Lord does give his recompense. The Lord does forgive even in the same measure as the individual does forgive the Lord's own offspring.

Thus, beloved, where there is nonforgiveness [on the part of the fallen angels],[23] there can be noncompromise on the part of the Lightbearer. For the unforgiving heart is truly the betrayer of the Sangha of the Buddha, the Dharma of the Buddha, the Guru who represents the Buddha, and the Buddha himself.[24]

Beloved ones, in this be it known that the fundamental and basic identity of the sons and daughters of God is the quality and the presence of the merciful heart. The Lord has not required you to extend mercy to the godless, to the evildoers, to the Watcher nor to the Nephilim. All of these are the "Nonforgivers," [for they have forgiven neither the Lord nor his own for the just judgments of the Law meted upon them]. Let the mercy of God that endures forever be understood as that mercy which endures unto the merciful.

You will discover, then, that mercy is a flame beyond reason or understanding or dissecting. Mercy is a flame in the mantra of Kuan Yin that does simply dissolve, as a universal solvent, all hardness of heart. Therefore, beloved, know that the foundation of all initiation is the loving heart of mercy that does stand firm and draw the line and keep the standard in oneself, the line of Christhood. There can be no other.

I call you to the heart of the living Buddhas on the path of the bodhisattva. None shall enter, no matter how extolled by others, none shall enter who have not the merciful heart. This is the dividing of the way.

Let us sing a mantra of Kuan Yin that you might know that each mantra recited in Love—Love sent forth to the most difficult person you know—is a bead upon the crystal rosary of yourself. May you one day find yourself draped in crystal rosaries unending, each bead a mantra that has become a song in your heart.

Gautama Buddha has drawn the line.[25] May all who desire to be on the right side of that line know that they may reenter the place of the Holy of Holies by the mantras of Kuan Yin. Let go, beloved. Let go and let Love be the song in your heart.

I work now with the third eye of each one. If you provide me not with sacred fire raised, there is little I can do to sustain progress or to open your inner sight to the highest octaves.

Come unto me, then, for I AM a Cosmic Teacher, tarrying this year to see what we may do for the Lord's Day.

"The Summit Lighthouse Sheds Its Radiance O'er All the World to Manifest as Pearls of Wisdom." This dictation was **delivered** by the Messenger Elizabeth Clare Prophet on **Wednesday, October 5, 1988,** 11:42 p.m.–12:19 a.m. MDT, during the six-day conference *The Harvest* held at the **Royal Teton Ranch, Park County, Montana.** Available with the dictation of the Goddess of Purity on 90-min. audiocassette K88031, $6.50 (add $.55 for postage), and on 90-min. videocassette HP88089, $19.95 (add $1.10 for postage). [**N.B.** Bracketed material denotes words unspoken yet implicit in the dictation, added by the Messenger under Cyclopea's direction for clarity in the written word.] Throughout these notes *PoW* is the abbreviation for *Pearls of Wisdom.* **(1)** Rev. 12; 13:2, 4; 16:13; 20:1–3. **(2)** In the service prior to Cyclopea's dictation, there was a video meditation to song 464, "Hail, Gautama Buddha!" in which images of Gautama Buddha were superimposed over scenes of the Inner Retreat. **(3) Three services.** 1988 *PoW,* p. 331 n. 3. **(4)** Matt. 12:25; Mark 3:24, 25; Luke 11:17. **(5) Kuan Yin's Crystal Rosary.** 1988 *PoW,* pp. 373 n. 13, 480 n. 7. **(6)** Matt. 25:1–13. **(7)** 1988 *PoW,* pp. 581–82, 583–84, 585, 586. **(8)** I Pet. 5:8. **(9)** Jude 13. **(10)** Pss. 2:1; 46:6; Acts 4:25. **(11)** Exod. 7:8–12, 15–21; 8:5, 6, 16, 17; Num. 17; Heb. 9:4. **(12)** Gospel of the Birth of Mary 5:12–17; 6:1–5; Protevangelion 8:6–12. **(13) Focus of Elohim at the Royal Teton Retreat.** The seven rays of the Elohim are enshrined at the Royal Teton Retreat, an ancient focus of Light congruent with the Grand Teton in Wyoming. The rays are concentrated and anchored in a large image of the All-Seeing Eye of God that is located in a council hall of the retreat. **(14) "Pay as you go."** "Every man shall bear his own 'economic' burden" (Gal. 6:5). See pp. 584–85, 597–98. **(15) 24 months.** El Morya, 1987 *PoW,* pp. 474, 480, quoted in 1988 *PoW,* p. 249 n. 7; 1988 *PoW,* p. 323. **(16) Dispensations of Alpha.** 1987 *PoW,* pp. 242–46, 384–86; 1988 *PoW,* p. 528. **(17) Deathless Solar Body.** 1988 *PoW,* pp. 17, 20 n. 5. **(18)** Gen. 3:7. **(19)** Matt. 19:17; Mark 10:18; Luke 18:19. **(20) Shrinking-man syndrome.** On January 1, 1980, Sanat Kumara explained that "there is no death but a succession of experiences whereby the soul may elect to become more of its own central sun or to squander the light of that central sun and to watch the diminishing of life in other souls and ultimately within itself. Beloved ones, when an individual puts out vast quantities of hatred upon other parts of life, and that life diminishes and the return of karma causes the diminishing of the individual who sent it forth, can you understand that the originator of the hatred might not be aware of the shrinking image of all who are involved in this group karma? Individuals have become less and less of the Godhead, yet who walks the earth saying today, 'I am not the man that I was yesterday or a century ago or ten thousand years ago'? People are what they are and they think they have always been what they are. But in fact, upon this earth many have been reduced to a lowly estate, without grace, by their own doings and dark deeds. It is the process of self-disintegration whereby the self that is in that process does not perceive the disintegrating self but only the self that remains. . . . Let us realize, then, the price that . . . must be paid by all of us ascended and unascended if together we would truly bring to the shrinking-man syndrome the awareness of expanding life, exalted life, transcendent life, and the unique I AM Presence, God Flame of each one." In his January 27, 1980 Pearl of Wisdom, Serapis Bey said that "the shrinking-man syndrome of which our Father spoke at the New Year's conference is indeed the syndrome of the synthetic self which senses the reduction of the life-force and the crystal cord as the judgment descends increment by increment" (1980 *PoW,* p. 18). **(21)** Aquarius/Leo, Taurus/Scorpio initiations of God-Love, God-Gratitude, God-Obedience, God-Vision. See 1988 *PoW,* pp. 479 n. 5, 463–80, 495, 535–38, 539. **(22)** I Cor. 13:13. **(23)** Matt. 19:28; Luke 22:30; I Cor. 6:3. **(24)** The Buddha, the Dharma, the Sangha (the **Three Jewels**). 1988 *PoW,* p. 447 n. 9. **(25) Gautama draws the line.** 1987 *PoW,* pp. 248–49; 1988 *PoW,* pp. 507–20.

Pearls of Wisdom®

published by The Summit Lighthouse

| *Vol. 31 No. 79* | *The Beloved Goddess of Purity* | *November 20, 1988* |

The Harvest

II

Spiritualization of Consciousness
The Weaving of the Deathless Solar Body
Seek and Find the Gifts of the Holy Spirit

From great heights of Cosmic Purity I descend. Hearts of pure fire, I am truly welcome. I AM the Goddess of Purity, and I form the descending point of an equilateral triangle and I am reinforced in the other points by the Goddess of Light and the Queen of Light.

We continue, then, the release of the Divine Mother from *FREEDOM 1988,* bringing to you in *The Harvest* the year's end [of dispensations] in the hour of the accumulation of all karma of acts, deeds, of the desire and the memory bodies.

The harvest, then, is truly plenteous in those who have given this year 1988 to the establishment of this figure-eight flow from the soul through the [heart] nexus of Maitreya, the Universal Christ, to the very living heart of God, to the heart of Buddha, from the heart of Mother below unto the Victory above.

Some did begin this year with the best of intentions to keep a white-fire discipline of the sacred energies of life. The very curse of forgetfulness that does come from the fallen ones, weakening the memory of the vow taken, has overtaken others.

Thus, to those who began and yet would desire to see a more intense coil appearing in their lives in this hour and do not, I say:

A new year awaits you, a year that will mark the final of this decade of the eighties. Let it be understood, beloved, that this [harvest of the decade] is the harvest to which we look, and we desire to see you make a most concerted effort to balance the karma of this entire decade by violet flame and rising sacred fire in your temple. Let this become your goal beginning now in this hour, for the harvest is the separation of the tares and the wheat.[1]

It is a propitious hour, then, to retain that which is the highest and to be willing to let go of that which is maya and illusion, for to take it with you is to endow it with importance and the importance of permanence as you borrow the Light of the Great Preserver[2] and seek, then, to retain that which is your desiring but which is [in Reality] illusion.

We come in this hour to all, without exception. Our Light pressing in gives you an optimum perspective in the separating out [of your soul] from that which is unreal, unnecessary and illusory. This is, then, in order to cause you to shed the weight of excess in all four lower bodies.

Ceasing thereby to feed those conditions of consciousness which have taken your Light and lifestream, and withdrawing the Light therefrom, you may then have an extraordinary momentum of Light now focused in the descending cascade, the waterfall of Light from on high, [with which] to endow only that [creation] which is [of] God-Reality.

It is our desire, beloved, to see you be in the very heart and in the very measure of that white-fire purity. It is our desire to be with you. It is our desire to place our equilateral triangle over you.

We come, then, with the Teaching. We come with that which does give to you the know-how in the soul of the weaving of the Deathless Solar Body.[3] I place before you the image of myself as the Divine Mother to show you how I weave—how I crochet, how I knit, then—the Deathless Solar Body, that you might enter into the cycles of the spinning and the spinning of the wheels of life and the very creation of the thread itself out of the chakras. Let it come forth, beloved, for it is indeed the hour when this Deathless Solar Body must progress and increase.

We therefore remind you that the white fire of Cosmic Christ obedience, which is alignment with the will of God in the Universal Mother, is the very beginning—the very beginning itself of a spiral that is formed as though in the threading of the eye of the needle you should begin to spin, as it were, a cocoon of Light. This is not only protection; it is the garment of the soul and the wedding garment. It is composed of mantra and of kindness, mantra and carefulness, mantra and entering in.

Thus, in the Presence of the Buddhas, in the Presence of the Divine One there is the sweetness, there is the refinement, there is the razor's edge as in the listening with the listening ear there is the taking in of more than the Word but the very Life and Light and Love and Consciousness of the Guru as Mother.

Know, then, beloved, that in this taking in and in this inner refining of the soul there is the means of the weaving. To be out of alignment with the Divine Buddha of oneself means false starts, beginning again and again as the thread does break, for it is not [a] fashioning out of the divine design. [Therefore the thread] is stretched where it ought not to be.

Blessed ones, obedience is to the true voice of God within. And so we know that the plight of humanity and of many who are of God is that they have lost the recognition of the true voice and there is a babbling of voices; and in some where the mind is so far astray in that rebellion there is a cacophony, O such a blasphemy of voices out of hell [assaulting the mind] as to truly make mad those who are already in the out-of-alignment state by the insanity of disobedience itself.

To love the will of God, to love the blue-flame chakra and the blue-throat Kuan Yin,[4] to love this very path of the way of the will of God, this is to enter in to that filigree blueprint that is already spun by the Starry Blue Mother, that does unfold and enfold you.

It unfolds before your very eyes as such a delicate filigree and yet of such precision and geometric design. It does surround you as the 'placenta' of the Cosmic Virgin, nourishing, imparting, radiating as a great sun disc. Blessed ones, this nestling in the heart of the will of God of the Divine Mother, O it is the relief and the surcease from struggle outside of that great sphere of oneness!

Our purpose declared at *FREEDOM 1988* is to prepare the Lightbearers for ages in transition, for the path of the ascension. Therefore, adding to all dispensations gone before, we come. We come delivering the opportunity to call upon us, to be with us that we might be with you, to take the Fourth Ray of Serapis Bey as a means to the strengthening of the Seventh and the First Rays, the Second, the Third, the Fifth and the Sixth.

As the white-fire core of Being does intensify in the chakras, it will thrust forward, then, the seven rays in the brilliance of color, creating ribbons of Light as pathways for souls in all dimensions and octaves to make their way to the heart of the Mother as Astrea, as Elohim, as Purity.

This confluence of the River of Life[5] within you does come about as you spiritualize consciousness and know that there is a true spiritual path. To enter therein is to enter in to the sacred fire and the white Light that is the heart of every ray.

Therefore, spirituality is not an automatic state of consciousness and the religious do not necessarily have this state. One, then, who has a spiritual consciousness is one who can easily transport the soul to realms of Light to commune with angelic hosts and saints in heaven. A spiritualization of consciousness is a world view that is not religious in the sense of ritual, though all these things are contained. Spirituality, then, contains all religion and all ritual and transcends them because it is transported beyond the form into octaves of Light.

That spiritual quality, therefore, is a holiness, and the holiness of God[6] does mark some but not others. Consider it, then, a quality of the Fourth Ray. Though there be many qualities that are admired, it is the lustre of holiness and of spirituality that does enable many to understand the mysteries of all of the seven rays.

But, above all, this spirituality is the mark of those who have not been forgetful in the weaving of the Deathless Solar Body. The nucleus of that body is Divine Love, and by Divine Love are the filigree patterns, the needlelike rays magnetized about the coil of being, even around the spinal altar.

Beautiful angels are gathering and you now feel the holiness and spirituality of their presence. Upon this meditate and receive that feeling of sacred fire, of Light movement in the body. Recognize yourselves as spiritual beings who dwell always in the etheric octave, a portion of the self below.

We desire to see a new sense of spirituality and holiness among the movement of Lightbearers of the world, that this quality outstanding of the pure in heart shall enable many to see God.[7]

For that God reflected in them may be seen by those who in so seeing may begin to desire to have that quality of purity, that freshness in springtime—the simplicity of a joy that is uncomplicated by the cares of this world, the freedom to breathe even the breath of the Holy Spirit—[to have] the inner desire, above all desiring, to be the bride of that Holy Spirit [and] to know that those nine gifts of the Spirit[8] are the greatest of treasures to be offered by God to those in embodiment.

We come to enhance not only your desiring for these gifts but your oneness with your Holy Christ Flame and Holy Christ Self that does enable you to receive these gifts as through the Lords of the Seven Rays the Maha Chohan does come to you. These [gifts] are not out of reach but you put them out of reach by inattention.

When you come to love the gift of faith, above all else you will note that faith is the key that opens the kingdom, that opens the kingdom of consciousness and of the mind and heart to the gift of wisdom [and the gift of self-knowledge], to the gift of the discernment of spirits, the gift of speaking in tongues and interpretation of tongues, as this is also the enlightenment and the comfort of the Holy Spirit. There are gifts of healing and gifts of miracles [and above all the gift of love—the love of the will of God and his Law].

What is this sense of unworthiness that does not seek and find, therefore, the means to be the instrument of the Holy Ghost? I tell you, beloved, when there is the misuse of the sacred fire in any manner in any of the chakras, so this does give unto the soul a sense of unworthiness.

I bid you, then, pursue your own self-appointed course in the righting of the chakras by the image and mantra of Kuan Yin, by songs to us if you will. For we three would also know you by the bija mantras,[9] by the white fire rising.

Let it come upon you, then, that the original joy of springtime and of eternal youth is when the Light, [i.e., the Threefold Flame] of the heart is rising. The Light of the spoken Word is the means whereby the soul, glorifying in her God, is buoyed up and carried into the very courts of heaven.

Purity, then, becomes the key and it is not so difficult to have, beloved. As you have determined to bind the creation of the not-self, so we come. Though much lies before you, the firm desire and the vow to accomplish this has enabled beloved Helios and Vesta to call us to your side that we might magnetize and magnify with you the power of the Great Central Sun Magnet to draw forth purity.

Seraphim celebrate, beloved, for there is a movement amongst you worldwide for that purity that does open the fount of Reality and take you to the very door and the heart's door of Alpha and Omega.

I counsel you, then, in pure *seeing,* pure *knowing,* pure *feeling,* pure *loving,* pure *desiring,* pure *speaking,* pure *entering in* to the secret chamber of the heart. In purity of service and ministration, all these things, then, shall give to you the power, ultimately, of the raising of the sacred fire of the Kundalini.

It is not only in meditation and recitation, it is in good works that build momentum of Cosmic Christ-Self awareness, of integrity which is integration with the Divine Mother [that the raising up of the white Light takes place]. And therefore, in the individualization of the God Flame the magnets of the upper chakras so purified draw the Light of the Mother in radiant stream of Divine Reality.

In our Presence, beloved, you are elevated, the energies of your temples are elevated, and you sense with what swiftness of God Mercury, with what serenity and, yes, even with what ease you may simply let go of all lesser forms and manifestations to rise into new dimensions of the holy image of the Christ Self now made manifest in the soul and the four lower bodies.

O interlaced chalices of Light, through my heart there does

descend Light of the Goddess of Light, Light of the Queen of Light. We come, then, and we touch the top three percent of the spiritual of the planet, of the holy.

It is our desire to so increase Light and Light's consciousness and Light's power to create and re-create and to preserve Light as to create a wedge for Kuan Yin, for beloved Alpha and Omega and for you that the miracles which come forth out of the God-mastery of the Mother Flame might descend—might clear the way, might open even the way for the miracle of God and God's intercession, if not for an entire planet then surely for the race of Lightbearers. May you be counted among these three percent, all of whom receive our angels ongoing.

It is the white Light, after all, beloved, when concentrated in the presence of the Great Central Sun Magnet, that can demagnetize from you the force of anti-Mother, anti-Buddha, anti-Father, anti-Son and anti-Holy Spirit. It is true, beloved, [that] to lend yourselves to the Fourth Ray does give impetus to the disengagement of all of your forces and resources from the negative and downward spirals initiated [through perversions on the seven rays] by you or others in your lifestream.

We are pressing in upon you now the very force of sacred fire, the very pressure of our auras, that you might receive truly a transfer from our Electronic Presence superimposed over you in the formation of this equilateral triangle [of Cosmic Purity], a measure of Light for the Victory, a measure of Light, a measure of Light so needed.

I seal it safely in the heart of the eight-petaled chakra. I seal it in the heart of your Holy Christ Self.

Drop by drop may this Light be to you always the difference between defeat and victory. May the drop of Light be that increment so needed, so essential in those moments when all of your forces must count for the Victory of Love.

I pray you, receive our Love and know that only Love could give to us so great, *so great* an electromagnetic field of *Light, Light, Light!*

O Dazzling Light, we command Light to convince the chelas of El Morya that you are worthy to save your Master by Light!

In the Trinity of the Divine Mother we seal you.

O Lightbearers of the world, be worthy of the name. We are with you unto the fulfillment of your inner name, even externalized as and in your spiritual and holy Deathless Solar Body.

This dictation by the **Goddess of Purity** was **delivered** by the Messenger of the Great White Brotherhood Elizabeth Clare Prophet on **Saturday, October 8, 1988,** 7:54–8:23 p.m. MDT, during the six-day conference *The Harvest* held at the **Royal Teton Ranch, Park County, Montana.** (For notes see Pearl no. 80.)

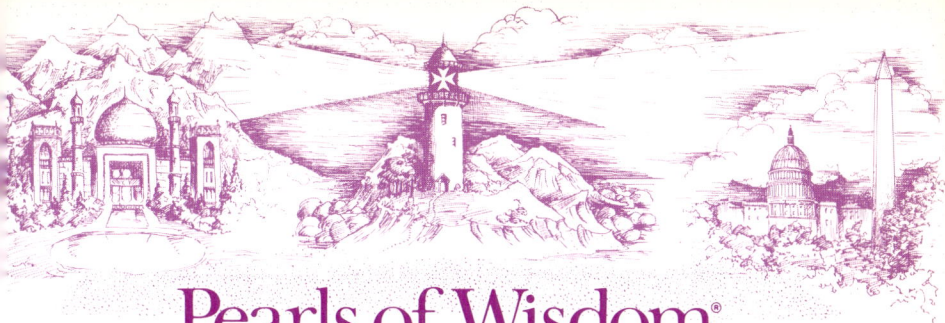

Pearls of Wisdom®
published by The Summit Lighthouse

| *Vol. 31 No. 80* | *Beloved Hercules* | *November 26, 1988* |

The Harvest
III
A Step of Attainment
The Chain of Hierarchy Moves On!
"Sustain and Raise Up That Pillar of Blue Flame Daily!"

Hail to Thee, Thou Divine Mother in heaven and on earth! Hail to thee, O Light shining in the temples of the Keepers of the Flame worlds without end!

To the Light above, to the Light below we bow.

Legions of angels of the First Ray of the Holy Will of God have preceded me to this place as with Amazonia *WE ARE, I AM THAT I AM,* the Alpha-to-Omega of the Elohimic God consciousness of the First Ray.

Therefore we have descended as the corridor [through the astral plane] has been cleared [by angelic hosts] and established [by the decrees of Keepers of the Flame].

Therefore we find room once again in the heart of a Messenger and of disciples becoming the incarnation of the Word of God of the First Ray.

Let it be known, therefore, that our bearing of the cross of the karmic burden of Keepers of the Flame and Lightbearers[1] has resulted in much good, individual by individual, and therefore of necessity [it has resulted in much good] in the Community of the Holy Spirit that is the Mystical Body of God upon this planet and extending beyond. (So the northern lights have illumined the way and mark the place of our descent from cosmic heights.[2])

We note, however, as is often the case when a portion of karma is borne for the individual, that in this same fourteen-month cycle the blessed Guru who is the sponsoring Master and the Chief of the

Darjeeling Council of the Great White Brotherhood, Lord Morya El, the Chohan of the First Ray, has lost the dispensation to intercede in many instances on behalf of his chelas.[3]

Therefore, as we have said that it is a two-edged sword, we would point out that not only is experience the best teacher but karma itself is the best teacher. For karma borne by the individual as dictated by the Law and by the Lords of Karma does provide a co-measurement of oneself [and one's attainment] against the backdrop of Threefold Flame, Holy Christ Self, I AM Presence, the Great White Brotherhood as well as one's peers upon the planet.

Thus, when the [karmic] weight lightens it is easy to assume that one has less karma and just as easy to forget that the lightness, at least in these fourteen months, has been caused by the bearing of the burden of your karma by this Elohim of the First Ray.

Thus [in your] taking for granted [such a dispensation], there does occur a forgetfulness concerning the devotion [that would ordinarily be] necessary to sustain the two-way street of Light between the heart of the chela, the chela of the will of God, and the heart of the Messenger of the will of God who is El Morya.

Blessed ones, I should have thought that my bearing of this cross would have allowed you to serve in a greater way the one who loves you most. El Morya truly is the eye of the needle that must be threaded by the thread of light from your heart.

Morya, then, is the keystone in the arch of The Summit Lighthouse. By his giving of his diamond and his mantle and his causal body to the founding of this activity in 1958, this blessed one did literally open the door through the Messengers and all who came after them to all other Ascended Masters and hierarchs who have sponsored this activity and all the Lightbearers who have been drawn to it.

Thus, beloved, it is not simply the loss of the intercession of a single hierarch most beloved [that you suffer from the Karmic Board's "no-new-dispensation-policy" for Morya in regard to his chelas] but it is a compromise [of the planetary service as well] of the very one who is responsible for the establishment of this activity.

You realize that El Morya stepped forward to sponsor these Messengers because Saint Germain himself had been denied new sponsorship by the Lords of Karma for having [had] so many [students and others] misuse the light of the violet flame and the dispensations that he had [been] given for the United States and Europe and to various individuals around the world.[4]

And so you see, beloved, there have been sponsoring Masters in these hundred years and more who have stepped forward [to assist certain ones or the planetary evolution] and then again you have not heard so often of them, thus signifying that they were able to accomplish only as much as those who would receive them would give unto them, would take the proffered gift, would multiply it, and would fulfill the law of the First Ray concerning the path of chelaship.

Thus, beloved, it is our concern that all have a centerpoise of realism—realism as to the absolute God-Reality that is unlimited potential for yourself to realize the Good, the God, and His Will and realism regarding the human consciousness that oftentimes will indulge itself as far as allowed by [the] authority or parent[al] figure.

Children in the playpen of life are some and some of you. Others more mature must watch, must be the watchmen on the wall and take care that the children maintain the standard whereby they lose not the contact with Reality through the sponsoring one, especially when they are taught and truly God-taught that the condition of the flesh on this planetary home is that 99 percent of the population are separated from the true and lasting and everlasting voice of the Holy Christ Self, for which reason Sanat Kumara has sent forth representatives of himself as a living Guru whereby the infant child humanity might sustain a tie through the heart of that Guru even to the heart of their Holy Christ Self.

Thus, envision the beloved El Morya, the right hand extended to your own, the left hand holding firmly the hand of [your] Holy Christ Self—and the pure will of God, and the Diamond Heart of that will within his own heart chakra, being the electrode and the nexus [sustaining the tie to your Holy Christ Self] until the thread from your heart should increase and thereby [allow you] to sustain that tie midst the turbulent astral seas and the moments when the sudden karmic descent may disrupt [your] individual communion [with your Real Self].

"*Master, save us or we perish!*"[5] Such was the cry of the disciples of Christ Jesus. "Master, save us or we perish!" And so it is the cry of some who are awake who know that it is the first order of this hour and every hour to seek once again the sponsoring of your Lord Morya El; for it is even by his sponsorship that I, Hercules, could also sponsor you.

Blessed ones, this Messenger has desired to see Morya restored by the hour of the Feast of the Epiphany,[6] when the three wise men did visit the Christ Child. Morya being somewhat more realistic and understandably a bit pessimistic, as anyone would be sharing his plight, has requested that the students might move toward his restoration to full opportunity by August 8 next.

Blessed hearts, Morya gives the date. I tell you the reason. It is because it is the very latest hour when your beloved Master may move and move again to assist you when you will require his assistance as you have never required it before. Thus, beloved, you may take the desire of the Messenger and work toward that date early in the new year and see what comes of your efforts, but I tell you, it will take [a] tremendous effort [to make it happen]. And now I shall unveil to you why of necessity the effort must intensify on the part of the Lightbearers.

Some weeks ago as the Messenger did stand offering invocation assisted by our servant, even before this very altar, we did reveal the opening of the pit,' the very pit itself in the Pacific Ocean, there beneath. I tell you, the prophecy of the opening of this pit is written in the Book of Life and that page is now open. Therefore, I tell you, out of that bottomless pit there does come, in that year noted by our Lord Alpha, upon planet earth and certain other planetary bodies that which has been stored there of the astral creation of all evolving lifewaves in that cycle preceding, long cycle.

Thus, Mercy's dispensation of [having long ago] sealed that place where the energy veil of mankind does dwell does become a new mercy—a mercy of the Law that does provide opportunity [(through the opening of the pit)] to the lifewaves who desire to ascend, to accelerate, to enter resurrection's coil, [and therefore to fulfill the requirement of the Law] to now stand, face and conquer in the very heart of the living Christ those conditions of their own human creation, those [karmic] conditions [of their own astral creation] which they must overcome if they would move up the spiral of being in the ascending process.

Thus, Mercy is as Mercy does. Mercy holds back for the benighted evolution, a humanity gone astray and children of the Light at play and sons of God who have not taken to heart to incarnate the Word after [the example] and in the footsteps of the Lord Christ [Jesus]. Thus all have to some extent indulged [themselves] while there was not a necessity to meet day by day that miscreation.

And this is the theme of my message to you, that though the mercy of the Law come to give time, time and a half a time to the individual and [to] a lifewave to attain to that Christhood, it is human nature, superimposed upon the soul, that the soul, then, does dally and tarry saying, "All things will continue as they were. I shall not fret. I shall not fret. I shall not fret."

Thus, blessed ones, the room given for personal Christhood is a room, [i.e., space in time], that has been occupied by those who have sought instead that Light inverted for all manner of sensual pleasure. And the history of the descent of the evolutions of this planet is clearly written. You know it well. Therefore, I say, the opening of the bottomless pit is the new mercy, the new covenant. As Morya and we of the First Ray put it simply, "Pay as you go."[8]

Now there does descend upon the earth, and there has been abuilding upon the earth in these numbers of weeks, a rising level of the muck and mire [of the astral sea containing] all manner of beast and creature and insect life and the most horrible forms of devil and entity. Truly the bowels of hell are outpouring.

And, beloved, the earth is now covered with this emission and only the areas of the high Himalayas where the true Masters abide and this area where we have established our Inner Retreat do retain the opening into the octaves of Light and the protection by walls of Light from this rising Darkness upon the earth.

And you who hear me may wonder, but I tell you, I speak to you out of the mouth of God* as *I AM THAT I AM ELOHIM* and as I AM sent to you in this hour.

You may comprehend, then, why it was the recommendation of Saint Germain that Keepers of the Flame leave the coasts.[9] It is because the weight of this effluvia is heavier at sea level [and more so] even as it does continue to rise. And we take note that it is far more difficult in this hour for Keepers of the Flame both at sea level and anywhere upon earth to maintain the same Light which they did keep three and five years ago.

But, beloved, the most awful sight to behold is to see how the mankind of earth do embrace these dark forms, do dance with them, move with them, do receive them, for they are of them and they [themselves] are out of the depths. They are from beneath even as you are from above, but not all.[10]

Therefore, beloved, understand how the Law does move and how all must enter in to the Law. Understand that *I may extend to you a dispensation for the bearing of your karmic burden only as you are able to sustain a rising coil of blue-flame will of God to the level of your own Christ Self.* To that end, though not known by the Messenger, the El Morya tapes have been begun.[11] I explain to you, then, that *I can and I shall, according to the Will and the Law of the LORD God, bear the burden, and a certain percentage of the karmic burden, of those Lightbearers who can sustain and raise up that pillar of blue-flame will of God daily.*

Ex cathedra: Latin, "from the chair" [of Peter]; by virtue of or in the exercise of one's office: with authority; i.e., out of the mouth of God.

Blessed hearts, I would acquaint you with this challenge by giving you a certain co-measurement. It has taken to this hour from the moment this prayer vigil began, as *The Harvest*, for yourselves assembled to clear and open the passageway to the octaves of Light of the abode of Elohim; and all of the calls [that have been made], and the clearing that has been done, have been to that end. And this was the requirement that we might both speak and offer our assistance so needed in this hour, not alone to yourselves; but in assisting you we do also assist our dear El Morya.

Now you may understand why we have called for the great crystal chalice of Elohim to be established in the Heart of the Inner Retreat as the open door and passageway [for angels descending and ascending[12]] from the Elohimic level to the Keepers of the Flame:[13] We have banked the fires of the resurrection and our Presence against the day and the hour when by cosmic law and the prophecy of the Book of Life this bottomless pit should be opened.

Thus, all manner of Darkness and dark and foul thing that does fly or creep or crawl on the face of the earth may be seen on the astral plane as a part of this rising tide. Therefore, beloved, the strengthening of that chalice, the sustainment of it by [daily] calls to the resurrection flame is most necessary.

This is the hour, beloved, when for some there shall be an understanding truly of what is the dark night of the soul when personal karma does cover the face of one's own world. Know, then, that the eclipsing of the Sun of the Mighty I AM Presence can come, [which is the Dark Night of the Spirit].[14] It can come to those who have not taken the opportunity of this thirty-year dispensation to build, to weave, to intensify a coil of fire from the soul in the seat-of-the-soul chakra unto the heart of Christ, unto the heart of succeeding levels of the universal consciousness of God.

It is for this reason that we say, let all of the dictations of this thirty-year spiral be published quickly and forthrightly. Let those who desire counseling receive it from us directly from the very first *Pearl of Wisdom* unto the last from *FREEDOM 1988*.

For if there be those who have not had the dispensation for thirty years on the outer, I tell you, this dispensation has been on the planetary body and you may have entered into its path and pursuit through other forms of meditation and worship which, though they did not contain the whole Truth or nothing but the Truth, did indeed serve you well to take steps of separating out from the miasma of the lower planetary astral consciousness.

Thus, beloved, to be able to retrace the footsteps taken by your Mark, who is truly a link to the heart of Morya, to be able to do so through his dictations and all the *Pearls of Wisdom* unto the present, this will afford you a systematic and step-by-step weaving of the Deathless Solar Body, which you are called and impelled to do to be true spiritual survivors in this age. Therefore plan well to have them even as we have counseled our Messenger to plan well to publish them.

Blessed hearts, we have left no stone unturned to provide these stepping-stones from the beginning to the ending of your thirty-year, thirty-cycle opportunity. The final three years, beloved, are your own alchemy for the victory of Christhood, building on the foundation that has been given.

Let us say, then, beloved, that to maintain this retreat and fortress of Light will require a vigilance and a diligence you have not comprehended before nor have you thought necessary. It is not that you have not given great portions of yourselves to the Light and to the Godhead. It is that the planet itself by comparison is in a greater state of the outpicturing of Darkness and a great heaviness does hang over every land. Peoples are agitated in every nation and this is the sign of the alchemicalization [that does take place at the end of an age and a dispensation].

This alchemicalization, beloved, will be enhanced as you use the violet flame cassette three, soon to be placed in your hands, we trust.[15] It is the challenge to the astral plane. But remember, beloved, as that violet flame dispensation goes forth it will be for some a license to miscreate as freedom's fires move across the land. May you heed the warning given by Saint Germain[16] and may you keep in the inner temple and the inner court of Morya the vigil of the blue flame, the vigil of your calls ratifying the judgments of Almighty God true and righteous, on earth as in heaven, through the heart of the Christ.[17]

And as you call for the binding of that beast of the not-self, known esoterically as the dweller-on-the-threshold, as you hold this balance for the Lightbearers even as you hold a balance as the "Great Teams of Conquerors"* go forth for the binding of the seed of the Wicked [One], you will see that that violet flame can create a blessed alchemy of universal freedom, but only because there be some who recognize that the balancing of the Threefold Flame of the heart is the very foundation of this endeavor and your success— your spiritual success on the Path.

The vigil to be kept with Elohim,[18] then, is to keep open the passageway to our octave so that in order to reach you instanta-neously we may not have to first send legions of our cosmic forces to

---

*Cosmic reinforcements in the service of Elohim engaged in the Battle of Armageddon on behalf of the Lightbearers of the galaxies. Call to them daily!

carve a pathway through the rising tide of the astral plane. Do you see, beloved? This balance of Alpha and Omega in the Northern Hemisphere from the Himalayas to the Northern Rockies does still provide the means of anchoring the Masculine and Feminine Rays in this octave.

Blessed ones, the physical area of Lake Titicaca is covered over with this astral substance, and therefore you see that this outpost, [i.e., the Royal Teton Ranch], of Lake Titicaca—of the retreat of the God and Goddess Meru and the focus of the Feminine Ray to the earth here in the Northern Rockies[19]—must suffice until the dark period of earth's travail does pass and a golden age may dawn—or at least a new age approaching a golden age—when by the very purging of the physical planet the weight will lighten.

Blessed ones, consider what fallout shelters or survival preparedness you make to be a crystal cave in the heart of the earth, a place of alchemy, even the tomb of the Lord Christ where you work out the problem of being as the alchemical changes take place on the surface, as there is the venting of the momentums of Darkness, as people are unable to deal with this rising tide of astral effluvia and therefore enter periods of insanity, profaneness and the blasphemy against God [which is prophesied in the scriptures of East and West for this Dark Cycle of the Kali Yuga].[20]

For they lose their sight in this astral smog and muck and they do not have discrimination to know who is the representative of Absolute God-Good and who is the representative of the Evil One, and one will appear as the other to them. And therefore, watch and pray that you judge righteous judgment,[21] that you enter into the heart of your own Christ Self.

You must plan to be prepared to keep the Flame [of God] unending while you have life and breath, that all who live upon this planet may make their choices in the final decade of this century whether to serve the Light with everlasting love or whether to serve the Darkness with an everlasting contempt for the Light and the Lightbearer.[22]

And the warning went forth and it was sounded through God's Messenger to the people: Beware the rising tide of Darkness. Preserve the Light. Preserve the Safety. Preserve the Community. Preserve the Word of God. For though this heaven and this earth may pass away, yet the Word of the Logos shall live forever in the hearts of the Lightbearers who keep the Flame.[23]

And my Word shall be engraven upon spindles threaded in gold, and upon this thread shall the everlasting Word be recorded so that at any hour this Word may speak in the heart—from all of the speakings of the Word since the Word did come forth to create from the heart of Brahman. And whatever is the need of the hour, that speaking of the Word shall be heard by the Lightbearer from within.

This prophecy written in the Book of Life, beloved, that I have read to you does point to the hour when the communication of God is through the Threefold Flame and the Holy Christ Self.

Now you have been given by the Lord Sanat Kumara and others of our bands a means and a method of ascending the fiery coil of being and the spiral [rising] from the seat-of-the-soul chakra, [your soul] making safe passage through the samsara of the electronic belt, through the desire body, tarrying at the level of the solar-plexus chakra to pass the test of the ten.[24]

Thus, I speak to you the tenth day of the tenth month of the year—and it is an omen for good, for your victory in the desire body and by that solar plexus becoming the instrument of rivers of water of Life[25] flowing through to heal and bless—for all of thy desiring is in his Law and in the meditation and in the Works and the Word of his Law day and night.

Thus, beloved, surfacing from [the seat-of-the-soul chakra] beneath the conscious awareness, one must then face the challenge in one's soul of the dominant carnal mind, the dominant mental body where the computer of that mental body, programmed by the prevailing educational systems [and the] parental and authority figures of the time, does become a dictator over the soul who would emerge.

This soul is sensitive yet not fully awakened, aware yet not possessing her full faculties of discrimination. The soul knows by an inner knowing and by a feeling but cannot always explain, for want of the fullness of the Logos within, the logical step-by-step explanation of her posture [vis-à-vis this tyrant].

Therefore the soul as the negative polarity of the I AM Presence is confronted by the intellect, which is the inversion of the positive polarity of the Mind of God in Christ. Thus, in the Matter spheres this plus-minus condition of consciousness is the situation in which the soul must find herself, must gain self-worth, self-recognition and know that the way of the inner sensitivity to the pulsation of Life is superior to the intellectual, rational methods of the computer mind.

Thus, the soul weaving her wedding garment and gaining skeins of Light must bypass this intellect that is subtle and clever and establish that fiery thread to the Mind of Christ. So the cry went forth: Let that Mind be in you which was also in Christ Jesus![26] To be carnally minded is the Death of the soul. To be spiritually minded is the eternal and everlasting Life and Peace of the soul.[27]

So let the soul be forewarned of the intimidations of this carnal mind, not alone within the temple of her abode, not alone within the entity called self, but in fallen angels and others such as mechanization man who have developed that intellectual mind to such extents as to be able to intimidate and belittle that soul who is about to become the handmaid of her Lord, her Saviour, her Holy Christ Self.

Though your souls have met their master in this [intellectual] mind in previous lifetimes, only to awaken [after passing from the screen of life] to this realization [thence] to be caught up, even if momentarily, in the heart of the Divine Mother, your souls have reincarnated again and again only to be put down [by the same carnal mind] as though under the weight not only of the cross but of the tombstone itself.

Blessed ones, I give you, then, a gift and it is to your soul the cumulative self-awareness—as though [you were] reading the story of your life, of many scenes—of each and every time you have been traduced, for you have allowed yourself to be traduced, by someone or another's intellect and that carnally minded consciousness which is of the flesh and of the physical-mental functioning of the outer self.

Thus, beloved, my gift is the cumulative awareness, the discernment [of the whys and wherefores of your soul's meanderings through the labyrinth of the carnal mind] and what your Teachers and the Great Gurus have taught you concerning [life's journey], those lessons learned and then forgotten.

This is a wise gift recommended by Solar Logoi, for if we may not carry all of your burdens, we may give you the most expedient means for you to rise beyond the entanglement with the not-self and the not-self reasoning, [thence to eliminate the cause of the burden].

You shall then be tutored by angels of Jophiel's band. You shall receive illumination. You shall no longer be naive or sleepful or slothful or allow yourself to take on the robes of [the] over-self-confidence of the ego mind. But you shall understand that you are an identity in God, yet a shorn lamb, but not all. And you are rising step by step, coil by coil up that pole of being.

You have one goal: union with Christ, union in the Living Flame of Love. Bypass all else, all byways. This is a key to your journey through the labyrinth of the subconscious and the electronic belt. Follow by the heart. Follow by the heart flame. Follow by your love of Saint Germain and Morya and Mary and Kuan Yin and Kuthumi and all who love you. Follow their heart by your heart sensitivity which you, then, must develop daily.

Follow straight as an arrow of Love to the heart of your Christ Self and know that my name is Hercules and by my name you can pass every test aright and, without inordinate pain of passage, [soar] to rarefied heights of consciousness.

You can do this if *only* you will attain a sense of co-measurement of the relationship of the soul to the untransmuted karmic self, to the electronic belt, to the dweller-on-the-threshold, to the Threefold Flame of the heart, to the Holy Christ Self, to the Community of the Holy Spirit, [and] to the entire Spirit of the Great White Brotherhood ascended.

The sense of the realism of self: glean it and call it forth from the heart of Lanello!

Mount [up] as with eagle wings but do not skip steps. For each step, though difficult, is the stepping-stone to the next and you need a sound and firm foundation in order to meet the challenges of the next. Some, listening, then, to the intellect, have cleverly skipped those steps, or so they thought or so they made it appear to others. Lacking the roots and the grounding or the humility to begin again and to begin again *and to begin again* where there is a weakness in the building, they have positioned themselves as though standing on air instead of [on] terra firma and upon the Rock of Christ.

Blessed ones, an attainment truly won, even if it be the first step, will not be taken from you by any, not through the ravages of astrological cycles or of clever thieves in the night. A step of attainment truly won can become the white stone and the white cube and even the chief cornerstone in the temple.

Fear not to perfect the first step. Fear not to go back. Fear not, for you build for eternity, and each stone you carve is a stepping-stone to the Central Sun. You create your path stone by stone which you then walk upon as star to star the markers of the homeward journey point the way to the heart of Alpha and Omega, to your Christ, my Christ.

Think on these things. Understand the usefulness of Community when all for one and one for all may build, may sustain, may defend a physical retreat that is meshed with the etheric octave as no other place on the planet. Defend it, yes, from astral encroachment of every kind.

Let the joy of the Lord sing in your hearts. May the melodies of heaven be not far from your throats. May your lips be formed about the mantras of Kuan Yin. May your bodies be light and your souls take flight.

I AM Hercules. Amazonia does stand in the heaven-world beneath. It is a congruency of the Divine Mother of Elohim of First Ray establishing a polarity with me in higher octaves from that place beneath you which you equate with the lower astral plane and Death and Hell.

As time and space and heaven and hell have no direction according to compass, yet for want of other expression, up is heaven, down is hell, so we say there are levels of density and levels of etherealization. [Therefore] Amazonia, her Mother Flame, does now take up the occupation of those lower worlds so that should you trip and fall and make your bed in hell, behold, you shall find, as the LORD hath said, *I AM there.*[28]

Thus, the Mother Elohim of all rays of Elohim do seek to sustain that heavenly realm in another dimension while the astral plane does rise. Never the twain shall meet, yet those who contain the heavenly consciousness of the Divine Mother shall abide under her shadow as under the shadow of the Almighty of Elohim of the Feminine Ray.

And therefore even in the midst of meeting and defeating old karma and old forms of consciousness, they may remember that the Divine Mother in the heart of the earth does truly abide and sustain [the Comfort Flame] for those who may reach her by the mantra, reach her by the Hail Mary, reach her through any heart of any Feminine being.

Thus know the requirement is the same in both directions: I, Hercules, bear the cross hourly and daily for those who reach me at the level of the Christ Self.

I wish you Godspeed. I send you all courage and encouragement. From the point of realism, then, accept the intercessions of Saint Germain and the violet flame Masters but take not for granted that freedom. For, for every gift received and used you will one day give answer to the Law of Love in being called upon to provide that very same gift from your causal body to another evolution that does follow you up the mountain.

Thus, to internalize the gift in the hour when there is yet time for God-mastery is truly the Word and Work of the wise ones: for they know that they shall have preserved in their cosmic bank account of the causal body that momentum whereby to stretch forth the right hand to the one beneath and to maintain the firm grasp to the one above.

Thus, the chain of Hierarchy moves on! And I, Hercules, pull up the entire chain of being of this planet by the Lightbearers who maintain consonance with my heart!

You who do, then, maintain your Holy Christ Self awareness and the clear tunnel of being as a cylinder of blue flame from your soul to that level of Cosmic Christ consciousness of your Holy Christ Self—you, then, shall be truly the open door which no man can shut[29] to the descent of Hercules and the ascent of souls who will tug upon your garments and, because you stand and still stand, will be strengthened, will make it, will enter in.

Thus, be patient and not impatient with them. Be tolerant and not intolerant, for you have been there before *when Lord Morya El pulled you up!*

I speak to the wise, the strong and the loving. To bring back El Morya to your side you now must become him as intercessor, not alone for the reasons declared but because when the hour comes for the consideration of his return to the front lines midst his chelas, he must gather those who have sustained his Electronic Presence and present all to the Lords of Karma and the Cosmic Council. And it is by you that he shall return to the place he loves most: to the heart and soul and mind of his chelas.

O Thou Divine Mother in heaven, O Thou Divine Mother in the earth, O Amazonia, *I AM, WE ARE ELOHIM of the Will of God!*

And so we sustain it for all of a cosmos, for all who will reach us through the Avatars sent, through the Buddhas sent, through the Bodhisattvas sent!

Purusha.[30] It is done.

THE TRIUMPH IS UNTO THOSE WHO LOVE SUPREMELY.

"The Summit Lighthouse Sheds Its Radiance O'er All the World to Manifest as Pearls of Wisdom." This dictation by **Hercules** was **delivered** by the Messenger of the Great White Brotherhood Elizabeth Clare Prophet on **Monday, October 10, 1988,** 11:11 p.m.–12:08 a.m. MDT, during the six-day conference *The Harvest* held at the **Royal Teton Ranch, Park County, Montana.** Available on 90-min. audiocassette K88032, $6.50 (add $.55 for postage); on videocassette with dictations of Heros and Amora and Mother Mary, 2 hr. 20 min., HP88091, $39.95 (add $1.10 for postage). [**N.B.** Bracketed material denotes words unspoken yet implicit in the dictation, added by the Messenger under Hercules' direction for clarity in the written word.] Throughout these notes *PoW* is the abbreviation for *Pearls of Wisdom.* **(1) Hercules carrying the cross of the burdens of the Lightbearers.** On August 10, 1987, Hercules announced, "I have strapped upon my back a wooden cross representing the burdens of the Lightbearers. Yes, I carry this cross. And you will see me as though I were a carpenter in his trade. And upon my back that cross shall remain for this fourteen-month duration, giving you the opportunity, as the karmic weight may be lifted from the Lightbearers, to draw them into the circle of their Mighty I AM Presence. Beloved ones, it is a two-edged sword: For when the Law no longer allows me to bear this cross, what then will come upon them when suddenly their karma returns again?...

"Therefore, beloved, those Lightbearers who are to come into this activity, let them come in the next fourteen months. For when that burden of karma descends upon you, unless some mighty miraculous dispensation occur from hearts of Keepers of the Flame, I tell you, they must have the wherewithal [of a Light invoked and sustained in their electromagnetic field] to meet it. It is as though there were a mini-dispensation. As Jesus Christ bore this cross for two thousand years, thus I may also bear it, but only for the Lightbearers, for those who have elected to bear the Light now for fourteen months. Thus, in a mini-cycle, beloved, many may come to understand those fourteen stations of the cross. And they may walk them. And they may emerge triumphant." 1987 *PoW,* pp. 442–43. **(2)** The **northern lights,** also known as the aurora borealis, is a luminous phenomenon thought to be of electrical origin which can be seen in the Northern Hemisphere at night, especially during the time of the equinoxes. On October 10, 1988, at about 1 a.m. there was a spectacular display of northern lights in the sky over the Royal Teton Ranch, which changed in intensity from moment to moment. The mountain ranges to the northeast were silhouetted in stark relief by a flow of white light suffusing into a layer of green light with shafts of ruby shooting upward. **(3) El Morya loses dispensation to intercede.** 1988 *PoW,* pp. 581–82, 583–84, 585, 586. **(4) Saint Germain's dispensations for Europe and the United States.** *Saint Germain On Alchemy,* pp. x, xv–xxvii, 137–38; *Saint Germain On Prophecy,* pp. 33–39; 1988 *PoW,* pp. 563, 570 n. 5. **(5) "Lord, save us: we perish."** Matt. 8:25; Mark 4:38; Luke 8:24. **(6) Epiphany,** January 6, 1989. **(7) Bottomless pit.** Rev. 9:1–12; 11:7; 17:8; 20:1–3. **(8) Pay as you go.** "Pay your karmic debts as you go and thus earn your dispensations." See El Morya, 1988 *PoW,* p. 584. **(9)** On Thanksgiving Day, November 27, 1986, Saint Germain said, "The divine experiment is past. Let the reality be now! Let those **Keepers of the Flame living on these coasts,** from Canada south, be no longer here beyond the end of 1988. Understand, beloved, the unpredictability of the carnal mind. There are no guarantees, even from our level, else life should be a predestination and all should sit and do nothing. Depending upon the vigilance as never before of our Keepers of the Flame, depending on the Light invoked, so shall the protection be and so shall be the forestalling of cataclysm as well." 1986 *PoW,* p. 651. **(10) "Ye are from beneath; I am from above:** ye are of this world; I am not of this world." John 8:23. **(11)** *El Morya, Lord of the First Ray: Dynamic Decrees with Prayers and Ballads for Chelas of the Will of God 1,* 94-min. audiocassette with booklet, B88125, $5.95 (add $.55 for postage); see Summit University Press 30th anniversary sale catalog, p. 18. When ordering, indicate slow or fast version. **(12)** "And he [Jacob] dreamed, and behold a ladder set up on the earth, and the top of it reached to heaven: and behold the angels of God ascending and descending on it." Gen. 28:12. **(13) Crystal chalice of Elohim.** 1988 *PoW,* p. 580 n. 1. **(14)** The **dark night of the soul** is the test of the soul's encounter with the return of personal karma, which, if she has not kept her lamps (chakras) trimmed with Light (Matt. 25:1–13), may eclipse the Light (Christ consciousness) of the soul and therefore its discipleship under the Son of God. It precedes the **Dark Night of the Spirit,** the supreme test of Christhood, when the soul is, as it were, cut off from the I AM Presence and must survive solely on the Light (Christ consciousness) garnered in the heart, while holding the balance for planetary karma.

The sixteenth-century mystic Saint John of the Cross described these initiations in his work "The Dark Night": "This night...causes two kinds of darkness or purgation in spiritual persons according to the two parts of the soul, the sensory and the spiritual. Hence the one night or purgation will be sensory, by which the senses are purged and accommodated to the spirit; and the other night or purgation will be spiritual, by which the spirit is purged and denuded as well as accommodated and prepared for union with God through love." Saint John writes of the initiation of the Dark Night of the Spirit: "Since the divine extreme strikes in order to renew the soul and divinize it (by stripping it of the habitual affections and properties of the old man to which it is strongly united, attached, and conformed), it so disentangles and dissolves the spiritual substance—absorbing it in a profound darkness—that the soul at the sight of its miseries feels that it is melting away and being undone by a cruel spiritual death; it feels as if it were swallowed by a beast and being digested in the dark belly, and it suffers an anguish comparable to Jonas's when in the belly of the whale. [Jon. 2:1–3] It is fitting that the soul be in this sepulcher of dark death in order that it attain the spiritual resurrection for which it hopes." *The Collected Works of St. John of the Cross,* trans. Kieran Kavanaugh and Otilio Rodriguez (Washington, D.C.: ICS Publications, 1979), pp. 311, 337.

For the Messengers' teachings on the dark night, including readings and commentary on the writings of Saint John of the Cross, see Elizabeth Clare Prophet, *Living Flame of Love,* 8-audiocassette album, 12½ hrs., A85044, $50.00 (add $1.65 for postage); "The Dark Night of the Soul," on two 60-min. audiocassettes, MTG7412, MTF7413, $13.00 (add $.95 for postage). See also Archangel Gabriel, *Mysteries of the Holy Grail,* pp. 173, 368–69. **(15) *Save the World with Violet Flame! by Saint Germain 1, 2, 3* and *4*** audiocassettes. 1988 *PoW,* pp. 400 n. 6, 560 n. 1; Summit University Press 30th anniversary sale catalog, p. 18. **(16) Fallen ones abuse dispensations of freedom.** Saint Germain, 1988 *PoW,* pp. 549–54. **(17) True and righteous judgments.** Rev. 16:7; 19:2. **(18) Elohim vigil.** El Morya, 1988 *PoW,* pp. 584–85. **(19) Royal Teton Ranch as outpost of the God and Goddess Meru's retreat.** On December 25, 1986, Jesus announced that the God and Goddess Meru had come from their retreat at Lake Titicaca to "establish a corridor of light from the etheric retreat over the Royal Teton Ranch to the etheric retreat of the Feminine Ray at Lake Titicaca. By this corridor of light, beloved, we open a highway whereby your calls may reach South America in time. This light sealed in the heart of the God and Goddess Meru will be released so as not to be requalified by the human but so as to liberate and enlighten. These Teachings published in the South American languages and preached to the people will be the vehicle to anchor that light. Pray God that many shepherds respond and cease their rivalry and come out from among them to deliver the Word of this age. . . . Blessed ones, the God and Goddess Meru tarry here now. Their great momentum of victory over witchcraft, Death, Hell, and black magic is brought to bear in this hour on the threat of suicide worldwide as an open door to the devastation of the Fourth Horseman approaching. They are ready to turn back and bind the entire momentum of this force in answer to your call. . . . The God and Goddess Meru, having stood thus far in etched profile in golden garments of light, have now placed themselves within golden white spheres. These spheres rise from this place to be sustained above it as their Presence with you." 1986 *PoW,* pp. 681, 682. **(20) Kali Yuga** is the Sanskrit term in Hindu philosophy for the "age of darkness." It is the last and worst of the four *yugas,* or world ages, comprising a cosmic cycle and is characterized by strife, discord and moral deterioration. The present dark age, or Kali Yuga, is believed to have begun on February 18, 3102 B.C. (with a duration of 432,000 years). For a different calculation of the duration of the yugas which sets the present age 285 years into the Dvapara Yuga, see Swami Sri Yukteswar, *The Holy Science,* 7th ed. (Los Angeles: Self-Realization Fellowship, 1972), pp. 7–20. See *The Lost Teachings of Jesus I,* pp. 82, 143, 359 n. 19; or pocketbook edition *The Lost Teachings of Jesus 1,* pp. 115, 189, 268 n. 19. **Dark Cycle.** See 1988 *PoW,* p. 561 n. 3. **(21) Judge righteous judgment.** John 7:24. **(22) Awake to everlasting life or contempt.** "And at that time shall Michael stand up, the great prince which standeth for the children of thy people: and there shall be a time of trouble, such as never was since there was a nation even to that same time: and at that time thy people shall be delivered, every one that shall be found written in the book. And many of them that sleep in the dust of the earth shall awake, some to everlasting life, and some to shame and everlasting contempt. And they that be wise shall shine as the brightness of the firmament; and they that turn many to righteousness as the stars for ever and ever." Dan. 12:1–3. **(23) My words shall not pass away.** Matt. 24:35; Mark 13:31; Luke 21:33; I Pet. 1:25. **(24)** The Ascended Master Djwal Kul teaches in his *Intermediate Studies of the Human Aura* that "the solar-plexus chakra has ten petals—five with the positive charge focusing the thrust of Alpha in the secret rays and five with a negative charge focusing the return current of Omega in the secret rays. Thus to the evolving soul consciousness, the solar plexus is the vehicle whereby the initiation of the **test of the ten** is passed. This is the test of selflessness which always involves the test of the emotions and of the God-control of those emotions through the Divine Ego which can come into prominence in the soul only as the result of the surrender of the human ego." See *Intermediate Studies of the Human Aura,* pp. 83–90, also published in Kuthumi and Djwal Kul, *The Human Aura,* pp. 161–69. **(25) Water of Life.** "In the last day, that great day of the feast, Jesus stood and cried, saying, If any man thirst, let him come unto me, and drink. He that believeth on me, as the scripture hath said, out of his belly shall flow rivers of living water." John 7:37, 38. "And he showed me a pure river of water of life, clear as crystal, proceeding out of the throne of God and of the Lamb." Rev. 22:1. **(26) "Let this mind be in you,** which was also in Christ Jesus: who, being in the form of God, thought it not robbery to be equal with God: but made himself of no reputation, and took upon him the form of a servant, and was made in the likeness of men: And being found in fashion as a man, he humbled himself, and became obedient unto death, even the death of the cross." Phil. 2:5–8. **(27)** "For they that are after the flesh do mind the things of the flesh; but they that are after the Spirit the things of the Spirit. For to be **carnally minded** is death; but to be **spiritually minded** is life and peace. Because the carnal mind is enmity against God." Rom. 8:5–7. **(28)** "Whither shall I go from thy spirit? or whither shall I flee from thy presence? If I ascend up into heaven, **thou art there:** if I make my bed in hell, behold, thou art there." Ps. 139:7, 8. **(29) Open door no man can shut.** John 10:7, 9; Rev. 3:8. **(30)** *Purusha/Parousia.* 1988 *PoW,* p. 228 note.

Notes from Pearl no. 79 by the Goddess of Purity:
Prior to the Goddess of Purity's dictation, the Messenger delivered teachings on the "Thirty-Three Manifestations of Avalokiteśvara as Kuan Yin" (manifestations 7, 12–22), 90-min. audiocassette B88129, $6.50 (add $.55 for postage). The dictation of the Goddess of Purity is available with that of Cyclopea on 90-min. audiocassette K88031, $6.50 (add $.55 for postage), and on 90-min. videocassette HP88089, $19.95 (add $1.10 for postage). **(1) Tares among the wheat.** Matt. 13:24–30, 36–43. **(2) The Great Preserver.** The Second Person of the Trinity, the Universal Christ, the Son of God, Vishnu, embodied as Lord Krishna. **(3) Deathless Solar Body.** Serapis Bey, "The Great Deathless Solar Body," in *Dossier on the Ascension,* pp. 154–59; 1988 *PoW,* p. 17; 1987 *PoW,* p. 622; 1984 *PoW,* pp. 2, 3–4, 564, 565, 568; Keepers of the Flame Lesson 30, p. 38. **(4) The blue-throat Kuan Yin** is one of thirty-three manifestations of Kuan Yin which have been venerated in China since the seventh century. The third section of mantras in *Kuan Yin's Crystal Rosary: Devotions to the Divine Mother East and West* released by Elizabeth Clare Prophet is based on these thirty-three manifestations. Some Buddhist scholars believe that the blue-throat Kuan Yin is modeled after Shiva, Third Person of the Hindu Trinity. According to legend, Shiva saved the world from destruction by swallowing the poison that issued from the mouth of the lord of serpents. The poison would have killed him had it reached his stomach but instead it remained in Shiva's throat, causing a blue spot on his white throat. The mantra to the blue-throat Kuan Yin is *Na-mo Ch'ing Ching Kuan Yin* (Hail! the blue-throat Kuan Yin, pronounced Nah-mo Ching Jing Gwan Een). In the Messenger's teaching on this mantra and manifestation of Kuan Yin (see note above), she explained that "in addressing Kuan Yin we tie into the power of her throat chakra whereby the divine Word is released in all of her mantras and manifestations. We tie into the absolute blue-flame will of God that is our protection even from every type of poison—the poisoning of the mind, the poisoning of the feelings . . . . The power of Kuan Yin is released in this mantra. You can see it as a mantra to give before you engage in public speaking, before you initiate new cycles in your life." She said this mantra "assists us to support El Morya" and "gives us a shaft of blue flame for the transmutation of all misuses of the sacred fire in the throat chakra." See *Kuan Yin's Crystal Rosary,* 3-audiocassette album, cassette III, booklet p. 36; 1988 *PoW,* pp. 373 n. 13, 480 n. 7. **(5) River of Life.** John 7:38; Rev. 22:1. **(6) Holiness unto the LORD.** Exod. 28:36, 37; 39:30, 31; Isa. 23:18; Jer. 2:3; Zech. 14:20, 21. **(7) Pure in heart.** Matt. 5:8. **(8) Gifts of the Holy Spirit.** I Cor. 12; Mark L. Prophet and Elizabeth Clare Prophet, *Lords of the Seven Rays: Mirror of Consciousness,* Book One; *The Lost Teachings of Jesus II,* pp. 151–293, or pocketbook edition *The Lost Teachings of Jesus 3,* pp. 107–285. For the Messenger's teachings on the gifts of the Holy Spirit charted on the Cosmic Clock, see "Darshan, Teachings and Dictations with Paul the Venetian and the Maha Chohan," 2 audiocassettes, 3 hr., A88103, $13.00 (add $.95 for postage). **(9)** A **bija** ("seed") syllable, or mantra, represents the essence of a cosmic being, a principle or a chakra. See "Bija Mantras to the Feminine Deities," no. 14, and "Bija Mantras for Chakra Meditation," no. 62, in *Mantras of the Ascended Masters for the Initiation of the Chakras,* pp. 4, 17, on audiocassettes B85135, B85137; Summit University Press 30th anniversary sale catalog, p. 18; 1988 *PoW,* p. 270 n. 6.

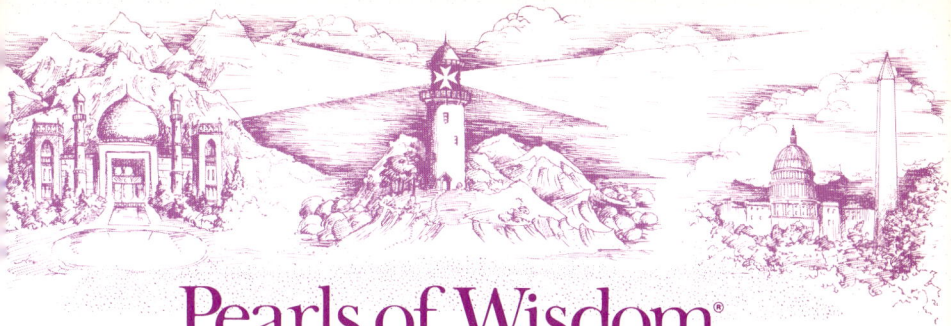

Pearls of Wisdom®
published by The Summit Lighthouse

| Vol. 31 No. 81 | Beloved Heros and Amora | November 27, 1988 |

The Harvest
IV
Our God Is Love
The Power of the Three-Times-Three of Elohim
A Child's Rosary and the Ruby Ray Judgment Call

Our God *is Love* and this *is* the religion of the golden age.[1]

Our God of Love has sealed within this very Community, within this very heart such a cornucopia of loveliness, of teaching, of mystery of God as to endure as the foundation and fulfillment of Aquarius. Now, beloved, this Word that has gone forth and this Work of the LORD [the Mighty I AM Presence][2] can no longer be contained by a planetary vibration that does increase in Darkness ere the Light come.

Thus, you are in, as you have been told, the cycle of the five secret rays[3] as the fire infolding itself[4] does draw you within— within to the heart to keep the Flame for life, within even in the heart of the earth, aye, to keep the Flame for life, to keep the thread of contact and of continuity of being from the center of the earth through the many spirals that are under the earth to the surface itself.

The northern lights come as a light without source, as an unfed flame. So does the heart ignite as it is ignited by Love, burn[ing] on and on and on. Therefore [do] the rays of Light* East and West [come as] the great gathering of the teachings of the Divine Mother of Lemuria and of all ages, some far, far distant in the past and the future. This is preserved. This is prepared. For the New Day shall dawn and a planet and a people purged of the density of the perfidy of ignorance shall emerge.

And when the angels of the Lord have gathered the tares and separated them from the wheat and bound them in bundles and

---

*i.e., the 'Alpha' and 'Omega' of the Universal Christ consciousness, 'East' and 'West'

removed them,[5] so you shall see that the good wheat shall prosper as the seed of Christ and those who may not have chosen to be that Christ in ages past shall emerge and see the Light. They shall hear the voice of the Lord [the Mighty I AM Presence] and the dead shall rise and they shall live—those who were dead to that voice—in this hour.[6]

Thus, beloved, we, Elohim of God-Love and God-Love's Third Ray, have moved about in the wind and the thunder and the water, in the turbulence and above it. For we have determined to answer every call of every heart of fire upon the planet, irrespective of affiliation. And we especially appreciate the calls unto the Ruby Ray and the Ruby Ray judgment through the heart of the Buddha of the Ruby Ray. For, beloved, we then become the instrumentation of the fiat of Five Dhyāni Buddhas who activate through your heart and the concentric spheres surrounding that heart chakra the action of the secret rays in this hour.

You will recall the mighty legions of angels of the Ruby Ray who did whirl and dance and spin at the Heart of the Inner Retreat at this summer's conclave.[7] These particular bands of angels of the Ruby Ray, beloved, wielding their Ruby Ray swords, have truly come from far-off worlds, have come to address a Mother's distress and that of her children, even the presence of the Guru Mother in the earth and all of the disciples such as ye are who follow that Mother Flame and are determined, ever more determinedly, to embody that Mother Flame as cosmic white-fire purity and as the Feminine Ray of God.

So we have come and so these legions have come by the direction of the Almighty One in the Great Central Sun. Thus, beloved, you find that these are intercessors. But intercessors of the Ruby Ray of the intensity of the Holy Spirit come closest to those who have accepted the message of the Maha Chohan to enter into the path of initiation, which initiation is always the judgment[8] as the judgment is defined as the separation of the Real from the Unreal within each and every individual.

Thus, beloved ones, as you have been admonished to seek the nine gifts of the Holy Spirit,[9] understand that these gifts show [in those who have received them] the balanced Threefold Flame; and they show the inner contact of the heart and Threefold Flame below with the heart [and Threefold Flame] of the Holy Christ Self [and] with the heart and Threefold Flame of the I AM Presence—the Power of the Three, times the Three, times the Three, beloved.* This, then, as a goal, as a resolve—resolute in the heart of each bodhisattva ye are—does become the means, the strengthening, the wise dominion, the everlasting Love in you

---

*The Power of the Threefold Flame of the heart multiplied by the Power of the Threefold Flame of the Holy Christ Self, multiplied by the Power of the Threefold Flame of the Mighty I AM Presence. Or, the Power of the Trinity times the Trinity times the Trinity focused as the Threefold Flame in the three bodies of man.

whereby we may work directly through you for the binding of those conditions that arise out of the pit itself.

Elohim of the Third Ray we are and our office does mandate that we deal with the inundation of planetary spheres with the karma of lifewaves. Thus, beloved, until you reach the hour of attainment in the Holy Spirit of this Power of the Nine, *know* that your call for the Ruby Ray judgment ratified on earth as in heaven is the means whereby we may go after those conditions which may have been directly caused by yourselves, thus assisting you in balancing, as only the Ruby Ray can balance, the misuses of the Light of* the Holy Spirit. Indeed, this is what the Ruby Ray is and is for: the balancing of the karma made through the misuse of the Light of the Holy Ghost.

Blessed ones, when it was spoken long ago that the sin of the Holy Ghost cannot be forgiven,[10] understand that this was a judgment upon the levels of nonattainment of a people who had not the attainment [of God-Self awareness] nor were they living in an age when the temple doors were opened for them to receive such initiation. Even the baptism by sacred fire of Holy Spirit[11] is but the beginning rather than the ending of the attainment of the Power of the Three-Times-Three.

Thus, acquiring gifts by self-mastery of Holy Spirit is, as it were, the capturing of nine stars that should form the belt of Heros and Amora. So you have heard of Orion's belt.[12] We also, then, have our belt and it is nine stars of Cosmic Threefold Flame, *the Power of the Three-Times-Three of Elohim!*

Know, then, beloved, that the Call is ever the key to your integrity and oneness with the God of Love in the Masters of the Third Ray. The key, beloved, begins with balancing the Threefold Flame below. And I tell you, precious hearts, Love is the key to that balance when love is true Love. For true Love infires and goads one to acquire illumination—and *illumination* as "illumined action" by wise dominion of self. True Love when it is true does love and adore the will of God whereby the power of God is vouchsafed to the individual, for the individual has proven himself in every possible way to be unwilling to give in to the temptation to misuse power.

O beloved hearts, if you would only know how the representatives of the Third Ray and of the Holy Spirit do test and continue to test and test souls of this planet [as to] whether when given the opportunity for certain power—temporal, spiritual, mental or whatever sort—that power is taken in the service and the glory of God and in profound humility or is seized as with pride the individual then does stand above his fellows in his own mind; for now he has acquired some power, some piece of land, some paltry sum of money, some this or that whereby he fancies himself better.

*i.e., the God consciousness of

Blessed ones, take heed, for those who pass the tests of the right use of* an increase in energy, in light, in consciousness, even in freedom from certain karma, do enter in and acquire O so much more than position among their peers. These, beloved, may receive, then, the initiations to have the gifts of the Holy Spirit. There is no greater power that could be desired and yet desirelessness itself is the key. And so the meek inherit the earth because they are desireless.[13]

Blessed ones, let us turn, then, to the dilemma, for we have turned to it, of this rising astral sea.[14] The key is the Ruby Ray and the Holy Spirit. And you will shorten the day and the distance between yourself and your congruency with this Ruby Ray by seeing to it that five Ruby Ray judgment calls[15] go forth [from your heart] each day for the clearing of all that gathers around any vortex of Light.

Now, you have understood that this vortex of Light of this Inner Retreat is intended to hold the balance in the West for the abode of the Masters of the Himalayas, yes, the true Masters who must keep the Flame [of the Divine Mother on earth] and hold it against the false hierarchy of India and the false gurus who come forth therefrom.

Blessed ones, you hold a citadel and a spiral of living flame of Love, a teaching and a sacred mystery that does keep the Flame against the false hierarchy of religion in the West and the false pastors and the false rabbis and the false priests. Know, then, beloved, that that fire is unto God. Let it be a pillar that burns clean, for you have kept open this cylinder, for you have sustained the Elohim chalice by resurrection flame,[16] for you have communed, for you have entered, for you have known the love of Christ in Jesus, in yourself, and you will not let go of the honor of Christ.

When all else seems wanting and you may think you have lost the thread of contact with your Holy Christ Self and Flame, remember the honor of Christ and you will have right thought, right action, right desire, right motive and purpose. The honor of Christ is always loving, kind, wise and tethered to the Law without compromise. The honor of Christ is the shaft of white fire. The first virtue of that honor is self-honesty and honesty toward all.

The Tempter comes but so does the Initiator. You may learn of me that the initiator does come to you in the person of your beloved Mother Mary. She, the Divine Mother, has a greater sternness than many conceive of. She does come, then, to prove and reprove you in honesty with self.

Blessed ones, our Father has sent Mary, the Blessed One, as Mediatrix of the Divine Wholeness, she being there so very close to the hearts of Lightbearers of the earth. You may know her as

*i.e., the righteousness of

one who yet abides very close to your souls and one, above all, who is dedicated to maintaining that string of pearls of rosary that does tie the soul to the Holy Christ Self.

Therefore understand, beloved, why we have introduced the Hail Mary to you and why it is O so important that you remember <u>to tarry and to conclude your morning prayers with the Child's Rosary.</u>[17] When you participate in concentration and visualize the strengthening of the cord, even the cord twixt the soul and the heart flame and the Universal Christ, you can know that this is one of the surest means of the very maintaining of that Holy Christ-Self awareness that <u>does guarantee to you each day that Hercules may bear your burden</u> and the burden that is lawful.[18]

You may know, when you strengthen that tie through the heart of Mother Mary and you feel that strengthening, that you will be able to take on the holding of the balance for those who are not able.[19] You will feel in yourself that you can carry first one and then another and you will look, of course, to the children who are in your tender care.

Blessed ones, <u>the difference in having Hercules and Amazonia bear the burden of karma and [in] not having them bear it is great,</u> and you may discover this if perchance in forgetfulness you do not enter in to those spirals early. And you will see that <u>the fifteen-minute rosary,</u> in addition to a disciplined self-awareness in Christ, <u>is a small requirement for so great an intercession as that available through Elohim.</u>

We then say to you that by the Ruby Ray judgment call you may satisfy [the Great Law on behalf of] yourself individually and as a Community to allow us to intercede for the binding of your contribution (the tributary of your lifestream) that has increased the weight of astral debris upon a planet, which does now come forth out of the bottomless pit.

Therefore, it is our goal to see the Lightbearers be the wayshowers. Those who bear the Light of the Christ in fulfillment of Hercules' requirement will also have through their Ruby Ray judgment calls a first priority on our daily list of the orders that we set in motion for the bands of Ruby Ray angels who wield their swords with delight and have aeons of momentum of binding the demons and discarnates on every planet and system of worlds where they have been sent.

It is our goal to see you freer and freer from the karmic weight. Thus, <u>that Ruby Ray call does make our day. May it make your day, beloved,</u> as you understand that to lighten the karma that you carry on the Third Ray is the necessity whereby you can increase [your success] in receiving and passing the initiations of the Holy Spirit through the Lord the Maha Chohan and through his blessed Sons, the Seven.

See, then, how great an opportunity. For if it is the requirement of the Law to balance the Threefold Flame by beginning with Love, then does it not follow as corollary that the love that you may begin with is the love that you have sown and reaped in the karma of good works? And the very good works of giving that [Ruby Ray] judgment call, being so critical and vital in this hour, do accrue to your lifestream as immediate blessing and as transmutation of your own banal past whereby the earth does now feel the weight of a planetary evolution.

To see the Lightbearers on top of such conditions is our goal. Thus, we have, with a great intensity accorded to us by the Great Law, occupied ourselves in all space and time dimensions since our dictation given at *FREEDOM 1988.* And we come this hour a little later than autumn equinox[20] for the equalization and balancing of that which can be balanced ere the cycles turn and the entering in to the challenges of the hierarchy of Scorpio does bring to you truly new, new, I say, as well as deliberate tests of the Law.

Thus, by the All-Seeing Eye of God you have the opportunity in these weeks ahead to bring God-Mastery and God-Control to the life-force within you such as you have not done before, to raise that sacred fire of the Mother to new levels of creativity in the heart, increasing the focus of the Great Central Sun Magnet of the heart and therefore magnetizing the soul up and up the spiral into the heart of the Christ Self.

There are many cosmic forces working toward your Victory. We come to deliver our message that you might know the equation of the challenge and that which is given to you as Opportunity.

May you find yourself during the day, when meeting the very challenges of that day, to speak the call to Elohim of the Third Ray, Heros and Amora, to speak the call to the Archangel Chamuel and Charity, to Paul the Venetian, the Maha Chohan and the Buddha of the Ruby Ray, but above all to call for cosmic legions of Ruby Ray angels to move in and to *Take command! Take command! Take command!* by the Holy Spirit of those conditions which would obstruct the Word and the Work of the LORD [your Beloved Mighty I AM Presence] from enduring even midst this period when other things shall pass away.

In your heart there is a drop of Ruby Ray.[21] For some it is a microscopic drop but nevertheless a drop. For those with developed Threefold Flame it shall so multiply that development. For those without a Threefold Flame it may be the single pearl of a drop that does magnetize and establish within you an integrating principle of Life whereby by the drop of Ruby Ray you may find yourself receiving through the instrument of the Lord Christ the quickening, truly the quickening whereby love in your heart may renew a magnet that can become—by your service, selflessness, unceasing surrender and sacrifice—a Threefold Flame.

Yes, beloved, all may move forward in this hour and progress toward the heart of the I AM Presence!

To Keepers of the Flame around the world I speak. May your abode be found in the heart of the Buddha and the Western Shamballa and may your abode be found in the crystal of the ruby, even in the heart of the Buddha of the Ruby Ray.

Our Presence as Elohim of Love is the greatest force that does repel the hate and hate creation that does ooze out of the realms of Death and Hell. May you, then, come to know and to value the action of the Elohim of the Seven Rays, to call us forth to maintain our vigil,[22] and to know that we are determined—and [determined] as Lightbearers are determined and meet us halfway—to see to it that every good and perfect gift,[23] even the gift of everlasting Life, everlasting Truth, everlasting Love shall be thine own here and now, most especially here and now for the pragmatic usefulness of the hour.

May the necessity of this hour of earth's evolution impel you to expand and develop the flame of the heart, for thereby millions shall be saved and you shall ascend.

We are Elohim of the Third Ray, perpetually in action. When you think of us think of Shiva. Think of the intensity of the Power/Wisdom/Love of the Holy Spirit to move systems of worlds and galaxies into alignment with the will of God. As you form that grid for planet earth that we might use, as you form it as Community, know that you can make a difference as to the levels of intensity which this planetary change that is ordained by God will take. Thus there is, as you would say, an upside and a downside. <u>Let us minimize planetary destruction. Let us maximize planetary harmony.</u>

The Ruby Ray is an intense fire, beloved. To bear it you must be ready. We are sealing this Community in the cosmic cross of the Ruby Ray. It does remain in the etheric octave and will descend as some are able to contain it and to maintain their harmony.

As we recede into the spheres of the five secret rays, your Blessed Mother, Mary, approaches to speak with you.

"The Summit Lighthouse Sheds Its Radiance O'er All the World to Manifest as Pearls of Wisdom." This dictation was **delivered** by the Messenger Elizabeth Clare Prophet on **Tuesday, October 11, 1988,** 12:53–1:27 a.m. MDT. Available with the dictation of Mother Mary on 90-min. audiocassette K88033, $6.50 (add $.55 for postage); on videocassette with dictations of Hercules and Mother Mary, includes slide meditation on galaxies, 2 hr. 20 min., HP88091, $39.95 (add $1.10 for postage). Throughout these notes *PoW* is the abbreviation for *Pearls of Wisdom.* **(1) God is Love.** I John 4:7, 8, 16. **(2) I AM THAT I AM.** Exod. 3:13–15. **(3) Serapis Bey's 14-month cycle in the secret rays.** 1988 *PoW*, p. 502 n. 6. **(4) Fire infolding itself.** Ezek. 1:4. **(5) Tares and the wheat.** Matt. 13:24–30, 36–43. **(6) They that hear shall live.** John 5:24, 25, 28, 29. **(7) Ruby Ray angels in the Heart.** Heros and Amora, 1988 *PoW*, p. 464. **(8)** On February 22, 1988, the Maha Chohan announced that he had come to deliver **the initiations of the Holy Spirit (as the judgment)** starting in the city of Los Angeles: "As the result of the consequences of the violation of the Holy Ghost in little children, in Nature and [in] the defilement of the body and the soul, you will see that *unless these things are turned around and a people invoke the Light of their God and fulfill the Law of Love, those things projected will come to pass.*" The Maha Chohan also invited us to enter the path of initiation: "I come to you with the same offer made to you by the Lord Christ: to receive you as my students. For as I serve as the Teacher of the Lords of the Seven Rays, I shall also desire to teach the pupils of the Lords of the Seven Rays. Traveling their sevenfold path back to my heart of the Holy Ghost, you will know, then, that *there is a way out* and that there is a transfiguration that awaits you, there is a transformation indeed." On July 4, 1988, the Maha Chohan said he had come to serve the Holy Spirit's Communion and explained that "our coming is [to the end] that by the action of the Emerald Matrix and the Communion you might be afforded the ability, the opportunity to enter a new path, a new highway of our God formerly not open to you . . . because knowledge is not a sufficiency to enter into this path but only initiation." 1988 *PoW,* pp. 225, 226, 542. (**9**) **Admonishments to seek the nine gifts.** 1987 *PoW,* pp. 160, 266; 1988 *PoW,* pp. 616–17, 634 n. 8. (**10**) **Blasphemy against the Holy Ghost not forgiven.** Matt. 12:31, 32; Mark 3:28, 29; Gospel of Thomas, logion 44. (**11**) **Baptism by fire.** Matt. 3:11, 12; Mark 1:8; Luke 3:16, 17; Pistis Sophia, bk. 3, chap. 115. (**12**) **Orion's belt.** Orion is the constellation on the celestial equator named for the mighty hunter of Greek mythology; his belt is marked by a row of three bright stars. (**13**) **Meek inherit the earth.** Matt. 5:5. (**14**) **Rising astral sea.** 1988 *PoW,* pp. 622–24, 625–26. On November 1, 1987, and January 3, 1988, Serapis Bey and Archangel Michael also warned that the weight of planetary karma would increase tenfold on January 1, 1988 (1987 *PoW,* p. 584; 1988 *PoW,* p. 90). (**15**) Decree 33.00, "The LORD's Judgment by the Ruby Ray through Archangel Chamuel and Charity," in *Prayers, Meditations and Dynamic Decrees for the Coming Revolution in Higher Consciousness,* Section III. (**16**) **Corridors of light.** On October 10, 1988, Hercules spoke of the clearing and opening of the "passageway to the octaves of Light of the abode of Elohim" which had been accomplished through the calls of the Messenger and Keepers of the Flame gathered for *The Harvest* class. Hercules also emphasized the importance of sustaining the **crystal chalice of Elohim** which had been established in the Heart of the Inner Retreat during the summer of 1987 (see 1988 *PoW,* p. 580 n. 1). On December 25, 1986, Jesus announced that the God and Goddess Meru had come to "establish a corridor of light from the etheric retreat over the Royal Teton Ranch to the etheric retreat of the Feminine Ray at Lake Titicaca. By this corridor of light, beloved, we open a highway whereby your calls may reach South America in time." On June 28, 1987, Nada said that "that highway of light to Lake Titicaca from the Retreat of the Divine Mother over the Royal Teton Ranch . . . is now extended to the retreat of the Lord Jesus over Saudi Arabia and the entire Holy Land and the Middle East. It is expedient, beloved. For I tell you the Light must flow to hold the balance against war." 1986 *PoW,* pp. 681, 691; 1987 *PoW,* p. 309. (**17**) In Hercules' October 10, 1988 dictation delivered prior to Heros and Amora's dictation, Hercules said: "Even in the midst of meeting and defeating old karma and old forms of consciousness [Lightbearers] may remember that **the Divine Mother in the heart of the earth** does truly abide and sustain [the Comfort Flame] for those who may reach her by the mantra, **reach her by the Hail Mary,** reach her through any heart of any Feminine being" (1988 *PoW,* p. 630). See *A Child's Rosary to Mother Mary,* 15-minute rosaries with scriptural readings from the New Testament for adults and children, four 3-audiocassette albums, 3 hr. each. Album 1: John, James, Jude; album 2: Hebrews; album 3: Galatians; album 4: Corinthians; $9.95 each (add $1.05 each for postage). Also included with "Watch With Me" Jesus' Vigil of the Hours, devotional service invoking the intercession of Jesus and the heavenly hosts, as the last half hour of the 93-min. cassette, which includes the adoration of the Blessed Virgin in the singing of "Ave Maria." On October 4, 1987, Jesus said, "It is my desire, then, that in 52 sessions with you, which I would like to be of 90-minute duration (or more), you might experience such renewal and such self-transcendence" (1987 *PoW,* p. 495). (**18**) **Hercules bearing karmic burden of Light-bearers.** On August 10, 1987, Hercules announced that he would carry the burdens of the Lightbearers as a cross upon his back for 14 months (see 1987 *PoW,* pp. 442–43, quoted in 1988 *PoW,* p. 632 n. 1). In Hercules' October 10, 1988 dictation delivered at the conclusion of the 14 months, the Elohim said he could continue to bear a certain percentage of our karmic burden only as "you are able to sustain a rising coil of blue-flame will of God to the level of your own Christ Self" and "raise up that pillar of blue-flame will of God daily" (1988 *PoW,* p. 623). (**19**) "I AM keeping the Flame for you until you are able." The Maha Chohan, Keepers of the Flame Lesson 2, p. 12. (**20**) At the conclusion of their June 30, 1988 dictation, **Heros and Amora** said, "Elohim have delivered a sufficiency of Love and we withdraw, for earth has reached the level of saturation until you yourselves increase the violet flame and the Astrea exorcisms. It would be **our desire to return in each quadrant of the year** to increase this action. May the autumn equinox find you ready to receive us again" (1988 *PoW,* p. 470). The autumn equinox occurred September 22. (**21**) **Drop of Ruby Ray.** 1988 *PoW,* pp. 535–38. (**22**) **Elohim vigil.** 1988 *PoW,* pp. 584–85, 625–26. (**23**) **Every good gift and perfect gift.** James 1:17.

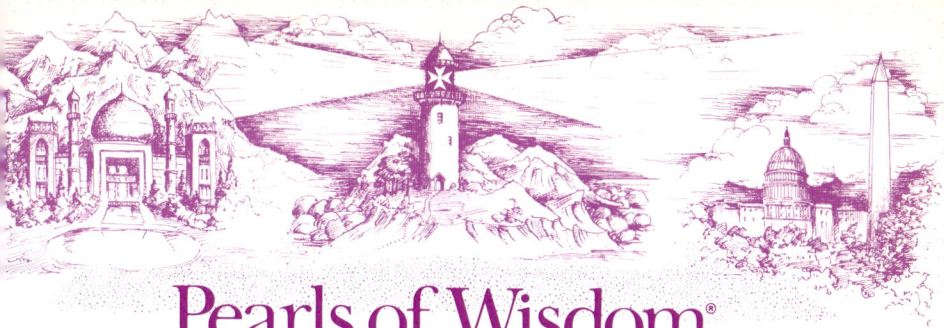

Pearls of Wisdom®
published by *The Summit Lighthouse*

Vol. 31 No. 82   *Beloved Mother Mary*   *December 3, 1988*

The Harvest
V
The Mediatrix of Divine Wholeness
Your Own Attainment Sustained by Your Heart Flame
"I Shall Not Leave Thee"

O beloved of my heart, remember that the Father did call me, and as Raphael and I were summoned to that throne and as I received the commission to enter the portals of birth on earth to give birth to the Christ, the Christ of Jesus, it was not alone to be delivered of that Son of God: But I was sent to go after each and every one who had come with Sanat Kumara, the Lightbearers originally anointed by God who had successively lost their sense of Self-awareness as that Christ, whose Self-worth had somehow receded by their brushing with fallen angels with a vacant heart.

Know, then, beloved, that the Father did send me as a Mediatrix[1] of the Divine Wholeness. And as I have been allowed to come nearer to earth, even to the point where my tears are seen on my statues and images,[2] you may understand that truly through my heart you may achieve a daily oneness with your Christ Self. Blessed ones, not without effort, however, for in this hour, and from this hour on, you see [that] this rising tide of [the sea of the] astral plane does make more difficult the raising up of that line, that lifeline to my heart, and my extending it [to you].

But I tell you, the power of the salutation to me "Hail, Mary! Hail, *Ma-Ray!*" and the mantra "In the Immaculate Heart of Mary I trust!" [is great]. These combined with the science of the spoken Word, the exercise thereof in the calling forth of the violet flame of the Holy Spirit, do so enhance your ability to maintain and strengthen the tie to my heart, [and] thus the tie to your Christ Self. Know, beloved, that my mission twenty-four hours a day is to restore to the Lightbearer and to the child of God's heart that oneness that is so needed.

I hope, and it is my fond hope and prayer and it is my prayer to the Father in your behalf, that you will so increase in your desire to be with me, to be my own sons and daughters in the very sense that Jesus is, that you will soon have such a presence of my aura around you that you can be the open heart whereby many can enter in.

I seek in the students of the Ascended Masters representatives who can bring the Lightbearers to a higher level of understanding than that which they are limited to in their orthodoxy and in the canopy of that orthodoxy that does limit their piercing through that skyey tent to all of the great hierarchies of heaven and to the ultimate awareness of being anointed to be that Christ.

Thus, beloved ones, I come to you in great comfort, but be mindful that the comfort is in the Law of the Comforter, which Law of the Holy Spirit has been explained to you from the heart of the Elohim of the First and the Third Rays. Even my intercession is subject to your obedience to the requirements of the Law, that the spoken Word of the rosary might be your instrument to and through my heart.

For those, then, who are unable to maintain the tie to the Holy Christ Self in any other way, I represent the point of recourse. Thus, I have given those words that many may pray to the Blessed Mother, saying:

> O Blessed Virgin, as we have recourse to thee, receive our souls and hearts and bind us to our living Saviour, Christ, the Lord of Jesus and the Lord of all who have ascended to my God and your God. O my Blessed Mother, hear me in this hour as I give thy rosary unto thee and through thy heart unto God and through thy heart on behalf of all Lightbearers of this darkened star.

Blessed are ye who have a momentum on [any] one or more of the seven rays on prayer and service and in the things of God, for it is your momentum that will multiply again and again your daily prayers [offered on each of the rays of God's Presence].

I would tell you, beloved, that to a certain extent all of the Archeiai of the Seven Archangels and Archangels of the secret rays and the Eighth Ray are very close in their intercessory power. But, then, you have been admonished to place your attention upon any Mother figure in the ascended realms and to develop your momentum through that Mother's heart.[3] This is because, beloved, for all evolutions in samsara, for all who must face [and] pass through the astral plane, and all Christed ones who with Jesus descend into hell for times and times again, it is the Presence [of the I AM THAT

I AM] of the Divine Mother personified in angelic hosts, in ascended and cosmic beings that does provide the means of entering in to the heart of the Trinity and to the highest octaves of Spirit.

Oneness with the Divine Mother as She does appear to you in our varied manifestations does establish within you the electromagnetic field of the divine polarity of the Mother; and that powerful magnet that does have the minus coefficient does then become to you the means of attracting the Father, therefore Divine Wholeness and therefore [the] escape from time and space, which does trap astral debris.

So, beloved, I am called the Mediatrix of Divine Wholeness, for healing of the Fifth Ray does always come when by my flame or the flame of the representative of the Divine Mother nearest to you, you do magnetize the presence of the Masculine Ray and of the Father and therefore have a circle of oneness whereby you are immune—immune to the conditions of the flesh, to the decay of the flesh and to death itself. And that immunity is a soul immunity which may extend to the very form as in the lives of the saints their bodies were preserved beyond transition, did emit perfume and did become a focus also to conduct that light of spiritual realms.

With Raphael we are one. And your call for the reinforcement of the dispensation of the anchoring here of Fátima and Fátima's retreat[4] will avail much as you keep the Flame and keep this physical property clear and clean, pure by your own consciousness and life for the maintenance of the Feminine Ray of a planet and a people until the focus of Lake Titicaca should become the focus of the Feminine Ray in the physical octave again. Of course, you know that the retreats of the God and Goddess Meru and the Lord Himalaya are not moved, are not changed and ever pulsate [the Masculine and Feminine Rays of the Godhead], but what is of greatest need in the earth in this hour is the sustainment in the physical octave of these rays.[5]

Not without forethought by Almighty God was the Retreat of the Divine Mother, that does appear to you even as the City Foursquare over this property, established here.[6] Thus, that retreat has magnetized you even as you have magnetized it, that in this place and in this earth that manifestation might be the balance that is needed for millions in the hour of their personal and planetary initiations.

With the Buddha in your heart and the Buddha in the Heart of the Inner Retreat[7] may you always remember and say, *"By the grace of God and by his grace alone, Mother Mary, we shall not fail!"* And, blessed ones, you may insert after my name the names of any Ascended Masters or angels or Elohim whose sweet presence is on your heart and mind and in whose name you can say with God within you, *"We shall not fail!"* It is a fiat, beloved. It banishes failure and creates the vacuum which only Victory does fill.

As it is our office, Raphael and I seal you now in the healing thoughtform.[8] May the healing mantras find you, as with the mantras of the Divine Mother, in a state of wholeness invoked from on high, that day by day will become your own attainment and [be] sustained by your heart flame, not alone by those of the heavenly Hierarchy.

This is the joy of past, present, future becomings, that all that you call forth from God as gift and grace is one day your own attainment, for you have seen and known the co-measurement spoken of by Elohim and you have set your sights on that co-measurement with those of our realms who have answered your calls daily until *you*, as the answered call, are in the state of attainment whereby the God above has become truly in manifestation as the God of your heart.

Even so, build concentric spheres of causal body round about this form and know that I the LORD thy God [the Mighty I AM Presence] in Father and in Mother shall not leave thee! *I shall not leave thee. I AM with you alway, even unto your fulfillment of the Feminine Ray.*

Now your Messenger does recede for the fulfilling of the promises, all promises, all promises vested in her keeping by the Hierarchy above and the disciples below who also know her heart as the nexus whereby you may enter in to your Christhood.

This dictation was **delivered** on **Tuesday, Oct. 11, 1988**, 1:32–1:50 a.m. MDT. Available on audio- and videocassette, see p. 641 note. Throughout these notes *PoW* is the abbreviation for *Pearls of Wisdom*. (1) **Mediatrix** [derived from Latin *medius* 'middle']: a female mediator; one who intervenes between parties at variance, esp. to reconcile; a go-between, messenger, agent, intercessor, intermediary. The Blessed Virgin Mary is known to Roman Catholics as the Mediatrix or Mediatress of all graces. St. Bonaventure described her role as Mediatrix "between us and Christ, as Christ is between us and God," and St. Francis called her "treasurer of graces," "advocate," and "collaborator in our salvation." Although Catholics believe they can pray directly to God the Father and God the Son, they have a deep devotion and confidence in the Blessed Mother as the one who will always intercede in their behalf. They believe she has great influence and favor with her son and that God loves and trusts her so much that he will never refuse her requests. It is also taught that Christ, in his role as Mediator between God and men, loves to grant men graces as they invoke his Mother's intercession through devotion to her Immaculate Heart. St. Bonaventure said that "whenever the most sacred Virgin goes to God to intercede for us, she, as Queen, commands all the angels and saints to accompany her and unite their prayers to hers." (2) 1988 *PoW*, p. 604 n. 14. (3) 1988 *PoW*, p. 495. (4) 1988 *PoW*, pp. 258, 442 n. 1. (5) **Focuses of the Masculine and Feminine Rays** of the Godhead are at the etheric retreats of Lord Himalaya and the God and Goddess Meru respectively. On Oct. 10, 1988, Hercules said that because the physical area of Lake Titicaca in the Andes (where the Feminine Ray should be anchored physically) is covered over with astral substance, the Royal Teton Ranch "must suffice" as "the [physical] focus of the Feminine Ray to the earth here in the Northern Rockies . . . until the dark period of earth's travail does pass." Because the Ascended and Unascended Masters of the Himalayas keep the Flame of the Masculine Ray, it is anchored physically in the Himalayas from Lord Himalaya's Retreat of the Blue Lotus. See 1988 *PoW*, pp. 623, 626. (6) On Dec. 15, 1985, Sanat Kumara announced that the **Retreat of the Divine Mother** was positioned above the entire area of the Royal Teton Ranch. 1986 *PoW*, pp. 70–72. (7) The **Western Shamballa**, Gautama Buddha's etheric retreat centered at the Heart of the Inner Retreat at the Royal Teton Ranch, Montana, is an extension of Shamballa, site of Sanat Kumara's original retreat located above the Gobi Desert, where the Lightbearers who accompanied him to earth first descended. 1981 *PoW*, pp. 226, 227; 1988 *PoW*, p. 519 n. 13. (8) 1988 *PoW*, p. 442 n. 2.

Royal Teton Ranch

Box A, Livingston, Montana 59047-1390   406/222-8300

November 1, 1988
All Saints' Day

Dearest Friends of the Ascended Masters,

One year ago today our beloved Jesus called us to enter
the path of personal Christhood in all earnestness. The Lord
said:

"Become that Christ! Receive your Lord and your God
into your temple. And I, Jesus, as your brother, will walk at your
side, will talk with you, will counsel you. And you will know me
in the Love that I shared with John, my beloved. You will know
the intimacy of Love's communion and Love's initiation."

And so on this day as we celebrate the victory of "All
Saints" of the Great White Brotherhood and our own overcoming victory, let us recapitulate the Master's admonishments to us
and the fruitage of the Watch we have faithfully kept with him in
our midst (as he promised he would be) in the ensuing year.

On Ascension Thursday, May 28, 1987, the Saviour called
us to receive him into our life for the quickening of our own
ascension. As a means to that end he also called us to become
world teachers and he asked you to assist me in gathering
10,000 Keepers of the Flame from across the North American
continent.

And so you sent me stumping for the Coming Revolution
in Higher Consciousness. City by city you welcomed me into
your hearts and you received the Lightbearers who came to
hear the message of their soul's reunion with God through the
violet flame and the dynamic decree of the Word which, to the
pure in heart, unfolds the mystery of eternal life.

By your effort, your outreach, and your prayerful intercession before the altars of God which you have raised up in your
homes and sanctuaries around the world, 2500 new souls have
joined the Keepers of the Flame Fraternity and now know the
direct, conscious, one-on-one sponsorship of Saint Germain and

Portia, hierarchs of the Aquarian age and dispensation, and that of the Lords of the Seven Rays, whose retreats they enter nightly.

Think of it! Because of you 2500 lifestreams have made a unique, soul-satisfying contact with the World Teachers, with the Divine Mother, East and West, through Mother Mary and Kuan Yin, with Maitreya through his Mystery School at the Inner Retreat, and with our dear sponsor Morya El. And we are 25 percent of the way toward achieving the goal of 10,000 hearts, who are to be the catalyst for a million violet flame decreers-- the number Saint Germain says it will take to work the alchemical change for the turning back of that personal and planetary karma which is "the handwriting on the wall" for the 1990s.

Alleluia, Praise the Lord! His saints are marching in!

Then on October 4, 1987, as he addressed you and all Lightbearers of the world in New York City, Jesus came to claim "my own disciples." He explained to us that the Father had opened his heart for the purpose of sending him to "call my own to a path whereby they shall embody my Word, my Teaching, my Flesh and my Blood."

I shall never forget the moment of inner knowing as I was fully embraced in the living presence of the Lord, his Sacred Heart pulsating with my own. The feeling of his love--his longing, his desiring, his urgency to receive each and every one of you and all Lightbearers of the world who have not yet heard the Call--was a fire in my heart. I saw the way cleared for all who would respond to the Lord with their whole heart and life, that they could and would achieve in this life apostleship in the fullest sense of the word. His words flowed on:

"I call you to my fold not in the general sense but in the specific sense of knowing that a Teaching, a Way of Life, a Spirit of the Resurrection cannot endure upon earth unless, truly, 10,000 determine in this hour of my appearing to embody the fullness of myself. . . .

"I would receive you, then, in my retreat in Arabia [on the etheric plane] to tutor you as I did tutor my apostles Paul and John and countless others through the ages who have come to be initiated in the secret rites given to those who are able to enter the inner circle.

"Blessed ones, that door is open to all who qualify."

Speaking out of the heart of Maitreya, Jesus said, "Discipleship in this age is the Call of the Cosmic Christ."

Thus the Lord's summoning to "Become that Christ" beginning in all earnestness on November 1 was the logical unfoldment of his prior calling to us to be world teachers and disciples that would intensify when in Lisbon, Portugal, he said:

"I call you not only to be my disciples, [but] I call you [also] to be shepherds and to feed my sheep, to quickly devour by the Holy Spirit the teaching that is already set forth and therefore to put on and receive the mantle of apostleship--that you might know yourselves as shepherds and feed the children of God mouthful by mouthful that morsel of bread, that cup of cold water in my name that does return to them the inner resource of Light, the fount of that holy Christhood and the Presence of the I AM THAT I AM.

"This must be done quickly, beloved, for the fallen angels know that they have but a short time, but a narrow few years in which to move against the world that is about to deliver the mandate of the Universal Christ nation by nation."

Thus, I for one--who have received from our Father and the Holy One of God knowledge of the cycles of earth changes--knew, as Jesus came to me in the fiery Spirit of the Resurrection this Easter past, why his rebuke to the fallen angels who deny not only the Divine Mother but also woman her proper place in the churches was so intense--as was his judgment upon the false hierarchy of Christianity--and why his admonishment to his own was delivered with an impatience warranted by their delay and the lateness of the hour.

"Blessed ones, the Way may be hard and each footstep up the mountain more difficult, but, beloved, the steps must be taken. . . . The breaking of the spell of Death and Hell in established religion, truly the hypnotic spell of orthodoxy, may only come by the living witness. And I, if I am lifted up in you, I will draw all Lightbearers unto you. Therefore, as a staff, raise up the Light in your temple.

"Heed my call! Deny me not! For the years pass: I come again, I deliver my message, and the Law requires an acceleration. . . . For too long have even my own in this Community heard this message without fully believing and drinking the cup and manifesting that Christhood. Do not weary us with delays and we shall not weary you with the repetition of our message. Thus, beloved, the hour is come and must be taken; and the world shall see and know that the Teaching is real because you and not another, but you have dared to embody my Word."

And I remembered how with a similar urgency for our youth and our civilization Jesus had cried out to us Easter 1987:

"Blessed hearts, long ago I said, 'Feed my sheep.' And this you will also do. But in this hour, I say, take up the sword of the Spirit and fight for my sheep ere they are lost to the clutches of the drug peddlers and the peddlers of deceit and annihilation. This is my cry and my plea."

Even so do I write to you today with Jesus' words of Thanksgiving last resounding in my very soul:

"I AM in the heart of hearts of all who call to me in this moment to be my disciples indeed. I make known to you once again: 10,000 Keepers of the Flame are needed. . . . Let us not rest until the magnet of the heart, the fire burning there, does truly draw into our ranks those who are already Keepers of the Flame at heart."

Now it is my turn to respond and to do so decisively and with dispatch. Therefore, to assist you in responding mightily to his Call, I am sending to you our Summit University Press catalogue celebrating 30 years of publishing the teachings of the Ascended Masters and 1.1 million of their books sold!

In this 38-page magazine you will find unprecedented reductions on books and tapes--up to 70 percent off of our retail prices on hundreds of items all earmarked for those 7500 Keepers of the Flame-to-be and the Lightbearers of the world who have heard Jesus' Call in their souls and are praying to know the Way to go.

This is my tangible expression of gratitude for your faithful and loving support and all you have personally done to make our mutual service truly an Ascended Master Jesus Christ God-success!

You will find our Lost Years--which alone has sold over 100,000 copies--and Lost Teachings of Jesus at 50 percent off. And our just-off-the-press pocket-size editions--a total of five of the most beautiful books we've ever released in this mass-market format--specially priced at $19.95 for the complete set.

These are the books I want you to give to all your Christian friends and relatives--and everybody who walked out of their churches and temples years ago in search of Christ Truth. These are the books you can afford to place in libraries, prisons, schools, colleges, hospitals, and homes for the elderly and infirm--and on our military bases.

And karmically speaking, we can't afford not to place them!

As you turn the pages you will see your favorite New Age classics--Corona Class Lessons, The Great White Brotherhood and Cosmic Consciousness--all 50 percent off! Climb the Highest Mountain is 40 percent off! Pearls of Wisdom volumes are up to 50 percent off and Saint Germain On Alchemy and Lords of the Seven Rays are 33 percent off--just so you can choose the perfect message for those you are leading into the paths of Higher Consciousness. In addition, our basic Stump message from San Diego is 40 percent off and our audiotapes that are over two years old are 25 percent off or more. These contain the priceless basic teachings that have been released in our 30-year history as your Messengers.

My most favorite pages are the centerfold, offering so many of our wonderful decree and song tapes at $2.95 each in quantities of ten or more. The old-time favorite music tapes are your perfect singing Christmas card to lighten up our world this holiday season. And the four Save the World tapes are a violet flame marathon for those who are building their momentum on the Seventh Ray as they step up their pace and their vibes for Aquarius with each succeeding cassette.

The rest of the Christmas goodies I'll let you discover for yourself. May you take this opportunity and run with it to polarize the revolutionaries of the world to the Light of God which never fails to give earth freedom now!--in answer to our call.

In conclusion let us remember that true Keepers of the Flame are born, not made. They have been keeping the Flame for lifetimes by their heart's allegiance to their Mighty I AM Presence and the cosmic honor flame. Thus a single book or tape can quicken the soul-memory of Saint Germain and of their role in Aquarius. They are there--with the Goddess of Liberty we must go and find them.

Thus I leave you with her telling and profound words spoken at FREEDOM 1988:

"What I would unveil to you is that you are not natives of this earth and one and all came for this purpose: to keep the Flame in the hour when such aliens of the Light should move against the children of the Sun and [the children of the Sun should] require you as defenders. It is to this moment of your physical and mental recognition of the threat [of aliens] that Jesus, the beloved Son of God, and Saint Germain have prepared you in the past year and that our dictations have prepared you for many a year.

"You have been called to your ascension, called to be the Christ, to be Shepherds. You have been called to magnetize 10,000 Keepers of the Flame. May you [now] understand how a Body of God and Light--you the Mystical Body of God, of holy Church--have conspired in the Holy Spirit at inner levels long ago with our Lord Gautama and Sanat Kumara to be here and now ready in this day and age to be equipped with the armour of Light and Community and oneness and one-pointedness, setting all other things aside for this one commitment:

"To keep the Flame of Cosmic Liberty upon earth until cosmic reinforcements should come by the very magnet of your being, to keep the Flame of Cosmic Liberty on earth on behalf of those of lesser evolution who could not stand in the day of the enemy's appearing.

"In the many thousands of years that you have tarried here, other tributaries of lesser goals have vied for your energy.

Thus, today your energy fills many pots, many causes and purposes and endeavors you are engaged in.

"There is a certain quotient of light [which flows from your Mighty I AM Presence] over the crystal cord [to keep the Threefold Flame of Liberty that burns on the altar of your heart]. [But this quotient of light] does not increase until you increase the Cosmic Christ consciousness of Liberty through the Threefold Flame of your heart. Thus, like the spigot of water, only so much may pass through at a time and in a given day. Wherever you direct portions of that energy, you have a little bit less for this assignment.

"As wise investors, consider, then, how you shall take of this crystal-clear stream, how you shall direct it; and know that the preservation of life in sanity and on the path of spiritual oneness with God is the most important reason for being. All other daily activities must support you in this goal. All other activities unessential that do not lead to this goal ought to be dispensed with.

"May you find yourself in my heart this day in meditation upon being a Cosmic Mother, a Cosmic Father of the Threefold Flame of Liberty unto the evolutions of Light of this earth and beyond.

"I have stood for you for aeons, beloved, my torch raised high. With all the fervor of my Being, having come from the depths of Nirvana, I pass to you a torch of Liberty which is Cosmic Christ Illumination multiplied by Love, multiplied by Power, squared by the Purity of the Divine Mother.

"May you endure to the end. May you be God-victorious in Cosmic Liberty that I AM THAT I AM!"

My Sons and Daughters of the Flame, let us resolve together to meet our commitments to the decade--and to the heart of Jesus Christ and Saint Germain. And, lest we forget, El Morya.

All my Love is with you--and my mantle--as you go forth sowers and multipliers of the Word.

Mother

Elizabeth Clare Prophet

Pearls of Wisdom®
published by The Summit Lighthouse

| *Vol. 31 No. 83* | *Beloved Jesus Christ* | *December 4, 1988* |

The Zeal of My House
Thanksgiving Day Address 1988
Keep the Flame of the Ark of the Covenant Blazing upon This Altar!

Hail to the Light of the holy ones of God here below who do reflect the Holy One of God above!

O Thou I AM THAT I AM, reveal thyself now in this form. Reveal thyself that all might know that the LORD God [the Mighty I AM Presence] has shone upon his own in this hour and he will not leave his people comfortless. For I send my Messenger before my face, saith the LORD.[1] And therefore, behold the Messenger of God and know that even as the Holy One of God above is of too pure eyes to behold iniquity,[2] so, beloved, your eyes cannot yet look, as they are of the flesh, upon the pure image of sacred fire of the I AM THAT I AM in this octave.[3]

Therefore, we send a Messenger of God to earth to proclaim the coming of that Presence in ye all. Therefore, while ye have that one with you, may you know the inner accord of the harmony of that divinity which is the Real Self above and recognize that it is a sign, even a signet unto the people of God that God does also dwell in your midst in this hour when, beloved, you must fulfill all things, all things of the Great Law, all things of the karmic condition and [when] all does come to bear upon the center of self as the coils of cause and effect infold, recoil and bring back to every point upon the aura, the electromagnetic field, [and] the four lower bodies that which has been sent forth.

Thus, people speak of pressure and they speak of stress. Let it be known, beloved, that this is returning personal karma though you may identify it as condition and circumstance or the result of another's hand.

Let it be known this day, beloved, that the violet flame raised up within you by love and by adoration is able to give you that sheath and armour, purple vein wherewith to consume that which comes from without and that which would erupt from within. Thus, the insulation of the violet flame as the additional skin of self, as an armour of substance as though metallic, impervious, out of the heaven-world, does give to you the soothing comfort of perpetual transmutation.

But, beloved, only that violet flame which is called forth in utter adoration and obedience to the inner Christ, to the Universal One, to the Holy One of God, the I AM THAT I AM, can afford you the living presence of the swaddling garment, as it were, of the God of the Seventh Ray.

Blessed ones, let Love endow every word and syllable. Let the attention flow to the heart of your I AM Presence and to my beloved Saint Germain, to Portia, to the entire Spirit of the Great White Brotherhood.

I *fear* lest you adopt the ways of the rote performance of ritual of mechanization man! I *fear* lest you take for granted the staff that is placed in the hand of the Messenger! It is a spiritual staff of which the one she does hold is outer sign and symbol. Therefore, let the rod of the Law be a comfort to my people! Let angels comfort you. And may you know, beloved, that it is an hour of O so close communion!

How I would desire to speak to you each week were you to find it possible to journey to this place. Blessed ones, we have much to accomplish ere this altar no longer serve us. I bid you decide in counsel with one another whether you will come here on the Sabbath, [which] we celebrate on Sunday, whether you will come to this place in full force that I, Jesus, might impart to you moment by moment of increment of sacred fire whereby those conditions within which resist the Light and those without may be broken.

It is urgent that the soul be prepared for union with God. How shall the soul provide a vessel unless I come to you day unto day unto day? Yet I do not condemn. I do not force. I do not compel. I do not love you less for any thing. But I would that I could love you more by your very physical presence. Is it not my physical presence in this Messenger as you see me in this very moment—is it not this congruency that you also desire even with your Holy Christ Self?

Yea, they are baptized once in a lifetime, dipped in water. The ceremony then is complete. I tell you, I would baptize you daily in the water of Life, in the living Word, in that which flows from the I AM Presence, beloved, that crystal-clear stream. I would be the instrument to you.

Come unto me, all ye who labor, all ye who are weary: I shall give you rest as restoration and re-creation and a re-infiring of the cells and the molecules of life and [of the] life-force within you.

Thus, beloved, while my Messenger is with you I can for you do many things. And if you forget and if you neglect so great an opportunity, beloved, then how can heaven help you? How can I deliver to you that intensity of fire of my heart that I would transmit?

O let the holy ones of God come forth and let those, then, who are possessed of those wandering demons that come after the Light be stayed. Let them not come hither, for they must be cleansed of these foul spirits by their own application unto the Law which they have once violated.

The Law, then, in this hour, beloved, is a dispensation that is not wide but narrow. And it does provide for those who desire to be the pure in heart and are the pure in heart and see, then, that there is a crack in the door where the dazzling fire of the Presence does tell that there is beyond that door, that barrier of karma, truly the entering in.

Thus, my beloved, I would draw you close to my heart. I would remind and confirm for you all words and statements ever made by the Brotherhood, especially in these several years, concerning the prophecy of coming events, including the delivery of our sermons, our Stump messages, yes, even the concept of the Coming Revolution in Higher Consciousness.

Will you not broaden your understanding to know that a revolution is indeed required not alone in every heart but throughout the planetary body—that the kingdoms of this world might truly be in physical manifestation the kingdoms of our Lord and of his Christ?

So Maitreya does live and so he does walk in your midst. Fear not, grumble not, worry not. Do not enter into a doomsday consciousness but recognize there has never been a moment in your personal history, and I speak to everyone here, to all Light-bearers of the world, to all Keepers of the Flame, when *you* could so intensify the inner coil of being!

I cry to you, beloved, that you do not perceive [the jeopardy] in the hour of the descent of your karma and the dark night of the soul![4] And therefore I come with a Light to lighten the very cave of your world that you might see and know that that karma shall pass but not without heroic effort and heroic measures.

Blessed ones, the door is cracked. I, Jesus, may open it to you. Therefore, be long-suffering with your own soul, but do not allow your soul to suffer or to be surfeited whether in pleasure or pain. Mount up as with eagle wings.[5] Mount the fiery coil of being and desire more Light than you have and know that it is that Light that will quench the Darkness.

Let the zeal of my house, then, come upon you in this hour! Let the zeal of the Holy Spirit come upon you![6]

I, Jesus, tell you that that zeal which I give to you is of the fire of the Sun. And though you may not have noticed, beloved, I have journeyed to the very Central Sun this week, there to fetch that fire of the Lord GOD that my own in the earth might have from me and from my own heart even a quickening, even a fervor—even seeing in my Presence and aura this day something you have never seen before, even the fires dripping from the altars of that very center of a spiritual Cosmos.

I, therefore, bring you tidings of Alpha and Omega. I bring you the presence of ring upon ring of seraphim of God to *shake you awake!* O I would to God you would understand how so great a salvation is at hand, how it is offered to you and how the Darkness that does descend does allow you to again and again and again so indulge these worn-out grooves of karmic consciousness!

Therefore, I say again of you, beloved: "Father, Mother, forgive them, for they know not what they do."[7] Yet, beloved, how long may I say this prayer of the enlightened ones who have been told and told again and yet in the hour of the descent of the very density of karma are enveloped by it and do enter even its degradation *and, beloved,* [this] after so long, so long being a part of this holy communion [the dictations of the Ascended Masters by the Holy Spirit] that we share.

Thus, my beloved, let it be known unto you this day that I, Jesus, have implored before Alpha and Omega [that they might] give me that fire whereby in the zeal of the LORD [the Mighty I AM Presence] and by the fire of that Presence with you, you should come to know the means and the wherewithal to endure spiritually and to be endued and empowered from on high[8] as our Messenger has been by my hand in this very week.

Blessed ones, so know the LORD. So know that some must qualify. And, beloved, thank God—thank God that one called is yet here; for I tell you, the hour of the dark night of the soul for you, each one, must be met: and that hour is now! And you may either weep and wail and depart and be divided and allow all of the venting of the anger in the subconscious or you may come and bend the knee and kneel before the altar and fasten yourself to the Flame of sacred fire burning thereon.

Blessed ones, that dark night of the descent of karma must come, for if it come not you cannot endure nor the Light [of the

Universal Christ consciousness] nor the Dark Night of the Spirit, [i.e., the absence of the Light], that shall come upon this planet ere the New Day shall appear.

And for the record, may you understand that the dark night of the soul is the period when the soul does groan in travail with her own karma, and it is meet. And in that hour you have reinforcement of angels and saints, myself and Ascended Masters and Cosmic Beings. It is an hour when you keep tethered to the Law; and if you do, beloved, you may be saved by the very Law that does demand [that] you right all wrong against that Law.

Thus, beloved, this path is known, the path of karma balanced by fervent hearts who have willed, *who have determined* to slay inordinate desire. For by this and this alone shall you suffer calamity.

Thus, beloved, take to heart the teachings of the Buddha, of Maitreya. And let all of thy desiring be this: to pass beyond those karmic conditions which at any moment by the condition of planetary, solar and galactic karma could sweep you from the very center of your First and Best Love.

So having passed this dark night of the soul, as ye all have observed the Messenger pass through in the long years of this service, so you come to the hour when you must have internalized that Christ and you must be able to sustain that momentum of Christhood. [This initiation of the Cosmic Christ is called the Dark Night of the Spirit.] And this is the eclipse of the Sun of the I AM Presence. And it does come about, beloved, precisely under the conditions in which you find yourselves upon this planet: the astral sea rising,[9] the outpouring [from the pit that is opened[10]] and the spewing of the astral consciousness, and you here below in physical embodiment.

And therefore, the astral plane does present that separation between the externalized self-mastery and the I AM Presence. And if there be no self-mastery for want of love of Christ and of me, your own Beloved, then in the Dark Night of the Spirit, beloved, you are cut off and it is the dark night when none may extend that hand, for your opportunity has been given to manifest a Light that never shone on land or sea.[11]

Thus understand, beloved, work while ye have the Light.[12] Work on your karma! Work on your zeal! Be not satisfied with your mediocrity! Work while you have a physical hand extended to you and know that that hand is the best hand we can offer you. And therefore, by that sustaining Love you may receive that imparting and that reigniting of the Word.

And there be some among you—and do not say, "Is it I,

Lord?"—who have scarcely a divine spark to sustain you. And yet you walk as the proud, as though by some prior heredity you are a favorite son, with no sense of co-measurement of the dire need of the soul to magnify the LORD, [the Mighty I AM Presence, in your members] as Mother, as Trinity in the heart—to expand and fan that fire by Love and Service, looking neither to the right nor to the left but giving and giving. For the Lord, the Holy Spirit, does attend you, even your beloved Maha Chohan, to breathe upon you again the breath of life, to fan that divine spark that it burst into a Threefold Flame once again.

Blessed ones, we speak not to cause you pain, but pain you shall have if you are not awakened! It is not the hours of service that I speak of, but the quality of heart and what does occupy the mind, what does occupy the feeling world, what are the true desires that compel you to lesser stars and to cast your anchor into the astral sea instead of into the infinite to catch a star of God's own destiny.

Therefore, I, Jesus, have done what I could do in the ultimate sense of my imploring, for it is to the Lightbearers, every one upon this planet, that I come this day. I come in a Divine Visitation and as I implore you, my Electronic Presence is before each and every one who does bear Light, who is of Alpha's seed, who does have a Threefold Flame, or once had it and allowed it to go out by neglect.

I stand before each and every one whose names have been read by the Keeper of the Scrolls there in the great throne room before me and before Alpha and Omega. And in answer to my imploring, beloved, so our Father, our Mother have sent me to you and to those upon this planet to whom the agenda of Alpha is open[13] and all who have recourse to the Central Sun through the blessed heart of Mary, my Mother, through the heart of Kuan Yin, through the entire Spirit of the Great White Brotherhood. And I trust they also have recourse to that heart through your own blessed heart expanded as a living fire.

Thus, observe the hierarchies of the weeks and understand the meaning of the seventy weeks[14] as seventy hierarchies of the Sun extended from the Central Sun through time and space. Thus, they define the cycles and the cycles of initiation. Thus, they deliver to the Lightbearers the test of the ten[15] in the seven outer rays of manifestation.

Seventy weeks, therefore, unto each Lightbearer is given. And what is the length of time and space? No man knoweth, for the cycles are shortened for those who elect[16] to embrace them and they are lengthened unto the agony not of the true cross of Light but of the *false* cross of the *false* crucifixion of the *false* Christ who is Antichrist.

Therefore, by inordinate desire you may be impaled on a cross with Antichrist—but I shall not be there. And by right desire and right reckoning of the cycles you may pass every test as though in microseconds. There is no limit to God-realization except to those who yet insist upon defining [and confining] self by laws of mortality.

Thus, take the seventy weeks and see that you waste not time or space or energy. I tell you, so great is the opportunity that there is not one among the body of Lightbearers—and I count you in that body, that Mystical Body of God on planet earth—no matter what age, who could not, if he would, fulfill the mandate and the requirement of the ascension in this life.

But, beloved, the extraordinary outreaching of the soul and the heart is something that many among you have not known or understood. And those who take their backward steps away from the Flame of the ark of the covenant blazing upon this altar, those who pursue the steps of Jungian psychology or any other means as a substitute for the living fire of Christ and my Sacred Heart, I say to you, *They shall not prevail!* They shall not prevail. And they are the rebellious ones and clouds without water[17] who have forsaken the divine spark and will not bend the knee to receive another [divine spark], which I should gladly give by a simple demonstration of a measure of the ritual of devotion.

There be some among you who since your entering this path have indeed kindled a divine spark when you had it not. All things are possible. But when you hear of the possibility of failure, you sink back into that sense of failure instead of realizing that the possibility of Victory is present whenever it is possible to fail.

Why, then, enter the negative assessment of oneself? Why not perceive with the inner sight? Why do you see with a flesh-and-blood consciousness and therefore curse yourself to that consciousness ad infinitum?

Let the holy ones of God truly be more holy. For those who do have that flame must make more rather than less effort until the Light so shine in you that your eyes are as stars and your aura so powerful that none can deny that truly a path of Christhood is won; and therefore the lesser endowed take hope to follow in your footsteps.

Cast down the idols of your flesh-and-blood consciousness, for those whom you worship are not the living Christ. Blessed ones, worship not but adore the Light. Adore the Light and do not set on a pedestal any human being. Ye do err, not knowing the scriptures.[18] Ye do err, sustaining the idolatry of self.

I come for the breaking of the pitchers.[19] I come for the breaking of the vessels that no longer serve you. I raise my staff and I say, let them be broken by the rod of fire! I, Jesus, decree it that you might come forth and stand God-free sons and daughters.

Blessed ones, *be pillars of fire in the earth!* Be pillars of fire in the earth, beloved, and *heed* the Call! Heed the Call of Light. Do not decide why you cannot be at Glastonbury in preference to anywhere else but decide how you *can* be there. Decide, beloved, that Community is your protection.

I AM walking through that land this day. For I would exorcise from it the demons that some of you have brought with you in your argumentation and your folly and your blindedness by energies that never ever should have passed through you. Let my rod through my Messenger disperse, then, all injustice, all that is dishonest, all that is unfair. Be willing to admit where you have wronged another. Settle your accounts. Do not defend your person but *be true to me.*

I, Jesus, speak to you and you know of whom and whereof I speak. And therefore, there are some who should be ashamed to stand in my Presence and there are others who have kept the Flame as saints of God.

Thus, I call you to the House of the LORD [your Mighty I AM Presence]. May you know now that Communion of my heart. May you know it, beloved.

This is, then, the last I may offer to you of the series of dictations begun in the hour of the Call to the ascension.[20] Thus, beloved, when the response is full, even full to that which I bring this day, I shall once again implore Alpha and Omega to assist you through the journey ahead and every step of the way.

Keep my Flame in this Community, beloved, for I have given more of myself than you will ever know to the very presence of my Church in this place. And it shall not be bestowed upon me that I may start anew or begin again. With Almighty God [and] all saints of heaven who have gone before you, I say: *in this Community we must not fail.*

Let there be not fragmentation or division, but know that your loyalty is to the Flame that burns upon the altar because the Lord God has sent to you a Messenger who is able, by his grace, to keep that Flame. And as you sustain your devotions the Flame is kept in this octave. It is a Light unto the world, beloved, and that sacred fire is your salvation in this octave.

Now let the forces of Death and Hell rage if they will, for

I shall be midst my own. And let the Love bond of Gautama Buddha[21] allow all to prefer one another[22] and this holy Community before all other passions, disputes, all other claims of Darkness, all other false prophets who say, "Go here and there, for the Messenger is no longer in her temple." I tell you, beloved, all of these most frightening claims and allegations may come, but let the true disciples of my heart who are the witnesses from the beginning unto the end of their own salvation by the grace of this dispensation *keep the Flame of the ark of the covenant blazing upon this altar!*

So I shall bear you witness. So I shall bear you witness: call unto me. And all who have asked for direct chastisement or initiation or soul-testing or rebuke from the Messenger, I, Jesus, will come to you. Listen for my footstep. Know my voice and know that I shall surely make known to you those conditions of consciousness or action, those desires or projects or goals which are truly not an acceptable offering to the Holy One of God, your I AM Presence.

Therefore, beloved, for the finishing of the Work, my Work, I withdraw this Messenger for a season to complete those publications while there is yet time. May you, then, implement, *truly implement* the Law that is given to "work out your own salvation with fear and trembling," as it is written,[23] for it is an hour when the whole world does fear and tremble. And you ought to have that awe before your God in the moment when the forces of Antichrist come to test and to test your soul.

Blessed ones, I AM there. I AM there in that hour and you have the wherewithal to put them to flight with a single fiat. Be alert, then, beloved, for by your Victory a world shall know a New Opportunity and a New Day. Gather in the mountain of your Mighty I AM Presence and be in the right place in the hour when his fulfillment is come.

I choose to remain with you, to be seated in your midst while Communion is served that you might know that I bless it and give it to you as substance from the altar of the Great Central Sun.

O fire of my Fire, heart of my Heart, you whom I have known forever, come into the foreverness of the everlasting arms of Alpha and Omega!

May you bring the little ones to be baptized. May you bring your hearts and tarry a moment, for I, Jesus, would surely impart myself to you.

Beloved, when the Law does require that I should withdraw from you for a little while that you in your aloneness might choose to be all that I AM, then remember, *O remember,* that my Fervor and my Love is waiting, waiting for your decision, that I might come close again.

For you see, beloved, there are some tests that you must pass in the aloneness of the aura and the electromagnetic field which you yourself have created. In that hour, then, I say, trust. Trust and do not forsake. Trust and remember, I AM thy brother.

I AM Jesus, thy Love, thy Perfect Love. And I AM watching from afar your Victory. O snatch it from the very teeth of the defeat of Death and Hell. Snatch your Victory, beloved! *Tear it!* from these fallen ones who would steal [in] in the night and steal it from you.

Blessed, all is in Divine Order for you to fulfill all things. Do it, I say. Do it for the sake of Our Love.

"The Summit Lighthouse Sheds Its Radiance O'er All the World to Manifest as Pearls of Wisdom." This dictation by **Jesus Christ** was **delivered** by the Messenger of the Great White Brotherhood Elizabeth Clare Prophet on **Thanksgiving Day, November 24, 1988,** 3:15–3:59 p.m. MST, at the **Royal Teton Ranch, Park County, Montana.** Available on 90-min. audiocassette B88145, $6.50 (add $.55 for postage); on 52-min. videocassette HP88097, $19.95 (add $1.10 for postage). [**N.B.** Bracketed material denotes words unspoken yet implicit in the dictation, added by the Messenger under the Master's direction for clarity in the written word.] Throughout these notes *PoW* is the abbreviation for *Pearls of Wisdom.* **(1) I will send my messenger.** Mal. 3:1; Matt. 11:10; Mark 1:2; Luke 1:76; 7:27. **(2) "Thou art of purer eyes than to behold evil."** Hab. 1:13. **(3)** Therefore the office of the Messenger is the shield protecting the eyes of the people from the direct gaze of the I AM THAT I AM. Thus, the Messenger goes before the face of the Presence, even as scripture declares that God sends his Messenger, the Holy Christ Self, before the face of the people that they might commune with the Son who is the Divine Mediator between the Absolute and the relative states of existence. **(4) Dark night of the soul and Spirit.** 1988 *PoW,* p. 632 n. 14. **(5) Mount up with wings.** Isa. 40:31. **(6) Zeal of thine house.** Ps. 69:9; John 2:17; Isa. 9:7; 59:17. **(7) Father, forgive them.** Luke 23:34. **(8) Endued with power.** Luke 24:49. **(9) Rising astral sea.** Hercules, 1988 *PoW,* pp. 622–24, 625–26. **(10) Bottomless pit.** Rev. 9:1–12; 11:7; 17:8; 20:1–3. **(11) Glory of God lights New Jerusalem.** Rev. 21:23. **(12) Work while ye have the Light.** John 9:4, 5; 12:35. **(13) Alpha's Agenda.** 1987 *PoW,* pp. 379–94; 1988 *PoW,* pp. 521–34. **(14) Seventy weeks.** Dan. 9:20–27. **(15) Test of the ten.** 1988 *PoW,* p. 633 n. 24. **(16) Days shortened for elect.** Matt. 24:22; Mark 13:20; Pistis Sophia, bk. 1, chap. 27, in G. R. S. Mead, *Pistis Sophia: A Gnostic Gospel* (Blauvelt, N.Y.: Spiritual Science Library, 1984), p. 31. **(17) Clouds without water.** Jude 12. **(18) "Ye do err, not knowing the scriptures."** Matt. 22:29; Mark 12:24. **(19) Breaking of the pitchers.** Judg. 7:16–22 (Matt. 9:16, 17; Mark 2:21, 22; Luke 5:36–38). **(20) Jesus' calls.** Starting on May 28, 1987, Jesus delivered a series of dictations in which he called us to the path of the ascension and to gather ten thousand Keepers of the Flame, to the path of discipleship and Christhood, and to become shepherds. On April 19, 1987, he also called us to "take up the sword of the Spirit" against peddlers of drugs and of deceit and annihilation. (See 1987 *PoW,* pp. 196, 269–76, 491–98, 577–82; 1988 *PoW,* pp. 290, 291, 294, 297.) During Jesus' October 4, 1987 dictation, when he called us "to be my disciples in the most serious effort of all of your incarnations, to recognize that in thy flesh thou shalt see God and be my Self," Jesus also asked us to renew our commitment to give his **"Watch With Me"** Jesus' Vigil of the Hours, promising: "I shall be in your midst, beloved, as you give this prayer service in my name weekly. You may give it alone, all-one with me, with the recording provided. . . . It is my desire, then, that in fifty-two sessions with you, **which I would like to be of ninety-minute duration (or more),** you might experience such renewal and such self-transcendence at the conclusion of a single year's Watch with me that you shall indeed know that I AM come into the earth to take my own in the grand ritual of the Resurrection and the Ascension." Jesus' Watch is part of the Wednesday evening healing service, one of the three weekly services Serapis Bey has admonished all Keepers of the Flame to participate in without fail. Available on 93-min. audiocassette B87096, $6.50 (add $.55 for postage), and in 44-page booklet, $2.00 (add $.60 for postage). Special offer: $5.00 for cassette and booklet in quantities of 5 sets or more (add $1.50 postage per 5 sets); additional booklets $20.00 a dozen (add $1.50 postage per dozen). **(21) Gautama's bonding of Love.** 1988 *PoW,* p. 518. **(22) Prefer one another.** Matt. 12:46–50; Mark 3:31–35; Luke 8:19–21; Rom. 12:10. **(23) Work out your own salvation.** Phil. 2:12.

Pearls of Wisdom®
published by The Summit Lighthouse

| Vol. 31 No. 84 | *Beloved Gautama Buddha* | *December 10, 1988* |

The Initiation of the Heart
The Alpha Thrust and the Omega Return
The Psychology and Karma of Child Rearing

Hail to the Chelas of the Will of God!
Hail to the Devotees of the Buddhic Light!
Hail to the Lovers of the Divine Mother!

So I AM your Gautama and I have returned. Having come in the Alpha Thrust to this city,[1] I bear the good tidings of the Omega Return[2] whereby I might fasten you, beloved, back to the heart of the point of origin. Thus I came and so I come again. And so I come in order to assess what is and what has been the response to my placing of a focus of the Threefold Flame of my heart over this place.

Beloved ones of the Light, know, then, and understand as you assess the path of your own lifestream in the year and then some that has passed since my coming [that] all that you have passed through of joy and of the very fervor and ardor of overcoming the not-self of being has been *the initiation of the heart*. I say this not alone to those who abide here and keep the flame of this city but to all Lightbearers of the world, for the extension of myself into octaves nearer the physical plane has been unto all who are of the Light an initiation of the heart.

Therefore, in this period you have or should have accelerated the sense of attunement of the inclination of the ear to the vibrations, five distinct vibrations of the Dhyāni Buddhas, of the secret rays and of Cosmos. And, of course, beloved, calling forth the violet flame with Mighty Cosmos' secret rays is surely the action whereby there does increase in you a permeation, a percolation through those five secret-ray spheres surrounding the heart chakra, spheres of the consciousness of Cosmos, spheres for the entering in not only to the innermost place of being, the secret chamber of the heart, but also to the Holy of Holies of the Most High God. This, then, is the goal of the path of this life.

Heed well, then, the call to internalize and outpicture the goal of individual Christhood on the seven rays, for upon this foundation of the rainbow rays of God, in this balance of the seven planes of being in your chakras here below, you are able first to balance the Threefold Flame and then to increase the Light of the Divine Mother rising that becomes the magnet of the Buddha descending.

These are not mere words, beloved. The initiation of the heart has meant a cataclysm in some lifestreams upon planet earth. Some have passed from the screen of life. Others have found the burning in the heart to be a pressure of Light and sacred fire consuming from within to the without the burdens of hardness of heart and the records of death that beset the heart chakra.

One is taken and another is left. Some by merit and deeds of good service have earned a new heart physically and spiritually while others have lost both by their neglect. And so the cycles of the years and of the weeks do turn in this planetary home.

Beloved, the heart is the seat of consciousness and the seat of Life. Guard the heart. Guard the heart, beloved. It is your citadel of the Central Sun here below.

Therefore, for the soothing of the heart, for the melting of the records of the unmerciful heart, beloved Kuan Yin has come to the fore and is in your midst. Even in this very hour, beloved, the blessed Kuan Yin, open door to the Amitābha, open door to the Five Dhyāni Buddhas, does move through this building, does place a special Electronic Presence of herself, unique to each individual's need, before you.

So, beloved, you have tarried many hours, and many hours you have given as I would before God and as the Lord Christ Jesus would also. So to you, beloved, we restore balance as the grace of the Law does allow, for the rule of Alpha, even as it is the call of Morya, is "pay as you go."[3] As you have given Light, so we return Light measure for measure according to that need, beloved.

We observe, therefore, that the great need of the hour is the balancing and the strengthening of the Threefold Flame of the heart. Therefore assess and measure as you approach winter solstice and a new year of opportunity and a new year of personal and planetary karma how you have related to circumstance of karma, conditions of daily life as pertains to the heart.

Out of the heart are the issues of Light. Let the pure in heart see God face to face. Purify the heart, beloved. Let it not be fatted. Let it not become obese with the weight of inordinate desiring whether of false appetites or whether of the bloated consciousness of the astral plane that is seething with toxins of those vices that deny the merciful presence of the heart of the Divine Mother within you toward all.

Behold, then, the fierceness of the eye of the Buddha that is borne as the Ruby Ray chastening unto the seed of the Wicked [One]. Behold the tenderness of the heart as you experience the balance of the merciful heart of Love and the laser beam of the Ruby Ray of the mind and the eye of God that can clear from you, once you have withdrawn all substance thereof, those momentums of desiring, and [the] desiring [of] those things to be drawn to oneself that simply have nothing whatsoever to do with the kingdom of God or of getting there swiftly.

Therefore, beloved, the heart that is expanding in the Divine Flame, the heart that is increasing in the spheres of the secret rays, this heart must not suffer the outrages of anger from without or within. Imagine creating the delicate and yet superstrong framework of a heart that endures all cycles and journeyings even unto the ascension in the Light itself. The heart that does endure the dark night of the soul and the Dark Night of the Spirit, this heart, beloved, in its formation as a crystal fiery heart of Light must be undisturbed.

Guard the heart. Do not allow it to be bombarded by [dissonant] sounds whether through the media or one's ill-chosen companions in life who do not contain the reverence of the heart of God with them.

Thus the profane, beloved, will defile the heart as they would steal the rhythm of the heartbeat of God and his sons and daughters and then play it with electronic sound and syncopated beat to disturb the very formative process even of the physical heart of the unborn within the womb. And as the soul begins to attune to the heartbeat of the Father-Mother, so that soul must already in the tenderness of the envelope of the fetus in the womb begin a process of self-defense against the misuse [of] and the tampering with the rhythm of the heartbeat of God that is to become the very pulsation of life within the newborn babe.

Such is the sacrilege of the forces of Death and Hell. Such is the misuse of the great inventions sent forth for Aquarius, for the amplification of the Word and the Work of the Lord by Saint Germain. Blessed hearts, the most magnificent dispensations out of the Cave of Symbols[4] afforded by Saint Germain for the very defense of life, the defense of America, the defense of freedom in every nation have been either aborted or misused, sold to the enemy to be misused again and again to destroy life instead of to defend that life.

Let us understand, then, that those who will endure are those who do not allow the encroachment upon the heart and who stop short of [expressing] the word, the vibration and the feeling that is a sharp and searing, tearing attack upon the heart of self and others. Love the flame of the heart above all self and self-defense, beloved, and then you shall see how a spark does become a Threefold Flame, how the very breath of the Holy Spirit as intense love does fan that fire and that Threefold Flame until so great a flame does reveal the manifestation of the Light-emanation of God in form.

You have nothing to fear, beloved, but fear itself, for fear is indeed the destruction of the heart and the delicate filigree membranes that are being formed and then rewoven and then mended by angels when they are torn again and again.

Blessed ones, there is an emotional rut! You must beware of it! It is the pitfall whereby the soul may fall into the desire body, into the same old trap again and again. Understanding the sine wave of your emotions and your feelings on a cyclic basis day by day according to the cycles of the moon, according to the movements of such as the planet Mars and others, where you have not that Christ-dominion in you, you are subject, as are all of the members of the race of *Homo sapiens,* beloved, to astrology, you are subject to the tides of the sea, to the lunar influences and to the planetary bodies that represent the lower order of evolution.

Take thy dominion over it, for the Divine Mother has shown you the way[5] and all these things she has placed under her feet.[6] Therefore, get the victory as God-mastery in illumination in the signs of Pisces and Virgo, of Gemini and Sagittarius and become not dullards and dense ones [through the] ignoring, by the surfeiting of yourselves in ignorant animal magnetism,[7] of the Great Law of Life. Thus, you are not, I say, victims of an astrology. You are mighty conquerors who will look upon that astrology as the initiation of the hour for which you are well-equipped, beloved.

Therefore, I say to those who would read the signs of the times in the charts of astrology of the Keepers of the Flame, you may not predict nor condemn my own according to your interpretations, whether of past karma or past failures. For no one must judge another and say that that which does befall one is the result of his karma. *You* do not know! Therefore do not be so presumptuous, for the signs of astrology are the signs of initiation. Take heed, then, lest you condemn a Christed one when that Christed one is bearing a cross for you and you and you!

I say to you, beloved, all must be tested. Do not walk about with the sadness of "sackcloth and mourning"[8] but rather rejoice to see that every difficult karma coming your way, which may or may not be heralded in the signs of your stars, must be seen as a path of initiation under Maitreya. Pass your tests, and if karma is a part of them, it shall be dissolved by the sacred fire, and if it be not, then woe to those who condemn another for having a so-called heavy karma! We have a right to test! You have a right to be tested.

And therefore I did initiate the testing of the heart. I did initiate the initiations of the heart in this place, for America must pass her tests. And, beloved, many in this nation not connected with a path of Light have simply flown from that initiation, have departed from it, have invented a false heart and with their false starts no longer have any substance whatsoever in their approach to life. They are unwilling to engage in the initiations of the heart with a Divine Reality, with a forging of a Christhood.

Do you see, beloved, how that state of consciousness has been represented ad nauseam in the speeches of the candidates who have pitted quip against quip and twerp against twerp in their vying for what was once the highest office in the land? Blessed ones, [there is] no substance, no engaging; for without a heart of fire one can only seek the support, the popularity of the mass consciousness. Yet an entire nation and a world was alerted to the emptiness, the frightening hollowness, the tomblike quality of those who come purporting to represent the living yet only representing the dead—and the "undead," who, though they have not passed from the screen of life, find themselves as whited sepulchres, full of dead men's bones.⁹

Now may you see how life is meaningless, how in the drama or the comedy that is played upon the screens of the media there is no real profound meaning or plot. There are no real characters engaged with Life in the highest sense, combating forces of Darkness while standing, if they must stand alone, for Light and Truth and Honor.

These fallen ones who have abandoned the heart of a Christ and a Buddha have naught to do with the Great White Brotherhood nor are they equipped to lead a nation under God and a holy people through the narrow straits, the very narrow straits that must lead to eternal Life. They have espoused the broad way of social programs in place of the spiritual defense. They have abandoned the Child, the Contra, people of every race and nation. They have abandoned the path of the creative heart and they soothe themselves and soothe others with words and more words that do not carry the comfort flame to a people. There is no trust in such leaders. There is no desire to vote for such leaders.

Blessed ones, I, for one, stand with El Morya holding [up] the profile [of the Christed one] to you and your own for those who must be raised up¹⁰ that there might still be a standard and a cosmic honor flame as one holds the Light of Saint Thérèse and another of Saint Thomas More and another of Becket or of Merlin or of Samuel, another of Krishna and another and another and another that the Lords of Karma might say the saints live today on planet earth, and in embodiment are those who are equal to and may bear the triangle, the equilateral triangle, here below of the saints of the etheric octave, the heaven-world and the absolute octaves of Light.

Blessed hearts, you are the counterparts of an invisible world. You are the counterparts-to-be of golden-age cities of Light and inner temples. So long as you walk the earth, your auras reflecting that higher playground of life where true initiation is realized, so long as there is a peep into the infinite through the electromagnetic field of yourselves—so long is there hope in the hearts of those who yet walk this planet. When there cease to be chelas in embodiment fulfilling that just requirement of the Law, I tell you, an entire planet can descend into lows of depression you know not of.

It is the Lightbearers of the world who keep that torch in the name of the Goddess of Liberty. Now more than ever let it not be compromised but let the sign of the torchbearers be also the sign of the initiates of the heart chakra who desire and dare to be one with my heart and who are willing to shed the fat that does prevent that union.

One cannot be a citizen of a spiritual cosmos and enjoy [i.e., indulge in,] the supposed benefits, all of them, of a physical earth in the throes of internalizing and regurgitating astral consciousness and effluvia. There is no question, beloved, it is a sick society in a comatose state that does remain riveted before the television, entering the world of unreality, the world of trompe l'oeil, the world that is the artificiality of the false hierarchy of Cyclopea and the All-Seeing Eye of God.

Thus, beloved, you watch your fellows slip into illusion. Though not drunk with alcohol, though not perverted whether by crime or misuse of the sacred fire or by drugs, they have a dazed and a glazed look that does tell and tell all that they are more in the astral plane and only as tree trunks [do they] remain in the physical.

Go not after them and above all do not respond to the demons and entities of glamour that extend their tentacles, their bonied arms and fingers, out from the holes in those hollowed-out tree trunks. They would lure you by any means to part with your Light. I say, depart this place! Depart this plane of consciousness for higher spheres. For as the Lord Christ has told you, never has opportunity been of [i.e., consisted of,] such a great encounter with your God.[11]

Now, beloved, in the guarding of the heart and the initiation thereof recognize that the heart is the twelve-petaled chakra, that these twelve petals must have something of your love and attainment, each and every one. Thus, by the work of the seven rays build upon them as though you were earning the badges of the honor flame of the Boy and Girl Scouts of America and the world. Contribute something of yourself to the strengthening of each and every one of the twelve petals, thereby passing through to the antechamber, the Eighth Ray chakra, the secret chamber of the heart.

Behold, the Lord cometh. Behold, I AM Gautama. I stoop this day. I bend to you. I incline my ear and my heart. In this mode, beloved, I come in one of my lower bodies and manifestations that you might know me in this hour as Brother and that you might also remember that your Brother, so near to you, also does occupy the office of Lord of the World.

I desire you to know me as Brother, not in the familiarity or the intimacy that breeds contempt or the taking for granted of my Presence but in the sense that one who has been accorded this office by Sanat Kumara and the Cosmic Council, being entrusted with the fate of all lifestreams of a planet, does also know you intimately as a chela of the heart of God's will, as a disciple and as one who yet must pass through even the burdens of the flesh, even the burdens of mortality.

Therefore, beloved, in this closeness to you in this hour may you know, even as you know through the love of a mother's heart, that there is understanding and compassion for the plight of the chela, for the distress of the burdens of the body and all temptations in this octave. May you know that though there be compassion, therefore, there [may] also be the correcting rod of the Ruby Ray and its laser beam.

We may understand, beloved. We may feel with you and understand your feelings, but by that very empathy we do not excuse. We rebuke and we remind you that, yes, this is the condition of the flesh and, *no!* you may not indulge it. No longer may you indulge these conditions, beloved! Time is up for those who do! And know that the Law comes down and it becomes the dividing of the way on the one side and the other—whether Failure or Victory!

It is always best in such troubled times of a planet and an age to assume that one's day, when the dawn comes, is one's last and to prepare to meet thy God and the Lords of Karma at the conclusion of that day, thus to put one's best foot forward, to do one's best and not plan on a future that does not exist. For where is the future when the present day is misused? There is no future, for this day must be lived again. And thus there are many on the planet who are perpetually in the present and have no sense of tomorrow's Victory being won by the ingredients of the moment.

Lie not. *Deceive* not! Belittle not, mock not the Christ in oneself or another, beloved, by the very depredation of the Light.

Take your stand, then, for the Victory of the moment and you will have the Victory of eternity. If you compromise the moment and procrastinate acts of Victory, I assure you there will be no tomorrow that can contain you and no tomorrow which you yourself can contain.

Take control, then, of the body and you will find that the body will be a faithful servant. Take control of the mind and the mind will serve you as a vessel for infinite thoughts. Let the desire body be the vessel of thy God and see what is the power of thy God-desiring.

I AM Gautama. I came with hope when I did place this Threefold Flame over this city. I come with hope again. Some must regroup forces to balance karma of lost opportunity since initiation began, while others may build and receive from me in this hour increment of fire to move on.

God-Harmony is the key. When thou dost love God-Harmony above all else, when thou dost know harmony in the discipline of the Law and even in the rebuke [of the soul by] the Inner Self and the Divine Teacher, when harmony is the means to a sacred-fire release that does realign forces, then harmony is the victor.

Understand, beloved, when a planet is so far out of alignment with the inner blueprint, then the definition of harmony may be cataclysm and the disruption [caused by] cataclysm. For, beloved, the next best thing to harmony is the restoration of harmony. And if a world must come tumbling down for harmony to be regained, then, you see, the means can be considered to be harmony though it be a harmony of a most forceful and abrupt kind. This must be understood as a chemicalization whereby the right chemistry is the desired result. All else being inharmony, there must be the means [—God-Harmony's means—] for the dissolution and the reassembling of the atoms of being.

Thus, beloved, the violators of the living Flame of God-Harmony, which is the Flame of the Mother on the six o'clock line (which is the sacred fire of the base-of-the-spine chakra), these violators as they continue to violate the Light of the Divine Mother create such karma that the Law of Harmony itself does break the mold, the vessel, and does therefore discontinue the very treasure and gift of Life lest the increased manifestation of inharmony should create for that one such a karma as to defy its balancing in the future.

Thus, beloved, in the matter of the psychology of child

rearing, in the matter of the opinions of so-called parents today that "harmony" is an absence of discipline or chastisement, these know not what they do! For they shall return again and again until [the Law does require that] those children—whom they have spoiled by a failure to raise up the rod of the Divine Mother in themselves and [by a failure] to wield that rod of sacred fire [on their behalf—be brought to them so that those parents who caused them to get] out of alignment [in the first place might have the karmic opportunity of drawing them] back into alignment again in future lifetimes. Thus you see, beloved, those who have not the self-discipline to obey the laws of the Divine Mother within their own temple can scarcely call themselves parents; and the disservice they do is not alone to a single lifestream but to an entire civilization.

O what a tangled web is woven by those who deceive themselves by their prating about love and kindness and harmony, and yet beneath the surface of that is the very hatred of the Child, the very hatred of the Father-Mother God as these defiant ones purvey their socialistic psychology that is the very undermining of their offspring.

Do you think we send Lightbearers to those who will not discipline the self first? I tell you nay. And it does not matter where such individuals are found, even in spiritual movements. The highest Lightbearers preparing to descend, beloved, await those who prepare themselves physically, spiritually, mentally, emotionally, psychologically. Those who have the purest desire for God-Good, therefore, receive the souls of highest attainment who also have the desire, the purest desire, for God-Good.

I say, therefore, there must be a judgment in this hour upon those parents who are literally spoiling the opportunity of their offspring for the Victory in this life. [Wherefore,] I, Gautama, will be in their hearts. I will be in the hearts of those children of the Light and I shall school them in the ways of inner self-discipline whereby one day they shall disapprove and disavow those parents who have done them wrong, but they shall overcome.

Be watchful, beloved. Therefore, let the Father-Mother God within you be the parents of your own soul, disciplining your soul and raising up the Mother Light, for without that strength and fire how can a Threefold Flame expand?

Is not the nourishment of Life from beneath [through] the Divine Mother and from above [through] the Divine Father? Is any child complete without the twain? The child shall miss the mother or the father. Therefore give equal and unfailing devotion and quickly challenge that psychology and that astrology that does not allow you to trust the Father-Mother God and therefore finally enter in to a true upbringing of your soul in trust of the Lawgiver, in trust of illumination, in trust of love.

I therefore trust that initiates of the heart will become my own initiates, will redeem the gifts of Morya and his Diamond Heart, will restore the fullness of opportunity to Saint Germain and will in the process never neglect the Call of the heart to be prepared and to survive. We desire to see you in embodiment in twelve years and twenty-four, having weathered the testings and the trials of a planet in the throes of alchemical change, waiting to give birth, travailing to give birth to the Universal Christ in the hearts of the Lightbearers.

I AM Gautama. Let the purpose to which this Teaching Center was founded in this city be fulfilled and let all who hear that call so contribute, for by the heart chakra of a nation and of a people shall Divine Intervention come in the hour of greatest need. And if the heart be not raised up, how shall the heavenly host descend for the rescue of the soul in the seat-of-the-soul chakra?

I AM Gautama Buddha. I claim you as my brothers and sisters. I ascend to the heart of the Western Shamballa. May you know me as I AM: the Keeper of the Hearts of the Faithful.

I seal you with the sign of the heart, the sign of the head, the sign of the hand, signifying that by the love of your heart the mind shall be illumined and by the illumination of the mind multiplied by the love of the heart the right hand in action shall be the Work of God in the Omega cycle that did descend to you in the beginning as the living Word [in the Alpha cycle].

Lo, I AM THAT I AM the Oneness, the Oneness, the Oneness of the Community, of the Teaching outpictured, delivered as example. I AM the Presence of the Buddha and the mantle of the Buddha upon the witness of the eternal Guru in the midst thereof.

This dictation was **delivered** on **Sunday, November 27, 1988,** 4:31–5:14 p.m. CST, at the Church Universal and Triumphant Community Teaching Center, **Chicago, Illinois.** Available on 90-min. audiocassette K88042, $6.50 (add $.55 for postage). Throughout these notes *PoW* is the abbreviation for *Pearls of Wisdom.* **(1)** In his Alpha Thrust Lord Gautama placed a focus of his heart, the **Threefold Flame of the Lord of the World,** over Chicago. Gautama Buddha, 1987 *PoW,* pp. 569–72. **(2)** "I AM Alpha and Omega, the beginning and the ending" (Rev. 1:8). The **Alpha Thrust** is the thrust of Spirit, the going out from God or descent of the soul by the Light of the Father, and the **Omega Return** is the coming in to God or the ascent of the soul by the Light of the Mother. Charted on the Cosmic Clock in Mother's teachings on sowing and reaping karma and the journey of the soul from the Great Central Sun through the planetary spheres and home again, the Alpha Thrust is from the 12 to 6 o'clock lines, the Omega Return is from the 6 to 12 o'clock lines (see note 5 below). **(3) Pay as you go.** Gal. 6:5. 1988 *PoW,* pp. 584, 608, 623. **(4) The Cave of Symbols** is Saint Germain's etheric/ physical retreat located at Table Mountain in the Rocky Mountains in Wyoming. See glossary in *Saint Germain On Alchemy,* p. 370; *The Lost Teachings of Jesus II,* p. 402, or pocketbook edition, Book 4, p. 133. **(5) Taking dominion over personal astrology.** 1988 *PoW,* p. 479 n. 5. **(6)** Rev. 12:1. **(7) Ignorant animal magnetism.** 1988 *PoW,* p. 339 n. 8. **(8) sackcloth:** a rough, dark-colored cloth usually made of goat's or camel's hair; customarily worn as a sign of mourning or penitence, often worn by prophets and captives. See Gen. 37:34; II Sam. 3:31; Esther 4:1–3; Isa. 15:3; 37:1, 2; Jer. 4:7, 8; 6:26; Lam. 2:10; Ezek. 7:18; Dan. 9:3; Matt. 11:21. **(9)** Matt. 23:27; Teachings of Silvanus 106:9–14. **(10) Profile of leadership.** El Morya, 1988 *PoW,* pp. 2–3, 6–8. **(11)** Jesus, 1988 *PoW,* pp. 652–53.

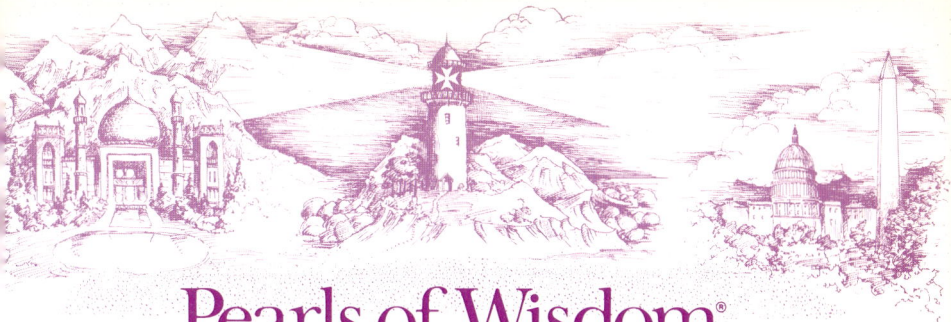

Pearls of Wisdom®
published by The Summit Lighthouse

| Vol. 31 No. 85 | *Beloved Lord Maitreya* | *December 11, 1988* |

The Sword of Maitreya
The Joy of the Flaming Ones
Building the Crystal Fortress of the Heart

Comes Maitreya, comes Lao Tzu.
Comes Gautama, comes Lanto.
In the flesh I AM here in that of my Messenger and [I AM] in the etheric body of the students of my Flame. You have heard many words passing through the needle and the eye of the needle. But it is a Flame that you have come to study—[it is] meditation upon the Flame, and beyond the Flame the smile and then the face that does contain the smile.

Thus, beloved, I AM Maitreya in all octaves—in my hand a Cosmic Egg and inside the evolution of Lightbearers born to earth. Thus in this egg there is gestation. There is the becoming of Buddha. There is the Buddha becoming, displacing the force of the anti-Buddha.

Is this not the way of the Mystery School? Is it not the way of Life? How joyous is the challenge of the five secret rays of Dhyāni Buddhas. How joyous is the one Padma Sambhava.

Let the prophecies be heard and known of that which was foreseen to come to pass in Tibet.[1] So also let the prophecies be known of that which shall surely come to pass in the West. It is necessary. For then, beloved, you shall see in the New Day how forms etheric become available to the sight, for the earth is cleansed and solar rings and sunspots play their role in inaugurating change.[2]

We force out the disreputable ones! All over the world we force them out. I have come with a sword this night. This is my night to wield and twirl the sword of Maitreya, of the Lord Buddha. I move with Ruby Ray angels and Buddha of the Ruby Ray.

Thus, when you speak [the word of the LORD's judgment] and

when you speak [it] before this altar there is a dividing of the way of the Real and the Unreal. And judgment may descend by your seeing [through the All-Seeing Eye of God]—by your separating, by your drawing of the line: *Thus far and no farther!*

Thus you have stripped the Lie of its virility. Continue. Let it be exposed. Let it be shredded. Let it be scorched. Let the Ruby Ray fire purge from our way and our path all that which would prevent the ascent up this very mountain of souls yet dwelling in the valley. Let them be lifted up, O Gautama, O Buddha in the heart, the secret chamber of the heart of the chela.

Let those Lightbearers whose destiny it is to fulfill a role here receive in this hour assistance by the momentum [which they may] glean from Summit University students and all Keepers of the Flame in this world [from the decree momentum they have delivered] during this fall quarter of the year. Let that Light go as ruby arrows. Let it go as armour and legions. Let it be used for the saving of the Lightbearer. This is our mission.

Therefore, by the rosary of Kuan Yin, rosary of the amethyst and gold, the repetition of the mantra is a softening for the opening of the heart. Some hearts have been sealed by hardness and ignorance. Thus their assessment of self and environment is not what is but what is not.

We would hasten and give a spin to electrons and chakras. We would even place our Electronic Presence with those who waver and falter in the Community worldwide. But, beloved ones, we know that those who receive the warmth of the sun oftentimes cannot sustain it when the sun does move on. Perhaps we shall do it that they might have a memory. But even the memory body is so cluttered to capacity that they cannot even record the impression of our coming and retain it.

Our mission, then, [is] to connect the line of our heart to the hearts of those who have built a fortress as the abode of Maitreya, waiting for my Homecoming. Blessed ones, I will enter the hearts of those who have prepared me room and I will say to all that this promise extends for long, long time into the future.

I give you almost unlimited time to do this. And I say the completion of the necessary crystal structure of Light is not something that is built in a day or three months. It is the result of long dedication, the purity of Light and the pure qualification of the crystal-clear stream of the River of Life that has allowed this crystal fortress to be built.

Thus, upon its completion I, Maitreya, enter the heart and enter to stay. For, beloved, I would be there as a presence to assist you by example, by vibration in externalizing your own Holy Christ Self somewhat after the pattern of my own Buddhahood.

I may speak these things to those who have heard all of my words, to those who have contemplated and allowed the golden fires of illumination to pass through.[3] For you will understand, you will know—you will be the crystallization of the God Flame.

Are you willing, students, to pay the price for true Christhood? ["Yes."] Then I say to you I shall exact that price daily and in response I expect you to pay it daily, and so long as this keeps up I shall remain your Mentor. And when you say "no more," then I pray you shall understand [that] I shall move on in the cycles of the sun. And my instruction to you in that hour shall be, whether you hear it or not, "Hold fast what thou hast received.[4] Retain at least this line you have gained. Therefore do not forsake the call to Archangel Michael to protect the God-estate."

There ought to be never a backward step. For it is a loss of time and energy, momentum. And one day by the regrouping of forces roads must be retraveled and once again you may come to the place where you once stood on ascension's hill.

Far, far away in a land you do not know there are devotees who have attained to certain levels of illumination. This land is in the etheric octave, beloved. Perhaps you may think of it as the Tushita heaven.

But, blessed ones, there does come a moment in levels of Victory when you may attend Maitreya's Mystery School beyond the physical. For you shall have balanced the karma of the physical and have no longer need to descend, for you shall have raised the sacred fire to levels of chakras above the heart and, in compassion rendered to all, [you shall] depart, depart this mortal scene of corpses and disease, of corpulence and those emaciated and all manner of humanity distorted so far from the true [Divine] Image as not to provide [in their current outpicturing even] a trace of the inner blueprint from which they were made.

Blessed ones, those things that you desire are waiting in this Mystery School. It is not so far away but it shall remain distant as long as you neglect the true mastery of the sacred fire in your being as well as the balance of karma.

O how you must understand how needful is the violet flame to your liberation from this world! How wondrous are these recordings going forth. How they enable you to tie in to the electromagnetic field of the earth and to anchor therein the Seventh Ray.

The service is so great, beloved, that it is almost easy to earn the balancing of karma by devotion to the violet flame and to do so, I pray you, on behalf of all students of the Buddha upon earth. For it is so needful that these Lightbearers in their comfortable niches of an ancient teaching be able to accept this key dispensation of my coming. Saint Germain has been my forerunner as have the Lords of the Seven Rays, and these Chohans who have gone before have cleared the way by violet flame and all other rays.

Timetables, then, have accelerated and my presence can be to you a wondrous activity so long as your aura is joyously filled with violet flame. Thereby many angels shall enter in. And if you allow the deep penetration of the violet flame, you will see how the dweller[-on-the-threshold⁵] can no longer hold [on to you]. There is no ability to grip the aura that is a blazing, dazzling violet flame. In this condition, beloved, it is also easy for Archangels to bind those portions of the not-self that you have seen through for the very act of invoking the violet flame that transmutes the propensity to *dwell upon* the dweller, the propensity to *dwell with* the dweller, the propensity to *sink with* the dweller.

The violet flame is a buoyant energy that by its very rising does begin to allow the spinning of the base chakra and the raising up of the Light. Blessed ones, this must be understood. For along the way the records are contacted by the sacred fire, opening, therefore, conditions of consciousness that are sealed.

As you hasten the day of your acceleration in the violet flame and the transmutation of these conditions that appear at every rung of the spinal ladder [on the way] up and mounting the chakras [from the base-of-the-spine to the crown], you will see that there will no longer be impediment to the raising of that Kundalini fire. You will see as you retain your diligence and perseverance with Astrea and the calls to Archangel Michael that day by day if you do not slip or falter or turn back or be sidetracked, *there is gain.* And this net gain, beloved, is the means whereby you pay the price for every initiation you require.

Let those who climb the mountain not dally, not tarry at a certain level long enough to be discovered by the cross hairs of the sinister force. Therefore I say, move on. Go up and be quick about it.

When you set your goal you do not make new decisions daily. You set the goal, take the path that leads to it, and then use all your energies to attain the goal instead of reconsidering, reevaluating and changing course with each new wandering fire that comes your way and then you say again, "Perchance is this my Presence beckoning me here and there?" Get out of Hell, I say. Get out of Death and all its consciousness! Get Home free!

Angels bearing the golden velvet robe that is the sign of the completion of Summit University level one now approach to place this robe upon you. Let all of my good students rise to receive that robe. [Summit University students rise.] You will note upon the right collar a five-pointed star of purple of Saint Germain. This star, then, is the focus of the violet flame you have invoked and does reflect the intensity of fire. Visualize its spin and know that the five-pointed star of the body of self does spin with violet flame. And Saint Germain's promise is true: by determination, by violet flame you can win and you can win the star in the crown in this life.

Henceforth wherever you go angels and all will note that you have attended here. You have endured. You have concluded your course with joy. And let all upon this planet know that I, Maitreya, am the sponsor of those who deal justly with their God and with all life, those who place Justice and Honor and Mercy as the standard of all interchange with life.

Let those who have known me deliver this my mandate to all and become it. Let the age of Maitreya be marked by the bearers of Freedom's Flame. Let earth be penetrated with violet fire.

As I speak, the mandate does impel the penetration of earth by violet flame angels. And we are beginning to see a fraction of a percentage of a lightening of the weight of the Lightbearers themselves. The momentum is beginning to build. May you look back in twenty years and know that your presence on earth and your momentum of the violet flame did make for all earth's evolutions an easier passage.

I come with my sword, then, and I come to you each one. And this sword does descend and there is a separation of the Real from the Unreal as I hold that sword with each one. And all my chelas may stand now to receive this. [Congregation rises.]

For this moment your God Reality stands before you intact and the not-self separated out. Now look and see, for in everyday life the soul has merged with both, and some, but not all.* Now understand the work of the ages for the soul to separate herself out from Unreality, to fully embrace Reality and to be prepared to forsake some cherished beliefs and concepts and other entrapments of the lesser personality as well as trappings. So, beloved, if Truth were so obvious and so desirable, this would be another planet.

The sword of Maitreya does hold you and separate you out from that Darkness. I, Maitreya, have one mission to fulfill for my chelas: to force out the Darkness that you might confront it. Be not afraid. My angels are ready. And if you are not, they will assist you. And you may pray, "Lord, I am ready. Help thou my unreadiness."

*In some of the chelas, but not all, the soul has merged with both her God Reality and the not-self. Compare John 13:10: "He that is washed needeth not save to wash his feet but is clean every whit: and ye are clean, but not all."

I, Maitreya, adjure you in this hour, there is and can be no further postponement of this course. I say *you must,* if you would survive as an integrity in God, say die to all that you can see and know that is not real within you and all that I will show you. And the time is short. When I say "you must," beloved, it is, of course, with the proviso that you must or you will be required to pay a price you cannot pay, for you will not be prepared.

If and when the hour comes of the paying of the ultimate price upon this planet, I, Maitreya, am here to see to it that you shall have so strengthened the mind and heart and will and light in all your cells that you shall be ready to pay even that price and survive in the integration with Universal Christhood.

The force of opposition to this my mandate will be as usual. Do not fall for it. *Charge! charge! charge!* I say. Move swiftly through maya and illusion and self-attachment—and *such* pride. Let it all go, beloved. For I promise you, you are ready. Your Christ Self is ready. And as though there were a great silence all heaven is poised and ready for your declaration of *Victory! Victory! Victory!* in the cups of time and space day by day. I promise you it will not be arduous forever.

And now is eternal joy. In sweet surrender to the heart of my Messenger in the heart of Padma Sambhava I reinforce the mantle,[6] for the embodied Guru must also smite the waters[7] of Hell.

Rejoice, for all things in Time come to a conclusion and Eternity opens, the mountain opens, the rock cleaves and there, behold, I step forth to take your hand.

Come with me to the Royal Teton Retreat this night. Let us begin and set the foundation of a tie and an allegiance to the inner Mystery School so that no outer condition can break the Loyalty, the Faith and the Vow of those who are Maitreya's.

My blessed, I AM thine own forever.

I will touch my own now quickly while there is time. Pass by me, beloved, and receive what I speak in your heart in this moment.[8]

This dictation by **Lord Maitreya** was **delivered** by the Messenger of the Great White Brotherhood Elizabeth Clare Prophet on **Sunday, December 11, 1988,** 9:13–9:43 p.m. MST, at the **Royal Teton Ranch, Park County, Montana.** It was the concluding address to the students of Summit University Fall Quarter 1988, sponsored by Lord Maitreya and the World Teachers. Throughout these notes *PoW* is the abbreviation for *Pearls of Wisdom.* **(1) Disasters prophesied to befall Tibet.** See 1988 *PoW,* p. 62 n. 5. **(2) Sunspot indicators of the potential for war.** 1988 *PoW,* p. 520 n. 18. **(3)** Summit University Fall Quarter 1988 studied 63 dictations delivered through the Messengers Mark and Elizabeth Prophet by Lord Maitreya September 18, 1960–June 30, 1988. **(4) "Hold Fast What Thou Hast Received"** is a motto of the Keepers of the Flame Fraternity. See Rev. 3:11. **(5) Dweller-on-the-threshold.** 1988 *PoW,* p. 170 n. 6. **(6)** Padma Sambhava bestowed the **mantle of Guru** upon the Messenger Elizabeth Clare Prophet in his dictation given July 2, 1977, "The Great Synthesis—the Mother as Guru," 90-min. audiocassette B7745, $6.50 (add $.55 for postage). **(7) Elisha smote waters with mantle of Elijah.** II Kings 2:5–15. **(8)** Following the dictation, Lord Maitreya blessed all as the Messenger touched the amethyst egg to the third eye of each devotee who passed by the altar.

Pearls of Wisdom®
published by The Summit Lighthouse

Vol. 31 No. 86 | Beloved Lanello | December 24, 1988

The Spirit of the Great White Brotherhood
A Candle in the Night
Christmas Eve Candlelight Service

Out of the star of the East I speak to you, beloved, for I have communed these weeks with unascended masters of the Far East, some of whom have come from the West to be in retreat in the Himalayas. And they speak of cycles and of *manvantaras*.[1] They speak of their coming and their going, entering into the world of form and maintaining the highest degrees of God-Mastery prior to the ascension as they abide in etheric octaves.

Thus the golden vision of the future is theirs, a not-too-distant future which many of you shall see in this life when the earth has been cleansed and once again the Divine Mother may sponsor these souls of Light who truly desire to incarnate, blessed ones—sweet souls, ancient souls, masterful souls. These envision the hour when after the cleansing of the divine rain and the divine fire there might come again the Community life, the holy family and the very attendant reduction in the lifewaves of Evil (these having passed their time and spent their space, being no longer allowed to incarnate upon earth) [and] thus an environment that you have not known for too, too long in earth's experience.

Behold Himalaya. Behold Meru. See how that balance is held for the earth.[2] Thus the Divine Mother must expel the dark ones and the dark seed to prepare the place for the coming of these ones, beloved, who have long ago chosen to attend that Divine Mother. And they have truly determined to forgo the ascension that they might thread the eye of the needle of a spiritualization of consciousness to come whereby the teaching you have received may be embodied by them and therefore conveyed to those who will be sent for new beginnings.

Thus, beloved, these are the true unascended masters of the Great White Brotherhood. They have naught to do with the false hierarchy and false gurus of India. And there be some who have emerged from the ancient lineage of those who were present when the Vedas were released from the heart of Sanat Kumara and his emissaries, beloved.

I bid you enter as a ceiling is lifted from you by the cumulative effect of your invocation of the violet flame in this entire year. Enter, then, into the sense of being truly a part of this Spirit of the Great White Brotherhood. The gift of my birthday, then, is to part this curtain that you might know that you have elder brothers and sisters who have taken the teaching which you have been given, applicable to all of the four lower bodies, and they have brought this teaching as a continuous thread from the heart of the Ancient of Days to a culmination and a fruitful effort whereby that mastery of God in them may shine forth when again they reembody.

Blessed ones, it should give you joy to know [this] and thus it is my desire to bring you this joy—the joy of the knowledge that there is a vast chain of Hierarchy upon earth. And there be some who are self-conscious in the way of this God-Mastery. And there be others of Light who have embodied with fiery hearts who lead by love, compassion and the Holy Spirit and who are drawn even as I was drawn early in my last incarnation to those who are a part of the Brotherhood, having no background in the ancient traditions such as is common in everyday life in India.

Thus, beloved, there are some who are a part of the Brotherhood who have not full conscious outer awareness and yet by their fiery hearts they are every [bit as] much a manifestation, an extension of that Brotherhood in their areas of service. Pray for them, beloved, for without the conscious outer contact they may only go so far in their own path of God-Mastery. For it does require at a certain point on the Path the physical contact with a representative of the Great White Brotherhood in order for the individual to make that certain progress which you yourselves have embarked upon.

Having a candle in the night is necessary when the full impact and vent of the unconscious and the not-self must be challenged. There must be wayshowers, beloved, and there must be someone physical and present who may hold the balance moment by moment in those hours of interior terror and aloneness. Upon some have come depression of the mind. Yet these too have been our chosen.

And therefore we speak of the lonely ones even as we speak in communion with Community who love and have one another. Treasure, then, this experience, for there be some whom we desire so profoundly to draw to this Community, some who could attain to the ascension, beloved, but they too must walk through the valley of the shadow of death, the experience of the dark night of the soul, ere that karma may be balanced, even the 51 percent. And if they will attain to 100 percent balance, they must know the initiation of the Dark Night of the Spirit.

We would lead them. I pray you, feed them and remember Alpha's Agenda.[3] All services, including Saint Germain's service, are dedicated to the cutting free of the Lightbearers of the world. They must be cut free, they must be sealed! Pray for them. Call for their tube of light as you call for your own. Envision them [sealed in their tube of light daily]. Call for Archangel Michael's cylinder of blue flame and the full power of Hercules and Amazonia.

I tell you, beloved, the fallen ones do not desire to see you made known through the international media, even as they would desire to destroy you through it. Thus it is a two-edged sword, for as you become known these isolated ones [i.e., the Lightbearers,] will recognize the true path no matter what is said or written.

But we do not desire to see this method used by the fallen ones but rather [the method of establishing] the inner network of light whereby you send forth the call and our angels are empowered to draw these souls [to the place] where they might have the support necessary to gain that ground whereby those [among them] who are fulfilling [i.e., concluding,] a lifetime might enter into the octaves of Light with the stupendous momentum of having begun [their course] in the physical, so continuing with the unascended masters of the Himalayas and so reembodying as fiery ones. Others may be cut free by your effort and your prayer for them to be liberated, even the final prayer on your lips as you place your body to rest at night. These may ascend in this life.

Thus every moment does count. As time is marked by the hourglass, so it is marked by the candle you hold. Thus when the wick of self is consumed, the allotment of a lifetime, unless the victory be won the soul must recommence.

Therefore Alpha's Agenda is for the saving of the Lightbearers. Blessed hearts, it is not a selfish concept. For if all the Lightbearers of the world be saved, if all the Lightbearers of the world be cut free from their involvements in materialism and [from following] other wandering stars, do you not see that the numbers of Lightbearers as Christed ones should turn a world in an upward spiral and momentum [so] as to facilitate the new religion of the New Age to become a universal recognition and awareness? And if there be present in the world saved Lightbearers, those in whom the Threefold Flame is now a divine spark, saved Lightbearers having that expanded heart fire, *then*, beloved, the religion of Aquarius will not be diluted as was Christianity.

There must be those who are the Christ who will stand and still stand when the powerful, the godless, recognizing that they have been defeated by the Teachings of the Ascended Masters— for the whole multitude is gone after the Christed ones—will then join them and attempt once again to dilute, distort, tear down, deny the Path while making a god of those who have been the founders. They have done it again and again! Thus every major thrust of religion does have its false hierarchy in the world today and its false teaching.

Understand, beloved, the promise of Jesus "Heaven and earth may pass away," [for] indeed they shall, "but my Word shall live forever."[4] The candle you hold does reveal, beloved, that indeed the flame in your heart is the Word that does live forever.

(I request the audience lights be not lit during the candlelight service, for I, Lanello, would give a teaching of the sacred fire and I desire meditation only upon the flame.)

Let the Light be raised up from the base unto the crown. May you hold very high above you now this candle. May you stretch the arm and then consider that to hold that flame at that height for five minutes or ten or fifteen does become strenuous. Therefore when it was required of Moses to hold up his arms for the turning back of the tide of the fallen ones, he did require assistance to the right and to the left, for he could no longer hold up his arms.[5]

Blessed ones, the effort that it does take for you to sustain the candle raised up—sustained, blessed ones—may give you a co-measurement of the effort that is required to raise up the sacred fire from the base to the crown, to keep one's consciousness raised and therefore to *compel*, to *require* of one's members that all be raised up, be accelerated; and that which is unreal and that which is misqualified substance therefore must be transmuted.

This is the value of [calling forth from the heart of your Mighty I AM Presence] resurrection's flame, beloved, in conso-nance with the violet flame and the invocation of Mighty Cosmos' secret rays,[6] that the upward movement of the Mother Flame [which is enhanced thereby], the turning [i.e., rotation,] of the base-of-the-spine chakra, all energy then rising, you see, [will therefore result in] that which is in the electronic belt passing into the fire.

This momentum of the upward current and the upward draft of a flame does move against what is called gravity. Thus you pull against the world when you determine that you shall raise on high that God consciousness. Thus, beloved, this is the effort [you must make]. I desire you to sense a co-measurement with the effort of moving against the grain of the downward pull [of earth and her evolutions].

The Goddess of Liberty peacefully contemplates so many of herselves in this room.[7] In love for you she does place now, with my own, her Electronic Presence over you.

Contemplate, then, as you look about you, so many candles lit, how a million members of the Great White Brotherhood upon earth as Christed ones are still one single flame of God. But O what a flame! O what an individualization of that God Flame!

Yes, you have projects. Yes, you have goals. Yes, you desire all things good to serve the Light. But I will tell you [that] the greatest service you can render is to raise up the Light in your temple. That Light raised up, beloved, is available to us twenty-four hours a day. By it we can save souls for Morya, for you. We can save twin flames for the Ascended Masters and for one another upon earth.

We are after the quality of the Light. We need, as Morya says, "good hearts." Therefore let those who work the works of God do so out of a heart chakra that is on fire. I say, you who have not felt the burning of the heart, you must prime the pump. You must get on fire in love for God. This fire must be an intense fire, beloved, an intense devotion.

It is by devotion that you will magnetize a sponsor in heaven who will share with you the heart fire of his God-Mastery. All may use the multiplication factor of an Ascended Master to kindle and rekindle, to increase, to intensify, to balance Love and Wisdom and Power.

Let devotion to the will of God increase! Let the desire to be in alignment with the heart of Gautama Buddha increase. Let the desiring of the heart, the imploring of the heart attract to you masterful beings who will enter a figure-eight spiral with you and assist you to increase that fire. It is the greatest need of earth in this hour, but above all it is *your* greatest need.

Take those moments, then, to contemplate the Master of your choice and truly offer more than self. Transcend oneself in this offering, beloved. For heaven stands waiting, and this night by sponsorship of Himalaya and the God and Goddess Meru these un-ascended masters of the Far East are also authorized and given the dispensation through the Four and Twenty Elders to assist you, to sponsor you and to be with you, for their oneness with you is great.

Their love is great for you, for they see in you the key to reach those who are caught in the [traps of the] world religions of the

East and the West. They see in the violet flame and your soul's
liberation from an orthodoxy or an intellectual or an emotional
religion without the sacred fire, they see in you, beloved, an
example and a way that many may follow. And they *will* follow
you, beloved, by the increase of the heart[-flame] and by the Light.

Thus for effort, for desiring to serve, you shall now count
among your ranks those who have been held in abeyance until you
should determine what many of you have now [determined]: that
the mastery of the physical body must be the goal if one is to be the
Master in that body.

Some of you have greater mastery in the spirit than you have
in form and thus that inner mastery does not wholly integrate with
the form because the form may not be the perfect instrument.
Thus you deprive yourself and your fellows of a greater God-
manifestation [by your neglect or failure to master the physical
body, as well as the etheric, mental and desire bodies]. But worst of
all, because you do not experience the inner Master that you are in
your Christ Self, you come to believe that you do not have that
mastery and that you are not that masterful presence.

Thus the condition of the body affects the consciousness of
the soul and soul-awareness. And as you can see the conspiracy
against the people of the West and of the whole world to destroy
their brains and bodies, you can know that though a Christ Child
be born among you, unless that Child have the adequate vessel the
Light will not shine as example. [Even] the best of Lightbearers in
embodiment, a child or a babe, may be subject to crankiness, to
excessive fatigue, to crying, to nondesiring to master that form
merely because of the [biochemical or other] imbalance.

Therefore, you see, these unascended masters in previous
lifetimes have paid attention to the path of physical self-mastery,
for they have seen the vision of the future and their own calling to
return again and again and again.

Look now as Babaji[8] has placed himself within the tree of
Christmas, there to remain in meditation throughout this conference through New Year's Day. He does come, beloved, in honor of
the one, the few and perhaps the many who so desire to be a part
of those bands and have been in previous lifetimes. Thus old
friends of his are here and the new may make his acquaintance.
If you have not known of him, you may read lightly of him in
Yogananda's *Autobiography of a Yogi.*

Thus a little bit of understanding of this chain of Hierarchy
amongst the Lightbearers of the East may bring to you true
enlightenment and a new sense of all who comprise the Spirit of the

Great White Brotherhood. They have come, beloved, and now they move among you. Some you have known in past embodiments in the East have since ascended. They too are here as Ascended Masters.

There is indeed a great gathering. Gathered from the four winds[9] do the Lightbearers of the earth come to consecrate, to place their Presence. For wheresoever is the Body of Christ there the eagles shall be gathered together.[10]

This evening we pause, then, and pause to consider who are we and who are our bands. And this New Year, then, does mark a conclave and a celebration here and in the Central Sun whereby those who are present physically and on the etheric plane, as well as the Ascended Masters, shall dedicate their service to this God-purpose that there might be a saturation of those in all octaves of Matter, especially those on the physical plane, of such Light of the Sun for the holding of the balance in the earth. May you rejoice, then, that your invocations and decrees have accrued to your lifestreams a momentum whereby these things which we have desired to see come to pass may now come to pass.

And thus I revealed to the Messenger this day even the desire of the Hierarchy to see earth so accelerate in the violet flame by your quickening and the sparks that fly to others, that earth should be then allowed to enter into a figure-eight flow with the violet planet and Omri-Tas and therefore to truly be accelerated by that spin of the violet planet which is now in a golden age due to the very violet flame her evolutions have invoked.

Our goal, beloved, is to see take place on earth that which is on the violet planet: 144,000 priests of the sacred fire, Masters of the violet flame, priests and priestesses, beloved. One hundred and forty-four thousand—surely this is not too hard for the Lord and the Lord's chelas!

Begin with yourselves, beloved. For I, Lanello, speak to you and in this hour I say, these 144,000 desire with all of the desiring of their hearts to have the opportunity to have for each of them one lifestream upon earth who will maintain that violet flame action sufficiently to be in a figure-eight flow between that priest and that one on earth. Were this to be accomplished in this age, beloved, that the full 144,000 candidates upon earth should be able to so sustain such a Light, it would be the beginning and the nucleus whereby that figure-eight configuration of the two planets should occur.

The violet planet is accelerated into another vibration, higher than that of earth. And thus you see how that momentum could draw up this planet into her rightful place. For earth's destiny [in this solar system] is to be Freedom's Star and Freedom's Star is the star of the Seventh Ray and the Seventh Age. This is precisely the purpose of Omri-Tas' coming in Washington, D.C., many years ago, releasing [the resurgent power of the violet flame focused in the nation's Capitol and] violet flame spheres which were physically visible in the skies.[11] It was to contact [chelas of Saint Germain and the seventh dispensation] and to increase the desire for freedom and the violet flame.

You have captured those spheres, the energy thereof, in your violet flame songs and decrees on tape. Let them increase. Let them be amplified. Let them be refined, for truly you create chalices whereby these priests of the sacred fire might find those ones, for they are known already, beloved. It is known in the cosmic computer of the Mind of God who upon earth are those [144,000] who could attain to that level. Think of it, beloved. And some of them include these unascended masters who desire to come into embodiment for this very purpose.

Yes, beloved, there is hope in heaven. There is hope in Cosmos. And this hope is born in great measure by your performance, especially in the final months of this year. These four months, beloved, of greater diligence on your part have seen the turning of the tide of opposition to chelaship as a [viable] path and to the chela of the will of God.

As you are stalwart and honest, serving devoutly, so much is consumed that has burdened El Morya. On behalf of my Guru and in my love for him I thank you for your service and I encourage you to do more and more, that swiftly he who also wears the winged sandals of God Mercury may do *something*, that *something* he desires to do to assist you.

O his heart, beloved! If you have known me and known my heart's love, then I say, know the heart of Morya through me, for he is an inspiration to evolutions of other planets and planetary systems. *El Morya, El Morya*, his name is known, beloved, far beyond this world. Yet he tarries here, for so many of you are not only his chelas but his dearest friends.

From the heart of Himalaya and the God and Goddess Meru our twin flames and your own enter now new dimensions of cosmic service on behalf of earth and the Christed ones. I seal you now, having so delivered myself of that message and intent.

Blessed ones, call for my Presence and my Heart. I give it freely, for we desire to give our Christhood to none other than those who have served with us many years in this life and in many centuries. You are our friends, our brothers and sisters, our family of Light.

We embrace you, and may the cumulative Christ conscious-ness of us all so weigh as a star of magnitude that does sing in the heavens for El Morya, for his Victory, for your own and for that becoming of that critical mass by this Community whereby even through you the Great White Brotherhood might know a million members strong, every one counted as [a candle in the night and] a candidate for the ascension.

Thus it shall be, for God has willed it so. It is the timing that remains in the free will of the hearts of the Keepers of the Flame—in the freewill hearts of the Keepers of the Flame.

May you, then, sing the "Immaculate Mary" as you attend your Mother's coming.

Immaculate Mary

Immaculate Mary, our hearts are on fire
Your title so wondrous fills all our desire.
Ave, Ave, Ave, Maria
Ave, Ave, Maria.

Immaculate Mary, your praises we sing
You reign now in splendor with Jesus our king.
Ave, Ave, Ave, Maria
Ave, Ave, Maria.

In heaven the blessed your glory proclaim
On earth we your children invoke your sweet name.
Ave, Ave, Ave, Maria
Ave, Ave, Maria.   (Sung seven times)

This dictation by **Lanello** was **delivered** by the Messenger of the Great White Brotherhood Elizabeth Clare Prophet during the Christmas Eve candlelight service, **December 25, 1988,** 12:23–1:03 a.m. MST, at the **Royal Teton Ranch,** Park County, Montana. Available with the dictation of Mother Mary on 90-min. audiocassette B88157, $6.50 (add $.55 postage). Throughout these notes *PoW* is the abbreviation for *Pearls of Wisdom*. **(1) Manvantara.** 1988 *PoW,* p. 208 n. 8. **(2) Focuses of the Masculine and Feminine Rays** of the Godhead are at the etheric retreats of Lord Himalaya and the God and Goddess Meru respectively. 1988 *PoW,* pp. 623, 626, 645, 646 n. 5. On Dec. 25, 1986, Jesus announced that the God and Goddess Meru had "placed themselves within golden white spheres" over the Royal Teton Ranch "to be sustained above it as their Presence with you." 1986 *PoW,* p. 682, quoted in 1988 *PoW,* p. 633 n. 19. **(3) Alpha's Agenda.** 1987 *PoW,* pp. 379–94; 1988 *PoW,* pp. 521–34. **(4) My Word shall not pass away.** Matt. 24:35; Mark 13:31; Luke 21:33. See 1988 *PoW,* pp. 446, 626–27; 1986 *PoW,* pp. 560–61; 1985 *PoW,* pp. 479–80; 1982 *PoW,* pp. 237–38, 276; 1974 *PoW,* pp. 210–11. **(5) Moses' hands held up by Aaron and Hur.** Exod. 17:8–13. **(6) "Mighty Cosmos' Secret Rays,"** decree 0.03 in *Prayers, Meditations and Dynamic Decrees for the Coming Revolution in Higher Consciousness,* Section I; no. 12 on *Save the World with Violet Flame! by Saint Germain 3* audiocassette. For teaching on Mighty Cosmos' secret rays, see 1988 *PoW,* p. 230 n. 7. **(7)** Each one in the congregation was holding a Christmas candle and had his right arm raised up high after the manner in which the Goddess of Liberty holds her torch. **(8) Babaji** dictated through the Messenger Elizabeth Clare Prophet on June 17, 1979, at Camelot, Los Angeles County, Calif. (see Radiant Word, 1987 *PoW,* pp. 463–64). **(9) Gathering elect from four winds.** Matt. 24:31; Mark 13:27. **(10) "Where the eagles gather."** Term used by the Brotherhood to signal the Inner Retreat as the place of the 'Body' of Christ where the sons of God gather. The Mystical 'Body' of the Universal Christ is the entire Spirit of the Great White Brotherhood ascended and unascended. Matt. 24:28; Luke 17:37. Title of the 1981 *Pearls* volume. **(11)** Following the July 6, 1963 dictation by Omri-Tas (see p. 682), conferees attending *The Goddess of Liberty's Freedom Class* in Washington, D.C., witnessed the physical precipitation of hundreds of **violet flame spheres** over the nation's capital.

THE RADIANT WORD

VIOLET FLAME SPHERES OVER THE NATION'S CAPITOL

Excerpt from a dictation given in Washington, D.C., July 6, 1963
by Beloved Omri-Tas through the Messenger Mark L. Prophet

We adore the violet fire and the violet fire adores us, serving us very well. And therefore tonight it has been requested by beloved Portia of your own great Karmic Board that we shall release the power of the violet fire from our planet to the planet earth in hope that the beneficiaries of our radiation will be those chelas who request from the great Karmic Board a release and cessation of the karma which they have builded through the centuries.

You have called forth, beloved and benign ones, violet fire for many years. Archangel Zadkiel, who frequently visits our planet, has told us of the tremendous calls which have been made by the people of earth who are familiar with the law of Saint Germain's freedom flame and the violet flame, and we are wholly in compassion with the need for your people to share this great blessing. Therefore, accept from my hands as a gift of divine love the resurgent power of the violet flame projected toward the earth.

Magnificent violet fire angels from Saint Germain's own band have volunteered to blaze a path through cosmic highways toward the earth planet and to focus it, beloved ones, upon your nation's Capitol, to which this sanctuary is so proximate. Beloved ones, the charge of violet fire shall utilize the Capitol dome as an electrode and it shall radiate out as from a great hub throughout the entire planet known as earth. Every chela of Saint Germain upon this planet shall be blest with the radiation which we shall pour forth. . . .

And now, beloved priests of the violet planet, I, Omri-Tas, say unto you: release your mighty power of light and build up the forcefield upon this great electrode of light that the people of earth may be blest this night with all of the beauty of the violet flame which we can release and convey to them. . . .

To complete our great experiment of light we shall now form beautiful, magnificent spheres of violet flame, and we are going to roll them down this cosmic highway in much the manner of a bowler attempting to knock down bowling pins. But we shall hit our mark. There are 144,000 of these spheres. Each one of the priests of the sacred fire here has one in command. These shall be released for the next twelve hours and each one shall come down the same highway of light we projected the great release of violet flame.

When these violet flame spheres contact the Capitol of your nation, they, too, shall shatter and diffuse and create a repetition of the same first charge, for these were specially prepared for this purpose. The reason the charge shall be the same is because the release which we made a few moments ago is sufficient, insofar as the violet flame substance is concerned, to mix with the radiation of each of these spheres and produce the selfsame results in each case. Therefore, for the next twelve hours there shall be a continual release, spaced by cosmic law, of violet flame from this planet.

Ladies and gentlemen, friends of freedom, friends of Saint Germain, friends of your own Mighty I AM Presence, may I convey to the planet earth the love, the compassion and the longing of our people to see you win your freedom by the proper use of the violet flame of Saint Germain. He is well known here, honored and loved. He came here long ago. Many, many years ago Saint Germain came here and formed with us a friendship of undying quality.

Pearls of Wisdom®
published by The Summit Lighthouse

| *Vol. 31 No. 87* | *Beloved Mother Mary* | *December 25, 1988* |

Reinforcement by Example
A Spiritual Path for Children
Christmas Eve Candlelight Service

How heaven does wait, beloved, for that reinforcement upon earth whereby the children, O the children, might have from birth, from infancy, a spiritual path whereby the internalization of that God Flame should bring them to the very same disciplines and initiations which were given to my Son Jesus.

Blessed ones, this Community is the hope of many, not alone these unascended masters of whom Lanello spoke to you[1] but very precious souls, Christ children, who may recognize a joint-heirship from childhood and truly expand the fullness of the Light to a Christhood and full Sonship as adults.

Therefore I would speak to you of the necessity of so caring for all children as though they were of such mettle and [of so] caring for all children as though they had a karmic burden, thus not becoming so enamored, shall we say, of that [Christ child] as to not consider how these children of the Light require every measure of the standards of love and discipline and inner learning and outer learning. For all these things must come back to that new consciousness, that new body-awareness, that new soul-awareness that is given [to the newborn child].

I cannot stress to you [enough], O parents and teachers and sponsors of our children, how necessary is reinforcement by example. Let your categorical imperative be as the byword "A child may be watching me. A child *is* watching me. A child will do what I do because I present myself as a Keeper of the Flame, as a member of this Community and a chela of the Ascended Masters."

Let everyone who hears or reads my words know that the example set for children is that which you shall reap as positive, good karma and rings of Light [added to your causal body] that never end or as negative, bad karma, beloved, that does cause you to return again and again for* the hurting of one of these little ones by a failure to tend the flame and to be sensitive [to the fact] that the child will follow those whom he sees and knows and that, unless and until otherwise [taught], the child does respect the adults and the older children around him.

As I have passed through your midst in the twenty-four hours prior to my coming, my ears have pained me from the sound, the vibration and the tone of voice which I have heard mother or father or teacher or someone use in conversing with a child. The tone of voice may be condescending, subtly condemnatory and containing elements of control rather than the uplift in conveying direction or the do's and don'ts of life, the uplift of the Holy Spirit whereby the child takes on the desire to do what is right because the support is the upward voice of resurrection's flame, is positive reinforcement but not degrading or disrespectful.

I speak now not merely of words, for the words may be all correct. It is the vibration of the voice and the feeling world. All these things enter in and become the chemistry of life for a soul.

Truly you know not what you do. Thus I come to teach you. For in the care of the child you make contact with your own soul and the child within that may have ceased to grow or to mature at some level on the way when by trauma or encounter with adults [that child] simply could not continue to unfold or to blossom.

Thus, in some areas, sometimes and usually in the emotional body but ofttimes in the mental, the growth has stopped and the individual must deal with himself as an adult in an adult world and yet [he] has not fully come to a maturity which can only be defined as we define it: a maturity that is a point of resolution. Thus the impact you may make upon a child may deny that child resolution with the cycles of life proceeding and ongoing, resolution with the karma returning, resolution with those around him.

Let there be, then, an attentiveness to one another and [to] the child within one another and the realization that all are parents to one another in Community and that in the sensitivity of the Five Dhyāni Buddhas and the five secret rays you can assist your neighbor, one with whom you may have a brief conversation, to get past a point of consciousness, a block, a knot in the psyche that has been there whether a decade or ten thousand years; and at that knot evolution of a certain portion of self has ceased. Perhaps the intellect has raced on, other achievements have been attained but one day the facing of that place along the Path must come. And I say, for every chela of the will of God that moment has come.

For some, you can go no further for nondevelopment of the

*because of

Threefold Flame; but then, why is it imbalanced? It is that point of nonresolution. Thus, let us treasure the newborn babe and the white page and let us desire in our hearts to write nothing there that must be erased, to place not the stumbling block that will have to be undone one day, painfully, by that child-man.

Building blocks, then, must be foundational from the years prior to conception to the conception of the child to the gestation and through the first seven. From the moment of passing, a lifestream may be assigned to a new mother and father who themselves may be the age of eight or ten. Thus, while out of embodiment the soul must prepare. And you yourselves anticipating having families in the future, as some of you do, ought to be praying for the healing, the resolution, the [violet-flame] transmutation concerning [the records of the lifestreams of] those souls who are assigned to you.

All may pray for those assigned to come to this Community and to all families of Light upon earth. Thus, praying for parents-to-be and teachers is most necessary; for, blessed ones, the question does come to mind, How can those who have not overcome themselves be a clear vessel for the children entrusted to their care?

Well, beloved, it may not be possible in other quarters but here you have [knowledge of] the call for the lowering of the Electronic Presence of the Holy Christ Self and the I AM Presence and of the Ascended Masters. Here you have a path of chelaship where if you are obedient to the inner divine blueprint, to your God Presence and to the voice of the Teacher (if you have one), then, you see, by being a chela and having that direct tie to the Master, the Master may override those conditions of consciousness which could inhibit or deny your being that clear vessel.

But, beloved, this does require the conscious determination and decision to have bound by the blue-lightning angels and to set aside those elements of the personality which you know to be detrimental to yourself, to your loved ones, to your cohorts on the Path. This is the profound value of the Guru-chela relationship under the Ascended Masters. And when you cannot hear or discern the Master's voice, the value of the Messenger is paramount.

Blessed ones, I desire to give you somewhat of the background of this Messenger as a chela in the East in India in many ancient times under the gurus there. Without [her] having learned or become lettered or tutored in all of these ancient texts [in this lifetime], yet by the mantle of Messenger today, you receive from her in the way* ancient wisdom gained through many embodiments under the various masters.

Thus, it is truly the voice of the Spirit of the Great White Brotherhood, [her] preparation and [her] Path in many climes and

*as you encounter her along the way

ways and under various systems that enables us to bring to you [instruction through her mantle] and to speak to you individually concerning your lifestream and your descent under the Manus and the root races or from other systems and other worlds.

Thus, value the Word and come to understand that as we are dedicated, so is it the deepest desire and dedication of this heart to bring you to the consummate reunion with your Real Self. You have a friend, beloved, who will spare nothing, not even her life itself to render this service to your heart and soul. And therefore we come in an attempt to reach as many hundreds and thousands of lifestreams at an individual level as is possible.

Blessed ones, your Messenger is able to be with you at inner levels by a dispensation of bilocation which [in her case] is more the dispensation of the sending of the Electronic Presence and the Holy Christ Self at will. Thus you *are* being tutored, and many of you know it consciously; and you are being mothered and cared for by one who yet shares with you the physical vibrations of a physical octave.

Be still and listen to the voice within and see the confirmation that we bring you through her. Know then, beloved, that as you correct each crooked way in the psyche and the self, you come more and more into that oneness where you may receive greater initiation and a course of greater self-mastery.

We, then, do encourage even as we laud the current efforts of faculty and parents and the Messenger herself to see to it that the very fundamentals and building blocks of language, both the language of the soul and the language in which the Ascended Masters deliver their messages, be established in the children from earliest time, even prior to birth.

Thus we have called one of our daughters to assemble this [information] and to present it to you at this New Year's conference, the very subject of the internalization of the Word, of language, the ability to read, to read not only the letters of words, beloved, and to know them but to know within the inner meaning of the word in the English language, the vibration of the letters, the fohatic keys. For these things do the souls who come to you have as inner awareness. Therefore, let them learn, for they are able. The Mind of God is with them and in them uninhibited, unlimited. They know no limitation, these babes in arm.

But let us dwell upon the Holy Spirit as the means of enlightenment and teaching and let us know that the geometry of God as the mathematics of God is assimilated as easily as the written and spoken word. And those who teach shall also find a transmutation through this science that while imparting it to children they themselves will know the healing power of the Word.

Blessed ones, giving the gift of speech, locution, elocution, understanding the meaning of sound, entering into the heart of the divine science of linguistics, these things, beloved, become, then, the foundation of the gifts of the Holy Spirit. And thus you find in your midst Sarasvati herself. For wherever wisdom is so extolled there she is and she has not left since the hour of the announcement of her appearing.[2]

Now, beloved, as you teach, the fire of compassion of your heart is kindled and with joy of the heart you communicate. But I must remind you that the child who must develop and balance the Threefold Flame will do it best by having the awakening of the quality of compassion, concern for life [the] lesser endowed, concern for life in pain and [the] aware[ness] that one can reach out to help those in need.

I bring to your attention, then, that children of all ages require a pattern of Threefold Flame decree momentum daily. We set one hour that must be filled by children with songs and decrees. The younger ones may sustain twenty minutes three times daily. You may contemplate their measures.

The Messenger has long ago called for physical exercise, balance and yoga itself to occupy children's bodies while they give their decrees. Decrees and songs of the violet flame and music to develop their rhythm and their bodies simultaneously must begin. Already the physical exercises included for brain development[3] have allowed children who enter into them to absorb more violet flame within the brain, the central nervous system and thereby to, yes, increase the capacity of the brain to be the chalice for the Mind of God.

These children, beloved, will take on the aura of the holy innocents and the holy angels and they will with facility, then, find the healing of their bodies in proper loving care and correct diet. They will pass easily into the new vibration of Aquarius and a golden age.

Be tender and positive, beloved. If you have not yet slain the beast of fear and torment within yourself, you may convey it to them. You must convey a fearlessness toward the future, a sense of overcoming victory and of conquering. Be careful, then, [of] your conversation in their presence. Be careful, beloved, and see that you approach the Path as one of moving toward the Sun, a golden path of light and initiation, and that which lies before you as simply a part of Maitreya's requirements [for the path of chelaship].

Let the doomsday consciousness be banished from this Community, for the children must not have it upon them. And may you pierce it within yourselves, for it does become a shame before the Lord Christ. The future is positive and bright with hope and you must pass through the Night victors entering into the fray as with the relish of Ruby Ray angels and blue-lightning angels.

You are the winners and you shall win because you have the diamond-shining Mind of God, the fiery steel, and the All-Seeing Eye. You will not fail if you will it so and if you surrender all lesser desires, all lesser baggage, all lesser tributaries of purpose.

To summon, then, the focalization of divine purpose in the heart comes Babaji and the unascended masters. May you know one-pointedness of Morya's Diamond Heart and my own, for it is the key to your victory. May you take, then, as your goal the goal-fitting and the goal-setting of Alpha unto Omega unto Maitreya unto Morya and my heart.

So the signs of the times are the signs in the heavens. See them written in the skies and in the sky of your own etheric body. Read the record of your life, of your birth and your transition. Enter fully into it and win.

I bless now the Christmas Eve Communion. I, Mary, with Raphael now charge this wafer and wine with healing substance, for I desire with Raphael to serve this Communion to you, each one. It is for healing, beloved, [the] healing of those conditions of consciousness which you dare not keep for the child or the children who take example from every level of being.

I have given to you the motivation of my heart to be overcomers this night. May you shine forth as the instrument of the star of your causal body, for at the level of the soul the child does read all.

Blessed are the children, they are the peacemakers.

Blessed are the children, they are the messengers of heaven.

Blessed are the children, for they believe in miracles and contain them.

Blessed are the children, for they are the joy of father and mother and all life.

Blessed are the children, for they are God with you.

Except ye become as a little child ye shall in no wise enter in.

I seal you in the hope of the Christmas Rose and the Christ Child. I AM Mary, Teacher, Prophetess, Archeia, Mother. I AM Mary, your Friend, and I AM your Friend most of all when you are the friend of the Child. Keep the Flame of the children for me, beloved, as I keep the Flame for the Child within you.

This dictation by **Mother Mary** was **delivered** by the Messenger of the Great White Brotherhood Elizabeth Clare Prophet during the Christmas Eve candlelight service, **December 25, 1988,** 1:14–1:44 a.m. MST, at the **Royal Teton Ranch, Park County, Montana.** Available with the dictation by Lanello on 90-min. audiocassette B88157, $6.50 (add $.55 for postage). Throughout these notes *PoW* is the abbreviation for *Pearls of Wisdom.* (**1**) Lanello, 1988 *PoW,* p. 673. (**2**) **Sarasvati,** the wife or consort of Brahma (the First Person of the Hindu Trinity), is the goddess of wisdom, eloquence, learning, and music as well as patroness of the arts. See 1987 *PoW,* pp. 241, 458. (**3**) A program of **physical exercises for brain development** designed by Glenn Doman and the staff of the Institutes for the Achievement of Human Potential was implemented at Montessori International school at the Royal Teton Ranch in the fall of 1988. The exercises, which consist of crawling, creeping, running and brachiating (swinging by the arms on an overhead ladder), improve the organization and functioning of various levels of the brain.

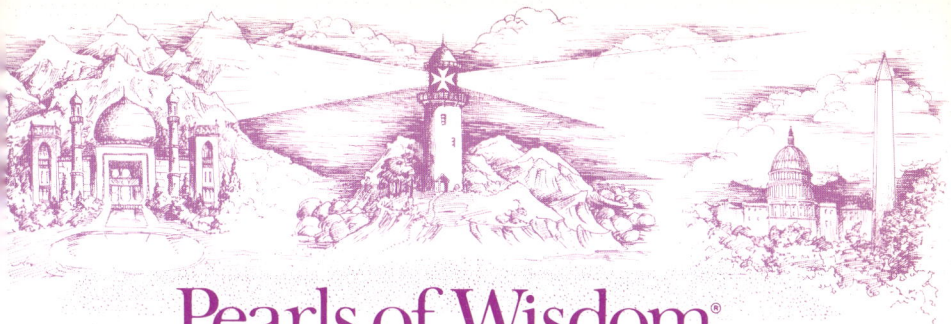

Pearls of Wisdom®
published by The Summit Lighthouse

Vol. 31 No. 88 | *Beloved Jesus Christ* | *December 26, 1988*

The Sanctification of the Heart
Giving Birth to the Divine Manchild Where You Are
The Lord's Christmas Address 1988

May the eye of the vestal virgin Pallas Athena be upon you always. For it is the age of Christ Truth and those who have my Truth have universal Life everywhere present in God.

Those who live for Truth, those whose auras bespeak the cosmic honor flame as a strength, as a pillar of fire, these move in the earth in the correctness of the Holy Christ Flame. These know that "as Above so below" the mirroring of the Great God Self within the soul must be accomplished.

Such as these are not otherworldly but know that daily deeds and thoughts and acts and words are the building blocks of the etheric reality. And therefore they are not satisfied with mere ideation, with mere contemplation. Their satisfaction must be the laying of the stone, even the white cube of the City Foursquare. Lives must be lived here and now, truly in the geometry of God.

Let us chisel anew the profile of your Christhood this night!

As Kuthumi and I come in the office of [the] World Teachers, so we bear the Alpha, the Omega of the lifestream Maitreya. Therefore, thou Cosmic Christ, we thy Sons come bearing gifts of thy illumination flame to these thine own who gather and tarry to lay the chief cornerstone of the will of God that upon it and out from it there might spring forth illumination's golden flame as the spark that crosses the night sky and illumines a plane and a planet.

We come also out of the East unto the West. For we too participate in the Temple of the Blue Lotus of Himalaya, in Maitreya's place and the place where all the Brothers of the Golden Robe are. It is for the increase of illumination's flame that the sons and daughters of Tibet are persecuted, brutalized and their community and their culture desecrated.

Blessed hearts, these are a lifewave and an evolution sponsored by the Great White Brotherhood as ye are. Thus, to add to the burden of El Morya is the plight of such as these, for they have carried the golden thread even continuously by reincarnation since the hour of Sanat Kumara. Let it be known, then, that you do hold the balance for them and they have received a certain flame of joy. As you have celebrated my birth in the violet flame[1] so I have chosen to pass that flame by an arc to the very heart of those individuals whom Morya calls chelas and to whom the adepts bow, bowing before the Light of the heart and the perseverance.

Pray for them, beloved, for in other times it is they who have held the balance for you and there is an inner tie and an inner connection. Let it be the golden thread of contact and let the golden lining be the interior garment that you wear, always remembering how my beloved Kuthumi, my Francis,[2] does love you.

The tangible sign of our love may be our Messenger but it is also your beating heart, your pulsating flame. For your flames do show the sign that the Master does tend his own, does tend the garden of the heart. I, Jesus, come again as the gardener in disguise. I come also tending the flowers of Dhyāni Buddhas.

O how in my journey to the East I did exult in the path and the teachings of the heart! Blessed ones, I was taken up into etheric and physical retreats of the Great White Brotherhood and of unascended masters. And there I did receive out of the heart of Maitreya truly the instruction, the initiation, the soul-testing whereby I was indeed required to go and challenge the corrupt ones of the day who hid the Light of religion[3] and did not give this blessed tie that binds the soul[4] to Hierarchy.

Blessed ones, I must perform deeds for the masters that I found in the East. Thus they sent me into the lairs [of the fallen ones], into the very dens of these who had all but put out the candle of self-knowledge unto those whom they considered beneath them and not even worthy of having the impartation of the flame.

In this day and hour the Great White Brotherhood, even led by El Morya, the Chief of the Darjeeling Council, is determined to give every opportunity to those who desire it and who will make use of that opportunity once again to reestablish the thread of contact with the Hierarchy of Light.

Thus, my beloved, not in mere instruction, not in the telling of the Word did I realize the fullness of that Christ of Maitreya with me, did I bring to fruition that which was begun and continued through numerous previous incarnations: I must go forth in confrontation. I must challenge. I must meet and sense even the armour and the shield of the dark ones and what it would take of my own sacred fire to part even the steel, as it were, of the mind-set of their fortresses gainst which the little people could not prevail.

But in this hour it is they who are arrayed against the people of Maitreya East and West. And thus, this people must also know the initiations of the heart which I endured. [For] the heart is not strengthened except in action.

Thus, the time does come when one knows surely that these fallen ones will lay every trap, will rant and rave—and they shall rage and they shall come. One will know it and one will thrust forward the sacred fire even to devour the hatred of the enemy before it descend.

Blessed ones, going within to commune with the Master, even in the secret chamber of the heart with Gautama, is for the understanding of what must be taken up in the outer in the day-to-day existence. Thus, this training I received. And the knowledge of the five planes of the five Buddhas and the spheres surrounding the heart made of me a devotee forever of the heart of Maitreya.

Thus, in the West my heart is spoken of as the Sacred Heart, and yet what I have realized and brought forth in my heart is something which you can do also. Your heart is the Sacred Heart, for God has made only sacred hearts, no other. The Threefold Flame of your heart is that sacredness. To be so felt and so acknowledged requires but the intensification of its dimension of that blazing sun of God-reality.

It is only in measure of increments whereby you think of my heart as the Sacred Heart and your own in a state of becoming, but I unveil to you the Threefold Flame of the heart of your Holy Christ Self. I unveil to you the Threefold Flame in the heart of your I AM Presence. This is the Sacred Heart and in divine reality it is your own, your very own heart.

Thus, the geometry of Truth which Pallas Athena would bring to you is the knowledge of the precipitation of these things [i.e., the Threefold Flame,] from the higher to the lower octave, that in the mirror of the soul the Great God Self might appear smiling in the foreverness of your being.

O ye of the Sacred Heart, O ye are sacred hearts! To even move in the self-knowledge of the sacredness of Life is to magnetize quickly and powerfully even the Sacred Heart just above.

Some have spoken to you of holiness, of the need for spirituality.[5] I come with a simple lesson that you might increase both and that is, by the maintaining of the sense of the sacredness of your heart and the knowledge that when you so acknowledge that sacredness of your Holy Christ Self with you the heart *must* expand, it *must* increase.

I, Jesus, come, then, speaking to you quietly as with the voice of the Buddha Gautama. As with the voice of Maitreya I come. For I come within in this hour rather than without. I speak to you from within your own heart that you might know that I, Jesus, your Brother, can and do choose to sanctify your hearts this night. And I ask you to seal that sanctification by your own affirmation, for I alone am not empowered by God to fully sanctify your heart. It is you who must participate [with me in this empowerment].

I give to you, then, my beloved, the Alpha Thrust of the sanctification of the heart. I ask you to give to me the Omega Return of the sanctification of the heart. And this return, beloved, is a daily and hourly ritual that occurs from within. And because it occurs, there is likewise the sanctification of the works of your hands, your walk with me and [with] the heavenly hosts. There is a consecration in ritual, in the rhythm of life whereby all that you do is sanctified because it comes from your heart which you and I have so sanctified.

My Power and Wisdom and Love to sanctify also comes from the works that the Father Maitreya, Gautama and I have worked together in my life on earth and beyond. This same Power, Wisdom and Love is yours whereby to sanctify [the heart] as the instrument of my work and the work of Maitreya and Gautama and Sanat Kumara. Through the hierarchical chain of being of this order of the Second Ray know, then, that you touch the heart of our Father in heaven even as the Divine Mother ensouling the earth does also reinforce your sanctification of the heart.

Blessed ones, you are unique in that many do not have a labor that is sacred. Your labor being sacred in the furtherance of the Teachings of the Ascended Masters, your avocation of discipleship does thereby enable you to see quite easily that the works of your hands do beget the holiness unto the LORD[6] unto millions.

Therefore, from you to whom I have given this great opportunity to bear the Teaching to the world I do expect much.[7] I do expect, then, that you shall entertain always the holiness of your physical and mental labors, of all that you do. And let the world know that aura of holiness not by word but by your sense of reverence for the flame within the heart of all whom you meet. They will sense that reverence when you speak, the form of your address and communication and caring and concern for physical completion of service.

Let the golden halo of each one shine brightly. Let the sweetness of the inner walk with God, let your communion with me in that Eighth Ray chakra, as with Gautama and Maitreya there, be upon you as a holy oil and a radiance whereby you sense that the outer service is an extension of the inner temple work, the inner temple meditation, contemplation, garnering of the Light. For it is also, beloved, in the secret chamber of the heart that you affirm the Word and wax strong in the power of the spoken Word.

The inner temple work for the establishment of these spheres is thine own now. And as you are taken to the etheric retreats of the Brotherhood, you who have passed through the steps of the seven rays do enter the inner court[8] while new students newly entering, coming newly out of the physical body to the etheric while they sleep at night, do take the very first steps of the seven rays.

Thus, there is the inner court. Knock. Knock and it shall be opened unto you. The knocking, beloved, is what you do each day to prove to the hierarch of the ray that you are indeed skipping no steps, seeking no side doors or byways, that you are determined to keep the flame of the ray each day of the week and in the fortnight you spend at these retreats of the Chohans.[9]

There, beloved, as you pass beyond the outer coloration of the ray, entering the chamber that is central in these retreats, you then come into the unity and the oneness of the white light. And this white light is the sphere of transition to the five secret rays.

In the unity of the seven, then, you come in to the Holy Spirit. And in the Holy Spirit that is the white fire, you seek and find the enlightenment of the Trinity. That enlightenment as the illumination flame of the Second Ray becomes the principal and central flame of your altar as you are communing for the Power, Wisdom and Love, for the initiation and the attainment of the five secret rays.

Thus, beloved, as you read of my journey to the East, the chronicles thereof, you will understand that that which was recorded was that which was seen by men, that which was known by those devotees where I did take my rest and abide for lengths of time to study their ways, their scriptures, their language, their needs and their hearts.

Blessed ones, if one spends seventeen years of one's life, all of one's nights out of the body studying in the temples of the Brotherhood of the Himalayas, I can assure you that much [much learning and soul-testing and sanctification] does accrue to the lifestream. And inasmuch as I had been in a continuity of purpose within those retreats for many thousands of years, I was able to bring back the most precious gift of all to the West, beloved. And yet I was allowed to bear it [only] as far as Palestine for that particular mission of three years.

It is the flame of Maitreya that I bore, his actual flame, beloved. This I carried in my heart and this to me was the personification of Father, for the concept of Father and Guru are one. Thus you understand, "I and my Father are one,[10] I and my Guru are one." And it is so this day, beloved. Thus, it did remain for my disciples and others to bring that flame of Maitreya to the West. And you have followed our Messengers to this place prepared for the flame of Maitreya.

Of course, I had many journeyings beyond the hour recognized as that of the resurrection in that life and did appear here and there around the world to the peoples that were waiting for the coming of the sign of the avatar of Pisces.

Blessed ones, the establishment of the Mystery School, therefore, at this retreat has been a profound completion and joy to my heart—and to see how you have gathered from ancient times, whether you knew me in my life in Palestine or in previous incarnations. You have followed my lead, my Presence, though at times you have not seen me nor even known if the guidance was mine, yet it was.

We come so far West, therefore, beloved, that West becomes East again. And in the great gathering of those from all corners of the earth,[11] so the prophecy is also fulfilled of the coming of Maitreya[12] to all people. Each and every heart representing the nations and the peoples of this planet who then [does] take up the path of the Ascended Masters, which is Maitreya's way, does therefore take into the karmic evolution that enlightenment.

Remember, then, that you have been taught to call for the cutting free of all those who [have] come down the ancestral tree of your background and [to] send [the call] into the very heart of those areas of the world that mark the points of your origin; [for there is where you must also send] the light and the teaching by dynamic decree, first and foremost, and if possible by the written and the spoken Word.

Thus, it is an hour of fulfillment for us, for Maitreya and for you. As Saint Germain has emphasized the meditation upon the heart, the expansion of the heart, so it is leading to this moment, beloved, when I must tell you that the initiation of the Sacred Heart is yours to claim. You must confirm and ratify whatever heaven does give to you. You must sanctify. This, then, is the step required, as it was required of me.

It is good that you should compare yourselves to me as Brother and Friend and not place so much distance between us in the sense that I am perfected and you are not. You must recognize that it is the quality of the inner man of the heart,[13] it is the quality of the soul and the spirit and then the determination to bring all these to fruition in the physical octave that is the making of the Christed one.

I desire you to be wed to Christ Truth this night and to receive Pallas Athena as my representative and spokesman to you for a time. For her momentum in Truth will cause you to desire Truth above all else—all compromise, all gray areas, all hidden dishonesties with self and others.

Pallas Athena, boldly anchoring the Light of Truth within you to amplify, will bring to you the awareness of the precipitation by the emerald ray of the Divine Image of the All-Seeing Eye of God.

Pallas Athena will teach you the precipitation of that cosmic cube, will enable you to be precise in your building and your preparedness and all things that must be completed as you complete the balancing of your physical karma.

So long as you retain physical karma, beloved, and physical ties, the Law may require reincarnation. But if you fulfill the mandates of the Law in the physical octave, the astral plane and the mental, you will find that there will be less cause for you to descend into realms of density.

Blessed ones, I speak to you of a Keeper of the Flame who did pass from the screen of life this Christmas morning. The circumstances surrounding this passing were [due to] an extreme out-of-alignment state. Thus, this individual, having not taken seriously the path of keeping the Flame, had not garnered the Light or the necessary self-discipline to keep out of harm's way. Thus it was entirely the fault of this individual that life was taken so suddenly from one so young.

Though the call was made at this altar to the legions of Archangel Michael and Astrea by the Messenger for this individual to be taken to his lawful place in the octaves, that one could not rise above the level of purgatory for want of momentum in Light, for utter compromise of Truth of many lifetimes and a failure to take seriously the meaning of the pledge to be a Keeper of the Flame.[14]

Thus, by the ultimate compromise one may lose one's opportunity to be in this plane. By not availing oneself of the path of discipleship and the decrees offered, one may not even be able to navigate out of the place where accident or sudden circumstance may take one from the screen of life. Thus, as the tree falls so it shall lie. And as this one passed, so he was at the moment the Messenger began her invocations. Thus, the angel of God did pronounce [that] this one could rise no higher than the "third level."[15]

Let it be understood, beloved, that among this Community it

is often the case that when one speaks of one as a Keeper of the Flame it does immediately connote someone who is a devotee, someone special. Indeed it should be but it is not always. Thus, merely to be a Keeper of the Flame, beloved, does not guarantee salvation, even as membership in a Christian church or responding to the altar call to be saved likewise guarantees nothing, nor do those who wear the cloth and call themselves ministers have any prior claim upon heaven. By words and acts and deeds alone, by initiation under the Hierarchy of Light is there won any victory at all.

Those who do not, then, acknowledge the Christ of me as the Christ of Maitreya may not receive the kingdom of God, for it is the chain of Hierarchy, and not an isolated favorite son that conforms to a fabricated orthodoxy, that can win [the victory] for the individual. Just as the denial of my Mother, Mary, is the denial of my own seed and incarnation through her, so, beloved, to think that flesh and blood can reveal that Christ or be that Christ is an error that does not convey salvation.

May you know, then, beloved, that a mere title, an acceptance or a sense of long affiliation with this movement will not [necessarily] afford the individual the momentum or the wings of Light to be at the right place in the time of transition.

You may wonder that I should deliver this message at Christmas, but it is at this hour of the year when the cycles turn that there is a harvest of souls. And you can note this in the events that occur in the winter as each year there are a certain number of souls who take their leave from this octave, for their opportunity with the conclusion of the year does run out.

Happy are ye, then, who have tarried in the God Flame, in the communion, in the oneness of our fellowship. May you understand, then, that an individual's demise by self-abuse is preordained by the individual. And by this individual's neglect of the Law and even the Teaching itself not a single Ascended Master by cosmic law could intercede.

Blessed ones, this is a measure [of the Great Law] that must be told and it is a comfort to all. For you see, beloved, inherent in the message of the possibility of failure is the message of [the possibility of] victory. If it is possible to fail a test, then it is possible to pass a test. And it can be known by given acts—if these acts had not been taken and other positive momentum built—that by the individual's own word and own work his salvation could have been attained. This you must understand and no longer leave as a gray area, a nebulous area [the notion] that another, whether myself, the Messenger or any angel in heaven or any friend upon earth, can guarantee for you your individual, hard-won, gracious victory in the Light.

Let the full weight of the recognition of the God Flame come upon you! Let the full weight of the Sacred Heart above you and the masterful Presence of Life, your *own* I AM Presence who *is* your True Self, come upon you in this hour as we *seal* the flame of Christmas 1988!

And as we *seal* it in your heart you may know that giving birth to the Manchild where you are and bringing that Manchild to the full Godhood and stature of being ordained by the Father-Mother God is your calling, which is possible, which is preordained but which you yourself must ratify—and if you do not, beloved, there can be no intercession [of] another doing it for you.

I give you this Teaching this night once again by way of exposing to you the lie that has crept into my Church, which is no longer my Church therefore. I give you this Teaching that you might leap with the joy of victory to know that as the victory is yours to claim it can be done. [You can give birth to the Divine Manchild because God has empowered you to do so by the sanctification of the heart!] God has sent you to do it and ordained you to do it and he has not sent me to do it for you in your stead, nor any other Master or friend. But you, beloved, contain in your being, as I did and as I do, all of the necessary ingredients to achieve the victory.

As I speak to you, my angels of golden illumination's flame are peeling from you centuries of ignorance and of ignoring the inner law of being. The lie has saturated the lower ethers of the planet that somehow something, someone, some institution, some government outside of yourself will supply percentages of your identity, your life, your happiness, your needs.

See how subtle is this lie because, beloved, it has invaded the plane of the five secret rays. This I tell you, beloved, so that you will understand what must be consumed, what must be burned off before the fullness of Mighty Cosmos' secret rays can manifest surrounding your heart. But, beloved, those secret rays do contain the power to consume all unlike themselves. Thus, rejoice that you have the call to Mighty Cosmos' secret rays.[16]

I open another door of another chamber. And in this chamber, beloved, which is a grand hall, there is one in this hour who does take his ascension. This lifestream, beloved, knew the walk with God through the Keepers of the Flame Fraternity. This lifestream, beloved, in this hour and in this moment is entering the ceremony of the ascension. Serapis Bey, Saint Germain and Lanello are present, and as we take our leave of you we shall also be present.

Blessed ones, one is taken in the victory of the ascension and another is left in purgatory where he shall experience his own sowings and come to grips with his own karma and receive the instruction that in so facing that karma at that level of the astral plane, in the flame of overcoming he too may transcend octaves and rise, but not shortly, beloved, not shortly. For this one had squandered the Light of the Threefold Flame long ago.

Therefore, two scenes, each illustrative of choices made by the individuals and none others. In each case, beings of Light and Darkness assailed, supported, entered the life of the individual. In one instance, the individual did follow the lead of Light in obedient love and Christ Truth and illumination. In the other, by pride and rebellion, that one did follow and agree with the condemnation of the Light and the Lightbearers over many centuries.

The outcome can be foreknown of your daily choices. You have but to look at them and to know that God has allowed a place to be prepared for every lifestream according to his choices. Therefore, in the astral plane are many compartments and gradations, moving from the physical to greater and greater darkness in the depths of the consciousness of the dark ones.

So El Morya, the wise man, does say, "As you live, so you shall die." May you take this wisdom and understand that as you are in this life, so you shall be in the next. And the guarantor of your victory is you, beloved, you sanctified in all planes of being. Let the victory path be begun by you this night in earnest by your consideration of my word for your own sanctification of the heart.

And it doth not yet appear what you shall be. But you know that when your Holy Christ Self shall appear to you, you shall be like him for you shall see him as he is[17]—reflected in the mirror of your soul.

I AM and I remain Jesus, your Brother, with you always when you call to me and when you maintain my vibration, which is the vibration of Maitreya. And a holy, holy night to all.

"The Summit Lighthouse Sheds Its Radiance O'er All the World to Manifest as Pearls of Wisdom." This dictation by **Jesus Christ** was **delivered** by the Messenger of the Great White Brotherhood Elizabeth Clare Prophet during the Christmas Night service, **December 26, 1988,** 12:45–1:35 a.m. MST, at the **Royal Teton Ranch, Park County, Montana.** Available on 90-min. audiocassette B88158, $6.50 (add $.55 for postage). [**N.B.** Bracketed material denotes words unspoken yet implicit in the dictation, added by the Messenger under Jesus' direction for clarity in the written word.] Throughout these notes *PoW* is the abbreviation for *Pearls of Wisdom.* (**1**) Keepers of the Flame held a Christmas Day **violet flame prayer vigil,** using the *Save the World with Violet Flame! by Saint Germain 1–4* audiocassettes, in the chapel at the Royal Teton Ranch and at sanctuaries around the world to hold the balance for the Lightbearers of the world and our Community of the Holy Spirit. (**2**) The Ascended Master **Kuthumi** was embodied as Saint Francis of Assisi. (**3**) **Jesus' challenges to the false priests** and their false teachings during his sojourn in the East from age 13 to 29 were chronicled by Buddhist historians in "The Life of Saint Issa," republished in Elizabeth Clare Prophet, *The Lost Years of Jesus,* 1984, pp. 197–207. (**4**) The word **religion** is derived from the Latin *religio* 'bond between man and the gods' or *religare* 'to bind back'. (**5**) **The need for spirituality and holiness.** Mother Mary and the Goddess of Purity, 1988 *PoW,* pp. 312, 313, 320, 322, 616; Mother Mary, 1987 *PoW,* pp. 395–400; Lanello, 1986 *PoW,* p. 670; Gautama Buddha and Lady Master Nada, 1984 *PoW,* pp. 37–39, 287–90; Jesus Christ, 1982 *PoW,* pp. 625–26; Archangel Raphael, March 23, 1978, audiocassette B7843; Mark L. Prophet and Elizabeth Clare Prophet, *The Lost Teachings of Jesus II,* pp. 502–4. (**6**) **Holiness unto the LORD.** Exod. 28:36, 37; 39:30, 31; Isa. 23:18; Jer. 2:3; Zech. 14:20, 21; Elizabeth Clare Prophet, 1986 *PoW,* pp. 279–88; 1985 *PoW,* pp. 509–10; Sanat Kumara, 1979 *PoW,* p. 88; Mark L. Prophet and Elizabeth Clare Prophet, *The Lost Teachings of Jesus II,* pp. 335–37. (**7**) **"Unto whomsoever much is given, of him shall be much required."** Luke 12:48. (**8**) **Inner court.** Ezek. 10:3; 40:19; Rev. 11:1, 2. (**9**) The Seven Chohans and the Maha Chohan are currently conducting classes at the **universities of the Spirit** now open at their etheric retreats. 1988 *PoW,* pp. 287 n. 5, 544 n. 11, chart p. 438. (**10**) **I and my Father are one.** John 10:30; 12:44, 45; 14:9–11, 20, 24; 17:21. (**11**) **Gathering together the elect from the four winds.** Matt. 24:31; Mark 13:27. (**12**) **Prophecy of Maitreya's coming.** 1988 *PoW,* p. 170 n. 2. (**13**) **Inner man.** Eph. 3:16; I Pet. 3:4. (**14**) At 4:17 a.m. Christmas morning a 26-year-old **Keeper of the Flame** (Lesson 7) who had been drinking on Christmas Eve **passed from the screen of life** when his car slid out of control and overturned. He was on the way to get chicken with a companion when he veered off the roadway. He was pronounced dead at the scene of the accident. His companion was injured but reported in satisfactory condition. According to police alcohol was a factor but it was not determined if he was legally intoxicated.

On Christmas Eve, the Keeper reportedly announced that he was taking down his altar and wasn't going to decree anymore. He and several friends went to a bar and returned home after midnight. When he and his friend left to get some chicken, the victim told another who had wanted to go along, "This ride isn't for you."

When the Messenger heard of the accident on Christmas morning and offered invocations on behalf of this lifestream, he was still at the scene of the accident, disoriented, unaware that the crystal cord was broken and his opportunity for incarnation in this round had been terminated tragically by his own actions. Only 12 hours earlier the Messenger had written in her December 24 letter to Keepers of the Flame Lesson 8 and above in good standing, "As I offer prayers for those who pass from the screen of life each week, whether they are of our Community or of the world body, I see so clearly how the persistent, relentless use of the violet flame has saved any number of souls from the necessity of tarrying in the astral plane (purgatory or worse) to balance their karma made at that vibratory level while on earth. Those who have not received this gift of Saint Germain's 'miracle pouch' or those who have it and do not 'hurl it' into the earth and into their electronic belts are the very ones who have no wind in their sails to buoy them up into etheric octaves and the retreats of the Great White Brotherhood and the Holy City when the hour of transition comes."

(15) **The "third level," purgatory, a level of the astral plane.** The astral plane has 33 levels in descending order of density where souls are required to "serve time" in order to pay debts of karma to life by experiencing some portion of the pain they have caused to life, before reembodying to take up the balancing of karma in the physical octave. Those at the lowest levels are waiting on "death row" for the time of their "second death" before the Four and Twenty Elders at the Court of the Sacred Fire. These, too, are required to experience some portion of the pain they have caused life before the end of opportunity come. **(16)** **"Mighty Cosmos' Secret Rays,"** decree 0.03 in *Prayers, Meditations and Dynamic Decrees for the Coming Revolution in Higher Consciousness,* Section I; no. 12 on *Save the World with Violet Flame! by Saint Germain 3* audiocassette; printed in 1988 *PoW,* p. 543. **(17)** **We shall see him as he is.** I John 3:2.

Save the World with Violet Flame!
3 and 4
by Saint Germain

December 24, 1988

Beloved Keepers of the Flame of My Heart,

On this eve of the celebration of the birth of our Lord, sent to earth by the Father to reignite the divine spark in his own, my <u>meditation</u> is <u>upon the sacred mystery of the Holy Spirit and His gifts and graces to us.</u> And my heart goes out to you each one through the Christmas Rose, our fairest Lord Jesus who came to save us by his example--we who are treading vales of karma on this earthly sphere.

<u>Winter solstice</u> has delivered to us the sacred fire of the Central Sun. It is a burst of flame not only to quicken the mind and heart, but also <u>to consume the dregs of a twelvemonth and centuries of karma.</u> Indeed the fire of solstice is Shiva, the Separator of Light and Darkness! It is the blaze of Kali, whose sword may split the very hairs of division within our members even while she, the Divine Mother, sweeps us up in her powerful arms!

'Tis the season to be merry in the harvest of good works spiraling upward into our causal bodies. And we watch Nature receive her King as snowflakes descend to cover all that is unredeemed with the whiteness of star-fire purity. And so blessed Hope carries me to wherever you are this Christmas Eve, lighting a candle, singing hymns and offering invocations in the living Word for <u>the raising up of the children of the Light through the star of Jesus' I AM Presence</u> and causal body <u>and your</u> <u>own.</u> Truly, they are raised through that star of the entire Spirit of the Great White Brotherhood, focal point of the Oneness and the Mission that is our joy to bear together!

This is the night we also remember that seventy years ago God sent to us his son born to humble parents in the little town of Chippewa Falls, Wisconsin. They named him Mark Lyle--"Mark of the Isles"--and their surname was Prophet. And so tonight at our candlelight service we celebrate <u>the birthday of a king and the birthday of his prophet!</u> Jesus, the King of

Box A, Livingston, Montana 59047-1390 (406) 222-8300

kings, whose message Mark, the Prophet, recorded when he was embodied as Mark the gospeler, as Origen of Alexandria and as Saint Bonaventure.

Yet our understanding was not fully reawakened to the sacred mysteries of our Lord until we knew him as Mark, the Messenger of the Great White Brotherhood, in his final incarnation when he was called to found The Summit Lighthouse by the Ascended Master El Morya to restore the lost Word.

Through Mark Prophet I first heard the dictations from my Lord, Jesus. From his lips the Holy Spirit poured the sound and the vibration of the Jesus I knew as a child and 2,000 years ago. O the miracle and the wonder of it all! And then to watch the Archangels step through the veil through him! It was the power of God descended like lightning, passing through his form into the earth--and his face shone with a heavenly radiance. O what a transcendent way we have walked with Mark and with the Ascended Masters all these years of our discipleship that have brought us together in the living flame of Love.

Today millions of people follow the Teachings of the Ascended Masters delivered by Jesus Christ through Mark's Messengership. But those same millions are also touched by the violet flame because you, Keepers of the Flame, have carried the torches of Pisces and Aquarius that have been passed to us by Jesus and Saint Germain through our beloved Mark. For truly he who was the nexus for the Sacred Heart of Jesus and his resurrection flame was also the open door for Saint Germain's message to America and the world and his gift of the violet flame.

Whereas the torch of the Piscean dispensation is the Sixth Ray of ministration and service whereby we put on that Christhood Jesus demonstrated before our very eyes, the torch of the Aquarian dispensation is the Seventh Ray of freedom and transmutation whereby we realize soul liberation in the unfolding divinity of our Great God Self. The flame of Pisces, the portion of the Son, is the resurrection flame. The flame of Aquarius, the portion of the Holy Spirit, is the violet flame. As we invoke these flames through the beloved Masters whose portraits flank the Chart of the Presence at the thousands of altars we have erected throughout the world, the redemption of our souls and our planet draweth nigh.

Today, as I look out the window and see the snow everywhere on the mountains and covering the forest which surrounds me, I commune with the saints in white who attend us and my thoughts are of you, the saints on earth who keep his flame. And my heart literally burns in the presence of Jesus and his own.

Beloved Keepers of the Flame, I loved you before I knew you. And so it was love at first sight when I saw you as God revealed you to me through the Messenger Mark as he was conducting a service in the Boston Ascended Master sanctuary in 1961. I saw you then as a million daisies scattered all over the world and I knew that I must go and pluck you to bring you to the heart of Jesus. For it was meant to be that through his Sacred Heart you might discover the flame of your Holy Christ Self, the divine spark by which your soul would receive the gift of immortality. Twenty-seven years later I still see you as daisies in the field of the Lord. But now I know you each one, your faces smiling in my memory as I have known you on inner planes and in the outer. O such happiness and blessings and healings and miracles we have known together in the circle of our oneness worldwide!

There is after all only one fire that ignites us all. Are we not, then, partakers of the One, rather than the many, as we come together to offer our decrees and mantras for the deliverance of all people? Indeed we are One. For wherever we are gathered together in the resurrection flame, in the violet flame there is Jesus in our midst and Saint Germain and El Morya, Mother Mary and Kuan Yin, Kuthumi--and always our precious Lanello.

Each time a child or any one of us takes up his decree book to invoke that Light, all hearts of Keepers of the Flame are linked. We are an endless chain of 'Christmas tree lights' all aglow--for the One is the fulfillment of the many. The strengthening bonds of our Jesus' Watch, our violet flame vigils with Saint Germain, and our adoration of the will of God through the heart of El Morya have indeed increased the powerful presence of the body of Keepers of the Flame and Lightbearers of the world.

Our presence is felt in the earth this night! We have made our mark on the ethers and the molecules--upon the souls of a people, the elementals, the trees and the waters! There is something to be said, something gained for the year's striving.

And so it is for the harvest of good works and for the transmutation of those not-so-good works that I am sending you Save the World with Violet Flame! by Saint Germain cassettes 3 and 4. Yes, I do know that many of you already have your own copies but I also know that not all of you have them and that all of you can surely use another. What with the wear you give these tapes and the fast pace of your lives, you need an extra tape and a couple of extra booklets so that you can fill the cycles and the hours of your Cosmic Clock and the lines of your astrology with Seventh Ray angels, cosmic forces of the seventh age and gnomes all dressed in violet, purple, pink!

It is the request of our beloved El Morya and the Darjeeling Council to honor Saint Germain and his faithful Keepers of the Flame by sending all who are current in their dues (Keepers of the Flame on lesson 8 and beyond in good standing) each new cassette of prayers, dynamic decrees, hymns, mantras, affirmations, invocations and ballads as they are released!

And so in this propitious hour when the sands in the hourglass for 1988 run out and we are called to transmute the records of the planetary karma of this decade each day throughout 1989, I am placing in your hands the most powerful releases of the violet flame that I know of recorded in an outer retreat of the Great White Brotherhood still accessible to all people on earth. These are for your use as you channel the Light of the Aquarian dispensation from your I AM Presence and your Holy Christ Self through your chakras to bless and heal! and bless and heal! and bless and heal! all life on earth.

I bear you witness that you who have diligently worked with our violet flame cassettes this year bear the very notice-able sign in your auras and electromagnetic fields of the Seventh Ray and dispensation of Aquarius. There is a violet glow around your heart chakras and a softening of karmic lines on your finer bodies and faces. Whereas before you did not, now you appear as a blip on the screen of the planetary aura regis-tering as a purple ovoid pulsating. This is the true meaning of holding the balance for world karma.

Keepers of the Flame, you have come of age! I have seen your stars not only in the East but all over the world as you have raised up the star of Pisces in Jesus' name (through the weekly "Watch With Me") and the star of Aquarius in Saint Germain's name. May you be encouraged by your efforts. May you know that you are making true progress on the Path toward the victory of your goal: the ascension in the Light. And may you not weary in this well-doing of freely letting the light of the violet flame flow through you (as well as the resurrection flame from Jesus' heart) as your offering upon the altar of God on behalf of his people.

As I offer prayers for those who pass from the screen of life each week, whether they are of our Community or of the world body, I see so clearly how the persistent, relentless use of the violet flame has saved any number of souls from the necessity of tarrying in the astral plane (purgatory or worse) to balance their karma made at that vibratory level while on earth. Those who have not received this gift of Saint Germain's "miracle pouch" or those who have it and do not "hurl it" into the earth and into their electronic belts are the very ones who have no wind in their sails to buoy them up into etheric octaves and the retreats of the Great White Brotherhood and the Holy City when the hour of transition comes.

As some of you have been serving the cause of the Great White Brotherhood for decades in this and previous lifetimes, you are nearing by percentages the balancing of that necessary 51 percent of your karma which will enable you to make your ascension upon your soul's transition from earth's schoolroom. When the violet flame is offered in love and combined with daily service to life and a reaching out to help all whom the Lord sends to you, that violet flame can make the difference for many--and it does make the difference--whether they shall return via reincarnation to balance their karma or whether they shall attain their soul's immortality at the conclusion of this life.

And this is the very purpose for which Saint Germain has sent his violet flame and his purple fiery heart to us in this century: that we might be the instruments of bringing all cycles of both personal and planetary karma to their fulfillment that the golden age might come and the world experience a New Day of freedom and enlightenment and peace.

Never has the world needed the violet flame more and never has the world needed you more as its effective instrument. For it is through the science of the spoken Word which is demonstrated on all of our decree and song tapes that the spiritual flame becomes physical in the world. It must be anchored through people and it must be invoked in full voice and in full joy with our chakras engaged, for only through the threefold flame of the heart can the flames of the seven rays burning on heavenly altars be sustained on earth.

This is what it means to be a Keeper of the Flame of Life, and the Flame that is yours to keep and balance and expand is the threefold flame within your heart, Christ's gift to us at Christmas and every day of the year as we elect to be the watchmen in the Dark Night of the Kali Yuga (Isa. 21:6; 62:6; Jer. 31:6; Ezek. 3:17; 33:7) keeping the watch with the Universal Christ each Wednesday at our vigil with Jesus--and hourly with Saint Germain.

There is one thing I know and this I will tell you, that if you make it your business and your resolution each day for the rest of your life to give forty-five minutes of adoration to the Christ of the violet flame through these decrees and songs, you can know joy and happiness all the days of your life and at the conclusion a Victory unparalleled, an Opportunity, a Mercy and, if all other karmic things in your life are tidied up, entrée into the Ascension Temple at Luxor. There you may be shown what requirements remain, if indeed there be any which remain, for you to be a candidate for the ascension or for some final and triumphant service yet to be rendered on earth or in heaven before that hour.

There is no question in my mind that <u>the greatest benefit from our year's worth of offering the violet flame to Saint Germain has been that which has accrued to the Keepers of the Flame themselves.</u> For this El Morya has told me and truly it is evident. To see what you have become in one year, it is simply stunning to imagine what you will be in stature and self-mastery, in co-measurement with the octaves of Light if you should fulfill this lifelong calling of tending the fires of the violet flame!

<u>Why, earth herself could be rejoined with the violet planet of Omri-Tas through a figure-eight flow</u> (yet to be granted by the Karmic Board) if Keepers of the Flame on earth were to finally achieve a momentum of violet flame sufficient for the earth to be cosmically juxtaposed with that violet planet. Do you know that 144,000 priests of the sacred fire together with the evolutions of that planet sustain such a momentum of violet flame that their planet is manifesting a golden age in the seventh dispensation of Aquarius right now, right while we're facing a planetary karmic retribution of cataclysmic proportions? And do you know that <u>we're facing what we face today because millions of Lightbearers of earth have not yet caught the spark of violet flame freedom and are not yet invoking that flame daily in dynamic decrees as you are?</u>

I can assure you that the evolutions of the violet planet rejoice to see Terra taking on that violet hue and yourselves outpicturing more and more of the grace, the ease, the freedom and the mastery which their ray imparts. And <u>the more we give the violet flame, the more the Lightbearers of the world are cut free,</u> literally drawn by the Great Central Sun Magnet of our oneness into the Seventh Ray vibration to follow the violet ribbons that go forth from our hearts to theirs forming pathways of light whereby they too might know the wonder and the miracle of our beloved Saint Germain.

And so, among the desires of my heart to be cherished in this moment is <u>the desire to give myself, and that we all might give ourselves, as a sapphire chalice to beloved El Morya even as he gave himself</u> on February 13 in San Francisco to be a sapphire chalice to the chelas of the will of God (see Pearls of Wisdom, vol. 31, no. 19, May 8, 1988, "A Sapphire Chalice"). El Morya told us that he desired to give of himself to demonstrate to us "the way of the Diamond Heart of God's will."

The Master said that in so doing "I give myself to be filled by my chelas with the wine, the purple wine of the rich grape of the harvest." He said: "Let it be, then, an intense wine of the Spirit that comes forth by your call to the violet flame. Let the chalice of my being, with you, be the wine-bearer of Aquarius, beloved, for something must be done. Something is needed, beloved! Therefore, I propose in my heart to give myself, for what else can one give?"

El Morya expressed his desire to be a chalice--and I express my desire to you today that each one of us might be for him a chalice--of violet flame for Saint Germain. He gave to us a vision of himself overflowing "with the wine that you distill by your meditations in the white light of the Holy Spirit" and "such intensity of the violet flame as to provide our beloved Saint Germain with an extraordinary portion, even a reservoir of such violet flame as to increase transmutation and therefore provide that measure of safety that is not now present in the earth."

"Let there be a turning of the tide," he said, "for God is able and God in you is able and I have seen what miracles my chelas have wrought in recent years and centuries. Therefore, it is never too late to begin.

"Thus, I AM become a chalice walking--a chalice running when you run! I come, beloved, in the full measure of my heart's devotion to my brother Saint Germain, your own beloved Master whose life, I tell you, is given for you. Therefore, let the full measure of this chalice be given daily, for each day I shall take that which you have deposited in this chalice and place it in the violet flame reservoir of light on the etheric plane. Therefore, beloved, fill and let it be emptied--fill it to overflowing.

"Thus, beloved, this my walk with Saint Germain may prove to be that stitch in time of Hercules and Amazonia. It may prove to be such a boon to chelas that they will at last transcend these planetary karmic cycles that have produced a density within them that is not to my liking.

"Therefore, pierce! pierce! pierce! O blue-flame sapphire light! Blue-lightning angels and devas of the Diamond Heart, come forth, then! For there must be a piercing of this density, that this overflowing wine of violet flame, Holy Spirit, may pour through the cracks and the fissures in the earth and yet give to elemental life the support so necessary. . . .

"O be quickened, O be quickened, beloved! For the victory is nigh. The angels stand guard. But a victory whose cup is not quaffed is not a victory--and there are not in-betweens. Blessed hearts, it is a choice for victory or utter defeat and self-humiliation.

"Let the light ascend and the soul will follow suit. Let the soul ascend and millions will follow. Have we not earned our blue-flame ribbons of light? Have we not seen and known the inspiration of millions because we have dared to ascend the mount Horeb and to know God face to face?

"Let the uncommon Light be kept by the uncommon souls who do dare to be different."

In recently preparing for you beloved El Morya's 8-8-88 dictation on the Light and the Beautiful published in the Pearls I took note that he referred to his February 13 announcement. He said, "Beloved, I did give myself to receive the violet flame and to give the violet flame. If you will remember that I determined to be that cup of violet flame, that reservoir of light, [then] remember me also, beloved, for I am the one that does repeatedly come to defend you. And you have become so accustomed to my intercession, O blessed hearts, that I am concerned that when the hour come and I am not allowed to give it that you will suddenly sense and say to yourself, 'Where is Morya? Why does this battle endure?'"

In retrospect one can understand El Morya's desire for us to so mount the momentum of violet flame in our souls and our auras that we would be prepared for the possibility of just such an announcement that the Master did finally have to make--that the hour had come that did mark for him "the termination of new opportunity" whereby he could offer "no new dispensation" for "the chelas of the will of God." Morya did refer to this period of no new dispensation to him from the Lords of Karma whereby he might intercede on behalf of his chelas in their karmic straits as his "being benched."

I am certain that he knew on February 13 that unless an extraordinary momentum of violet flame were to be invoked and the leaders of the nations respond to the call and the prophecies of Saint Germain, such a curtailment could indeed come upon him as Chief of the Darjeeling Council of the Great White Brotherhood, for he has indeed sponsored the governments and the economies of the nations and they have indeed misappropriated the energy allotment of his causal body.

And it is this misappropriation--a planetary debt which fell due August 8, 1988--that now becomes and is the Master's karma: a grievous burden which we his chelas so desire to help him bear. For it is he, the Beloved Darjeeling Master, who has borne the cross of _our_ karma for centuries. Without him many of us would have surely perished.

And therefore for the karma of the world's neglect of the message and teachings of the Ascended Masters as well as for the misuses of prior dispensations (or the failure to ratify them) on the part of some chelas, our dear Morya must have anticipated that the hour could come when we would need him and need him desperately and he might not be allowed to give the assistance to which we have become so easily accustomed.

On August 8 El Morya did also remind us that there is one exception which people sometimes make for themselves for which the violet flame by cosmic law cannot compensate. The Master explained: "If you are outside of the Law, whether human or divine, you must quickly confess your sins to the appropriate persons, make rectitude, correct such states and come into alignment. For the sin not confessed, the illegal posture not acknowledged, though none may know about it, does prevent the karma from descending and therefore [does prevent] the expiation of that karma--even if you give the violet flame decrees daily."

Thus it has been for us a period of soul-searching and introspection, of going deep and bringing to the Flame of the ark of the covenant that burns upon our altar those sins that must go beforehand into the Flame (see I Tim. 5:24, "Some men's sins are open beforehand, going before to judgment; and some men they follow after") so that we might be the full expression of our Holy Christ Self here on earth even while we yet are treading those vales of planetary karma.

The plight of our beloved El Morya in this very moment is the most compelling reason I know of--if there were no other-- why we must offer our hearts as chalices for the violet flame at the level of the forty-five minutes daily (one side of a cassette) to "unbench" our beloved Master. Referring to El Morya as "the eye of the needle that must be threaded by the thread of light from your heart," beloved Hercules said on October 10:

"Morya, then, is the keystone in the arch of The Summit Lighthouse. By his giving of his diamond and his mantle and his causal body to the founding of this activity in 1958, this blessed one did literally open the door through the Messengers and all who came after them to all other Ascended Masters and hierarchs who have sponsored this activity and all the Lightbearers who have been drawn to it.

"Thus, beloved, it is not simply the loss of the intercession of a single hierarch most beloved [that you suffer from the

Karmic Board's 'no-new-dispensation-policy' for Morya in regard to his chelas] but it is a compromise [of the planetary service as well] of the very one who is responsible for the establishment of this activity.

"You realize that El Morya stepped forward to sponsor these Messengers because Saint Germain himself had been denied new sponsorship by the Lords of Karma for having [had] so many [students and others] misuse the light of the violet flame and the dispensations that he had [been] given for the United States and Europe and to various individuals around the world.

"And so you see, beloved, there have been sponsoring Masters in these hundred years and more who have stepped forward [to assist certain ones or the planetary evolution] and then again you have not heard so often of them, thus signifying that they were able to accomplish only as much as those who would receive them would give unto them, would take the proffered gift, would multiply it, and would fulfill the law of the First Ray concerning the path of chelaship.

"Thus, beloved, it is our concern that all have a center-poise of realism--realism as to the absolute God-Reality that is unlimited potential for yourself to realize the Good, the God, and His Will and realism regarding the human consciousness that oftentimes will indulge itself. . . .

"Thus, envision the beloved El Morya, the right hand extended to your own, the left hand holding firmly the hand of [your] Holy Christ Self--and the pure will of God, and the Diamond Heart of that will within his own heart chakra, being the electrode and the nexus [sustaining the tie to your Holy Christ Self] until the thread from your heart should increase and thereby [allow you] to sustain that tie midst the turbulent astral seas and the moments when the sudden karmic descent may disrupt [your] individual communion [with your Real Self].

"'Master, save us or we perish!' Such was the cry of the disciples of Christ Jesus. 'Master, save us or we perish!' And so it is the cry of some who are awake who know that it is the first order of this hour and every hour to seek once again the sponsoring [by the Lords of Karma] of your Lord Morya El; for it is even by his sponsorship that I, Hercules, could also sponsor you.

"Blessed ones, this Messenger has desired to see Morya restored by the hour of the Feast of the Epiphany, when the three wise men did visit the Christ Child. Morya being somewhat more realistic and understandably a bit pessimistic, as anyone would be sharing his plight, has requested that the students might move toward his restoration to full opportunity by August 8 next.

"Blessed hearts, Morya gives the date. I tell you the reason. It is because it is the very latest hour when your beloved Master may move and move again to assist you when you will require his assistance as you have never required it before. Thus, beloved, you may take the desire of the Messenger and work toward that date early in the new year and see what comes of your efforts, but I tell you, it will take [a] tremendous effort [to make it happen]."

Therefore in the name El Morya I implore you, stalwart Keepers of the Flame, to keep the violet flame and the violet flame chalice for him as he has made himself a sapphire "chalice walking--a chalice running when you run" for beloved Saint Germain.

Let us determine that we shall not fail in the heart of beloved Mother Mary and Kuan Yin to provide the necessary personal and planetary transmutation whereby El Morya can intercede with unlimited dispensation from the Father of Lights, Sanat Kumara, on behalf of all Lightbearers of the world. For we so need him--more than we know--in this hour and in the hour when our need for him will be paramount by August 8, 1989.

As Saint Germain's gratitude is boundless for your offering of "those violet flames" (see Pearls of Wisdom, vol. 31, no. 72, Saint Germain's FREEDOM 1988 Fourth of July dictation), so my gratitude for you and your service to the Light on earth is registered in the heart of Alpha and Omega this day. May we think of each other in the fondness with which our dear El Morya holds us as we pour forth our gratitude to him, to Saint Germain, to Lanello, by joyously offering the violet flame each day throughout the coming year. And may we know that the strength of our Union is in the violet flame that erases the boundaries of time and space.

My forty-five minutes I promise you--do you promise me yours? Yes, let our gratitude for these our beloved Ascended Masters be the release to the Lightbearers of the whole world of that sacred fire of Christ's rebirth in our hearts. For it is these saints in white who have unveiled to us the true and living Saviour, the Ascended Master Jesus Christ, and his Blessed Mother Mary. Through the Sacred Heart of Jesus and the Immaculate Heart of Mary in which we trust, may we know God face to face.

On this Holy Night I send you all my love for the new year and may you tick off the years from '89 on with Victory! Victory! Victory! Victory! Victory! in the violet flame until the earth is swallowed up in violet flame and Death and Hell are cast into the lake of sacred fire, and until an earth transcendent is seen transformed in octaves of Light. <u>This Victory in the Seventh Ray dispensation of Aquarius will happen because Keepers of the Flame shall have chosen by free will, by the enlightenment of the Holy Spirit, by oneness with the beloved I AM Presence and Holy Christ Self to keep that flame blazing come what may.</u>

I love you with an everlasting Love,
that loved us before we loved one another,

Mother

P.S. Be sure to send for your precious copies of the <u>Only Mark 15</u> and <u>16</u> albums: four 90-minute cassettes per album. Number 15 contains dictations from Saint Germain, the Goddess of Liberty, Zarathustra, the Great Divine Director, Casimir Poseidon, Hercules, Archangel Gabriel, God Harmony, El Morya, Kuthumi, Chananda and Rose of Light delivered July 4, 1969–October 5, 1969. Number 16 contains dictations from Hercules, Godfre, the Great Divine Director, Archangel Gabriel, Listening Angel, Cuzco, Nada Rayborn, Archangel Zadkiel, El Morya, Jesus, Lord Lanto, Archangel Michael, Pallas Athena and Lord Maitreya delivered February 9, 1969–July 4, 1969, $26.00 per album. We are also pleased to announce the release of two new sets of <u>Discourses on Cosmic Law</u> by Mark L. Prophet (without album covers to save time). Be sure to get your copies of <u>Discourses 14,</u> which includes "How to Develop the Christ Consciousness," "Transition," "I AM the Way--the Mystery of Being" and "The Triumphant Order," and <u>Discourses 15,</u> including "The Role of the Spiritual Teacher," "The Role of the Spiritual Order in Life" and "An Anthology of the Great White Brotherhood," $12.95 each.

Special offer to Keepers of the Flame who keep current in their dues: Get a 25 percent discount when you buy all four albums. That means you'll get the two <u>Only Mark</u> albums for only $19.95 each and the two <u>Discourses</u> albums for only $9.95 each. Your price for all four is $59.80--a savings of $18.10!

Appendix

Letters and Articles on the
Montana Department of Health and Environmental Sciences'
Environmental Impact Statement
on Church Universal and Triumphant

Royal Teton Ranch

Box A, Corwin Springs, Montana 59021   406/848-7381

November 18, 1987

Dear Friends,

Since September 1981 we have been working hard to establish our self-sufficient community in the making here at the Royal Teton Ranch. Located just north of Yellowstone National Park and stretching all the way to the town of Livingston over forty miles away, the Inner Retreat has grown to include some 33,000 acres of South Central Montana's beautiful Paradise Valley.

Today the land is being well cared for and used successfully for many of the traditional activities carried on here since pioneer days. We raise sheep, cattle, turkeys and chickens. We have a 90-acre produce farm and dairy. We grow wheat, barley, oats, corn, carrots, potatoes and other grains and root crops. Our mountains, valleys, streams and forests are not being over-hunted, over-fished, over-farmed, over-grazed or logged out. We've striven both to emulate and improve upon the example of those who've lived here before us.

We've also gone about the process of doing exactly what we came here to do and what many others have only dreamed of accomplishing: to establish a self-sufficient religious retreat and community as an outpost of the Brotherhood and to serve as a living example of our spiritual principles and way of life. And despite apprehension by some in the local area, things have gone well here and we've learned to respect and get along with our new neighbors while working to earn their respect.

Over the 4th of July holiday last year we announced the news of the sale of Camelot--our California base of operations for eight years--and our decision to re-establish the Church's headquarters at the Inner Retreat in Montana. Mother and I worked with our Engineering and Planning Department all summer and fall to evaluate alternatives, choose the ideal site along the beautiful Yellowstone River for our new campus community, and design the infrastructure and buildings to be placed there. Because Camelot had to be completely vacated by the end of 1986, plans for water and sewer systems were quickly submitted to the State Water Quality Bureau, a number of modular buildings were purchased for housing, classrooms, offices, cafeteria, etc., and tentative arrangements were made with a contractor to start construction on our new Chapel of the Holy Grail.

Then in November 1986, at the insistence of several local environmental groups and other residents, the State Water Quality Bureau decided that an Environmental Impact Statement (EIS) should be prepared to address questions and concerns being expressed over the scope and extent of our project before making a final decision on our permit applications for water and sewer systems. While it meant a delay in starting construction on our new headquarters, we agreed at that time to cooperate fully with this comprehensive study and to work to mitigate any possible impacts to the environment. In the meantime, Church departments have been functioning out of temporary quarters and the re-opening of Summit University has been delayed for over a year.

The EIS being conducted by professionals in the Montana Department of Health and Environmental Sciences is all encompassing and will involve an examination of all possible impacts to the physical and human environment--including such things as water quality, air quality, wildlife, fisheries, historical and archeological sites, geology, soils, vegetation, roads, utilities, county services, local tax base, schools, social values, aesthetics, Yellowstone geothermal resources and many others. Not only has this study taken time, but it has also cost us a substantial amount of money. So far, we've spent the following approximate amounts on expert consultants chosen with the approval of the state to gather information for parts of the EIS:

Wildlife Study	–	$ 3,000
Fisheries Study	–	3,000
Vegetation Study	–	3,000
Cultural Resource Survey	–	12,000

LaDuke Hot Spring Well Study	–	5,000
Road Engineering Report	–	1,500
Soil Tests, Engineering Reports	–	3,500
		$31,000

All of this is in addition to the extensive research and design work accomplished by our own engineering staff on water systems, sewage treatment systems, utilities, roads, architectural and building plans submitted to the state, as well as the numerous state and federal agencies with expertise in particular disciplines that have provided input for the report.

The Draft EIS is now almost finished and is scheduled for release next month. Once it is, a period of 30–45 days will be allowed for public comment and one or two additional public meetings. This input will be taken into account by the state in issuing the Final EIS together with a decision on our permit applications.

However, it appears that some of the same people who last year were urging the state to conduct an EIS are now gearing up to challenge the results when they are released in the coming month (see copies of enclosed articles). In a fund raising letter recently sent out by the "Upper Yellowstone Defense Fund" (copy enclosed), this group claimed that "The ecosystem of Yellowstone National Park. . .is being threatened" and that "the culprit in all this is a wealthy and aggressive group from California known as the Church Universal and Triumphant."

The letter uses such scare tactics as warning of the destruction of wildlife and habitats, impacts to Yellowstone's geothermal features, and threats to the aesthetics and water quality of the Yellowstone River--but the group has never offered any facts or evidence to show that these fears are warranted. All of these subjects are to be covered by the EIS and have been carefully considered by us in designing our facilities--but this group doesn't seem satisfied to wait for the results. Funds are already being raised by them to cover anticipated legal expenses to challenge the EIS and to help create national publicity.

Even worse, the "Defense Fund" is exaggerating and misrepresenting the facts with claims that we have proceeded with development work without permits (when we haven't) and that the Church's headquarters is designed for "several thousand students" (rather than the 596 staff and students it is actually designed for). Such misrepresentations and scare tactics have recently been addressed by me and repeated by members of the Defense Fund in several editorial letters published in the newspaper (copies enclosed).

I have written to you on this occasion to apprise you of these developments and to request your assistance in meeting the challenge. This group of supposedly concerned citizens apparently views the EIS as nothing more than a stall tactic and is already preparing for further appeals and legal action before they have even seen the results.

We need your support in decrees and prayers to meet the spiritual challenge, and financially to establish our own defense fund--The Inner Retreat Defense Fund--to protect and sustain our right to be doing what we are doing. Private property rights are under assault all across America, and it is important that we establish our rights now to the reasonable use of our land free from the harassment of groups such as these.

We didn't come here to spoil the environment or to attempt to change the character of this area. On the contrary, we came because we cherish the beauty and quality of nature in this land. The very elements which make it ideal for our use are those which this group says we are about to defile. The truth is, we want the land to remain the way it is just as much as our neighbors do. In fact, keeping the Inner Retreat wild and pristine is essential to our long-term purpose here. Yellowstone Park with all of its natural wonders--wildlife, geysers, rivers and forests--should remain intact and unimpaired for future generations. This can and will be done in harmony with our religious community and wise use of the land.

Your financial support will be used to meet this challenge, counter misinformation put out by groups like the "Defense Fund," and pay the expenses related to the preparation of the EIS and ongoing legal and professional assistance. Remember, each time we collectively take a stand to defend our freedom and liberty wherever it is being assaulted, we are taking that stand for every American citizen who may later come under the same kind of attack. The results of our fight--and our victory--can set important precedents for the future.

Please act now to defend our right to be who and what we are--to live free in conscience, mind and body, and to enjoy life, liberty and the pursuit of happiness on this beautiful retreat which God gave to all of us through the loving and sacrificial gifts of Keepers of the Flame and friends of Saint Germain. Together we have forged and won it, united we shall stand to preserve and defend it!

Sincerely,

Edward L. Francis
Vice President and Business Manager

Enclosures

P.S. Mother and I look forward to being with you to celebrate Thanksgiving in our nation's capital, and we hope you will make every possible effort to get there and keep a Prayer Vigil for America and our Church with Beloved Saint Germain.

When we were in Washington, D.C. for my Senate Subcommittee testimony on July 14, 1987, Beloved Godfre gave a dictation at the Teaching Center in which he said: "Blessed ones, while there is hope we dare not desert this place [our nation's capital]. Let it be filled, then, with Lightbearers. And let Keepers of the Flame hear my call. For Saint Germain and I with El Morya would see you gather here once more this fall. Therefore, let the Keepers of the Flame be summoned. And let it be such an outpouring of light that the evidence is forthcoming in physical manifestation by the year's end that there is indeed a turning of the tide.... Let all Keepers of the Flame gather in this city when and where the arrangements can be made. And make haste that it be before the end of this year. For thereto have I sent my Messenger to be in this city and you, also, bearing the light from the Heart of the Inner Retreat."

See you there!

CUT claims Park County watchdog group using 'scare tactics'

By MIKE MALES
Chronicle Staff Writer

About 30 Gardiner and Paradise Valley residents have formed the Upper Yellowstone Defense Fund to oppose what they see as threats to the area caused by the Church Universal and Triumphant's extensive developments.

CUT Vice President Edward Francis said this week that the group is using "scare tactics" and "blatantly untrue statements" regarding church plans.

The group started meeting last winter out of concern about the environmental effects of CUT's plans to build housing, commercial plants, schools and other facilities as it moves its church headquarters from California to Park County, Defense Fund spokeswoman Julia Page of Gardiner said Wednesday.

Page, who operates the Yellowstone Raft Co. in Gardiner, said in a recent fund-raising letter that CUT "is a wealthy and aggressive group" whose developments threaten wildlife habitat, Yellowstone National Park thermal features and the Yellowstone River.

The Defense Fund is a loosely organized group of "local citizens mostly from the Gardiner-Paradise Valley area who are working to preserve the environment and natural values which make this area so special," the letter said.

The Defense Fund will use any money raised for legal assistance to participate in the environmental review of CUT developments now being performed by the state Department of Health and Environmental Sciences and to see that state laws governing development are enforced and strengthened, the letter said.

"What we do will depend on what shows up in the EIS (environmental impact statement)," Page said. "We want to be ready when it comes out."

The draft EIS on the church's proposed developments should be ready for public distribution by December, Tom Ellerhoff, technical writer for the state DHES, said Wednesday.

"I think this group is misleading people with its fund-raising device," Francis said Thursday of the Defense Fund's letter.

Francis said a statement in the letter that the church is building housing for up to 600 staff members and a university which could accommodate several thousand students each semester was "a gross misstatement of fact."

Francis said the church is building housing for a total of 596 people, including all staff, students, family members and 200 people who are already living on church-owned property.

"A lot of what they say is just scare tactics," Francis said. "All of our planned development will take place on just 1 percent of our property.

"These are the same people who convinced the state to do an EIS on our developments, and we agreed to accept the results and make any changes necessary," Francis said.

"What I fear with this group is that the EIS was merely a stalling tactic. They're saying now that they're raising money to challenge the EIS, and the EIS results aren't even out yet."

CUT owns about 30,000 acres in southern Park County and has 400-500 staff members in the area, Francis has said.

livingston
enterprise

Livingston, Mont., Monday, October 26, 1987

Group opposed to CUT's plans

By AL KNAUBER
Enterprise Staff Writer

Gardiner area residents have banded together in the newly formed Upper Yellowstone Defense Fund to challenge planned land development by the Church Universal and Triumphant.

Calling CUT "a wealthy and aggressive group from California," Gardiner resident Julia Page said Monday that the Defense Fund is asking for donations to cover anticipated legal expenses and to help create national publicity on CUT's proposed developments along the upper Yellowstone River valley.

She explained that any challenges to the state Water Quality Bureau's Enviromental Impact Statement on CUT's activities would require money for legal assistance.

The EIS, scheduled for release in mid November, will address the overall impact to the area from CUT's planned developments.

"That is where we would anticipate burning up a lot of money," she said of possible legal challenges to the EIS.

"My concern is purely land use," she said.

CUT's developments for the area are called a threat to the aesthetics and water quality of the region, in the solicitation for funds which was sent to numerous area residents.

Ms. Page, who said she has operated a summer business in Gardiner for seven years, said the Defense Fund is "a loose association of people who have talked together" last winter and this summer. The group has about 30 members, she said.

The solicitation letter notes that Defense Fund members are "working to support and prod state and local officials to enforce that laws do exist regarding these (CUT) developments.

"Also, we must work to strengthen these laws to prevent developers such as (CUT) from circumventing their intent," she said.

Ms. Page said the Defense Fund's request for financial assistance was sent out last week to Livingston and Gardiner residents as well as other out-of-state people.

"We are trying now to get ready to respond when the EIS comes out," she said.

The letter asking for donations states that of the 30,000 acres which CUT owns, 11,000 of those acres are contained in the former Malcolm Forbes Ranch, which adjoins Yellowstone National Park.

Because the former Forbes Ranch shares a nine mile border with YNP, she is concerned what impact any developments on the ranch would have on the ranch's grizzly bear habitat and winter range for bighorn sheep, antelope and elk which migrate from YNP.

Ms. Page claimed that both YNP's wildlife and geothermal features are threatened by CUT.

CUT recently drilled a well to tap into LaDuke Hot Springs, which may be linked to the geothermal features in Yellowstone Park.

While the well has been capped, Ms. Page stated that CUT hoped to use the hot water for a planned university and housing complex.

"My concern is what is being done here will have a huge impact on this valley.," she said.

"We are responding to very rapid growth and growth that no one has had a say in."

Growth in Park County goes largely unchecked as the county does not have zoning regulations to control construction.

She said people who are upset by CUT's developments have not had an organization to which they could bring their concerns.

The Defense Fund will "give people some way to focus their energies," Ms. Page said.

letters

Scare tactics

Editor:

Recent newspaper articles and radio reports have detailed the efforts of a group calling itself the "Upper Yellowstone Defense Fund" to raise money for publicity and legal assistance to oppose the efforts of Church Universal and Triumphant to establish its religious community, church and school near Corwin Springs. I believe that statements made by the Defense Fund's representative Julia Page deserve a response.

First of all, it is undisputed that this group has just as much a right to exist and become involved in the state permitting process as anyone else. There is no question on that.

But just as a few outspoken members of the group have repeatedly stressed that the Church must be honest and accurate in presenting details, answering questions and following state environmental guidelines in the establishment of its religious community, the same is rightfully to be expected of them.

Unfortunately, recent actions by the Defense Fund have created a serious question as to whether they are willing to practice what they have been preaching.

For example, the fund-raising letter recently sent out by Julia Page for the Defense Fund contains several gross misstatements of the facts of the Church's proposed project, including the following:

— The letter says the Church proposes to erect housing for up to 600 staff plus a university which could accommodate "several thousand students each semester." That just isn't true by any stretch of the imagination. Our plans in fact propose to accommodate a total of 596 people including students, staff and their famillies, and also including all the pre-existing facilities on the ranch. The actual added capacity is only about 320 people.

—The letter also contends that the Church is moving forward with construction in violation of an agreement with the state. That isn't any more true now than it was last spring when they made the same claim and were proven wrong. It also ignores the fact that we have continued to work to complete projects for which permits were received several years ago.

— This is a group which uses such scare tactics to raise money as warning that "the ecosystem of Yellowstone Park is being threatened" and implying that all sorts of wildlife and habitats will be destroyed by the Church, but fails to ever mention that all of the planned development (including pre-existing facilities) will use less than one percent of the land owned by the Church in the Corwin Springs area alone — with the rest planned to remain in agricultural use, wildlife habitat and other open space. Is a one percent use really so unreasonable, and couldn't a lot of worse things have happened to this property in the hands of a more conventional developer?

These kinds of distortions are inappropriate in a process that is supposed to be ascertaining facts and scientific data in an unbiased manner to determine the real, not imagined, environmental impacts of a project and hopefully to help point out better ways of doing things.

Members of the Upper Yellowstone Defence Fund are the same folks who last year insisted that an Environmental Impact Statement should be prepared by the state in examining the Church's plans. Though it cost us a great deal in time and money, we agreed to submit to that examination and to abide by the results reached by the state.

We've also agreed to be flexible in altering our plans to mitigate possible impacts that are pointed out by the study. That's what the purpose of an EIS is all about.

But before the results are even out, some of the same ones who wanted the EIS to begin with are already engaged in criticizing the state's conduct of the study — and are now raising money avowedly to legally challenge the EIS when it does come out.

That's not only putting the cart before the horse, but it tends to show that — at least for some — the EIS may have been viewed as a stall tactic to begin with.

To put things in perspective, we want to make it clear that we don't think that most people who are concerned about the effects of the Church's community in Park County, or who may even oppose it outright, fall into the above category. There are lots of legitimate concerns and issues to be addressed and clarified, and the EIS being prepared under the provisions of the Montana Environmental Policy Act has turned out to be the best way to exa-mine them in detail for all the public to see and comment on.

It may turn out that impacts will be identified which need to be mitigated, and that some plans will need to be modified or improved. If so, we've indicated we will accept the results and make every effort to satisfy the concerns expressed.

The question is, will the Upper Yellowstone Defense Fund accept the results of the study they insisted on having? Or is an EIS for them only a means to an end, with the inevitable appeals, legal action and other obstruction tactics to follow?

Only time will tell. But in the meantime, it appears people are possibly being misled as to the true motives of this group.

Edward L. Francis
Royal Teton Ranch
Corwin Springs MT

LIVINGSTON **ENTERPRISE**, Wednesday, November 4, 1987

letters

No attack

Editor:

The letter I received from the Upper Yellowstone Defense Fund soliciting assistance hardly qualifies as a "vicious attack." In fact, John Turnquist seems not to have read the letter as nowhere in it is Old Faithful mentioned. His question about shouts,of "Fire!" is a little garbled but we don't have to look far to find smoke — it's in Ed Francis's letter on the same subject.

How close is 600 to 596? That's Ed's own number in his own letter. When folks raised questions last spring about the ongoing construction the answer wasn't that nothing had happened, but that no technical violation of the law had occured. The physical facts are standing there on the ground. Ed and his organization have freely waved thir lawyer in people's faces for some time so he shouldn't be so defensive, or surprised, when he receives the same treatment.

I am sure that we are all relieved to hear that CUT intends to live with the EIS results, whatever they may be. I don't know what conclusions the EIS will draw but I am sure glad that soembody is raising money to examine those conclusions carefully. I won't promise to accept, sight unseen, the contents of an incomplete document.

I was at the front urging that an EIS be prepared because it was clear that the original proposal had more holes in it than a swiss cheese, a conclusion born out by the numerous changes that Ed points to with pride. Mr. Francis' letter just sounds like a repeat of that old line, "Trust me!"

Richard C. Parks
Box 196
Gardiner

letters

Not a bad idea

Editor:

In regards to Ed Francis's letter of Oct. 30, I agree that the EIS should be the public forum for debate. We who are involved with the Upper Yellowstone Defense Fund didn't choose to use our recent letter as a public forum — that was Mr. Francis's move. Which isn't a bad idea anyway.

CUT is better organized and funded than any prior threat to this unique area. We feel that we need to modify that balance of power; hence our letter.

Mr. Francis questions our figures on occupancy of the ranch. However, the application for permit for kitchen facilities at the Spring Creek site is for 3,000 meals per day. That, in addition to facilities at the Ranch Kitchen, the old ranch headquarters, and the Trestle Ranch constitutes expectation of several thousand, wouldn't you agree?

In closing, let me quote Mr. Francis. "Only time will tell. But in the meantime, it appears people are possibly being misled as to the true motives of this group."

Linda Collins
Box 201
Gardiner, Mont.

Doesn't add up

Editor:

Richard Parks' arithmetic and his memory as displayed in his twice-published letter have left me a little bit confused. Let's see, 600 is pretty close to 596 — the total number of staff and students as stated in the plans for our headquarters and other facilities at the Royal Teton Ranch.

But, as if he didn't notice, 600 isn't the number at issue from the Upper Yellowstone Defense Fund's letter. According to the fund-raising letter signed and sent all over the country by Julia Page, she incorrectly claimed the plans to be for "600 staff" plus "several thousand students." By my calculation, those two figures add up to at least 2,600 people — and that's a long way from 596. By a factor of over four times in fact.

Richard better brush up on his arithmetic.

This only helps point out the fact of the rest of the exaggerated claims and dire scenarios painted up by this group in the past. If they can't even keep track of the most basic numbers involved in a project, how can they ever be relied upon to give out accurate information on what the true impacts might be? Another reason why professionals ought to be the ones doing the EIS.

With this kind of bookkeeping, one is only left to ponder whether they'll be able to keep accurate account of any money that might be given to them for carrying on their crusade.

Edward L. Francis
Royal Teton Ranch
Corwin Springs, Mont.

letters

There you go!

Editor:

The effort by Linda Collins to justify the Upper Yellowstone Defense Fund's propaganda line of "several thousand" people at the Royal Teton Ranch reminds me of the Reagan-Carter debate of some years ago. "There you go again!"

While I don't doubt Linda's sincerity and honest belief in her conclusions, they are based upon a superficial examination of the facts. Most likely, she is going on what someone else has told her they saw in an application.

The information she is referring to is not an "application for permit for kitchen facilities" at all, but is in fact included in Engineer's Reports submitted to DHES covering public water and sewer systems at the church's planned headquarters. Also included with these documents is a detailed statement of existing and planned development of all our property along the Yellowstone River near Corwin Springs. That includes the other facilities referred to by her together with the numbers of people that can be accommodated at each.

This statement shows that as of last spring the existing facilities included a residential occupancy of 256 people on approximately 48 developed acres. The proposed addition of the church's headquarters and housing at Corwin Springs adds an additional residential occupancy of 340 people on 70 developed acres. That's a total of 596 people on 118 acres — well less than 1 percent of all our land in the area.

The church's planned headquarters includes both residential and day use facilities, such as our school, a church building, cafeteria and offices. According to DHES design circulars which must be followed by all engineers in designing water and sewer systems, residential and day use facilities must be accounted for separately and cumulatively in establishing design flows. And the system must be designed for maximum possible use during a 24-hour period (i.e., with everything full), even though this may rarely if ever be the case.

Thus, in designing our system, the engineer had to assume full residential occupany, all offices in use, school in session, a full cafeteria and a packed church in session all day — all at the same time. The unlikelihood of this is obvious. But since it's possible, it must be designed for. That ensures that the system can never be pushed beyond its capacity.

As for the 3,000 meals referred to by Linda, that assumess the chapel, school and offices all full at the same time — such as could possibly be the case for a few days during a church conference with visitors in the area — with all the people eating in our cafeteria. And, of course, that also assumes that all the people are eating three meals per day — so we're talking about way less than a thousand people on a day use basis in addition to the ranch residents.

That's the facts. And it still doesn't come anywhere close to the 600 plus "several thousand" referred to by the Defense Fund — even allowing for some sloppiness or journalistic license on their part.

By comparison, the town of Gardiner ranges seasonally from 500-800 residents. But do you think its sewer system is only designed for that number?

If you were to allow for all the houses, motels, restaurants, business establishments, churches, meeting halls and the school to be filled at the same time, you'd end up with a total of three or four thousand people. And any engineer worth his salt, if he were designing a new system for the town, would have to look at the possibility of everything being full all at once.

However, if a group of people were to then push the panic button and start running around spreading rumors that the engineer was proposing to expand the town to three or four thousand people, what would you think of them?

I hope the above will help explain the misconceptions now being aired concerning our future plans, the the complexities of information which an EIS must examine in detail. That's even more of a reason to wait for the results of the EIS to be published before flying off in a cocked hat with all sorts of rumors and exaggerated conclusions.

I, for one, am tired of the inaccurate information being bandied about before any definitive results are even published. Once they are, there'll be plenty of time for more input, clarifications, questions, public meetings, objections, etc. before the final EIS is released.

Why don't we see if a better level of communication and understanding can't be achieved through this process before trying to kill it at the outset? We certainly intend to try. And to the extent that the Defense Fund is preparing to review EIS results with an open mind, I'm still hopeful we can both learn to meet each other half-way.

Edward L. Francis
Royal Teton Ranch
Corwin Springs

****

****

Response Requested   April 8, 1988

CHURCH UNIVERSAL AND TRIUMPHANT
DRAFT ENVIRONMENTAL IMPACT STATEMENT

BACKGROUND INFORMATION

On February 19, 1988, the Montana Department of Health and Environmental Sciences ("the Department") released its Draft Environmental Impact Statement ("EIS") on projects proposed by Church Universal and Triumphant ("the Church") in Park County, Montana.

The 160-page Draft EIS document is the culmination of 15 months of data gathering that began in November 1986. This study was conducted by the Department under the provisions of the Montana Environmental Policy Act ("MEPA") and the regulations adopted thereunder to determine the potential impacts of development projects principally associated with the establishment of the headquarters of the Church on the Royal Teton Ranch at Corwin Springs and other locations in Park County.

The determination to conduct an EIS was originally made by the Department in the wake of the unexpected sale of the Church's headquarters in California and decision to relocate to Montana, and as the result of our filing of several applications to construct water and sewer facilities followed by a letter-writing campaign from local residents insisting that an EIS be prepared.

Since that time we have cooperated fully with the Department to disclose all known or proposed projects, information, plans, specifications and technical data to aid in completing the study. In addition, experts were retained with the Department's approval to study and submit reports on possible impacts to wildlife and wildlife habitats, fisheries, vegetation, rare and endangered species, historical and archeological sites, LaDuke Hot Spring and Yellowstone Park geothermal features, and road dust control methods. A sociologist from a private university also wrote a sociological report on the history and activities of the Church in Park County that was incorporated into the document.

A summary of the principal findings of the EIS, as stated verbatim in the draft report, is as follows:

Wildlife

-- Some of the small, nonmobile wildlife have, and will be, displaced by construction activities.

-- It appears the migration routes of the larger, mobile wildlife in and out of Yellowstone National Park (YNP) should not be greatly affected by the Church's proposals since the activities are occurring in or near areas of established development.

-- Fencing will restrict domestic livestock to specific areas.

-- Waste material that could attract wildlife will be properly disposed.

-- Hunting and fishing on Church property will continue to be on a permission basis.

Fish

-- By using proper construction techniques, it is unlikely the proposed developments will impact the fishery in the Yellowstone River and its tributaries.

-- The aquatic life in several of the streams could improve if the Church and state and federal agencies can form agreements to maintain minimum stream flows.

Water

-- By having plans and specifications for public water and wastewater systems approved by the Department, water quality in the area will be maintained.

-- Based on long-range scientific projections, wastewater will have an "unmeasurable" effect on the aquatic life in the Yellowstone River.

Aesthetics

-- The area near Corwin Springs will appear more urban, but the new facilities at the Spring Creek site should not be visible to travelers along U.S. Highway 89.

Unique Environmental Resources

-- Until the Church decides to use its water well across from LaDuke Hot Spring, there probably will not be any concerted effort to investigate the possible impacts on the geothermal resources in YNP.

Historical and Archeological Sites

-- A thorough survey of the Church's property and adjacent land in the Corwin Springs area resulted in the identification of a number of historical and archeological sites.

Economic Considerations

-- The Church is the fourth leading taxpayer in Park County. It and its members do use public services, even though the Church provides some comparable services. It also does a considerable amount of business in Park County.

Transportation

-- The Church is working with the county to upgrade unsurfaced roads and control dust.

-- If the Corwin Springs Bridge across the Yellowstone River can eventually be upgraded, the heavy vehicles that now must use the county road between Gardiner and the ranch (west of the river) will be able to cross at Corwin Springs.

Planning

-- Park County residents have chosen not to implement any form of comprehensive county plan or special planning district in the Corwin Springs-Gardiner area.

Four alternative choices for the Department's action on the Church's permit applications are identified in the Draft EIS. These include: (1) denial, (2) unconditional approval, (3) requirement for modification of plans, or (4) approval subject to mitigation measures. The Department is recommending the selection of Alternative #4.

The document then sets forth a 16-point Mitigation Plan that its approval would be conditional upon, including the following:

– Site planning that will allow housing and other facilities to be clustered in small units, minimizing loss of productive land, impacts on wildlife and preserving aesthetics of the area

– Implementation of a road improvement and dust control program, car pooling and other methods of common transportation

– Solid waste and composting should be removed from the Corwin Springs area

– Domestic sheep should not be allowed to use the winter range of the bighorn sheep herd on Cinnabar Mountain

– Construction of a bearproof fence around the tree farm and the root crop fields

– Implementation of a sediment control plan

– Minimum instream flows be maintained in Reese Creek, Mol Heron Creek and Cedar Creek for fisheries

– A catch-and-release program be developed with the assistance of the Department of Fish, Wildlife and Parks for the upper section of Mol Heron Creek during that time of the year when the outdoor conference will be held

– Best management practices be utilized in all aspects of agricultural production

– The geothermal well drilled to tap the aquifer serving LaDuke Hot Spring should not be utilized until a change in the point of diversion and place of use is approved under Montana Water Law

– Monitoring of the groundwater impact and flows at all wastewater systems and sand lining of the drainfield trenches for several proposed wastewater systems

Finally, the study concludes that "it is the Department's opinion that while implementation of the proposed development plan will obviously be a change for the area, and the Corwin Springs area in particular, the environment will be adequately protected by the review and approval of specific projects provided by the Department and the implementation of the mitigative measures."

Most of these mitigative measures have in fact already been implemented by us or incorporated into our plans. And we have indicated to the Department that the plan would be acceptable to us subject to certain clarifications and conditions, such as the protection of established water rights and additional bearproofing options other than fencing.

PUBLIC COMMENT PERIOD

A 60-day public comment period has been allowed by the Department to give an opportunity for interested persons to express their opinions on the draft document and to provide any additional factual input. The purpose of issuing a draft and providing an opportunity for comment, as stated in the document, is to "compile a factual record to aid the Department in making an environmentally informed decision and provide a means for public information and comment. The draft gives interested parties an opportunity to submit substantive information to expand the body of knowledge and correct factual material."

Public comment to the Department is open until April 21, 1988. In addition, a public hearing was held on March 21, 1988 in Gardiner. This marathon session lasted from 7:00 p.m. until after 1:00 a.m. and included testimony from more than 40 people, including representatives of Yellowstone National Park, environmental groups, numerous local residents and the Church.

Most of the hearing took the form of a well-coordinated assault on the plans, intentions and integrity of the Church and on the accuracy and credibility of the Draft EIS. The majority of these comments emanated from an extreme environmentalist perspective, but were often liberally laced with anticult-type remarks and sarcastic comments alluding to the Church's religious beliefs. And in perhaps what amounts to an implied threat, a representative of Earth First! (the activist group that has been involved in acts of sabotage against loggers, miners, etc.) appeared and lambasted the study.

However, events preceding the public hearing and much of the testimony given there now lead to the conclusion that an orchestrated campaign is being carried out by those who oppose the establishment of our religious community to try to convince the Department that the Draft EIS is flawed and that there is overwhelming public opinion against it. We believe that a carefully planned strategy has been devised to employ false statements and allegations, misinformation, scare tactics, a narrow spectrum of public opinion, and the EIS process itself as a stall tactic to deny us the right to use our land--regardless of what the actual environmental impacts are or might be.

Some of the evidence leading to this conclusion is as follows:

1. Most of the same Gardiner residents who participated in a letter writing campaign in 1986 insisting that the Department conduct an EIS banded together several months later to form the "Upper Yellowstone Defense Fund."

2. In late 1987 and prior to the release of the Draft EIS, the Upper Yellowstone Defense Fund sent out letters attempting to raise money to legally challenge the EIS when it did come out. In effect, many of those who insisted on having an EIS in the first place were now organizing to try to discredit it before the results were even out.

3. Immediately after release of the Draft EIS, the Upper Yellowstone Defense Fund quietly mailed out a newsletter condemning the results of the study. But the wording of the newsletter turned out to be the same as an "EcoAction" newsletter released by the Bozeman-based Greater Yellowstone Coalition environmental group. In fact, the same word processor was used and all copies from both groups were mailed from Bozeman.

4. The newsletters contained blatantly false and misleading statements about the Draft EIS, such as:

- That the EIS "totally fails to disclose or mitigate anticipated impacts." This is an outrageous statement, because it ignores the entire content of the study and the 16-point mitigation plan.
- That the EIS "fails to include site-specific descriptions of development projects and associated human activity." This totally ignores the first ten pages of the report and six detailed area and site maps.
- That the EIS has "no data on traffic projections." This acts as if a four-page section in the document, which is backed up by a lengthy report and analysis, doesn't even exist--an outright lie.

5. At the Gardiner public hearing, a total of 32 people spoke out against the content and/or conclusions of the Draft EIS. Of that number, at least 23 (72%) demanded that the document be done over and re-issued for public comment again--a highly unusual procedure. Could this possibly be just a coincidence?

At the public hearing and in the newsletters released since the Draft EIS was issued, a pattern of inaccurate criticisms--both vague and specific--of the Church, the EIS and even of private landowners in general, has begun to emerge. Taken together, these amount to a disinformation campaign which is calculated to lead inexorably to the conclusion that the Draft EIS and its current findings are wrong and must be re-done and that the Church must be stopped at all costs from proceeding with its plans.

Also implicit within the newsletters, which have been mailed out of state, as well as many of the statements made at the public hearing, is the idea that this is now an issue which is national in scope and that a national call to action is needed to bring every kind of pressure to bear to try to stop this use of private land from occurring--whether it be legal, political, legislative or even physical action.

Because of the falsity of many of the statements and allegations that have been made, and because the opposition themselves have now sought to expand the forum outside of Montana, it is essential that those who are in a position to know the facts provide their comments to the Department whether or not they are residents of this area.

False and inaccurate statements and misrepresentations of public opinion should not be allowed to stand unchallenged. Therefore, this Priority Alert is being provided to inform you of both the false statements, impressions and information being pushed, together with true facts which should be recognized by the Department and the public at large. Included are comments given at the public hearing as well as from other sources since the release of the Draft EIS. These are quoted from an unofficial but reasonably accurate transcript of a recording of the meeting and are organized under several broad categories for simplicity's sake. **(Note: Statements printed in bold in the following sections are the Church's explanations or responses.)**

ATTACK ON PRIVATE LANDOWNER RIGHTS

Many of the comments made at the public hearing and in environmentalist mailings about the Church's land use are actually assailing the rights and prerogatives of all land-owners--particularly farmers and ranchers. This attitude is sometimes subtle and hidden. But the overriding message is clear: private landowner rights must now be subordinated to public values such as wildlife and "ecosystem" concerns--and

even many traditional land uses such as agriculture are now to be looked at as damaging. More land use restrictions and regulations are seen as the solution.

*   *   *

"Major environmental impacts in this ecologically and aesthetically sensitive area are expected as a result of an influx of hundreds of people, whose activities include farming, ranching cattle and sheep, dairy and poultry farming and processing...."

– Environmental Group Newsletter

"Why plant and irrigate highly attractive forage only 300 yards from the Park border which then draws Yellowstone's remnant pronghorn herd out of the Park, then when so-called damage occurs, the Church...gains permission from the Montana Department of Fish, Wildlife and Parks to have the animals killed?"

– Yellowstone National Park Representative

[Note: The "highly attractive forage" is alfalfa and grass hay, the most common crop grown for livestock feed in the region. The pronghorn antelope herd now numbers about 500 and is at its highest level since before World War II. The fact is that virtually all of the animal herds inside Yellowstone have been growing unchecked for decades and therefore--far from being lured out--are increasingly being forced to range outside of the Park to avoid starvation. Because of Yellowstone's strict adherence to a let-nature-run-its-course internal policy, the only effective game management is provided through public hunting allowed by the state and private landowners outside of Park boundaries. This has forged a de-facto balance which is helping to keep overgrazing problems to a minimum inside the Park.]

"Why establish a commercial truck farm which produces 200,000 pounds of root crops that are highly attractive to bears within one-half mile of the Park border? This industrial crop does not give the ranch self-sufficiency since two-thirds of it is sold to nationwide distributors."

– Yellowstone National Park Representative

[Note: In the last two years we've produced an average of 185,000 lbs. of potatoes and carrots (an "industrial crop" in YNP parlance) per year, and sold only 46,000 lbs. per year-- an average of less than 25%. What's wrong with a farm selling its crops anyway? In our six years of growing carrots and potatoes at the ranch we've never had a single bear problem in the crop yet. And if this is so bad, why has Yellowstone Park itself been providing a 2–3 acre un-bear-proofed, irrigated garden area for employees several miles inside the Park for years?]

"Why completely de-water Reese Creek for a month at a time thus largely destroying the value of one of the few remaining good cutthroat trout spawning streams on the Yellowstone River?"
                                    – Yellowstone National Park Representative

[Note: Our private water rights on Reese Creek date back to 1883, preceding the expansion of Yellowstone Park into Montana by half a century. For over 100 years, including the 50 years since the Park acquired land along Reese Creek, the stream has been de-watered for irrigation practically every year and by every successive landowner--and the Park has raised no objections until now. Why?]

"Their work includes many nontraditional uses of ranch land, such as schools, church services, lectures, seminars and conferences."
                                    – Local Resident

[Note: Practically every large ranch in the county has an old schoolhouse or church on it. And in the former settlements of Aldridge, Electric and Corwin Springs on the Church's land there were at least two former schoolhouses, two churches, a 72-room hotel, meeting halls, a power generating plant, stores, housing for at least 2,000 people, etc. And whoever said that freedom of assembly is something that is "nontraditional" anywhere in America?]

". . . the airstrip was constructed with a takeoff and approach pattern over the Yellowstone River posing hazards to wintering and mating bald eagles as well as the potential for chemical spill."
                                    – Local Resident

[Note: The ranch airstrip is actually a flattened out portion of an abandoned railroad grade used by one private plane for an average of less than one flight per week. The gravel strip is located over 500 feet from the Yellowstone River. By comparison, the nearby Gardiner Airport is located closer to Yellowstone Park and closer to the river, has at least 20 times the traffic and is even used by government airplanes for Park business.]

"While the DEIS recognizes the need to segregate domestic sheep from the bighorn sheep, yet there's nothing to prevent the conflict with cattle. They must also compete with Church cattle grazing along the river. . . . The fence erected to keep cattle in is still going to make it an obstacle for the bighorn. . . . The fence is an additional source of stress on a herd that does not need any more stress. . . . The cattle should live in an area further downstream from habitat critical to Cinnabar bighorns."

– Local Resident

"Section 7 of the Endangered Species Act and subsequent court decisions provide the necessary authority to protect threatened and endangered species in their habitat on private land." (Emphasis Added)

– Local Resident

"This inadequacy of the DEIS is evident in the discussion of the grey wolf as well. . . . I truly believe it is only a matter of time before the wolves will return to the Yellowstone ecosystem."

– Local Resident

[Note: Wolves will be returned to the Yellowstone area only if environmentalists get their way and only if landowners and residents fail to object. If they are returned, it will mean more livestock killings and will create another excuse to grab more private land and enact more restrictions to protect the new "wolf habitat."]

"Bighorn sheep:. . . No heart monitors have been used to see if indeed stress is a factor. Why not?"

– Local Resident

In referring to our private property, one government employee even said, ". . . I would say that why should any special interest group be given preference to degrade a unique natural area that should be able to be enjoyed by all members of the American public."

– Yellowstone Park Employee

"Given the uncertainty which still exists over what the future holds for CUT development, local land use regulations, specifically zoning, is not only reasonable but an absolute necessity."

– Ben Berto, County Planning Director

LANDOWNER PERSPECTIVE

One local rancher not connected with the Church had the courage to stand up at the public hearing and expose these radical attitudes for what they really are--and what they can mean to all landowners.

* * *

"What will the development be? Mostly agricultural. In the Coalition and Defense Fund's letters, both contend that this ag-development is a threat to the environment, that activities such as farming, ranching, cattle and sheep and dairy and poultry farming and processing will result in major environmental impacts. It is ironic that the very backbone of this state is a threat environmentally. . . . They have made it into a viable ag-unit. This is to be praised, not admonished.

"Comments concerning water usage depleting streams is invalid. . . . A landowner can use up no more than his right decrees. And any landowner has the right to irrigate his ground with his water if his water rights allow it. CUT rights are all senior decrees preceding all others, just as mine are on my place. If the State starts telling ranchers, farmers or any other landowners that the water needs to be turned back to streams in favor of irrigating pastures, it violates constitutional rights.

"I think the demand for an EIS was met successfully by the state. It bothers me that people are trying to fashion a lot of restrictions in response to CUT being here. They don't totally realize, or maybe they do, that much of what they oppose or complain about is in direct conflict with any property owner, CUT or not. One gets the feeling after reading the statements of the Coalition and Defense Fund that their main complaint is that property owners have any rights at all.

"Finally, they would be satisfied if. . . they saw all rights stripped and delegated by a special interest group. That's too damn bad because there is room for all of us here if we cooperate in an open and fair way."

— Local Rancher

ATTACK ON CHURCH BELIEFS, PRACTICES AND LIFESTYLES

Negative comments regarding the Church were usually woven into the text of other environmental concerns and questions, but were nevertheless frequent. It appears that for many the environmental rhetoric is the means, but the end is "we don't want your Church moving into our area."

* * *

"I don't want. . . [to] advance the interests of a religious group that I don't wish to support. . . ."

— Local Minister

". . . the Church chooses to be a somewhat closed society."

— Local Resident

"The numbers of people being located on church property are the staff of a business setup that's successful enough over the years to buy 33,000 acres in Park County. . . . The moneymaker is Elizabeth Clare Prophet and the selling of her words, and this is managed by that large staff whose presence is bringing the problems of urbanization to this fragile and ecologically important land. . . . CUT is a business. It should be evaluated as a business and held responsible for the impacts it will cause."
– Local Resident

"Who are we kidding? Everyone knows the Rajneesh episode is a national issue--a small, insignificant town in Oregon taken over by a group of people calling themselves 'religious.'

"I also object to the fact of the explanations of CUT's theology being included in an EIS. This is nothing more than propaganda and I don't care what they believe or who they worship. It is inappropriate. . . a diversionary tactic. . . Elizabeth Clare Prophet's late husband Mark telling her from his deathbed to take the Church to Montana because of the grassroots of America's kind of people. Was she to go there after she tried Colorado and Idaho?. . . could she just maybe have settled on Paradise Valley, Montana because of the lack of zoning ordinances? The intelligence of the residents of Park County has been insulted by the inclusion of such soap opera scenes in print.

". . . are you planning to examine the work of other religious sociologists not recommended by Mr. Francis concerning the social impact of the cult?. . . strong parallels between Rajneeshpuram and CUT. . ."
– Local Resident

". . . the ongoing and proposed developments of the Church will. . . degrade the aesthetic experience of thousands of tourists traveling to Yellowstone National Park from the north, and of the fishermen and boaters who use the Yellowstone River. . . ."
– Environmental Group Newsletter

COMPLAINTS AGAINST CHURCH SUMMER CONFERENCE SITE (HEART OF THE INNER RETREAT)

The annual summer conference in the Heart of the Inner Retreat was chosen as a particular bone of contention by those commenting on the EIS. While the use of the Conference Site is not even the subject of any pending applications for permits or licenses from the state, it was included in the EIS as a collateral issue. The Draft EIS found no significant impact, but individuals at the public hearing spoke of alleged impacts to wildlife, vegetation and even public health.

* * *

"Conferences brought thousands into the narrow confines of upper Mol Heron Creek. Traffic and dust in the canyons deteriorated the aesthetics of the area."
– Local Resident

"The impact of 2,500 people shows a great deal of stress on the animals which can only increase the odds against their survival."
– Local Resident

"What happens during the conference with 2,500 persons walking on the land? How long will good grasslands remain stable? These animals. . .have to deal with human encounters during summer feeding, the conference. . . .Should this area not be under strict control?"
– Local Resident

"From personal experience I can tell you that the entire Cinnabar Basin is impacted by the conference, not just the 60 acres near to the Mol Heron."
– Local Resident

[Note: Cinnabar Basin is over seven miles by road from the Conference Site in the Mol Heron valley, and is separated from the area by an 8,500-foot-high mountain range.]

"Especially with their yearly massive communal gathering each Fourth of July, we have a lot of influx of different people coming in that could bring different diseases from across the whole United States. This is why my great concern is that we are leaving a lot of children here in the Gardiner area unprotected."
– Local Resident

COMMUNITY OF GLASTONBURY

The Community of Glastonbury was likewise mentioned as the subject of alleged environmental impacts at the public hearing. The Draft EIS briefly discussed Glastonbury but did not analyze it in detail. There are no pending applications by the Church for permits or licenses there that have not already been approved by Park County and/or the Department under state subdivision laws, such as the Golden Age Village. Development at Glastonbury is largely in the hands of private parcel owners, not the Church. Interestingly, while many were demanding that the impacts of "unregulated development" at Glastonbury be included in a new Draft EIS, others were calling for the Church's planned headquarters to be moved there and away from Yellowstone Park. This insistence that all of Glastonbury be included in a new EIS amounts to an effort to have MEPA improperly used as a substitute for county planning and zoning. Glastonbury residents and landowners will likely want to comment to the Department on these allegations and demands.

*   *   *

"Is it good public policy to have 100 to 200 homes situated where there is no guaranteed access for fighting fires or controlling unlawful activities?"
                                                    – Local Resident

[Note: Easements for roads in the Community of Glastonbury are platted and provide guaranteed legal access to every parcel and lot in the Community. This includes emergency access for fires and law enforcement. As of this date, at least nine Glastonbury residents are participating members of the Chico Volunteer Fire Department.]

"The ridge has been desecrated, although I remember promises from the C.U.T. that homes would be built out of sight, secluded and sequestered from public view. . . . Promises made and promises broken."
                                                    –Local Resident

[Note: No such promises have ever been made or broken. This resident may be referring to the plan for the Golden Age Village, which stated that buildings would not be visible to adjoining property owners outside of Glastonbury or from highways and county roads--a promise that has been kept. Decisions on where to build or not on individual parcels are up to the owner of each parcel.]

"I would like to know, are there families at Glastonbury sharing wells and/or septic tanks? How many cases are there of more than one dwelling on a 20-acre lot? Is not the practice of sharing the costs of a 20-acre lot, then--developing that parcel with more than one dwelling without any kind of review--an evasion of the intent of the subdivision law?"
                                                    – Local Resident

[Note: This is a clear example of attempting to have MEPA improperly used as a substitute for county planning and zoning regulations which do not exist. Many of the comments regarding Glastonbury and the Church's projects fall into this category.]

". . . we, the county, are allowing the development pattern at Glastonbury that can be a future liability against both the economy and attractiveness of tourists to Park County. . . . The Environmental Impact Statement should take the opportunity to educate the county about the costs of unregulated development."
— Local Resident

". . . by leaving out Glastonbury the EIS is failing to recognize that it is different from other real estate promotions because the Church has a built-in market consisting of people who are willing to invest their savings to build there even though they are not getting marketable title. The EIS ignores the fact that the people living there have practically no chance of being integrated into the local economy other than the economy of the Church itself."
— Local Resident

". . . serious defect to have omitted from your scrutiny the Community of Glastonbury, 4,500 acres. . ."
— Local Resident

"Glastonbury North and South. . . we feel it is incumbent on the state to explain why these two areas with perhaps the greatest intrinsically negative land use impacts are not being reviewed. Even a cursory examination of the covenants for Glastonbury reveals that CUT wields nearly absolute authority over every aspect of community life, including whether individuals may occupy the land they paid for. Given the impacts of this haphazard, sprawled housing development and the continuing controlling presence of CUT, any comprehensive EIS should address Glastonbury."
— Ben Berto, County Planning Director

[Note: Last year the same individual referred to the Glastonbury covenants as inadequate and filled with loopholes at a public meeting.]

ECONOMIC IMPACTS

It was repeatedly implied at the public hearing that the Church's presence in Park County is of little economic benefit to area residents, and that it will actually create a drain on the local economy and on the county treasury, school system and tax base. These claims ignore not only the purchase of large amounts of goods and services locally and increases to the county tax base from the Church directly, but also the increased local commerce and taxes being paid on new houses, etc. from Church members in the area.

* * *

"I know that members of the Church do purchase a certain amount of goods locally. But do they purchase enough to offset the impact that they have had on the local employment situation?"

– Local Resident

"Taxes: again, what, if anything, will CUT be paying in terms of taxes on its new facilities?. . . . Park County appears to be about to shoulder the additional impacts of development with very little counterbalancing tax benefits."

– Ben Berto, County Planning Director

"Far from being as CUT states in the EIS Draft an ongoing windfall income for the local public school system, CUT's impacts are more akin to an albatross."

– Ben Berto, County Planning Director

"CUT does not provide jobs for anyone but their members. They have people on welfare and the Church is not generating funds that the county can use. Sure, they pay taxes. But the majority of their members rent, thus they do not pay property taxes. There also are very clear indications that a number of cult children are in need of special education or in learning disabilities programs. This, too, comes out of the taxpayers' dollar."

– Local Resident

"Demands on government services is an area of special concern. On a personal level CUT has placed tremendous pressure on my office both in terms of trying to meet the demands that they specifically generate and in what their hundreds of members individually do. The sanitarian is also experiencing additional demands."

– Ben Berto, County Planning Director

[Note: The Church and Glastonbury owners in fact paid total property taxes in Park County in 1987 of $145,381.63. This amount represents a total of approximately 2.4% of all taxes paid in Park County including Livingston and 15% of all taxes levied in the Gardiner area. In terms of annual taxes paid in unincorporated Park County, the Church and

Glastonbury have already increased the tax base on the properties they have acquired since 1981 by approximately $71,399.60 (193%). This is new tax money for the county. And most of the new facilities planned to be built in the future will also be taxable--only the actual church and school buildings themselves will qualify for exemption under state law. Any local government services received have been amply paid for. How can it be said that the Church and its members don't pay their fair share and haven't contributed to the local economy?]

YELLOWSTONE NATIONAL PARK AND ENVIRONMENTALIST DEMANDS

The bottom line of all of the adverse comments and opinions was a chorus of demands from Yellowstone Park and the environmental groups to radically alter, restrict, move or prevent the Church's establishment of its headquarters and religious community on the Royal Teton Ranch and to redo the EIS. These are the key demands that must be countered.

* * *

"The proposed CUT development would be yet another blow to the long-term biological integrity of the Greater Yellowstone Ecosystem."
– Earth First! Representative

". . . anything that happens to Yellowstone Park or the surrounding community is an issue not only for Wyoming residents or Montana residents but it's also of national significance."
– Yellowstone Park Employee

"How many people will be coming to these church services and conferences? How often? We have to know this. . . ."
– Environmental Group Representative

". . . In view of the fact that no baseline data are available on fish populations and invertebrates for Mol Heron and Cedar Creek. . . . Complete baseline data needs to be gathered on these streams to evaluate the impact of these and future developments."
– Local Resident

"If CUT will only sell Glastonbury to members, so it should be treated as part of this EIS process."
– Local Resident

"As a result of the inadequacies that we discussed, we are requesting that the agency will fully revise the EIS. . .and resubmit this document in draft form for full public review and comment."
– Environmental Group Representative

"There are enough serious problems with this document as it stands that we the Park County Planning Board and the planning office feel there should be another draft document issued."
– Ben Berto, County Planning Director

"I believe there are a number of alternatives which the state should require to lessen or alleviate the impact. Why wasn't an alternative Conference Site identified? Surely within the 33,000 acres owned by the Church, a site more equal to the needs of 2,500 people and not within Situation I grizzly habitat could be found. Why can't an alternative date for the conference be required, say in August. . .?"
– Environmental Group Member

"Why isn't human management stressed by moving the site or the time of the conference or by confining the activities of the conferees?"
– Environmental Group Member

"[There is] no information in the document provided by the Church or the state which gives a financial, religious, legal, moral, practical or historical reason why the headquarters complex and other buildings couldn't be located on another site north of Yankee Jim Canyon. . . ."
– Environmental Group Representative

"[The] headquarters [should] simply be moved to a location somewhere in the Emigrant area on the property which they already own."
– Environmental Group Representative

"The Draft EIS does not evaluate alternative locations for ranch development such as northern Paradise Valley and we request this be done in the final version. . . . We strongly urge the Royal Teton Ranch to select another portion of its extensive holdings for these subdivision activities and then submit new plans to the State of Montana for approval."
– Yellowstone National Park Representative

[Note: This sounds like zoning without lawful regulations or due process. If these arguments are valid, and when the residents in the northern Paradise Valley also object, then

why couldn't the Church be forced to relocate its headquarters outside of Park County, or even the State of Montana-- or better yet--to another country?]

"We do not want massive development threats on Yellowstone's border and the people of the United States will not stand for it."
– Yellowstone National Park Representative

[Note: It is indeed ironic that Yellowstone Park has put itself in the forefront of complaining about the establishment of our agriculturally based religious community, when the Park is the one that is responsible for the largest influx of people and ongoing development in the area. Government statistics show that over 2.6 million people and 892,000 vehicles visit the 2.2-million-acre Park annually--more than one person per acre each year. There are facilities, housing, campgrounds and RV parks for up to 17,000 residents and visitors in the Park at any one time--plus the restaurants, gas stations, stores, etc. There are at least six "towns" inside the Park, including Mammoth, Canyon Village, Lake, Grant Village, Old Faithful, and Roosevelt. And now the Park is even planning several large additions, including the building of 488 new lodging units at Canyon Village. This compares with additions in the border town of Gardiner in the last two years alone of three large motels (total of over 100 units), a new mobile home park and 40,000 gallons of sewage per day from a new laundry operation inside Yellowstone Park to the Gardiner community sewage system, which is leaking and not operating properly. By contrast, we are talking about 600 permanent residents plus perhaps 5–6,000 visitors annually on a total of 15,000 acres on the Royal Teton Ranch--less than half the density as in Yellowstone Park itself. If Yellowstone Park and Gardiner--where most of these complaints are emanating from--can successfully handle this kind of activity and new development and still remain pristine and unspoiled, then so can we!]

WHAT YOU CAN DO NOW

The opportunity for public comment on the Draft EIS is open until April 21, 1988. You are free to write to the Department to express your opinions on the Draft EIS, comment on statements made about the Church and the EIS by others, and add additional factual information that may be relevant. This may include, for example, personal observations made by you while on Church property, at the summer conference in the Heart, as a resident living at Glastonbury, etc.

The Department needs to know that there are people who agree with the job they've done on the EIS and who don't agree with these environmentalist demands. Specifically, they need to know if:

1. You don't think it's necessary for a new Draft EIS to be done or re-issued for public comment;

2. You don't think the Church should be forced to move its headquarters to some other property not of its choosing;

3. You don't think it's reasonable to ask that the summer Conference Site and dates be changed--and why;

4. You don't think Glastonbury ought to be included in an EIS;

5. You don't think it's fair to create unreasonable restrictions on the Church and its land that no one else in this area has to live with;

6. You don't think MEPA should be used as a substitute for county planning and zoning; or

7. You do think the same standard should be applied to the Church's land use rights as for everyone else--not the double standard which these environmentalists are pushing for.

DEADLINE

The deadline for submitting your written comments to the Department on the Draft EIS is April 21, 1988. Be sure to get your letters off well in advance as the mail deliveries in this area can sometimes take up to five days to reach their destination.

livingston
enterprise
A Yellowstone Newspaper

Vol. 77—No. 130, Livingston, Mont., Friday, Feb. 19, 1988—Thirty Five Cents

EIS gives CUT initial go-ahead for developments

Enterprise photo by Tom Shands

The first overview of the Church Universal and Triumphant's development within Park County was revealed in the church's E.I.S.

Document termed thorough by state Water Quality staff

By AL KNAUBER
Enterprise Staff Writer

Without significant public protest, the stage appears to be set allowing the Church Universal and Triumphant to proceed with its proposed development plans if precautions are taken to minimize the impacts.

The long-awaited Environmental Impact Statement, assessing the overall impact of the church's activities, was released late Thursday in Helena. The EIS, ordered 16 months ago, was prepared by the state Water Quality Bureau.

CUT Vice President Ed Francis said he had not had time to review the EIS "with a fine-tooth comb," but said the document looked "complete and comprehensive.

"I think they did a good job," Francis said.

He said he did not see anything in the document that suprised him.

Francis added that he anticipated there would be extensive public comment on the EIS, both for and against the document.

"We may submit additional comments," he said.

He said the EIS probably was needed because of "misinformation" in the community surrounding the church's activities.

He said the document "gets the facts out in the open" regarding the church.

"I think it was appropriate because of the fact that there were legitimate concerns on the part of many people," he said.

Steve Pilcher, Water Quality Bureau chief, said the report "is probably as thorough as any document, draft EIS, that we have been associated with."

In a prepared statement, he noted that "the diverse nature of the church's development combined with a location adjacent to our nation's oldest national park has made this review one of the most difficult tasks we have faced."

The 160-page draft version was made available to several public libraries, including those in Park County.

Pilcher said he was not suprised by the length of the EIS, and added "it was obvious early in the game that it would be a fairly lengthy document."

The drive south along U.S. 89 through the Paradise Valley, from Livingston to Yellowstone National Park, is a tour of CUT's vast land acquistions.

The church purchased several thousand acres in 1981 when it acquired the 12,000-acre Forbes Ranch, which borders the park. In both outright ownership and under contract, CUT has about 33,209 acres.

Many Park County residents believed an overall review of the church's activies was necessary and the state Health Department concurred, ordering an EIS in November 1986.

The document contained four alternatives: either deny or approve all licenses and plans; modify all plans; or approve the proposed developments subject to reducing potentially adverse effects.

The Water Quality Bureau offered 16 recommendations to minimize the impact from CUT's proposed developments. Included among those recommendations were:

— Maintaining housing and work units in clustered areas to minimize impacts on wildlife, loss of productive land and preserve the aesthetics of the area.

— Not developing a geothermal well, tapping the aquifer serving La Duke Hot Springs, until a change in the point of diversion and place of use is approved by the Department of Natural Resources and Conservation.

— Implementating of a road improvement and dust control program in conjunction with Park County officials. Mass transportation, such as car pooling, also should be used.

— Constructing a bear-proof fence around the tree farm and root crop fields. Also recommended was the removal of composting vegitation to other church property to avoid bear problems.

— Preventing domestic sheep from using the bighorn sheep herd winter range on Cinnabar Mountain. This would minimize the potential for spreading disease.

— Implementing sediment control plans for developed areas near streams where natural vegetation is removed.

— Maintaining minimum flows in Reese Creek, Mol Heron Creek and Cedar Creek. A catch-and-release pro-gram was to be developed, in cooperation with the state Department of Fish, Wildlife and Parks, for the upper portions of Mol Heron Creek when the church holds its annual outdoor conference.

— Monitoring of the groundwater impact from all wastewater disposal systems, both existing and planned.

— Removing solid waste from the slaughterhouse operation at the conclusion of processing, to a licensed disposal area outside the immediate area of the facility.

The EIS noted that the recommended alternative for dealing with CUT's proposals provided many of the benefits without the environmental sacrifices associated with an unconditional approval of CUT's planned developments.

"By and large, this document probably embodies the best information available" on the impact from CUT's proposed developments, said EIS technical writer Tom Ellerhoff.

Ellerhoff said much of the EIS addressed the impacts to wildlife and to both the social and cultural concerns. "Those are the things we thought were the most germane. We tried to get the best information available to tried to be as thorough as possible."

Public comments on the document will be taken by the Water Quality Bureau until March 21 when a public hearing is scheduled to be held in the multi-purpose room of the Gardiner High School. The hearing will start at 7 p.m.

If there are enough additional concerns that were not addressed in the draft version, a final EIS may be written.

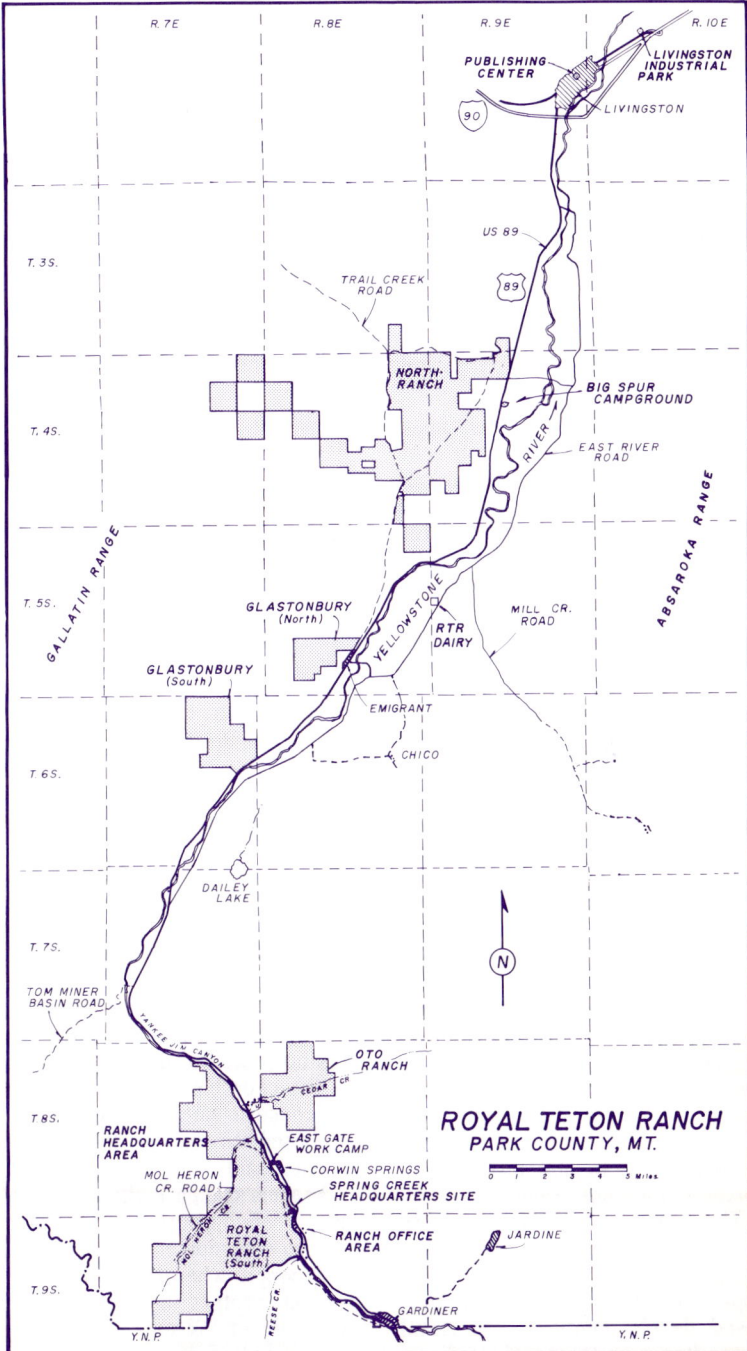

MAP I

ROYAL TETON RANCH
PARK COUNTY, MT.

State can't force CUT to move developments away

By **MIKE MALES**
Chronicle Staff Writer

The state of Montana doesn't have the power to force the Church Universal and Triumphant to move its developments farther away from Yellowstone National Park as park officials would like, a state health official says.

"The department is not in a position to dictate to the applicant (CUT) the location of their development," Steve Pilcher, chief of the state Health Department's Water Quality Bureau, said Wednesday.

CUT vice president Edward Francis said Wednesday that park officials' statements that the church should move its development were "outrageous, and as far as we're concerned, completely unacceptable."

Francis said the park service's request "is tantamount to condemning our land without paying for it. It's socialized, centralized planning."

"If it's such a great idea, why not close the town of Gardiner and move it up next to Livingston?" Francis said.

A statement by Yellowstone Park Superintendent Robert Barbee, delivered by his management assistant Steve Iobst to a public hearing in Gardiner Monday night, said that CUT should move its planned developments to its property in northern Paradise Valley.

The hearing was called by state health officials to take public comments on the draft environmental impact statement on CUT's proposed developments on its Royal Teton Ranch northwest of Gardiner.

The church proposes to build a slaughterhouse, religious and administrative buildings, agricultural facilities, and housing to accommodate eventually several hundred workers on the ranch, most within a couple of miles of the park.

"We do not want massive development threats on Yellowstone's border, and the people of the United States will not stand for it!" Barbee's statement said. "We strongly urge the Royal Teton Ranch to select another portion of its extensive holdings for these subdivision activities and then submit new plans to the state of Montana for approval."

Barbee's statement requested that the state Health Department's final EIS "evaluate alternative locations for ranch developments (such as northern Paradise Valley)," which the draft EIS did not do.

Barbee's statement argued that Yellowstone is a unique international treasure, "the icon of our public lands."

Park and many other local and environmental group speakers stressed the largely intact nature of the Yellowstone area and its value in terms of recreation, fisheries, water and air quality and wildlife.

However, Pilcher said the state has no power to demand relocation of the church's projects. "We have to concern ourselves on what is proposed to us by the church," Pilcher said.

Francis said park officials were "a bunch of hypocrites" to criticize church developments involving 600-700 people when the park brings 2 million visitors annually into the area, maintains extensive developments of its own, and "clogs the roads around here with traffic."

"They ought to be managing their park right rather than criticizing what their neighbors do," Francis said.

Pilcher said he disagreed with a lot of things park officials said, including Barbee's observation that "the draft EIS does not address the cumulative impacts of Royal Teton Ranch development on the aesthetic and biological values of the greater Yellowstone area," which the park service called "enormous."

"We keep hearing that this area is so critical to the Yellowstone ecosystem," Pilcher said. "I have to at the cumulative impact of the church's activities and other past and planned developments on the park and surrounding ecosystem, "I have some real problems personally dealing with cumulative impacts," Pilcher said.

"What do you include? Where do you draw the line?" he said.

Pilcher cited as examples the Gardiner wastewater treatment system, which has been cited as inadequate, and the Gardiner airport.

"We heard criticisms that the church's airstrip might dump diesel

---

'Past mistakes offer no justification for making more in the future.'
—Bob Barbee

---

wonder why, if it is so critical to the park, Yellowstone didn't buy that land when it was available?"

Federal officials, saying they couldn't get the money, rejected an offer to buy the old Forbes Ranch before CUT purchased the 12,000-acre property for its Royal Teton Ranch in 1981.

Pilcher said he was frustrated by many of the criticisms of the draft EIS voiced by most of the 45 speakers in the audience of 400 people at the hearing. Most in attendance opposed the document's conclusion that CUT's developments would be environmentally acceptable if subjected to certain conditions.

"Many of the comments we heard were of such a general nature and represented personal preferences: they don't want the church there," Pilcher said.

"Well, I may not want the church there either, but I have to evaluate specific impacts," he said.

While many of the speakers faulted the draft EIS for not looking fuel and cause pollution of the Yellowstone River, but the Gardiner airport handles 20 times more traffic and is equally close to the river, and that's OK," Pilcher said.

Moving the church's activities to its 15,000-acre North Ranch, about 10 miles south of Livingston, "might be more acceptable to the residents of Gardiner or Yellowstone National Park, but not to the residents of Paradise Valley," Pilcher said.

Barbee's statement acknowledged that past developments within and adjacent to the park had shortcomings but said, "Past mistakes offer no justification for making more in the future."

Pilcher said the state was not inclined to withdraw the draft EIS, as many speakers at Monday's hearing requested, "but we don't rule out anything." State officials will take public comments on the draft EIS until April 21 and then prepare either a final EIS or an amended draft EIS he said.

Bozeman Daily

CHRONICLE

Volume 78 — Number 64   Wednesday, March 15, 1989, Bozeman, Montana   35¢

CUT gets OK on development

By MIKE MALES
Chronicle Staff Writer

HELENA — Acknowledging that the decision "will not satisfy everyone," state health officials today gave the Church Universal and Triumphant the final go-ahead to proceed with its extensive developments in southern Park County, but with some modifications to protect the environment.

"With the mitigation plan agreement that has been developed, the environmental concerns in this sensitive area will be addressed while allowing reasonable development to take place," Sidney Pratt, acting director of the Montana Department of Health and Environmental Sciences, said this morning in releasing the final environmental impact statemeht on CUT's developments.

The final EIS also sends a clear message to Park County residents, planning agencies and environmentalists concerned about the impact of CUT and other large developments locally and on the Yellowstone-area ecosystem: If you want more controls, they must be implemented through local land-use measures and agreements with private property owners such as CUT, not through state health or environmental laws.

The EIS released today culminates a 2½-year DHES review of the environmental impacts from CUT's 1985 decision to move its California headquarters and 500 employees to the Gardiner-Corwin Springs area. The move has drawn protests from local residents.

Nearly 500 people and organizations testified or wrote letters to DHES on the CUT developments in

The EIS released today culminates a 2½-year review of the environmental impacts from CUT's 1985 move to the Gardiner-Corwin Springs area.

the 13 months since a draft EIS, which made nearly the same recommendations as the final EIS, was released in February 1988.

Critics included nearby residents, National Park Service, Montana Department of Fish, Wildlife and Parks, the Bozeman-based Greater Yellowstone Coalition and the Fishing and Floating Outfitters of Montana.

Critics cited extensive environmental and social concerns from CUT developments and charged that the draft EIS failed to identify impacts or assure they will be addressed.

But the final EIS re-asserts that most of the harmful environmental impacts of CUT's buildings and other projects — including housing developments, agriculture and food processing operations, and religious, educational and commercial developments — can be reduced or eliminated with mitigating measures.

Many of these projects have been placed "on hold" by CUT, which owns 31,500 acres in Park County, including its 12,000-acre Royal Teton Ranch at Corwin Springs, and is the county's fourth largest taxpayer.

Chief impacts and mitigating measures identified in the EIS are:

● Wildlife impacts. "Migration routes of the larger wildlife in and out of Yellowstone National Park (YNP) should not be greatly affected," the EIS concludes.

The EIS requires that CUT design a site plan to minimize the effects of developments on wildlife, dispose of garbage properly and fence crop areas to avoid attracting animals, and fence its domestic livestock in confined areas away from wildlife winter range.

● Fish. "By using proper construction techniques, it is unlikely the proposed developments will impact the fishery in the Yellowstone River and its tributaries," the EIS concludes.

The EIS requires CUT to implement a sediment control plan, maintain minimum in-stream flows in creeks, enforce a catch-and-release policy for fishing during its summer conferences, and monitor groundwater and river quality subject to DHES supervision and corrective measures.

"Based on long-range scientific projections, wastewater will have an 'unmeasurable' effect on the aquatic life in the Yellowstone River," the EIS concludes. "Water quality in the area will be maintained."

● Aesthetics. "The area near Corwin Springs will appear more urban," the EIS states. Other CUT developments will not be visible to travelers along U.S. Highway 89, it says.

The EIS requires that the CUT site plan cluster housing and work facilities in small areas, reducing visual and land-use impacts.

"There is no local land use planning or control" to allow greater restrictions, Pratt notes. "Neither MEPA (the Montana Environmental Policy Act) nor the DHES reviews can be used as a de facto means for instituting local land-use planning," the EIS adds.

● Geothermal resources. Despite fears raised by environmental and Park Service spokespersons about the effect of CUT use of LaDuke Hot Spring on Yellowstone geysers "is not an issue at this time," the EIS concludes.

The EIS recommends that CUT's geothermal well at LaDuke not be used until approval is obtained under state water law, a process which requires environmental review and possibly public hearings.

● Transportation. The EIS requires CUT to implement a road improvement and dust control plan with Park County authorities and to use carpools and buses where possible.

● The "Yellowstone ecosystem" concept. The EIS rejects state authority to implement the "Yellowstone ecosystem" concept advocated by environmental groups to measure and control the cumulative impacts of development in the Yellowstone region as a whole.

The concept may work where only government land is concerned, but "it is a much different matter when attempting to apply the idea to private property, particularly in areas which have historically resisted community planning, such as Gardiner," the EIS says.

Unless local groups can reach a consensus on land-use controls, including agreements with private property owners, little can be done to advance the ecosystem concept, the EIS concludes.

Church Universal, state agree on mitigation plan

Final EIS on development released

By MIKE DENNISON
Associated Press

HELENA — Church Universal and Triumphant's extensive developments in Park County should proceed as long as the church abides by conditions designed to limit impacts on water and wildlife, the state Health Department announced Wednesday.

An agreement between church officials and the state was included in a long-awaited final environmental impact statement (EIS) released Wednesday by the Health Department.

"It is our opinion that with the mitigation plan agreement ... the environmental concerns in this sensitive area will be addressed while allowing reasonable development to take place," said Dr. Sidney Pratt, the department's acting director.

The church owns about 33,000 acres in Park County, including the 15,000-acre Royal Teton Ranch-South that borders Yellowstone National Park.

At the urging of area residents, the state began the EIS process in late 1986, after the church announced it was moving its international headquarters from California to the ranch. Residents said they were concerned the development might harm the area's abundant wildlife, water quality and rural nature.

Planned developments at the ranch near Corwin Springs include a housing project for about 260 people, a school, dining hall and chapel, and a new ranch headquarters.

Ed Francis, church vice president, said Wednesday that he was satisfied with the EIS and the church will abide by the agreement signed with the state.

"The mitigation plan agreement should help resolve many ... concerns," he said. "While it is a voluntary agreement, it is a legally enforceable agreement. And, we are willing to maintain a dialogue with all interested parties."

Several parties that have been critical of church projects and the state's draft EIS said Wednesday they would wait until later this week to comment, after they had reviewed the final document.

Steve Pilcher, director of the state Water Quality Bureau, said the main difference between the draft EIS, released in February 1987, and the final document was the latter's inclusion of the signed mitigation plan agreement.

"We are committing ourselves to unannounced and announced inspections to make sure there is compliance with the agreement," he said.

The 16-point mitigation plan calls for, among other things, monitoring the effects that wastewater systems have on ground water; keeping housing and work facilities in small units; keeping domestic sheep out of the winter range of bighorn sheep on Cinnabar Mountain; implementing a sediment-control plan for areas where natural vegetation is removed; maintaining minimum stream flows on three creeks running through the property; and delaying development of a geothermal spring at Corwin Springs until further approval by the state Department of Natural Resources and Conservation.

Coalition sues state over CUT development

HELENA (AP) — A coalition of four environmental groups has sued the state over its document allowing the Church Universal and Triumphant to proceed with extensive developments north of Yellowstone National Park.

"The state simply should not be able to get away with an inadequate EIS (environmental impact statement) and not have it challenged," Sherm Janke of the Sierra Club told the Livingston Enterprise on Monday.

The Sierra Club's Montana chapter was one of four groups to challenge the EIS, which was released March 15. The document said the church can go forward with its development plans if it agrees to limit impacts on water and wildlife.

Steve Pilcher, head of the state Water Quality Bureau, said Monday that the lawsuit comes as no surprise.

"I have said that the critics will not be satisfied as long as the church is allowed to locate anywhere near the park," he said.

Developments addressed by the EIS are several miles north of the park. Portions of church property include winter range for park herds of elk, bison and bighorn sheep.

The suit against the state Department of Health and Environmental Sciences was filed Friday in district court at Helena. The other three plaintiffs are the Upper Yellowstone

> **The lawsuit says the EIS is inadequate under state law because it failed to "fully address all of the environmental consequences caused by the church's proposed development."**
> — *Attorney for plaintiffs*

Defense Fund, the Greater Yellowstone Coalition, and the National Parks and Conservation Association.

The groups want a preliminary injunction to block the state from issuing any water or wastewater permits to the church. A hearing before District Judge Jeffrey Sherlock is scheduled April 12.

The lawsuit says the EIS is inadequate under state law because it failed to "fully address all of the environmental consequences caused by the church's proposed development," said Jack Tuholske, a Missoula attorney representing the plaintiffs.

He said the plaintiffs want to force the state to prepare a new EIS.

The church plans to build a

community near Corwin Springs that includes housing for 260 people, a chapel, dining hall and school. Headquarters for its Royal Teton Ranch would be nearby. The church owns about 33,000 acres in Park County.

The EIS included an agreement signed by church officials, in which the church agreed to a 16-point plan to mitigate impacts of church developments.

Ed Francis, vice president for the church, said Monday he was disappointed that groups opposed to the development are refusing to abide by the EIS process.

"I don't think they ever intended to abide by the results unless they got the result they wanted, which is to deny all permits," he said. "I view it as kind of an abuse of the process."

He pointed out that some of the groups that brought suit were the ones who asked for the EIS in late 1986.

Francis said building plans were scheduled to begin next week, and that any delay beyond then will be a hardship for the church.

The lawsuit said the Department of Health did not consider all reasonable alternatives to the development near the park, such as requiring the church to move its developments to property outside the Corwin Springs area. The church owns additional ranchland about 12 miles south of Livingston.

Janke said the EIS lacks proper data to determine whether environmental impacts will result from the church development.

CUT's Francis says environmental suit won't force church to move

HELENA (AP) — Regardless of the outcome of a lawsuit challenging a state review approving development plans for the Church Universal and Triumphant, a top church official says the religious group intends to keep its headquarters in southcentral Montana near the border of Yellowstone National Park.

"We have a very strong belief that we are intended to be where we are," said Ed Francis, vice president and business manager for the church.

Francis was joined by several officials from the state Department of Health and Environmental Sciences Water Quality Bureau who testified Thursday at a district court hearing in Helena in defense of the state environmental impact statement. The hearing continues this afternoon.

A coalition of four environmental groups has asked District Judge Jeffrey Sherlock to order a halt to construction on the church's property near Corwin Springs at the northern edge of Yellowstone until controversy over the state's environmental impact statement is resolved.

The environmentalists contend the EIS should be redone because it doesn't adequately address potential environmental impacts from church development, including impacts on grizzly bears and other wildlife.

If the state ultimately disapproves CUT's development plans, the church would seek other alternatives to resolve the problem, Francis said.

While he did not know what those alternatives would be, he said, "Things change over time. Nobody can foresee what can happen over a period of time."

Francis said nothing indicates the state would not reach the same conclusion that development should proceed, even if a new review is ordered. In addition, he said no one has suggested the church take additional measures to reduce possible impacts on the environment other than to relocate its headquarters, which is an unacceptable option.

"We're already there operating in cramped makeshift facilities," Francis said. "Our intention would be to just stay there."

Francis testified during the hearing that if the church decided to expand development beyond what was covered in the state review, church officials would notify the state and do what was needed to comply with regulations.

Church plans call for construction of housing for 260 people, a dining hall, chapel, school, ranch headquarters and a maintenance shop on its 12,500-acre Royal Teton Ranch-South. The church bought the

Montana property in 1981 and moved its headquarters from Los Angeles in 1986.

James Melstad, an environmental engineer with the state health department, testified that state approval for a wastewater system at a site on the east end of the ranch could be issued in about a week if the state EIS is approved.

Helena attorney Stan Kaleczyc, who represents the church, urged the judge to dismiss the coalition's lawsuit.

"The church has a very vested interest in maintaining a very sensitive area," he said. "It's their home."

Park biologists testified Wednesday that the state review failed to adequately address impacts on grizzly bear habitat and migration patterns of elk, pronghorn antelope, deer and bison.

But Kaleczyc told the judge Thursday that the needs of humans must be balanced with those of wildlife, and he stressed that the park biologists agreed that other wildlife experts could come to different conclusions about the effects on wildlife.

"The church is demonstrating its sensitivity and its commitment to the environment. Enough is enough ... and more than enough has been done," he said.

Sherlock said he had not heard testimony that would dispute the conclusions by the wildlife experts who testified Wednesday. He said he believed the state review adequately covered potential problems from population growth on church property, but he remained mostly concerned with possible impacts on wildlife.

State water quality division officials testified Thursday they relied on experts within the Department of Fish, Wildlife and Parks in preparing the state review and reiterated their belief that it was thorough.

livingston
enterprise

A Yellowstone Newspaper

Vol. 78—No. 178, Livingston, Mont., Tuesday, May 2, 1989—Thirty Five Cents

EIS trial draws to a conclusion

State says it is not responsible for land-use planning in valley

HELENA (AP) — A state district judge says he may rule by next week on the request to block the Church Universal and Triumphant's development north of Yellowstone National Park and order a new environmental review of the project.

District Judge Jeffrey Sherlock of Helena said final documents are due by next Tuesday on the case, and that he hopes to rule as soon as possible.

Much of the church's planned developments near Corwing Springs have been on hold for more than two years, waiting for completion of a state environmental impact statement.

The EIS was issued in March, but a coalition of environmental groups sued the state three weeks later, claiming the document was inadequate.

On Monday, an attorney representing the groups said the EIS should be redone because it overlooked legitimate concerns about environmental impacts of the development.

"We're talking about one of the most environmentally sensitive pieces of real estate in the country," said Jack Tuholske of Missoula. "A lot is at stake here. Redoing the environmental impact statement (EIS) is not just a paper exercise.... Additional disclosure of information could result in more mitigation measures."

Lawyers for the state and CUT said the lawsuit should be dismissed and that the development allowed to proceed under constraints outlined by the EIS. They said its critics are asking the state to go beyond its legal duty in evaluating the church development.

"We are not a land-use planning agency," said Frank Crowley, an attorney for the state Department of Health and Environmental Sciences. "We are not a de facto police officer of the Paradise Valley."

Crowley said the state's environmental review adequately addressed concerns about impacts on wildlife and water quality in the area bordering Yellowstone Park.

"We consulted many, many people," he said. "If this document is not (complete), I don't know what is."

The arguments wrapped up four days of testimony before Sherlock, spread over more than two weeks.

The church plans to build a housing project for 260 people, a dining hall, school, chapel and ranch headquarters. It also has sheep, cattle, orchards, gardens and a food-processing facility on the property.

The area is considered prime winter range for elk, bison, bighorn sheep and pronghorn antelope, and critical habitat for grizzly bears.

Stan Kaleczyc, a Helena lawyer representing the church, said Monday that the real intent of those seeking a new EIS is to stop any development by the church in the Corwin Springs area.

He said the bulk of their case depends on opinions of Yellowstone Park wildlife biologists and researchers, who view the area as pristine.

"The rest of us in Montana live in a world where development co-exists with the natural world," he said.

He pointed out that the church has agreed to numerous mitigation measures and has already carried out several.

Yet Tuholske said the state failed to follow its own rules, which say the final EIS must include responses to "substantive comments" made on the draft EIS.

"That didn't happen here," he said. "There is no evaluation of the (National) Park Service's comments, or the Greater Yellowstone Coalition's comments.... Those concerns are ignored."

The EIS also did not contain enough information to back up its claim that there will be little impact on grizzlies and other wildlife, he said.

Bozeman Daily

CHRONICLE

Sunday, May 14, 1989, Bozeman, Montana

Judge gives CUT the go-ahead

State's EIS on Corwin Springs development upheld; action denied

By SCOTT McMILLION
Chronicle Staff Writer

LIVINGSTON — A Helena judge has refused to halt Church Universal and Triumphant's planned developments at Corwin Springs, giving the controversial church the green light to build a 600-person religious community there.

In what he called a difficult decision, District Judge Jeff Sherlock on Thursday ruled that the state's Environmental Impact Statement (EIS) was legal and denied a request for a permanent injunction filed by a consortium of environmental groups, including the Montana chapter of the Sierra Club and the Greater Yellowstone Coalition.

> 'They wanted to treat us differently from everybody else.'
>
> — *Ed Francis*

"The duty of this Court in this case is to determine whether Montana state law on the preparation of (the EIS) was followed," wrote Sherlock in his 48-page decision. "The court is not to determine whether or not the proposal of the church is a good idea."

The plaintiffs sought to halt proposed CUT developments on the northern edge of Yellowstone Park, saying that they pose a threat to the environment and to wildlife, particularly ungulates and grizzly bears.

CUT's development plans, with several mitigations imposed by the state, were OK'd in March by the Montana Department of Health and Environmental Sciences. The state approval came in an environmental impact statement issued after an often stormy preparation process that lasted 2½ years.

The church plans to build sewage and water treatment facilities, housing, church headquarters and other projects.

The plaintiffs argued that the EIS was inadequate, particularly on wildlife issues.

"We're obviously very pleased with the results," said Ed Francis, CUT vice president and business manager. "The plaintiffs have expected too much out of the process all along. They wanted to treat us differently from everybody else."

Francis said it would be several months before construction starts.

The Health Department stressed in the EIS that its role was limited to CUT's specific proposals, and the judge agreed with that position.

State health officials have also maintained that if people want more control over developments by CUT or any other developer, measures must be taken at the local level, not at the state level.

"It is sad beyond belief that CUT chose to develop this area the way they have," said Julia Page, president of the Upper Yellowstone Defense Fund, another of the plaintiffs. "Lawsuit or no, win or lose, that worries us."

Page said CUT's developments still threaten critical wildlife winter range even though the injunction was denied. Thousands of ungulates leave Yellowstone Park every year to winter on CUT property.

Scientists from the park testified before Sherlock that CUT developments could threaten Yellowstone's wildlife, disagreeing with the state's wildlife managers that the effects would be minimal.

Sherlock ruled that a difference of opinion between experts does not invalidate an EIS.

He also ruled that restricting the scope of the EIS to CUT's south ranch was reasonable, as was the range of alternatives considered by the state.

Secondary and additional impacts of the developments were also reasonably discussed, Sherlock ruled.

He also said that the state's responses to comments on the draft EIS "while not heroic, are adequate."

While conceding that the EIS could have contained much more information, Sherlock said that the plaintiffs must prove "by a preponderance of evidence that the EIS process was flawed" and that they did not accomplish this.

The other plaintiffs were Page as an individual and the National Parks Conservation Association.

livingston
enterprise

A Yellowstone Newspaper

Vol. 78 — No. 204, Livingston, Mont.; Thursday, June 8, 1989 — Thirty Five Cents   (2 sections)

Appeal of CUT plans dropped

Given High Court's makeup, case could set bad precedent

By AL KNAUBER
Enterprise Staff Writer

A coalition of four environmental groups has decided not to appeal a Helena district court ruling supporting the environmental impact statement on the Corwin Springs developments of the Church Universal and Triumphant.

Missoula attorney Jack Tuholske, who represents the environmental groups, said Thursday the decision against appealing the ruling by Judge Jeffrey Sherlock is not because the group's believe the judge's decision was correct, but because of the composition of the Montana Supreme Court where the appeal would be filed.

"The court's record on (the Montana Environmental Policy Act) in the past is not very encouraging," Tuholske said.

Tuholske said losing such a case at the state's highest court may create future problems for others who challenge the EIS process under MEPA.

The next time the state performs an EIS, it could be challenged on the same grounds that were presented to Sherlock and other district court judges would not feel obligated to follow Sherlock's ruling, Tuholske said.

If the EIS on the church is appealed to the Supreme Court, Tuholske said the higher court ruling would bind all district court judges in Montana.

An unfavorable ruling could set a "really bad" precedent, he added.

Tuholske said it is difficult to overturn an agency decision such as that contained in the EIS.

The state Water Quality Bureau released the EIS on the church in March after 2½ years of preparation. The document allows the church to develop its Corwin Springs property, but outlines certain conditions to which the church must abide.

The EIS was challenged in Helena district court by the Upper Yellowstone Defense Fund, the Montana Chapter of the Sierra Club, the Greater Yellowstone Coalition and the National Parks and Conservation Association.

Sherman Janke with the Montana Chapter of the Sierra Club in Bozeman said the decision not to appeal was difficult.

He said the groups will now watch CUT's development to make sure they follow conditions outlined in the EIS.

Janke supports a bill by U.S. Rep. Wayne Owens, D-Utah, to have the Forest Service purchase from CUT about 12,000 acres — adjacent to Yellowstone Park — that is slated for development under the EIS.

"There is no question ... all of us would clearly like to see that real estate in the public domain and properly managed," he said.

Representatives for the Upper Yellowstone Defense Fund and the Greater Yellowstone Coalition could not be reached for comment on the decision not to appeal.

Index to 1988 *Pearls of Wisdom*

For an alphabetical listing of many of the philosophical and hierarchical terms used in the 1988 *Pearls of Wisdom*, see the comprehensive glossary, "The Alchemy of the Word: Stones for the Wise Masterbuilders," in *Saint Germain On Alchemy: For the Adept in the Aquarian Age.*

mine," 585; cooperating with karmic cycles, 563; does bring fruit to the Master, 513; fervent, 606; Great White Brotherhood does choose its, 512; and Guru, 589; humble heart of a, 607; understanding and compassion for the plight of the, 663; unprofitable, 511–12. *See also* Chelaship; Disciple(s); Guru-chela relationship; Initiates

Chelaship: Ascended Master sponsorship of, 512–13; opposition to, 680. *See also* Chela(s); Discipleship

Chicago, Threefold Flame over, 666n.1

Child: division between parent and, 522; Gautama Buddha on child rearing, 664–66; what every child must be reared with, 530; within, 684. *See also* Children

Children: bringing forth, 593–94; judgment of the violators of, 465–66; Mother Mary on, 683–88; must be their own person, 596–97; in the playpen of life, 621; in this Community, 597. *See also* Child

China, desecration of war upon, 478

Chinese, your effort to chant in, 478

Chohan(s): desirous of your coming to their retreats, 542; fortnight you spend at retreats of the, 693; Kuan Yin served as, 428n.3. *See also* El Morya; Lords; Paul the Venetian; Saint Germain; Serapis Bey

Choices, a place prepared for every lifestream according to his, 698

Cholesterol, 593

Christ: Body and Blood of, *following* p. 580 *(in Sept. 19, 1988 letter)*; as initiator, 593; mirror reflection of the, 590; union with, 629; you have been called to be the, *following* p. 646 *(in Nov. 1, 1988 letter)*. *See also* Christ Self; Christed one; Christhood; Jesus

Christ Self: call for the Electronic Presence of, 506n.2, 685; Christ-Self awareness, 639; communication of God through the, 627; congruency with your, 648; cylinder of blue flame from your soul to your, 631; daily oneness with your, 643–44; El Morya holding the hand of your, *following* p. 700 *(in Dec. 24, 1988*

letter); Electronic Presence of your, 504; externalizing your own, 669; focus the inner eye upon your, 460, 460n; fusion of the soul with the, 480n.7; as Mediator, 656n.3; new dimensions of the, 617; 99 percent of the population separated from the voice of the, 621; standard and wisdom of the, 473; Threefold Flame of the, 636. *See also* Christ; Christhood

Christed one, making of the, 695. *See also* Christ

Christhood: descent of your, 475; emergent, 396; given to the world increment by increment, 432; increase of your own, 558; Jesus called us to enter the path of personal, *following* p. 646 *(in Nov. 1, 1988 letter)*; price for true, 669; profile of your, 689; on the seven rays, 658; supreme test of, 632n.14; time given for personal, 623; time to attain to, 622; won, 653; your, 399. *See also* Christ; Christ Self

Christianity, diluted, 676. *See also* Church; Orthodoxy

Church: lie that has crept into, 697; Satan given 75 years to destroy the, 462n.13. *See also* Christianity; Orthodoxy; Religion(s)

Church Universal and Triumphant: communicant of, 509; and the Environmental Impact Statement, *following* p. 700 *(in Nov. 18, 1987 and April 8, 1988 letters)*. *See also* Community; Royal Teton Ranch; Summit Lighthouse, The; Summit University; Summit University Press catalogue

City, Holy, 463

City Foursquare, 409

Civilization, must enter a period of self-transcendence, 395

Clare of Assisi, biography of, 416

Cloud, of Light, 441

Cloven tongues, of fire, 435, 436

Co-measurement, 629; spoken of by Elohim, 646

Coasts: Keepers of the Flame living on the, 632n.9; recommendation of Saint Germain to leave the, 623

Coil, of white fire, 441

Communion: Holy, 432; of the Holy Spirit, 540, 541–42, 642n.8; from Mary and Raphael, 688; Pearls of

Elementals: love the violet flame, *following* p. 438 *(in June 14, 1988 letter);* trying to figure out why violet flame keeps walking with your shoes, 545; when they receive too much violet flame, 549; who shall earn a threefold flame, 469–70. *See also* Elemental beings; Elemental life

Elephant, and Ganesha, 501n.6

Eleven o'clock line, 599

Elocution, 687

Elohim: chalice of, *following* p. 438 *(in June 1, 1988 letter),* 440, 580n.1, 624, 638, 642n.16; chalice sustained by, 579; re-creation by, 608; servants of, 470; their focus at the Grand Teton, 608, 612n.13; their words to El Morya, 584–85; those who will stand as chalices of, 585; vigil of, 641; vigil to be kept with, 625. *See also* Amazonia; Apollo and Lumina; Astrea; Hercules; Heros and Amora

Emerald ray, 540

Emotional body, sometimes growth has stopped in the, 684. *See also* Astral body; Emotions

Emotions: sine wave of, 660; test of, 634n.24. *See also* Emotional body; Feelings

Enemies, to be defeated, 396. *See also* Enemy

Enemy, your worst, 460–61. *See also* Enemies

Enoch: judgment of the Watchers pronounced through, 492n.3; judgments prophesied in the Book of, 552

Entities, suicide, 456. *See also* Demons

Entity, diseases have a companion, 451. *See also* Demons

Environmental Impact Statement (EIS), 561n.4, *following* p. 700 *(in Nov. 18, 1987 and April 8, 1988 letters)*

Error, repetitive, 566

Etheric octave: a land in the, 669; meets the land at our retreat, 410; physical retreat meshed with the, 629–30. *See also* Octaves

Europe: crowned heads and others of, 403; and the INF Treaty, 534n.10

Evil, reduction in the lifewaves of, 673. *See also* Darkness

Evil ones, encounter with, 585

Ex cathedra, def., 623n

Example: immense opportunity to set an, 509; set for children, 683–84; your, 477

Excalibur: in *Le Morte d'Arthur,* 400n.4; steel of, 396; sword, 457

Exercise, for children while they give their decrees, 687

Exorcism, 441; at the Friday night Ascension Service, 607–8

Eye: All-Seeing Eye lent to El Morya and his devotees, 607; "eye magic," 451; fire of the, 594; inner, 460; "If thine eye be single . . . , *following* p. 438 *(in June 1, 1988 letter),* 442n

Fail: potential to, 597; "we shall not fail," 645–46. *See also* Failure

Failure, 600–601; possibility of, 653, 696; repetitious, 510; which you accept, 407. *See also* Fail

Fallen angels: come to you for one purpose, 605; curtailed through your judgment calls, 553; intimidate and belittle, 628; Jesus' rebuke to the, *following* p. 646 *(in Nov. 1, 1988 letter);* lot of, 599; not-self of the, 428n.5; pity them not, 412; psychic projection from, 607; their judgment pronounced through Enoch, 492n.3; their round-the-clock attempt to manipulate the mind, 525; threatened, 452; who have bound you for aeons, 472. *See also* Fallen ones

Fallen ones: in Church or State, 479; disintegration of, 568–69; jealousy and envy of, 517; judgment calls are the only way to slow down the, 558; judgment of the Trinity upon, 523; see the Lightbearers as the maximum threat, 602; seek to be embodied through Lightbearers, 593; tactics of, 550; who plot their devices, 528; whom Jesus was required to challenge, 690–91; whose time has come, 506; will lay every trap, 691. *See also* Antichrist; Fallen angels; False hierarchy; Impostor(s); Laggard; Malevolent forces; Nephilim gods; Watchers; Wicked

False hierarchy: have as tenet the nonrecognition of Victors, 452; of religion, 638. *See also* Fallen ones

Family, future plans that have to do with, 594. *See also* Ancestral tree; Parent(s)

Father, and Guru, 694

Fátima: anchoring here of Fátima's retreat, 645; arcing of, 441; Light of, anchored in the Heart of the Inner Retreat, 439, 442n.1; prophecies may be turned back, *following* p. 438 *(in June 14, 1988 letter);* prophecies of war from, 396

Faults, highly exaggerated, 567

Favorites, hierarchy of, 609

Fear, 404

Fearlessness, 404

Feelings: harboring of intense, 606–7; hurt, 451; we understand your, 663; weigh down the Light of the Mother, 605. *See also* Emotions

Feminine Ray, 423; focus of the, 626, 646n.5, 681n.2; sustainment in the physical octave of the, 645

Fetus, in the womb, 659

Figure-eight flow, 602

Fire(s): of gold and pink and white from Maitreya, 445; from Maitreya, 447; on the mountain, *following* p. 438 *(in June 14, 1988 letter);* out of the mouth of the Two Witnesses, 453; those sealed in a spiritual, 565–66; threatening the Royal Teton Ranch, 603n.2; out of your mouth, 426. *See also* Flame(s); Sacred fire

First Ray, why we have so emphasized calls to the, 551–52. *See also* Blue flame(s)

First strike, by the Soviets, 538n.10. *See also* War

Five o'clock line: of the Cosmic Clock, 604n.26; El Morya on the, 599

Flame(s): be prepared to keep the, 626; blazing upon this altar, 655; can have consciousness, 547–48; diligence in the, *following* p. 438 *(in June 1, 1988 letter);* "I AM keeping the Flame for you . . . ," 642n.19; tends to rise, 483; that burns in all directions, 503; that burns upon the altar, 654; that does not ascend each twenty-four hours, 545–46; that literally walk with you, 545; upward draft of a, 676; in your heart, 676. *See also* Fire(s); God Flame; Threefold Flame

Flattery, ego, 572

Flesh-and-blood consciousness, idols of, 653

Flirting, 572

Foreheads, sealing of the servants of God in their, 408

"Forget-me-not," 462n.1

Forgetfulness, 613

Forgiveness: from the one you have wronged, 515; and separation from Alpha and Omega, 522; withholding of, 555. *See also* Mercy; "Nonforgivers"

Founding Fathers, *following* p. 438 *(in June 14, 1988 letter)*

Four Cosmic Forces, 440n

Four lower bodies. *See* Astral body; Bodies; Body; Desire body; Emotional body; Mental body; Physical body

Four Noble Truths, 496n.3; and nonattachment, 518n.9

Fourteen-month cycle(s), 495; of Hercules' bearing the karmic burden of Lightbearers, 619–20, 632n.1; of Serapis Bey, 502n.6, 527

Fourteen months, cycles of the, 542

Fourth Ray: holiness as a quality of the, 616; to lend yourselves to the, 618; as a means to the strengthening of the rays, 615. *See also* White light

Francis of Assisi, Saint: Kuthumi was embodied as, 699n.2; momentum of, bequeathed to you, 460–61; and Saint Clare, 416

Free enterprise, misreading of, 408n.1

Free will: cosmos is a place of, 596; in the hands of the fallen ones, 551

Freedom: individual, 414; take it not for granted, 630; true, 446. *See also* Freedoms; Liberty

FREEDOM 1988, *following* p. 438 *(in June 1 and 14, 1988 letters);* the Call to be present at, 572; in the Heart of the Inner Retreat, 406; purpose at, 615; sponsoring Master of, *following* p. 438 *(in June 1, 1988 letter)*

Freedom's Star, earth's destiny to be, 679–80

Freedoms, sacred, 452

Friday night: aftermath of the Friday night vigil, 609; Friday night Ascension Service, 607–8; surgery of cosmic dimensions each, 608

Fruit, that the chela does bring to the Master, 513

Future: fearlessness toward the, 687; golden, 603; golden vision of the, 673; and present, 663–64; those who have never visited the, 579

Gabriel, Archangel: before all the unresponsive ones, 602; as Guru, 498; lilies planted by, 497–98; retreat of, 501n.3; in San Diego, 431. *See also* Archangel(s)

Ganesha, in the teachings of Hinduism, 501n.6

Gates, of the seven planes of heaven, 428n.9

Gautama Buddha, 419n; coming of Padma Sambhava foretold by, 544n.2; consciousness of God-purity held by, 447n.5; face and posture of, 404; in the hearts of children, 665; his 'Inner Retreat', 397; his mantle upon the Messenger, 508; his meditation, 605; Keeper of the Flame, *following* p. 438 *(in June 1, 1988 letter)*; to personally initiate the heart chakra, *following* p. 438 *(in June 1, 1988 letter)*; retreat of, 519n.13, 646n.7; shall intercede for you, 515; statue of, 519n.13; tied to the threefold flame of every heart, 555; and Wesak, 421; your Brother, 663. *See also* Buddha(s)

Gemini: hierarchs of, 572; hierarchy of, 566–67

Genetic code, of the Lightbearers, 484

Genetic engineering, 525

Genetic manipulation, 486

Genetic violations, 496

Geopolitical configuration, understanding of the planetary, 569

Glasnost, 562n.10

Glastonbury, 594, 597, 654

Goal: goal-fitting, 531; most important, 488; set your, 670

Gobi Desert, *following* p. 438 *(in June 1, 1988 letter)*; etheric retreat over the, 519n.13, 646n.7; Shamballa over the, *following* p. 438 *(in June 1, 1988 letter)*

God: Father-Mother, 404, 665–66; "get right" with, 515; as Mother, 414; opportunity of a great encounter with your, 662; potential to be, 490; if you right your heart with, 517.

See also Brahman; God Self; Godhead; Godhood

God Flame: snuffed out, 611; thy, 446. *See also* Flame(s); Threefold Flame

God Reality, stands before you, 671

God-realization, no limit to, 653

God Self: ministrations of your, 516; mirroring the, 689. *See also* I AM Presence

God Star, representatives of the, 530–31

Godfre, calling to, 530

Godhead, four Principles of the, 502n.9. *See also* God

Godhood, accountability to pursue thy, 491. *See also* God

Gog and Magog, forces of, 525

Golden pink glow-ray, 445, 446, 452

Golden white spheres, of God and Goddess Meru, 580n.2, 633n.19

Gorbachev, Mikhail, 554, 562n.10

Gossip, concerning the Messenger, 508

Government: continuity of God-government, 530–31; reins of your, 395; representative, 530; representatives of this, 568. *See also* Leaders; Leadership; President of the United States; State

Grace, by which ye are saved, *following* p. 580 *(in Sept. 19, 1988 letter)*

Grand Teton: descent of the root races at the, 577; focus of Elohim at the, 608. *See also* Royal Teton Retreat

Gratitude, 445; God-gratitude, 477–78

Great Central Sun Magnet: to draw forth purity, 617; of the Seventh Ray, 546; of the Threefold Flame of Liberty, 481; and the white Light, 618

Great Divine Director: Great Causal Body of the, 507; retreats of the, 570n.4; on the twelve o'clock line, 518n.1, 586, 599

Great White Brotherhood: all who comprise the Spirit of the, 678–79; entire Spirit of the, 548, 681n.10; path of the, 477; physical contact with a representative of the, 674; relationship that you enjoy with the, 512; those sponsored by the, 690. *See also* Ascended Master(s); Hierarchy

Guru(s): and chela, 589; embodied, 672; false, 454, 674; and Father, 694; mantle of, 513, 672n.6; office of, 511; sight of the, *following* p. 438 *(in June*

1988 letter), 442n; if tempted to believe you have no need of, 491; those who have an inner rebellion against the, 476; and the Three Jewels, 447n.9; who gave their chelas intense discipline, 590. *See also* Guru-chela relationship; "Guru Ma"

Guru-chela relationship, 447; access to the Master's causal body in the, 514; bane of the, 406–7; fundamental definition, 513; message of Gautama Buddha on the, 578; profound value of the, 685; standard that is set for the, 511–12; this, 477; those who have profound need of the, 476. *See also* Chela(s); Guru(s)

"Guru Ma," *following* p. 438 *(in June 1, 1988 letter)*

Hail Mary, 643; recite it with the OM MANI PADME HUM, 415

Harmony: Gautama Buddha on, 664; internal, 536

Harvest: of the decade, 613–14; of souls at the conclusion of the year, 696

Hatred: forces of, 465; put upon other parts of life, 612n.20. *See also* Animosities

Healing, 441; Communion for, 688; healing angels, 439, 439n, 441, 498; healing matrix imbedded in the psyche of the planet, 439–40, 442n.2; healing service, 455; healing thoughtform, 442n.2, 646; pillars of, 451; within the psyche, 522; of the soul, 456; and the willow branch, 480n.11

Health: conspiracy against, 558; good, 593

Heart: appreciation of the, 539; burning of the, 677; capacity of the, 471; clearing of the, 592–93; development of the, 404; follow by the, 629; Gautama Buddha on the, 657–61, 662–63, 666; human, 473; initiation(s) of the, 657, 658, 661, 691; merciful, 606, 610–11, 659; opening of the, 668; purification of the, 472–73; purple fiery, 559; sanctification of the, 692, 697, 698; strong and virtuous, 475; twelve petals of the, 475. *See also* Chakra(s); Heart meditation(s); Immaculate Heart;

Sacred Heart; Secret chamber of the heart

Heart meditation(s), of Saint Germain, 472, 495, 559

Heartbeat, of God, 659

Heaven, must have instruments, 433

Hercules: and Amazonia bear the burden of karma, 639; bearing the cross daily, 630; bearing the karmic burden of Lightbearers, 619–20, 623–24, 642n.18; calls to, 549; carrying the cross of the burdens of Lightbearers, 632n.1; descent of, 631. *See also* Elohim

Heroism, that is called for, 398

Heros and Amora: belt of, 637; desire to return in each quadrant of the year, 470, 642n.20; retreat of, 409. *See also* Elohim

Hierarchies, of the sun, 473. *See also* Solar hierarchies

Hierarchy: chain of, 674, 678–79, 696; gifts of, 580. *See also* Ascended Master(s); Great White Brotherhood

Highway: of light to Lake Titicaca and the Middle East, 642n.16; of our God, 542

Himalaya, Lord: retreat of, 646n.5; Temple of the Blue Lotus of, 689

Himalayas, retain the opening into the octaves of Light, 623

Holiness, 691; of all that you do, 692; Goddess of Purity on, 616

Holy Ghost, sin against the, 637. *See also* Holy Spirit

Holy Spirit: balancing the misuses of the Light of the, 637; Communion of the, 540, 541–42; descent of, 435; gifts of the, 616–17, 636–37, 638, 687; initiation(s) of the, 414, 429, 435, 437, *following* p. 438 *(in June 1, 1988 letter)*, 639, 641–42n.8; key to Victory in the secret rays, 500

Homecoming, requirements for your, 531

Homo sapiens, 567; self-sufficient, 474

Honduras, United States dispatched troops to, 560n.2

Honor, of Christ, 638

Hope, Archeia, retreat of, 501n.3. *See also* Archangel(s)

Horse, black, 601. *See also* Horseman

Horseman, Fourth, 633n.19. *See also* Horse

See also Kuan Shih Yin
Kumaras: in Hindu tradition, 580n.3; Seven Holy, *following* p. 438 *(in June 1, 1988 letter)*, 576n
Kundalini: awakened, 574n.5; coil of white fire fashioned of the, 441; pulling upon the, fire, 426; raising of the, 442n.3, 617, 670; rising, 410; shall rise, 460; you become the, 412
Kuthumi: emerald matrix of, 463; on the four o'clock line, 586; his final incarnation, 461n.1; in the office of World Teacher, 689; was embodied as Saint Francis of Assisi, 699n.2

Labor, that is sacred, 692
Ladder, life is a, 411
Lady Master, intense devotion to one Ascended, 495
Laggard, a Cosmic Christ assigned to each, 506n.5. *See also* Fallen ones
Lanello: "best man," 456; call for his Presence and Heart, 680; calling to, 530; jaw of your, 514. *See also* Messenger(s); Prophet, Mark L.
Language, building blocks of, 686
Law: edict that comes forth out of the, 510–11; galactic and intergalactic, 524; an hour when you keep tethered to the, 651; is just, 429, 586; if you are outside the, *following* p. 700 *(in Dec. 24, 1988 letter)*
Leaders: in Church and State, 472; infamous, *following* p. 438 *(in June 1, 1988 letter);* nations bereft of great, 397; not equipped to lead a nation, 661; of vision, 396; who have betrayed and who shall betray, 529; world, 573. *See also* Government; Leadership; State
Leadership: could not pay the enormous karmic debt of the loss of America, 570n.7; of this nation, 563–64, 565. *See also* Government; Leaders; State
Lemmings, def., 570n.13
Lemuria: Mystery School upon, 436; those who tended the altars on, 397
Leo, Dark Cycle in, 561n.3
Lesson, learned and earned, 596
Liberty: commitment to keep the Flame of Cosmic, 487; Cosmic Christ consciousness of, 488; Cosmic Threefold Flame of, 481–82,

483, 486; Flame of Cosmic, *following* p. 646 *(in Nov. 1, 1988 letter);* flame of, is the threefold flame, 452; reactions to the celebration for the Statue of, 408n.1. *See also* Freedom
Liberty, Goddess of: giant manifestation of, 484; her Electronic Presence over you, 677; her Temple of the Sun, 408n.1; tenfold karma for the violation of, 483–84. *See also* Liberty, Mother
Liberty, Mother, her statue in New York Harbor, 401–2. *See also* Liberty, Goddess of
Lie(s): big, 399; of the fallen ones, 460; stripped, 668
Life, leading to the ascension, 474
Light: ability to assimilate, 514; conserved, 411; day by day transfer of, 432; of the Divine Mother raised up, 605; does bring to the surface all manner of records, 608; drop of, 618; extraordinary momentum of, 614; fallen ones move in to take the, 504; far more difficult to maintain, 623; grid of, 440; raised up, 412, 676, 677; raising up of the, 442n.3, 665, 670; rising, 617; saturation by, 430; a seraph assigned to each one who keeps the, 431–32; squandering of, 418, 608; stepped down and distributed, 433; transfer of, 434; when capitalized, 417n; when you raise up, 496; where you must send, 694; which flows over the crystal cord, 488; will turn and serve you, 430
Lightbearer(s): all of heaven have their attention upon the, 610; be worthy of the name, 618; in a confrontation with the seed of the wicked, 517; cutting free, 557, 675; final opportunity for many, 508; 5 percent who responded, 587; Hercules bearing the karmic burden of, 619–20, 623–24, 642n.18; Hercules carrying the cross of the burdens of, 632n.1; of highest attainment, 665; lightening of the weight of the, 671; network of, 440; progress on the part of some, 516; receive assistance, 668; rescue every, 531; saved, 675–76; unreached and untapped, 478; who had come with Sanat Kumara, 643; who have not responded to the Call

571, 572, 674; highest degrees of God-Mastery, 673; inner, 678; pursue God-mastery, 453–54; science of God-mastery, 573; you shall be called upon to demonstrate God-mastery, 528. *See also* Attainment
Materialism, 397
Mathematics, 686
Maturity, defined, 684
Mechanization man, 567; intimidate and belittle, 628; metallic, 472; psychology of, 473–74; race of, 483
Media: drama or comedy in the, 661; international, 675
Mediatrix: def., 646n.1; of Mercy, 427. *See also* Intercessor
Mediocrity, 406–7
Medjugorje, 396
Mental body: dominant, 627; psychological self centered in the, 590; sometimes growth has stopped in the, 684. *See also* Mind(s)
Mercy, 532; elixir, 423; greatest gift of, 444; invoke Mercy's flame, 585; new, of the Law, 622–23; that endures forever, 611; true and profound heart of, 555; your heart's own, 546. *See also* Forgiveness
Meru, God and Goddess: golden white spheres of, over the Royal Teton Ranch, 580n.2, 633n.19; retreat of, 415n.6, 626, 646n.5; Royal Teton Ranch as outpost of the retreat of, 633n.19; spheres of, 576
Messenger(s): alignment with the, 586; authority in the mantle worn by the, 487; burden of awareness borne by, 482–83; call made by the, 587; to complete publications, 655; denial of that office of, 607; does assist you in bearing your karma, 513–14; function of the, 512–13; Gautama's mantle placed upon the, 508; "get right" with this, 515; of the God Mercury, 459; her preparation and Path, 685–86; her words to El Morya, 587; knelt before Mary and Raphael at Fátima to give their Christhood, 432; long history of your relationship to this, 512; mantle of, *following* p. 438 *(in June 1, 1988 letter)*, 442n, 583; mantle of Guru upon the, *following* p. 438 *(in June 1, 1988 letter)*, 672n.6; mantle on the, 513; mantle

that Gautama placed upon the, 511; most physical work that has ever been accomplished through the, 610; office of, 656n.3; passed through the dark night of the soul, 651; Path of this, 599–600; physical aura of the, 510; role of the, 509; short-circuiting of the cosmic circuits in the, 490; step-down transformer in the aura of the, 433; with you at inner levels by a dispensation of bilocation, 686; your, 646. *See also* Lanello; Prophet, Mark L.; Two Witnesses
Micah, Angel of Unity, 538n.20
Michael, Archangel: calls to, 467, 504, 550–51, 553; his aura, 503; Pope Leo XIII's prayer to, 462n.13; retreat of, 415n.6; why we have so emphasized the calls to, 551–52. *See also* Archangel(s)
Middle East, highway of light extended to the, 642n.16. *See also* Mideast
Middle Way, 410
Mideast, turbulence in the, 516–17, 519n.17. *See also* Middle East
Million(s): inspiration of millions, *following* p. 700 *(in Dec. 24, 1988 letter)*; invoking the violet flame daily, *following* p. 438 *(in June 14, 1988 letter)*; a million souls as devoted as this nucleus, 467; a million violet flame decreers, *following* p. 646 *(in Nov. 1, 1988 letter)*
Mind(s): attrition of the intelligence of the Universal, 568; of Christ, 628; demons possessing the, 451; desperate need for the restoration of the, of God, 567; fallen ones seek to control, 527; is but a portion of self, 590; manipulation of, 565–66; round-the-clock attempt of fallen angels to manipulate the, 525; take control of the, 664. *See also* Carnal mind; Consciousness; Intellect; Mental body; Mindless; Subconscious
Mindless, those who are, 569. *See also* Mind(s)
Miracles, 618; demonstration of, 403
Mirror, of Kuthumi's inner garment, 460–61
Misfits, prior to our ascension, 474
Money: money beast, 587; squandered, 608; those who control you

Padma Sambhava, 491; bestowed the mantle of Guru upon the Messenger, 672n.6; biography of, 544n.2; lineage of, *following* p. 438 *(in June 1, 1988 letter);* mantra of, 540, 544n.2; office of Guru from, 511

Pallas Athena, 695; Truth which she would bring, 691; twin flame of the Maha Chohan, 460

Parent(s): Divine and human, 521–22; division between child and, 522; God Parents, 522–23; learn the art of sacrifice, 597; in the Old and New Testament, 593–94; to one another in Community, 684; praying for parents-to-be, 685; who have brought forth lifestreams not assigned to them, 593

Parenting, future plans that have to do with, 594

Parvati, and Ganesha, 501n.6

Path: give it a diligent try for six months, 516; is precipitous, 510; sponsorship on this, 509–10; that is a spiral, 410–11; those who made initial progress on the, 589; unreal picture of oneself on the, 510

Paul the Venetian, emerald and rose cape of, 540. *See also* Chohan(s); Lords

Pay, "pay as you go," 584, 608, 623, 658

Peace, inner, 591

Pearl, of great price, 514

Pearl(s) of Wisdom: are Holy Communion, *following* p. 580 *(in Sept. 19, 1988 letter);* counseling from the, 624. *See also* Teaching(s)

Perestroika, 562n.10

Perfection, tenth, 518–19n.9

Permanent seed atom, 575

Personal Impersonality, 496, 502n.9

Personal Personality, 496, 502n.9

Personality: lesser interchanges of the world's personality cult, 572; Personal and Impersonal, 496, 502n.9; which you know to be detrimental, 685. *See also* Ego

Physical body: balance in the, 527; mastery of the, 678. *See also* Bodies; Body

Pisces: flame of, *following* p. 700 *(in Dec. 24, 1988 letter);* hierarchs of, 572; Mother of, 424; sign and hierarchy

of, 453n. *See also* Age

Pit: astral debris out of the bottomless, 639; opened, 624, 651; opening of the bottomless, 622–23

Place Prepared, *following* p. 438 *(in June 1, 1988 letter);* in the wilderness, 418. *See also* Inner Retreat; Royal Teton Ranch

Plagues, last, 552. *See also* Diseases

Pleiades, 436; arcing of the, 441

Pope Leo XIII, his prayer to Saint Michael, 462n.13

Portia, *following* p. 438 *(in June 14, 1988 letter);* over every place where two or three are gathered to give violet flame, *following* p. 438 *(in June 14, 1988 letter);* Goddess of Opportunity, 421n.3; in support of Saint Germain, 565

Power: abusers of, 554; abuses of, 550; black, 553; opportunity for, 637–38

Prajna boat, 446; def., 447n.8

Prayer(s): answer to, 414; daily, 644. *See also* Hail Mary; Rosary

Preferences, hierarchy of, 609

Presence, dazzling fire of the, 649. *See also* I AM Presence

Present, and future, 663–64

Preserver, Great, 634n.2

President of the United States, mantle of the office of, 529–30, 538n.18. *See also* Government; Leaders; Leadership

Price, paying of the ultimate, 672

Pride, spiritual, 450, 491

Priests: 144,000, of the sacred fire, 679, 680, *following* p. 700 *(in Dec. 24, 1988 letter);* of the violet planet, 682

Prince, 490; "cometh and findeth nothing in me," 454

Problems, that have seemed unsolvable, 464

Profile: of the Christed one, 661–62; of your Christhood, 689

Progress: as the balancing of karma, 405; since Wesak last, 516

Projection, psychic, 607

Prophecies: final opportunity to mitigate, *following* p. 438 *(in June 1, 1988 letter);* may be turned back, *following* p. 438 *(in June 14, 1988 letter);* mitigated and averted, 519n.18; of Mother Mary, 413; of that which

Watchers: Great Silent, 428n.9; judgment of the, pronounced through Enoch, 492n.3; know that they are spending their last hours, 552–53. *See also* Fallen ones

Watchmen, of the night, 395–96

Water, rising fount of, 418

Water glasses, those who fill, 430–31

Wave, of Light, 417

Weariness, everywhere upon the planet, 427

Wedding day, of the soul, 456

Wedding garment, 456–57, 614; gold and purest white, 591

Wesak: celebration of, 507; day of, 419; explained, 421; progress since last, 516

West, sleepfulness of the, 396

West Coast, Keepers of the Flame on the, 431

Western Shamballa, 573; Gautama's 'Inner Retreat', 397; at the Inner Retreat, *following* p. 438 *(in June 1, 1988 letter)*, 519n.13, 646n.7; Open Door to the abode of the Buddhas, 574; secret chamber of the heart maintained in the, 409. *See also* Inner Retreat

White fire, coil of, 441

White light: trailing the Ruby Ray, 433; transition to the secret rays, 693. *See also* Fourth Ray

Wholeness: attracting Divine, 645; invoked from on high, 646; Mediatrix of Divine, 643, 645; sevenfold, 498

Wicked: checked by your calls, 529; judgments upon the seed of the, 517, 552; their reaction to the lifting of the burden of karma, 549. *See also* Fallen ones

Will of God: bracing the violet flame by the, 551; the call(s) to the, 583, 584; embodying the, 549–50; light of the, 449–50; nestling in the heart of the, 615; ray of the, 602

Willow branch, and healing, 480n.11

Wind, great, 535

Wisdom: gone out of you, 577–78; wisdom cross, 572; wisdom cross on the Cosmic Clock, 574n.6

Within, going, 691

Woes: knowledge of the threatening, 524; that shall descend, 526

Woman, and her seed, 462n.16

Wonderman of Europe, 403, *following* p. 438 *(in June 14, 1988 letter)*

Word: "In the beginning was the Word . . ." parallels Hindu teachings on *Vāc*, 501–2n.8; incarnate within thee, 574; of the Logos shall live forever, 626–27. *See also* Spoken Word

Work(s): of the ages, 671; sanctification of, 692

World Teachers, 689

Worthlessness, 491

Year(s): fifty and one hundred, 526; harvest of souls at the conclusion of the, 696

Yellowstone, 415

Yoga(s): four, 569n.1; karma, 569n.1, 570n.2

Youth. *See* Teenagers

Zadkiel, Archangel, 682. *See also* Archangel(s)

Zarathustra, 403

Zeal, of the fire of the Sun, 650

FOR MORE INFORMATION

Write or call for information about the dictations of the Ascended Masters published weekly as *Pearls of Wisdom*, the Keepers of the Flame Fraternity with monthly lessons, the Ascended Masters' study center nearest you, and Summit University three-month retreats, weekend seminars and quarterly conferences that convene at the Royal Teton Ranch. At this 33,000-acre self-sufficient spiritual community-in-the-making adjacent to Yellowstone National Park in Montana, Elizabeth Clare Prophet gives teachings on the Divine Mother, the parallel paths of Christ and Buddha, Saint Germain's prophecies for our time and the exercise of the science of the spoken Word as well as dictations from the Ascended Masters and initiations of the Great White Brotherhood. These teachings are published in books and on audio- and videocassette. We'll be happy to send you a free catalog when you contact Summit University Press, Box A, Livingston, Montana 59047-1390. Telephone: (406) 222-8300.

All in our community send you our hearts' love and a joyful welcome to the Royal Teton Ranch!

Reach out for the **LIFELINE TO THE PRESENCE.** Let us pray with you! To all who are beset by depression, suicide, difficulties or insurmountable problems, we say **MAKE THE CALL!** (406) 848-7441